Shared Prosperity and Poverty Eradication in Latin America and the Caribbean

Shared Prosperity and Poverty Eradication in Latin America and the Caribbean

Louise Cord, María Eugenia Genoni,
and Carlos Rodríguez-Castelán, editors

WORLD BANK GROUP

Contents

Boxes

Figures

Maps

Tables

Foreword

The Latin America and the Caribbean Region has seen marked and critical progress for its people over the last decade. Extreme poverty has been halved; inequality has declined; and the growth rate among the bottom 40 percent of the population in the region eclipses the performance of that group in every other region in the world. These are all great strides that have helped transform the socioeconomic makeup of the region and grow the middle class to unprecedented levels.

Continuing with the status quo, however, will not be enough, and the last decade's progress is at risk in the face of the global economic slowdown and declining incomes across the region. Moreover, with 75 million people still living in extreme poverty and nearly two-thirds of the population either poor or vulnerable to falling into poverty, the region has not yet enabled and harnessed the full potential of all of its people. A persistent lack of opportunities, quality basic services, and good jobs has kept many of the poor in poverty, and made it harder to break the cycle of poverty and vulnerability between generations.

The region's overall advances mask significant differences between countries, with strong performers canceling out some of the losses of those that were perhaps less successful in reducing poverty and boosting the welfare of the least well off. And, even in countries where progress has been substantial, poverty is often persistent and geographically concentrated. Take Peru, for example, one of the countries that has done quite well in reducing poverty over the last 10 years. Just one-third of the country's population lives in rural areas; however, those same areas account for half of the poor and 80 percent of the extreme poor.

It is important to keep in mind that Latin America and the Caribbean includes countries with varying levels of development, and thus the composition of the bottom 40 percent and the impact of growth on this group may look markedly different from country to country. Some of the strongest performers, Argentina, Bolivia, Brazil, and Panama, saw income growth rates among the bottom 40 at well over 7 percent. Compare this to some of the weakest performers, Guatemala and Mexico, which saw growth rates among the bottom 40 of −1.0 and 1.3 percent, respectively.

Shared Prosperity and Poverty Eradication in Latin America and the Caribbean takes a closer look at the region, presenting eight country case studies to better understand where poverty persists and how best to design policies and programs that will reach the least well off both today and in the years to come. This country-specific approach helps offer tailored analysis for countries, taking into account their socioeconomic structure, progress on the World Bank Group's twin goals, and level of development, rather than applying the region's overall good performance to each country uniformly.

As the World Bank Group continues to work with its partners to end poverty by 2030 and boost shared prosperity around the world, knowing who remains poor and vulnerable and how to increase the welfare of the bottom 40 percent in each country will be crucial. Policies and programs, to be effective, cannot be designed with no evidence to support them, or targeted solely on the basis of what we think might work. This study will help policy makers do a better job of building on the last decade's progress, promoting growth and incomes regardless of the global slowdown, and moving forward into an even more successful decade to come for the people of Latin America and the Caribbean.

Jorge Familiar
Vice President, Latin America
    and the Caribbean
World Bank Group

Ana Revenga
Senior Director,
    Poverty Global Practice
World Bank Group

Acknowledgments

This set of country case studies has been produced by World Bank experts working in the Poverty Global Practice (GPVDR), Latin America and the Caribbean Region, the World Bank.

The coordination of the country studies has been led by Louise Cord, María Eugenia Genoni, and Carlos Rodríguez-Castelán. The core team members are Giselle Del Carmen, Stephanie Majerowicz, and Daniel Valderrama. The team benefited from valuable inputs provided by Alan Fuchs, Santiago Garriga, Lea Giménez, María Ana Lugo, and Martha Viveros. Administrative support was supplied by Karem Edwards. Robert Zimmermann conducted editorial reviews. Publishing and distribution support was assured by Mark Ingebretsen, Patricia Katayama, and Marcela Sánchez-Bender. The work was carried out under the direction of Louise Cord, Augusto de la Torre, Humberto López, and Ana Revenga.

The peer reviewers were Francisco Galrão Carneiro, Wendy Cunningham, Samuel Freije-Rodríguez, Michele Gragnolati, Magnus Lindelow, Kathy A. Lindert, Gladys López-Acevedo, Luis F. López-Calva, Julian Messina, Zafer Mustafaoglu, Jamele Rigolini, Peter Siegenthaler, Emily Sinnott, Miguel Székely, and Renos Vakis. The team also received useful observations from Javier E. Báez and Daniel Lederman, and it benefited from internal discussions with members of Poverty Global Practice, Latin America and the Caribbean Region.

The authors of the chapters would like to express their appreciation of the following: Javier E. Báez, Augusto de la Torre, Daniel Lederman, Julian Messina, Ana Revenga, and Miguel Székely (Overview); Pablo Acosta, Louise Cord, Zafer Mustafaoglu, Rafael Rofman, Emily Sinnott, and Trang Van Nguyen (Argentina); Rita Almeida, Oscar Barriga Cabanillas, Louise Cord, Michael Drabble, Cornelius Fleischhaker, Magnus Lindelow, Luis F. López-Calva, Miriam Müller, Elizaveta Perova, Carlos Rodríguez-Castelán,

Philip Schellekens, Joana Silva, Emmanuel Skoufias, and Anna Wellenstein (Brazil); Tania Díaz-Bazán, Patricia Caraballo, Giselle Del Carmen, Louise Cord, Mauricio Cuellar, Eric Dickson, María Eugenia Genoni, Samuel Freije-Rodríguez, Stephanie Majerowicz, and Mary Alexander Sharman (Colombia); Pablo Acosta, Oscar Calvo González, Kathy Lindert, Mateo Salazar, Liliana D. Sousa, and Miguel Székely (El Salvador); Louise Cord, Wendy Cunningham, Samuel Freije-Rodríguez, Gladys López-Azevedo, Luis F. López-Calva, Carlos Rodríguez-Castelán, Isidro Soloaga, and Miguel Székely (Mexico); Louise Cord, María Eugenia Dávalos, Carolina Díaz-Bonilla, Michele Gragnolati, Jesko Hentschel, Rafael de Hoyos, Dante Mossi, Zafer Mustafaoglu, and Rossana Polastri (Paraguay); Amparo Ballivian, Malva Baskovich, Livia Benavides, Oscar Barriga Cabanillas, Louise Cord, María Eugenia Dávalos, Tania Díaz-Bazán, Santiago Garriga, Stephanie Majerowicz, Karina Olivas, Gustavo Perochena, Adam Kahn Ratzlaff, Megan Rounseville, Kinnon Scott, Peter Siegenthaler, Renos Vakis, and Nobuo Yoshida (Peru); and Louise Cord, Carolina Díaz-Bonilla, Luis F. López-Calva, Zafer Mustafaoglu, Cristina Savescu, and Emily Sinnot (Uruguay).

About the Editors and Authors

About the Editors

Louise Cord is practice manager in the Poverty Global Practice for the World Bank's Latin America and the Caribbean Region, leading a diverse program on poverty, equity, and gender equality. Prior to her experience in Latin America, Louise was the poverty sector manager in the central unit of the Poverty Reduction and Economic Management (PREM) Network, where previously she had been a lead economist working on pro-poor growth, aid effectiveness, rural poverty, and poverty reduction strategies in Africa. Before coming to the PREM Network, she worked for seven years in the World Bank's rural development group of the Latin America and Caribbean Region on rural poverty, agricultural trade and price policy, and rural finance. She has published several articles and reports on poverty and agricultural policy in Mexico, Eastern Europe, and Central Asia, and more recently on pro-poor growth, inequality, and political economy. She holds a PhD in development and economic policy from the Fletcher School of Law and Diplomacy, Tufts University.

María Eugenia Genoni is an economist in the Poverty Global Practice at the World Bank, working in the Latin America and Caribbean Region. Currently, she leads the poverty and equity program in Peru and co-leads the program in Bolivia. She also has contributed to the World Bank's poverty and equity agenda in Central America and to the Regional Gender Impact Evaluation Initiative. Her research has focused on development economics and applied microeconomics, particularly on survey design, poverty and inequality, migration, and risk management. She received her PhD in economics from Duke University.

Carlos Rodríguez-Castelán is senior economist in the Poverty Global Practice at the World Bank, working in Latin America and the Caribbean Region. Currently, he leads the poverty and equity program in Colombia and co-leads the Global Solutions Area on Markets and Institutions for Poverty Reduction and Shared Prosperity. He also has contributed to the World Bank's poverty and equity agenda in Chile, Mexico, Paraguay, and Uruguay and to the corporate activity of Data for Goals. Prior to joining the World Bank, he was a postdoctoral fellow in the Foreign Policy and Global Economy and Development programs of the Brookings Institution. His research has focused on development economics and applied microeconomics, particularly on poverty and inequality analysis, noncompetitive market structures, social protection, education, and risk management. He received his PhD in economics from Cornell University.

About the Authors

Javier E. Báez is senior economist in the Poverty Global Practice of the World Bank, where he specializes in poverty analysis and impact evaluation. He holds a PhD in economics from Syracuse University and an MA in development economics from Harvard University.

Oscar Barriga Cabanillas is a PhD candidate in agricultural and resource economics at the University of California, Davis. Previously, he worked at the Poverty Global Practice of the World Bank as a junior professional associate.

Kiyomi Cadena is a consultant in the Poverty Global Practice of the World Bank, where she has conducted poverty and social impact analyses for projects in Central America, the Latin America and Caribbean Region, and Mexico.

Santiago Garriga is a junior professional associate in the Poverty Global Practice of the World Bank. He is part of the team for statistical development in the World Bank's Latin America and Caribbean Region, where he has conducted data analysis on poverty and inequality.

Lea Giménez is an economist in the Poverty Global Practice of the World Bank, focusing on poverty measurement, institutional and statistical capacity building, social impact, and activities supporting evidence-based policy making.

Marina Gindelsky is a consultant in the Poverty Global Practice of the World Bank, where she has conducted research on poverty and inequality for projects in Iraq and Uruguay.

Luis F. López-Calva is lead economist and regional poverty adviser in the World Bank's Europe and Central Asia Region and was previously lead economist in the Poverty Unit in Latin America and the Caribbean Region. He holds a PhD in economics from Cornell University.

María Ana Lugo is an economist in the Poverty Global Practice of the World Bank, specializing in equality of opportunities, poverty, and multidimensional poverty analyses. She holds a PhD in economics from the University of Oxford.

Alejandro Medina Giopp is a senior monitoring and evaluation specialist at the Poverty Global Practice of the World Bank. He holds a PhD in management sciences from the Escuela Superior de Administración y Dirección de Empresas, Barcelona.

Miriam Müller is a research analyst in the Poverty Global Practice of the World Bank, where she specializes in gender. She is currently a PhD candidate in the sociology program at Humboldt University of Berlin.

Aude-Sophie Rodella is an economist in the Poverty Global Practice of the World Bank, focusing on urban poverty analysis and inclusive growth. She holds a PhD in microeconomics from the Centre for Studies and Research on International Development, Université d'Auvergne.

Megan Rounseville is a consultant in the Poverty Global Practice of the World Bank, where she specializes in econometric impact evaluation and poverty analyses. She has worked with projects in several countries in Latin America and the Caribbean.

Mateo Salazar is a junior professional associate in the Poverty Global Practice of the World Bank. He has coauthored various analytical reports on the measurement, monitoring, and diagnosis of the causes and nature of poverty in several countries in Latin America and the Caribbean.

Kinnon Scott is a senior economist in the Poverty Global Practice of the World Bank, specializing in social mobility and poverty analyses. She holds a PhD in economic and social development from the University of Pittsburgh.

Ali Sharman is a junior professional associate in the Poverty Global Practice of the World Bank, where she has worked on conducting data analysis and research for projects in Brazil, Colombia, the Dominican Republic, and Ecuador.

Emmanuel Skoufias is lead economist in the Poverty Global Practice of the World Bank, with experience working on targeting and the impacts of social transfers, child malnutrition, risk management among the poor, and the impacts of climate change on welfare. He holds a PhD in economics from the University of Minnesota.

Liliana D. Sousa is an economist in the Poverty Global Practice of the World Bank, where she is the co–task team leader of the team for statistical development in the Latin America and Caribbean Region. She holds a PhD in economics from Cornell University.

Erwin R. Tiongson is a professor in the Walsh School of Foreign Service at Georgetown University. Previously, he was senior economist, World Bank, focusing on poverty analysis. He holds a PhD in economics from the George Washington University.

Daniel Valderrama is a junior professional associate in the Poverty Global Practice of the World Bank, where he has conducted data analysis on poverty, inequality, and shared prosperity for projects in several Latin American countries.

Martha Viveros is a consultant in the Poverty Global Practice of the World Bank, where she has conducted data analyses on poverty, inequality, vulnerability, and shared prosperity in Brazil and in Latin America and the Caribbean.

Abbreviations

BF	Bolsa Família (family allowance program) (Brazil)
BRIC	Brazil, Russian Federation, India, and China
BSM	Brasil sem Misería (Brazil without Misery plan) (Brazil)
CONEVAL	Consejo Nacional de Evaluación de la Política de Desarrollo Social (National Council for the Evaluation of Social Development Policy) (Mexico)
DANE	Departamento Administrativo Nacional de Estadística (National Administrative Department of Statistics) (Colombia)
ENIGH	Encuesta Nacional de Ingresos y Gastos de los Hogares (Household Income and Expenditure Survey) (Mexico)
FONDEN	Fondo de Desastres Naturales (National Disaster Fund) (Mexico)
GDP	gross domestic product
HOI	human opportunity index
IDP	internally displaced person
INDEC	Instituto Nacional de Estadística y Censos (National Institute of Statistics and Censuses) (Argentina)
INEGI	Instituto Nacional de Estadística y Geografía (National Institute of Statistics and Geography) (Mexico)
IPEA	Institute for Applied Economic Research (Brazil)
IPS-8	Índice de Privación Social (recortado) (adjusted social deprivation index) (Mexico)
MCS-ENIGH	Modulo de Condiciones Socioeconomicas (Socioeconomic Conditions Module of ENIGH) (Mexico)

MESEP	Misión de Empalme de las Cifras de Pobreza y Mercado Laboral (Colombia)
MPI	multidimensional poverty index
OECD	Organisation for Economic Co-operation and Development
PANES	Plan de Atención Nacional a la Emergencia Social (Uruguay)
PISA	Program for International Student Assessment (OECD)
PPP	purchasing power parity
SEDLAC	Socio-Economic Database for Latin America and the Caribbean
SPI	shared prosperity indicator

Note: All dollar amounts are U.S. dollars ($) unless otherwise indicated.

CHAPTER 1

Overview

Louise Cord, María Eugenia Genoni,
and Carlos Rodríguez-Castelán

Introduction

In 2013, the World Bank adopted two overarching goals to guide its work: (1) to end extreme poverty or to reduce the share of people living in extreme poverty to 3 percent of the global population by 2030 and (2) to promote shared prosperity in every country through a sustainable increase in the well-being of the poorer segments of society, roughly defined as the lowest 40 percent of the income distribution (the bottom 40).[1] The adoption of these complementary objectives is helping to renew the focus of the global development community on the welfare of those at the bottom of the income distribution. Moreover, these goals provide a line of sight that development agencies and countries may use to prioritize actions and funds.

Over the last decade, the Latin America and Caribbean region achieved important progress toward the twin goals by cutting extreme poverty in half and realizing the highest income growth rate among the bottom 40 across all regions of the world in absolute terms and relative to total population. These gains have transformed the configuration of the socioeconomic groups in the region. In 2012, more than one-third of the bottom 40 in the region was comprised of vulnerable households (those that have moved out of poverty, but do not have enough income to be considered part of the middle class); this compares with 2003, when the bottom 40 was exclusively comprised of households living in poverty. The inclusive nature of the growth process in the region has also been evident in the decline in the region's notoriously high levels of inequality, which dropped from a Gini coefficient of 0.56 in 2003 to 0.52 in 2012. Some projections estimate the share of households that will be living in extreme poverty ($1.25 a day) in the region in 2030 at 3.1 percent, down from 4.6 percent in 2011, and thus reaching the World Bank's goal of 3 percent by 2030 (World Bank 2015b).[2]

Despite this impressive performance, social progress has not been uniform over this period, and certain countries, subregions, and even groups have participated less in the growth process, thereby constraining opportunities for poverty reduction and shared prosperity in countries and the region. More than 75 million people are still living in extreme poverty in the region, half of them in Brazil and Mexico, and extreme poverty rates (using the $2.50-a-day per capita line) are above 40 percent in Guatemala and reach nearly 60 percent in Haiti.[3] This means that extreme poverty is still an important issue in both low- and middle-income countries in the region. The recent slowdown in economic activity and the decline in the pace of inequality reduction pose additional barriers to rapid progress toward the institutional goals (Cord et al. 2014; de la Torre et al. 2014).[4] According to a recent study by Narayan, Saavedra-Chanduvi, and Tiwari (2013), the shared prosperity indicator (SPI) is highly correlated with growth in average incomes, but, if inequality is high, mean income growth will not accrue proportionally to the bottom segment of the distribution.

The purpose of this overview is to assess the performance of the region in reducing poverty and boosting shared prosperity during the last decade, while using a simple asset-based framework to highlight some of the key elements affecting the capacity of less well-off households to generate income. The descriptions presented in this chapter set the stage for the eight country studies that follow and that assess the heterogeneous advances toward the goals and identify some of the key policy variables that have affected the outcomes within the countries.

The first part of this chapter provides a baseline analysis of the region in terms of the institutional goals, while emphasizing the diversity of outcomes. This analysis takes advantage of comprehensive harmonized household survey data from the Socio-Economic Database for Latin America and the Caribbean (SEDLAC) database; such data are key for cross-country comparability.[5] These data cover 17 countries in Latin America and the Caribbean and account for about 90 percent of the population in the region.[6]

The second part of the chapter illustrates an asset-based framework. The framework identifies the main elements that contribute to household income generation and that can be intuitively related to poverty reduction and shared prosperity. The simple framework depicts the realization of household market income as a function of four major components: (1) the capacity of households to generate income based on the productive assets they own, (2) the private transfers—the monetary value of domestic and international private contributions—they receive and the public transfers that are incorporated as a policy variable, (3) the set of prices of the basket of goods and services that the households consume, and (4) the external shocks that generate variability in the incomes. The capacity of households to generate income based on the productive assets they own can be further disaggregated into the interaction between the role of assets (human capital, housing, and capital and land), the intensity of asset use (participation in labor and financial markets, agency), and the returns to assets (labor demand factors, including uneven returns by race, gender, and location).

This asset-based approach integrates macroeconomic and microeconomic dimensions so that growth and the incidence of growth can be understood as mutually determined processes. The framework considers the distribution of assets as a given in the short run; thus, changes in the income generation capacity of households depend mostly on macroeconomic variables that affect the demand for labor across sectors, relative prices (returns and consumer prices), and the intensity of the use of assets over the economic cycle. In the long run, the main drivers of income growth will be the level and distribution of assets—human, physical, financial, social, and natural capital—that people own and accumulate, as well as the intensity with which they are used and the associated returns, which will reflect asset productivity.

The third part of the chapter relies on the asset-based framework to characterize the bottom 40 in terms of their capacity to generate income relative to the top 60 percent of the distribution (the top 60). The analysis focuses mainly on describing the capacity of households to generate labor income given the importance of this source of income in total income and as a driver of trends in poverty and shared prosperity in the past decade. Exploring the asset composition of households can provide information important to understanding the factors that contribute to boosting the capacity of individuals to generate income, climb out of poverty, and avoid the risk of downward mobility.

Finally, the chapter links the twin goals to four fundamental policy areas that have a direct impact on the capacity of households to generate income, but with a particular focus on those households that are poor and that belong to the bottom 40. These four broad policy areas, which have also been defined in previous studies (World Bank 2013a, 2014a), are (1) equitable, efficient, and sustainable fiscal policy and macroeconomic stability (direct and indirect taxes and transfers, inflation targets); (2) fair and transparent institutions capable of delivering universal, good-quality basic services (a greater and better supply of public goods, protection of property rights); (3) well-functioning markets (improved connectivity to markets, competition policy); and (4) adequate risk management at the macro and household levels (macroprudence, safety nets). The country study cases presented in the rest of this volume organize the discussion around these four policy areas in a way that is relevant for poverty reduction and the promotion of shared prosperity.

Transformational Change in Living Standards in the Region

Recent trends in poverty reduction and shared prosperity

Poverty reduction

Over the past decade, the Latin America and Caribbean region experienced remarkable reductions in extreme poverty.[7] According to extreme poverty

Table 1.1 Extreme Poverty Rates, Developing Regions, 2002 and 2011

Region	Extreme poverty rate, $1.25 a day			Extreme poverty rate, $2.50 a day		
	2002	2011	Change, %	2002	2011	Change, %
Sub-Saharan Africa	57.1	46.8	18.0	84.2	78.0	7.4
South Asia	44.1	24.5	44.4	86.7	74.5	14.0
East Asia and the Pacific	27.3	7.9	71.0	62.4	31.9	48.8
Latin America and the Caribbean	10.2	4.6	54.7	27.1	13.3	51.0
Middle East and North Africa	3.8	1.7	55.9	31.9	22.1	30.7
Europe and Central Asia	2.1	0.5	77.0	11.6	3.8	67.2

Source: World Bank calculations using PovcalNet (online analysis tool), World Bank, Washington, DC, http://iresearch.worldbank.org/PovcalNet/.
Note: The poverty data on Latin America and the Caribbean differ slightly from the data in the SEDLAC database because of variations in the methodology used to calculate poverty rates.

measures using an income-based aggregate and an international poverty line of $1.25 a day in 2005 prices, the extreme poverty rate fell from 10.2 to 4.6 percent between 2002 and 2011. Based on a higher international poverty line of $2.50 a day calculated from an average of national poverty lines in the region to identify the extreme poor, the headcount fell by half, from 27.1 to 13.3 percent over the same period (table 1.1).

Compared with other developing regions, Latin America and the Caribbean also performed well in reducing extreme poverty over the last decade. Based on a $1.25-a-day poverty line, the region's extreme poverty reduction of about 55 percent surpassed South Asia and Sub-Saharan Africa, but lagged Europe and Central Asia and East Asia and the Pacific. Based on the $2.50-a-day poverty line, the region's extreme poverty reduction of 51 percent exceeded the declines observed in all other regions except Europe and Central Asia, which cut this rate by 67 percent.[8]

The improvements in living conditions in Latin America and the Caribbean dramatically shifted the socioeconomic composition of the population. In 2012, more Latin Americans were living in the middle class than in total poverty, 34.4 versus 21.2 percent in 2003 (figure 1.1, panel a). Moreover, whereas in 2003, 6 in 10 people in the bottom 40 were among the extreme poor, by 2012, only 3 in 10 were in this condition. In 2012, the vulnerable (people earning between $4 and $10 a day) made up a third of the bottom 40 in the region (figure 1.1, panel b).[9]

Shared prosperity

The reduction in poverty rates and the significant expansion in the middle class observed in Latin America and the Caribbean has been accompanied by strong growth in the incomes of the bottom 40. Between 2003 and 2012, the average income of the bottom 40 in the region increased by 5 percent a year, from $2.10 a day per capita in 2005 prices to $3.30 a day. This growth rate was greater than the corresponding rate observed for the whole population, which was 3.3 percent a year (from $8.80 a day per capita to

Figure 1.1 Socioeconomic Composition of the Population, Latin America and the Caribbean, 2003 and 2012

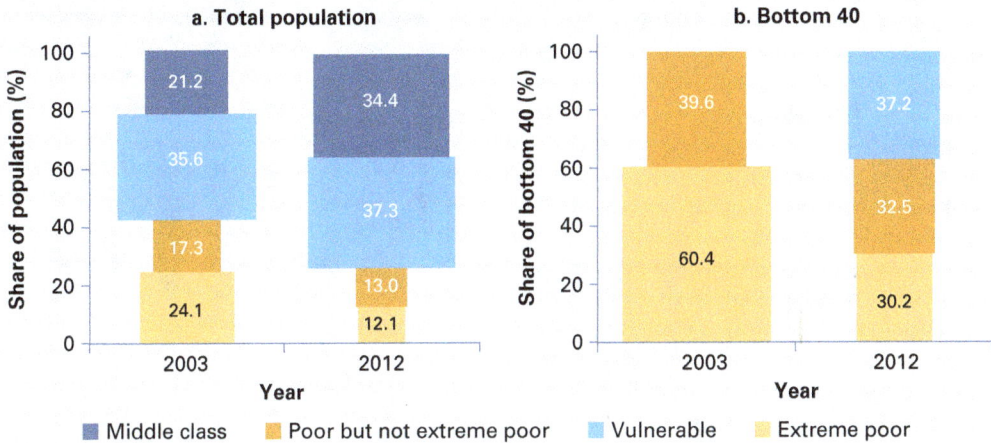

a. Total population

b. Bottom 40

Middle class   Poor but not extreme poor   Vulnerable   Extreme poor

Source: Calculations based on data in the SEDLAC database.
Note: The estimates of poverty, vulnerability, and the middle class are population-weighted averages of country estimates. The extreme poor are people living on less than $2.50 a day; the poor but not extreme poor are those living on $2.50 to $4.00 a day; the vulnerable are those living on $4.00 to $10.00 a day; and the middle class are those living on $10.00 to $50.00 a day (all in 2005 purchasing power parity [PPP] international U.S. dollars).

$11.70). The region's performance in shared prosperity was also positive compared with that of other regions. Between 2006 and 2011, the average growth rate per year in the mean income of the bottom 40 across countries in the region was approximately 5.2 percent. This was the highest rate in all regions (figure 1.2, panel a). Moreover, the region's bottom 40 enjoyed the most rapid income growth relative to the total population; thus, based on these indicators, Latin America and the Caribbean has been the most inclusive region in the world over the last decade (figure 1.2, panel b).

Demographic changes and the composition of the bottom 40

Over the last decade, the observed progress in poverty reduction and shared prosperity has been accompanied by a transformational change in the basic demographic characteristics of households in the region (table 1.2). Households in Latin America have become smaller and more likely to be headed by older, more well educated, and women household members. These trends are similar among households in the bottom 40 and households in the top 60. Despite the similar trends, households in the bottom 40 are significantly different from those in the top 60, and the gaps have not changed substantially. Households in the bottom 40 are younger, larger, and more likely to be headed by women and less well-educated individuals. For instance, the education gap of household heads was approximately three years between the two groups in 2012. Moreover, 2 in 3 households in the bottom 40 resided in urban areas, compared with 9 in 10 among the top 60.

Figure 1.2 Shared Prosperity: Annualized Income Growth, Developing Regions, around 2006–11

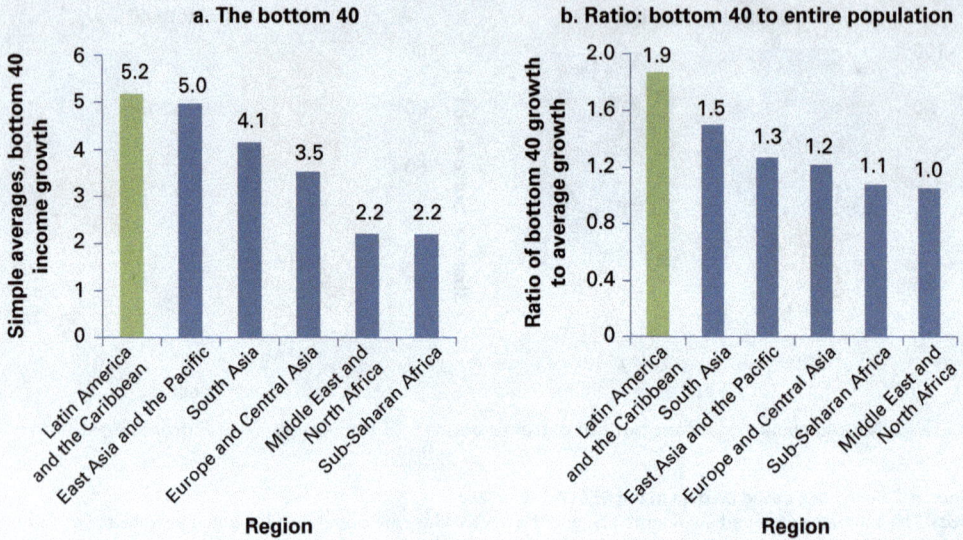

a. The bottom 40

b. Ratio: bottom 40 to entire population

Source: GDSP (Global Database of Shared Prosperity), World Bank, Washington, DC, http://www.worldbank.org /en/topic/poverty/brief/global-database-of-shared-prosperity.
Note: The data are simple averages across countries in the regions calculated using household surveys. They may not be strictly comparable because some regions use expenditure survey data, while Latin America and the Caribbean uses income data.

Table 1.2 Bottom 40 and Top 60: Household Characteristics, Latin America and the Caribbean, 2003 and 2012

Indicator	Bottom 40		Top 60	
	2003	2012	2003	2012
Average age, household head, years	43.3	45.3	48.2	50.0
Woman-headed households, %	28.1	36.3	27.4	34.7
Average education, household head, years	4.7	5.8	8.0	8.9
Average household size, number	4.4	4.1	3.4	3.0
Urban households, % of total	66.6	66.2	86.3	87.5

Source: Calculations based on data in SEDLAC.
Note: The data represent population-weighted averages across countries in the region.

Transformational change reflects strong growth and significant redistribution

Strong growth and a significant narrowing in the region's high level of income inequality drove the gains in poverty reduction and shared prosperity between 2003 and 2012. The combination of prudent macrofiscal economic policies, global liquidity, and positive terms of trade because of

Figure 1.3 Average GDP Growth Rates, Latin America and the Caribbean, 1990–2013

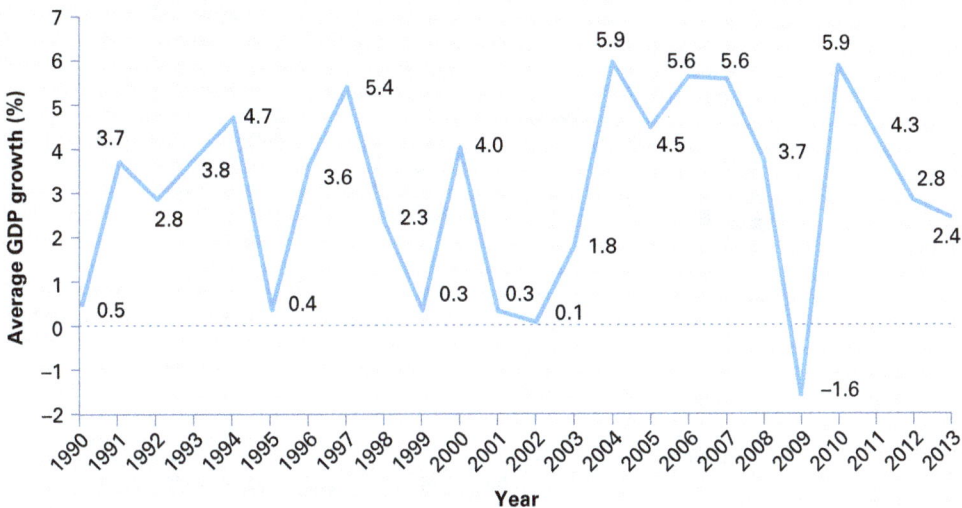

Source: WDI (World Development Indicators) (database), World Bank, Washington, DC, http://data.worldbank
.org/data-catalog/world-development-indicators.
Note: The regional average is the regional aggregate of the countries in the region, excluding high-income
countries.

the commodity boom helped foster a decade of strong growth in the region, which was largely able to weather well the financial crisis. In particular, during the past decade, real incomes rose by more than 25 percent across the region; annual gross domestic product (GDP) increased at an average of 3.2 percent. Moreover, growth proved resilient across the region: many countries maintained positive growth rates throughout the global financial crisis of 2008.[10] However, while GDP growth was an important driver of poverty reduction and shared prosperity, it did not seem to be the only force behind the progress. In fact, while the region's GDP growth during the 2000s was high, the region did not grow much more quickly relative to the previous decade (figure 1.3). GDP growth was 3.1 percent during the 1990s, compared with 3.2 percent during the 2000s.[11] Despite similar growth rates, the region's performance in poverty reduction was different in the 1990s and 2000s. While poverty fell less than 1 percent a year during the 1990s, poverty rates decreased at a much higher rate in the 2000s, approximately 6 percent a year.[12] The different poverty gains across two decades with similar levels of growth highlight the importance of the nature of growth and the redistributive policies applied.

An important difference between the 1990s and the 2000s was the region's progress in narrowing household income inequality. While the Gini coefficient barely changed during the 1990s, it fell from 0.56 to 0.52 between 2003 and 2012 (figure 1.4). This trend was widespread: income inequality declined in all 17 countries for which frequent household survey

Figure 1.4 Trends in the Gini Coefficient, Latin America and the Caribbean, 2003–12

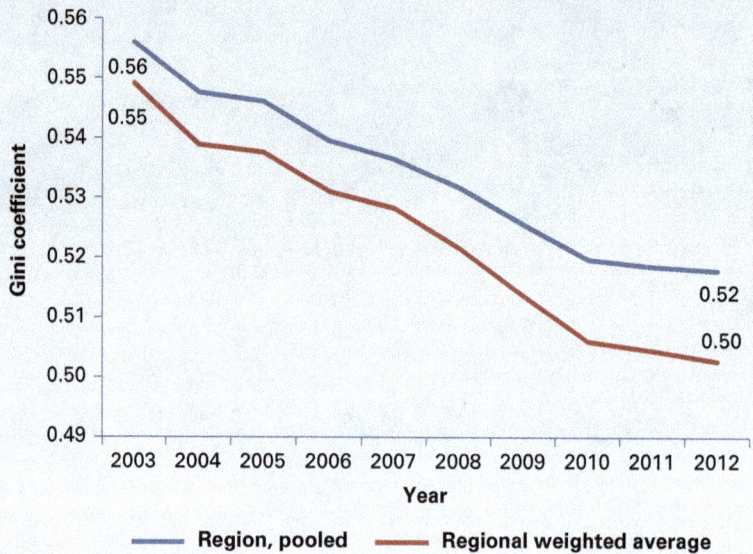

Source: Cord et al. 2014.
Note: Because the Gini coefficient does not satisfy group decomposability, the regional Gini coefficient is computed based on pooled country-specific data for 17 countries. To test the robustness of the results, the unweighted average is also presented.

data are available.[13] Even though this decline likely reflects a combination of pro-poor social policies and growth, there is still debate about the specific drivers behind it. Recent evidence highlights the change in the distribution of labor income as the main factor behind the progress, followed by the expansion of government transfers and, for the countries in the Southern Cone, the broadening of pension coverage (Cord et al. 2014; López-Calva and Lustig 2010; Lustig, López-Calva, and Ortiz-Juárez 2013). The decline in labor income inequality is largely explained by a fall in the skill premium, that is, a reduction in the wage differential between more highly educated workers relative to less highly educated workers. This reduction seems to reflect a combination of lower excess demand for skilled labor and improved access to education that increased the supply of skilled workers (Gasparini et al. 2011). In particular, the expansion of education coverage over the period implied a rise in the share of new students at lower socio-economic status, which may have reduced the average quality of education. A deterioration at the margin of the quality of educational institutions may have also accompanied this trend (de la Torre et al. 2014). One potential demand-side explanation of the observed narrowing in wage inequality is the effect of the commodity boom, which promoted growth in the nontradable sectors and, in this way, raised the demand for unskilled workers relative to skilled workers.

In sum, during the past decade, both growth and redistribution contributed toward the progress achieved in eradicating extreme poverty and promoting shared prosperity. Two-thirds of the observed decline in extreme poverty in the region between 2003 and 2012 can be explained by economic growth, while the rest is explained by changes in income distribution (World Bank 2014a).

Progress was heterogeneous across countries

While the region's progress on the twin goals was substantial during the period, the averages mask significant heterogeneity across and within countries. While certain countries took advantage of a decade of high growth rates to drive steep declines in poverty and boost shared prosperity, such as Bolivia, Brazil, and Peru, others grappled with lackluster growth, such as Guatemala and Mexico. Other countries achieved substantial growth, but struggled to convert the gains into better livelihoods among the poorest. One clear example is the Dominican Republic, where GDP per capita grew by 53 percent from 2000 to 2012, while extreme poverty remained stagnant (box 1.1).

The region still presented wide disparities in extreme poverty rates. In 2012, about 4 in 10 people in Guatemala and Honduras were living in extreme poverty. In contrast, 3 in 100 people were among the extreme poor in Chile and Uruguay (figure 1.5). Nonetheless, there is evidence of a regional convergence in poverty rates: countries with high poverty rates at the beginning of the decade experienced large reductions thereafter. Some of the top performers were the Andean countries and Brazil. Notable exceptions were Guatemala and Honduras, which both had high initial extreme poverty rates; Guatemala even saw a subsequent rise in extreme poverty.

In addition, even among the strong performers, there were significant geographical disparities, including pockets of high and persistent poverty. For instance, Peru, one of the best performers on the twin goals in the region, presented strong disparities in poverty across its 1,800 districts. In 2007, almost half the extreme poor were concentrated in approximately 11 percent of the districts (map 1.1, panel a), while these same 11 percent of districts accounted for a third of the total population. In addition, in 2013, the rural areas of Peru contained 33 percent of the country's population, but accounted for half of the poor and 80 percent of the extreme poor. Meanwhile, in Bolivia between 2001 and 2011, approximately half the municipalities reduced extreme poverty substantially. However, some areas were still lagging in 2011, particularly small rural municipalities where the poverty rates had been higher at the beginning of the decade. In 2011, nearly a third of Bolivia's municipalities still showed an incidence of extreme poverty greater than 50 percent (map 1.1, panel b). In the case of Colombia, historically large disparities between urban and rural areas persist, and the rate of income convergence across the country's *departamentos* has been limited over the past decade. According to official data, the difference between the departamento with the highest poverty rate and the departamento with the

Box 1.1 Poverty Trends in the Caribbean

Even though the improvement in economic conditions was significant throughout Latin America, progress was sluggish and limited in the Caribbean. Extreme poverty rates in the Dominican Republic have remained stagnant despite the strong economic growth over the past decade (World Bank 2014b). Between 2000 and 2012, the extreme poverty headcount ($2.50 a day) fell less than 1 percentage point (from 15.7 to 14.6 percent) below the regional average. In Jamaica, poverty rates based on official figures reached 17.6 percent in 2010, compared with 12.3 percent in 2008. The country was negatively affected by the global crisis, as well as rising food and energy prices, and this hindered poverty reduction (World Bank 2014c).

Similarly, while extreme poverty in Haiti—based on a consumption aggregate and a national poverty line of $1.23 a day—dropped from 31 to 24 percent between 2001 and 2012, the gains appear to have been linked to the greater aid flows, particularly into urban areas, and higher remittances, which soared after the earthquake (World Bank and ONPES 2014). In addition, the moderate poverty rate remains high (58.5 percent in 2012).

The lack of official poverty and inequality data in the eastern Caribbean makes it challenging to evaluate trends in poverty there. Nonetheless, the patterns of asset ownership and the high rates of unemployment and underemployment suggest that social disparities have been exacerbated by the 2008 financial crisis (World Bank, forthcoming). The evidence from household survey data suggests that the financial crisis had significant negative and long-lasting impacts on household welfare in St. Lucia. While the unemployment rate was around 16.9 percent among all welfare quintiles from early 2008 through late 2009 (according to an asset-based welfare measure), the unemployment rate among the bottom 40 (29 percent) was nearly double the rate among the two highest quintiles (15.7 percent) from 2011 to 2013.

Prior to the crisis, the characteristics of the bottom 40 and the top 60 were relatively similar in St Lucia, while, since the crisis, there has been a widening gap between the two groups. For example, in 2008, although they were more likely to be self-employed and less likely to be working in the professional services sector, the bottom 40 were virtually indistinguishable from the top 60. By 2013, however, the bottom 40 were significantly more likely to be unemployed (by 11 percentage points), significantly less likely to be an employee or an employer, had significantly less educational attainment, showed a higher probability of residing in urban areas, typically had smaller households, and were more likely to be living in woman-headed households. By 2013, relative to the top 60, they were twice as likely to be working in the agricultural sector, were more likely to be working in construction or manufacturing, and were significantly less likely to be working in education, health care, or social or professional services.

These outcomes are not surprising given that the economies in the Caribbean greatly depend on industries such as tourism, agriculture, and financial services that rely heavily on the external demand of the developed economies where the crisis originated. In addition, most Caribbean countries suffer from substantial national debt and lack a stable financial sector to channel financial resources efficiently. These challenges make especially difficult the establishment of the social protection mechanisms necessary to shield the vulnerable from the relatively large shocks faced by the region.

lowest rate was 38 percentage points in 2002, whereas, in 2014, the difference was 53 percentage points. (See the country chapters.)

Levels of development differ across Latin America, which implies that levels of income and other characteristics of the bottom 40 in each country may also differ, especially because participation in this population segment is measured in relative terms. In some countries, there is a large overlap

Figure 1.5 Extreme Poverty Rates, Latin America and the Caribbean, 2003–12

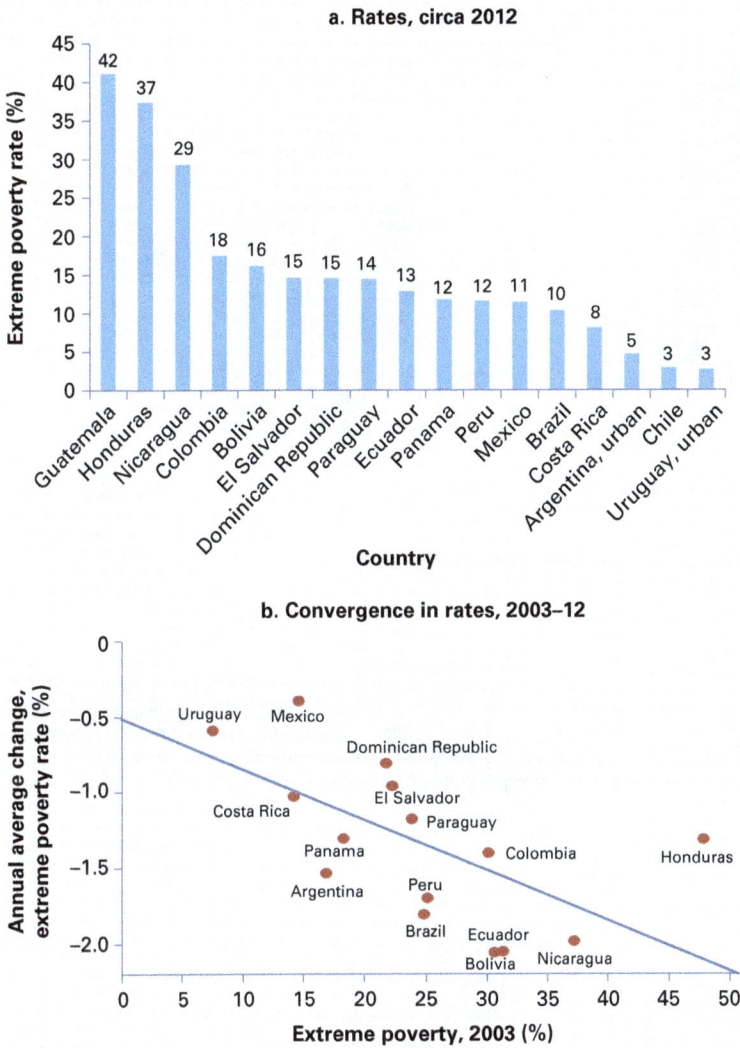

a. Rates, circa 2012

b. Convergence in rates, 2003–12

Source: Calculations based on data in SEDLAC.
Note: The extreme poverty rate is calculated using a $2.50-a-day poverty line. Panel b excludes Guatemala, which is the only country in the region in which extreme poverty grew over the period.

between the bottom 40 and the extreme poor (for example, Guatemala, Honduras, and Nicaragua), while, in other countries, the bottom 40 is mainly comprised of people living above the poverty line (such as Chile and Uruguay). The heterogeneous progress over the past decade in shared prosperity can also be illustrated through changes in the composition of the bottom 40. For instance, while 8 in 10 people in the bottom 40 in

Map 1.1 Heterogeneity in Living Standards, Bolivia and Peru, 2007 and 2011

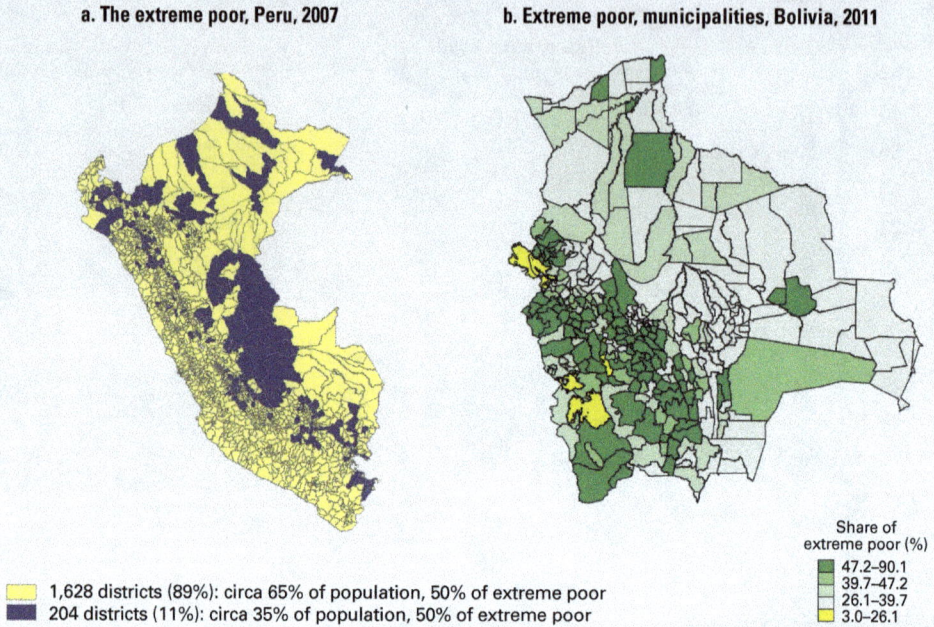

a. The extreme poor, Peru, 2007

b. Extreme poor, municipalities, Bolivia, 2011

Share of
extreme poor (%)
- 47.2–90.1
- 39.7–47.2
- 26.1–39.7
- 3.0–26.1

☐ 1,628 districts (89%): circa 65% of population, 50% of extreme poor
■ 204 districts (11%): circa 35% of population, 50% of extreme poor

Source: Calculations using monetary poverty maps of Bolivia and Peru.
Note: District poverty maps in Peru are based on consumption using data from the 2007 National Household
Survey and the 6th National Housing Census and 11th Population Census (both 2007). The municipal poverty
map of Bolivia is estimated based on income using data from the 2011 Household Survey and the 2012 National
Census of Housing and Population. The computation of poverty rates follows the official poverty methodologies
of the countries. Both maps have been estimated using the Elbers, Lanjouw, and Lanjouw (2003) small area
methodology.

Ecuador were among the extreme poor in 2003, only 3 in 10 were in this
condition in 2012. In contrast, in several Central American countries, such
as Guatemala, Honduras, and Nicaragua, an overwhelming proportion of
the bottom 40 continued to be composed of the extreme poor, with little
change (figure 1.6).

While the average income of the bottom 40 grew approximately 5 percent a year across the region between 2003 and 2012, the heterogeneity
was significant in shared prosperity by country. The strongest performers,
Argentina, Bolivia, Brazil, and Panama, with income growth rates among
the bottom 40 well over 7 percent, far outpaced the weakest performers,
Guatemala and Mexico, with growth rates among the bottom 40 of –1.0
and 1.3 percent, respectively. Guatemala was the only country in the region
in which the incomes of the bottom 40 declined over the decade (figure 1.7).

For most countries in the region, income growth among the bottom
40 outpaced the average growth among the population over the decade (figure 1.8). However, the size of the gap also varied. In some countries, such as
Argentina, Bolivia, and Nicaragua, the growth rate was significantly higher

Figure 1.6 Composition of the Bottom 40, Latin America and the Caribbean, 2003 and 2012

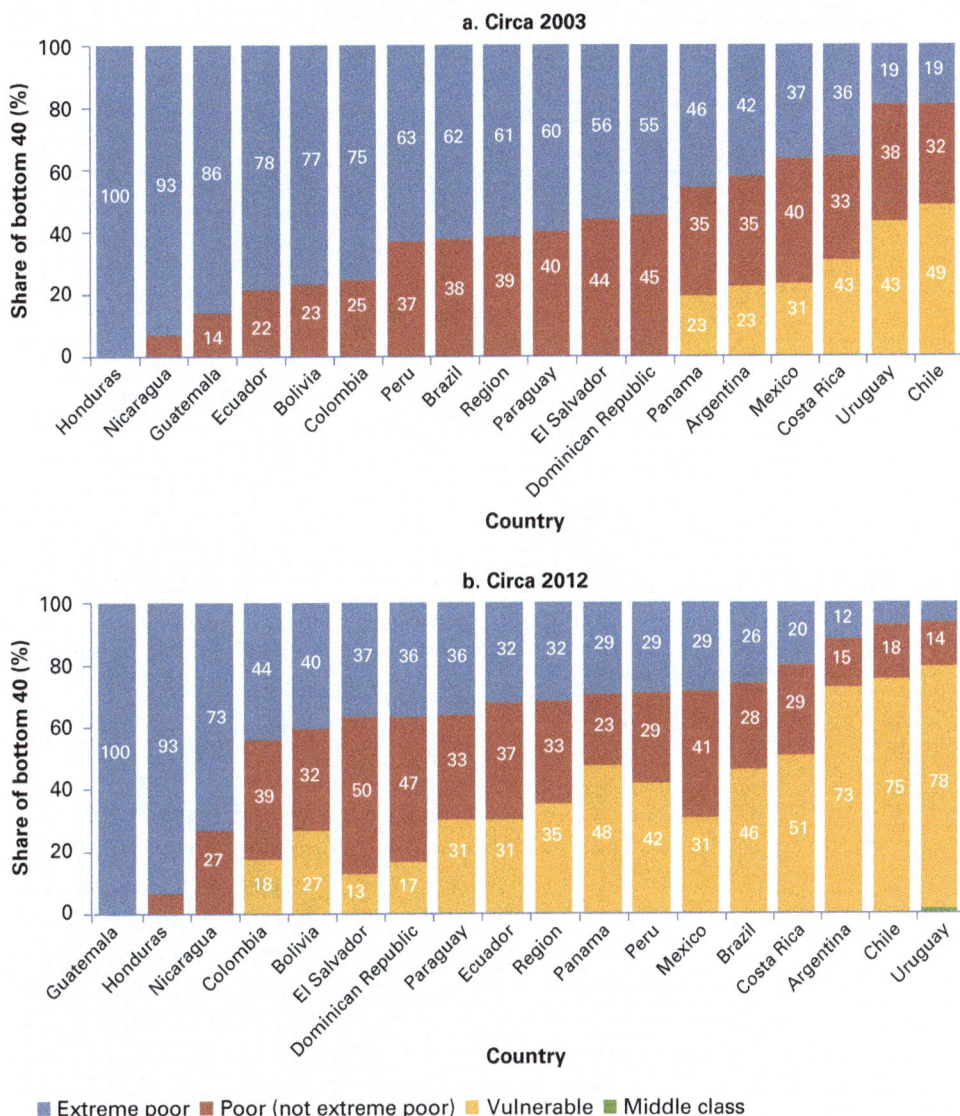

a. Circa 2003

y-axis: Share of bottom 40 (%)

Country	Extreme poor	Poor (not extreme poor)	Vulnerable
Honduras	100		
Nicaragua	93		
Guatemala	86	14	
Ecuador	78	22	
Bolivia	77	23	
Colombia	75	25	
Peru	63	37	
Brazil	62	38	
Region	61	39	
Paraguay	60	40	
El Salvador	56	44	
Dominican Republic	55	45	
Panama	46	35	23
Argentina	42	35	23
Mexico	37	40	31
Costa Rica	36	33	43
Uruguay	19	38	43
Chile	19	32	49

x-axis: Country

b. Circa 2012

y-axis: Share of bottom 40 (%)

Country	Extreme poor	Poor (not extreme poor)	Vulnerable
Guatemala	100		
Honduras	93		
Nicaragua	73	27	
Colombia	44	39	18
Bolivia	40	32	27
El Salvador	37	50	13
Dominican Republic	36	47	17
Paraguay	36	33	31
Ecuador	32	37	31
Region	32	33	35
Panama	29	23	48
Peru	29	29	42
Mexico	29	41	31
Brazil	26	28	46
Costa Rica	20	29	51
Argentina	12	15	73
Chile	18		75
Uruguay	14		78

x-axis: Country

■ Extreme poor ■ Poor (not extreme poor) ■ Vulnerable ■ Middle class

Source: Calculations based on data in SEDLAC.
Note: Estimates of poverty, vulnerability, and the middle class in the region are population-weighted averages of country estimates. The poor are defined as people living on less than $4 a day; the vulnerable are those living on $4–$10 a day; and the middle class are those living on $10–$50 a day (all in 2005 PPP international U.S. dollars).

among the bottom 40, while, in Costa Rica, Guatemala, and Mexico, the rates were almost the same. Colombia was the only country in the set that was analyzed in which average income growth among the bottom 40 did not surpass the income growth of the total population.

Figure 1.7 Income Growth among the Bottom 40, Latin America and the Caribbean, around 2003–12

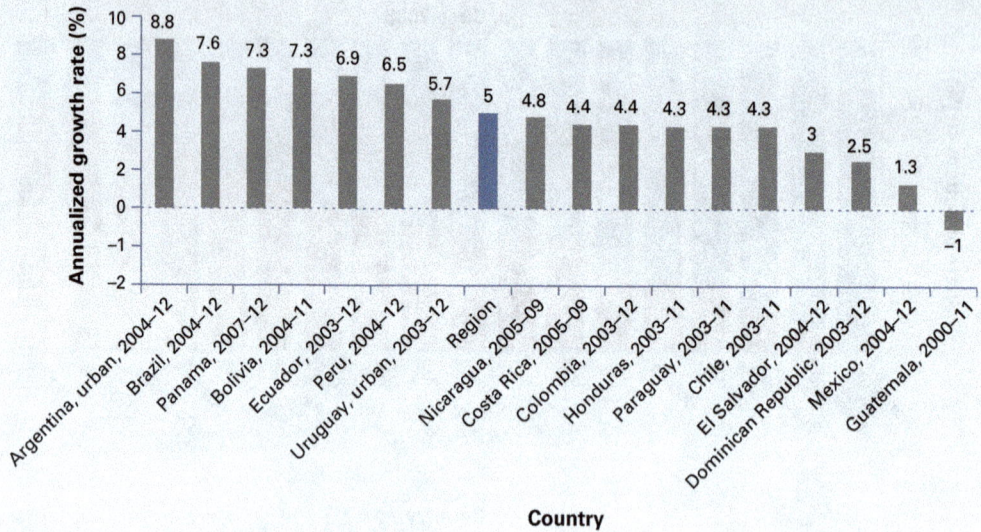

Source: Calculations based on data in SEDLAC.
Note: Annualized growth rate of the income of the bottom 40. The numbers for the region are calculated using pooled data of countries. To analyze the same set of countries every year, interpolation has been applied if country data were not available for a given year.

Even though there was a positive correlation between total income growth and income growth among the bottom 40 during the last decade, the relationship was not perfect. Some countries, such as Chile, Colombia, Costa Rica, Honduras, and Paraguay, had similar growth rates in the average income among the bottom 40, but different overall income growth rates. Other countries, such as Argentina, Brazil, and Colombia, experienced similar total income growth rates, but performed differently in the mean income of the bottom 40. This heterogeneity indicates that the outcomes in shared prosperity were dependent not only on growth, but also on the sources of growth and specific policies and redistribution efforts.

Similarly, the responsiveness of poverty to growth was heterogeneous in the region. For instance, Mexico showed low GDP growth over the period (about 0.7 percent a year), but poverty levels were responsive to this growth (about 2 percent of poverty reduction for each 1 percent in GDP growth). In contrast, the Dominican Republic experienced high GDP growth, but this did not translate into a commensurate reduction in poverty (about 0.2 percent of poverty reduction for each 1 percent in GDP growth).

There was also significant variation across countries in the relative importance of redistribution and growth for poverty reduction. Thus, in Colombia, poverty reduction was only driven by growth, while in other

Figure 1.8 Income Growth, Bottom 40 and the Entire Population, Latin America and the Caribbean, around 2003–12

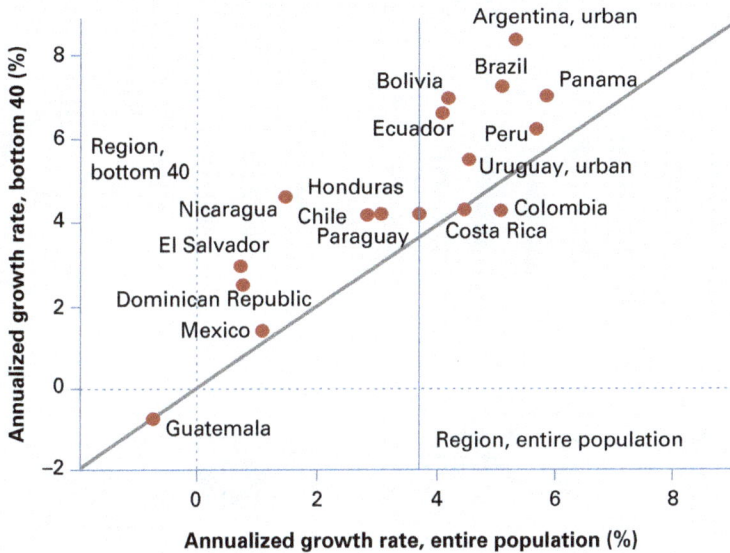

Source: Calculations based on data in SEDLAC.
Note: Blue line = the 45° line. The data on the region are calculated using the pooled data on the countries.

countries, such as the Dominican Republic, El Salvador, and Nicaragua, redistribution was almost exclusively responsible for the reductions in extreme poverty. Most countries fell somewhere in between: important components of poverty reduction were attributable to growth, but others were associated with redistributive policies such as the expansion of social safety nets (figure 1.9).

The sustainability of the social gains achieved by most countries in the region may be jeopardized by less positive prospects for economic growth and by stagnation in the pace of the reduction in income inequality. According to de la Torre et al. (2014), growth in Latin America and the Caribbean has been decelerating since 2012 relative to the significant growth rates that characterized the region during the golden precrisis years. According to the latest projections, GDP growth in the region will reach only 1.7 percent in 2015 and 2.9 percent in 2016 (World Bank 2015c). Moreover, Cord et al. (2014) find evidence of stagnation in the pace of the reduction in income inequality in Latin America since 2010 (box 1.2).

To identify opportunities to maintain the progress toward achieving the twin goals of ending extreme poverty and boosting shared prosperity, the next section presents a conceptual framework that is useful for understanding the factors that may contribute to boosting the capacity of individuals

Figure 1.9 Contributions of Growth and Redistribution to Falls in Extreme Poverty, Latin America and the Caribbean, around 2003–12

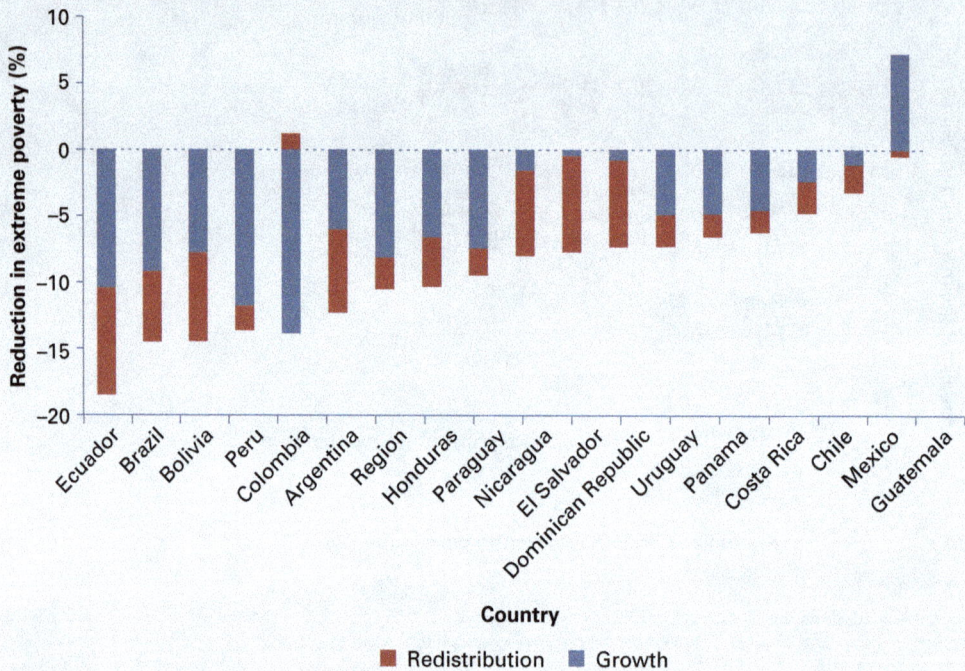

Source: Calculations based on data in SEDLAC.
Note: The figure shows a Datt-Ravallion decomposition. Changes in extreme poverty are decomposed into changes associated with economic growth (or mean income) in the absence of changes in inequality (or income distribution) and changes in inequality in the absence of growth. For more information about the method, see Datt and Ravallion (1992).

to generate income, climb out of poverty, and avoid the risk of downward mobility. The framework takes account of the concept of sustainability and the interaction of macro- and microeconomic variables in achieving and sustaining the goals socially, economically, and environmentally.

The Asset-Based Approach to Gauging Household Income

The World Bank goals of reducing extreme poverty and boosting shared prosperity have three important characteristics in common. First, both are measured using a monetary welfare indicator, such as income or consumption, as a proxy for the capability of individuals to achieve a certain standard of living.[14] The extreme poverty rate measures the share of individuals currently living below the $1.25-a-day threshold, while the shared prosperity goal aims to capture a relevant sustainable increase in income among the poorer segments of society, roughly defined as the bottom 40. Second, both

Box 1.2 Stagnation in the Contraction of Income Inequality in the Region

The within-country trends in income inequality are significantly different in Latin America and the Caribbean if one views the last decade as two periods, 2003–10 and 2010–12 (figure B1.2.1). Such a split is useful because it showcases the stagnation in the pace of the contraction in income inequality in the region after the global financial crisis of 2008 (see Cord et al. 2014). Of the 17 countries on which data are available for 2003–10, 15 exhibited a decline in the Gini coefficient; Colombia and Costa Rica were the only exceptions. Since 2010, 4 of the 15 countries on which data are available experienced a rise in the Gini coefficient (Costa Rica, Honduras, Mexico, and Peru), while Panama showed no change. The rise of the Gini coefficient in Honduras was substantial, from 0.53 to 0.57 in 2010–12. Meanwhile, the increase in the Gini from 0.48 to 0.49 in Mexico in 2010–12 explains a good part of the recent regional slowdown in the decline of income inequality.[a] At the same time, while inequality reduction continued in 10 countries after 2010, the pace of the decline weakened in Brazil, the most populous country in the region.[b]

Figure B1.2.1 Gini Coefficient: Annualized Changes, Latin America and the Caribbean, 2003–10 and 2010–12

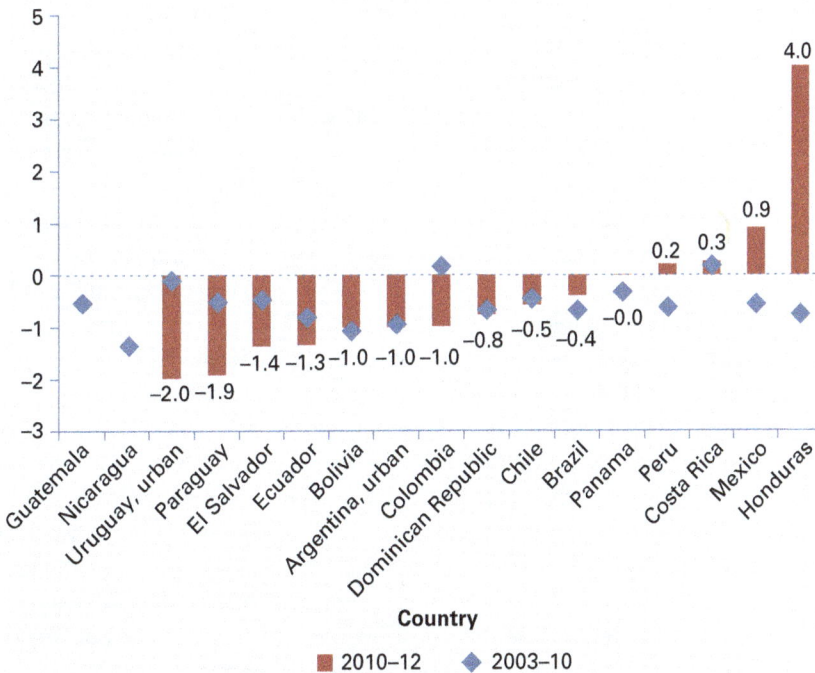

Source: Cord et al. 2014, based on data in SEDLAC.
Note: The figure shows changes in the Gini coefficient between 2003–10 and 2010–12, or the nearest years, in case data for these years are not available. Data on Guatemala and Nicaragua are available only for the first period.

Cord et al. (2014) find that the declines in inequality before 2010 were driven by labor markets in the Andean and Southern Cone subregions, including Brazil, while in parts of Central America and Mexico, the decline was mainly determined by equalizing nonlabor income sources and the impact of

(continued)

Box 1.2 Stagnation in the Contraction of Income Inequality in the Region *(Continued)*

the financial crisis, which especially affected the incomes of the top end of the distribution. They also find that the stagnation experienced since 2010 reflects, to a large extent, the subsequent recovery in Central America and Mexico. Moreover, even in countries in which income inequality continued to fall, this was mostly driven by zero or negative growth among the top of the income distribution, rather than greater growth among the poorest.

---

a. The Gini coefficients in this study are calculated using the SEDLAC database, a regional harmonization effort. The effort generates income aggregates that are comparable across countries and, as a result, often differ from official income aggregates. The trends in Mexico's Gini coefficient are comparable with the trends in the Gini calculated by Mexico's National Institute of Statistics and Geography (INEGI) using the traditional Household Income and Expenditure Survey (ENIGH). The latter Gini increased from 0.435 to 0.440 between 2010 and 2012, while the Gini calculated by Mexico's National Council for the Evaluation of Social Development Policy (relying on the socioeconomic conditions module of the household survey) fell from 0.509 to 0.498.
b. Brazil is home to 37 percent of the total population of the 17 countries under analysis.

focus on the welfare of those at the bottom of the income (or consumption) distribution; the poverty rate is an absolute measure, while shared prosperity is a relative concept. Third, both track economic progress by focusing on trends in household welfare.

Based on these three shared characteristics of the twin goals, this section presents a simple asset-based approach as a macro-micro framework to guide the discussion in the following section, which describes key aspects of the capacity of households in the bottom 40 in Latin America and the Caribbean to generate income compared with the top 60 in the region. The framework is an extension of a model presented by Attanasio and Székely (2001) and Bussolo and López-Calva (2014) and that aims to unpack the elements of the market incomes of households to shed light on the potential determinants of outcomes in poverty and shared prosperity.[15]

In the framework, the realization of household market income is a function of four main components: (1) the capacity of households to generate income based on the assets they own; (2) the private transfers households receive, which may include domestic and international remittances and in-kind transfers from other households; (3) the set of prices of the basket of goods and services that the households consume; and (4) a positive probability of being affected by the realization of (negative or positive) shocks (health, natural disasters, crime, and loss of employment) (figure 1.10).[16]

The capacity of households to generate income based on the assets they own can be disaggregated into three additional elements: (1) the stock of income-earning assets owned by each household member, which may include human capital (such as educational attainment and years of experience in the labor market), financial and physical assets (such as ownership of machinery or financial assets such as stocks and bonds), social capital (such as the set of norms and social networks that facilitate collective action; see Putnam 1993), and natural capital (such as land, soil, forests, and water); (2) the rate at which these assets are utilized by each household member to produce income (this may include labor market participation, the use of

Figure 1.10 The Asset-Based Approach to the Generation of Household Market Income

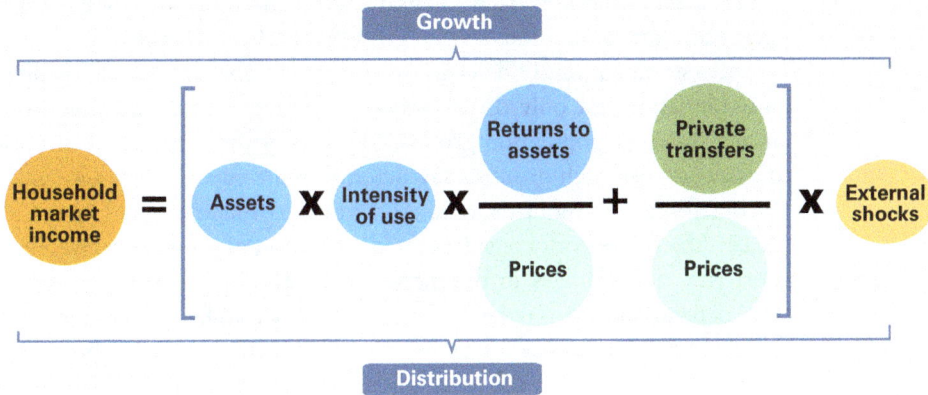

machinery, and the exploitation of land through agricultural production); and (3) the returns to assets (such as the price of factors of production, including wages and interest rates).

For ease of illustration, the elements of the asset-based framework are sometimes presented somewhat independently of each other. However, the elements do interact with each other as part of the dynamics of household income generation. For instance, nominal wages and the number of hours of work are important in decisions to participate in the labor market, and consumer prices may impact income earnings through the returns to the assets of producer households (Bussolo and López-Calva 2014; López-Calva and Rodríguez-Castelán 2014). Moreover, in the framework, both the observed accumulation of income-earning assets and the observed rate at which these assets are used by individuals are assumed to incorporate the desire of individuals to realize their aspirations, one of the manifestations of agency. Some examples of how a lack of aspirations may prevent households from accumulating assets and participating in productive activities include suboptimal investment in human capital and production technologies or the abandonment of the search for employment in formal sector firms.[17]

Furthermore, actual household market income may differ from potential household market income because of shocks that may affect private transfers and the income from the use of assets. There are multiple external risks, including macroeconomic crisis, extreme climate-related events, health-related shocks, and crime and violence, that individuals and societies face and that can have pernicious consequences for the income generating capacity of households (World Bank 2013b). Risks turned into negative shocks could potentially lead to asset loss, disinvestment, unemployment, malnutrition, and child labor if people lack the means to manage and cope with them. A large body of empirical evidence shows that the poor are often more vulnerable to the negative consequences of shocks. Thus, in the framework, the probability of being affected by external shocks is expected to be greater among low-income households.

The asset-based approach integrates both the macroeconomic and the microeconomic dimensions so that growth and the incidence of growth can be understood as jointly determined processes. The framework facilitates an explanation not only of the ways macrofactors affect income growth among different population groups, but also of the ways the distribution of assets across such groups may determine the capacity of these groups to contribute to overall growth. According to Bussolo and López-Calva (2014), the framework considers the distribution of assets as a given in the short run, and changes in the income generating capacity of households thus depend mostly on the macroeconomic variables that influence the demand for labor across sectors, relative prices (returns), and the intensity of the use of assets over the economic cycle. In the long run, the main drivers of income growth will be the level and distribution of the assets—the human, physical, financial, social, and natural capital—that people own and accumulate, as well as the intensity with which the assets are used and the volume of the associated returns, which will reflect the productivity of the assets.

Finally, the asset framework allows for a cohesive description of intra- and intergenerational economic mobility, chronic and transient poverty, and between-group inequities (the poor and the nonpoor, the bottom 40 and the top 60, minorities, and so on) that potentially thwart the possibility of certain vulnerable populations to participate in and benefit fully from the development process.

In the next section, the asset-based framework is used to describe trends in selected central components of the income generating capacity of households in the bottom 40 relative to the top 60 to shed more light on the significant progress achieved in poverty reduction and underscore the substantial heterogeneity of the countries of Latin America and the Caribbean.

The Income Generating Capacity of the Less Well Off

Data from household surveys across the region show that labor makes up a significant majority of income across all countries among the bottom 40 and the top 60 (figure 1.11). Labor income accounts for 60 to 80 percent of total income among households in the bottom 40, while the corresponding share is even higher among households in the top 60. It has been the main driver of poverty and inequality declines over the past decade. The majority (60 percent) of the decline in extreme poverty in the region is explained by higher labor incomes. Higher earnings among women were responsible for 22 percent of the decline, while the earnings of men accounted for 38 percent (figure 1.12). Similarly, labor incomes explained approximately two-thirds of the total poverty reduction and about 45 percent of the inequality reduction between 2003 and 2012.

Figure 1.11 Labor Income, Bottom 40 and Top 60, Latin America and the Caribbean, around 2012

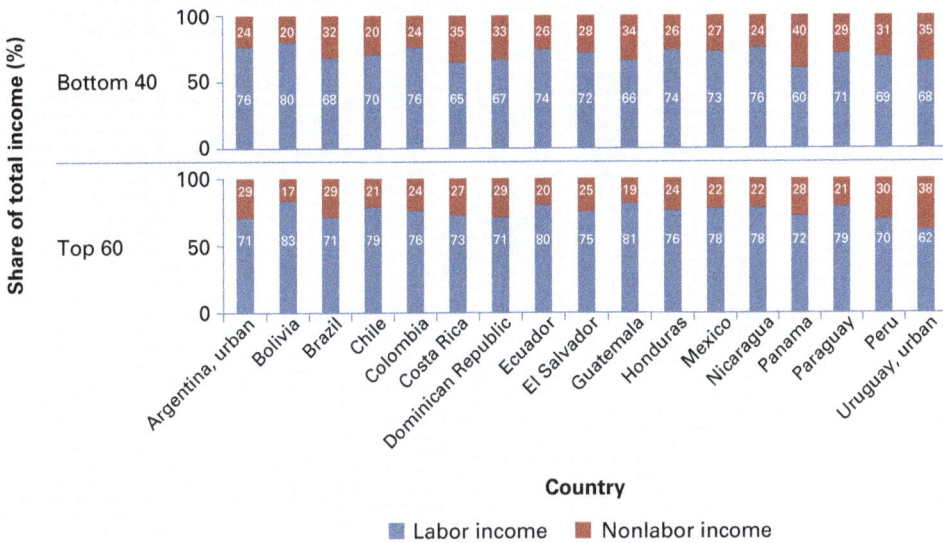

Source: Calculations based on data in SEDLAC.

Given the importance of labor income as a share of total income among the less well off, a description of how the capacity to generate labor income has evolved over the past decade across the region can promote a better understanding of the progress and divergence of countries with respect to the twin goals. In particular, this section focuses on the ability of the bottom 40 to generate labor income and explores the asset stock, intensity of use, and returns that determine labor income. It then illustrates the importance of private transfers, prices, and exposure to external shocks in determining the market income of households. It concludes with a brief discussion of how policies can be linked to the capacity of households to generate income through the asset-based approach.

The stock of assets: human capital

Human capital is generally defined as the stock of knowledge, competencies, and personal attributes that determine a person's capacity to perform in a labor market. It can be built up through education or training, but also includes intrinsic talents and skills, such as creativity and discipline, that are more difficult to measure. Human capital is the main asset that allows individuals to generate labor income. Hanushek and Woessmann (2012) find that differences in human capital can account for half to two-thirds of the variations in income between Latin America and the rest of the world. In large part, this is driven by differences in educational attainment and in the

Figure 1.12 The Reduction in Extreme Poverty, by Income Component, Latin America and the Caribbean, 2003–12

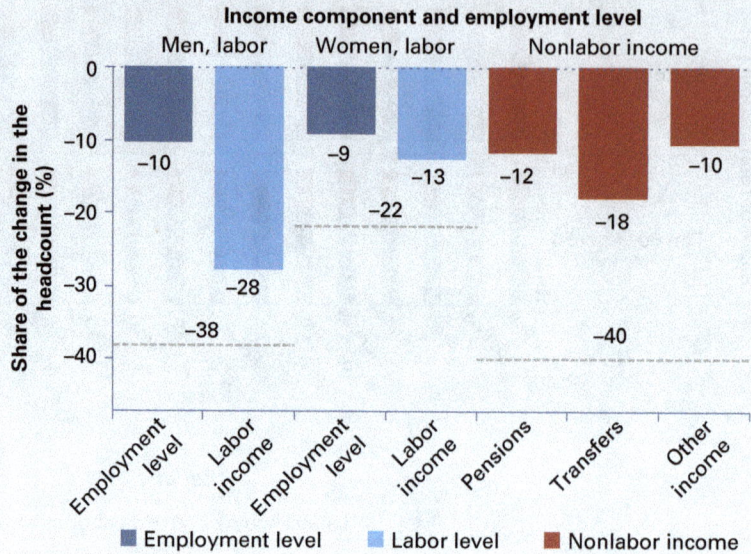

Source: Calculations based on data in SEDLAC.
Note: Estimates of poverty at the regional level are population-weighted averages of countries. The figure shows the Shapley Decomposition of poverty changes between 2003 and 2012 by components of the income aggregate. See Azevedo, Sanfelice, and Nguyen (2012) for details about the decomposition technique.

quality of schooling. Educational attainment is an imperfect, but important measure of human capital. In the past decade, there have been substantial improvements in educational attainment among the bottom 40 across the region, but the group continues to lag the top 60 (figure 1.13).

Most countries in the region have achieved nearly universal coverage in primary education. With a few exceptions in Central America, the gaps in access to primary education between the bottom 40 and the top 60 have practically closed. While progress has also been made in access to secondary education (above 80 percent in most countries), access to tertiary education remains a privilege of the wealthier top 60, with more persistent gaps between the bottom 40 and top 60, and achieving universality among either group is a distant goal. For instance, in Uruguay, while access to secondary education was at 86 percent among the bottom 40 and 95 percent among the top 60 in 2012, access to tertiary education among these two groups was 21 and 55 percent, respectively.

Despite the improvements in access and educational attainment, the quality of education remains an important challenge across the entire income distribution in Latin America and the Caribbean. There is signifi-cant variation in the quality of education within the region, which is heavily

Figure 1.13 Educational Attainment, Bottom 40 and Top 60, Latin America and the Caribbean, around 2003–12

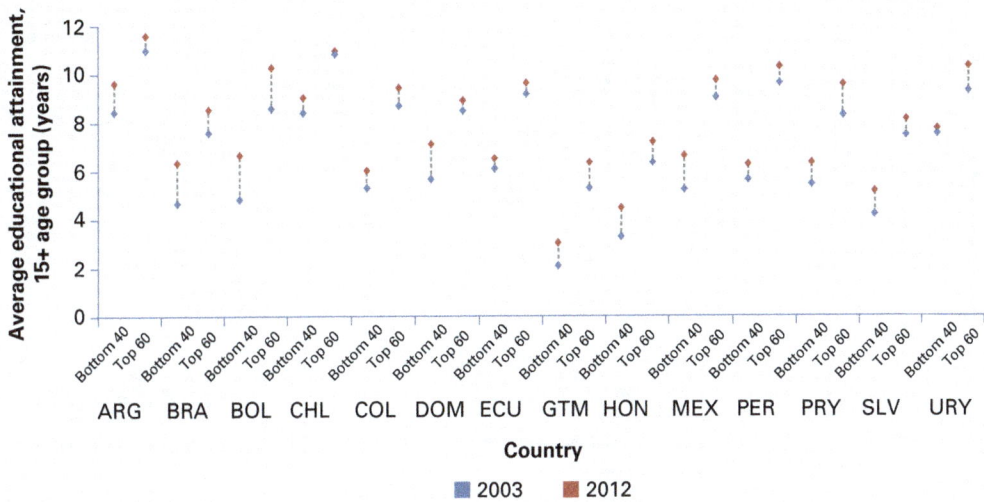

Source: Calculations based on data in SEDLAC. Country codes are ISO 3166 standard.

correlated with top 60 or bottom 40 status. While the rate of completion of the sixth grade on time has improved, especially among the bottom 40, there is still evidence of gaps across socioeconomic groups (figure 1.14). As of 2012, the gap in the completion of sixth grade on time between children in households in the bottom 40 and children in households in the top 60 was widest—more than 20 percentage points—in Colombia, the Dominican Republic, and Nicaragua.

Internationally comparable measures of educational quality such as the scores of the Program for International Student Assessment (PISA) of the Organisation for Economic Co-operation and Development (OECD) demonstrate that the region lags all other regions except Sub-Saharan Africa in learning outcomes. The assessment scores have improved among some countries in the region that apply the test, most notably Brazil and Peru and, to a lesser extent, Chile and Uruguay. However, overall performance is significantly behind the performance of the OECD countries. Thus, the average student in the region scores 100 points lower than the average OECD student in mathematics, which is equivalent to two full years of education in mathematics (Bruns and Luque 2015).

Intensity of use: labor force participation

To turn human capital into labor income, the poor and bottom 40 need access to the labor market. This includes not only the ability to participate in the labor market, but also sufficient labor demand so that the bottom 40 are able to work an adequate amount of time. The labor force participation

Figure 1.14 Completion of Sixth Grade on Time, Latin America and the Caribbean, 2000–12

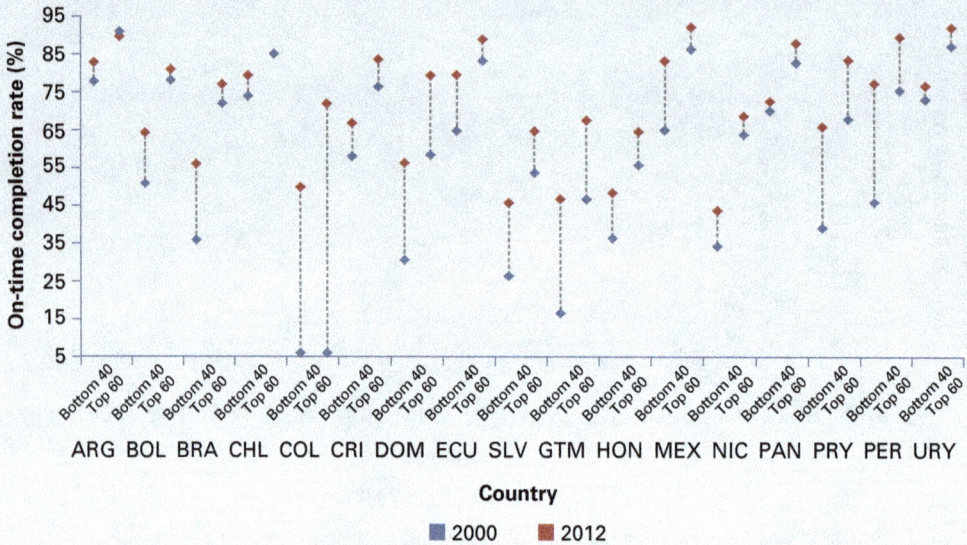

Source: Calculations based on data in SEDLAC.
Note: The figure reflects a simulation for 12- to 16-year-olds. For Brazil, Guatemala, and Nicaragua, the simulation represents 13- to 17-year-olds because primary education starts one year later in these three countries. Country codes are ISO 3166 standard.

rate in the region was slightly above 65 percent between 2003 and 2012. However, regional trends in labor force participation diverged among individuals in the bottom 40 and individuals in the top 60: the rate increased from 66.7 to 68.6 percent among the latter, but fell from 62.8 to 59.4 percent among the former.

This phenomenon, which was related to a decline in the use of productive assets among the less well off between 2003 and 2012, was the norm in many countries in Latin America (figure 1.15). With the exception of a few countries in Central America, the Dominican Republic, Mexico, and Paraguay, the share of the bottom 40 participating in the labor force dropped during these years. The trends were similar among men and women except in Chile and Uruguay, where labor force participation narrowed among men and widened among women. Moreover, in the countries in which the labor force participation of the bottom 40 increased, female labor force participation drove the change. Labor earnings among women can thus make a key contribution to poverty reduction and greater shared prosperity. Indeed, female labor market participation grew by 15 percent in Latin America from 2000 and 2010, which contributed to the substantial drop in poverty rates observed across the region (World Bank 2012a). Among the

Figure 1.15 Gaps in Labor Force Participation, Bottom 40 and Top 60, Latin America and the Caribbean, 2003–12

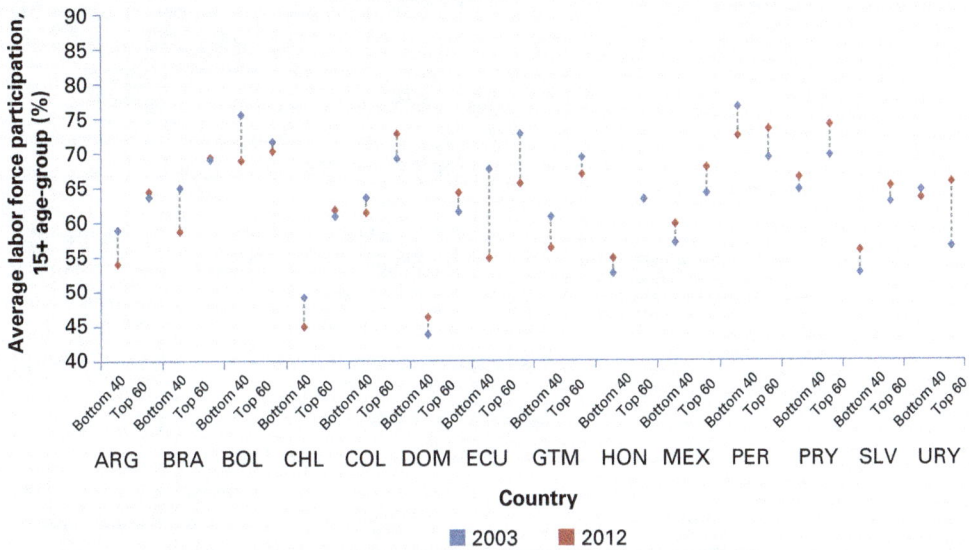

Source: Calculations based on data in SEDLAC. Country codes are ISO 3166 standard.

top 60, labor force participation rose in most countries, mainly also driven by the higher participation of women in the labor market.

The higher labor force participation rates of the top 60 relative to the bottom 40 is somewhat endogenous, but is nonetheless indicative that the bottom 40 may face higher barriers or enjoy fewer opportunities or incentives to access labor markets. The decline in the share of the bottom 40 participating in the labor force suggests that the reduction in poverty and in the promotion of shared prosperity observed in the region would have been even more dynamic had the labor participation among the bottom 40 risen in more countries. Achieving a better understanding of the constraints faced by the bottom 40 in participating in labor markets is thus critical to efforts to enhance the inclusiveness of growth and the ability of the bottom 40 to contribute to growth. Box 1.3 discusses several hypotheses that may explain the decline in labor force participation among the bottom 40 in many countries in Latin America.

Over the past decade, there have been important gains in access to housing and communications infrastructure that, all else being equal, may have enhanced the access to markets and allowed for greater use of productive assets by households. Recent studies have found that greater access to electricity services among informal women entrepreneurs and wider access to financial markets through mobile phone services can have positive effects

Box 1.3　Explaining the Decline in Labor Force Participation among the Bottom 40

There may be several reasons for the drops in labor force participation among the bottom 40 in Latin America and the Caribbean. According to one hypothesis, younger segments of the population are delaying their participation in the labor market to invest in education. This would represent a potential trade-off involving a sacrifice of short-term gains in poverty reduction and shared prosperity for greater long-term human capital improvements. This hypothesis is consistent with the falloff in labor force participation among 15- to 20-year-olds in many countries in 2012 and the rise in enrollments in secondary and tertiary education among the poor in the region. This was evident in, for example, Bolivia, Brazil, Colombia, and Ecuador.

According to a second hypothesis, the high unemployment rates observed among younger age-groups discourage labor force participation. This is consistent with data indicating that persistent shares of youth are out of school and out of work (Cárdenas, de Hoyos, and Székely 2014). Recent demographic trends have pushed youth above the threshold for working age, while the workforce, especially potential workers with less education or poorer-quality education, may not be able to take advantage of employment opportunities.

A third hypothesis is related to the potential effects on labor force participation at the margin, particularly among the 25–65 age-group, caused by newly expanded social protection systems across the region, including conditional cash transfer programs, universal health insurance schemes, and unemployment insurance initiatives. This hypothesis is consistent with the findings of recent studies on the negative labor market outcomes generated by social protection schemes instituted in parallel to established social security programs for the formally employed (for instance, see Levy 2008 on the case of Mexico). Argentina, Brazil, and Ecuador may offer examples of this phenomenon.

A fourth hypothesis focuses on the decline in labor force participation among the 65+ age-group. Because of the aging of the population, smaller, younger cohorts are unable to replace the older cohorts that are retiring, thereby cutting into overall participation rates. Moreover, the expansion of noncontributory pension programs and skills obsolescence among older workers, especially in the context of the demands of new information technologies, may also be contributing to a reduction in the labor force participation rates among the 65+ age-group.

on the productive use of assets by households (Demombynes and Thegeya 2012; Dinkelman 2011). Box 1.4 presents evidence on access to services in Latin America that can be associated with the greater use of the productive assets of households, particularly among the poor and the bottom 40.

Returns: wages

Despite the drop in labor force participation among the bottom 40, there has been improvement in hourly wages among the bottom 40 in most of the countries of the region over the past decade.[18] The rise in hourly wages has been especially strong in Argentina, Bolivia, and Brazil, while the rise has been more moderate in Chile, Colombia, Nicaragua, Paraguay, Peru, and Uruguay. The rest of the region has seen smaller increases in hourly wages among the bottom 40. In contrast, except for Honduras, the top 60 has enjoyed a smaller expansion in hourly wages (figure 1.16). This indicates that an important force behind the rise in the incomes of the bottom 40 has been higher returns in the labor market rather than greater labor market

Box 1.4 Connectivity Infrastructure in Latin America and the Caribbean

While not a perfect indicator of connectivity to markets, access to electricity and new information technologies are a good proxy for the transaction costs and barriers associated with accessing markets. Access to electricity, cell phones, and the Internet allows individuals to connect to markets to employ their assets and obtain returns.

Access to electricity has improved across Latin America and the Caribbean over the past decade, and regional disparities have shrunk substantially (figure B1.4.1). Bolivia and Peru have made the biggest advances in expanding electricity coverage among the bottom 40. However, substantial disparities still exist within and across countries. While less than 70 percent of the population in Nicaragua has access to electricity, Brazil, Chile, and Uruguay have achieved almost universal coverage. Many countries have closed the electricity gap between the bottom 40 and the top 60, but the gap is sill large in Bolivia, many Central American countries, and Peru.

Figure B1.4.1 Electricity Coverage Rates, Latin America and the Caribbean, 2000–12

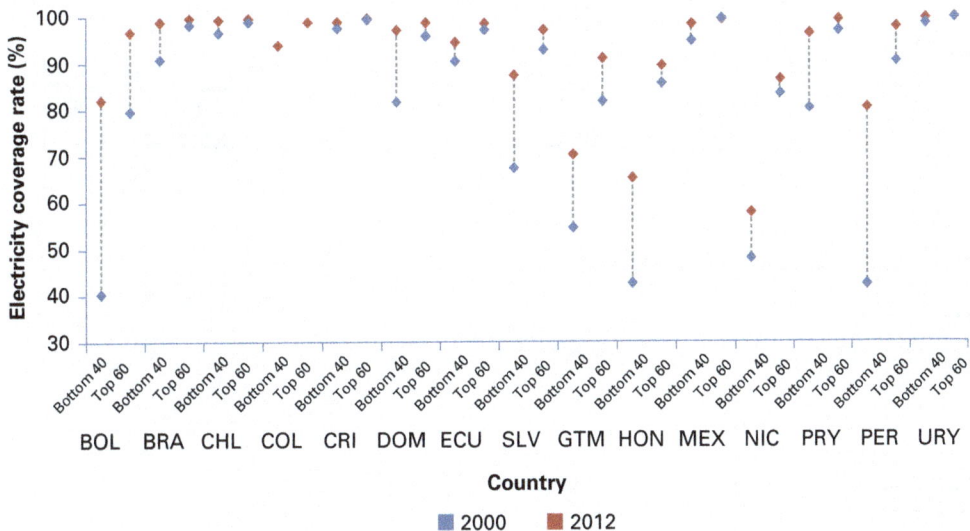

Source: Calculations based on data in SEDLAC.

As of 2012, access rates to cell phones were high in the region among both the bottom 40 and the top 60 (figure B1.4.2). The large gaps between the bottom 40 and top 60 observed at the beginning of the decade had been nearly erased 12 years later in countries such as Brazil and Chile. However, coverage gaps of over 20 percentage points between households in the top 60 and the bottom 40 persist in Mexico, Nicaragua, and Peru, and this limits access to markets and information among the poorest.

Internet access rates are much lower across the region, and there is significant heterogeneity (figure B1.4.3). Available data suggest that countries have made enormous leaps in Internet connectivity over the past decade. Coverage rates in Brazil and Chile rose from low levels to 21 and 25 percent of the bottom 40, respectively. However, unlike electricity and cell phone coverage, which is now almost universal across the region, even the wealthiest Latin American countries barely reach 50 percent in Internet coverage, while coverage does not exceed 10 percent in Bolivia and in Central America.

(continued)

Box 1.4 Connectivity Infrastructure in Latin America and the Caribbean *(Continued)*

Figure B1.4.2 Cell Phone Coverage Rates, Latin America and the Caribbean, 2000–12

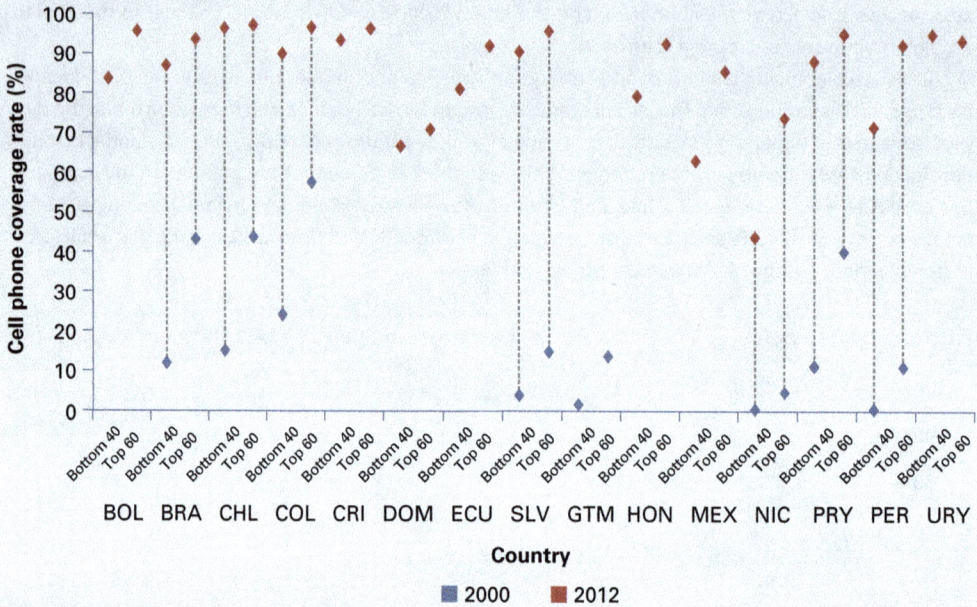

Source: Calculations based on data in SEDLAC.

Figure B1.4.3 Internet Coverage Rates, Latin America and the Caribbean, 2000–12

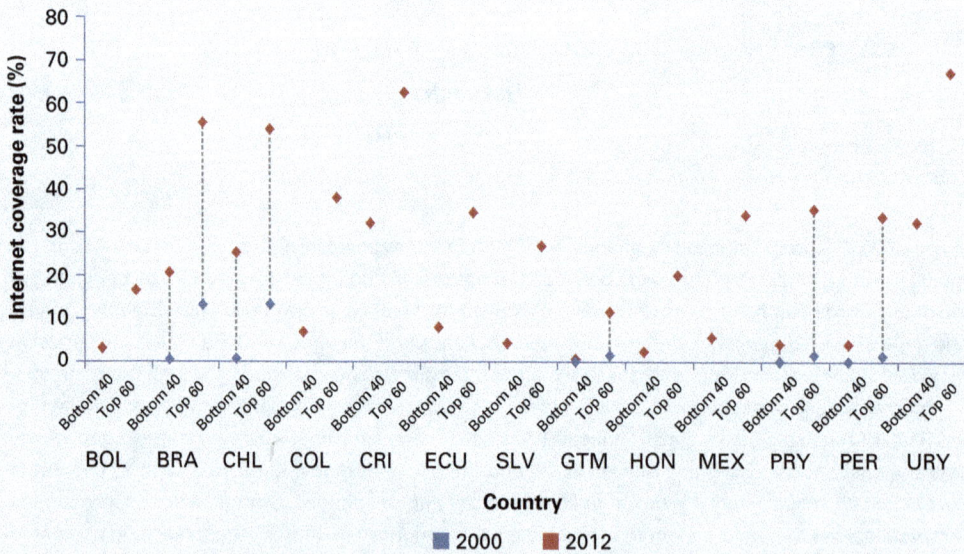

Source: Calculations based on data in SEDLAC.

Figure 1.16 The Rise in Hourly Wages, Bottom 40 and Top 60, Latin America and the Caribbean, 2003–12

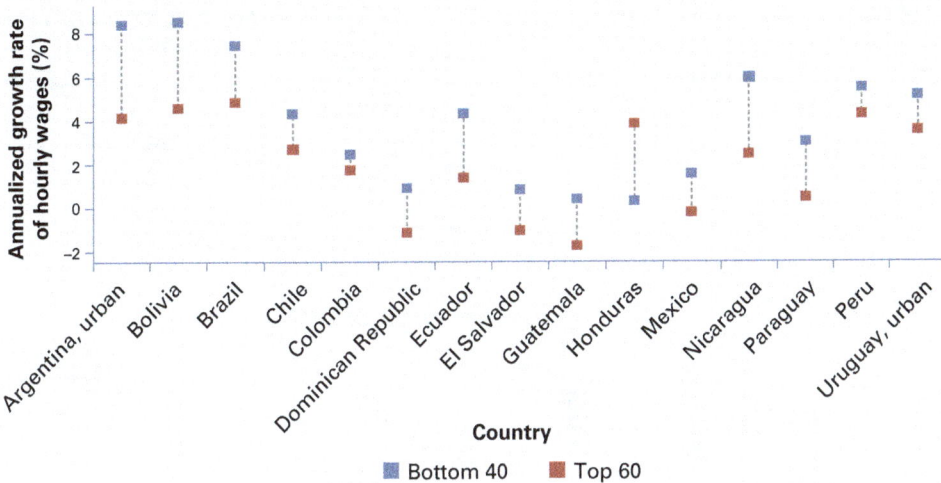

Source: Calculations based on data in SEDLAC.

participation, which is consistent with the falling skill premiums noted in many studies during the first decade of the 21st century.

Despite the gains among the bottom 40, some population groups are lagging in wage compensation. Thus, for example, according to a recent report of the World Bank (2012a), women and men may not be compensated on par. After controlling for education, age, and the share of workers in each occupation between 2000 and 2010, the report finds evidence of a large and persistent wage gap affecting women in Brazil, Chile, Mexico, and Peru that is especially marked among the top-paid professions.

One of the advantages of the simple asset-based framework is the framework's suitability for the analysis of the capacity of various socioeconomic and demographic groups to generate income. Box 1.5 describes poverty rates and the capacity to generate income among indigenous populations based on a subset of countries on which household survey data on ethnicity are available.

Private transfers

In some countries and among some households, private transfers, such as remittances and in-kind transfers from other households, can be a major source of income and a determinant of household well-being. In the region, total transfers represent about 10 percent of total household income. Moreover, the share of private transfers in total household income tends to be larger among the bottom 40 than among the top 60. However, the

Box 1.5　The Asset-Based Approach: Indigenous Populations

Poverty reduction

The poverty reduction in Latin America and the Caribbean between 2000 and 2012 was also evident among most indigenous groups. For instance, the share of indigenous people living on less than $2.50 a day in Bolivia and Ecuador (extreme poverty) fell 19 and 17 percentage points, respectively. In both cases, the decline was higher than the decline among the total population. In contrast, the share of indigenous people living on less than $2.50 a day in Guatemala rose from 45.7 to 54.9 percent over the period.[a]

Figure B1.5.1　$2.50- and $4.00-a-Day Poverty Rates, Indigenous Populations, Latin America and the Caribbean, 2000–12

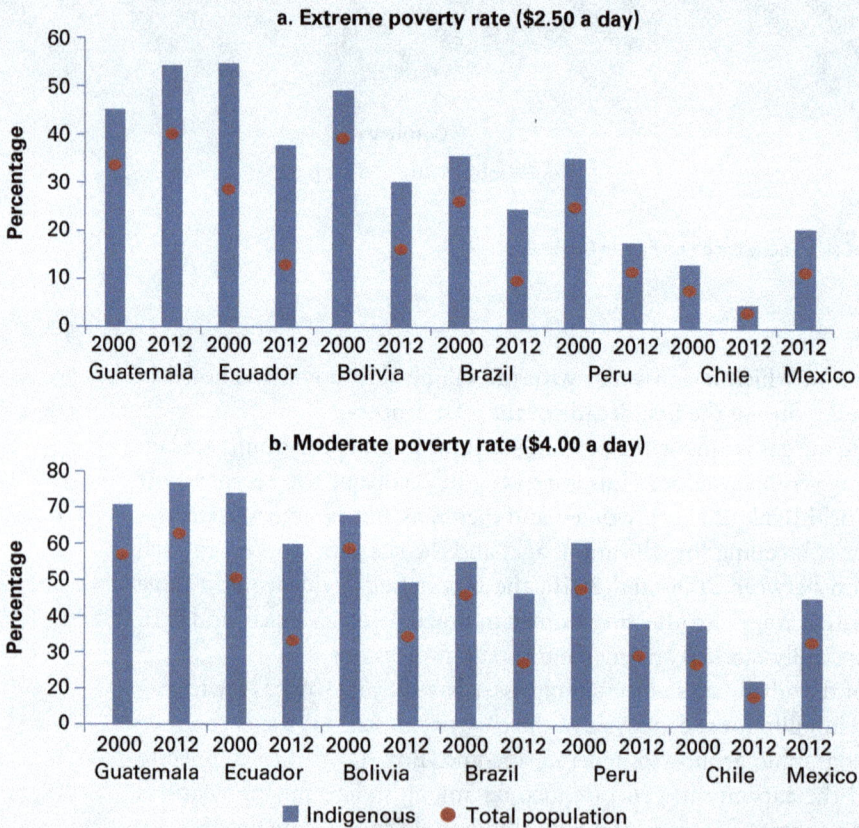

Source: Calculations based on data in SEDLAC.
Note: The nearest year to 2000 or 2012 is used for countries on which data are not available in that year. Ethnic identity is based on self-reported data. Because the data presented here are based on SEDLAC, a regional data harmonization effort that increases cross-country comparability, they may differ from official statistics reported by governments and national statistical offices. All monetary values are reported in 2005 PPP international U.S. dollars.

(continued)

Box 1.5 **The Asset-Based Approach: Indigenous Populations** *(Continued)*

Level of assets: human capital

The positive changes in poverty reduction in the past decade have been accompanied by improvements across various education measures on indigenous populations in the region. Among relevant groups in Brazil and Ecuador, school enrollments among 6- to 15-year-olds rose 9 and 10 percentage points, respectively. In 2000–12, the groups in Brazil also showed the greatest increase in average years of schooling—1.5 additional years—among people aged 18+ years. Guatemala experienced the greatest gains in the literacy rate (12 percentage points) and school enrollments among 6- to 15-year-olds (18 percentage points) during the period. Nonetheless, indigenous groups continue to lag the total population in human capital accumulation. As of 2012, Bolivia, Ecuador, and Guatemala had the widest gaps in educational attainment. Indigenous groups in Ecuador exhibited an average of four years less schooling than the total population. Similarly, in Bolivia, the literacy rate among indigenous groups was 13.7 percentage points lower.

Intensity of asset use: labor force participation

Trends in labor force participation rates among indigenous groups was heterogeneous in 2000–12. In Bolivia, participation rates among indigenous groups expanded by 3.6 percentage points, greater than the 1 percentage point increase among the total population and the largest rise among the countries in the analysis. Enhancements in human capital accumulation and employment have translated into greater poverty reductions in Bolivia. In contrast, labor force participation among indigenous groups in Ecuador declined by 10.7 percentage points, deeper even than the 7.2 percentage point fall among the overall population. The drop occurred mainly because of female labor force participation in both groups, which narrowed by nearly 16 and 10 percentage points, respectively, during the period.

Despite the progress, indigenous groups still lag in the region, and this is hindering advances in shared prosperity and poverty reduction.

---

a. The share of the indigenous population living on less than $1.25 a day in Guatemala increased from 17.3 to 18.5 percent over the period. However, this was smaller than the rise among the total population (11.8 to 13.7 percent).

significance of private transfers as a share of total transfers varies widely across countries and between the bottom 40 and the top 60 (figure 1.17, panel a). Private transfers are especially important in countries in Central America, such as El Salvador and Guatemala, where they account for more than 80 percent of total households transfers.

Evidence indicates that the positive effects of remittance flows include greater macroeconomic stability, higher savings, better access to health care and education, more entrepreneurship, and reductions in poverty and social inequality. The money migrant workers send back to their home countries is linked to lower poverty rates and enhancements in education and health indicators (Fajnzylber and López 2008). Between 2002 and 2008, remittance flows rose substantially each year, at an average rate of 17 percent. However, in 2006, the growth rate, though high, began slowing, and, because of the economic crisis in 2008, remittances fell more than 15 percent in the final two quarters of 2009. Given the importance of these flows for the recipient households, migrants adjusted their spending habits to continue to send money home despite the economic uncertainty. The year

Figure 1.17 Transfers, Bottom 40 and Top 60, Latin America and the Caribbean, 2003–12

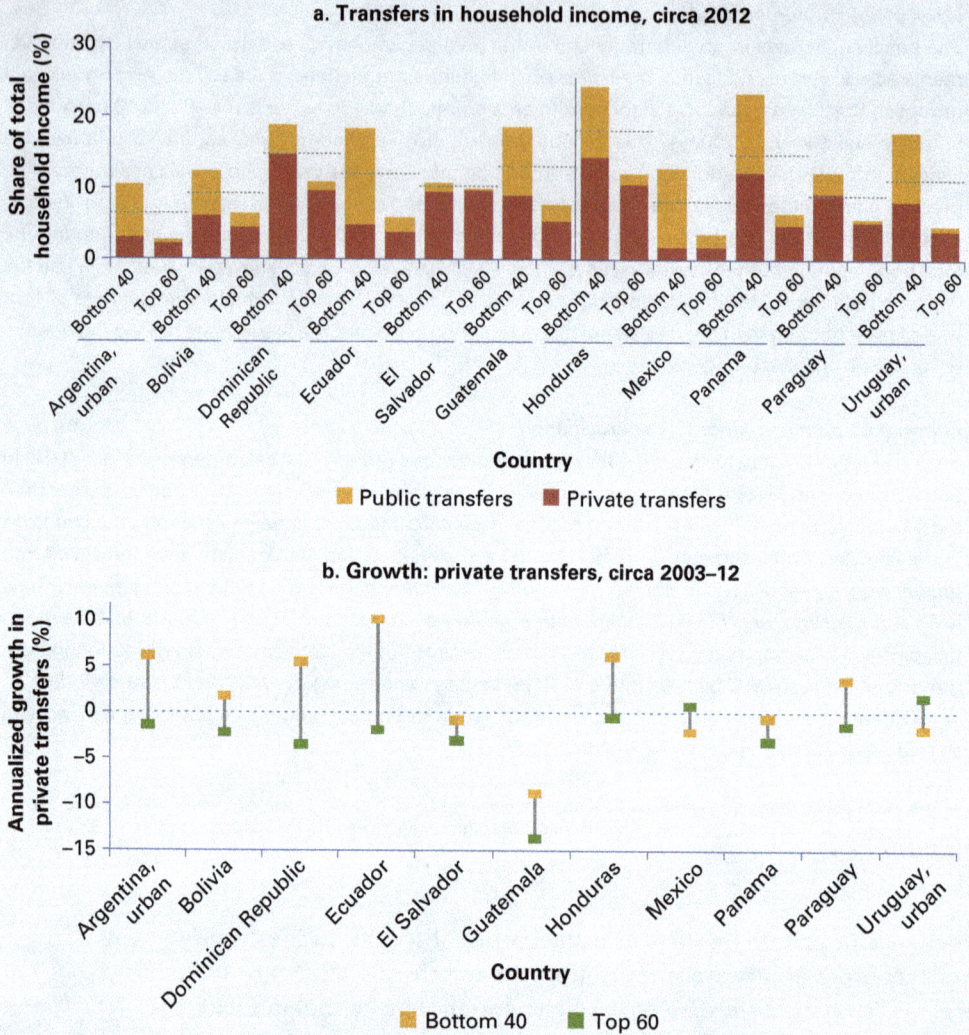

a. Transfers in household income, circa 2012

Public transfers   Private transfers

b. Growth: private transfers, circa 2003–12

Bottom 40   Top 60

Source: Calculations based on data in SEDLAC.
Note: The figure covers only countries where data on private transfers are available and comparable.

2010 marked the start of an upward trend lasting throughout that year and reaching an annual positive growth with respect to the previous year. The flows in 2011 exceeded the amounts sent the previous year by 6 percent, the largest positive growth rate of the previous four years (Maldonado, Bajuk, and Hayem 2012).

Over the past decade, the trends in the growth of private transfers, which includes remittances and other in-kind transfers, varied by country and among the top 60 and the bottom 40 (see figure 1.17, panel b). However, in most countries, private transfers grew more quickly or fell more slowly among the bottom 40. The only two countries in which private transfers grew more slowly among the bottom 40 were Mexico and Uruguay. Among the top 60 in most countries on which data are available, private transfers showed negative growth rates.

In El Salvador, one of the largest remittance-receiving countries in the region, private remittances played a major role in poverty reduction. In 2012, private remittances accounted for over 16 percent of GDP, a more than 10-fold increase since 1990. Remittances expanded in both size and scope. In 2000, 4 percent of households received remittances; by 2012, one in five households was receiving remittances, while the amount per migrant rose by almost a third between 2000 and 2010. Remittances do not necessarily go to the poorest households in El Salvador; the average per capita income in households receiving remittances is $8.90 (2005 U.S. dollars), compared with $3.10 among poor households. Reliance on remittances exposes countries to the business cycles of the countries in which the migrants reside. In El Salvador, this means a strong reliance on the U.S. economy because 88 percent of Salvadoran migrants reside in the United States.[19] The sharp decline in remittances that occurred because of the 2008 financial crisis highlights the vulnerability associated with this dependence.

In Paraguay, family transfers may not be an important driver behind the change in the incidence of poverty, but still play an important role in alleviating poverty and as a household mechanism for coping with adverse shocks. Without these transfers, the extreme poverty rate in rural areas would be 4 percentage points higher. The elderly and woman-headed households receive substantially larger family transfers, suggesting that migration is a household income diversification and coping mechanism.

Prices of goods and services

The market income of households is also directly affected by the prices of the goods and services they consume. During the past decade, macrostability has translated into lower inflation rates, which has helped maintain the purchasing power of households relative to the situation in the 1990s. However, fluctuations in food prices have been an important source of vulnerability among some households in the bottom 40. Evidence shows that households in the lower deciles of the income distribution consume a higher share of food with respect to their total basket of goods, and these households are thus more exposed to changes in food prices (figure 1.18).[20] Estimates based on the latest recorded worldwide increase in food prices, in 2011, show that high, volatile food prices pushed 44 million people further into poverty primarily in low- and middle-income countries (World Bank 2011a). Box 1.6 presents an interesting case of the potential negative effects of high food prices on poverty reduction.

Risk and external shocks

Uninsured risks often have permanent effects on the welfare of households by aggravating poverty traps because low-income people—the poor or the bottom 40—are often more vulnerable to the negative consequences of shocks

Figure 1.18 Food Consumption in Total Consumption, Latin America and the Caribbean, around 2010

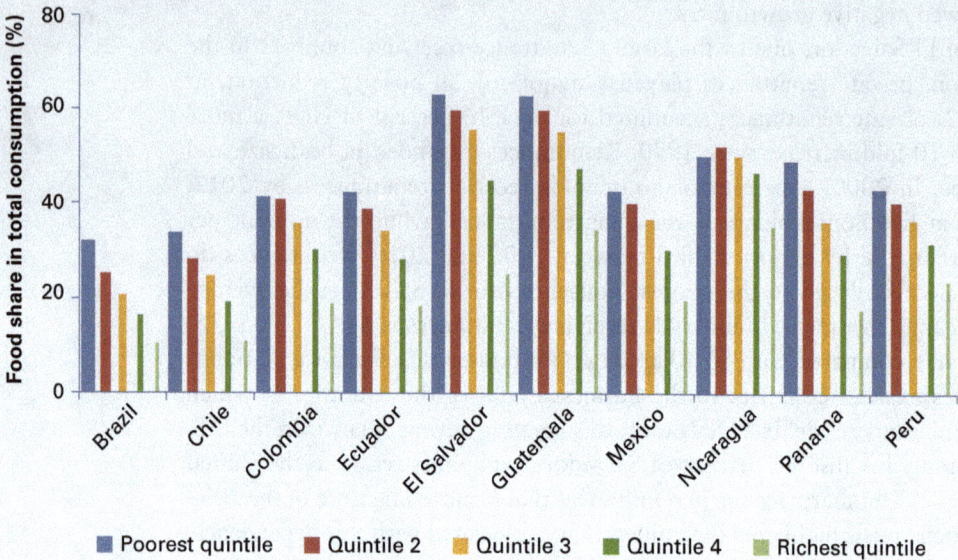

Source: Calculations based on data in SEDLAC.

(Barro 2006; Becker 1968; Carter et al. 2007; Dercon and Christiaensen 2011). Specifically, negative shocks can directly affect all components of the income generating capacity of households. For instance, the assets of any individual or household could be destroyed by a natural disaster, and such a disaster could also affect household decisions on the accumulation of certain assets. Uncertainty in the realization of shocks may likewise affect the intensity of the use of assets; for example, an expected drought (or flood) could reduce the utilization of land for agricultural activities. Risk is also captured by relative prices similar to the interest rate, which certainly captures the sovereign risk of an economy as a whole. Finally, macroeconomic contagion can cause a fiscal crisis that may reduce a government's capacity to provide social assistance to the poor by reducing the coverage or the size of cash transfers.

One increasingly important source of risk is climate change, which is expected to raise the frequency and severity of extreme weather events. The Latin America and Caribbean region has already experienced the greater variability, frequency, and strength of natural disasters in recent years. In particular, there appears to be a positive correlation between natural disasters in the region and a worsening trend in welfare indicators (figure 1.19). Poor and vulnerable populations tend to be more prone to episodes that result in the loss of income or assets. Poor households may be exposed not only to large, unusual shocks, but also to smaller high-frequency events that may prevent the households from escaping poverty.

Box 1.6 The Poverty Effects of High Food Prices, Paraguay

Between 2003 and 2013, economic growth and improvements in income distribution combined to contribute to a large reduction in moderate poverty in Paraguay, from 44.0 to 23.7 percent. However, because the extreme poverty line is determined solely based on the price of a selected food basket, the reduction in the extreme poverty rate became less dynamic when food prices began rising at a higher rate than general prices. This was particularly evident in 2003–11, when extreme poverty fell by only 3.2 percentage points. In contrast, a slowdown in food price inflation in 2011–13 was an important contributing factor in the 7.9 percentage point decline in the extreme poverty rate during those years (figure B1.6.1, panel a).

Figure B1.6.1 Changes in the Extreme Poverty Rate, Paraguay, 2003–11 and 2011–13

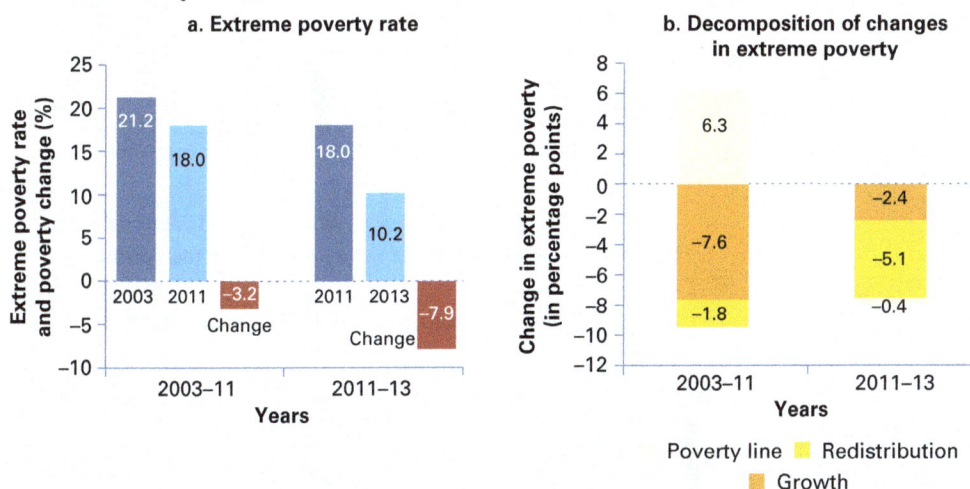

Source: World Bank calculations based on data from the Permanent Household Survey for 2003, 2011, and 2013.

A quantification of the effects of economic growth, redistribution, and an extreme poverty line based solely in food prices helps unpack the changes in extreme poverty over the last decade in Paraguay. Together, high economic growth rates and improved income distribution accounted for a decline by 9.5 percentage points in extreme poverty in 2003–11, while rapidly rising prices for the food items in the basket relative to general prices slowed the reduction in the extreme poverty rate by 6.3 percentage points (figure B1.6.1, panel b), leading to a net decline of only 3.2 percentage points in the rate. Thus, the food price rise relative to general prices cut into the positive effects on poverty reduction of significant economic growth and gains in redistribution.

In contrast, since 2011, all three forces have been trending in the same direction. The deceleration of the increase in food prices between 2011 and 2013 meant that, in real terms, the extreme poverty line—updated using food price data of the Banco Central del Paraguay—was marginally lower in 2013 than in 2011. As a consequence, prices played a limited, but positive role in the drop-off in the extreme poverty rate, whereas the enhanced income distribution reflected in the widening of the distribution was responsible for 65 percent of the total change in the headcount (5 percentage points out of close to 8), and average income growth (the shift to the right in the distribution) explains the remaining 35 percent of the fall.

An additional contributing factor behind the sensitivity of the extreme poverty line to food prices is the fact that a large share of the population lives in households with incomes near the extreme poverty line. Because of this clustering, even slight shifts in the poverty line can have noticeable impacts on poverty rates.

Figure 1.19 Incidence and Poverty Effects of Natural Disasters, World Regions and Latin America and the Caribbean, 1970–2009

a. Incidence, by region, 1970–2008[a]

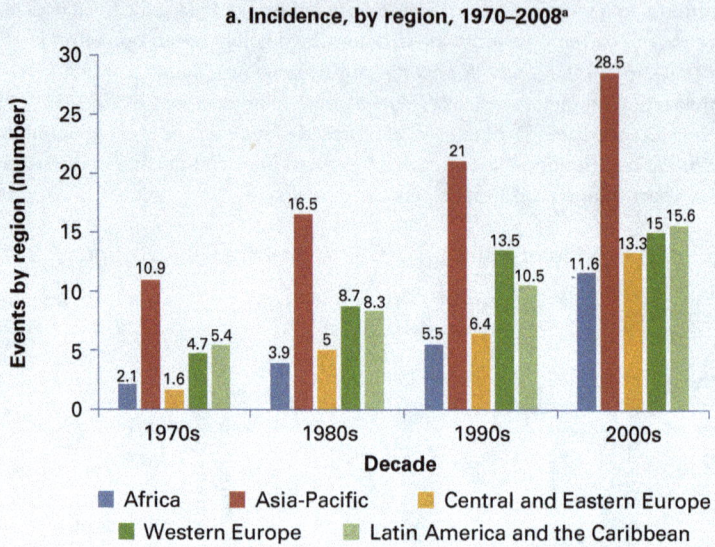

Legend:
- Africa
- Asia-Pacific
- Central and Eastern Europe
- Western Europe
- Latin America and the Caribbean

b. Correlation with poverty, Latin America, 2009

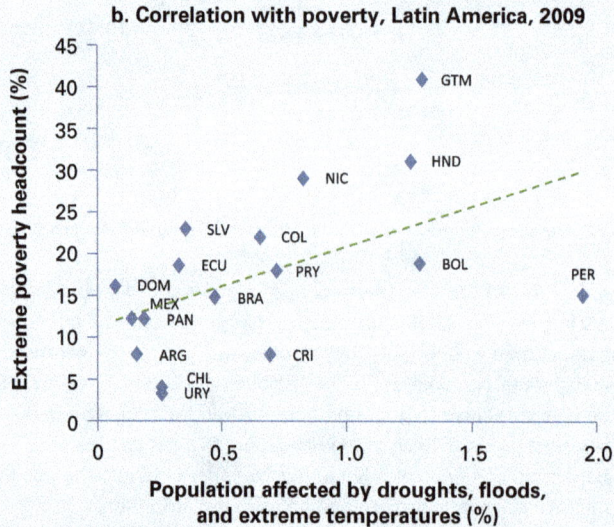

Sources: Cavallo and Noy 2011 based on data in, for panel a, EM-DAT (International Disaster Database), Centre for Research on the Epidemiology of Disasters, Université Catholique de Louvain, Brussels, http://www.emdat.be/database; and, for panel b, SEDLAC for the poverty headcount; and WDI (World Development Indicators) (database), World Bank, Washington, DC, http://data.worldbank.org/data-catalog/world-development-indicators, for population impacts.
a. The years for Latin America and the Caribbean in panel a are 1970–2012.

Báez, de la Fuente, and Santos (2010) show that disasters produce deleterious impacts on education, health, and many income generating processes. They also highlight that, in most disaster events, the poorest carry the heaviest burden of the effects. For instance, in Peru, while 30 percent of

Figure 1.20 Shocks Reported by the Bottom 40 and Top 60, Peru, 2013

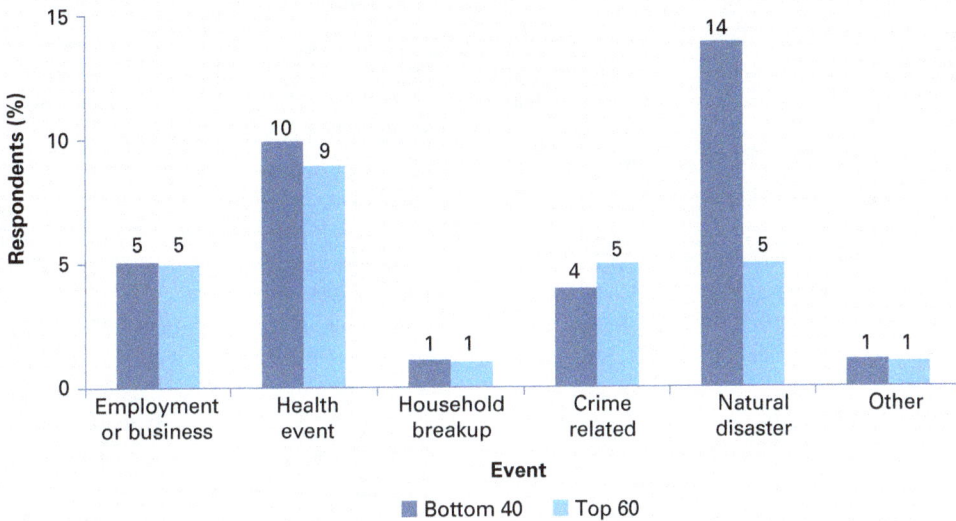

Source: Calculations based on data from the National Household Survey.
Note: The events resulting in the loss of income or assets were self-reported within the previous 12 months.
Employment or business = an episode involving job loss or the loss of a family business by a household
member. Health event = a household member was sick. Natural disaster = drought, flood, storm, infectious
disease or epidemic, and so on. Crime related = a household member was robbed or assaulted. Household
breakup = household head left the household. The data on natural disasters are statistically different.

households in the poorest decile reported experiencing a shock that translated into a loss of income or assets, only 14 percent of households in the
richest decile did so. Poor households are especially vulnerable to weather-
related events in Peru. While many events that cause shocks affect the bottom 40 and top 60 similarly, households in the bottom 40 are substantially
more likely to report they are affected by natural disasters and weather-
related crises (figure 1.20). Box 1.7 presents the relevant case of Haiti.

Another source of risk among many households in the region is crime
and violence. Ongoing crime and violence across Central America and
Mexico affect all aspects of development and intensifies inequities. They
influence investment in human capital, raise the security costs of businesses,
divert funds to combating crime, and discourage domestic and international
investment because they impact the general investment climate (Cárdenas
and Rozo 2008; Dell 2014; Powell, Manish, and Nair 2010; World Bank
2014d).

For instance, the costs of crime and violence in El Salvador are high.
Acevedo (2008) estimates that the costs of crime and violence represented
almost 11 percent of GDP there in 2008.[21] There is ample evidence of the
effects of crime and violence among individuals and firms. Over 45 percent
of men and 40 percent of women in El Salvador alter their shopping habits
because of fear of crime and violence; 15 percent have moved; and over

Box 1.7 Shocks, Coping, and the Impact on Household Welfare, Haiti

The recent history of Haiti is characterized by a combination of shocks and slow economic growth. In 2004, political and extreme weather events led to a 5 percent contraction in GDP. In May 2004, Hurricane Jeanne killed some 3,000 people, left a quarter of a million people homeless, and generated economic losses estimated at nearly $300 million (Zapata Martí 2005). In 2008, four hurricanes (Fay, Gustav, Hanna, and Ike) led to a combined economic contraction of 1 percent of GDP per capita. The associated floods destroyed more than two-thirds of the country's crops, resulting in child malnutrition and death. In 2010, a severe earthquake brought about the largest per capita GDP contraction in Haiti's history, at 5.5 percent, and a death toll of over 300,000. In 2012, hurricanes Isaac and Sandy had a significant economic impact: the former destroyed nearly $250 million in crops, and the latter devastated 90,000 hectares of cropland leading to a fall in per capita GDP of 1 percent.

A recent study (World Bank and ONPES 2014) includes the results of an analysis of the relationship between poverty incidence and shocks produced by natural disasters in Haiti using a survey of living conditions—the *Enquête sur les Conditions de Vie des Ménages après le Séisme* (postearthquake household living conditions survey)—collected through a partnership between the World Bank and the government of Haiti. The study also considers household risk coping mechanisms, such as using savings, receiving transfers from friends, changing nutritional inputs, or taking children out of school.

The study finds that a typical Haitian household faces multiple shocks annually and that nearly 75 percent of households are economically impacted by at least one idiosyncratic shock each year. Households in poverty are more likely to experience shocks: 95 percent of households in extreme poverty experience at least one economically damaging shock annually. Although households impacted by climatic shocks are more likely to be affected by agricultural setbacks or covariate economic shocks, there are no clear patterns indicating that certain types of shocks occur together.

The study also finds differences in the use of coping mechanisms by both the type of shock experienced and the poverty status of the household. Most households are able to cope with idiosyncratic shocks without resorting to changes in nutritional inputs. However, nutritional inputs are less well protected if a household experiences a covariate economic or weather shock. If there is a covariate economic shock in the community, a staggering 56 percent of households in extreme poverty change their nutritional profile, compared with 37 percent among resilient households (that is, the nonpoor and nonvulnerable). The study also shows that shocks are more likely to impede the future economic activities of households because households are forced to sell assets or take on debt to cope; this also affects households in extreme poverty more frequently than resilient households. Relative to households in extreme poverty, resilient households are two times more likely to rely on nonloan monetary help supplied by outsiders.

5 percent have changed jobs out of concern of being victimized. In 2010, over 85 percent of firms paid for security, which is 25 percentage points above the regional average, and slightly more than half of all firms identified crime, theft, and disorder as the major constraint to doing business, which is also substantially higher than the regional average.

In 2011, the homicide rate reached 90 per 100,000 deaths in Honduras, three times the level in Mexico and higher than the rate in El Salvador, which had the second highest rate. If crime were reduced by 10 percent in Honduras, then GDP could increase by 0.7 percent (World Bank 2011b). In 2012, the majority of Hondurans and Salvadorans reported crime and violence as the number one problem in their countries (Lagos and Dammert 2012).

Mexico has experienced an increase in the number of drug-related homicides, from 28 to 73 percent of total homicides from 2007 to 2011, respectively (SNSP 2012). Enamorado, López-Calva, and Rodríguez-Castelán (2014) find a negative impact of drug-related crime on income growth in municipalities in Mexico from 2005 to 2010 and no significant effect of non–drug-related crime on economic growth. Moreover, Enamorado et al. (2014) contend that a 1 percentage point rise in the Gini coefficient translated into an increase of more than 10 drug-related homicides per 100,000 inhabitants between 2006 and 2010.

Despite a lack of data on households, an analysis of municipal data suggests the relationship between poverty and crime in Mexico was convex in 2010: homicide rates were higher in both the poorest and richest municipalities (World Bank 2012b). This may arise because criminal organizations were diversifying their activities into richer municipalities through kidnapping and extortion or because of an effective security strategy in areas with high concentrations of crime and poverty. Using the World Bank (2012b) methodology, the United Nations Development Programme (UNDP 2013) finds parallel results in Brazil in 2011. In Colombia, the results suggest a contrast: the higher homicide rates occur in municipalities with the highest rates of multidimensional poverty.

Drug-related violence is also associated with higher unemployment and poorer school performance and can have long-run detrimental consequences in human capital accumulation (Arias and Esquivel 2012; Caudillo and Torche 2014; Michaelsen and Salardi 2013). Similarly, Velásquez (2014) finds that the violence associated with the Mexican drug war may also have long-term consequences on the wealth and welfare of Mexican households. Not only does the evidence suggest drug-related crime hinders economic growth, but the costs of combating drug trafficking are estimated at $9 billion a year, nearly as much as the Mexican government spends on social development (Keefer and Loayza 2010).

Links to policies

The asset-based framework represents a valuable way to approximate the heterogeneity in shared prosperity in the region. The capacity to accumulate assets, use them intensively, and obtain returns from the assets are systematically different among households in the bottom 40 and households in the top 60, and there are large variations across countries. The framework helps highlight how some macro and external variables that are not under the control of households may affect poor and less well-off households differently, such as food prices, climate change, or crime. The specifics largely depend on the context in each country and are examined in the country chapters.

In particular, a meaningful discussion of effective policy interventions to further shared prosperity requires a more detailed analysis within countries to understand the potential determinants of the diversity. The policy framework described below represents a systematic, concrete method to analyze the links between policies and the income growth of the bottom

40. Interventions in specific policy areas can be weighed for their potential impact on the accumulation of assets, the intensity of asset use, and the returns to assets and on final market incomes. This can help gauge how the policies may eventually allow the less well off to contribute to growth. Thus, this subsection elaborates on the connection between the policies and household market income to provide a road map for profiting from the country chapters.

The asset-based framework assumes that all agents are rational, that markets function perfectly, and, thus, that all individuals can take advantage of the full potential of their assets. However, in reality, the main factors that affect the income generating capacity of households include, for instance, inequality in opportunities, risk, and market failures that explain why some individuals are able to accumulate more productive assets, while others are prevented from doing so. Based on an examination of interventions that address institutional and market imperfections and that are generally used in microeconomic theory, the asset-based approach can be linked to four fundamental policy areas that have a direct impact on the capacity of households in an economy to generate income, but with a special focus on households in the bottom 40. The policies have also been identified in previous studies (World Bank 2013a, 2014a). They are (1) equitable, efficient, and sustainable fiscal policy and macroeconomic stability; (2) fair and transparent institutions capable of delivering good-quality basic services; (3) well-functioning markets; and (4) adequate risk management at the macro and household levels (figure 1.21). The policies can influence the realization of the total income of households by directly affecting the private income generating capacity of households through asset accumulation,

Figure 1.21 Policy Areas That Affect Household Income Generating Capacity

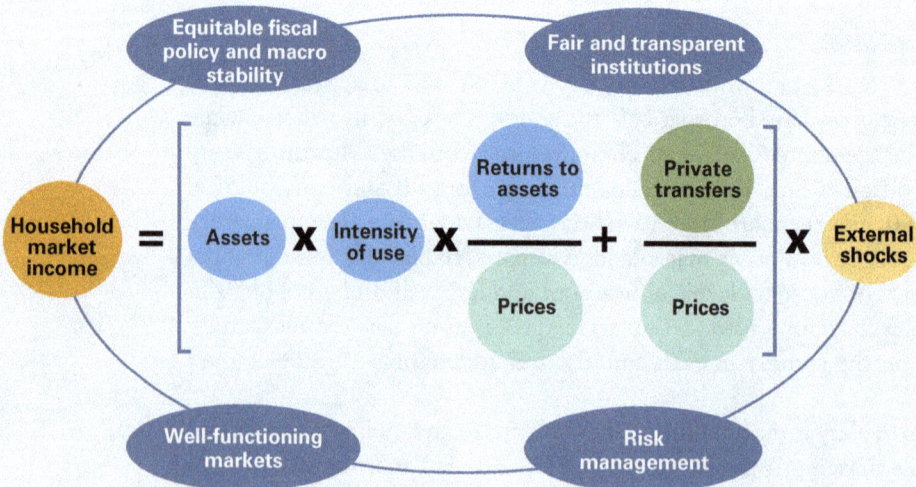

asset use, returns to assets, and increases in the size of private transfers or adding public transfers, while mitigating the negative effects of external shocks.[22]

First, equitable and sustainable fiscal policy has an impact on income generating capacity through direct taxation; it also affects the decisions of individuals about the intensity of the use of assets by influencing returns through direct taxes and public transfers. Indirect taxes, such as the value added tax, can have an immediate effect on consumer prices and, thus, have an impact on the relative returns of households. Although there is evidence that fiscal policy has a limited impact on inequality in Latin America and the Caribbean, the expansion of cash transfers and noncontributory pension programs in the region in the last decade has provided a safety net that has pulled people out of poverty by boosting their incomes directly and helping to protect them from falling back into extreme poverty if they are hit by external shocks (World Bank 2014a). While direct cash transfers complement household income directly, these programs assist in incentivizing the accumulation of human capital by making the transfers conditional on school attendance and health care checkups. This also forces governments to supply the schools and clinics necessary to meet the increased demand for these services, thereby boosting human capital.

Moreover, the parameters of monetary policy related to macroeconomic stability, such as inflation targets linked to interest rates, directly affect relative prices in an economy and, thus, the income generating capacity and productive choices of households. For instance, prudent macropolicies have allowed countries in the region to control inflation rates and achieve lower, steadier inflation rates for more than a decade. This regional improvement in the ability to control inflation impacts the real return on household assets. High inflation erodes the purchasing power of household wages, which effectively lowers the real returns on human capital and other types of assets. Prudent fiscal and monetary policies that are conducive to sustainable and acceptable trends in fiscal deficits and inflation are also important in mitigating potential external shocks such as fiscal and financial crises.

Overall, fiscal policies have efficiency and equity implications in both the short and the long run that can differentially affect the bottom 40 and the top 60. In the short run, the net system of fiscal incentives can reinforce or offset market income gaps. In the long run, they can impact decisions related to asset accumulation and use—as in the case of labor force participation or hiring decisions by firms—and may induce factor misallocations or affect the size distribution of firms.

Second, fair and transparent institutions capable of delivering good-quality basic services may directly affect the decisions of individuals to accumulate assets. In particular, strong institutional capacity linked to the delivery of good-quality services in education and health care can enhance the ability of poorer households to improve their accumulation of net assets. More and better health care services and employment systems are fundamental for mitigating the risks that households face from health-related shocks and the consequences of employment loss. Basic services such as running water, electricity, and sewerage are important contributors to human capital accumulation, particularly among the poor. Over the past decade, there has been a large expansion in access to education, water, improved sanitation, and health care services across the region. However, coverage remains uneven across and within countries and is positively correlated with income levels. The services are often inadequate in quality and only weakly coordinated with other key services, which undermines the overall impact, especially among the bottom 40.

Governance failures can also act as a barrier to progress in achieving the twin goals by imposing constraints on economic growth and job creation. Institutions can promote the protection of property rights and thus improve the investment climate in an economy by boosting the availability of well-paid employment opportunities and affecting the returns to factors of production. Strong regulatory entities are also crucial in overseeing private market behaviors, thereby minimizing the risk of financial and sectoral macroeconomic crises. On a global scale, weaknesses in institutions influence the competitiveness of an economy. Robust competition policy that reduces entry barriers for new firms to certain markets directly affects the relative prices faced by all households by reducing consumer prices. While weak institutions are not considered a binding constraint on growth, there is evidence that they play a negative role. Overall, since the bottom 40 has more limited options, such as a lack of practical access to high-quality services in the private market, governance failures can fundamentally constrain the capacity of the bottom 40 to build their human capital assets or to take advantage of economic opportunities, which undermines shared prosperity.

Third, directly linked to better connectivity and competition, well-functioning markets are central to any effort to reduce the barriers to a more efficient utilization of household productive assets and can help grow the relative returns to assets. Enhanced transportation infrastructure that allows disadvantaged groups to connect to markets is an example of an opportunity to raise the utilization of assets that can create additional income. Poor-quality infrastructure adds to the negative effects of distance between regions and limits the connection of local markets with national and global markets. Infrastructure deficits can also have a negative impact on the investment climate and can compromise the ability of an economy to expand to its full potential. An extensive and well-functioning transportation and communications infrastructure network is a necessary condition for access from poorer areas to major markets and services. Inequalities in coverage across regions limit the returns to other development initiatives such as investments in education, health care, and social programs. Noncompetitive business environments and poor-quality infrastructure limit productivity growth, the labor demand that creates good jobs, and, therefore, the ability of the labor market to translate economic growth into higher incomes among the bottom 40.

Access to financial markets is also important for the income generating capacity of the poor in at least three ways. First, access to savings accounts and investment opportunities allows individuals to employ financial assets (such as savings) to obtain returns (interest rates) and thus complement labor incomes. Second, by encouraging and facilitating savings, access helps mitigate the impact of shocks and therefore protect against risks. If they have access to savings, the poor no longer need to sell assets or underinvest in human capital (by pulling children out of school) if an unexpected crisis strikes. Third, access to financial institutions that include access to credit allows individuals to finance small businesses or invest in fertilizer, physical assets, or human capital and thereby improve the level and intensity of their use of human capital and physical assets.

Finally, adequate risk management can reduce the exposure to and impact of shocks among all households in an economy, but particularly the poor and vulnerable, who usually have a higher probability of risk and are thus forced to engage in negative coping mechanisms. Public safety nets such as public cash transfer schemes that are flexible so they may be scaled up during crisis and scaled down during recovery may be important instruments for supplying temporary income support to households affected by external shocks.

Final Remarks

Latin America and the Caribbean has experienced remarkable absolute and relative gains in achieving the twin goals. Moderate growth, combined with falling inequality, has propelled reductions in poverty and income growth among the bottom 40. Between 2002 and 2011, extreme poverty ($2.50 a day per capita) was cut in half, and higher incomes changed the demographic composition of the bottom 40. In 2003, everyone in the bottom 40 was poor, and almost two-thirds of the bottom 40 were among the extreme poor, but, by 2012, only two-thirds of the bottom 40 were poor, and only 30 percent were among the extreme poor, while the largest group were the vulnerable (at 37.2 percent). These trends are reflected in higher household incomes, mainly from higher wages. Greater human capital accumulation, economic growth, and falling inflation rates have been major factors behind the higher real-wage levels. Private and public transfers contributed almost 20 percent to the reduction in poverty. Some projections, drawing on the promising trends of the last decade in the region, estimate the share of households that will be living in extreme poverty ($1.25 a day) at 3.1 percent in 2030, down from 4.6 percent in 2011 (World Bank 2015b).

Despite this impressive performance, extreme poverty is still a salient issue in middle- and low-income countries in the region. More than 75 million people are still living in extreme poverty in the region, half of them in Brazil and Mexico, and extreme poverty rates (based on the $2.50-a-day per capita line) are above 40 percent in Guatemala and reach nearly 60 percent in Haiti. Moreover, combining the share of the poor and vulnerable in the region suggests that nearly two-thirds of the region's population is either poor or vulnerable to the risk of falling back into poverty. As growth wanes and progress in reducing the region's high levels of inequality slows, it will be more important than ever for governments to focus policies on inclusive growth. For example, understanding the drivers behind the falling labor force participation rates among the bottom 40 will be critical to ensuring the inclusiveness of growth, especially in a lower growth context that could limit labor market returns. Focusing on expanding the assets and market participation of indigenous households will also be crucial in closing the gaps between the bottom 40 and the top 60. In addition, the specter of climate change suggests that severe weather events may become more frequent, which, the evidence indicates, are likely to affect the poor and the vulnerable more than the middle class.

The goal of this chapter is to provide a baseline description on the standing of the region in the effort to achieve the twin goals and information on a framework that can contribute to a better understanding of the components of the income of households that are directly linked to the monetary elements of the twin goals. The country studies presented in the rest of this book provide a more detailed discussion of recent trends, policy areas, and challenges related to the income generating capacity of the less well off. The presentation in each chapter is organized around four important pillars that are linked directly to the asset-based framework: (1) equitable, efficient, and sustainable fiscal policy and macroeconomic stability (direct and indirect taxes and transfers, inflation targets); (2) fair and transparent institutions capable of delivering universal, good-quality basic services (a greater and better supply of public goods, protection of property rights); (3) well-functioning markets (improved connectivity to markets, competition policy); and (4) adequate risk management at the macro and household levels (macroprudence, safety nets). This comprehensive framework can be useful in approximating the diversity of results in poverty and shared prosperity observed over the past decade and in helping to identify the challenges ahead in the effort to reduce poverty and boost shared prosperity.

Notes

1. The extreme poverty rate is measured by the number of people whose income or consumption falls below an international poverty line of $1.25 a day in 2005 purchasing power parity (PPP) international U.S. dollars, a poverty line that corresponds to an average of the national poverty lines of the 15 poorest developing countries. Because the aim is to end chronic poverty and because frictional poverty—poverty stemming from unexpected economic fluctuations in poor countries, political conflict, and war—cannot be brought to an end yet, the first goal is formalized as a target of bringing the number of people living below the $1.25-a-day poverty line to less than 3 percent of the world's population (Basu 2013).

The second goal, boosting shared prosperity, places explicit attention on the least well off in a society by focusing on fostering the well-being of the bottom 40 in every country. Specifically, progress toward reaching the goal is assessed by measuring income or consumption growth among the bottom 40 in each country. According to the World Bank (2015a, 10):

> One way to think about the . . . shared prosperity goal is as an alternative to average income as the benchmark of development progress. Instead of assessing and measuring economic development in terms of the overall average growth in a country, the shared prosperity goal places emphasis on the bottom 40 percent of the population. In other words, good progress is judged to occur not merely when an economy is growing, but, more specifically, when that growth is reaching the least well off in society.

Although the shared prosperity indicator (SPI) focuses attention on the poorest segments of a country's population, it does not completely ignore the other segments. People above the bottom 40 may fall back into poverty if growth occurs only among the bottom 40 (Basu 2013).

2. In the region, most countries measure poverty using an income-based aggregate; this implies that it will always be reasonable to expect a positive extreme poverty rate because of frictional factors such as unemployment. For more details about the projections, see Ravallion (2003) and World Bank (2015a).

3. The poverty rate in Haiti is calculated using consumption instead of income as in the case of all other countries in the region for which data are available and harmonized. In the Latin America region, given the level of economic development, analysts use poverty lines that are higher than the global $1.25-a-day line. A $2.50-a-day extreme poverty line (an average of national extreme poverty lines) is considered more appropriate for the region.

4. According to recent World Bank studies (2013a, 2014a), the growth of gross domestic product (GDP) in the region declined from about 6.0 percent in 2010 to an estimated 2.5 percent in 2013, while the Gini coefficient was stagnant between 2010 and 2012.

5. See SEDLAC (Socio-Economic Database for Latin America and the Caribbean), Center for Distributive, Labor, and Social Studies, Universidad Nacional de La Plata, La Plata, Argentina and World Bank, Washington, DC, http://sedlac .econo.unlp.edu.ar/eng/statistics.php.

6. These countries are Argentina, Bolivia, Brazil, Chile, Colombia, Costa Rica, Dominican Republic, Ecuador, El Salvador, Guatemala, Honduras, Mexico, Nicaragua, Panama, Paraguay, Peru, and Uruguay. Regional poverty rates are population-weighted averages of country-specific poverty rates using international poverty lines. Whenever possible, annual household surveys from 2003 to 2012 have been used to estimate annual poverty rates. However, many countries do not conduct such surveys. To overcome this limitation, regional poverty rates have been estimated by generating artificial surveys using macroeconomic information on private consumption growth rates from the WDI (World Development Indicators) (database), World Bank, Washington, DC, http://data.worldbank.org/data-catalog/world-development-indicators.

7. The World Bank measures poverty rates according to the number of people whose income or consumption falls below a given threshold. To estimate the number of people living in extreme poverty, it currently uses an international poverty line of $1.25 a day in 2005 PPP international U.S. dollars, a poverty line that corresponds to an average of the national poverty lines of the 15

poorest developing countries. In Latin America and the Caribbean, given the level of economic development, analysts use poverty lines that are higher than the global $1.25 a day. A $2.50-a-day extreme poverty line (an average of national extreme poverty lines) and a $4.00-a-day total poverty line are more appropriate for the region.

8. In Latin America and the Caribbean, poverty is measured using income, while, in other regions, the World Bank uses consumption as the welfare aggregate. Consumption is typically assumed to be a better measure of current living standards given that it does not fluctuate as much as income. Consumption is usually more readily measured than income in countries with more informal labor markets. Relative to consumption measures, income measures usually imply that a larger share of households report zeroes and are thus classified as extreme poor.

9. The recent World Bank regional flagship report, *Economic Mobility and the Rise of the Latin American Middle Class* (Ferreira et al. 2013), characterizes the middle class based on the concept of economic security. A defining feature of membership in the group is household economic stability, which implies a low probability of falling back into poverty. The study defines a household as vulnerable if it faces more than a 10 percent likelihood of falling back into poverty over a five-year interval, which, surveys show, is approximately the average probability in countries such as Argentina, Colombia, and Costa Rica. This yields an income threshold of about $10 a day per capita (2005 PPP international U.S. dollars) for the middle class. The report defines three economic classes: (a) the poor (people who have a per capita income below $4 a day), (b) the vulnerable ($4–$10 a day); and (c) the middle class ($10–$50 a day), all in 2005 PPP international U.S. dollars. The remainder, people with more than $50 a day in income, makes up less than 3 percent of the region's population.

10. Nonetheless, the crisis had a significant negative effect on economic growth and income inequality in the Caribbean, Central America, and Mexico. In Central America and Mexico, labor market incomes and remittances dropped as a direct consequence of the recession in the United States, whereas the Caribbean countries suffered losses in incomes because of a decline in tourism and the higher prices of food imports.

11. The precise growth rates for the decades are sensitive to how the decades are defined. If the year 1990 (2000) is picked as the starting point rather than 1991 (2001), the respective growth rates for the two decades are 2.75 and 2.99 percent.

12. Calculations based on data in SEDLAC.

13. The decline has been documented in several studies using alternative sources of data, time periods, and income and inequality measures (see de la Torre et al. 2014; Gasparini et al. 2008; López-Calva and Lustig 2010; Lustig, López-Calva, and Ortiz-Juárez 2013).

14. Ravallion (2012) constructs a poverty measurement framework that is consistent with the utility theory and can capture the multidimensional aspect of poverty.

15. The proposed asset-based conceptual framework has been supported by academic research and has also been extensively applied in other studies that have analyzed the determinants of progress in poverty reduction and shared prosperity around the world (for example, see Attanasio and Székely 2001; Carter and

Barrett 2006; Székely and Montes 2006; World Bank 2014a). For a more formal presentation of the framework, see López-Calva and Rodríguez-Castelán (2014).

16. The framework represents private transfers as independent of household income-earning assets, but these, particularly international remittances, may be correlated with access to markets and the probability that households will migrate.

17. Studies that discuss the role of aspirations in household decision making include Diecidue and Van De Ven (2008), Mookherjee, Ray, and Napel (2010), and Ray (2006).

18. Because the distribution of the wages of the top 60 is likely skewed to the right by the top earners, while the bottom 40 is truncated, the average wage may be misleading. So, we use the median wage. The trends hold for average wage as well, although the gaps are larger because the average wage among the top 60 is higher than the median wage.

19. See "Topics in Development: Migration, Remittances, and Diaspora," World Bank, Washington, DC, http://go.worldbank.org/0IK1E5K7U0.

20. The net effect of changes in food prices needs to be further investigated in light of the fact that poorer households are also more likely to be food producers. For instance, Cuesta et al. (2010) study the distributive repercussions of the 2008 food price crisis in the Andean countries and find substantive poverty impacts ranging from 2 to 6 percentage points, although these results are sensitive to the net consumer (or producer) position of the households.

21. The estimate includes health costs (actual and loss of productivity), the costs of security and judicial procedures in the public sector and among households and firms, and the associated material costs (property loss).

22. Although the asset-based framework and its interaction with policy variables is presented statically, it is important to recognize that the interaction between policies and the elements that define the income generation capacity of households is dynamic. Moreover, government interventions that are associated with these policy areas and that are implemented today may have positive effects on the accumulation and use of assets, the returns to assets, consumer prices, and risk management in the future.

References

Acevedo, Carlos. 2008. "Los costos económicos de la violencia en Centroamérica." National Council of Public Security, Presidency of the Republic, San Salvador, El Salvador.

Arias, J., and G. Esquivel. 2012. "A Note on the Side Effects of the War on Drugs: Labor Market Outcomes in México." Unpublished working paper.

Attanasio, Orazio, and Miguel Székely, eds. 2001. *Portrait of the Poor: An Assets-Based Approach"*, Washington, DC: Inter-American Development Bank; Baltimore: Johns Hopkins University Press.

Azevedo, João Pedro, Viviane Sanfelice, and Minh Cong Nguyen. 2012. "Shapley Decomposition by Components of a Welfare Measure." Unpublished working paper, World Bank, Washington, DC.

Báez, Javier E., Alejandro de la Fuente, and Indhira Santos. 2010. "Do Natural Disasters Affect Human Capital? An Assessment Based on Existing Empirical Evidence." IZA Discussion Paper 5164, Institute for the Study of Labor, Bonn, Germany.

Barro, Robert J. 2006. "On the Welfare Costs of Consumption Uncertainty." Scholarly Articles 3224745, Department of Economics, Harvard University, Cambridge, MA.

Basu, Kaushik. 2013. "Shared Prosperity and the Mitigation of Poverty: In Practice and Precept." Policy Research Working Paper 6700, World Bank, Washington, DC.

Becker, Gary S. 1968. "Crime and Punishment: An Economic Approach." *Journal of Political Economy* 76 (2): 169–217.

Bruns, Barbara, and Javier Luque. 2015. *Great Teachers: How to Raise Student Learning in Latin America and the Caribbean*. With Soledad De Gregorio, David Evans, Marco Fernández, Martin Moreno, Jessica Rodriguez, Guillermo Toral, and Noah Yarrow. Latin American Development Forum Series. Washington, DC: World Bank.

Bussolo, Maurizio, and Luis F. López-Calva. 2014. *Shared Prosperity: Paving the Way in Europe and Central Asia*. Europe and Central Asia Studies. Washington, DC: World Bank.

Cárdenas, Mauricio, Rafeal E. de Hoyos, and Miguel Székely. 2014. "Out of School and Out of Work Youth in Latin America: A Persistent Problem in a Decade of Prosperity." Working paper, Brookings Institution, Washington, DC.

Cárdenas, Mauricio, and Sandra Rozo. 2008. "Does Crime Lower Growth: Evidence from Colombia." Commission on Growth and Development Working Paper 30, World Bank, Washington, DC.

Carter, Michael R., and Christopher B. Barrett. 2006. "The Economics of Poverty Traps and Persistent Poverty: An Asset-Based Approach." *Journal of Development Studies* 42 (2): 178–99.

Carter, Michael R., Peter D. Little, Tewodaj Mogues, and Workneh Negatu. 2007. "Poverty Traps and the Long-Term Consequences of Natural Disasters in Ethiopia and Honduras." *World Development* 35 (5): 835–56.

Caudillo, Mónica L., and Florencia Torche. 2014. "Exposure to Local Homicides and Early Educational Achievement in Mexico." *Sociology of Education* 87 (2): 89–105.

Cavallo, Eduardo, and Ilan Noy. 2011. "Natural Disasters and the Economy: A Survey." *International Review of Environmental and Resource Economics* 5 (1): 63–102.

Cord, Louise, Oscar Barriga Cabanillas, Leonardo Lucchetti, Carlos Rodríguez-Castelán, Liliana D. Sousa, and Daniel Valderrama. 2014. "Inequality Stagnation in Latin America in the Aftermath of the Global Financial Crisis." Policy Research Working Paper 7146, World Bank, Washington, DC.

Cuesta, José, Suzanne Duryea, Fidel Jaramillo, and Marcos Robles. 2010. "Distributive Impacts of the Food Crisis in the Andean Region." *Journal of International Development* 22 (7): 846–65.

Datt, Gaurav, and Martin Ravallion. 1992. "Growth and Redistribution Components of Changes in Poverty Measures: A Decomposition with Applications to Brazil and India in the 1980s." *Journal of Development Economics* 38 (2): 275–95.

de la Torre, Augusto, Eduardo Levy Yeyati, Guillermo Beylis, Tatiana Didier, Carlos Rodríguez-Castelán, and Sergio Schmukler. 2014. "Inequality in a Lower Growth Latin America." Semiannual Report (October), Latin America and Caribbean Region, World Bank, Washington, DC.

Dell, Melissa. 2014. "Trafficking Networks and the Mexican Drug War." Working paper, Department of Economics, Harvard University, Cambridge, MA.

Demombynes, Gabriel, and Aaron Thegeya. 2012. "Kenya's Mobile Revolution and the Promise of Mobile Savings." Policy Research Working Paper 5988, World Bank, Washington, DC.

Dercon, Stefan, and Luc Christiaensen. 2011. "Consumption Risk, Technology Adoption, and Poverty Traps: Evidence from Ethiopia." *Journal of Development Economics* 96 (2): 159–73.

Diecidue, Enrico, and Jeroen Van De Ven. 2008. "Aspiration Level, Probability of Success and Failure, and Expected Utility." *International Economic Review* 49 (2): 683–700.

Dinkelman, Taryn. 2011. "The Effects of Rural Electrification on Employment: New Evidence from South Africa." *American Economic Review* 101 (7): 3078–3108.

Elbers, Chris, Jean O. Lanjouw, and Peter Lanjouw. 2003. "Micro-Level Estimation of Poverty and Inequality." *Econometrica* 71 (1): 355–64.

Enamorado, Ted, Luis F. López-Calva, and Carlos Rodríguez-Castelán. 2014. "Crime and Growth Convergence: Evidence from Mexico." *Economics Letters* 125 (1): 9–13.

Enamorado, Ted, Luis F. López-Calva, Carlos Rodríguez-Castelán, and Hernán Winkler. 2014. "Income Inequality and Violent Crime: Evidence from Mexico's Drug War." Policy Research Working Paper 6935, World Bank, Washington, DC.

Fajnzylber, Pablo, and J. Humberto López, eds. 2008. *Remittances and Development: Lessons from Latin America*. Latin American Development Forum Series. Washington, DC: World Bank.

Ferreira, Francisco. H. G., Julian Messina, Jamele Rigolini, Luis F. López-Calva, María Ana Lugo, and Renos Vakis. 2013. *Economic Mobility and the Rise of the Latin American Middle Class*. Washington, DC: World Bank.

Gasparini, Leonardo, Guillermo Cruces, Leopoldo Tornarolli, and Mariana Marchionni. 2008. "A Turning Point? Recent Developments on Inequality in Latin America and the Caribbean." Working Paper 81, Center for Distributive, Labor, and Social Studies, Facultad de Ciencias Económicas, Universidad Nacional de La Plata, La Plata, Argentina.

Gasparini, Leonardo, Sebastián Galiani, Guillermo Cruces, and Pablo Acosta. 2011. "Educational Upgrading and Returns to Skills in Latin America: Evidence from a Supply-Demand Framework, 1990–2010." Working Paper 127, Center for Distributive, Labor, and Social Studies, Facultad de Ciencias Económicas, Universidad Nacional de La Plata, La Plata, Argentina.

Hanushek, Eric A., and Ludger Woessmann. 2012. "Schooling, Educational Achievement, and the Latin American Growth Puzzle." *Journal of Development Economics* 99 (2): 497–512.

Keefer, Philip, and Norman V. Loayza. 2010. *Innocent Bystanders: Developing Countries and the War on Drugs.* Washington, DC: World Bank.

Lagos, Marta, and Lucía Dammert. 2012. "La Seguridad Ciudadana: El problema principal de América Latina." Corporación Latinobarómetro, Santiago, Chile.

Levy, Santiago. 2008. *Good Intentions, Bad Outcomes: Social Policy, Informality, and Economic Growth in Mexico.* Washington, DC: Brookings Institution Press.

López-Calva, Luis F., and Nora Lustig. 2010. "Explaining the Decline in Inequality in Latin America: Technological Change, Educational Upgrading, and Democracy." In *Declining Inequality in Latin America: A Decade of Progress?,* edited by Luis F. López-Calva and Nora Lustig, 1–24. New York: United Nations Development Programme; Baltimore: Brookings Institution Press.

López-Calva, Luis F., and Carlos Rodríguez-Castelán. 2014. "Pro-Growth Equity: A Policy Framework for the Twin Goals." World Bank, Washington, DC.

Lustig, Nora, Luis F. López-Calva, and Eduardo Ortiz-Juárez. 2013. "Declining Inequality in Latin America in the 2000s: The Cases of Argentina, Brazil, and Mexico." *World Development* 44: 129–41.

Maldonado, René, Natasha Bajuk, and María Luisa Hayem. 2012. "Remittances to Latin America and the Caribbean in 2011: Regaining Growth." Multilateral Investment Fund, Inter-American Development Bank, Washington, DC.

Michaelsen, Maren M., and Paola Salardi. 2013. "School's Out: The War on Drugs and Educational Performance in Mexico." Working paper, Department of Economics, Ruhr University Bochum, Bochum, Germany.

Mookherjee, Dilip, Debraj Ray, and Stefan Napel. 2010. "Aspirations, Segregation, and Occupational Choice." *Journal of the European Economic Association* 8 (1): 139–68.

Narayan, Ambar, Jaime Saavedra-Chanduvi, and Sailesh Tiwari. 2013. "Shared Prosperity: Links to Growth, Inequality, and Inequality of Opportunity." Policy Research Working Paper 6649, World Bank, Washington, DC.

Powell, Benjamin, G. P. Manish, and Malavika Nair. 2010. "Corruption, Crime, and Economic Growth." In *Handbook on the Economics of Crime,* edited by Bruce L. Benson and Paul R. Zimmerman, 328–41. Cheltenham, United Kingdom: Edward Elgar.

Putnam, Robert D. 1993. *Making Democracy Work: Civic Traditions in Modern Italy.* Princeton, NJ: Princeton University Press.

Ravallion, Martin. 2003. "Measuring Aggregate Welfare in Developing Countries: How Well Do National Accounts and Surveys Agree?" *Review of Economics and Statistics* 85 (3): 645–52.

———. 2012. "Poor, or Just Feeling Poor? On Using Subjective Data in Measuring Poverty." Policy Research Working Paper 5968, World Bank, Washington, DC.

Ray, Debraj. 2006. "Aspirations, Poverty, and Economic Change." In *Understanding Poverty,* edited by Abhijit Vinayak Banerjee, Roland Bénabou, and Dilip Mookherjee, 409–22. New York: Oxford University Press.

SEDLAC (Socio-Economic Database for Latin America and the Caribbean), Center for Distributive, Labor, and Social Studies, Universidad de La Plata, La Plata, Argentina; World Bank, Washington, DC. http://sedlac.econo.unlp.edu.ar/eng/index.php.

SNSP (Mexico, Secretariado Ejecutivo de Sistema Nacional de Seguridad Pública). 2012. "Estadísticas y Herramientas de Análisis de Información de la Incidencia Delictiva (Fuero Común, Fuero Federal, 1997–actual)." SNSP, Mexico City.

Székely, Miguel, and Andrés Montes. 2006. "Poverty and Inequality." In *The Long Twentieth Century*, edited by Victor Bulmer-Thomas, John H. Coatsworth, and Roberto Cortés-Conde, 585–646. *The Cambridge Economic History of Latin America*, vol. 2. Cambridge: Cambridge University Press.

UNDP (United Nations Development Programme). 2013. *Informe Regional de Desarrollo Humano 2013–2014, Seguridad Ciudadana con Rostro Humano: diagnóstico y propuestas para América Latina.* New York: UNDP.

Velásquez, Andrea. 2014. "The Economic Burden of Crime: Evidence from Mexico." Job Market Paper, Department of Economics, Duke University, Durham, NC.

World Bank. 2011a. "Food Price Watch." February, World Bank, Washington, DC.

———. 2011b. "Crime and Violence in Central America: A Development Challenge." Poverty Reduction and Economic Management Unit, Sustainable Development Department, Latin America and the Caribbean Region, World Bank, Washington, DC.

———. 2012a. "The Effect of Women's Economic Power in Latin America and the Caribbean." Poverty and Labor Brief (August), Latin America and Caribbean Region, World Bank, Washington, DC.

———. 2012b. "Costs and Impacts of Crime and Violence in Mexico." Brief, World Bank, Washington, DC.

———. 2013a. "Shifting Gears to Accelerate Shared Prosperity in Latin America and the Caribbean." Poverty and Labor Brief, Report 78507 (June), Latin America and Caribbean Region, World Bank, Washington, DC.

———. 2013b. *World Development Report 2014: Risk and Opportunity, Managing Risk for Development.* Washington, DC: World Bank.

———. 2014a. "Social Gains in the Balance: A Fiscal Policy Challenge for Latin America and the Caribbean." Poverty and Labor Brief, Report 85162 rev (February), Latin America and Caribbean Region, World Bank, Washington, DC.

———. 2014b. "When Prosperity Is Not Shared: The Weak Links between Growth and Equity in the Dominican Republic." Report 85760, World Bank, Washington, DC.

———. 2014c. "An Assessment of the Poverty Methodology in Jamaica: A Consolidated Technical Note." World Bank, Washington, DC.

———. 2014d. "Avoiding Crime in Latin America and the Caribbean." Enterprise Surveys, Latin America and the Caribbean Series Note 7, World Bank, Washington, DC.

———. 2015a. *A Measured Approach to Ending Poverty and Boosting Shared Prosperity: Concepts, Data, and the Twin Goals.* Policy Research Report. Washington, DC: World Bank.

———. 2015b. *Global Monitoring Report 2014/2015: Ending Poverty and Sharing Prosperity.* Washington, DC: World Bank.

———. 2015c. *Global Economic Prospects, January 2015: Having Fiscal Space and Using It.* Washington, DC: World Bank.

————. Forthcoming. "The Aftermath of the 2008 Global Financial Crisis in the Eastern Caribbean: The Impact on the St. Lucian Labor Market." Report, World Bank, Washington, DC.

World Bank and ONPES (Haiti, National Observatory of Poverty and Social Exclusion). 2014. "Investing in People to Fight Poverty in Haiti, Overview: Reflections for Evidence-Based Policy Making." World Bank, Washington, DC.

Zapata Martí, Ricardo. 2005. "The 2004 Hurricanes in the Caribbean and the Tsunami in the Indian Ocean: Lessons and Policy Challenges for Development and Disaster Reduction." Estudios y Perspectivas 35, United Nations Economic Commission for Latin America and the Caribbean, Mexico City.

CHAPTER 2

Shared Prosperity and Poverty Reduction in Urban Argentina

Santiago Garriga, Emmanuel Skoufias, and Liliana D. Sousa

Introduction

Argentina rebounded following the severe crisis of 2001–02. The poverty rate fell sharply, from 31.0 percent living on less than $4.00 a day in 2004 to 10.8 percent in 2012; inequality narrowed; and incomes among the bottom 40.0 percent of the income distribution in the population (the bottom 40) expanded appreciably. As of 2011, more than half the population could be counted among the middle class, and, by 2012, the share of the population living on less than $2.50 a day was below 5 percent. Measured according to the Gini coefficient, income inequality was at 0.43, substantially lower than the 0.52 in the Latin America and Caribbean region. While Argentina has a significant social safety net, the impressive gains of the past decade have been largely driven by improved labor market outcomes. Greater labor earnings and a higher level of employment explain nearly 75 percent of the drop in poverty between 2004 and 2012. These gains were mainly generated by increases in earnings among men, particularly among the low skilled, and enhancements in the quality of jobs: the informality rate among wage earners fell from 58 percent in 2004 to 46 percent in 2012.

Argentina has had a strong recovery, developed a considerable social safety net, and made meaningful progress in poverty reduction, but inequality is still evident in the outcomes between men and women in the labor market, across the regions of the country, and in the access of children to essential goods and services, especially sanitation and good-quality education. Large dividends have been achieved through greater earnings and higher employment levels, but labor market outcomes among women lag the corresponding outcomes among men, and women are experiencing higher unemployment rates. Signs of strain are also visible in the nation's broadening social safety net. For example, even while more households are receiving benefits, the neediest recipients of public transfers are still living in extreme poverty. There are also telling reasons to question the sustainability of the accomplishments in the face of deteriorating macroeconomic conditions.

Changes in policy are needed to protect the advances that have been realized. Thus, for instance, additional investment is essential to boost the quality of schooling, which has important long-term implications for equity and growth. Meanwhile, weaknesses in innovation and competition may be limiting market resiliency and development, particularly in the labor market and the credit market. The fiscal health of the nation is paramount in protecting the population from dramatic declines in welfare such as those experienced during the crisis of 2001–02. Yet, expenditure growth has outpaced the growth of revenue over the past decade so that the commodity-fueled surpluses of the postcrisis period have now become deficits. Addressing this crucial issue will require revisiting many of the public spending choices of the past decade.

Background

Between 2004 and 2012, Argentina underwent a period of strong and inclusive growth, yielding substantial declines in poverty (reducing urban poverty from 31.0 to 10.8 percent) and a notable narrowing in inequality. These breakthroughs came on the heels of the country's powerful macroeconomic crisis of 2001–02, which resulted in a reduction of welfare on the order of 25 percent of gross domestic product (GDP) and led to a one-year increase of 56 percent in extreme poverty and 34 percent in moderate poverty (Sandleris and Wright 2014) (figure 2.1).[1] Subsequent growth and policy changes resulted in a recovery not only from the crisis, but also from the rise in inequality of the 1990s (Gasparini and Cruces 2009).

Following three years of economic recession, the 2001–02 crisis led to a sovereign default, a severe currency devaluation, and political instability. It generated serious job destruction and falling real wages; more than 6 in 10 households suffered from a fall in real income of more than 20 percent (McKenzie 2004). Though unemployment expanded widely during this period, nearly three-quarters of the reduction in household labor income was caused by declining real wages rather than fewer earners in households (McKenzie 2004). The crisis impacted people at the bottom of the income distribution disproportionately. Private sector workers with less educational attainment, whether wage workers or the self-employed, were the most vulnerable to job loss (Corbacho, Garcia-Escribano, and Inchauste 2007). Evidence suggests that the crisis caused food insecurity among people who had not completed secondary schooling (Bozzoli and Quintana-Domeque 2014).

Figure 2.1 Poverty Rates and the Share of Income Held by the Bottom 40, Argentina, 1991–2012

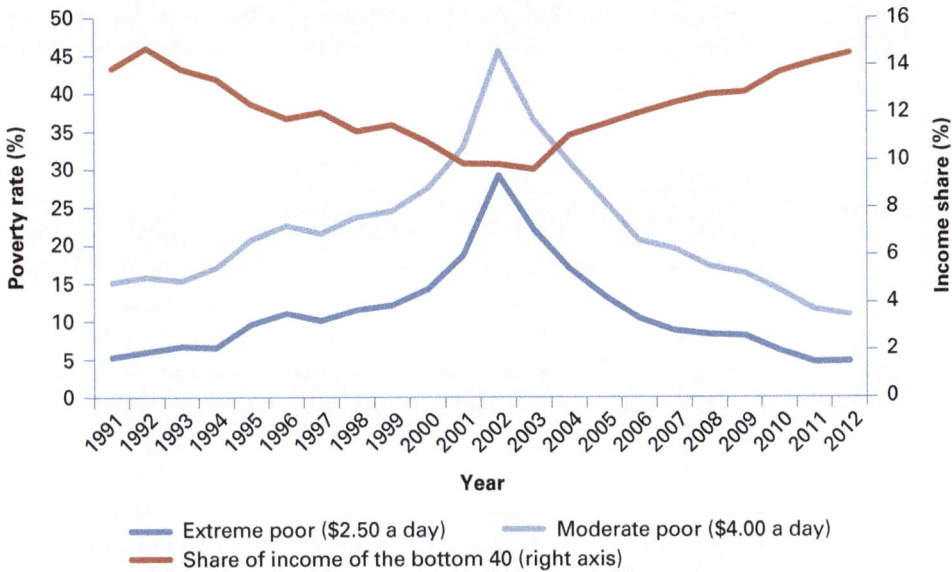

Source: Calculations based on data in Socio-Economic Database for Latin America and the Caribbean (SEDLAC).

However, beginning in 2003 and largely because of favorable macroeconomic conditions, including high commodity prices and a weaker peso, GDP rebounded and grew at an annualized rate of 7.9 percent between 2003 and 2006.[2] While the recovery was largely spurred by economic growth and poverty reduction arose mainly from improvements in the labor market, the postcrisis period has also been characterized by strengthened labor institutions and the implementation of more redistributive policies (Gasparini and Cruces 2009). The minimum wage was raised multiple times beginning in July 2003 and surpassed the precrisis value in September 2004 (Khamis 2013). Public transfers were also augmented, notably through the *Jefes y Jefas de Hogar* Program (a public transfer program introduced in 2002 and aimed at unemployed household heads), the universal child allowance, and the pension moratorium.

These policy changes were accompanied by a jump in public spending: total government spending rose from 30 percent of GDP in 2003 to 43 percent by 2009, and social spending accounted for half the government spending (Lustig and Pessino 2014). This expansion in spending was largely financed through tax collection, which increased by 10 percentage points of GDP between 2003 and 2009, mainly from three sources: a tax on financial transactions, taxes on primary exports, and employee contributions to the social security system (Lustig and Pessino 2014).

As commodity prices have fallen and economic growth has slowed in the region, the poverty gains in Argentina have diminished and now arise more from changes in income distribution than from income growth. While Argentina's poverty and shared prosperity indicators remain strong relative to the regional average, it is unclear whether the progress can be continued or even preserved over the medium term.

Diagnostics

Argentina has witnessed large advances in shared prosperity over the past decade. The urban poverty rate dropped from 31.0 percent in 2004 to 10.8 percent in 2012, and the middle class—people with incomes of between $10 and $50 a day—had expanded to more than half the urban population by 2011.[3] The decline in poverty and the growth of the middle class reflected a strong recovery from the severe 2001–02 crisis and the inclusive social policies enacted over the past decade. However, despite the achievements, 10.8 percent of the urban population is still living in poverty (less than $4 a day), and another 33.0 percent is vulnerable to the risk of falling back into poverty in the event of an adverse shock because they are living on only $4 to $10 a day (López-Calva and Ortiz-Juárez 2011) (figure 2.2).

While monetary poverty rates are only available for the 60 percent of the population that lives in larger metropolitan areas, nonmonetary indicators

Figure 2.2 Poverty Headcounts, Urban Areas, Argentina, 2004–12

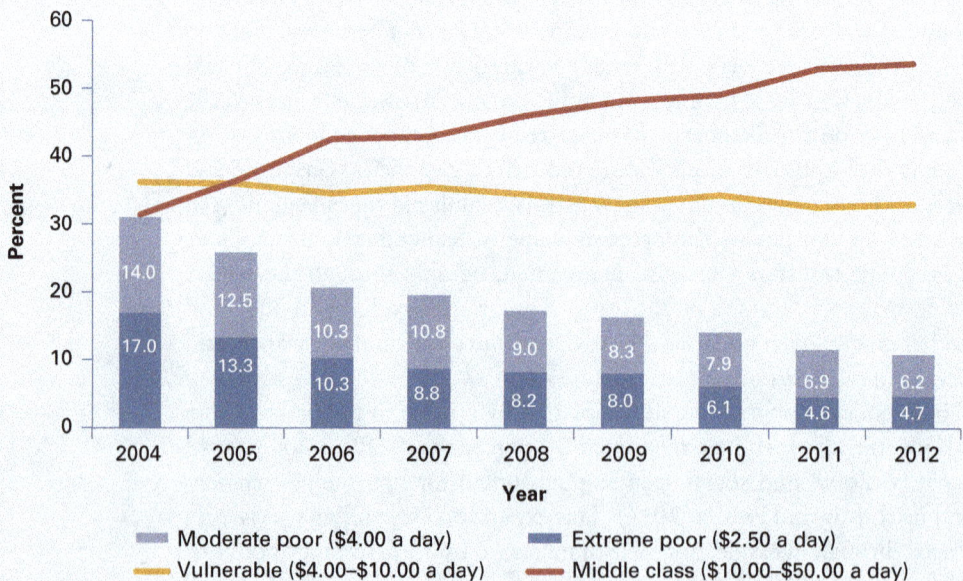

Source: Based on data in SEDLAC.
Note: Poverty lines are represented in 2005 purchasing power parity (PPP) U.S. dollars.

Figure 2.3 Annualized Income Growth Ratio, the Bottom 40, Urban Argentina vs. Region, 2003–12

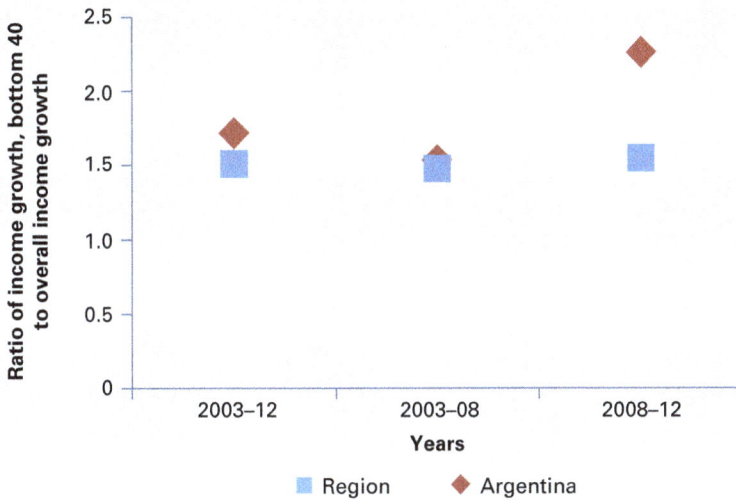

Source: Based on data in SEDLAC.
Note: The growth of per capita household income is calculated in 2005 purchasing power parity (PPP) U.S. dollars. Because of data limitations, the 2003 values for Argentina are based on 2004 data.

from the population census suggest that poverty rates are higher outside the larger urban areas.[4] Among the population, 12 percent had at least one unsatisfied basic need in 2010, including over 20 percent of the residents of Chaco, Corrientes, Formosa, Salta, and Santiago del Estero, provinces located in regions in the northwest and northeast of the country. The corresponding shares are also particularly high among people living in small towns (with less than 2,000 inhabitants) or rural areas, which, together, accounted for 11 percent of the population in 2001. While data are unavailable for 2010, the 2001 census showed that 36 percent and 24 percent of rural residents and inhabitants of small towns, respectively, had at least one unsatisfied basic need, far greater than the 16 percent of the rest of the population that had at least one unsatisfied basic need (World Bank 2010).

Argentina's strong economic growth since the 2001–02 crisis has been more propoor than the average growth in the Latin America and Caribbean region. Relative to the mean income, the income of the bottom 40 in urban areas in Argentina grew more quickly than the income of the bottom 40 in the region (1.7 times more quickly in Argentina versus 1.5 times in the region) (figure 2.3). Even within the bottom 40, income growth in Argentina since 2004 has substantially and consistently favored the poorest: the annualized growth rates were more than twice as high among the bottom decile than among the top decile. The differential in growth rates among the bottom 40 between Argentina and the region was particularly pronounced

Figure 2.4 Trends in Inequality, Urban Argentina and the Region, 2004–12

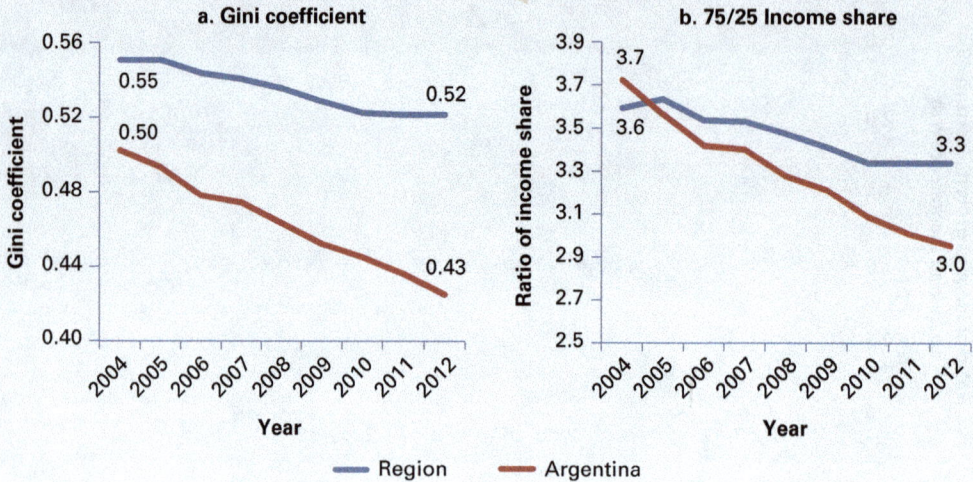

Source: Based on data in SEDLAC.

in the second half of the period: relative to the respective growth rate in overall income, the income growth rate among the bottom 40 in Argentina was more than double (2.3 times the mean income growth) compared with the income growth rate among the bottom 40 in the region (1.6 times the mean income growth).

As a result, the narrowing of inequality among the urban population in Argentina since 2004 has eclipsed the strong performance of the region (figure 2.4). In 2012, the Gini coefficient in urban Argentina was 0.43, much lower than the 0.52 in the region. During the period, income inequality fell by 15 percent in urban Argentina, substantially greater than the 5 percent decline in the region. Similarly, large reductions in inequality are evident in the ratio of average household income among the bottom quartile and among the top quartile of the population (the 75/25 income share). In 2004, the top 25 percent of the urban population in Argentina had an average income 3.7 times that of the bottom quartile, larger than the gap in the region. Since then, however, Argentina has strongly outperformed the region: in 2012, the average income of the top quartile was 3.0 times that of the bottom quartile, while the ratio was 3.3 in the region.

While some of the gains since 2004 reflect a continuation of the recovery from the crisis, including adjustments associated with the process of unpegging the peso from the dollar, and the expansion of the social safety net, the impressive performance in urban poverty reduction over the past decade has been largely driven by improved labor market outcomes (Gasparini and Cruces 2009). The depression in real wages following the crisis, combined with the strong economic recovery, led to more job creation; changes in the relative price of labor benefited unskilled labor-intensive industries, thus

Figure 2.5 Employment Profile, Argentina, 2004–12

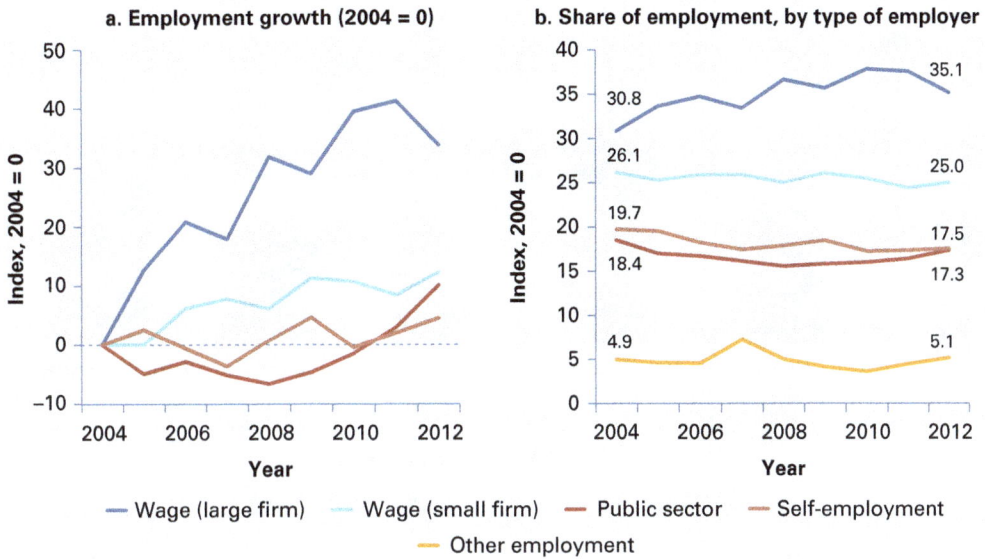

a. Employment growth (2004 = 0)   b. Share of employment, by type of employer

— Wage (large firm)   — Wage (small firm)   — Public sector   — Self-employment
                        — Other employment

Source: Based on data in SEDLAC.
Note: Data are based on the main employers of employed individuals between the ages of 16 and 65. Employers and unpaid workers are only reported in panel b; these two groups accounted for 5 percent of employment in 2004 and 2012. Small firms = firms with five or fewer employees.

generating more unskilled jobs; and slower technological upgrading relative to the surge in the adoption of new technologies in the 1990s (partially caused by the higher relative cost of imports and uncertainty because of the crisis and social unrest) led to expansion in labor-intensive industries (Gasparini and Cruces 2009). Between 2004 and 2012, improved labor outcomes (in both earnings and the level of employment) accounted for nearly 75 percent of the drop in total poverty; higher earnings alone explain 54 percent of the poverty reduction.[5]

The postcrisis period saw a sharp rise in the quantity and the quality of jobs. Overall, the number of employed adults was 18 percent higher in 2012 than in 2004. Employment expansion was accompanied by enhancement in the quality of jobs, particularly evident in the decline in the rate of informality. While employment grew across all firm types, the number of adults whose primary jobs were in firms with more than five workers each rose the most, increasing by 34 percent between 2004 and 2012 and accounting for 35 percent of all employed adults in 2012 (figure 2.5). The public sector also played a key role in job creation, especially after 2008, when there was a steep recovery in hiring in the sector following the cuts earlier in the decade. Because of the greater employment in large firms and in the public sector, the informality rate among wage earners, measured as the share of wage earners without the right to pensions or retirement

Figure 2.6 Average Monthly Earnings, by Gender and Educational Attainment, Argentina, 2004 and 2012

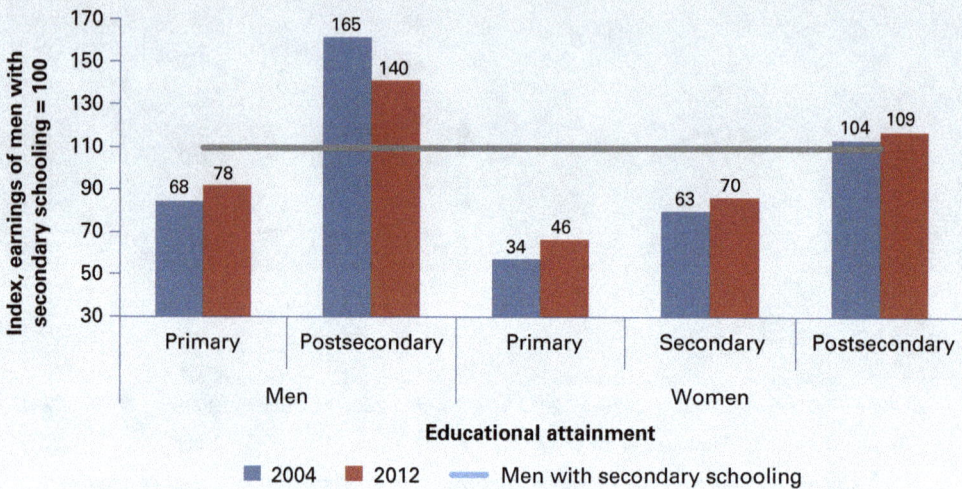

Source: Based on data in SEDLAC.
Note: The figure reports average monthly earnings for all employed individuals aged 15 years or older.

benefits, fell from 58 to 46 percent between 2004 and 2012. In Argentina, obtaining a formal job is three times more likely than obtaining informal employment to bring a family out of poverty (Beccaria et al. 2013).

While earnings grew at all skill levels, the boost was particularly strong among low-skilled men because the earnings premium of education had fallen among men (figure 2.6). The earnings of men who had not completed secondary school rose to 78 percent of the earnings of men with secondary schooling. Similarly, the monthly earnings of women across all skill-groups increased more quickly than the earnings of highly skilled men even as the gender hourly wage gap widened slightly between 2004 and 2012 for all women except those with tertiary education. The climb in earnings among the low skilled was associated with a rise in the minimum wage, which resulted in wage increases among low-skilled formal and informal workers, as well as changes in the sector of employment (Khamis 2013). Between 2004 and 2012, low-skilled labor shifted to construction, which augmented its share of low-skilled employment by 3 percentage points to reach 16 percent of employment among workers who had not completed secondary school, as well as to the hospitality sector, transportation, and private households.[6]

Since the crisis, the government has engaged in a considerable expansion of the social safety net. Three programs are worth highlighting:

- The Jefes y Jefas de Hogar Program was a critical source of income for lower-income households during the crisis and in the early period of the recovery. Spending on this program was approximately 1 percent of GDP in 2003, but fell appreciably as the unemployment rate declined (Lustig and Pessino 2014).

- A leading source of poverty reduction since 2007 has been the widening access to pensions, primarily through the pension moratorium instituted in the mid-2000s.[7] This program significantly expanded access to pensions by introducing a mechanism by which pensioners who did not contribute the full 30 years to the national pension system could still receive a pension. It had provided pensions to approximately 2.2 million beneficiaries by 2009 at an estimated cost of 2.4 percent of GDP (Lustig and Pessino 2014).

- The coverage of conditional cash transfers was broadened to include the children of parents in the informal sector through the introduction of the universal child allowance program in 2009. The previous conditional cash transfer was limited to low-income formal sector workers, with the exception of the Jefes y Jefas program, which was a temporary program more akin to unemployment insurance. In 2010, the transfer program cost 0.6 percent of GDP (Lustig and Pessino 2014).

Social spending helped cut poverty largely through positive changes in pensions, especially after 2007, the year the pension moratorium was fully implemented. Despite their significance, cash transfer programs did not lead to additional poverty reduction between 2004 and 2012. While the coverage rate of public transfers expanded, there was a drop in the share of household income from transfers. Among the bottom quintile, for example, the share of household income from transfers fell from 23 percent in 2004 to 12 percent in 2012. However, some of the poverty reduction attributable to labor force increases may be partially attributable to public transfer programs. For example, the Jefes y Jefas de Hogar Program required that recipients engage in training or community service or work for a private company benefiting from an employment subsidy, potentially leading to better employment outcomes among low-income households.[8]

Not all groups have benefited equally in the gains in poverty reduction and shared prosperity. Outcomes in the north of the country and among rural residents, women, and children lag along some dimensions. Substantial regional disparities persist. Thus, the northeast and the northwest trailed in several indicators of well-being. Although the extreme poverty rate among the urban population in the northeast was cut by three-quarters between 2004 and 2012 (from 34.1 to 7.7 percent), it was still higher than the national rate and double the rate in sparsely populated Patagonia, the region with the lowest extreme poverty rate (3.4 percent). At 5.6 percent, the extreme poverty rate in the northwest was also higher than the national average. While half the bottom 40 among the urban population lives in Greater Buenos Aires, and another fifth in the Pampeana region, the most populous parts of the country, the majority of the urban population in the northeast and northwest are in the bottom 40. There are also disparities in health outcomes. In Jujuy Province, 165 deaths per 100,000 live births are attributed to maternal-related causes, while the rate is only 18 in Buenos Aires.[9]

Figure 2.7 Improved Sanitation: Disparities in the HOI and Coverage, by Location and Region, Argentina, 2012

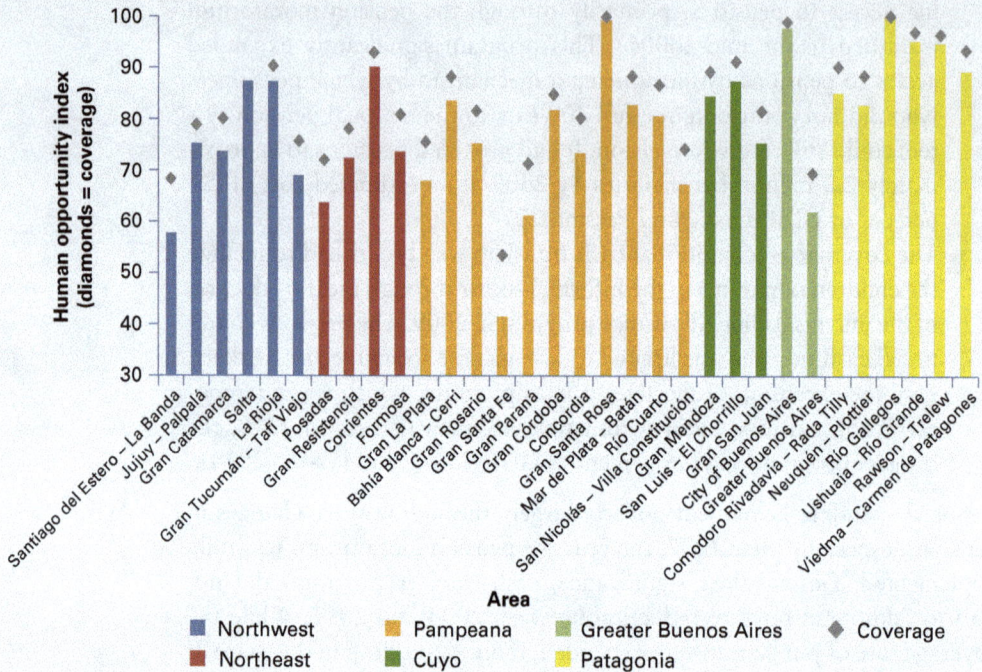

Source: Based on data in SEDLAC.
Note: These areas are defined using _aglomerados_ (metropolitan areas that may include more than one city). HOI = human opportunity index.

Notwithstanding the public transfer programs targeting them, children are disproportionately poor. Almost one in five children (19.0 percent) under the age of 15 was living in poverty in 2012, nearly double the overall poverty rate of 10.9 percent. Although more than half the urban population is in the middle class, only 37 percent of children were living in middle-class households. Households are more likely to fall into poverty if they include children, and, once poor, such households are less likely to exit poverty (Beccaria et al. 2013). This means households with children suffer from longer spells of poverty.

An analysis of the human opportunity index (HOI) and the relevant coverage rates indicates that inequalities persist in access to good-quality schooling and improved sanitation because of circumstances at birth, such as parental educational attainment and parental income.[10] Disparity in access to improved sanitation is wide across the country; the northeast, the Pampeana region, and the northwest lag. Access to improved sanitation among urban children varies from a low of 41.5 percent in the Gran Santa Fe area to universal coverage in Río Gallegos in Patagonia (figure 2.7). Nonetheless, access to improved sanitation is more prevalent in urban areas. Based on 2010 census data that include rural households and households in smaller towns, a starker picture emerges: only 18.6 percent of households in Misiones in the northeast and 21.9 percent of households in Santiago del Estero in the northwest had access to improved sanitation.[11]

Entries into poverty and exits out of poverty are largely determined by labor market events. Job loss is the primary driver of households falling into poverty (Beccaria et al. 2013). Though all groups have experienced declines in unemployment since 2004, women continue to exhibit higher unemployment rates, including women heads of household. Unemployment rates plunged across the board, but women face higher levels of unemployment than men in all groups defined according to educational attainment except for the lowest skilled, that is, people who have not completed primary school. In 2012, women in the middle of the skills distribution—those who had completed primary school, but had not pursued postsecondary education—showed an unemployment rate of 12 percent, double the unemployment rate of similarly educated men. Women with postsecondary education also had higher unemployment rates than similarly educated men: 7 versus 4 percent in 2012. This pattern holds among heads of household: women household heads with primary and secondary schooling had unemployment rates of 8 and 6 percent, respectively, in 2012. Similarly educated men household heads had unemployment rates of only 3 percent. Female unemployment poses a serious challenge not only because it puts households at higher risk of poverty, but also because it has implications for the economic independence and agency of women.

Policy Discussion

While Argentina has experienced a strong economic recovery, developed a broad social safety net, and made notable progress in poverty reduction, inequality in outcomes is still evident in the labor market, across the country's regions, and in the access of children to improved sanitation and good-quality education. More significant still is the question of sustainability: to what extent are the gains sustainable in the face of deteriorating macroeconomic conditions?

Two key sources of income underlie the progress in poverty and shared prosperity witnessed between 2004 and 2012: improvements in labor market outcomes, especially among low-skilled labor, and the greater coverage of pensions and public transfer programs. This section takes a closer look at the policies and risks influencing each and assesses the prospects for continued improvements in shared prosperity.[12]

Drivers of labor market outcomes: productivity growth and human capital

Sustaining the reduction in poverty requires continued resilience and growth in the labor market. While meaningful advances in shared prosperity have been achieved through higher earnings and better employment levels, particularly among the low skilled, the labor market outcomes of women lag those of men. The gender wage gap has not changed among people without tertiary education, and women are facing higher unemployment rates. Additionally, 18 percent of youth between the ages of 15 and 24 years are neither working nor in school.[13] Improving labor market outcomes requires short-term strategies, such as addressing higher unemployment among women and younger workers. It also requires long-term strategies, especially investing in productivity growth through increased human capital and the creation of an environment of well-functioning labor and credit markets to feed productivity growth.

Long-term labor market development depends on productivity growth, an area in which Argentina's performance has historically lagged, but has recently shown much improvement. The growth in employment in larger firms since 2004 suggests that workers have been moving toward more productive activities. Indeed, beginning in the 1990s, total factor productivity rose and, in 2010, was higher in Argentina than in Brazil or Colombia and approximately the same as in Chile. Despite these dividends, total factor productivity in Argentina was only 60 percent that of the United States in 2010.[14] A barrier to more productivity growth is the weak business climate. Business managers cite high tax rates (19.6 percent of respondents), poor access to finance (15.1 percent), excessive labor regulations (14.3 percent), and political instability (13.9 percent)—four areas directly influenced by the government—as the top obstacles impeding enterprise growth.[15] Access to credit is a particular challenge faced by the private sector. While the volume of private sector credit represents 50 and 80 percent of GDP in Brazil and Chile, respectively, it is only 13 percent of GDP in Argentina, where it is lower now than it was before the 2001–02 crisis.[16] A lack of access among firms to technology and financing and weak market competition, especially in nonexport sectors, has resulted in low investment in research and development in Argentina.[17]

The high labor productivity—$23,000 in value added per worker—is attributable to high capital intensity rather than efficiency improvements. The median firm uses $10,000 in capital (more than the corresponding average in Brazil, Chile, Mexico, or Uruguay).[18] Adjusted for capital use and sector, firms in Chile and Uruguay show similar labor productivity levels.[19] Meanwhile, in Argentina, labor costs have climbed from 37 percent of the value added in the median firm in 2006 to 48 percent in 2010 even as capital-adjusted productivity has remained steady.[20] Between 1995 and 2012, the value added per worker grew twice as quickly in the manufacturing, utilities, transportation, and communication sectors as in the overall economy although, measured by educational attainment, the most highly skilled workers are found disproportionately in services (public administration and defense, education, and social and health care services) (figure 2.8).[21] Combined, these findings suggest that a continued expansion in labor income and employment may not be sustainable without greater productivity and efficiency in the labor force.

The future of labor productivity will depend on the quality of human capital generated among youth today. Yet, the childhood opportunities

Figure 2.8 Sector of Employment, by Educational Attainment, Argentina, 2012

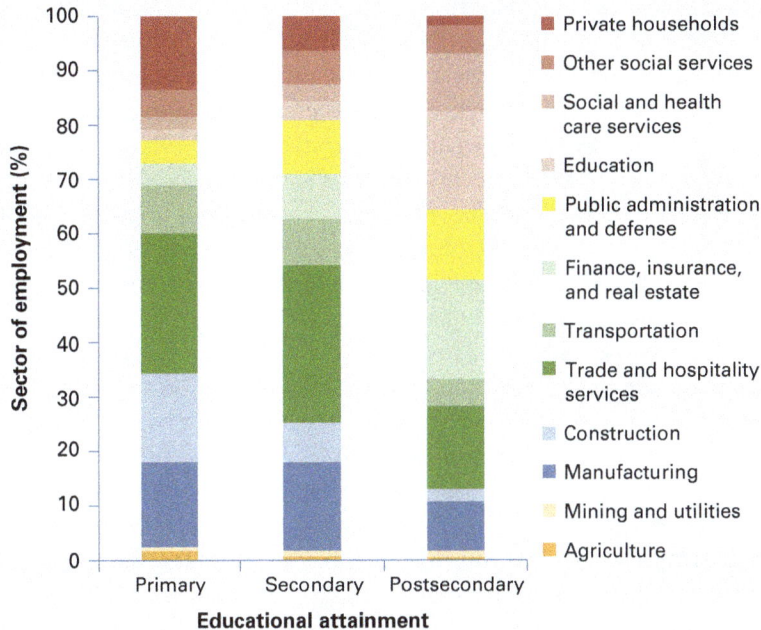

Legend:
- Private households
- Other social services
- Social and health care services
- Education
- Public administration and defense
- Finance, insurance, and real estate
- Transportation
- Trade and hospitality services
- Construction
- Manufacturing
- Mining and utilities
- Agriculture

Y-axis: Sector of employment (%)
X-axis: Educational attainment — Primary, Secondary, Postsecondary

Source: Based on data in SEDLAC.
Note: Data are based on the main employers of employed individuals between the ages of 16 and 65.

essential for human capital creation, particularly good schooling and access to housing with proper sewerage (important for childhood health), continue to lag. In 2012, over a quarter (28 percent) of children in urban areas did not have access to improved sanitation in their homes (World Bank 2014).[22] Moreover, though public spending on education grew from 3.4 percent in 2003 to 5.6 percent in 2009 (Lustig and Pessino 2014), this did not lead to improved education outcomes. Only about half the students who took the Program for International Student Assessment (PISA) tests in 2006 or 2009 showed a basic ability to apply the subject matter to real-world situations in reading or science, and only 40 percent were able to do so in mathematics.[23] The 2012 PISA scores indicate that little progress has been made in the quality of schooling outcomes since then: the rates have remained about the same as in previous years.

Access to these two important childhood opportunities—sanitation and good-quality schooling—is unequal. Access to improved sanitation is relatively lower among rural residents and the population in the poorer northern provinces. Moreover, international test scores reveal that the quality of schooling among children is largely determined in Argentina by parental socioeconomic background. PISA scores adjusted for equity using the HOI methodology indicate that unequal access to good-quality schooling is a significant problem in the region, and Argentina is no exception. For example, while 52 percent of Argentine students scored a 2 or higher on the PISA reading test, the HOI for reading is only 44, indicating that there is a substantial penalty associated with unequal outcomes across groups identified according to their circumstances (World Bank 2014).[24] Differences in the educational attainment of parents and the occupations of fathers account for more than half the difference in test scores across groups of children. This is also reflected in the significant variations in the outcomes among public and private school students. Students in private schools are two times more likely to achieve a passing score relative to students in public schools.

Differences in childhood access to basic services such as good-quality schooling and sanitation have long-term effects on inequality because they reinforce limited intergenerational upward mobility in Argentina. Because children in households with lower socioeconomic status exhibit worse educational outcomes, they can expect to have less success in the labor market as adults, all else being equal. Upward mobility has been substantial in Argentina in recent years; at least 42 percent of the poor in 1994 had escaped poverty by 2009. However, mobility across generations is less significant (Ferreira et al. 2013). Thus, while the income distribution has shifted toward less poverty, the outcomes of each generation continue to be highly correlated with the outcomes of the previous generation. Aside from issues of fairness, the lack of access to such opportunities can also hurt a nation's growth prospects because potential human capital is left untapped and underutilized.

Public spending: fiscal health and household resiliency

Social spending directly benefited 44.6 percent of the urban population in 2009, including 91.9 percent of the extreme poor and 78.8 percent of the moderate poor (Lustig and Pessino 2014). Public spending in Argentina is largely progressive; that is, it leads to a reduction in income inequality. All social spending programs in 2009 were progressive. Additionally, over a third of public spending on food, direct household transfers, and noncontributory pensions benefit people with incomes below $2.50 a day (Lustig and Pessino 2014).

However, indirect subsidies, which largely favor the middle class, doubled in value from 2.5 percent of GDP in 2003 to 5.6 percent in 2009, a year in which nonpension cash transfers accounted for 0.8 percent of GDP and noncontributory and moratorium pensions accounted for an estimated 5.3 percent (Lustig and Pessino 2014) (figure 2.9). Social spending programs—both direct transfers and indirect transfers through education and health care spending—are progressive; that is, lower-income groups receive a disproportionate share of the benefits, thereby leading to a reduction in inequality. However, subsidies are not progressive (Lustig and Pessino 2014). Subsidies going to agriculture, manufacturing, and airlines are regressive; that is, the benefits accrue disproportionately to higher-income households, while transportation and energy subsidies are progressive only

Figure 2.9 Government Spending as a Share of GDP, Argentina, 2003 and 2009

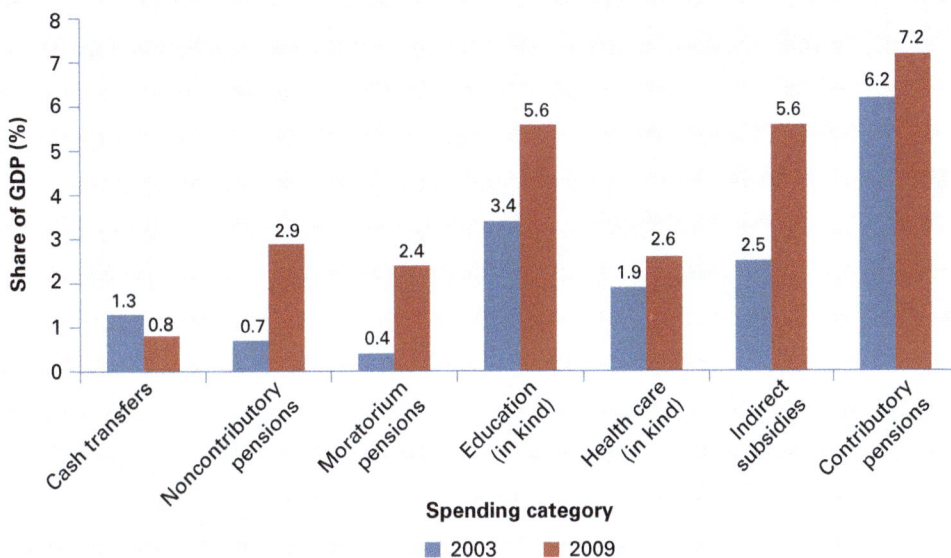

Source: Lustig and Pessino 2014.

in relative terms because, while they favor higher-income households, they are more progressive than the distribution of income. As a result, the government has begun taking steps to cut subsidies by announcing reductions in utility subsidies (in March 2014). Further subsidy cuts may be one way for it to trim public spending without diminishing the support for the poor and vulnerable.

The receipt of pensions was appreciably enlarged in 2006 and 2007 because of the pension moratorium, which granted pensions to beneficiaries who had not contributed the full 30 years of contributions into the system. The share of urban households with at least one member eligible for pensions—age 60 or above among women and age 65 or above among men—who was not receiving some income from pensions halved between 2006 and 2012, from 28 to 13 percent (figure 2.10, chart a). Bosch and Guajardo (2012) find that, while the moratorium generated overall employment declines among older men and women of 4.5 and 5.0 percentage points, respectively, it may also have led some older workers to switch to informal employment so as to continue receiving pensions.

As a result of the broadening in pension access and the frequent adjustments in pension benefits, poverty rates have continued to decline among households with pensioners (figure 2.10, chart b). Between 2006 and 2007, poverty among households with no pension income fell by 5 percent as poor households began to receive pensions and move out of poverty. In 2007, the extreme poverty rate began to fall among households with pensioners,

Figure 2.10 The Impact of the Pension Moratorium on Pension Coverage and Poverty, Argentina, 2004–12

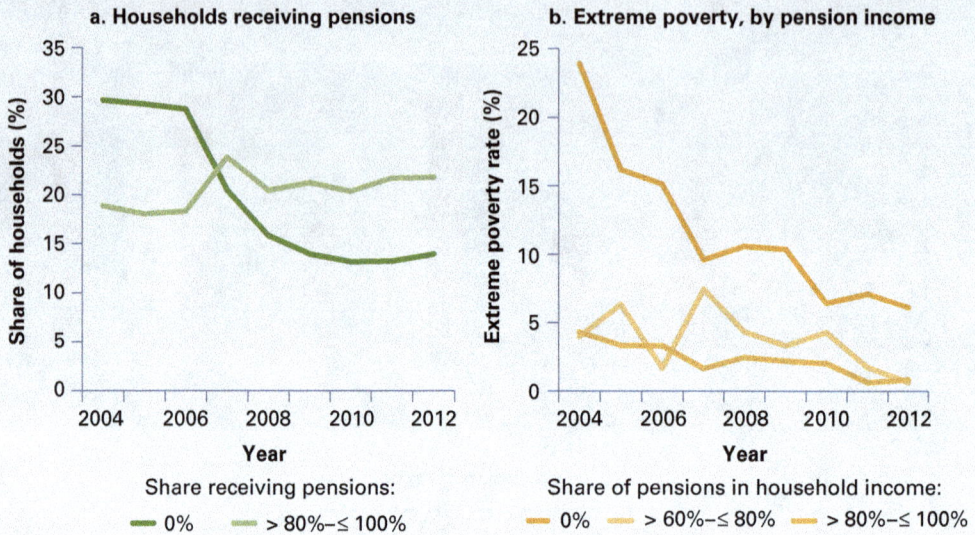

a. Households receiving pensions

b. Extreme poverty, by pension income

Share receiving pensions:
— 0% — > 80%–≤ 100%

Share of pensions in household income:
— 0% — > 60%–≤ 80% — > 80%–≤ 100%

Source: Based on data in SEDLAC.
Note: The data refer to households with members of pension age.

such that fewer than 1 percent of households receiving at least 60 percent of their income from pensions were in extreme poverty in 2012. The relatively high extreme poverty rate among households not receiving pensions indicates that some pension-aged individuals are without access to pensions. A new pension moratorium program was announced in June 2014, expanding coverage to anyone who made pension contributions between 1994 and 2003. Care should be taken to address the high transaction costs associated with accessing these pensions. These costs may inhibit a share of the older population from obtaining the benefit, particularly individuals with lower educational attainment.

While the rise in pension access has led to a notable reduction in poverty, the growing coverage of public spending has not. The share of households receiving income from public sources increased from 42 to 50 percent between 2004 and 2012.[25] However, this has been largely limited to households receiving less than 20 percent of their incomes from public sources, that is, households with less need. Meanwhile, beginning in 2010, benefits across various types of income from public sources have not risen at the same rate; thus, the minimum pension has climbed more quickly than the minimum wage or the minimum universal child allowance.[26]

Even though public spending has increased, some of the neediest recipients are still in extreme poverty. Consider the households most likely to need public transfers: households with low educational attainment and child dependents.[27] The majority of such households were not recipients of

Figure 2.11 Public Transfers, Households with Children and Low Educational Attainment, Argentina, 2004–12

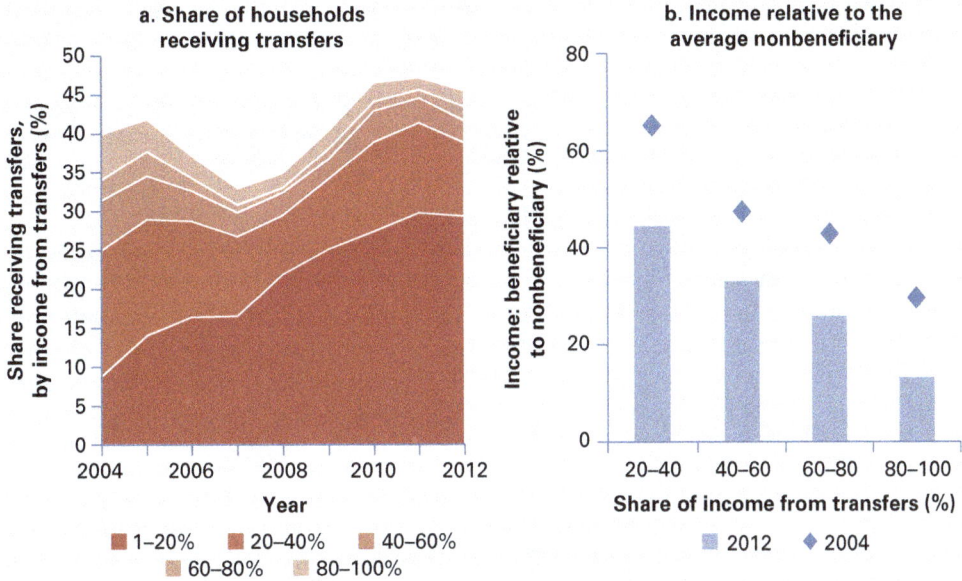

Source: Based on data in SEDLAC.
Note: The data refer to households (beneficiary and nonbeneficiary) with low educational attainment and children under the age of 18. A household has low educational attainment if none of the adult members has completed secondary schooling.

direct public transfers, while transfers accounted for less than 20 percent of the incomes of two-thirds of the households that did receive transfers (figure 2.11, chart a).[28] However, among households characterized by low educational attainment, dependents, and a heavy reliance on public transfers, the extreme poverty rate is still high; 94 percent of households receiving more than 80 percent of their incomes from social transfers were living in extreme poverty in 2012, along with more than 70 percent of households receiving at least 40 percent of their incomes from social transfers: public transfers are not sufficient to keep these households from living in extreme poverty.

As a result, while poverty rates have fallen significantly among some beneficiaries of social spending, notably pensioners, the incomes of the recipients of public transfers with low income from other sources have declined relative to the incomes of nonbeneficiaries. Households receiving more than 80 percent of their incomes from transfers in 2004 reported per capita incomes equivalent to 29 percent of the corresponding incomes of similar nonbeneficiary households; by 2012, the share was only 13 percent (figure 2.11, chart b). Beccaria et al. (2013) find that the exits from poverty related to nonlabor income between 2003 and 2008 arose primarily because of the receipt of pension income, while the receipt of public transfers did not translate into transitions out of poverty. This suggests a closer look at the nation's social spending programs is needed: more antipoverty gains might be possible if spending were reallocated from households with less need to households living in extreme poverty.

Because of the size and scope of Argentina's social programs, maintaining many of the gains in poverty and shared prosperity realized since 2004 must rely on the continued fiscal sustainability of these programs. Yet, this sustainability is being weakened by rising fiscal deficits as expenditure growth outpaces GDP growth (Lustig and Pessino 2014). Since 2011, the International Monetary Fund has been reporting and predicting annual primary budget deficits on the order of between –0.5 and –0.9 percent of GDP through 2019 (IMF 2014).[29] To accommodate spending increases, tax collection and social security contributions were rising throughout the period, reaching 29.5 percent of GDP in 2012. Nonetheless, expenditure growth has outpaced revenue over the past decade as the commodity-fueled surpluses of the postcrisis period became deficits more recently. Without spending cuts, especially to regressive subsidies, the current fiscal position means there is minimal flexibility to address shocks.

Protecting the postcrisis advances and investing in future progress require that macroeconomic and fiscal conditions must not deteriorate. Several crucial macroeconomic and fiscal challenges face the country in the near to medium term. Primary among these is the decline in growth relative to the past decade because of weak global demand, slowing growth in Brazil and China, Argentina's two largest trading partners, and restrictive domestic measures. Facing tighter access to international capital markets, the government's dollar reserves are the only source of financing for external debt servicing. These reserves have deteriorated quickly, dwindling from $52.2 billion in 2010 to $30.6 billion in 2013. High inflation, estimated at 16.4 percent for the first six months of 2014, also continues to be a challenge (INDEC 2014). Additionally, because of the importance of labor income in poverty reduction, a business climate and labor market outlook that are dimmed by restrictive policies can restrict future poverty cuts.

According to the *World Development Report 2014*, a variety of financial tools are necessary for effective household risk management (World Bank 2013b). Among these are savings instruments and a reliable and accessible banking sector that allows individuals to save in good times to smooth out consumption during bad times. However, banking and savings rates are low in Argentina. The country trails other upper-middle-income countries and other countries in the region in the share of adults with accounts at formal financial institutions, particularly among adults who have completed secondary schooling (37 percent in Argentina compared with 46 percent in the region) (Demirgüç-Kunt and Klapper 2012). Saving is severely discouraged by high inflation rates; hence, maintaining a low inflation rate can be an important risk management tool for raising household savings. Another important tool is access to credit, which, in the absence of savings, can also be used to smooth consumption and boost investments in human capital (such as through educational loans) and productivity (such as the purchase of a vehicle or business input). Also, access to emergency public transfer programs, such as the Jefes y Jefas de Hogar program, is a key safety net; this program accounted for nearly 40 percent of all household income among the bottom quintile in October 2002 (McKenzie 2004).

Above all, protecting the social gains and insuring against another crisis require prudent macroeconomic and fiscal management. The significant currency devaluation during the 2001–02 crisis, combined with the freezing of bank accounts, showed that household savings and access to credit are insufficient in the face of a major crisis (Gasparini and Cruces 2009). Argentina's vulnerability to fiscal and macroeconomic shocks is evident in the frequency of crises experienced by the country since the 1980s and the severity of the 2001–02 crisis (Gasparini and Cruces 2009). Even prior to the 2001–02 crisis, Argentina surpassed all countries in the region in volatility, as well as the regional averages in East Asia and Sub-Saharan Africa (Fatás and Mihov 2003). This turbulent history, along with the bleak macroeconomic prospects confronting the region, suggests a need for cautious spending policies and extra care in fortifying the risk mitigation tools available to households.

Notes

1. In this chapter, all data attributed to calculations based on the Socio-Economic Database for Latin America and the Caribbean (SEDLAC) rely on a harmonized version of the urban-only household survey, the *Encuesta Permanente de Hogares-Continua*. The survey is collected quarterly by the Instituto Nacional de Estadística y Censos (National Institute of Statistics and Censuses, INDEC), though the results included in this chapter rely only on the last two quarters of each year. The survey is representative of the 61 percent of the population living in the 31 largest urban areas in the country. The harmonization undertaken for the database increases the comparability of household surveys across countries in the Latin America and Caribbean region, allowing for internationally comparable indicators. All monetary measures, including poverty rates, are adjusted to 2005 purchasing power parity (PPP) U.S. dollars using official inflation estimates prior to 2007 and private estimates in later years. Because the microdata have been harmonized, poverty is reported using only international poverty lines. See SEDLAC (Socio-Economic Database for Latin America and the Caribbean), Center for Distributive, Labor, and Social Studies, Universidad Nacional de La Plata, La Plata, Argentina and World Bank, Washington, DC, http://sedlac.econo.unlp.edu.ar/eng/statistics.php.

2. Information based on tabulations using data from WDI (World Development Indicators) (database), World Bank, Washington, DC, http://data.worldbank.org/data-catalog/world-development-indicators.

3. Because of changes in survey methodology, data from before 2004 are not strictly comparable with data from later years. As a result, much of the analysis included in this chapter covers a period beginning in 2004.

4. Information based on INDEC tabulations using the National Census of Population, Households, and Housing 2010 ("Resultados definitivos," Serie B, N.2, Tomo 1). Five measures of deprivation rates (unsatisfied basic needs indicators)

were calculated from the census: (a) overcrowding: more than three people per room; (b) housing conditions: unsuitable or precarious housing; (c) sanitation: lack of a bathroom; (d) education: at least one school-aged child (6–12 years of age) not attending school; and (e) high dependency ratio: four or more people per employed household member, and the household head has less than three years of primary schooling.

5. The calculation is based on a Shapley decomposition of poverty changes using data in SEDLAC. Also see Azevedo, Sanfelice, and Nguyen 2012; Barros et al. 2006. Extreme poverty is measured at $2.50 a day (2005 PPP U.S. dollars).

6. Tabulations based on data in SEDLAC.

7. Argentina has a noncontributory pension program that covers elderly people who are ineligible for contributory pensions.

8. Pi Alperin (2009) finds that the Jefes y Jefas de Hogar Program had an unclear impact on job creation, while Galasso and Ravallion (2003) find that employment rose among participants through flows from both unemployment and inactivity.

9. See "Advierten que reducir la mortalidad materna es uno de los desafíos centrales en salud reproductiva," Pan American Health Organization, Buenos Aires, June 2008, http://www.paho.org/arg/index.php?option=com_content&view= article&id=107&Itemid=259.

10. The differences across the coverage rate, the proportion of children who have access to a particular good or service, and the human opportunity index (HOI) are the penalty for unequal access across groups defined according to circumstances. For example, if a service were evenly distributed across all groups so defined, the relevant HOI and the coverage rate would be equivalent.

11. Tabulations based on National Census of Population, Households, and Housing 2010, Subsecretaría de Planificación Territorial de la Inversión Pública. Programa Argentina Urbana, Avance II, Plan Estratégico Territorial, 2011.

12. The areas examined here align closely with the four policy areas identified by the World Bank (2013a) as essential for boosting and sustaining shared prosperity: (a) strengthening fair, transparent institutions that deliver high-quality goods; (b) enabling an environment of well-functioning and accessible markets; (c) maintaining equitable, efficient, and sustainable fiscal policy; and (d) developing instruments to improve risk management at the macro and household levels.

13. Tabulations based on data in SEDLAC.

14. See "Total Factor Productivity Level at Current Purchasing Power Parities for Argentina," FRED (Federal Reserve Economic Data) (database), Federal Reserve Bank of St. Louis, St. Louis, http://research.stlouisfed.org/fred2/series /CTFPPPARA669NRUG. See also Feenstra, Inklaar, and Timmer (2013).

15. Data for 2010 in Enterprise Surveys (database), International Finance Corporation and World Bank, Washington, DC, http://www.enterprisesurveys.org.

16. Calculations based on 2011 data in FinStats (internal database), World Bank, Washington, DC.

17. Calculations based on 2010 data in Enterprise Surveys (database), International Finance Corporation and World Bank, Washington, DC, http://www .enterprisesurveys.org.

18. Calculations based on data in Enterprise Surveys (database), International Finance Corporation and World Bank, Washington, DC, http://www.enterprisesurveys.org.

19. Calculations of technical efficiency based on data in Enterprise Surveys (database), International Finance Corporation and World Bank, Washington, DC, http://www.enterprisesurveys.org.

20. Calculations of technical efficiency, value added, and labor costs based on 2010 data in Enterprise Surveys (database), International Finance Corporation and World Bank, Washington, DC, http://www.enterprisesurveys.org. Similarly, Frenkel and Rapetti (2012) decompose the rise in labor costs between 2002 and 2010 and find that wages grew more than productivity.

21. Calculations based on data of INDEC and the Groningen Growth and Development Center, Economics Department, University of Groningen, Groningen, Netherlands.

22. Access to running water is defined as the availability in the dwelling of piped water from a public water source. Access to sanitation is defined as the availability in the dwelling or on the property of a bathroom or latrine that is connected to a sewerage system or a septic tank.

23. PISA is a worldwide study in member and nonmember nations carried out by the Organisation for Economic Co-operation and Development (OECD) among 15-year-olds to gauge their scholastic performance in mathematics, reading, and science. Passing in the text refers to achieving a score of 2 or higher, the threshold indicating a basic ability to apply the subject matter to real-world situations. In 2012, 77 percent of children in the OECD scored a 2 or higher on the mathematics section (OCED 2014).

24. The rates reported here are not identical to those reported in the OECD reports because, to calculate the HOI, the OECD observations involving incomplete data on the circumstances of the children have been dropped. The circumstances used to calculate the HOI are gender of the child, parental education, school location (region), father's occupation, and a household wealth index based on the composition of household assets.

25. Public income sources include direct cash transfer programs (unemployment insurance, the Jefes y Jefas de Hogar Program, the Programa Familias, the universal child allowance, and scholarship programs), pensions (both contributory and noncontributory), and wages from public employment (the main employer only).

26. Conclusions based on analysis of Argentina's published legal code.

27. Specifically, households with dependents in which no adult has completed secondary education and in which there is no pension access.

28. The transfers include unemployment insurance, the Jefes y Jefas de Hogar Program, the Programa Familias, the universal child allowance, and scholarship programs.

29. The primary deficit excludes net interest payments.

References

Azevedo, João Pedro, Viviane Sanfelice, and Minh Cong Nguyen. 2012. "Shapley Decomposition by Components of a Welfare Measure." Unpublished working paper, World Bank, Washington, DC.

Barros, Ricardo Paes de, Mirela De Carvalho, Samuel Franco, and Rosane Mendoça. 2006. "Uma Análise das Principais Causas da Queda Recente na Desigualdade de Renda Brasileira." *Revista Econômica* 8 (1): 117–47.

Beccaria, Luis, Roxana Maurizio, Ana Laura Fernández, Paula Monslavo, and Mariana Álvarez. 2013. "Urban Poverty and Labor Market Dynamics in Five Latin American Countries: 2003–2008." *Journal of Economic Inequality* 11 (4): 555–80.

Bosch, Mariano, and Jarret Guajardo. 2012. "Labor Market Impacts of Non-Contributory Pensions: The Case of Argentina's Moratorium." IDB Working Paper IDB-WP-366, Inter-American Development Bank, Washington, DC.

Bozzoli, Carlos, and Climent Quintana-Domeque. 2014. "The Weight of the Crisis: Evidence from Newborns in Argentina." *Review of Economics and Statistics* 96 (3): 550–62.

Corbacho, Ana, Mercedes Garcia-Escribano, and Gabriela Inchauste. 2007. "Argentina: Macroeconomic Crisis and Household Vulnerability." *Review of Development Economics* 11 (1): 92–106.

Demirgüç-Kunt, Asli, and Leora Klapper. 2012. "Measuring Financial Inclusion: The Global Findex Database." Policy Research Working Paper 6025, World Bank, Washington, DC.

Fatás, Antonio, and Ilian Mihov. 2003. "The Case For Restricting Fiscal Policy Discretion." *Quarterly Journal of Economics* 118 (4): 1419–47.

Feenstra, Robert C., Robert Inklaar, and Marcel P. Timmer. 2013. "The Next Generation of the Penn World Table." University of Groningen, Groningen, Netherlands. http://www.rug.nl/research/ggdc/data/pwt/.

Ferreira, Francisco H. G., Julian Messina, Jamele Rigolini, Luis F. López-Calva, María Ana Lugo, and Renos Vakis. 2013. *Economic Mobility and the Rise of the Latin American Middle Class.* Washington, DC: World Bank.

Frenkel, Roberto, and Martin Rapetti. 2012. "External Fragility or Deindustrialization: What Is the Main Threat to Latin American Countries in the 2010s?" *World Economic Review* 1: 37–57.

Galasso, Emanuela, and Martin Ravallion. 2003. "Social Protection in a Crisis: Argentina's Plan Jefes y Jefas." *World Bank Economic Review* 18 (3): 367–99.

Gasparini, Leonardo, and Guillermo Cruces. 2009. "A Distribution in Motion, the Case of Argentina: A Review of the Empirical Evidence." Research for Public Policy, Inclusive Development ID-06–2009, Regional Bureau for Latin America and the Caribbean, United Nations Development Programme, New York.

IMF (International Monetary Fund). 2014. "Public Expenditure Reform: Making Difficult Choices." Fiscal Monitor, World Economic and Financial Surveys, IMF, Washington, DC.

INDEC (Instituto Nacional de Estadística y Censos). 2014. "Índice de Precios al Consumidor Nacional urbano, base IV trimestre 2013=100." August 15, INDEC, Buenos Aires. http://www.indec.mecon.ar/desaweb/uploads/informes-deprensa/ipc_08_14.pdf.

Khamis, Melanie. 2013. "Does the Minimum Wage Have a Higher Impact on the Informal Than on the Formal Labour Market? Evidence from Quasi-Experiments." *Applied Economics* 45 (4): 477–95.

López-Calva, Luis F., and Eduardo Ortiz-Juárez. 2011. "A Vulnerability Approach to the Definition of the Middle Class." Policy Research Working Paper 5902, World Bank, Washington, DC.

Lustig, Nora, and Carola Pessino. 2014. "Social Spending and Income Redistribution in Argentina in the 2000s: The Rising Role of Noncontributory Pensions." In "Analyzing the Redistributive Impact of Taxes and Transfers in Latin America," ed. Nora Lustig, Carola Pessino, and John Scott, special issue, *Public Finance Review* 42 (3): 304–25.

McKenzie, David J. 2004. "Aggregate Shocks and Urban Labor Market Responses: Evidence from Argentina's Financial Crisis." *Economic Development and Cultural Change* 52 (4): 719–58.

OECD (Organisation for Economic Co-operation and Development). 2014. "PISA 2012 Results in Focus: What 15-Year-Olds Know and What They Can Do with What They Know." Overview, OECD, Paris.

Pi Alperin, María N. 2009. "The Impact of Argentina's Social Assistance Program *Plan Jefes y Jefas de Hogar* on Structural Poverty." *Estudios Económicos* (special issue): 49–81.

Sandleris, Guido, and Mark L. J. Wright. 2014. "The Costs of Financial Crises: Resource Misallocation, Productivity, and Welfare in the 2001 Argentine Crisis." *Scandinavian Journal of Economics* 116 (1): 87–127.

SEDLAC (Socio-Economic Database for Latin America and the Caribbean), Center for Distributive, Labor, and Social Studies, Universidad de La Plata, La Plata, Argentina; World Bank, Washington, DC. http://sedlac.econo.unlp.edu.ar/eng/index.php.

World Bank. 2010. "The Invisible Poor: A Portrait of Rural Poverty in Argentina." Report 54035, World Bank Country Study. World Bank, Washington, DC.

———. 2013a. "Shifting Gears to Accelerate Shared Prosperity in Latin America and the Caribbean." Poverty and Labor Brief, Report 78507 (June), Latin America and Caribbean Region, World Bank, Washington, DC.

———. 2013b. *World Development Report 2014: Risk and Opportunity, Managing Risk for Development.* Washington, DC: World Bank.

———. 2014. "Social Gains in the Balance: A Fiscal Policy Challenge for Latin America and the Caribbean." Poverty and Labor Brief, Report 85162 rev (February), Latin America and Caribbean Region, World Bank, Washington, DC.

CHAPTER 3

Poverty and Shared Prosperity in Brazil: Where to Next?

Javier E. Báez, Aude-Sophie Rodella, Ali Sharman, and Martha Viveros

Introduction

Brazil has succeeded in significantly reducing poverty in the last decade. It has nearly eliminated extreme poverty, which fell from a rate of almost 10 percent in 2001 to 4 percent in 2013. About 60 percent of Brazilians climbed to a higher economic group, that is, a higher level of income, between 1990 and 2009. Overall, approximately 25 million Brazilians escaped extreme or moderate poverty; this represented one in every two people who escaped poverty in the Latin America and Caribbean region during the period. The evolution of monetary and nonmonetary poverty across the states of Brazil has been a systematic process of poverty convergence: poverty is falling more rapidly in those states that had higher poverty rates before 2001.

Brazil has also shown strong income growth among the bottom 40 percent of the national income distribution (the bottom 40), indicating that economic progress has been leading to shared prosperity. The income growth among the bottom 40 averaged 6.1 percent annually from 2002 to 2012, well above the growth of mean income in the country (3.5 percent). In light of the positive evolution of the shared prosperity indicator (SPI), it is not surprising that income inequality has declined rapidly in Brazil. The Gini coefficient, a standard measure of income or consumption concentration, fell from 0.59 in 2001 to 0.52 in 2013, similar in magnitude to the reduction across the region.

What is behind these positive trends? At least three forces stand out as the main explanatory factors. First, Brazil enjoyed relatively stronger and more stable growth after 2001 than in the two preceding decades. At an average real annualized growth rate of 2.3 percent per year from 1999 to

2012, per capita income grew more rapidly in Brazil than in the region (1.8 percent) and more rapidly than in previous decades in Brazil (0.18 and 0.80 percent in the 1980s and 1990s, respectively). Overall, a standard decomposition analysis of the changes in poverty because of growth and redistribution suggests that economic growth explains two-thirds of the drop in poverty in Brazil from 2001 to 2012.

The second force that enhanced a growth process that favored the poor is the stronger policy focus on poverty. The government reinvigorated poverty and inequality reduction through the active use of redistributive policies. Reforms in social assistance transfers resulted in the establishment of large-scale noncontributory unconditional and conditional cash transfer programs targeted at low-income families that helped accelerate poverty reduction.

The third force is the dynamic labor market. Largely as an outcome of strong growth, the labor market has performed at record levels in the last decade (annex 3A). Healthy job creation has been accompanied by a rise in labor force participation and employment rates. The quality of jobs has also improved significantly. In 2012, nearly 60 percent of all jobs were in the formal sector, superseding the share of informal employment for the first time. Additionally, the economy has seen a large expansion in real wages, partly fueled by periodic boosts in the minimum wage.

While Brazil has made laudable progress in reducing poverty and inequality and in fostering economic and social inclusion, the task has not yet been carried to completion. Around 18 million Brazilians are still living in poverty, and over one-third of the population has not yet joined the middle class, remaining instead in a condition of economic vulnerability and lacking the assets, skills, and employability necessary to abandon vulnerability permanently. Inequality in Brazil is still above the average in Latin America and the Caribbean, a region that is already associated with substantial income disparities. The richest 1 percent of the population in Brazil receives 13 percent of total income, more than the income accrued by the bottom 40 (11 percent).

Sustaining and deepening the inclusive growth agenda will require challenges to be addressed in fiscal matters, service delivery, and productivity. Bringing prosperity to the less well off and sustaining the gains that have been achieved will demand policy action on at least three fronts. Key to this agenda will be enhancements to the progressivity of the fiscal system to ensure that public resources continue advancing social goals.

There also needs to be a focus on improving the quality of basic services. Despite the expansion in the coverage of and equitability of access to a range of services in the last decade, quality remains low and uneven across the parts of the country and across population groups. Poor quality is affecting low-income households disproportionally.

Finally, bolstering inclusive and sustainable growth will require a boost in productivity, especially among the poor and vulnerable so that they are able to contribute to and benefit from the growth process. The country has seen practically no gain in labor productivity since the late 1990s, and most of the growth has been fueled by an increase in labor supply, itself boosted by a demographic trend toward a larger share of the population of working age. Underlying the stagnation in productivity is a low rate of investment, underdeveloped infrastructure, skill shortages and mismatches, rigidities in the labor market, financial exclusion, and a business environment that is not entirely conducive to private sector development and to competition.

The Impressive Pace of Poverty Reduction

In line with global and regional trends, Brazil made considerable progress in reducing poverty between 1999 and 2013. Based on poverty lines derived from the Bolsa Família (family allowance, BF) conditional cash transfer program and the Brasil sem Misería Plan (Brazil without Misery, BSM), estimates show that poverty fell from 24.7 to 8.9 percent in 2001–13 (box 3.1). Extreme poverty also declined sharply during the period, dropping from 9.9 to 4.0 percent (figure 3.1, chart a). By 2013, over 17 million and 8 million people were counted among the poor or the extreme poor, respectively, corresponding to 23.5 million fewer individuals in poverty relative to 2001.

Poverty fell more quickly in Brazil than in the Latin America and Caribbean region, and this contributed substantially to poverty reduction regionally. Calculations based on internationally comparable poverty lines uncover the same trends observed in the national lines and also reveal that both moderate and extreme poverty declined more quickly in Brazil than in the region.[1] In 1999, the extreme poverty rates of Brazil and the region were similar, at around 26.0 percent. While the rate in the region had fallen to 12.0 percent by 2012, the drop in Brazil was to 9.6 percent. Additionally, while the region and Brazil shared similar moderate poverty rates in 1999 (about 43.0 percent), the rate in Brazil had declined to 20.8 percent by 2012, which was below the regional rate, at 25.0 percent (see figure 3.1, chart b). Given the size of the country and the speed of the poverty reduction there, Brazil has contributed substantially to the progress in poverty in the region, where the population living in poverty narrowed from 120 million to 67 million people during the period. According to internationally comparable methodologies, the 27 million Brazilians who rose out of poverty in 1999–2012 accounted for half of the people who abandoned poverty in the region.

Location is a key element to understanding poverty and equity in the country. The incidence of poverty has traditionally shown a strong correlation with geographical borders. Thus, for example, trends in income poverty have been heterogeneous across the five macroregions of Brazil. The states in the north and northeast macroregions face levels of poverty above those at the national level. In 2012, poverty rates (measured using the BF-BSM poverty lines) in the south and southeast macroregions were 3.4 and

Box 3.1 Poverty Measurement in Brazil

Brazil does not have an official poverty line. Most poverty measurements are derived from an absolute poverty line constructed using monthly household income. Several unofficial lines exist. They include lines constructed as a fraction of the official minimum wage (one-quarter or one-half, for example), regionalized monetary lines that reflect variable costs of living in different areas of the country, and a food basket price index based on minimum calorie-intake recommendations of the Food and Agriculture Organization of the United Nations and the World Health Organization.[a] The lines produced by the Institute for Applied Economic Research (IPEA) were long considered de facto poverty lines in Brazil and were used as such in the World Development Indicators database of the World Bank.[b]

In recent years, R$70 (extreme poverty: *indigência*) and R$140 (poverty: *pobreza*) per capita per month, which are administrative poverty lines for the Bolsa Família (family allowance, BF) program and the Brasil sem Misería Plan (Brazil without Misery, BSM) plan, are increasingly taking the place of official poverty lines. Monitoring poverty rates using these administrative lines is crucial, particularly in studies of trends in poverty in the country. According to an agreement with Brazilian authorities, these lines are now applied by the World Bank in data on Brazil in the World Development Indicators database.

The international $1.25-a-day extreme poverty line is also used on occasion in Brazil, notably in relation to the Millennium Development Goals. Indeed, complementary to the lines set in Brazil, the lines applied by the World Bank—$1.25, $2.50, and $4.00 a day at purchasing power parity (PPP) U.S. dollars—serve to harmonize the measurement and comparison of poverty and the identification of trends in poverty across countries. The choice to use one or another of these lines may reflect the objectives of an analysis or international comparison or the definition of a public policy. As a result of methodological differences in the computation of lines and income aggregates, there are sometimes small differences between government and World Bank estimates. However, the poverty trends revealed in Brazil are broadly consistent across methodologies.

Whenever possible, this chapter reports poverty rates using the Brazilian administrative poverty lines. In international comparisons, the analysis relies on the Socio-Economic Database for Latin America and the Caribbean, which includes a compilation of harmonized household survey data on 24 countries in the region and data on the international poverty lines applied by the World Bank and described above.[c]

a. Based on consumption baskets established for each of the nine metropolitan areas and Brasília, respective values are also derived for 15 urban and rural areas in various parts of the country, thereby establishing a total of 25 extreme poverty lines and poverty lines. The monetary amounts are adjusted relative to a reference date each year according to the varying prices for each product in the basket, based on the national consumer price index set by the Brazilian Institute of Geography and Statistics. Concerning the regional poverty lines, see Rocha (2006).
b. In December 2013, IPEA updated its extreme poverty and poverty numbers for the period ranging from 2009 to 2012, but no updated data on the regional lines relied on are available. For 2012, IPEA has put the extreme poverty rate at 5.3 percent and the overall poverty rate at 15.9 percent. See the IPEA website, at http://www.ipeadata.gov.br. See also WDI (World Development Indicators) (database), World Bank, Washington, DC, http://data.worldbank.org/data-catalog/world-development-indicators.
c. See SEDLAC (Socio-Economic Database for Latin America and the Caribbean), Center for Distributive, Labor, and Social Studies, Universidad Nacional de La Plata, La Plata, Argentina and World Bank, Washington, DC, http://sedlac.econo.unlp.edu.ar/eng/statistics.php.

4.0 percent, respectively, while, in the north and northeast macroregions, the corresponding rates were 15.6 and 18.4 percent, respectively.

Despite the significant heterogeneity in poverty headcounts across states, poverty convergence has been systematic across Brazil. For the most part, poverty rates have fallen more rapidly in states that had higher poverty rates before 2001. This may be observed in figure 3.2, where the vertical

Figure 3.1 Poverty Lines, Brazil, 1999–2013

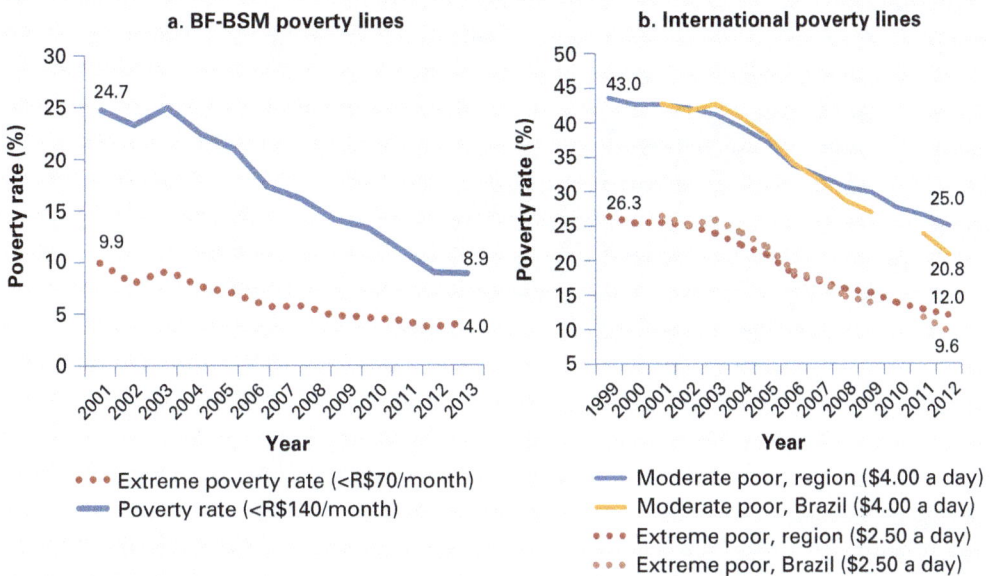

a. BF-BSM poverty lines

- ••• Extreme poverty rate (<R$70/month)
- —— Poverty rate (<R$140/month)

b. International poverty lines

- —— Moderate poor, region ($4.00 a day)
- —— Moderate poor, Brazil ($4.00 a day)
- ••• Extreme poor, region ($2.50 a day)
- ••• Extreme poor, Brazil ($2.50 a day)

Sources: Chart a: Calculations based on Pesquisa Nacional por Amostra de Domicílios 2001–12 (National Household Sample Survey), Brazilian Institute of Geography and Statistics, Rio de Janeiro, http://www .ibge.gov.br/home/estatistica/pesquisas/pesquisas.php. Chart b: Based on data in SEDLAC.
Note: BF–BSM = Bolsa Família (family allowance)–Brasil sem Miseria Plan (Brazil without Misery)

distance between the poverty headcounts in 2001 (the bars) and those in 2012 (the diamonds) is significantly greater in the northeastern and most of the northern states than in the rest of the country. The average absolute drop in the poverty headcount in the northeastern states was 28.0 percentage points in 2001–12, while in the southeastern states, the absolute fall was 13.3 percentage points.

While the incidence of poverty is significantly greater in rural areas, the majority of the poor are now living in urban centers. Measured using the BF-BSM poverty lines, the incidence of rural poverty was more than double the incidence of urban poverty; moderate and extreme poverty rates were 24.0 and 9.2 percent, respectively, in rural areas in 2012, compared with 6.2 and 2.6 percent in urban areas. There was some convergence in the gap between rural poverty and urban poverty: the difference in the rates dropped from 30.3 percentage points in 2001 to 17.7 percentage points in 2012. Moreover, Brazil has been experiencing substantial urbanization: 84.8 percent of the population was living in urban areas in 2012. As a result, despite the lower incidence of poverty in urban areas, the largest share of the poor live in cities. As of 2012, 60 percent of the nation's poor, almost 18 million people, were residing in urban areas.

The fall in income poverty has been matched by a steady decline in nonmonetary poverty over the last decade. Monetary-based indicators of human welfare can miss significant aspects of poverty. Thus, measures

Figure 3.2 The Reduction in Poverty, by State, Brazil, 2001–12

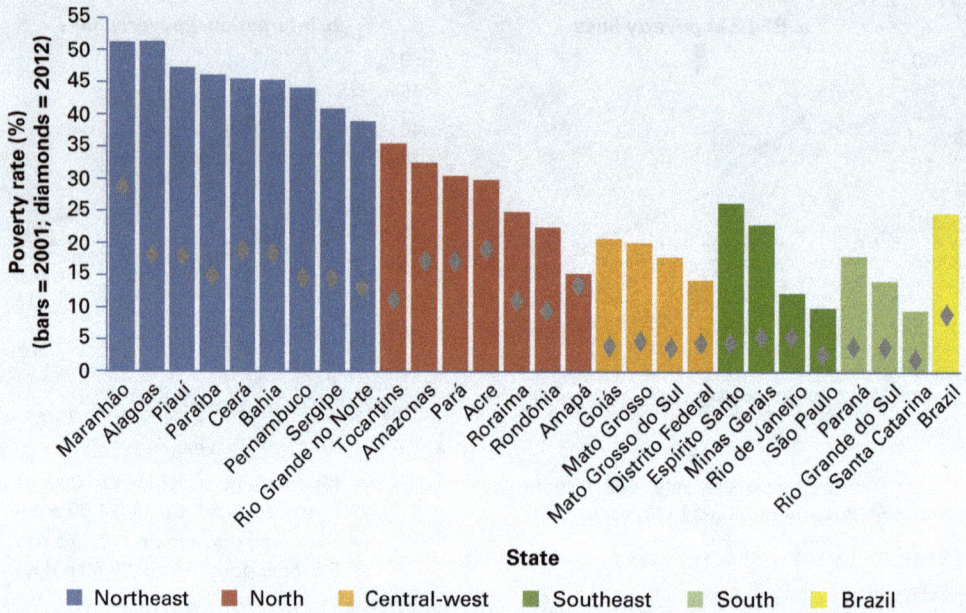

Source: Calculations based on Pesquisa Nacional por Amostra de Domicílios 2001, 2012 (National Household Sample Survey), Brazilian Institute of Geography and Statistics, Rio de Janeiro, http://www.ibge.gov.br/home /estatistica/pesquisas/pesquisas.php.
Note: The poverty line is R$140 a month per capita.

that take into account different types of nonmonetary deprivation and the intensity of such deprivation help provide a more comprehensive portrait of poverty and can be used to assess the ability of individuals to escape poverty and move up the socioeconomic ladder. Looking at changes in the prevalence of deprivation in education, inadequacies in access to basic services (safe water, sanitation, and electricity), housing characteristics, living conditions, and asset ownership, Castañeda et al. (2012) find that the head-count ratio of the poor in at least four of these dimensions (k = 4) in Brazil fell from 4.0 percent of the population in 2004 to 0.7 percent in 2012. Overall, while high levels of deprivation in access to improved sanitation remain a challenge, access to services has widened as monetary poverty has narrowed, thereby raising the quality of lives, investments in human capital, and shared prosperity.

Because of these various trends, the share of the chronically poor, that is, those people who are simultaneously poor in a monetary and nonmonetary sense, was reduced substantially. By combining monetary and nonmonetary measures, one may achieve a more comprehensive understanding of the poor and identify the kind of services most needed by each group within the poor (figure 3.3). The incidence of chronic poverty—defined to include people who are both income poor (based on the R$70 and R$140-a-month

Figure 3.3 Matrix of Multidimensional and Income Poverty, Brazil, 2004 and 2012

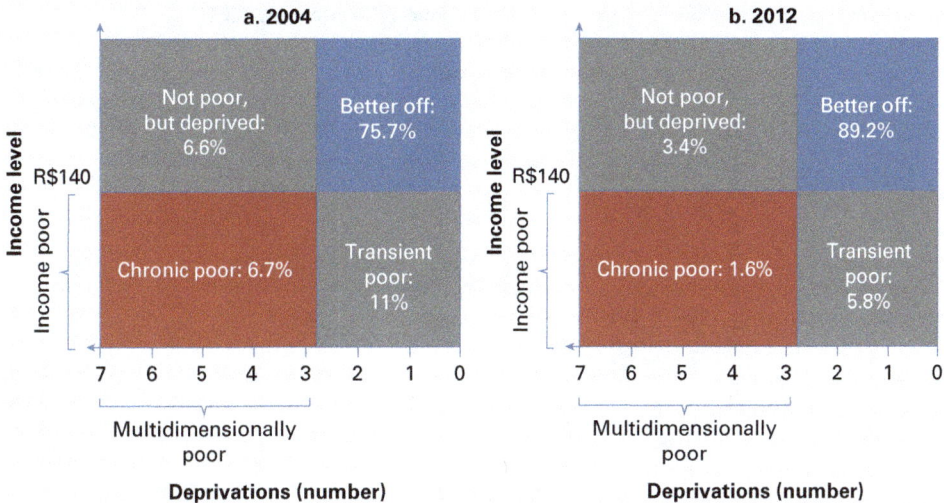

a. 2004

Income level

R$140

Income poor

| Not poor, but deprived: 6.6% | Better off: 75.7% |
| Chronic poor: 6.7% | Transient poor: 11% |

7   6   5   4   3   2   1   0

Multidimensionally poor

Deprivations (number)

b. 2012

Income level

R$140

Income poor

| Not poor, but deprived: 3.4% | Better off: 89.2% |
| Chronic poor: 1.6% | Transient poor: 5.8% |

7   6   5   4   3   2   1   0

Multidimensionally poor

Deprivations (number)

Source: Castañeda et al. 2012.
Note: The figure is based on the national monetary poverty lines of R$70 and R$140 a month for, respectively, extreme poverty and poverty. For the multidimensionally poor, the number of deprivations (k) = 3.

poverty lines) and nonincome poor (people suffering from three or more deprivations)—has fallen appreciably (by close to 80 percent) over the last decade. In 2004, 6.7 percent of the population was income and multidimensionally poor. By 2012, the share had fallen to 1.6 percent. The trend is clear if one focuses on the changes among those people who experience high-intensity income poverty, that is, the extreme poor (Castañeda et al. 2012).

Geographical factors are closely involved in determining the pace of the reduction in income and multidimensional poverty in Brazil. The trends in multidimensional poverty confirm the evidence for a convergence displayed by the changes in income poverty across the macroregions of Brazil. The states that exhibited the highest income and multidimensional poverty headcounts in 1999 were the same states that realized the largest reductions in multidimensional poverty during the next decade (figure 3.4).

The remarkable rise in the incomes of the poor and of people who risk falling back into poverty has led to substantial upward economic mobility over the past 20 years. A look at the ability of individuals and families to improve their economic status over time or across generations is crucial to assessing the equity of a society. Used in the absence of longitudinal data on one possible dimension of mobility, shifts in incomes among individuals over time, a synthetic panel methodology shows that there has been significant intragenerational upward mobility. Close to 60 percent of Brazilians moved out of poverty or from a condition of vulnerability in 1990–2009. Brazil ranks third in the region after Chile and Costa Rica and well above the regional average (41 percent) in this indicator (figure 3.5). Moreover,

Figure 3.4 Convergence in Poverty Reduction, Brazil, 2004–13

Income poverty headcount, 2004–13

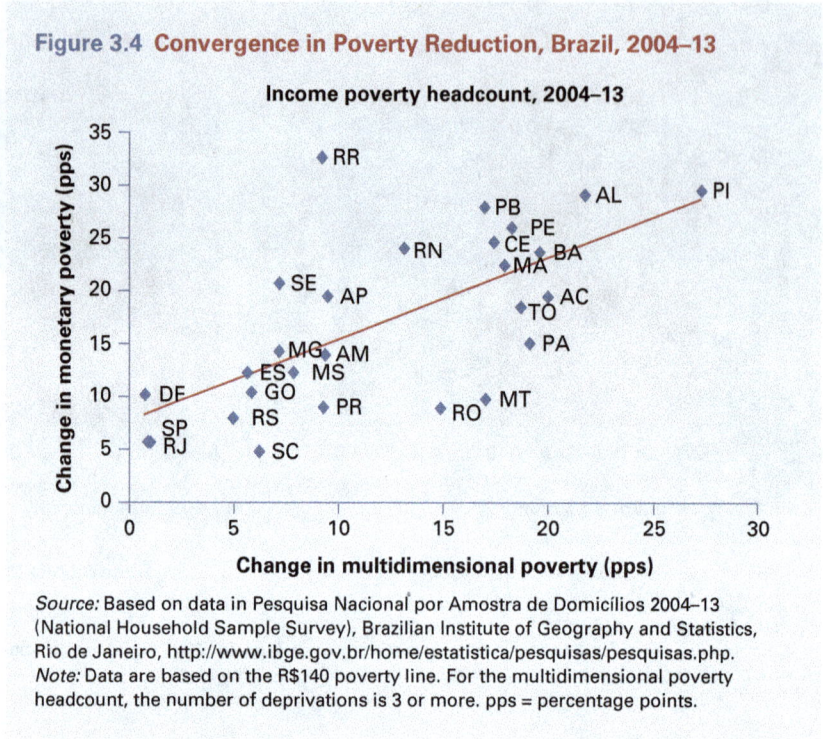

Source: Based on data in Pesquisa Nacional por Amostra de Domicílios 2004–13 (National Household Sample Survey), Brazilian Institute of Geography and Statistics, Rio de Janeiro, http://www.ibge.gov.br/home/estatistica/pesquisas/pesquisas.php. *Note:* Data are based on the R$140 poverty line. For the multidimensional poverty headcount, the number of deprivations is 3 or more. pps = percentage points.

Figure 3.5 The Poor, the Vulnerable, and the Middle Class, Brazil and the Region, 2004 and 2012

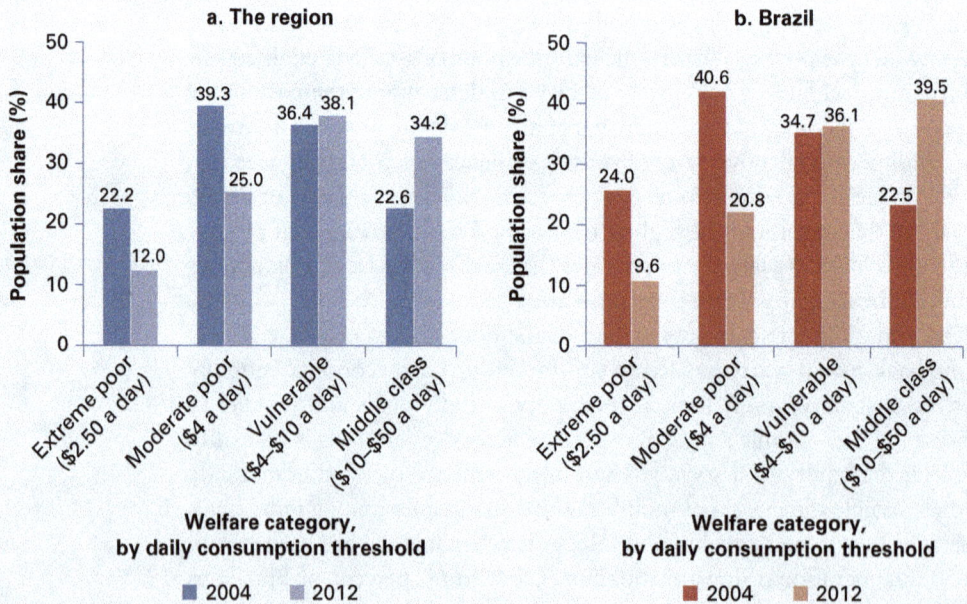

Source: Based on data in SEDLAC.

Table 3.1 Profile of the Extreme Poor, the Poor, and the Nonpoor, Brazil, 2012
percent unless otherwise indicated

Indicator	Extreme poor	Poor	Nonpoor
Share of population	3.6	9.0	91.0
North	11.0	14.8	7.9
Northeast	56.7	57.8	25.3
Southeast	22.7	18.4	43.5
South	6.0	5.5	15.4
Central-west	3.5	3.5	7.9
Access to water connection in the household	74.2	74.8	95.4
Household connected to sewerage network	50.1	46.4	78.5
Own home	66.2	67.7	70.9
Schooling attained by household head, years	5.26	4.73	7.43
Informal jobs among 15+ age-group	98.9	85.5	27.5

Source: Based on data in SEDLAC.
Note: Following the Bolsa Família (family allowance)–Brasil sem Miséria Plan (Brazil without Misery) (BF–BSM) poverty lines, the extreme poor are defined as people living on less than R$70 a month per capita; the poor are people living on less than R$140 a month per capita; and the nonpoor are people living on more than R$140 a month per capita. The values in the poor column combine data on both the extreme poor and the moderate poor (people living on R$70–R$140 a month per capita).

Brazil achieved the highest real median income growth in the region during this period, at almost 150 percent. However, some groups are less economically mobile than others. There is still a strong correlation between upward economic mobility and educational attainment, the gender of the household head, race, location of residence, and type of employment (formal versus informal) (Ferreira et al. 2013).

Despite the notable pace of poverty reduction, about 18 million Brazilians remain poor, and many of these individuals lack the assets and skills to escape poverty. Over half the 7.3 million Brazilians still living in extreme poverty (incomes under R$70 a month as of 2012) are located in the northeast macroregion, followed by the southeast (22.7 percent) and the north (11.0 percent). The average number of years of education attained by the heads of households among the poor is 4.7, in comparison with 7.4 among the heads of nonpoor households (table 3.1). Moreover, less than half of all the poor live in dwellings connected to sewerage networks, and about two-thirds have water connections, while the corresponding shares among nonpoor households are 78.5 and 95.4 percent, respectively. The vast majority of the poor work in informal jobs, in contrast with 27.5 percent of the nonpoor.

Another key challenge for Brazil is vulnerability. While it has decreased over the past decade, vulnerability is stubbornly pervasive. In 2013, over 27 million people, or about 14 percent of the population, while not poor, had incomes insufficient to take them into the middle class. According to the BF-BSM poverty lines, this means that a fourth of the population is either poor or vulnerable. The vulnerable face a high risk of falling into poverty in the event of economic shocks given the predominant role of labor income in their household finances. Additional challenges include the high share of the vulnerable working in the informal sector. Addressing vulnerability is thus a major problem in the effort to sustain and deepen the gains in shared prosperity achieved over the past decade.

A Positive Performance, but Challenges Remain

Growth has benefited the bottom 40 significantly in Brazil, which is a positive sign for shared prosperity. A look at the measure used by the World Bank to track trends in shared prosperity—income growth among the bottom 40—shows that improvement in this indicator has been substantial: incomes among the bottom 40 increased at an average annualized rate of 6.5 percent from 2002 to 2012. This is almost double the rate of growth of the mean income of the country, which was 3.6 percent during the same period, evidence that economic progress was favoring the poor more than proportionally. The depth of pro-poor growth in Brazil has also been remarkable relative to the performance in Latin America and the Caribbean. Brazil's bottom 40 recorded the fourth most rapid growth rate among this group in the countries of the region, which saw an average growth rate of 4.8 percent in 2002–12.

The states having the largest shares of individuals counted among the country's bottom 40 are concentrated in the northeast macroregion. Over half the populations in most north and northeastern states are included among Brazil's bottom 40. Thus, in Maranhão, the share is 70 percent (figure 3.6). The smallest shares occur in states in the southeast and south, such as Santa Catarina, where the share is only 16 percent.

The relatively larger-than-average gains in income among the poor and vulnerable are a common denominator across almost all states. This suggests that growth was pro-poor at the subnational level. Indeed, relative to the upper segment of the income distribution in each state, real income per capita grew more quickly among individuals counted among the country's bottom 40 in every state except Roraima (where the growth rate was the same), Maranhão, and Tocantins. Moreover, in many states, including some with higher initial levels of poverty, the absolute difference in growth rates between the bottom 40 and the mean of the entire population was notable (figure 3.7). For instance, annually between 2002 and 2012, incomes in Pernambuco and Piauí grew 6.7 and 7.3 percent more quickly, respectively, among low-income individuals than among the entire state population (4.1 and 5.6 percent, respectively).

The trend in the Gini coefficient, a standard measure of inequality, has shown a rapid, significant, and sustained reduction since 1999. It fell by six points, from 0.59 in 2001 to 0.53 in 2012. This narrowing in inequality is comparable with the decline of five points in the Gini across Latin America and the Caribbean, which had a Gini coefficient of 0.52 in 2012 (figure 3.8, chart a).[2] The reduction in inequality has been evident in urban and rural

Figure 3.6 Shares of the Country's Bottom 40, by State and Macroregion, Brazil, 2012

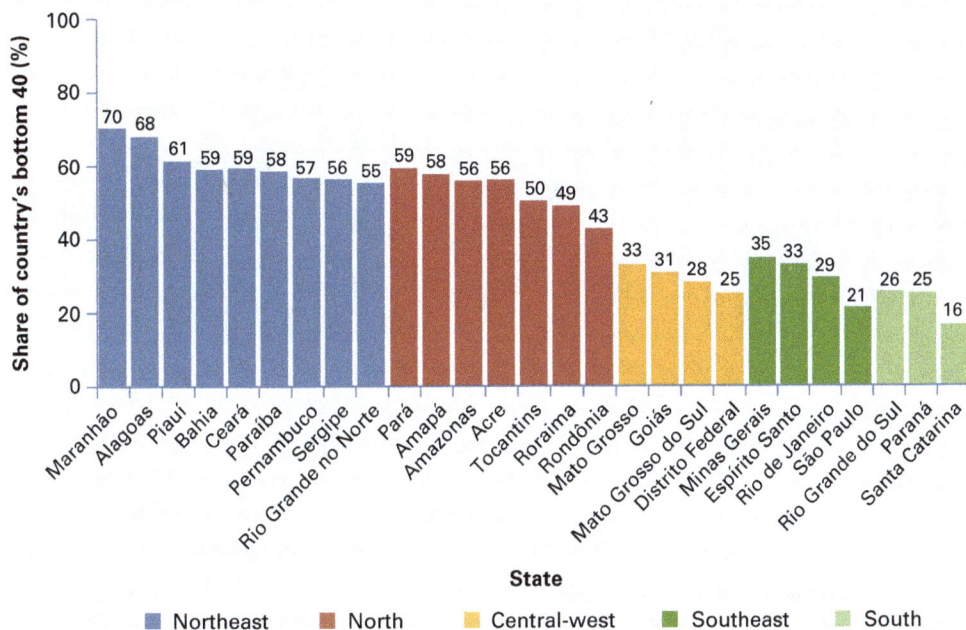

Source: Calculations based on Pesquisa Nacional por Amostra de Domicílios 2012 (National Household Sample Survey), Brazilian Institute of Geography and Statistics, Rio de Janeiro, http://www.ibge.gov.br/home/estatistica /pesquisas/pesquisas.php.

settings and seems to be converging (figure 3.8, chart b). However, inequality is wider in urban areas than in rural areas in Brazil; as of 2012, the Gini in urban areas was 0.52, compared with 0.49 in rural areas.

Despite important advances in reducing inequality, Brazil, like most of the region, continues to be highly unequal. Inequality in Brazil is above the average in a region that is already associated with large income disparities. As of 2011, when comparable data exist for a large number of countries in the region, Brazil was the fourth-most unequal country in the region after Honduras, Guatemala, and Colombia. Moreover, as data for Brazil for 2012 show, 10.7 percent of total income was accrued by the bottom 40, in contrast to 12.6 percent of the total income concentrated among the richest 1 percent of the distribution. Similarly, looking at income accumulation across socioeconomic groups, one sees that the poor account for 3.7 percent, the vulnerable 17.6 percent, the middle class 52.2 percent, and the rich (the top 4 percent of the population) 26.5 percent (figure 3.9). Benchmarked against the BRIC countries (Brazil, the Russian Federation, India, and China), inequality measured through the Gini coefficient is also higher in Brazil than in Russia (0.40 in 2009), India (almost 0.35 in 2010), and China (0.43 in 2009).[3]

Figure 3.7 Income Growth, Bottom 40 and Overall Population, by State, Brazil, 2002–12

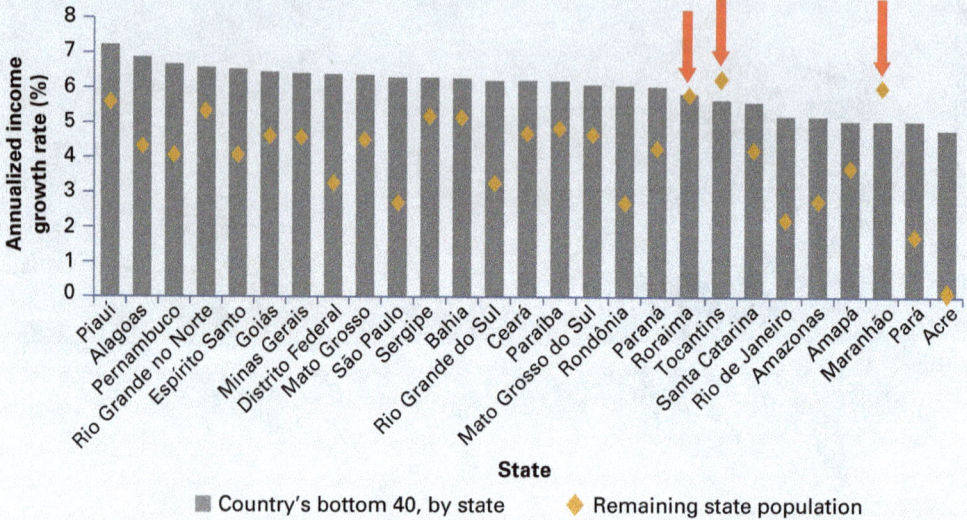

Source: Calculations based on Pesquisa Nacional por Amostra de Domicílios 2002, 2012 (National Household Sample Survey), Brazilian Institute of Geography and Statistics, Rio de Janeiro, http://www.ibge.gov.br/home /estatistica/pesquisas/pesquisas.php.

Figure 3.8 Trends in Inequality, Brazil, 2001–12

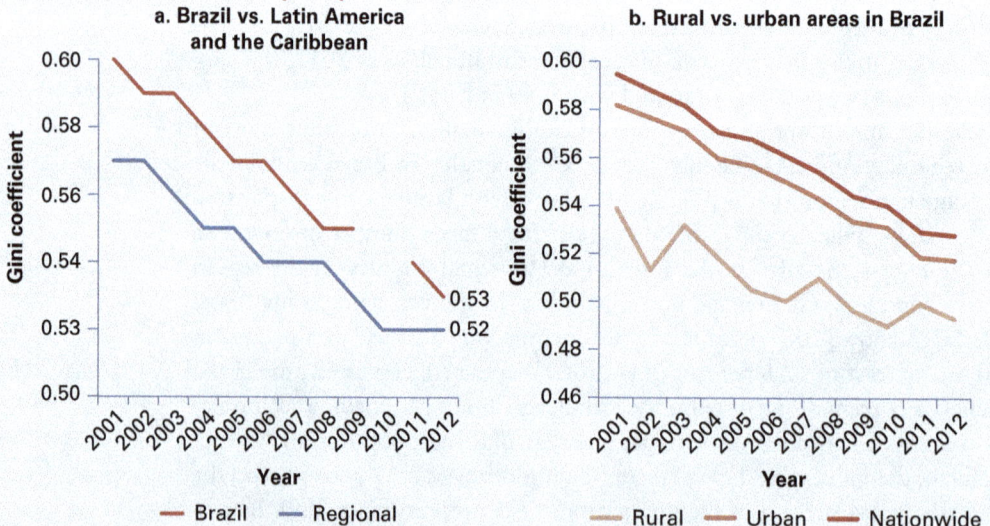

Sources: Chart a: Based on data in SEDLAC. Chart b: Calculations based on Pesquisa Nacional por Amostra de Domicílios 2001–12 (National Household Sample Survey), Brazilian Institute of Geography and Statistics, Rio de Janeiro, http://www.ibge.gov.br/home/estatistica/pesquisas/pesquisas.php.

Figure 3.9 Income Distribution, Brazil, 2012

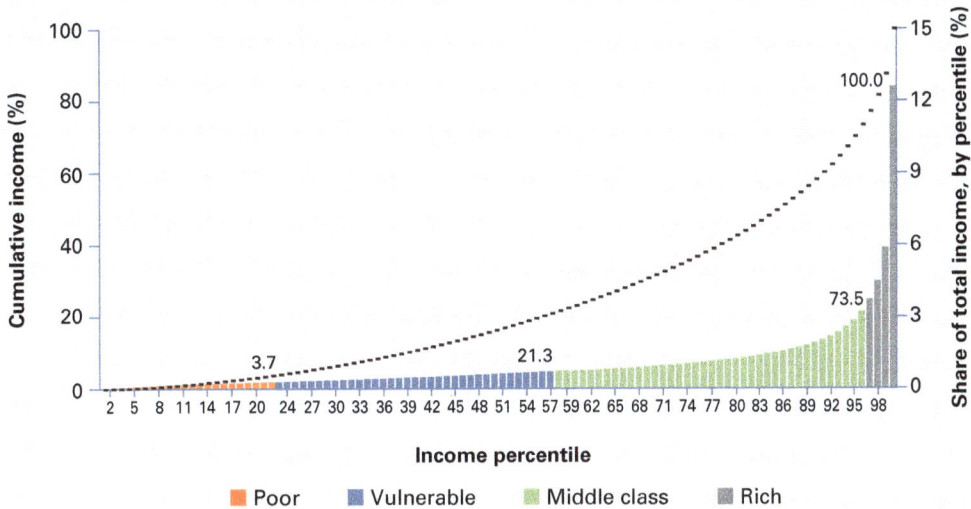

Source: Based on data in SEDLAC.

What Is Behind the Rapid Reduction in Poverty?

Modest, but strong and stable economic growth has been the main driver of poverty reduction in Brazil. Real gross domestic product (GDP) grew annually, on average, by 3.4 percent between 1999 and 2012, below the performance of the other BRIC countries (9.9, 6.9, and 5.1 percent in China, India, and Russia, respectively), but above the average in Latin America and the Caribbean (3.2 percent). Per capita income in Brazil grew at an average real annualized rate of 2.3 percent during the period, slightly more quickly than the regional average (1.8 percent) (figure 3.10). While still modest, this relatively stronger and more well-sustained economic performance diverges from the relatively weak and volatile growth level that Brazil had recorded in previous decades. Average annual real GDP per capita growth in the 1980s and 1990s was 0.18 and 0.80 percent, respectively. Growth decompositions show that the service sector has been the main contributor to the positive performance of the economy over the last decade.

Growth incidence analysis also suggests that economic growth played a leading role in the reduction in poverty. Growth incidence curves, which plot income per capita growth rates across percentiles of a baseline distribution, can be used to visualize differences in growth rates across the population. The curve for Brazil shows that the evolution of income resulting from economic growth has been pro-poor. Per capita income among individuals in the bottom 20 and the bottom 40 grew annually by 6–7 percent in 2001–12, nearly twice as quickly as the mean growth rate of the whole population (3.4 percent) (figure 3.11). Moreover, decompositions that

Figure 3.10 Annualized GDP per Capita Growth Rate, Latin America and the Caribbean, 1999–2012

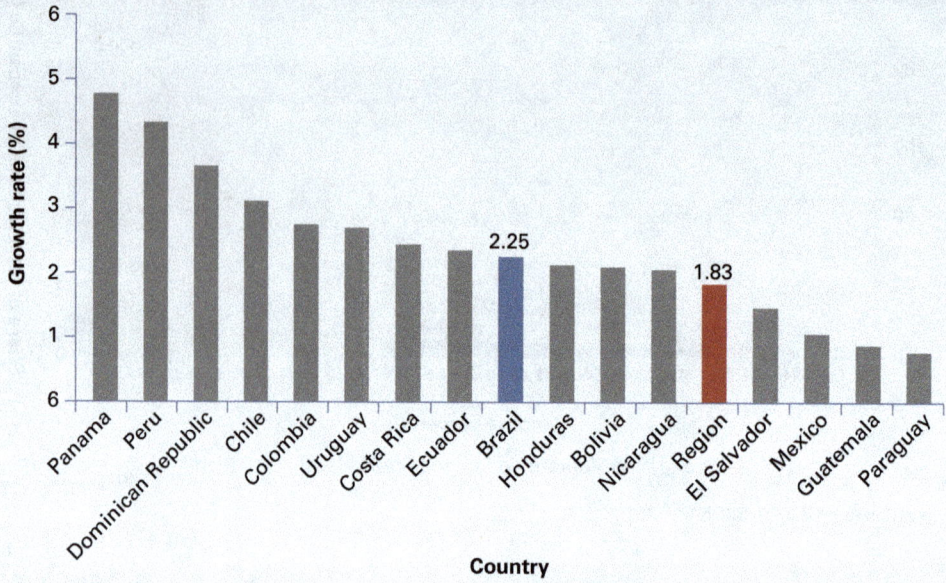

Source: Based on data in SEDLAC.

Figure 3.11 Annualized Growth Incidence Curve, Brazil, 2001–12

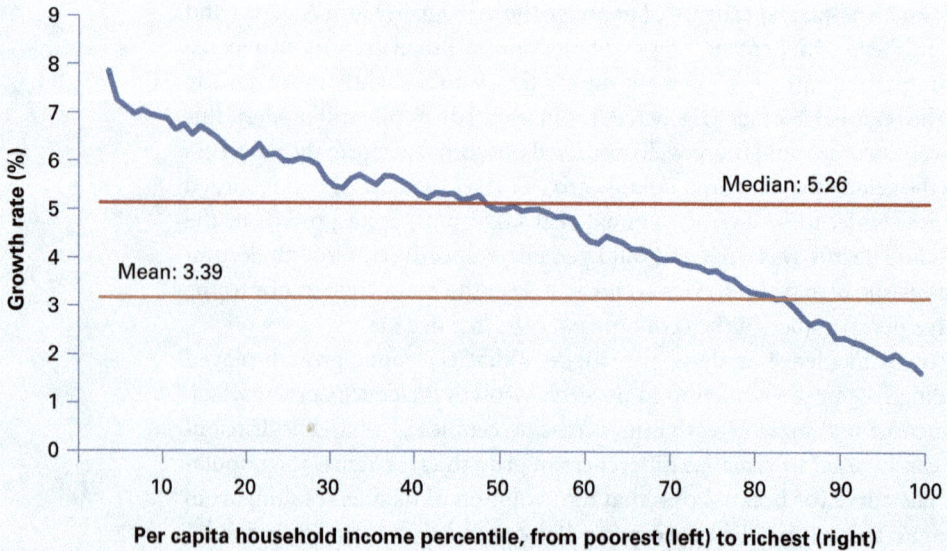

Source: Based on data in SEDLAC.

disentangle changes in poverty into balanced (that is, distribution-neutral) income growth and changes exclusively in the income distribution show that economic growth explains nearly two-thirds of the fall in poverty over the period. This is comparable with the portion of the fall in poverty that is explained by economic growth in the Latin America and Caribbean region.

Building on the stability in the macroeconomy and in growth, the government accelerated poverty reduction by implementing ambitious, progressive, and effective social policies. In the 1990s and 2000s, it advanced substantial reforms in social assistance policy. The reforms included the design and implementation of noncontributory unconditional and conditional cash transfer programs targeted at low-income families, among which the BF conditional cash transfer program and the noncontributory pension program Benefício de Prestação Continuada (continuous cash benefit) are the largest (box 3.2). A more active redistributive policy contributed to shaping the advances in poverty reduction and the promotion of shared prosperity. The relationship between annualized GDP growth and poverty reduction in 2002–12 suggests that poverty (measured by the $4.00 PPP poverty line) fell

Box 3.2 The Bolsa Família Program, Brazil

Created in 2003, the Bolsa Família (family allowance, BF) is the largest conditional cash transfer program in the world, serving almost 14 million families, 38.8 percent of all families in the country. In 2011, Dilma Rousseff's government adopted a new strategy to eliminate extreme poverty, the Brasil sem Misería (Brazil without Misery, BSM) plan, with which the BF was integrated. Through the strategy, the government deposits monthly cash transfers for beneficiary households that are aimed at helping the households secure minimum standards of education, health care, and nutrition. Households among the poor and the extreme poor are defined as households living on less than R$140 and R$70 per capita a month, respectively. The amount of the transfer depends on the size of the household, the age of its members, and the income level. The financial assistance is also conditional on household behavior and commitments, including vaccination and medical checkups among children 7 years old and younger, prenatal care among pregnant mothers, and mandatory school attendance among children 7 to 16 years of age. In 2013, to address the remaining cases of extreme poverty, the government launched Brasil Carinhoso (Brazil Cares), an integrated program focused on children and youth up to 15 years of age.

Several positive outcomes have been attributed to the BF program. Extensive evaluation research has shown that the BF contributed to reducing the dropout rate in primary and secondary education and improving the school promotion rate by grade among beneficiaries. López-Calva and Rocha (2012) also attribute to the BF a key role in the country's progress in leveling educational attainment across the population. A rise in the average number of years of schooling led to a decline in educational inequality, which, according to the authors, has been at the historical root of labor inequality and, ultimately, income inequality. IPEA (2010) argues that the BF accounted for about 13 percent of the total reduction in the Gini coefficient between 1997 and 2009. The BF program is also associated with a reduction by 19.4 percent in under-5 mortality rates. Similarly, pregnant beneficiary women recorded 1.6 more prenatal visits, and their children weighed more, on average, than the children of nonbeneficiaries (Jannuzzi and Pinto 2013). Evaluations of the effects of the BF on labor market outcomes have ruled out the possibility that program benefits discourage the labor supply of participants. Other important indirect impacts have also been found, including reductions in domestic violence and teenage pregnancies among BF beneficiaries (see Perova, Reynolds, and Müller 2012).

Figure 3.12 Formal and Informal Jobs, Brazil, 2001–11

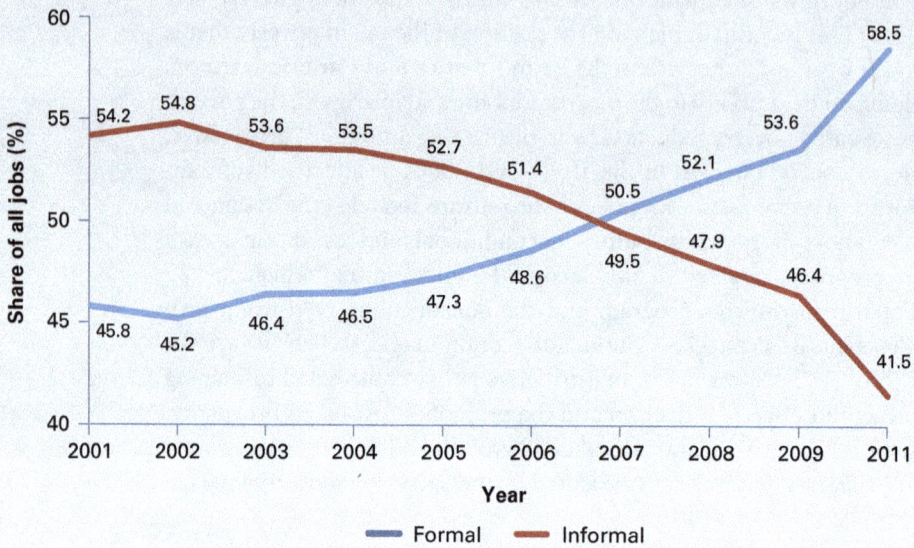

Source: Chahad and Pozzo 2013.
Note: Formal includes workers who contribute to social protection programs, including *militaries* (military personnel) and *estatutários* (statutory civil servants governed by specific labor legislation). Informal covers workers who do not have signed contracts (*sem carteira assinada*).

annually by 2.5 percentage points for each percentage point increase in GDP per capita. This elasticity is greater in Brazil than in other countries in the region: 1.4 in Colombia and Peru, 1.5 in Mexico, 0.8 in Panama, and 1.7 in the region.[4] Poverty decompositions also show that a more equitable income distribution is associated with 35 percent of the fall in moderate poverty in Brazil. In particular, income from transfers (public and private) accounted for 22 percent of the fall in moderate poverty, signaling the important role of public noncontributory programs in poverty alleviation.

A context of stronger, more well-sustained growth has translated into a more dynamic labor market, thereby raising employment and improving the quality of jobs. Over the past decade, Brazil has seen substantial job creation. Labor force participation and employment indicators were at record levels in the first decade of the 2000s. Nearly 20 million Brazilians joined the labor force between 2000 and 2011, representing an increase of 23 percent (Estevão and de Carvalho Filho 2012). According to the Brazilian Institute of Geography and Statistics, unemployment fell from 12.3 percent in 2003 to 5.5 percent in 2012. The creation of new jobs also translated into more formal jobs; after 2007, the proportion of jobs in the formal sector began to exceed the share of informal employment for the first time in recent years (figure 3.12).

Along with the decline in unemployment and the higher rates of formality, real wages grew remarkably. On average, real wages rose 26 percent between 2002 and 2011. A possible factor behind this trend was the greater

Figure 3.13 Income Components in the Decline in Poverty, Brazil, 2003–12

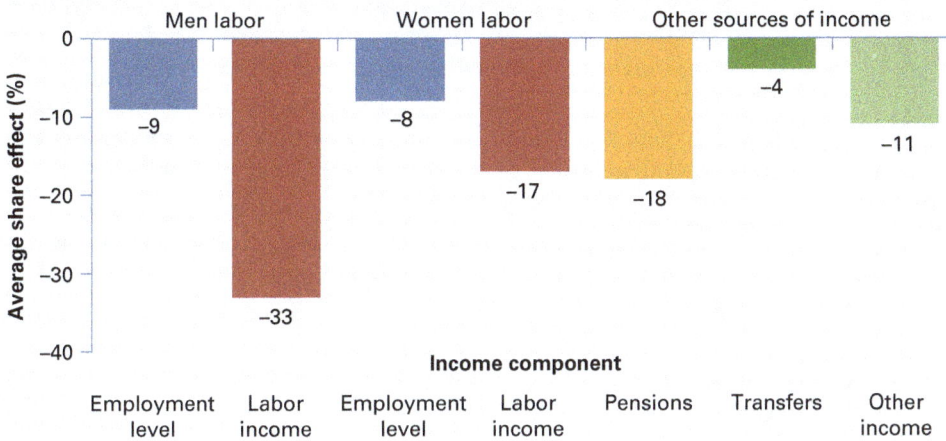

Source: Based on data in SEDLAC.

equality in the returns to schooling. The expansion in the demand for goods and services (particularly nontradable goods and services) likely raised the demand for unskilled workers and, consequently, the relative labor earnings of these workers. In addition, an active minimum wage policy boosted the official minimum wage by 76 percent in real terms between 2003 and 2013.[5] As a result of the significant job creation, a widespread surge in skills (including more highly skilled labor supply among the vulnerable), and a substantial rise in female labor force participation, labor markets now feature more and better jobs, higher incomes, and lower unemployment.

The positive labor market outcomes of the last decade help explain why labor earnings have been the main driver of poverty reduction. A decomposition of the changes in poverty by income source based on the international $4.00-a-day poverty line indicates that over two-thirds (67 percent) of the decline in total poverty between 2003 and 2012 was associated with improvements in labor income. Around 37 percent of the changes are attributable to labor income among women, which has been driven by greater female labor force participation and higher incomes generally (figure 3.13). These trends are in line with what has been observed throughout the region, where a similar share of the fall in poverty (69 percent) has been found to derive from labor incomes in which the earnings of women are also playing a prominent role.

The Challenges Ahead and the Role of Policy in Poverty Reduction

Stronger, but still modest economic growth, supplemented by well-targeted, effective social policies, has contributed greatly to the success of Brazil in reducing poverty and raising shared prosperity. A package of policy reforms initiated in the mid-1990s sought to achieve macroeconomic stability and fiscal prudence and to reinvigorate international trade. Largely as a result of the new policy regime, the government managed to bolster the macro-economic fundamentals, including by controlling inflation and fiscal deficits and lowering the vulnerability to domestic and external shocks. This led to greater, though still modest economic growth over the last decade, which contributed significantly to the reduction in poverty. The more favorable macroeconomic environment was accompanied by an expansion in the federal government's social assistance spending, most notably through the noncontributory pension program, unemployment insurance, and the BF conditional cash transfer program so that the entire income distribution benefited, while redistributive policies allocated more resources to the poor.

As the global and domestic economic context becomes more complex, Brazil and other countries in the region will face challenges in deepening the gains in poverty reduction and shared prosperity. Growth has slowed since 2011 and has been well below the rates recorded during the periods of rapid growth earlier in the decade. The demand for Brazilian exports has fallen as growth has eased in key market destinations. While not approaching the levels during the hyperinflation of the 1980s, inflation has been consistently above target in recent years. The slower growth has represented a drag on tax revenue, which has been outstripped by expenditure growth, and managing the fiscal balance has become more difficult. Moreover, stagnant productivity, low investment rates, underdeveloped infrastructure, inadequate basic services, gaps in access to financial services, and a regulatory environment that constrains the creation of firms and jobs could represent a barrier to the ability of the country to continue promoting more inclusive growth. A rapidly aging population, with direct implications for pensions and health care, will also be a key factor in determining the sustainability of the gains achieved.

This section discusses in more detail how past economic performance and policies have contributed to the shared prosperity agenda in Brazil and examines the key challenges along the path ahead. The analysis is structured around the three main channels through which growth and equity reinforce each other so that the gains of economic prosperity become more evenly distributed, as follows: (1) equitable, efficient, and sustainable fiscal policy; (2) fair and transparent institutions and the effective provision of public goods; and (3) well-functioning and accessible markets.

Equitable, efficient, and sustainable fiscal policy

Over the past decade, substantial growth and large increases in tax revenue have enabled successive government administrations to expand fiscal spending. Despite the size of public expenditures, which reached 40 percent of GDP in 2012, Brazil's fiscal stance has been characterized by fiscal prudence and primary surpluses in recent years.[6] The country enjoyed primary surpluses in the fiscal account that averaged 3 percent of GDP in 2003–13;

however, this has declined recently, falling from 3.1 percent in 2011 to 1.9 percent in 2013. Fiscal prudence has also facilitated the control of inflation within the target range of 2.5–6.5 percent. After a peak of 14 percent in 2003, Brazil managed to keep inflation within the 4–6 percent range, except in 2005, 2011, and 2013.

Because of the higher tax revenues and stronger macrofundamentals, the government was in a good position to increase public expenditures, including the allocation of more resources to targeted social spending. From 2000 to 2013, general government expenditure as a share of GDP rose from 35 to 40 percent (Azevedo et al. 2014). Social spending has also been rising and accounted for about 16 percent of GDP in 2009 (Higgins and Pereira 2013).[7] Of this, 4.2 percentage points corresponded mainly to non-contributory pensions, but also to cash social transfers (Lustig, Pessino, and Scott 2013). The sharper focus on social investment, a policy objective of the government, has roots in the 1988 Constitution, which made the state responsible for guaranteeing a minimum income to all citizens regardless of their capacity to contribute to social security (Barrientos 2013).

The more active use of redistributive policy led to the establishment of several large social assistance transfer programs that had sizable positive effects on poverty and inequality. Government-subsidized social assistance interventions have included a range of direct cash transfer programs, pension programs, education spending, and health care programs that have contributed to an improvement in social welfare. The largest of the non-contributory schemes is the continuous cash benefit pension program, followed by the BF conditional cash transfer program. In 2011, in an effort to eradicate extreme poverty, the government launched the BSM plan (box 3.3). The BSM builds on the country's social assistance system to guarantee a minimum income to all people, boost service access, and foster productive inclusion. The gains in poverty reduction achieved through the BF were expanded through the BSM plan, which, through a variety of social interventions, targeted 16 million people living in extreme poverty. Overall, the emphasis of the last decade on redistributive policies yielded large payoffs in poverty and inequality reduction. For instance, the continuous cash benefit program and the BF jointly accounted for almost one-fifth of the reduction in the Gini coefficient between 1997 and 2009 (IPEA 2010).

The increasingly tight fiscal space constitutes a concern moving forward. While primary expenditures rose by 2 percentage points of GDP in 2008–12, tax revenues have been diminishing because GDP is growing more slowly. As a consequence, the recurring primary surplus (adjusted for unusual revenues) has been progressively shrinking. The sustainability of curent social expenditures could create new fiscal pressures in the short and medium term. Because more Brazilians are now reaching retirement age, the rising commitments of the public service pension system (*regime geral de previdencia social*) are expected to exert additional pressure on the fiscal space in the long term.[8] On the revenue side, there is not much room to raise taxes because of political considerations, the relatively high taxation levels

Box 3.3 The Brasil sem Misería Plan

In June 2011, President Dilma Rousseff launched a new plan, Brasil sem Misería Plan (Brazil without Misery, BSM), to eradicate extreme poverty by 2014. Under the plan, the government set the goal of lifting 16 million individuals out of poverty. President Dilma's announcement was accompanied by the release of official statistics on extreme poverty based on the 2010 census of the Brazilian Institute of Geography and Statistics. Over 16 million Brazilians were living on less than R$70 a month (about $35), half of them under 19 years of age, and 40 percent of these people were in the northeast macroregion. The plan thus has an explicit focus on people who have not been reached by social policies in the past: the poorest of the poor.

The objective of the BSM is to lift these 16 million individuals from extreme poverty through a three-pronged approach, as follows:

- An income guarantee: the provision of cash transfers.
- Access to services: enhancing the access to public services among the poor and the vulnerable so as to close the existing coverage gaps in basic services such as education, health care, and sanitation.
- Productive inclusion: promoting activities in rural and urban areas aimed at raising the productivity of families in extreme poverty, through employment and income generation. In urban areas, productive inclusion articulates actions and programs that facilitate insertion into the labor market through formal employment, entrepreneurship, or small enterprises. In rural areas, where 47 percent of the BSM target population lives, the goal is to strengthen family farming among households that are among the extreme poor by increasing their productive capacity and facilitating the entry of the products of their labor into markets through guidance, technical support, and the supply of raw materials and water.

An overarching element of the BSM is the active search (*busca ativa*) for the extreme poor who are currently not included in the *cadastro único* (the single registry, or *CadUnico*). The *CadUnico* is the gateway to BSM programs and other federal government programs.

in Brazil relative to the region (overall tax collection is 33 percent of GDP in Brazil, close to the average among countries of the Organisation for Economic Co-operation and Development [OECD]), and economic concerns such as negative side effects on job creation, competitiveness, and growth.

Fiscal policies aimed at enhancing the progressivity of the system can help reduce fiscal pressures and sustain and extend poverty reduction and shared prosperity. Close to half of tax revenue is levied through indirect taxes on goods and services in Brazil. This contrasts with 32.5 percent in OECD countries. The heavier reliance on indirect taxes burdens poorer households disproportionately because much of the income of these households is spent on basic goods; the burden is even heavier on poor urban households, which are more dependent on the cash economy. Research based on the incidence analysis methodology has compared market income (before taxes and transfers) and postfiscal income (after direct and indirect taxes and subsidies) and found that, in Brazil, whereas direct taxes and transfers reduce income inequality, the net effect of indirect taxes and subsidies reverses some of the gains in inequality reduction. The overall redistributive effect of the fiscal policy—without considering in-kind transfers such as free

Figure 3.14 The Gini Coefficient before and after Government Transfers and Taxes, Brazil, 2009

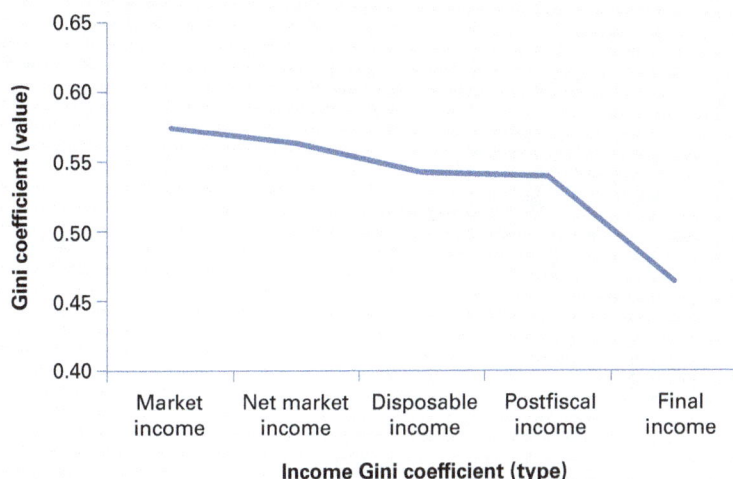

Source: Higgins and Pereira 2013.
Note: Market income refers to wages and salaries, income from capital, and private transfers before government taxes, social security contributions, and transfers. Subtracting direct taxes and employee contributions to social security from market income gives net market income. Adding direct transfers results in disposable income. Once indirect subsidies have been added and indirect transfers subtracted, the result is postfiscal income. Adding cash and in-kind transfers results in final income.

or subsidized government services in education or health care, net of payments—is modest. The Gini coefficient based on postfiscal income falls by only 0.03 points compared with the Gini coefficient calculated using market income (Higgins and Pereira 2013; World Bank 2014a) (figure 3.14).

There is also room to improve the progressivity of the tax burden. The share of total tax revenue collected from those in the bottom decile of the income distribution is 1.5 times greater than the share of this decile in total market income (World Bank 2014a). Other estimates show that the poorest 20 percent of the population lives in households that, on average, pay more in taxes than they receive in government transfers (figure 3.15).

Institutions and the provision of public goods and services: the quality challenge

During its recent history, Brazil has undertaken significant efforts to expand the delivery of basic services. Public expenditures on education and health care have increased substantially. During the 2000s, public spending on education has risen from 4.0 to 5.8 percent of GDP, while public spending on health care has grown from 2.8 to 4.2 percent of GDP.

In education, the government explicitly sought to equalize the average spending per pupil across macroregions by assigning additional resources to municipalities in need and reducing school costs for underprivileged

Figure 3.15 Ratio of the Share of Taxes Paid to the Share of Total Market Income, Brazil, 2009

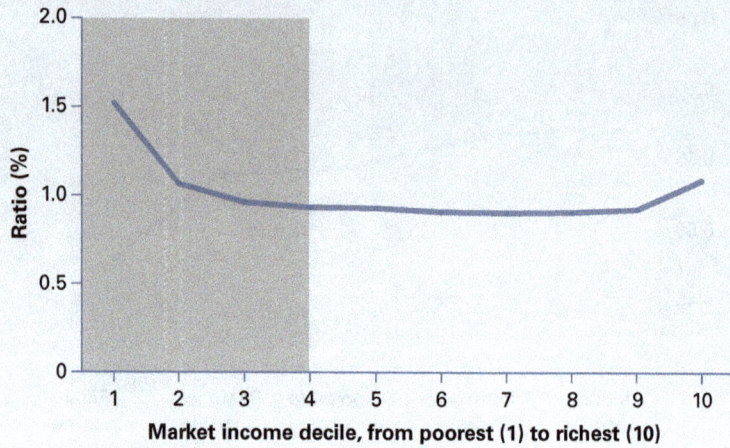

Source: World Bank 2014a.

children through transfer programs. However, annual public expenditure per student for all levels of education combined remains below the OECD average. Additionally, the allocation of funding across education levels is uneven: the government currently spends four times more per student in tertiary education than in primary or secondary education. Continuing the policies initiated through FUNDEF (Fundo para Manutenção e Desenvolvimento do Ensino Fundamental e Valorização do Magistério, Fund for Maintenance and Development of the Fundamental Education and Valorization of Teaching, launched in 1996) and FUNDEB (Fundo de Manutenção e Desenvolvimento da Educação Básica e de Valorização de Profissionais de Educação, Fund for the Development of Basic Education and Appreciation of the Teaching Profession, established in 2007), the National Education Plan seeks to increase public investment in education to 10 percent of GDP by 2024 (box 3.4). Relevant legislation allocates 75 percent of drilling royalties from the newly discovered presalt oil fields toward education.[9]

The delivery of primary health care has been enhanced through investments in health infrastructure and human resources to extend the free-of-charge, publicly funded *sistema único de saúde* (unified health care system) to remote communities facing major health care shortages. Since the implementation of the system, public per capita financing for health care has increased substantially, more than doubling since the early 1980s, although, as a share of GDP, Brazil spends less than the 6 percent threshold recommended by the Pan American Health Organization (Gragnolati, Lindelow, and Couttolenc 2013). Health indicators such as the infant mortality rate have shown positive trends, falling from 60.3 to 17.3 deaths per 1,000 live births between 1985 and 2009 (a decline of 71.3 percent), exceeding the average reduction

> **Box 3.4 The National Education Plan, Brazil**
>
> There have been several important legislative initiatives in the education sector recently. Chief among them is the approval, on June 25, 2014, of the National Education Plan for 2014–24. The plan is a strategic policy framework developed by the Ministry of Education to guide policy making and the development of education programs in the states, the federal district, and municipalities. It outlines 10 broad policy orientations, complemented by 20 objectives, each including a set of strategies. Targets and timelines have been included to measure the progress toward the achievement of each objective. The higher-level objective of the plan as outlined by the ministry is to reduce inequality and promote the inclusion of minorities such as students with disabilities, indigenous peoples, and *Quilombolas* (descendants of Afro-Brazilian slaves) by guaranteeing the right to quality basic education through universal literacy and the expansion of schooling and other educational opportunities. Four objectives are associated with significant targets in the education system: (a) universal access to preschool (ages 4–5 years), (b) at least 50 percent of children enrolled in crèches, (c) at least 50 percent of public schools providing full-time education, and (d) a substantial increase in teacher salaries.

in the region (33.2 percent) and in middle-income countries (28.5 percent) (Gragnolati, Lindelow, and Couttolenc 2013). Child mortality evolved similarly, and life expectancy at birth increased by 9.8 years, from 63.3 years in 1985 to 73.1 years in 2009. These gains were made primarily through improvements in outcomes among the bottom 40, though poor children still die at a higher rate than their wealthier peers. The decline in infant and child mortality has been attributed in part to the expansion of the coverage of the unified health care system, particularly the flagship Family Health Program, which is also associated with improved school enrollments and with augmented labor supply among adults in rural areas (Macinko, Guanais, and Fátima Marinho de Souza 2006; Rocha and Soares 2010).

Efforts to boost the access to services and render it more equal have helped expand the economic opportunities among low-income people, enabling them to capitalize on their productive potential. The human opportunity index (HOI) offers a way to quantify changes in the coverage and equity of access to key goods and services (Molinas Vega et al. 2012). The index measures how fairly the coverage of a set of opportunities (proxied by access to basic goods and services) is distributed across, for instance, the youth population aged 16 years or less. Calculations of the index for Brazil show that the coverage of services such as electricity and education is virtually universal. Improvements in the access to safe water and sanitation are also evident, though access is still lacking in many households (figure 3.16). Disparities in access to such vital services are especially worrisome in states in the north and northeast such as Acre and Maranhão, where roughly only a third of households have access to water, while access is almost universal in the central-west, south, and southeast macroregions.

Despite the greater, more equitable opportunities in access, the quality of services remains a challenge. Larger, more equal access to education is constrained by quality issues, for example. Even though school enrollment is nearly universal in virtually all states and macroregions, age-grade

Figure 3.16 Trends in Selected Opportunities, Service Coverage, Brazil, 1981–2012

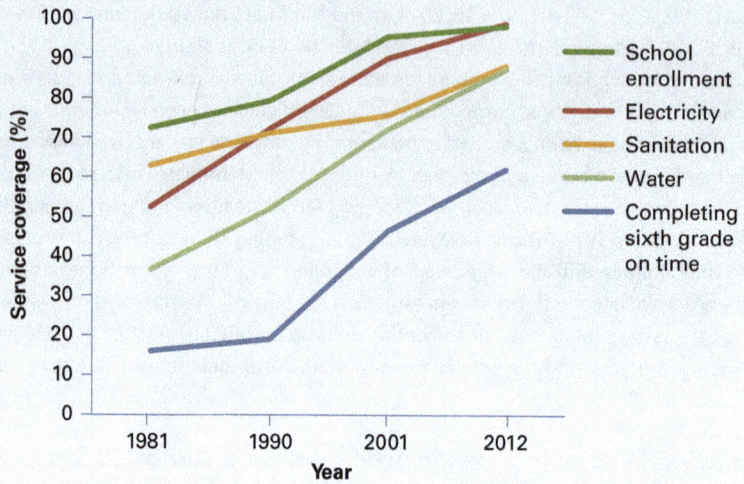

Source: World Bank 2014a.

distortions are significant. The HOI for completing sixth grade on time shows a major gap between coverage and grade progression, which may indicate problems in school quality (figure 3.17). Although the performance gains recorded in Brazil since 2003 are among the largest, the results in standardized tests of the 2012 OECD Program for International Student Assessment (PISA) place Brazil last after Mexico, Russia, the United States, and the average among OECD countries. Even though Brazil's scores have been improving in the past decade, there are still considerable gaps with students in OECD countries: students 15 years of age or above in Brazil are more than two years behind their OECD counterparts in mathematics, reading, and critical thinking skills (OECD 2012a, 2012b). Compounding this situation, high repetition rates are a costly characteristic of the education system. The Índice de Desenvolvimento da Educação do Estado de São Paulo (education development index of the state of São Paulo), an index that measures the quality of education in schools administered by the state of São Paulo, has revealed that learning outcomes among middle-school students are stagnant, while learning outcomes among high-school students have worsened over time.[10] These results are echoed by the 2013 Índice de Desenvolvimento da Educação Basica (index of the development of basic education), a key education indicator created in 2007 that has also significantly contributed to increasing transparency and accountability in the sector. While efforts to improve service quality have been undertaken, notably in the education sector, the widespread protests in June 2013 are a sign that social discontent with the quality of services more broadly is substantial and that efforts need to be sustained.[11]

Figure 3.17 The HOI for Completing Grade 6 on Time, by State, Brazil, 2012

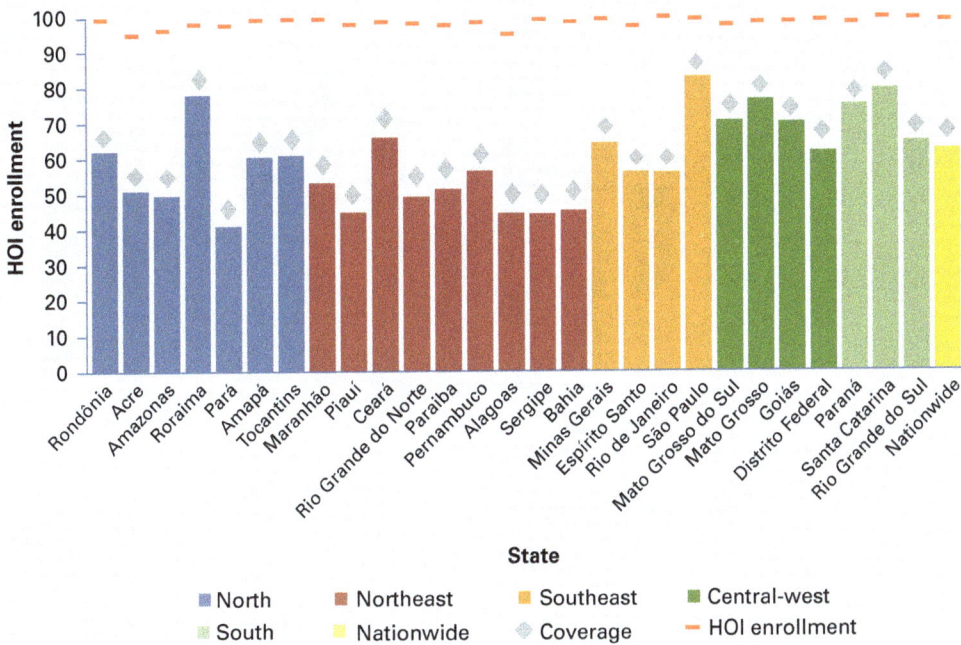

Source: Based on data in SEDLAC.
Note: The diamonds indicate the coverage of schools, that is, the inequality-unadjusted rates of completion of sixth grade on time. The bars indicate the inequality-adjusted rates of completion (the HOI). HOI = human opportunity index.

Outcomes such as the maternal mortality ratio may provide an indication of quality shortcomings in the health care sector. Official figures indicate that maternal mortality is not only high, but that it has been flat for the last 20 years even though more than 90 percent of births are delivered in professional health centers or hospitals.[12] At 75 deaths per 100,000 live births, adjusted maternal mortality ratios in Brazil are below the average in Latin America and the Caribbean, but well above the ratios in Chile and Turkey (26), Malaysia (31), and China and Russia (38–39) (Gragnolati, Lindelow, and Couttolenc 2013). Such challenges are compounded by the growing burden that chronic conditions and injuries, the aging population, and the rise of the middle class are placing on the health system, exposing weaknesses in the quality of primary care, gaps in the availability and quality of medium- and high-complexity care, and poor coordination across the service delivery network.

Given that they weigh more heavily on low-income households, quality problems in service delivery limit the ability to sustain poverty reduction and the gains in shared prosperity. The HOI for learning outcomes in school measured by the results of Brazil in the 2012 OECD Program

Figure 3.18 Attendance in Secondary School, 13–17 Age-Group, by Income Decile, Brazil, 2012

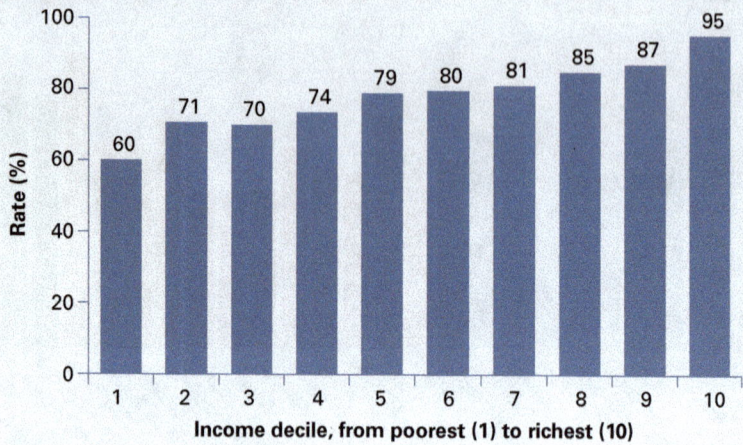

Source: Based on data in SEDLAC.

for International Student Assessment reveals large inequities in academic performance. Brazilian children benefit from the higher quality in education and thus perform better on academic tests if their parents are more well educated, have better jobs, and have accumulated more wealth or if the household is located in an urban area. Similarly, the gap between inequality-unadjusted rates of completion of sixth grade on time (diamonds) and the inequality-adjusted rates of completion (bars) in figure 3.17 suggests that high-quality education, which is probably associated with normal progression through school, is unequally distributed nearly everywhere in Brazil. Consequently, deprived students are less likely to finish elementary and secondary school or to pass admission tests in public universities. Similarly, although disparities in health outcomes have fallen geographically and across socioeconomic groups, gaps still exist in the north and the northeast.

Unequal coverage and the unequal utilization of basic services are also factors constraining economic and social inclusion. Children in households at the bottom of the income distribution still exhibit lower rates of attendance in secondary and tertiary education. While nearly all adolescents between 13 and 17 years of age in the richest 10 percent of the population are enrolled in secondary school, only 60 percent of the poorest 10 percent are enrolled (figure 3.18). Similarly, only 40 percent of the poorest households have access to basic sanitation, while the corresponding share is over 80 percent among the richest decile (figure 3.19).

Well-functioning, accessible, and equitable markets

Labor markets in Brazil have shown strong performance, particularly in the generation of more well-paying formal jobs. The unemployment rate

Figure 3.19 Households Connected to Sewerage Networks, by Income Decile, Brazil, 2012

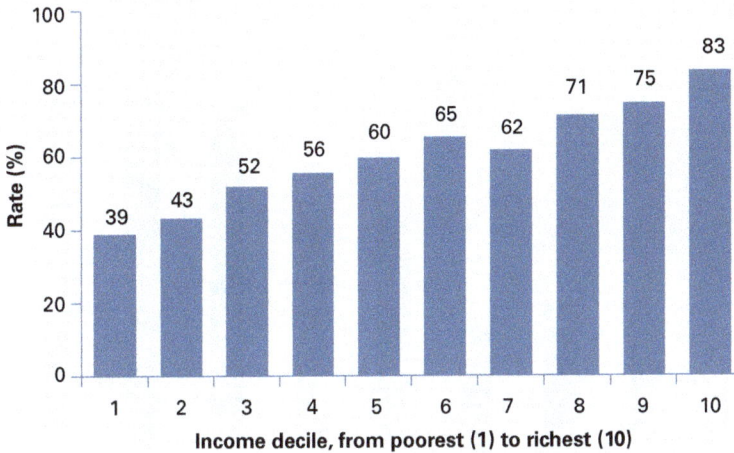

Source: Based on data in SEDLAC.

fell from over 12.0 percent in the early 2000s to 5.5 percent in 2012. This performance has continued although growth has slowed in recent years. The majority of employment growth has occurred through formal job creation. Since 2007, formal employment has outpaced informal employment, and this trend has increased over time (see figure 3.12). Thus, the share of formal jobs rose from 45.8 percent in 2001 to 58.5 percent in 2011.

However, not all groups have benefited equally. The majority of the 10.1 million net formal jobs created during the 2000s were generated among the upper quintiles of the wage distribution (Comin, Barbosa, and Carvalhaes 2012). Consistent with this, the share of the more well educated—defined as people who have attained 11 or more years of education—among the employed rose from 30.3 to 46.4 percent in 2002–11 (Chahad and Pozzo 2013). Likewise, the differences in real hourly wages across income groups are not only large, but have been widening. While the hourly wages of the more well off (people in the middle class and above) in 2003 were 6.3 and 4.1 times greater than those of the extreme and moderate poor, respectively, the respective ratios had risen to 7.9 and 4.4 by 2012.

Informality also varies greatly across socioeconomic groups and macro-regions. It is more prevalent among the poor and vulnerable as well as among workers in rural areas. At 52.7 percent, labor market informality is nearly twice as prevalent in rural areas; in urban and metropolitan areas, the corresponding shares are 22.0 to 26.0 percent. There are also big disparities across income groups. The large majority of workers among the extreme and moderate poor (99 and 83 percent, respectively) are working without formal contracts, and half of the total employment among the

Figure 3.20 Share of Informality, by Location and Welfare-Consumption Group, Brazil, 2012

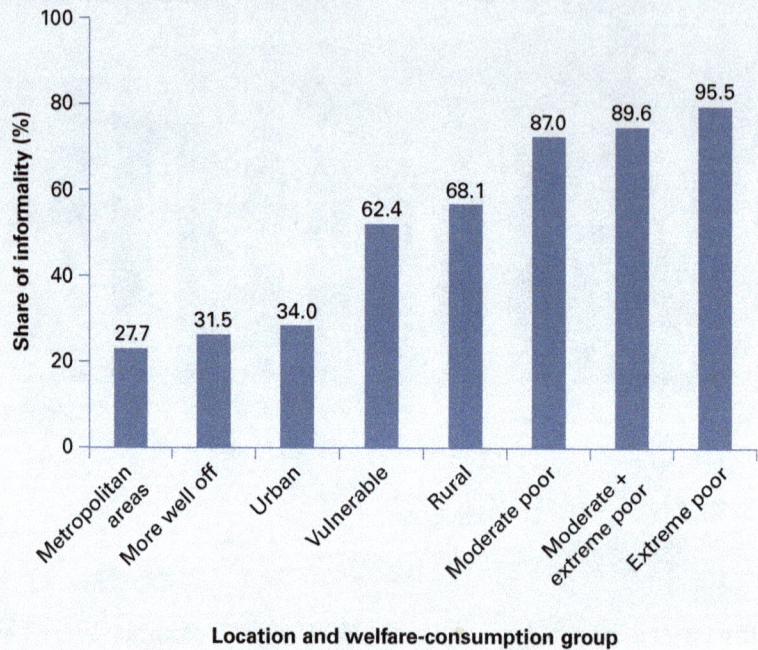

Source: Calculations based on Pesquisa Nacional por Amostra de Domicílios 2012 (National Household Sample Survey), Brazilian Institute of Geography and Statistics, Rio de Janeiro, http://www.ibge.gov.br/home/estatistica/pesquisas/pesquisas.php.

vulnerable is accounted for by informal workers (figure 3.20). While informality offers an opportunity for firms and workers to operate with less regulatory control and lower wage costs, it is often associated with inadequate insurance and retirement savings among the workers, excessive regulation, unfair competition, and noncompliance with tax collection, and, ultimately, informality creates a drag on productivity and growth (Perry et al. 2007). Furthermore, the uneven incidence of informality may undermine efforts to mitigate inequality and foster shared prosperity.

Labor markets have been dynamic, but stagnant productivity is still a key challenge if Brazil is to sustain inclusive growth. Because the demographic dividend that resulted from the availability of a larger working-age population is vanishing, the only option for boosting growth is to raise productivity. Productivity growth has partially recovered in the decades since the crisis of the 1980s, but it is still modest. Physical capital, a key driver of productivity growth, has stayed virtually flat in the 2000s. Human capital, another critical factor, has expanded, but skill shortages and the comparatively low quality of education are an issue. The lack of robust infrastructure and bottlenecks in the business environment that hinder competition are other impediments to the realization of productivity gains.

Figure 3.21 Labor Productivity per Person Employed, Selected Countries and Regions, 2012

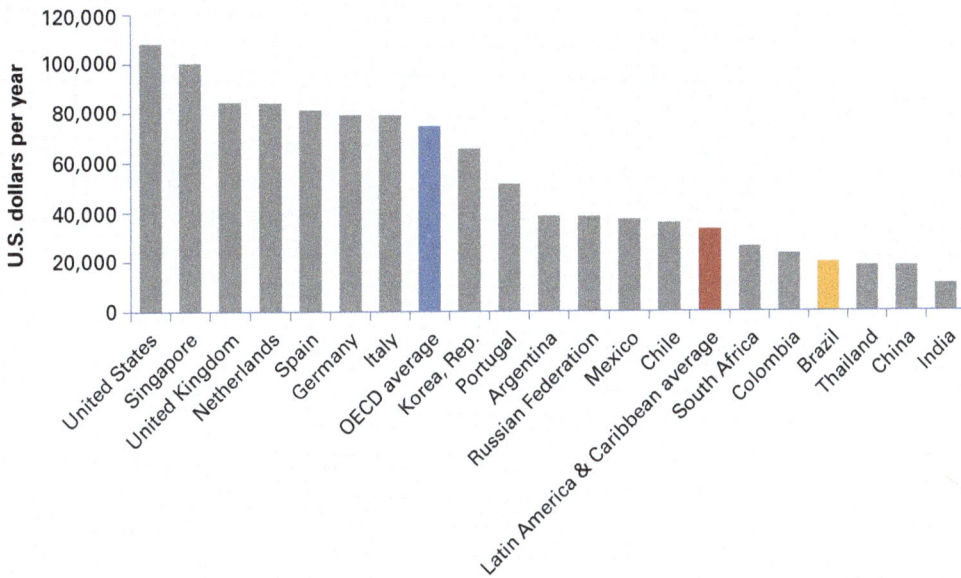

Source: Data of the Conference Board.

Gaps in labor productivity constitute a major drag on overall productivity in the economy. As of 2012, labor productivity measured as GDP per person employed ($19,899) was not even one-fourth of the OECD average ($74,874), nearly half the labor productivity in Mexico ($37,181) and Chile ($35,812), and 60 percent of the average labor productivity recorded across the Latin America and Caribbean region ($33,209) (figure 3.21). There have been no significant gains in labor productivity since the late 1990s, partly because of the nature of labor reallocations across sectors and industries. Labor shifted from high- to low-productivity industries, mainly toward services, where labor productivity growth was practically zero between 2007 and 2012. Moreover, within industries, labor was reallocated from large firms, often with higher productivity, to smaller, lower-productivity firms (World Bank 2014a). Other factors, such as skill mismatches and shortages, high labor market turnover, and rigidities in the labor market mostly because of labor regulation, have also hindered labor productivity growth.

A business environment that is not conducive to private sector development and that lacks competition is also a constraint to productivity. Brazil ranks 116th among 189 countries in the overall ease of doing business index and below other countries in the region, such as Chile (34), Peru (42), Colombia (43), Mexico (53), Panama (55), and Guatemala (79).[13] Brazil performs well below the average of the region in the number, amount of time, and costs of the formal procedures required to start a firm and to export and import goods, as well as in terms of the burden of taxes and mandatory contributions. Brazil's regulatory framework undermines the effectiveness of the regulatory and judicial system to enforce contracts and resolve other commercial disputes, including bankruptcy. Public policies to keep fuel and electricity prices artificially low and public lending at subsidized rates generate additional distortions in the economy.

Infrastructure and transportation systems are not adequate to sustain the country's growth and shared prosperity. Currently, only 1.5 percent of GDP is invested by public and private entities into infrastructure, while the long-run global average is 3.8 percent.[14] Brazil ranks 107th in 144 countries in the Global Ranking of Quality of Infrastructure, exposing major infrastructure bottlenecks and barriers in the efforts necessary to enable economic development through enhanced systems such as airports, ports, railroads, and highways (Schwab 2013). Similarly, public transportation and urban mobility were at the heart of the June 2013 protests. In metropolitan settings, lengthy commuting times and other constraints on mobility limit access to services and the opportunities of households and individuals, but particularly the most vulnerable groups living in periphery areas far from or with difficult access to productive centers.

In addition to weakening the microeconomic environment, stagnant labor productivity poses challenges in sustaining inclusive growth and socioeconomic progress. Individuals who belong to low-income groups, are poor, or are at risk of falling into poverty are more likely to be employed informally in low-skilled, low-productivity sectors. They are also more likely to have received an education of relatively lower quality, which limits their capacity to work in higher-productivity sectors. While the growth of real wages has fueled income growth and poverty and inequality reduction in the last decade, productivity has not been the driving force behind this process. Indeed, between 2004 and 2014, the increase in real wages (39 percent), particularly wages indexed to the minimum wage, which increased by 65 percent, significantly outstripped the productivity gains over the same period (13 percent), raising concerns about the sustainability of such trends (figure 3.22). An agenda aimed at boosting productivity may require more skill-intensive growth, the geographical clustering of economic activities, and a restructuring of the sources of growth, all of which could accentuate disparities across socioeconomic groups and macroregions.

Expanding financial system access to include people who are now excluded could also contribute to the shared prosperity agenda. Complete, well-functioning financial markets play an important role in development by promoting growth and reducing poverty and income inequality. Financial markets help households save, take loans, make payments, and adopt optimal risk management strategies.[15] However, global data consistently show that the poor, women, and rural households are more constrained in participating in the formal financial sector. While financial penetration in Brazil is above the regional average, there are disparities across socioeconomic groups (figure 3.23). For instance, 41 percent of adults in the bottom 40 report that they have accounts at formal institutions, compared

Figure 3.22 Labor Productivity, the Real Average Wage, and the Minimum Wage, Brazil, 2004–14

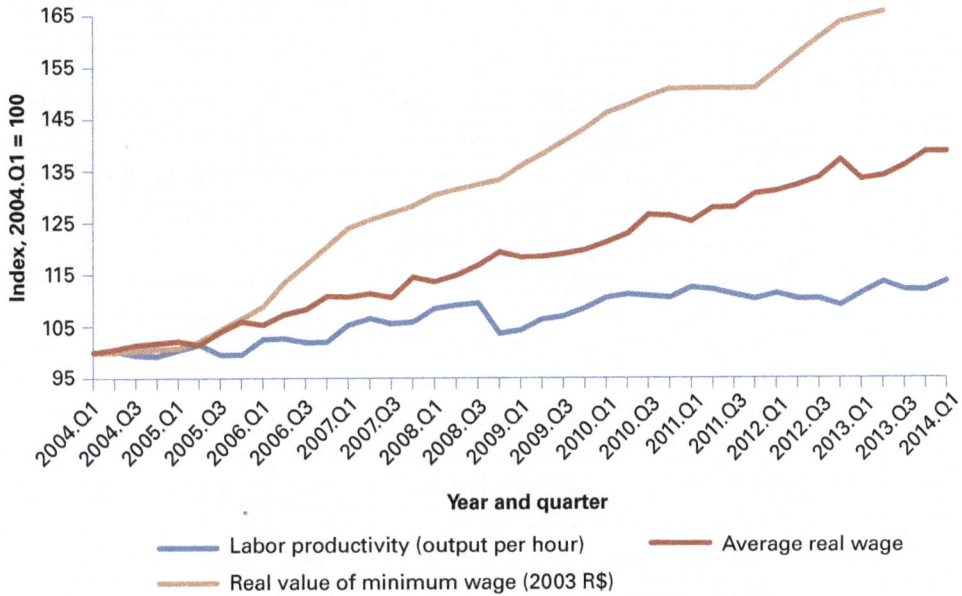

Source: World Bank and OECD calculations based on data of the Central Bank of Brazil.

Figure 3.23 Use of Financial Instruments, Region vs. Brazil, 2011

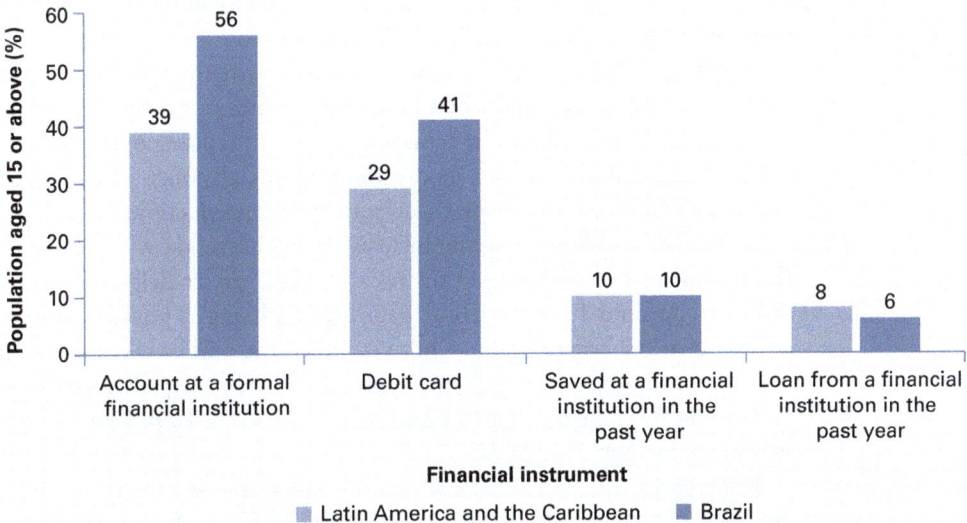

Source: Global Financial Inclusion (Global Findex) Database, World Bank, Washington, DC, www.worldbank.org /globalfindex.

with 65 percent among the top 60, and the ownership of bank accounts is nearly 10 percentage points lower among women and rural households than among men and urban households.

Final Remarks

In the last decade, Brazil experienced a remarkable reduction in poverty and inequality that boosted shared prosperity. At 4 percent in 2013, down from almost 10 percent in 2001, extreme poverty has now been almost eliminated from the country. Overall, around 25 million Brazilians have been able to escape extreme or moderate poverty, representing one in two people who escaped poverty in Latin America and the Caribbean during this period.

Signaling a process of convergence, poverty has fallen more rapidly in the states that had higher poverty rates before 2001. This has translated over the long term into robust economic mobility. Nearly 60 percent of Brazilians climbed to a higher economic group between 1990 and 2009. Furthermore, in a positive development for shared prosperity, growth has more than proportionally benefited the bottom 40. As a result, income inequality has declined.

Redistributive and minimum wage policy, along with more dynamic labor markets, has helped accelerate poverty reduction in a context of stronger and more stable, but still modest economic growth. At an average real annualized growth rate of 2.3 percent a year from 1999 to 2012, per capita income grew more quickly in Brazil than the average in Latin America and the Caribbean (1.8 percent) and more quickly than the growth recorded in Brazil in previous decades. Largely as a result of stronger and more stable growth, labor markets have performed at record levels in the last decade, leading to strong job creation, employment formalization, and real wage increases. Economic growth explains two-thirds of the fall in poverty between 2001 and 2012. However, Brazil's growth performance is still modest relative to its potential and the performance of the BRIC countries. To enhance the capacity of the economic system to reduce poverty, the government successfully implemented significant social policies that targeted low-income families and helped accelerate poverty reduction.

Sustaining and deepening the inclusive growth agenda will require that the challenges are addressed in the fiscal system, service delivery, and productivity. Around 18 million Brazilians are still living in poverty, and over one-third of the population has not yet joined the middle class, remaining instead in a condition of economic vulnerability. The inequality gap in Brazil is wider than the average in Latin America and the Caribbean, a region with large income disparities.

Bringing prosperity to the less well off and sustaining the gains already achieved demand policy action on at least three fronts. Key to this agenda will be enhancing the progressivity of the fiscal system to ensure that public resources continue to advance social goals. There also needs to be a focus on improving the quality of basic services. Despite the government's achievement in establishing greater and more equitable access to a range of services in the last decade, quality is low and uneven across macroregions and the population, and the poor quality is affecting low-income households disproportionally. Bolstering inclusive and sustainable growth requires boosting productivity, especially among the poor and vulnerable so that they may contribute to and benefit from the growth process. Brazil has basically seen no gains in labor productivity since the late 1990s, and most of the country's growth has been fueled by an increase in labor, itself boosted by a demographic trend toward a larger working-age population. Underlying the stagnant productivity is a low rate of investment, underdeveloped infrastructure, skill shortages and mismatches, rigidities in the labor market, financial exclusion, and a business environment that is not fully conducive to private sector development and competition.

There is also a need to reenergize Brazil's growth over the medium and long term and prepare the country to manage new challenges. Growth is traditionally the main force behind poverty reduction, explaining two-thirds of the fall in poverty in Brazil. Yet, in recent years, the country has been on a path of slow growth, which is being aggravated by diminishing external support factors such as weaker global demand and falling commodity prices. An effort to raise growth through enhanced productivity will require that the economy be exposed to greater external and internal competition, a restructuring in the sources of growth, a shift toward skill-intensive growth, reforms in the tax and labor regulatory environment, improvements in the business environment, and, possibly, a spatial concentration of economic activities. This process may create additional inclusiveness challenges that accentuate greater skills and geographical and income disparities and add pressures favoring income inequality. This will call for a renewed emphasis on social protection and risk management systems for benefit of the poor and vulnerable.

Annex 3A Labor Market Characteristics, Brazil

Table 3A.1 Labor Market Characteristics, Brazil, 2004 and 2012
percent

Indicator	Bottom 40		Top 60		Overall	
	2004	2012	2004	2012	2004	2012
Female labor participation	54.0	47.3	64.9	67.7	61.1	60.2
Male labor participation	83.0	77.0	85.9	85.6	85.0	82.8
Employee	46.6	54.4	64.9	71.1	59.1	65.9
Employer	0.6	0.6	5.0	4.5	3.7	3.4
Unpaid worker	15.3	11.5	5.2	2.9	8.4	5.6
Unemployed	15.8	13.1	6.1	3.4	9.2	6.4
Self-employed	21.7	20.4	18.7	18.0	19.6	18.8
Public	5.2	6.3	14.2	15.0	11.6	12.5
Private	94.8	93.7	85.8	85.0	88.4	87.5

Source: Based on data in SEDLAC.

Notes

1. Moderate poverty is measured at $4.00 a day, while extreme poverty is measured at $2.50 a day in 2005 purchasing power parity (PPP) U.S. dollars. The poverty data on Latin America represent a population-weighted average of Argentina, Bolivia, Brazil, Chile, Colombia, Costa Rica, Dominican Republic, Ecuador, El Salvador, Guatemala, Honduras, Mexico, Nicaragua, Panama, Paraguay, Peru, and Uruguay.

2. Because it does not satisfy group composability, the regional Gini coefficient is calculated based on pooled country-specific data.

3. The data are from the WDI (World Development Indicators) (database), World Bank, Washington, DC, http://data.worldbank.org/data-catalog/world-development-indicators.

4. Annualized rates for Panama and Peru have been calculated for 2007–12 and 2004–12, respectively.

5. The minimum nominal wage rose from R$200 to R$678 between 2002 and 2013, representing an increase in real terms of about 70.5 percent and covering more than 10 million workers and 900,000 retirees who were receiving one minimum salary each (SAE 2013). The rise in the minimum wage has had a positive effect on income distribution through two channels: labor income, which accounts for two-thirds of the gains in income inequality, and parallel increments in social transfers, which are tied to the minimum wage (López-Calva and Rocha 2012).

6. Budgetary policy focuses on the primary balance (government revenues, minus expenditures, excluding expenditures on interest payments).

7. This includes social assistance (direct cash transfers, noncontributory pensions, food transfers, unemployment benefits, and so on), health care and education spending, and spending at the federal, state, and municipal levels.

8. Between 1960 and 2010, the share of the elderly (the 60+ age-group) nearly doubled, from 5.2 to 10.3 percent of the population, an increase especially marked in the center-west and south. It is anticipated that, by 2050, the share will be 49 percent because of a rise in life expectancy to 81 years (Gragnolati et al. 2011).

9. The additional resources going to education from oil royalties are estimated at over $100 billion.

10. On a scale of 0 to 10, the index at the high-school level fell from 1.9 in 2012 to 1.8 in 2013, while, at the middle-school level, it was 2.5. The 2030 goals are 5.0 and 6.0, respectively. See "Programa de Qualidade da Escola," Secretaria de Estado da Educação, Governo do Estado de São Paulo, São Paulo, http://idesp.edunet.sp.gov.br/o_que_e.asp.

11. The efforts include measures to improve the educational attainment and salaries of teachers as well as the extension of full-day schooling. A 1996 law requires teachers in primary and secondary education to have a college degree. FUNDEF has also contributed to improving the salaries of teachers by earmarking 60 percent of education spending for teacher remuneration. In addition, since 2008, a minimum wage for teachers has been introduced, increasing income by more than fourfold, from R$415 in 2008 to R$1,567 in 2013. However, individuals with tertiary-level qualification continue to earn significantly more in nonteaching positions, resulting in challenges to attract and retain talented individuals to teaching. The government has also been pushing forward

with reforms to increase the time spent in school. The daily school attendance of children aged 4–17 has been estimated at 3.47 hours, significantly below international standards (IFB and EESP/EPGE–FGV 2008). Evidence shows that increasing instruction time has a positive effect on student performance, but, as of 2012, only 8.3 percent of children enrolled in primary and secondary education were receiving full-day schooling. Full-day schooling also represents an opportunity to offer additional good-quality extracurricular activities, besides focusing on teaching key academic subjects and providing remediation and tailored support for at-risk students.

12. Studies looking at this issue attribute the stagnant rate to improvements in the identification and recording of maternal deaths (Gragnolati, Lindelow, and Couttolenc 2013). While adjustments using statistical techniques show significant reductions in maternal deaths over the last 20 years, from 140 to 75 deaths per 100,000 live births, the rate is still at a relatively high level.

13. See Ease of Doing Business Index (database), World Bank, Washington, DC, http://data.worldbank.org/indicator/IC.BUS.EASE.XQ/.

14. McKinsey Global Institute estimates the total value of Brazil's infrastructure at 16 percent of GDP (Dobbs et al. 2013). Other big economies average 71 percent. To catch up, Brazil would have to triple annual infrastructure spending for the next 20 years. See "Infrastructure: The Road to Hell," *Economist*, September 28, 2013.

15. A growing body of evidence shows that the greater use and ownership of bank accounts and banking products raise consumption, productive investments, and savings, improve liquidity management, and help empower women (Aportela 1999; Ashraf et al. 2011; Dupas and Robinson 2009; Lusardi, Mitchell, and Curto 2010).

Bibliography

Aportela, Fernando. 1999. "Effects of Financial Access on Savings by Low-Income People." Unpublished working paper, Research Department, Banco de Mexico, Mexico City.

Ashraf, Nava, Diego Aycinena, Claudia Martinez, and Dean Yang. 2011. "Remittances and the Problem of Control: A Field Experiment among Migrants from El Salvador." Documentos da Trabajo SDT 341, Departamento de Economiá, Universidad de Chile, Santiago, Chile.

Azevedo, João Pedro, Antonio C. David, Fabiano Rodrigues Bastos, and Emilio Pineda. 2014. "Fiscal Adjustment and Income Inequality: Sub-national Evidence from Brazil." Policy Research Working Paper 6945, World Bank, Washington, DC.

Barrientos, Armando. 2013. "Transferências de Renda para o Desenvolvimento Humano no Longo Prazo." In *Programa Bolsa Família: Uma década de inclução e cidadania*, edited by Tereza Campello and Marcelo Côrtes Neri, 419–33. Brasília: Institute for Applied Economic Research.

Barros, Ricardo Paes de, Mirela De Carvalho, Samuel Franco, and Rosane Mendoça. 2010. "Markets, the State, and the Dynamics of Inequality in Brazil." In *Declining Inequality in Latin America: A Decade of Progress?*, edited by Luis F. López-Calva and Nora Lustig, 134–74. New York: United Nations Development Programme; Baltimore: Brookings Institution Press.

Bezerra de Siqueira, Rozane, and José Ricardo Bezerra Nogueira. 2013. "Taxation, Inequality, and the Illusion of the Social Contract in Brazil." Paper prepared for the International Association for Research in Income and Wealth–Brazilian Institute of Geography and Statistics conference, "Income, Wealth and Well-Being in Latin America," Rio de Janeiro, September 11–14.

Bruns, Barbara, David Evans, and Javier Luque. 2011. *Achieving World-Class Education in Brazil: The Next Agenda.* Report 65659. Directions in Development: Human Development. Washington, DC: World Bank.

Castañeda, Raul A., Anna Fruttero, Samantha Lach, Luis F. López-Calva, María Ana Lugo, Rogerio B. Santarrosa, and Jordan Solomon. 2012. "Poverty Dynamics in Brazil: Patterns, Associated Factors, and Policy Challenges." Policy report, World Bank, Washington, DC.

Cerqueira, Daniel R. C., Alexandre X. Y. Carvalho, Waldir J. A. Lobão, and Rute I. Rodrigues. 2007. "Análise dos Custos e Consequências da Violência no Brasil." Texto para Discussão 1284, Institute for Applied Economic Research, Brasília.

Chahad, José Paulo Zeetano, and Rafaella Gutierre Pozzo. 2013. "Mercado de Trabalho no Brasil na Primeira Década do Século XXI: Evolução, Mudanças e Perspectivas; Demografia, Força de Trabalho e Ocupação." *Boletim Informações FIPE* (May): 13–32, Fundação Instituto de Pesquisas Econômicas, São Paulo.

Comin, Alvaro A., Rogério J. Barbosa, and Flavio O. Carvalhaes. 2012. "Manufacturing Jobs: Economic Cycles, Job Creation, and Structural Change." Draft report (June), Economic & Social Research Council, Swindon, United Kingdom, and Warwick Institute for Employment Research, Coventry.

Dobbs, Richard, Herbert Pohl, Diaan-Yi Lin, Jan Mischke, Nicklas Garemo, Jimmy Hexter, Stefan Matzinger, Robert Palter, and Rushad Nanavatty. 2013. *Infrastructure Productivity: How to Save $1 Trillion a Year.* New York: McKinsey Global Institute.

Dupas, Pascaline, and Jonathan Robinson. 2009. "Savings Constraints and Microenterprise Development: Evidence from a Field Experiment in Kenya." NBER Working Paper 14693, National Bureau of Economic Research, Cambridge, MA.

Estevão, Marcello M., and Irineu E. de Carvalho Filho. 2012. "Institutions, Informality, and Wage Flexibility: Evidence from Brazil." IMF Working Paper WP/12/84, International Monetary Fund, Washington, DC.

Ferreira, Francisco H. G., Julian Messina, Jamele Rigolini, Luis F. López-Calva, María Ana Lugo, and Renos Vakis. 2013. *Economic Mobility and the Rise of the Latin American Middle Class.* Washington, DC: World Bank.

Gragnolati, Michele, Ole Hagen Jorgensen, Romero Rocha, and Anna Fruttero. 2011. *Growing Old in an Older Brazil: Implications of Population Ageing on Growth, Poverty, Public Finance, and Service Delivery.* Directions in Development Series. Washington, DC: World Bank. http://hdl.handle.net/10986/2351.

Gragnolati, Michele, Magnus Lindelow, and Bernard Couttolenc. 2013. *Twenty Years of Health System Reform in Brazil: An Assessment of the Sistema Único de Saúde.* Directions in Development: Human Development. Washington, DC: World Bank.

Higgins, Sean, and Claudiney Pereira. 2013. "The Effects of Brazil's High Taxation and Social Spending on the Distribution of Household Income." CEQ Working Paper 7 (January), Commitment to Equity, Inter-American Dialogue,

Washington, DC; Center for Inter-American Policy and Research and Department of Economics, Tulane University, New Orleans.

IFB (Instituto Futuro Brasil) and EESP/EPGE–FGV (Escola de Economia de São Paulo and Escola de Pós-Graduação em Economia–Fundação Getúlio Vargas). 2008. "The Quality of Education in Brazil." January, Inter-American Development Bank, Washington, DC.

IPEA (Brazil, Institute for Applied Economic Research). 2010. "PNAD 2009, Primeiras Análises: Distribuição de Renda entre 1995 e 2009." Comunicados do IPEA 63 (October 25), IPEA, Brasília.

Jannuzzi, Paulo de Martino, and Alexandro Rodrigues Pinto. 2013. "Bolsa Família e seus Impactos nas Condições de Vida da População Brasileira: Uma síntese dos principais achados da pesquisa de avaliação de impacto do Bolsa Família II." In *Programa Bolsa Família: uma década de inclusão e cidadania*, edited by Tereza Campello and Marcelo Côrtes Neri, 179–92. Brasília: Institute for Applied Economic Research.

López-Calva, Luis F., and Sonia Rocha. 2012. "Exiting Belindia? Lesson from the Recent Decline in Income Inequality in Brazil." Report 70155, Poverty, Gender, and Equity Unit, Latin America and Caribbean Region, World Bank, Washington, DC.

Lusardi, Annamaria, Olivia S. Mitchell, and Vilsa Curto. 2010. "Financial Literacy among the Young: Evidence and Implications for Consumer Policy." *Journal of Consumer Affairs* 44 (2): 358–80.

Lustig, Nora, Carola Pessino, and John Scott. 2013. "The Impact of Taxes and Social Spending on Inequality and Poverty in Argentina, Bolivia, Brazil, Mexico, Peru and Uruguay: An Overview." Tulane Economics Working Paper 1313 (April), Department of Economics, Tulane University, New Orleans.

Macinko, James, Federico C. Guanais, and Maria de Fátima Marinho de Souza. 2006. "Evaluation of the Impact of the Family Health Program on Infant Mortality in Brazil, 1990–2002." *Journal of Epidemiological Community Health* 60 (1): 13–19.

Molinas Vega, José R., Ricardo Paes de Barros, Jaime Saavedra Chanduvi, and Marcelo Guigale. 2012. *Do Our Children Have a Chance? A Human Opportunity Report for Latin America and the Caribbean*. With Louise Cord, Carola Pessino, and Amer Hasan. Report 65656. Directions in Development: Poverty. Washington, DC: World Bank.

OECD (Organisation for Economic Co-operation and Development). 2012a. "Programme for International Student Assessment (PISA), Results from PISA 2012: Brazil." Country Note, OECD, Paris.

———. 2012b. "Education at a Glance, OECD Indicators 2012: Brazil." Country Note, OECD, Paris.

Paim, Jairnilson, Claudia Travassos, Celia Almeida, Ligia Bahia, and James Macinko. 2011. "The Brazilian Health System: History, Advances, and Challenges." *Lancet* 377 (9779): 1778–97.

Perova, Elizaveta, Sarah Reynolds, and Miriam Müller. 2012. "Towards a More Comprehensive Domestic Violence Policy in Brazil." World Bank, Washington, DC.

Perry, Guillermo E., William F. Maloney, Omar S. Arias, Pablo Fajnzylber, Andrew D. Mason, and Jaime Saavedra-Chanduvi. 2007. *Informality: Exit and Exclusion*. Latin American and Caribbean Studies. Washington, DC: World Bank.

Porsse, Alexandre A., Marianne Z. Stampe, Marcelo S. Portugal, and Eduardo S. de Almeida. 2012. "Demographic Change and Regional Economic Growth in Brazil." Regional and Urban Economics Lab, University of São Paolo, São Paulo.

PREAL (Partnership for Educational Revitalization in the Americas). 2009. "Overcoming Inertia: A Report Card on Education in Brazil." Inter-American Dialogue, Washington, DC; Corporation for Development Research, Santiago, Chile.

Rocha, Romero, and Rodrigo R. Soares. 2010. "Evaluating the Impact of Community-Based Health Interventions: Evidence from Brazil's Family Health Program." *Health Economics* 19 (S1): 126–58.

Rocha, Sonia Maria Rodrigues Da. 2006. *Pobreza no Brasil: Afinal, de que se trata?* Rio de Janeiro: Editora FGV.

SAE (Brazil, Secretaria de Assuntos Estratégicos). 2013. "Classe Média e Emprego Assalariado." *Vozes da Nova Classe Média* Caderno 4 (August), SAE, Brasília.

SEDLAC (Socio-Economic Database for Latin America and the Caribbean), Center for Distributive, Labor, and Social Studies, Universidad de La Plata, La Plata, Argentina; World Bank, Washington, DC. http://sedlac.econo.unlp.edu.ar/eng/index.php.

Schwab, Klaus, ed. 2013. *Insight Report: The Global Competitiveness Report 2013–2014*. Geneva: World Economic Forum.

Sonnenschein, Jan. 2013. "Opinion Briefing: Brazilians' Growing Discontent." *Gallup World* (June 26). http://www.gallup.com/poll/163229/opinion-briefing-brazilians-growing-discontent.aspx.

Waiselfisz, Julio Jacobo. 2011. *Mapa da Violência 2012: Os novos padrões da violência homicida no Brasil*, vol. 1. São Paulo: Instituto Sangari.

World Bank. 2013a. "Making Brazilians Safer: Analyzing the Dynamics of Violent Crime." Report 70764, World Bank, Washington, DC.

———. 2013b. "Review and Research Agenda on Results-Based Management in Brazilian States." Report 82592-BR, World Bank, Washington, DC.

———. 2013c. "Shifting Gears to Accelerate Shared Prosperity in Latin America and the Caribbean." Poverty and Labor Brief, Latin America and Caribbean Region, World Bank, Washington, DC.

———. 2014a. "Social Gains in the Balance: A Fiscal Policy Challenge for Latin America and the Caribbean." Report 85162 (February), World Bank, Washington, DC.

———. 2014b. "Implications of a Changing China for Brazil: A New Window of Opportunity?" Economic Report 89450, World Bank, Washington, DC.

CHAPTER 4

Toward Shared Prosperity in Colombia

Lea Giménez, Carlos Rodríguez-Castelán, and Daniel Valderrama

Introduction

Between 2002 and 2013, Colombia experienced strong, sustained economic growth. The annualized growth rate of per capita real gross domestic product (GDP) averaged 3.3 percent, more than 1 percentage point above the Latin America and Caribbean regional average during the period. Colombia also achieved an impressive reduction in moderate, extreme, and multidimensional poverty and narrowed the inequality gap.[1] The declines in poverty and inequality in those years were driven primarily by an increase in labor income, greater labor market participation by household members, and transfers. The observed poverty reduction associated with transfers coincided with the expansion of conditional cash transfer programs such as Familias en Acción that boosted nationwide coverage to nearly 25 percent of all households.[2]

Nonetheless, poverty levels are high. Approximately one household in three is considered poor, and another one in three is considered vulnerable, which means that a sizable segment of the population is at risk of falling back into poverty. The middle class represents only one-fourth of the population, lagging the average size of the middle class in other countries in the region, including Argentina, Brazil, Chile, and Mexico. Moreover, Colombia is the seventh-most unequal country in the world and ranks second in comparison with other countries in the region and upper-middle income countries, registering a rate of income inequality similar to Angola, Haiti, and South Africa. The share of total income belonging to the bottom 10 percent of the income distribution is around 1.1 percent, while the top 10 percent of the distribution controls over 42.3 percent of total income.

Similarly, the historically large disparities between urban and rural areas persist. Both moderate and extreme poverty are significantly higher in rural areas relative to the main urban areas (the 13 largest cities). Furthermore, the welfare gap between the country's rich and poor departments has not improved and has widened in some cases. Inadequate infrastructure exacerbates these differences. Less than 12 percent of the road network is paved, limiting economic opportunities among rural populations and less well-developed departments. Improving the connectivity between rural and urban areas not only makes sense for the promotion of growth, it would also be an important factor in eliminating the persistent disparities one may observe across Colombia.

There are substantial gaps in access to basic services, such as water, sanitation, the Internet, and education, that, apart from their status as basic necessities, constitute important inputs in the production of human capital. In terms of educational assets, for example, 15-year-olds in Colombia in 2012 had below-average scores in all three areas covered by the standardized tests of the Program for International Student Assessment (PISA) of the Organisation for Economic Co-operation and Development (OECD).[3]

In an effort to address the significant problem of inequality, the government introduced the *Prosperidad para Todos* Development Plan in 2010 and, through the plan, the December 2012 tax reform.[4] While the 2012 reform is expected to boost employment, including formal employment, its impact on inequality is anticipated to be only moderate. Additional reductions in inequality require deeper fiscal reforms that encompass higher, more progressive taxes, more generous and more effectively targeted social transfers, and greater sustained effort to widen access to high-quality education and to ensure universality in the coverage of basic services. The implementation of such reforms makes sense from an equity point of view, but is also a good prescription for more rapid, more sustainable growth that is beneficial for all.

Background

Colombia experienced remarkable economic growth in 2002–13 that was coupled with large declines in poverty. It was able to sustain relatively high GDP growth rates despite the global financial crisis and continues to consolidate its position in the Latin America and Caribbean region as one of the strong performers, with stable economic growth, low inflation, and declining unemployment. Nonetheless, it still faces substantial poverty, unemployment, and disparity.

Despite the 2008 global financial crisis, Colombia maintained positive growth throughout 2008–13. Indeed, the average growth rate during this period was similar to the precrisis average. At the same time, the annualized growth rate of real per capita GDP averaged 3.3 percent, more than 1 percentage point above the regional average. While emerging markets experienced a growth slowdown throughout 2013, Colombia ended the year with a growth performance above the regional average. Boosted by a rise in construction, financial, and retail activity, economic growth increased during the last quarter of 2013, reaching an estimated annualized rate of 4.3 percent, while the region grew 2.4 percent.

The public sector deficit narrowed in 2002–13 and is currently below 1 percent of GDP. Inflation reached a record 50-year low in 2013 as prices rose 1.9 percent year-on-year, slightly below the Central Bank's target range of 2.0–4.0 percent. In 2013, Colombia also registered the lowest unemployment rate in 12 years, at 9.6 percent. This was likely associated with incentives generated by the 2012 tax reform that were aimed at reducing informality in the labor market. Despite these improvements, the rate of unemployment and the incidence of informality are among the highest in the region, representing a barrier to higher economic growth rates (DANE 2013a).

Growth was accompanied by substantial changes in the structure of production, especially the expanding participation of resource extraction in the past decade. Growth has been consistently driven by nontradable services. Oil and mining have played a widening role, while manufacturing has been gradually losing significance. These patterns have generated small changes in the composition of the economy. The value of resource extraction rose from 2.2 percent of GDP in 1976 to almost 8.0 percent in 2012, while manufacturing fell from 18.0 percent to 12.0 percent.

The first term of President Juan Manuel Santos was capped by a strong record of important macro, social, and structural reforms, such as the Fiscal Responsibility Law, the Fiscal Rule, and a comprehensive tax reform. The reelection of President Santos in 2014 should facilitate continuity in projects and policies aimed at strengthening economic performance and reducing inequalities, although peace negotiations with the Revolutionary Armed Forces of Colombia–People's Army, an irregular military organization, continue to be the focus of the current political agenda. By May 2014, 18 months after the start of the negotiations, agreements had been reached on three of five topics: rural development (June 2013), political participation (December 2013), and illegal drugs (May 2014). The two pending topics are ending the conflict and the status of victims. The dividends of a peace agreement are expected to be significant.[5] Following this positive development, Colombia was invited to start the ascension process to OECD membership. The country's risk rating has also been upgraded by all major rating agencies.

The strong economic performance has been accompanied by large drops in poverty. Between 2002 and 2013, the moderate poverty rate fell from 49.7 to 30.6 percent. Growth accounted for 84.1 percent of this reduction.[6] Additionally, during 2008–13, the growth elasticity of poverty was almost –0.6, meaning a 1.0 percent change in average GDP per capita was associated with a nearly 0.6 percent reduction in poverty rates. This emphasizes the key role growth has played in poverty declines in Colombia.

These positive outcomes have translated into higher levels of shared prosperity. Between 2008 and 2013, the growth rate of the incomes of the bottom 40 percent of the income distribution (the bottom 40) rose at a 6.6 percent rate, significantly above the 4.1 percent average across the distribution. This was reflected in a narrowing in income inequality at the end of the decade related to the expansion of social programs and better labor market conditions. Moreover, in 2008–12, the bottom 40 experienced an income growth rate (6.02 percent) that was higher than the regional average (4.25 percent).[7]

Poverty reduction was driven in 2002–13 primarily by a boost in labor income, greater labor market participation by household members, and transfers. During the precrisis years, real per capita income growth benefited the higher end of the income distribution and the middle class more than the poor; however, this pattern was reversed in 2008–13, when growth was relatively more pro-poor. One factor that may explain this result is a more rapid pace in the drop in the unemployment rate among the less well-off. In addition, the observed poverty reduction associated with transfers coincided with the expansion of conditional cash transfer programs. The coverage of one such program, Familias en Acción, rose from around 515,000 households in 2005 to approximately 2.9 million households in 2013, which amounts to nearly 25 percent of households nationwide. The findings suggest that the enlargement of social safety net programs was well targeted and effective in cutting into poverty, particularly extreme poverty.

Notwithstanding the robust economic growth and decreasing poverty rates during the period, Colombia is one of the most unequal countries in the world and suffers from persistent disparities relative to other countries in the region. The moderate and extreme poverty rates are significantly higher in rural areas relative to urban ones. The share of total income among the bottom 10 percent of the income distribution is around 1.1 percent, while the top 10 percent accounts for over 42.3 percent. The country also shows important gaps in the equality of access to basic services, such as water, sanitation, the Internet, and education.

Building the Foundations of Shared Prosperity: Recent Trends

Poverty reduction was remarkable in 2002–13

Colombia has made impressive strides in poverty reduction (figure 4.1). Extreme poverty fell from 17.7 percent in 2002 to 9.1 percent in 2013, which amounts to an annual average drop of 0.78 percentage points. Moderate poverty fell from 49.7 percent to 30.6 percent during the period, representing an annual average decline of 1.73 percentage points.[8] The notable cutback in moderate poverty translated into an absolute decrease of almost 6.0 million in the number of poor people, from over 19.9 million in 2002 to about 14.0 million in 2013. The multidimensional poverty index (MPI) also fell significantly, from 49 percent in 2003 to 24.8 percent in 2013, indicating that the country managed to cut by half the

Figure 4.1 The Reductions in Moderate, Extreme, and Multidimensional Poverty, Colombia, 2002–13

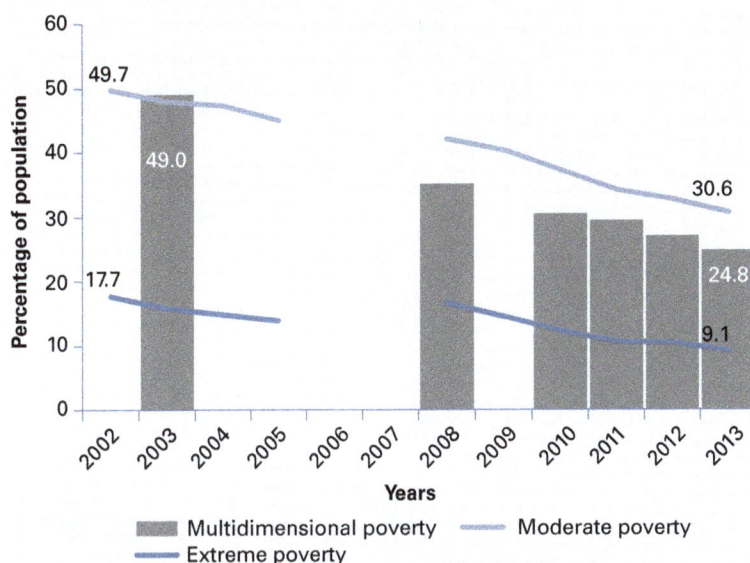

Sources: World Bank calculations. Monetary poverty: data of Estadísticas por Tema: Pobreza y Condiciones de Vida (database), Departamento Administrativo Nacional de Estadística (DANE), Bogotá, https://www.dane.gov.co/index.php/estadisticas-por-tema/pobreza-y-condiciones; and Misión de Empalme de las Cifras de Pobreza y Mercado Laboral (MESEP). MPI in 2003–08: data of Promoción de la Equidad y Reducción de la Pobreza (database), National Planning Department, Bogotá, https://www.dnp.gov.co/. MPI in 2010–13: data of Estadísticas por Tema: Calidad de Vida (database), DANE, Bogotá, https://www.dane.gov.co/index.php/estadisticas-sociales/calidad-de-vida-ecv.
Note: Monetary poverty estimates are based on the official poverty line. The MESEP committee decided not to report monetary poverty estimates for 2006 and 2007 given the methodological changes that took place in those years. The committee deemed that only estimates based on the 2002–05 and 2008–13 series are comparable.

proportion of the multidimensionally poor in the population.[9] The key advances behind this decrease in the MPI were improvements in health care and education, while long-term unemployment and access to sanitation and drinking water worsened during the period.

Poverty reduction was accompanied by a widening in the size of the middle class so that the nonpoor face a relatively lower risk of falling again into poverty. During 2002–12, the size of the middle class rose by 12.1 percentage points, representing a total increase of 80.0 percent.[10] Now, one household in four is considered in the middle class. Nonetheless, Colombia lags other countries in the region in the size of the middle class. In the region, about one household in three is classified as vulnerable; thus, a substantial share of the population in the region runs the risk of falling back into poverty (box 4.1).

Despite the advances, Colombia's ranking in terms of poverty with respect to the region remained the same in 2002 and 2012. Comparable World Bank poverty estimates show that moderate poverty in Colombia

Box 4.1 The Growth of the Middle Class in Colombia and the Region

The middle class in Latin America and the Caribbean grew at a more rapid pace in the past decade than in the 1990s. Despite significant variations across countries, the middle class in the region achieved overall positive growth in 2002–12 (figure B4.1.1). The region had more people in the middle class than in poverty for the first time in 2011, and 2012 saw a continuation of the trends of declining poverty and a growing middle class (World Bank 2013).

Figure B4.1.1 The Growth of the Middle Class, Latin America and the Caribbean, 2002–12

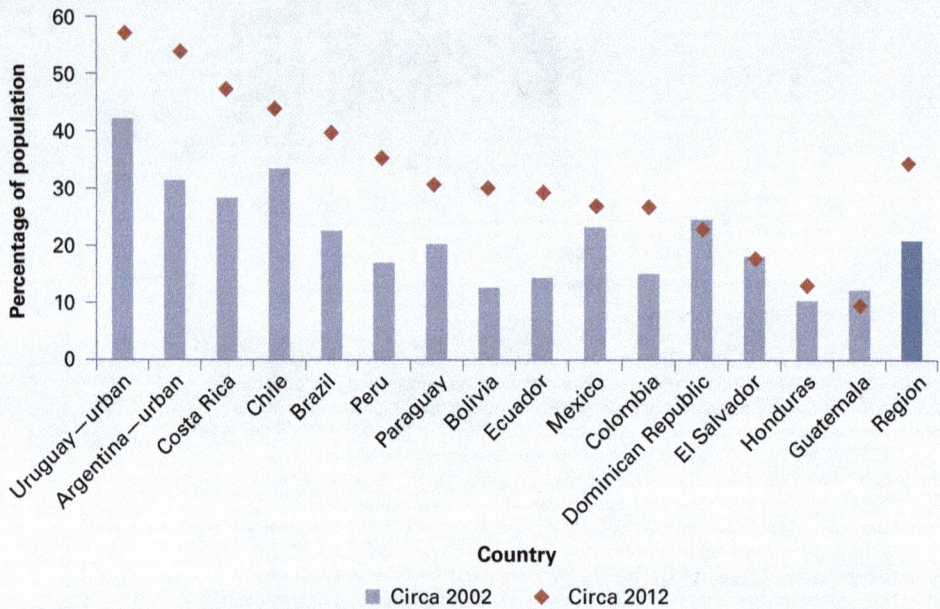

Source: Calculations based on data in SEDLAC.
Note: Circa 2002 = 2000 for Guatemala; 2003 for Chile, Ecuador, and Paraguay; and 2004 for Argentina and Peru. Circa 2012 = 2011 for Chile, Dominican Republic, Guatemala, Honduras, and Paraguay. The definition of middle class is based on Ferreira et al. (2013).

In transitioning the poor and the vulnerable into the middle class, Colombia was similar to its regional peers with comparable middle-class populations in 2002, for example, Bolivia and Ecuador. However, several countries outperformed Colombia, including Brazil, Chile, Costa Rica, and Peru. By 2012, Colombia had the fifth-smallest middle class in the region.

dropped an average 2.3 percentage points per year between 2008 and 2012, a much higher rate than the regional average of 1.4 percentage points per year.[11] Nonetheless, Colombia has yet to regain its 2002 moderate poverty ranking relative to other countries in the region. Meanwhile, Brazil and Mexico achieved comparable poverty reduction at relatively smaller rates of GDP growth.

Who and where are the poor?

Compared with the vulnerable population and the middle class, the poor in Colombia have lower educational attainment; poor men and poor women are less likely to work; and poor households have more members and are more likely to be headed by women (World Bank 2014).[12] Poorer households also have higher dependency ratios because of the larger number of members who are between 0 and 14 years of age or above 70 years of age. Although the dependency ratio declined in 2002–13 among the three socioeconomic groups under examination, it remained significantly higher among the less well-off relative to the middle class.

Meanwhile, ethnic minorities and internally displaced persons (IDPs) face high poverty rates (Cárdenas, Ñopo, and Castañeda 2012). According to Angulo, Díaz, and Pardo (2011), indigenous households exhibited both the highest rates of multidimensional poverty (58 percent in 2010) and the lowest rates of poverty reduction (in 2003–10). Similarly, among IDPs in 2010, the poverty rate was 96.7 percent and the extreme poverty rate was 66.4 percent, implying that at least one in four people in extreme poverty was an IDP in 2010 (CODHES 2010).

The large historical disparities in poverty between the main urban areas and rural areas persist. Despite the substantial nationwide decline in the incidence of poverty, the incidence of moderate and extreme poverty is significantly greater in rural areas (figure 4.2). Thus, between 2002 and

Figure 4.2 The Incidence of Poverty and Extreme Poverty, by Population and Urban or Rural Location, Colombia, 2002–13

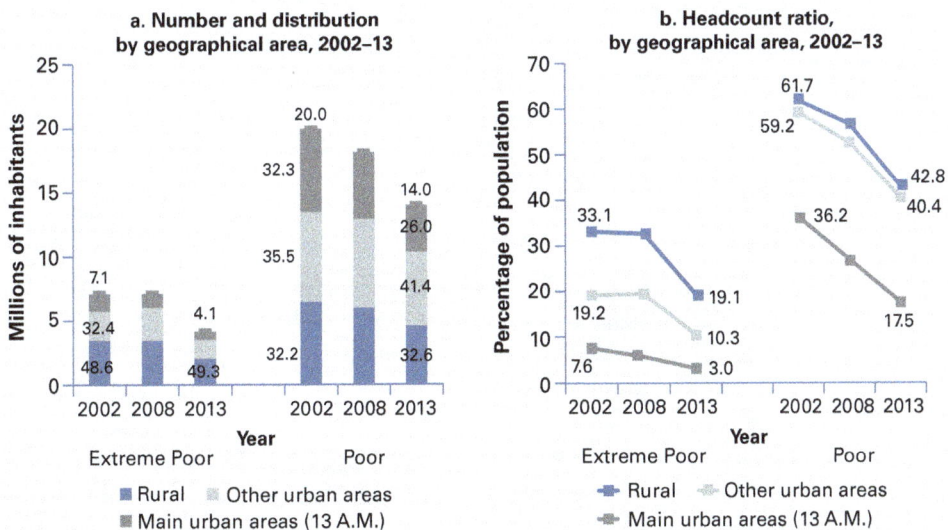

Source: Calculations based on data from the Departamento Administrativo Nacional de Estadistica (National Administrative Department of Statistics, DANE) and Misión de Empalme de las Cifras de Pobreza y Mercado Laboral (MESEP).
Note: A.M. = áreas metropolitanas [metropolitan areas].

2013, the extreme poverty rate in rural areas fell from 33.1 to 19.1 percent, whereas, in the main urban areas, it dropped from 7.6 to 3.0 percent. In 2013, extreme poverty was still more prevalent in rural areas than it had been in the main urban areas in 2002. Similar patterns are evident in moderate poverty.

Nonetheless, in absolute terms, moderate and extreme poverty is more concentrated in urban areas (mainly in the smaller urban areas) relative to rural ones (see figure 4.2). In particular, throughout the decade, roughly one extreme poor individual in every two was residing in an urban area, and two moderate poor individuals in every three were residing in an urban area. Meanwhile, among urban areas, the second-order cities are increasing their participation in total poverty. Moreover, the relative differences across the country's departments became more pronounced over the period. In 2002, the difference between the department with the highest poverty rate (Huila) and the one with the lowest poverty rate (Bogotá Capital District) was 37.8 percentage points, whereas, in 2013, by which year Choco had displaced Huila as the department with the highest poverty rate, the difference was almost 52.9 percentage points (DANE 2013b).

These findings suggest that poverty reduction was biased in 2002–13 toward the main urban areas and high-income departments (see annex 4A). In particular, measured according to the Huppi and Ravallion decomposition (1991), about 57 percent of total poverty reduction occurred in high-income departments and Bogotá, departments that represent approximately 50 percent of the population.[13] The poverty reduction in low-income departments, where approximately 20 percent of the population resides, accounted for only 13.9 percent of the total poverty reduction observed throughout the period. The decomposition also shows that male-headed households or household heads with primary education experienced higher poverty reduction during the period. An increase in the level of education of the household head was also associated with poverty reduction (see the intrasectoral component in annex 4A). Nonetheless, recent data that would permit more accurate analysis are lacking.[14]

Shared prosperity and reductions in inequality

The World Bank measure of shared prosperity, the shared prosperity indicator (SPI), is defined as the growth in per capita income among the bottom 40 (Basu 2013).[15] In 2013, three-fourths of the bottom 40 in Colombia consisted of the poorest households, while vulnerable households accounted for the other fourth.

Qualitative differences in the distribution of the benefits of economic prosperity in Colombia can be identified if one compares the precrisis period (2002–08) and the subsequent period (through 2013). Between 2002 and 2008, the real income per capita of the bottom 40 grew by 2.7 percent, which was below the mean growth rate of about 3.1 percent (figure 4.3). However, between 2008 and 2013, the bottom 40 benefited more than proportionately from economic growth, achieving a real income per

Figure 4.3 Annualized Growth Rate in Income, the Bottom 40 and the Mean, Colombia, 2002–13

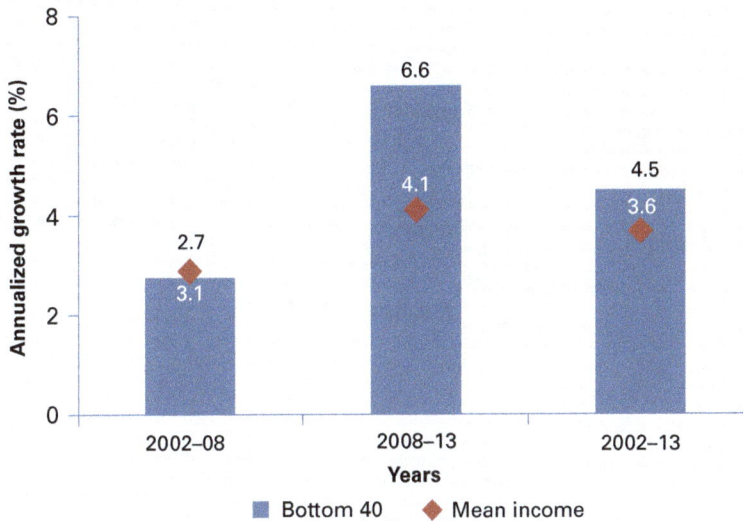

Source: World Bank calculations based on DANE-MESEP data.

capita growth rate of 6.6 percent, substantially higher than the 4.1 percent average.

The observed performance in shared prosperity at the national level was robust across departments (figure 4.4). This resulted in the narrowing of the income gap between the less well-off and the average person across departments. While the annualized growth rate of the mean per capita income was generally higher than the SPI in 2002–08, the reverse was true in 2008–13.

Despite the significant income growth among the less well-off, Colombia showed a blend of poverty reduction and persistent inequality. It has one of the highest inequality levels in Latin America and the Caribbean, the most unequal region in the world (World Bank 2014). In 2013, the year showing the lowest level of inequality, the richest 20 percent of the population held about 58 percent of total income, while the bottom 40 held around 10 percent. The general stagnation in inequality over the period was robust to several inequality measures (table 4.1). For example, the Gini coefficient and the Theil index remained practically stagnant during the main part of the period and declined only marginally during the most recent years (2010–13).[16] During these years, the annual reduction in the Gini was by a factor of two relative to the reduction in 2008–10 and six times the reduction in 2002–08. Additionally, the decline was linked to a rise in the SPI with respect to mean income. This was reflected in an increase in the participation of the less well-off in total income.

The stagnation in inequality in Colombia ran against the general declining trend in inequality in the region during the first decade of the 2000s

Figure 4.4 Improvements in the SPI, by Department, Colombia, 2002–13

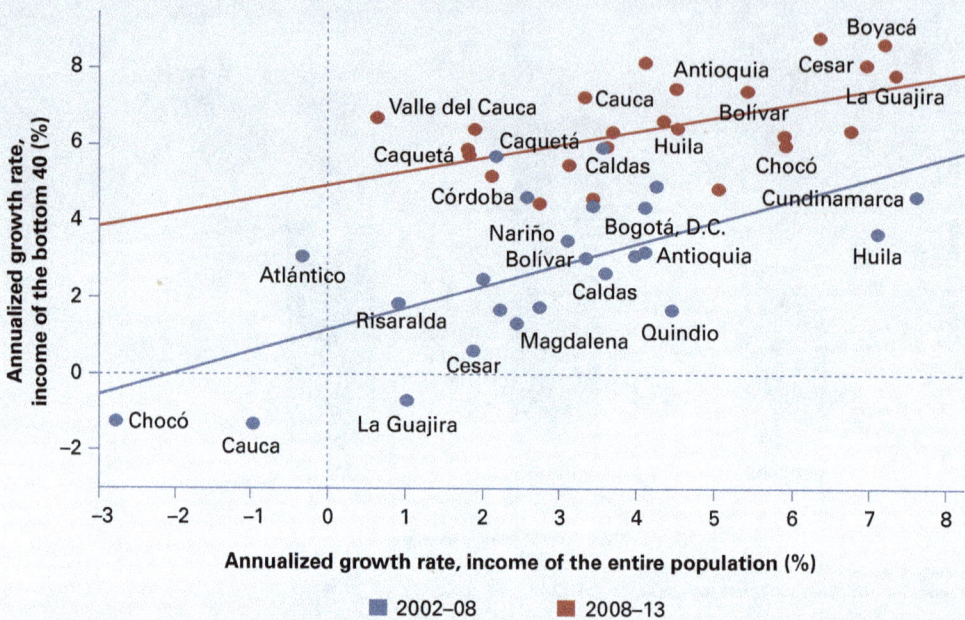

Source: Calculations based on DANE-MESEP data.
Note: SPI = shared prosperity indicator.

Table 4.1 Indicators of Inequality, Colombia, 2002–13

Indicator	2002	2008	2010	2013
Gini coefficient	0.572	0.566	0.560	0.539
Theil index	0.692	0.651	0.641	0.586
90th percentile/10th percentile	13.4	14.4	13.0	12.1
75th percentile/25th percentile	3.6	3.8	3.7	3.6
Annual changes				
Gini points	n.a.	−0.099	−0.325	−0.680
Theil points	n.a.	−0.674	−0.528	−1.832
90th percentile/10th percentile	n.a.	0.174	−0.675	−0.325
75th percentile/25th percentile	n.a.	0.038	−0.074	−0.046

Source: World Bank calculations based on DANE-MESEP data.
Note: n.a. = not applicable.

(Lustig, López-Calva, and Ortiz-Juárez 2013). Even countries with comparable or higher levels of inequality at the beginning of the 2002–12 period, such as Bolivia and Brazil, achieved better results in reducing relative income inequality over the 10-year span (figure 4.5).

Overall, the persistently high levels of inequality are a concern because they limit the positive effects of economic growth on poverty reduction.[17] Indeed, redistribution was not fully exploited as a means to reduce poverty in Colombia in 2002–13 and began to play a role only at the end of the

Figure 4.5 The Gini Coefficient, Selected Countries, Latin America and the Caribbean, 2002–12

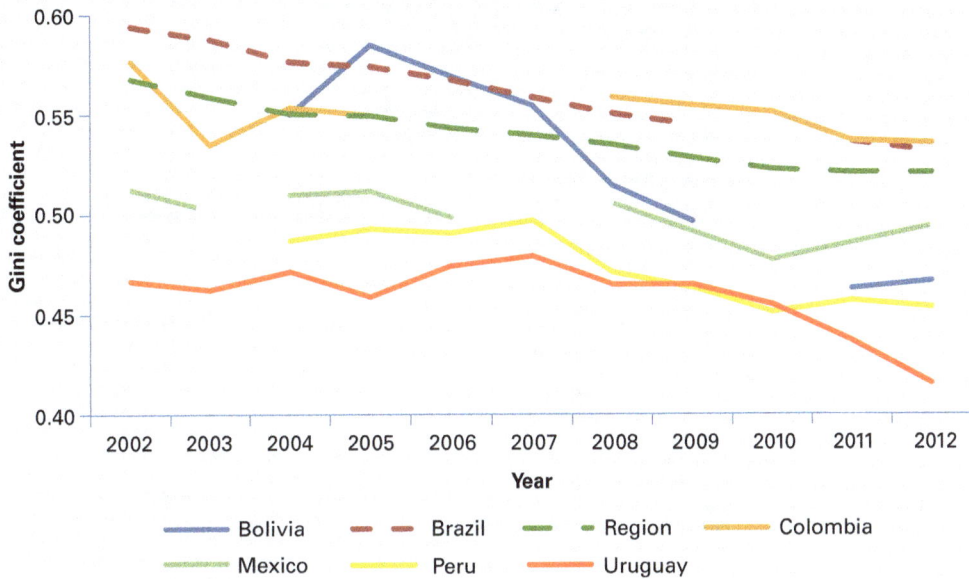

Source: Based on data in SEDLAC.

period. A decomposition of changes in poverty suggests there were qualitative differences in the underlying drivers of poverty reduction between the earlier and later parts of the period (Datt and Ravallion 1992). It reveals that, in 2002–08, the reduction in extreme and moderate poverty was mostly explained by the growth component. In particular, 95 percent of the total reduction in moderate poverty derived from growth, and only 5 percent from redistribution. Furthermore, the redistribution component had a negative effect on the reduction of the extreme poverty headcount during the period. This trend changed dramatically in the second half of the decade, when redistribution began to play a key role, especially in the reduction of extreme poverty (explaining 43 percent of the reduction), within a context of more rapid poverty reduction. Simulation results show that poverty would have declined more had the country experienced a more equitable redistribution of economic growth.[18]

The Drivers of the Observed Changes in Poverty and Inequality

In this section, we apply the asset-based framework as a first step to understanding the main drivers of the improvement in enhancing shared prosperity and reducing poverty in Colombia over time.[19] We examine the trends in each underlying component of income and decompose the distributional changes in income over 2002–13. The insights provided by this analysis are intended to contribute to the evidence base for policy making in Colombia going forward. However, the analysis does not allow causal effects to be identified, though it does help focus attention on the elements that are most important quantitatively in describing the recent changes in poverty and inequality.

Evaluating the dynamics of the sources of income

The fluctuations observed in the levels of poverty and inequality can be attributed partly to shifts in the demographic characteristics of households (age composition, fertility rates, labor force participation rates), changes in the share of economically active adults (access to labor markets), changes in labor incomes (rewards and the distribution of skills), and changes in nonlabor incomes (such as transfers, housing, and pensions).

Changes in labor income are likely to have led to significant modifications in the overall distribution of income. The data show that labor income constitutes a major share of total income across time and across all quintiles of the income distribution. In 2013, for example, labor income accounted for about 65.2 percent of the total income of the lowest quintile (the poor) and 71.3 percent of the total income of the highest quintile (the rich). Over the years, incomes from transfers increased considerably among the poor, suggesting that transfers played an important role in the observed reduction in extreme poverty. In particular, while the income from transfers accounted for 5.7 percent of income among the bottom quintile in 2002, it represented 17.2 percent of the income of the same group in 2013. Beyond the lowest two quintiles (the bottom 40), the value of transfers rose only slightly and was a relatively negligible source of income throughout the period.

Other sources of income are unlikely to have been important drivers of poverty reduction. They account for only relatively small shares of total household income, and these shares are rather stagnant (see annex 4B, the bottom panel of figure 4B.1). Overall, the changes observed in household incomes over time are related to the growth in transfers (especially at the lower end of the income distribution) and the relative growth of labor income.

The growth incidence curves presented in annex 4B, figure 4B.2 highlight the qualitative differences between the earlier and the later part of the period.[20] In 2002–08, the growth in real per capita income benefited the more well-off and the middle class more than the poor. This effect is related to the stagnation in the level of inequality and the low income growth among the bottom 40. In 2008–13, growth was somewhat more pro-poor because people below the 15th percentile were experiencing the largest relative increases in per capita income. These increases were associated with improvements in labor income and transfers. The latter played a significant role, particularly in the growth of the lower end of the distribution of real per capita income.

Accounting for the participation of income sources in poverty reduction

Similar to the more general experience in the region, poverty reduction in Colombia was driven primarily by labor market changes, such as increases in labor income (or the returns to the main asset of the poor, human capital) and the greater participation of household members in the labor market, which implies an expansion in the intensity of use of human capital assets (World Bank 2013). Annex 4B, figure 4B.3 shows that the rise in average labor incomes among working household members (the asset value of the poor in the labor market) explained approximately 43.0 percent of the decline in moderate poverty, while higher earnings among women were responsible for 13.6 percent of the drop, and earnings among men accounted for 29.4 percent. The share of active household members is a measure of the intensity of participation of poor households in the labor force. The expansion in the share of employed members in poor households explained about 28.3 percent of the variation in moderate poverty. Thus, more than 70.0 (60.0) percent of the decline in moderate (extreme) poverty was related to changes in labor market incomes and labor force participation.

The expansion of well-targeted public transfers (the policy component in the asset framework) proved effective in reducing poverty. The change in poverty associated with the increase in transfers among the less well-off was 16.8 percent in the case of moderate poverty and 39.7 percent in the case of extreme poverty, whereas the corresponding changes in the region were 13.0 percent and 23.0 percent, respectively (World Bank 2013). This suggests that the expansion in safety nets over 2002–13 was effective in reducing poverty, particularly extreme poverty, and that it was well targeted.[21]

The increase in the relative size of the incomes from transfers coincided with the expansion in conditional cash transfer programs. According to Escobar and Olivera (2013), public transfers as a proportion of public spending rose significantly, from 10.3 percent in 2003 to 13.6 percent in 2010. Similarly, during the latter part of the 2002–13 period, there was a large expansion in social programs, such as Familias en Acción, the coverage of which rose from around 515,000 households in 2005 to almost 2.9 million households in 2013 (nearly 25 percent of all households in the country).[22]

Relative to the region as a whole, the contribution of pensions to poverty reduction in Colombia was low (World Bank 2013). In particular, while the change in the poverty rate associated with pensions in Colombia was –2.8 percent for moderate poverty and 0.1 percent for extreme poverty, the analogous numbers for the region were –13.0 percent and –15.0 percent, respectively (annex 4B, figure 4B.2). The country's pay-as-you-go pension system, which has 1.4 million beneficiaries, almost exclusively at the upper end of the income distribution, is greatly responsible for this outcome.

Understanding the sources of inequality

Various sources of income played a role in two trends in inequality over the past decade: stagnation and the recent decline. Figure 4.6 illustrates

Figure 4.6 Inequality, by Income Source, Colombia, 2002–13

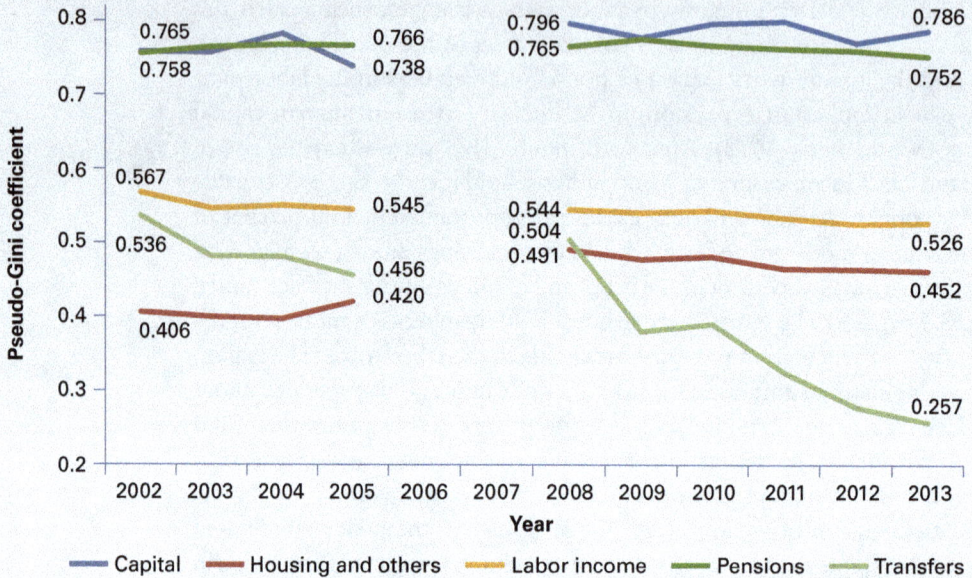

Source: Calculations based on DANE-MESEP data.
Note: The pseudo-Ginis have been computed following Yitzhaki and Lerman (1985). The weighted average of these pseudo-Ginis reproduces the total income Gini coefficient. Thus, the change in the pseudo-Gini of the income source *x* has an effect in the same direction on the change in the total income Gini.

the level of inequality linked to each source of income as measured by the pseudo-Gini coefficient, the weighted average of each pseudo-Gini in a given year (see Yitzhaki and Lerman 1985). Throughout 2002–10, labor income remained stagnant and did not help narrow the inequality gap; the relevant pseudo-Gini was around 0.54 across the period. Meanwhile, transfers contributed more to inequality reduction during the period, when the associated pseudo-Gini fell from 0.536 to 0.380. Moreover, as figure 4.6 highlights, pension and capital income accrue primarily to people in the higher income deciles; the relevant pseudo-Gini was around 0.75 over the period.[23]

Declines in inequality in 2010–13 reflected the more active role of labor income and transfers, which were the two most important drivers of the observed reduction in inequality over the period. Labor accounted for nearly 70.0 percent of total income, while transfers accounted for less than 5.0 percent of total income. Labor income and transfers represented 54.8 percent and 28.6 percent, respectively, of the observed decline in the Gini coefficient. Thus, given their relative shares in total income, every 1.0 percent of income originating from transfers was associated with a 5.7 percent decline in inequality, whereas every 1.0 percent of income originating from labor was associated with a nearly 0.8 percent decline in inequality.[24]

Two factors contributed to the relatively high elasticity of inequality to changes in transfers. During the latter part of the period (2008–13), transfers not only grew at a high rate relative to other sources of income, but they also benefited people the most at the lowest end of the income distribution (see annex 4B, figures 4B.1 and 4B.2). As a result, the pseudo-Gini of transfers declined by more than 50 percent over 2002–13, from 0.536 to 0.257. Overall, the growth and pro-poor development of transfers have had a positive and relatively large impact on the reduction of income inequality over the past decade.

Despite the large contribution of labor income to total income, the elasticity of inequality to changes in labor income was relatively low. Like the Gini of total income, the pseudo-Gini corresponding to labor income declined only marginally, falling from 0.567 in 2002 to 0.526 in 2013, and primarily during the latter part of the 11-year period. The highly unequal distribution of labor income, coupled with the fact that labor income represented more than two-thirds of total income throughout 2002–13, explains the persistently high level of inequality.

Boosting Shared Prosperity

This section examines contextual factors and policies that can help us better understand the forces that influence the short- and middle-run poverty and equity outcomes observed in Colombia over the past decade. Four important policy channels that facilitate the promotion of a more equitable society could enhance the capacity of an economic system to accelerate shared prosperity: (1) maintaining equitable, efficient, and sustainable fiscal policies; (2) strengthening fair, transparent institutions that deliver high-quality public goods; (3) enabling an environment of well-functioning and accessible markets; and (4) developing instruments to improve risk management at the macro level and within households. Focusing on the case of Colombia, the next paragraphs provide a brief discussion of the status of each of these four policy channels and, where possible, center on specific policy actions taken by the government.

Maintaining equitable, efficient, and sustainable fiscal policies

Colombia has exhibited strong economic performance and resilience to global shocks in recent years because of sound policy management and the favorable external environment. Relatively limited openness to trade and restrained inclusion in global financial markets has narrowed the exposure to shocks. Although growth slowed from 6.6 percent in 2011 to 4.0 percent in 2012, it was strong, above the regional average (3.6 percent), and close to the rate in emerging global markets (5.5 percent) (DANE 2012; IMF 2011). Despite robust economic growth and declining poverty rates, Colombia is the seventh-most unequal country in the world and is second relative to countries in the region and upper-middle-income countries. It did not experience the same sort of reduction in inequality that its neighbors in Latin America experienced over the course of the 1990s and 2000s. Such high levels of inequality can hinder economic growth and poverty reduction.

Figure 4.7 The Impact of Fiscal Policy on the Gini Coefficient, Four Countries in Latin America, 2009

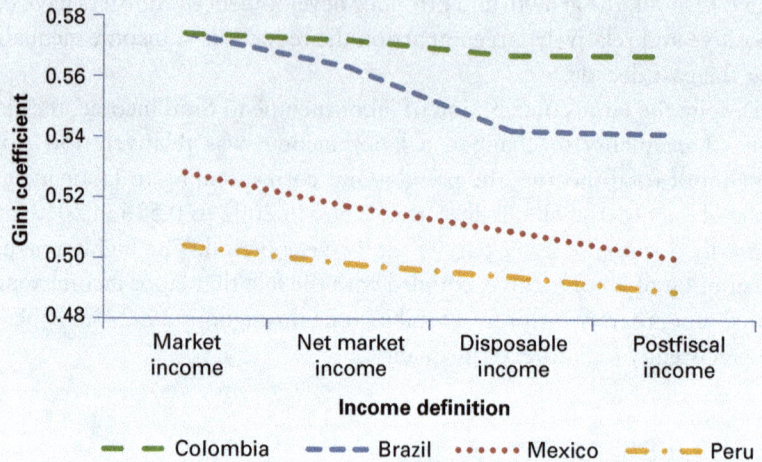

Sources: Higgins and Pereira 2014; Jaramillo 2014; Lustig and Meléndez 2014; Scott 2014.
Note: The figure shows the Gini coefficients calculated using each of the four income definitions of the Commitment to Equity. For a complete overview of the methodology, see Lustig and Higgins (2012). The data for Mexico refer to 2010. Dashed lines represent the change in the Gini coefficient attributed to in-kind transfers, which, unlike the other income definitions, are based on noncash transfers. For postfiscal income, see the text.

The tax and transfer structure prevailing in Colombia in 2002–12 had a limited impact on the high levels of inequality observed during the period. Tax revenues were relatively low, representing 17 percent of GDP, compared with 20 percent in the region and 34 percent in OECD countries (OECD, ECLAC, and CIAT 2014). The redistributive capacity of the fiscal system was limited in Colombia relative to similar countries in the region (Hurtado, Lustig, and Meléndez 2013). For example, Brazil and Colombia, two of the most unequal countries in the world, showed an almost identical level of inequality (0.574 and 0.575, respectively) measured by market income; however, if we take into account the current structure of taxes and transfers prevailing in each of the countries, we find that Brazil's Gini coefficient dropped considerably more than Colombia's (figure 4.7).[25] Indeed, in 2000–10, if direct and indirect taxes, transfers, and subsidies are taken into account, the Gini coefficient of postfiscal income was 0.541 in Brazil and 0.569 in Colombia.[26]

Two factors have contributed to the relatively low redistributive capacity of fiscal policy in Colombia. First, targeting mechanisms suffer from substantial errors of inclusion and exclusion (Joumard and Londoño Vélez 2013a, 2013b). For example, Hurtado, Lustig, and Meléndez (2013) report that, despite the significant expansion in coverage in the latter part of the 2002–12 period, the country's main conditional cash transfer programs—Familias en Acción and *Adulto Mayor*—distributed 37.8 percent of their

Figure 4.8 The Distribution of Monetary Transfers, by Income Decile, Colombia, 2010

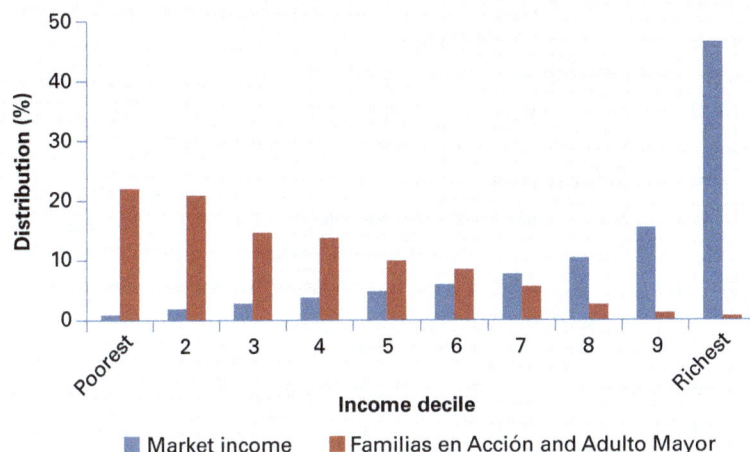

Source: Hurtado, Lustig, and Meléndez 2013.

funds to individuals who were not considered poor (figure 4.8).[27] Second, although generally progressive, several key components of social spending are regressive in Colombia, including indirect taxes and spending on tertiary education and housing subsidies (figure 4.9).[28]

To address the high levels of inequality, the government introduced the *Prosperidad para Todos* Development Plan in 2010. The plan calls for

Figure 4.9 The Concentration Index of Public Spending, Colombia, 2010

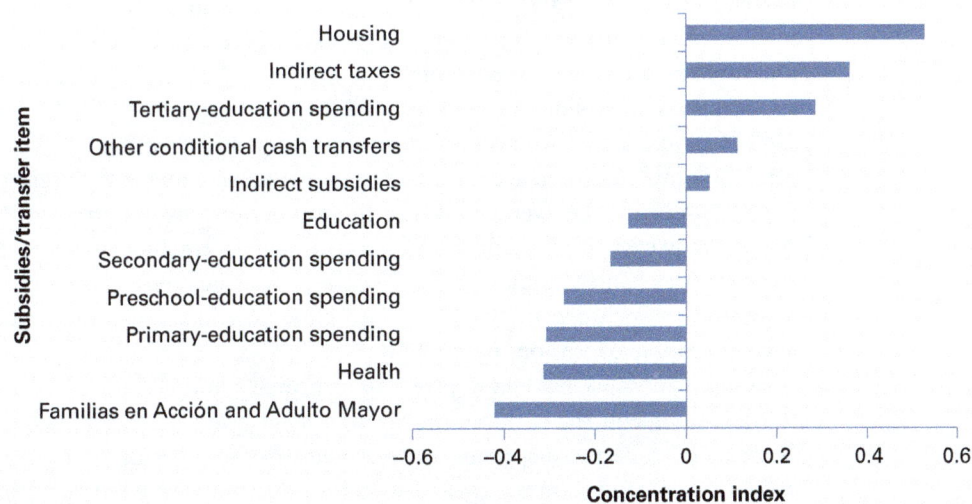

Source: Hurtado, Lustig, and Meléndez 2013.

sustainable economic growth, but also for growth accompanied by positive distributional and social effects. The plan has served as an umbrella for the introduction of a tax reform, which was launched in December 2012. The aim of the reform is to change the distributional impact of the tax system and reduce informality in the labor market. The goal is in line with the objectives of the World Bank's twin goals of economic growth among the bottom 40 (shared prosperity) and the eradication of absolute poverty by the year 2030. However, a recent study by the World Bank (2013) shows that, while the reform is expected to have a positive impact on poverty reduction and raise employment and wages, the reduction in inequality and tax revenues is anticipated to be only moderate. Overall, since the reform, there has still been significant room for boosting the influence of fiscal policy on the reduction of inequality.

Seeking an optimal fiscal policy mix, Moller (2012) compares the effects of various fiscal policy options on the promotion of shared prosperity in Colombia, focusing on the redistributive and revenue effects. Similar to the tax reform, Moller proposes a reduction in tax incentives, benefits associated with personal incomes, and value added taxes, coupled with the introduction of a tax declaration for independent workers. Unlike the tax reform, Moller also proposes an expansion in conditional cash transfer programs to achieve a fiscally neutral reduction in the Gini by 4.6 percentage points.[29] Apart from the expectation that such programs would have inequality reducing effects, the expansion of the programs is projected to have a positive effect on other dimensions of welfare, such as greater school enrollments and attendance and improved health and nutritional status among the targeted population.[30]

Strengthening fair, transparent institutions that deliver high-quality public goods

Ferreira (2012) estimates that over 20 percent of total income inequality in Colombia is attributable to inequality in the access to basic services as measured by the human opportunity index (HOI).[31] In terms of the dynamics of the HOI, Molinas Vega et al. (2012) show that, between 1997 and 2008, Colombia's HOI registered clear improvement, increasing by 17 percent. Colombia also did well in relative terms, placing above the regional average and near the average HOI of the top-performing countries in the region. However, it still exhibits important gaps in equality of access to basic services (water, sanitation, the Internet, and education); the main circumstances explaining the inequality are parental educational attainment and geographical location (figure 4.10).

While Colombia has made progress in primary and secondary educational attainment, the distribution of attainment levels has been unequal. Moreover, while the dispersion or inequality in the years of educational attainment narrowed in the region, it increased substantially in Colombia. The dispersion contributed to the widening in labor income inequality in

Figure 4.10 **The HOI, Colombia, 2012**

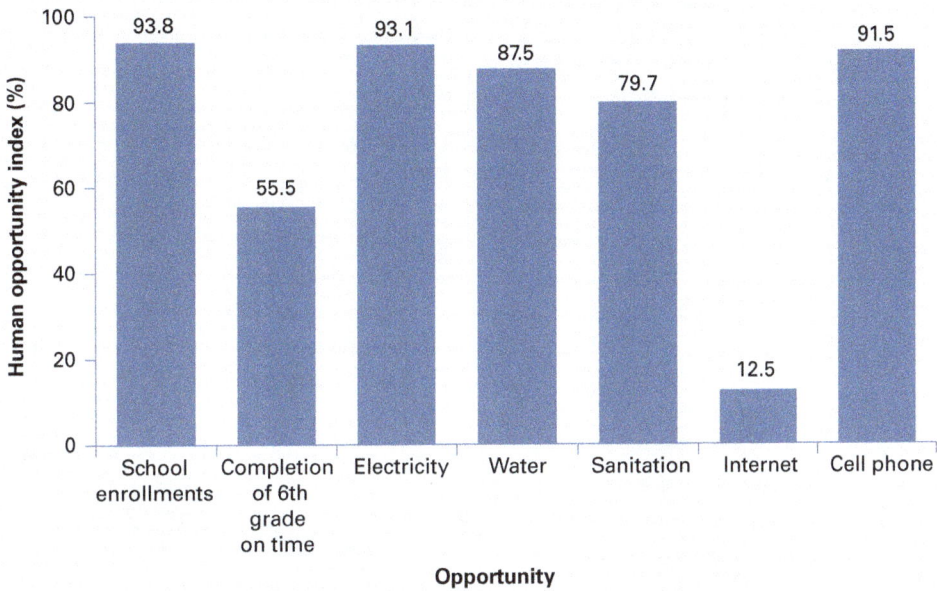

Source: Calculations based on data of GEIH (Gran Encuesta Integrada de Hogares 2012) (integrated household survey 2012) (database), Archivo Nacional de Datos, Departamento Administrativo Nacional de Estadística, Bogotá, http://formularios.dane.gov.co/Anda_4_1/index.php/catalog/77.
Note: The circumstances used in the analysis are the gender of the child, parental educational attainment, household per capita income, number of siblings, presence of both parents in the household, gender of the household head, and urban or rural residence.

the country, thereby diminishing the reduction achieved in income inequality because of changes in the returns to skills (Azevedo et al. 2013).

PISA scores for 2012, which show Colombia's below-average performance in all three subjects tested, highlight the challenges that must be faced to improve access to quality education (OECD 2014). If we use the standardized PISA scores as a gauge of the access to quality education, we find that Colombia lags relative to other countries in the region in basic mathematics (27 percent), reading (50 percent), and science skills (45 percent). Similarly, Colombia is among the countries with the lowest PISA HOI.

Several studies have characterized poor education as an inhibitor of intergenerational mobility in Colombia, suggesting that the outcomes in education have important implications for equity and shared prosperity. For example, Ferreira and Meléndez (2012) estimate that between 18 and 24 percent of inequality in Colombia in adult labor outcomes—that is, in labor incomes or in per capita household incomes—is explained by characteristics that are beyond the control of the individual and that the most important among these is parental educational attainment. Similarly, Ferreira et al. (2013) find that, in Colombia, 3.5 additional years of parental education is, on average, associated with more than 2.5 additional years of schooling in the next generation. The corresponding statistic—known as education persistence—on Peru, the country with the highest value in the indicator among the countries the authors consider, was slightly over 3.0 years of schooling in the next generation, while on Ethiopia, the country with the lowest value in the indicator, education persistence was less than 0.5 years of schooling in the next generation. Ferreira et al. (2013) also report that, in relative terms, Colombia ranks seventh among the 42 countries—rich and poor—in the correlation of educational attainment across generations.

Overall, the empirical evidence suggests that additional improvements in education are likely to translate into significant reductions in inequality, to have a larger welfare-enhancing impact among the less well-off, and to have positive spillover effects on health outcomes.[32]

Colombia has attained nearly universal access to basic services such as school enrollments, electricity, and cell phones. However, differences in access to water, sanitation, and the Internet and in school completion rates are substantial across all departments (figure 4.11).[33] Although a majority of the departments showed progress in the coverage of water and sanitation services, most were still below the national average for this indicator in 2012. Furthermore, even in 2012, nearly one department in five (5 of 24) showed coverage at under 90 percent in sanitation, whereas the coverage of water services in one in three (8 of 24) was below the national average (90 percent). The departments of Chocó, Córdoba, and La Guajira showed significantly lower coverage in water services (less than 61 percent), and

Figure 4.11 Index of Relative Service Coverage, Colombia, 2008 and 2012

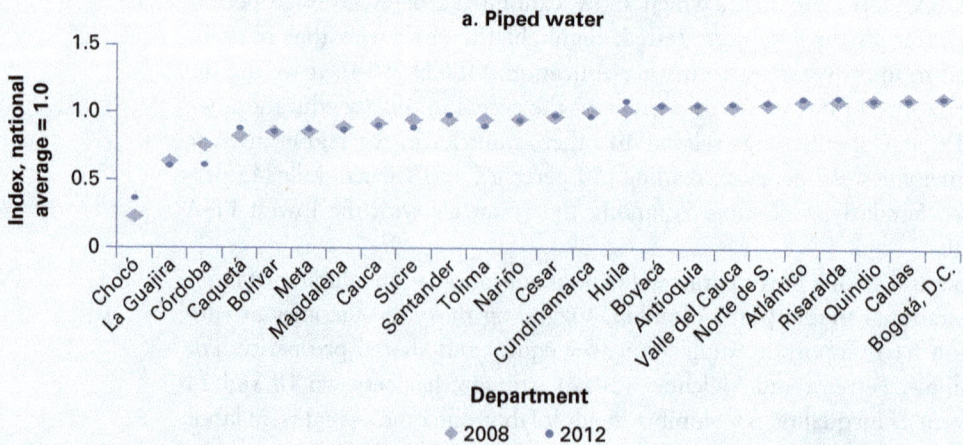

a. Piped water

(continued)

Figure 4.11 Index of Relative Service Coverage, Colombia, 2008 and 2012 *(Continued)*

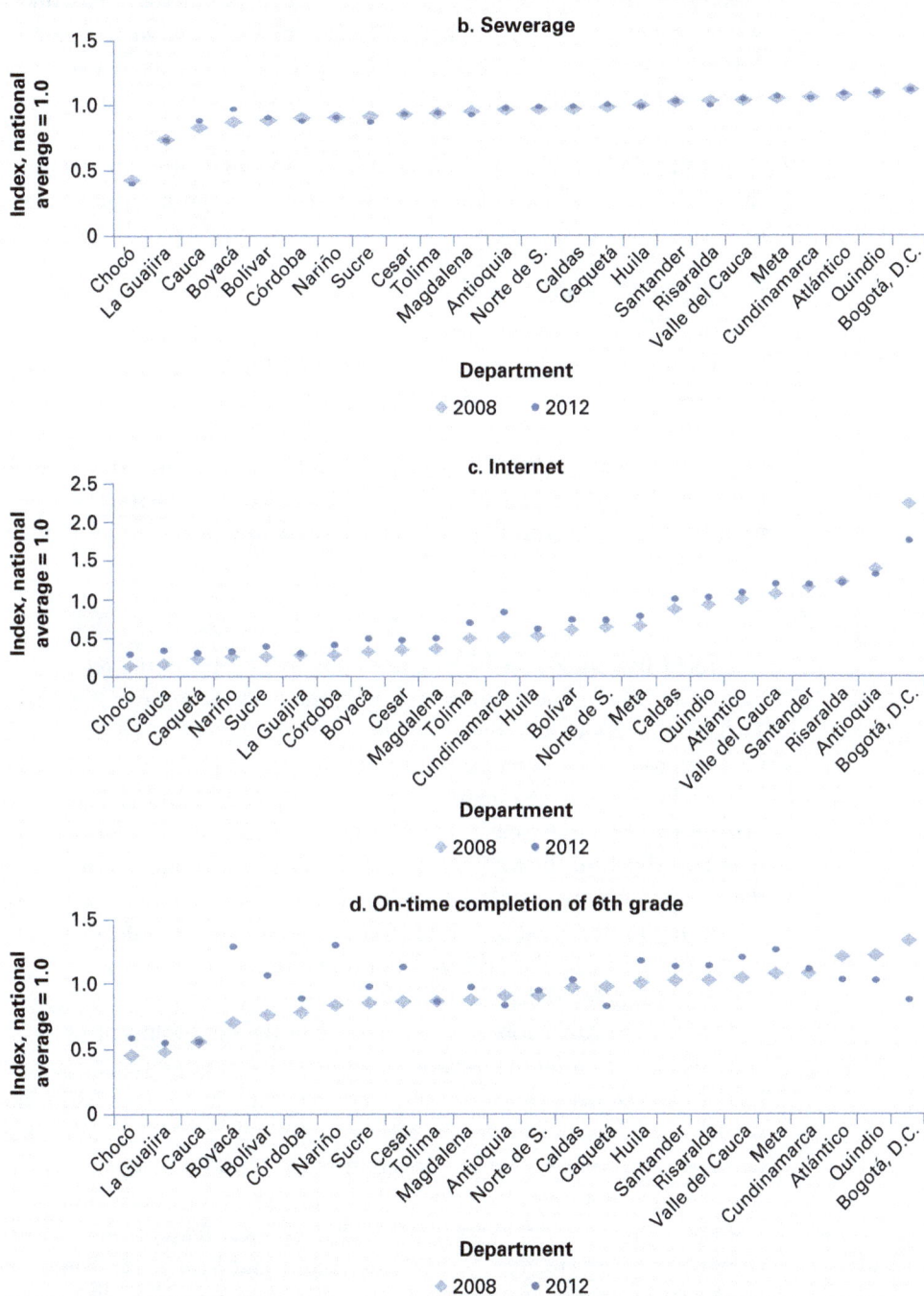

b. Sewerage

c. Internet

d. On-time completion of 6th grade

Source: Calculations based on data of GEIH (Gran Encuesta Integrada de Hogares 2008 and 2012) (integrated household survey 2012) (database), Archivo Nacional de Datos, Departamento Administrativo Nacional de Estadística, Bogotá, http://formularios.dane.gov.co/Anda_4_1/index.php/catalog/77.

Chocó and La Guajira also showed substantially lower coverage than other departments (less than 74 percent) in access to sanitation.

Internet coverage exhibited the largest disparities across departments. While improvements in the access to Internet services were greatest in 2008–12 (an 8 percent average rise in coverage across the departments), one department in every two (12 of 24) had coverage rates under 70 percent in 2012, and one department in four (6 of 24) showed coverage rates under 40 percent. Considering the impact of this new tool on growth and human capital, the unequal access to Internet services may imply persistent inequality in outcomes in the future.

Enabling an environment of well-functioning and accessible markets

Well-functioning markets ensure that skills are matched to employment, that competition and innovation are fostered through appropriate incentives and regulations, and that supply meets demand efficiently. Market conditions that foster the creation of good-quality jobs, trouble-free channels from education and training to labor markets, inclusive and accessible credit markets and financial institutions, and critical infrastructure linking market players are crucial to economic growth and poverty and inequality reduction.

Labor markets

Colombia has one of the highest unemployment rates in the region (10.4 percent in 2012); unemployment among the extreme poor reaches nearly 19.8 percent. Moreover, the poor who are working tend to be employed in the low-productivity informal sector, where their opportunity to move into better jobs is limited (Santa María, Prada, and Mujica 2009). These statistics are particularly troublesome because labor income represented more than two-thirds of the total income of the average Colombian throughout the decade, and it was also the main driver of poverty reduction. Overall, the high rates of labor income inequality (see above), informality, and unemployment that characterize labor markets are major obstacles to poverty and inequality reduction in the country.

One way to foster job creation is through the establishment of market conditions that promote hiring and incentivize worker participation in the formal market. Instead, in Colombia, as Cuesta and Bohórquez (2011) find, workers are likely to transition between informal and formal labor markets based on contributive and noncontributive social security mechanisms that incentivize informality and worker preferences for informal jobs.[34] In a study of the effect of reductions in payroll taxes (*parafiscales*) on total employment, job creation, and wages, Antón and Leal (2013) show that the 2012 tax reform tended to raise salaried employment (by 3.7 percent) and total employment (0.3 percent), while cutting informal employment (−5.3 percent).[35] Moreover, they find that the introduction of a corporate tax to offset lost revenues because of the payroll tax cuts yields results that are similar to the payroll reduction alone, but leads to a smaller expansion in salaried employment (3.4 percent) and a marginally larger rise in total employment (0.5 percent). Wages are expected to climb 4.9 percent among formal wage earners, 3.0 percent among informal wage earners, 4.0 percent among employers, and 2.8 percent among own-account workers. Without the corporate tax, the rise would be slightly higher among all workers, but not among employers. Increases in wages and total employment are likely to be poverty reducing, while expansions in formal employment are likely to be equity enhancing as the quality of jobs improves.

Efforts to prepare the workforce adequately for employment that are likely to enhance labor market outcomes among vulnerable groups should be supported. Similarly, policies with the goal of advancing human capital formation, particularly policies aimed at expanding access to good-quality education and promoting higher educational attainment, can help support beneficial labor market outcomes, reduce persistent inequality, and boost the relatively low rate of productivity growth among workers (Ferreira and Meléndez 2012; Joumard and Londoño Vélez 2013a).

Financial inclusion

Colombia has made substantial progress in promoting financial inclusion, but there are still large challenges. Especially the poor and vulnerable have only limited access to financial services. In 2011, while more than 90.0 percent of adults in OECD countries had accounts at formal financial institutions and differences in access to formal financial institutions between the bottom 40 and the rest of the population were small, only 30.4 percent of adults in Colombia had accounts at formal financial institutions, and only 15.5 percent of the bottom 40 had accounts.[36] Colombia's performance in access to financial services was also poor relative to other countries in the region (figure 4.12, chart a).

Similarly, banking penetration is low in Colombia. Though the number of bank branches is similar to the number in other countries, the number of automated teller machines is lower in Colombia than in other countries with a similar number of commercial bank branches (figure 4.12, chart b). Moreover, more than 40 percent of accounts at formal financial institutions are not used on a monthly basis, and two-thirds of banking correspondents handle fewer than five transactions a day or only accept bill payment transactions.[37] A survey conducted in Bogotá reveals that 70 percent of the unbanked respondents earn less than the minimum wage, are three times more likely than those who use banks to be unemployed, and have lower levels of education (Solo and Manroth 2006). The survey also highlights the challenges that low-income people face, which include the fees banks charge (an average 5–10 percent of a monthly minimum wage), high balance requirements for basic services such as savings accounts, the need for extensive documentation to obtain services, and the shallow penetration of banks in low-income neighborhoods.

Figure 4.12 Indicators of Access to Financial Institutions, Selected Countries of Latin America

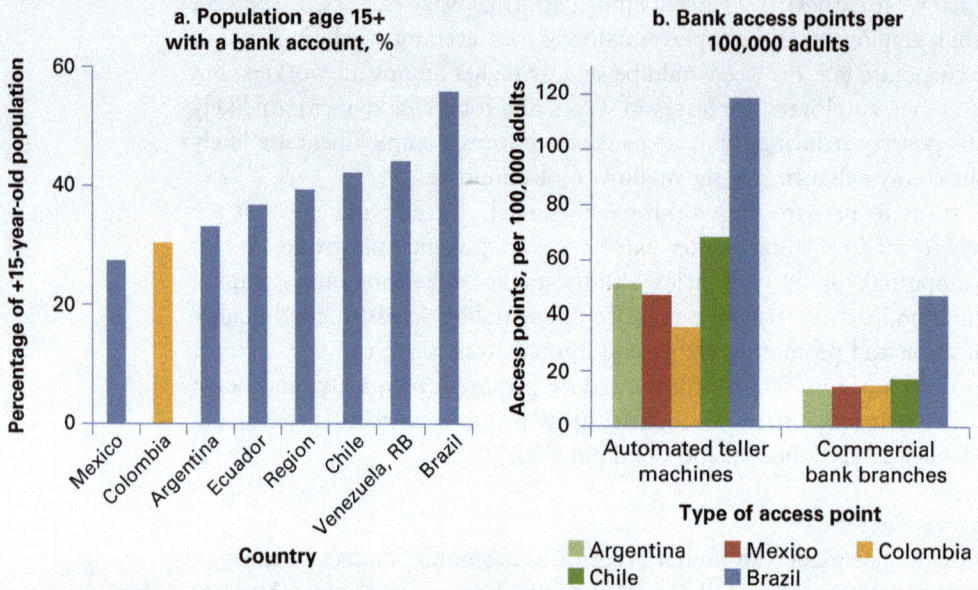

a. Population age 15+ with a bank account, %

y-axis: Percentage of +15-year-old population (0, 20, 40, 60)

x-axis (Country): Mexico, Colombia, Argentina, Ecuador, Region, Chile, Venezuela, RB, Brazil

b. Bank access points per 100,000 adults

y-axis: Access points, per 100,000 adults (0, 20, 40, 60, 80, 100, 120)

x-axis (Type of access point): Automated teller machines, Commercial bank branches

Legend: Argentina, Mexico, Colombia, Chile, Brazil

Sources: Chart a: Data in Global Financial Inclusion (Global Findex) Database, World Bank, Washington, DC, http://www.worldbank.org/globalfindex. Chart b: Data in FAS (Financial Access Survey) (database), International Monetary Fund, Washington, DC, http://fas.imf.org/.

Financial exclusion makes it more difficult for low-income families to save, build credit, and have a secure place to keep money, and limited access to financial services affects the growth of the economy as a whole because less money is available for investment. Colombian authorities have thus made financial inclusion a core element of enabling policies to promote socioeconomic development. In 2006, the government created Banca de las Oportunidades to support financial inclusion through regulatory reforms, financial capability initiatives, and incentives so that providers would meet the demand for banking services among low-income consumers. The government has also promoted access to bank accounts among the vast majority of beneficiaries of the Familias en Acción conditional cash transfer program. Policies have likewise been implemented to ease the regulations and tax treatment associated with low-balance accounts, including exempting them from the 4 × 1,000 (0.4 percent) tax and introducing simplified account opening procedures. Furthermore, the regulatory and supervisory environment for microcredit has been strengthened. A financial education decree was approved in 2014, and a committee on financial education has been created. Among the policy recommendations to address the remaining challenges are the lowering of taxes on financial transactions, employing subsidies to make up for high transaction costs, leveraging low-cost technologies such as automated teller machines, providing financial education to raise awareness among the unbanked, and fostering the access to and use of financial services, particularly in rural areas.

The competitive business environment and access to road infrastructure

Colombia ranked first in the Ease of Doing Business indicators in 2014 across all countries in the region and among the top 25 percent of countries globally. Nonetheless, the country still lags in road infrastructure. Given the high transportation costs that the lack of road infrastructure generates, this reduces the international competitiveness and growth potential of local markets.[38] These logistics costs also raise the cost of final products to consumers and affect equity by passing along a burden to poor people in the form of higher prices for basic consumption goods, including food. In Colombia, where the quality of the road infrastructure is ranked 108th among 142 countries and food makes up close to 50 percent of the total consumption among the poorest decile, the high logistics costs are likely to place a significant burden on the poor (Schwab 2012; World Bank 2011).

Less than 12 percent of the country's road network of 214,399 kilometers is paved, and, except for the access corridors to major cities and ports, which are predominantly under concession, road quality is poor (Yepes, Ramírez, and Villar 2013). Poor road conditions and the lack of roads to link rural areas to markets and major metropolitan areas represent important barriers to rural populations in gaining access to public services, selling their products, and taking advantage of economic opportunities. Improving the connectivity between rural and urban areas makes sense for growth and is crucial to overcoming persistent departmental disparities. To address these challenges, policy makers can streamline investment planning and project structuring and management at the subnational level to complete the decentralization of the road network and to ensure the connectivity of buyers, intermediaries, suppliers, and the broad population in isolated departments (World Bank 2012).

Risk management at the macro and micro levels

Between 1970 and 2010, natural disasters caused an average annual loss of $177 million in Colombia. Over 62 percent of these natural disasters were related to excessive rainfall, and the associated landslides caused the greatest number of deaths and flooding and the largest loss of property (Sánchez and Calderón 2012a, 2012b). Areas of settlement that cannot provide adequate housing support for inhabitants, such as informal settlements, which are populated primarily by the poorest members of society, accounted for more than half the housing loss caused by natural disasters between 1970 and 2011; 51 percent of the residential buildings destroyed by natural disasters were destroyed because the location was not suitable for housing (Campos et al. 2011; Van Gelder 2013).

More recently, rising climate variability, often linked to the occurrence of the El Niño and La Niña phenomena, has led to significant losses in Colombia (Campos et al. 2011). Massive flooding during the 2010–11 rainy season alone (*ola invernal*) impacted 4 million people, causing 423 deaths and economic loss reaching $5.1 billion (2 percent of Colombia's GDP), including damage to over 560,000 homes, flooding on close to a million hectares of productive farmland, the death or displacement of over 1.5 million head of cattle, and severe disruption on 98 major roadways, leading to delays in food distribution and to food price increases.[39] In response to this unprecedented destruction, the president of Colombia signed Law 1523, which established a national system for disaster risk management that will address some of the risks the country faces.

While this is a timely initiative, the risks related to climate change are secondary to the inadequacy of territorial, sectoral, and private sector risk management in dealing with the growing risks of disaster. According to Campos et al. (2011), four factors contribute to the accumulation of disaster risk. First, risk conditions are exacerbated because the relationship between disaster risk management and sustainable development has not yet been assimilated by public policy and management. Second, poor municipal land use policies and inadequate watershed management have led to the continued accumulation of risks in cities and rural areas. Third, rising levels of exposure to risk and vulnerability resulting from the ineffective application of disaster risk management policies in sectoral planning threaten the sustainability of investments in the productive and service sectors. Fourth, fiscal costs are rising because of the lack of a clear policy defining the responsibilities of the various actors in the prevention of and response to disasters.

To address these challenges, Colombia would benefit from enhancement of the governance structures in disaster risk management. The focus should be on consolidating government policies aimed at strengthening the local capacity for land use planning, improving the coordination of government entities in watershed management, defining the responsibilities of sectoral stakeholders, and promoting the participation of public and private actors, thereby contributing to reducing the state's fiscal vulnerability to disasters. This might involve adopting regulations to reinforce Disaster Risk Management Law 1523 (2012) and its institutional framework and implementing the national disaster risk management plan (Plan Nacional de Gestión del Riesgo de Desastres).

Through these integrated actions, the effectiveness and efficiency of risk management investments would be supported by strategic planning, coordination across territorial levels, and monitoring and supervision. Meanwhile, regulations on flood and landslide control and management, technical standards for risk assessment and mitigation, and a strategy for implementation should also be adopted. To achieve this objective, coordination among the various agents responsible for watershed management will be central to reducing the risk of flooding and landslides through planning, investment, and monitoring and supervision. Through these strategies, the formulation and implementation of watershed management plans (*Planes de Ordenación y Manejo de Cuencas Hidrográficas*) should be accelerated and incorporated as a determining instrument in municipal land use plans.

Final Remarks

Colombia enjoyed strong economic performance during 2002–13. It also achieved an impressive decline in the incidence of moderate, extreme, and multidimensional poverty. Despite qualitative differences between the first and the second half of the period, the less well-off benefited more than the average population from income growth. Today, more households are part of the middle class than ever before, and conservative estimates show that the size of the middle class should surpass the size of the poor segment of the population in 2015.

Notwithstanding this progress, however, there are important challenges. The poverty rate is still high for an upper-middle-income country. Colombia continues to lag other countries in the region in the size of the middle class, and a large share of the population—more than one household in three—is vulnerable to falling back into poverty. Moreover, income inequality is more severe in Colombia than many other places in the world. In terms of regional trends, large historical disparities between the main urban areas and the rest of the country (semiurban and rural areas) persist, and the gaps between rich and poor departments is widening because the pace of poverty reduction has been more rapid in high-income departments and the main cities. Empirical evidence suggests that poverty would have declined more over the past decade had the country experienced more equitable economic growth, implying that a more robust reduction in inequality is likely to lead to significant welfare gains.

To address some of these challenges, in 2010, the government introduced the Prosperidad para Todos development plan. The plan calls for sustainable economic growth, but also for growth accompanied by positive distributional and social effects. This has represented an important step forward in the effort to promote shared prosperity. Nonetheless, the existing empirical evidence and the analysis presented in this chapter suggest that the associated tax reform is expected to have only a moderate impact on income inequality. Thus, continued inequality reduction will require deeper fiscal reform, including more progressive taxes, more generous and well-targeted social transfers, and sustained and significant initiatives to expand the access to high-quality education and to ensure the universality of the coverage of basic services among the less well-off. Similarly, in response to sociodemographic developments, the focus of policies should not only be on poverty eradication, but also on protecting vulnerable populations. Lastly, to address persistent departmental disparities in outcomes and access, mainstreaming the integration of rural areas and low-income departments into the growth process through local investments, infrastructure, and transfers will be essential for more poverty reduction. These recommendations not only make sense from an equity point of view, but are also a good prescription for achieving more rapid, more sustainable growth that is beneficial for all.

Annex 4A Decomposing Poverty Reduction

Table 4A.1 Participation in Poverty Reduction, Intrasectoral Effect and Intersectoral Effect, Selected Household Characteristics, Colombia, 2002–13

Household characteristics	Distribution 2002	Distribution 2013	Intrasectoral effect Components	%	Intersectoral effect, %	Interaction effect, %
By department level of income[a]						
Bogotá capital district	16.2	16.7	18.3	99	0.8	0.2
High	33.8	31.7	38.7			
Medium	29.9	30.9	28.2			
Low	20.1	20.7	13.9			
Economically active, household members, %						
Less than 25	33.2	22.7	22.6	73	29	−2.00
25–50	50.1	50.1	42.2			
Over 50	16.7	27.2	8.2			
Economically active, household members, number						
None or one	43.8	41.6	41.8	98.1	2.1	−0.16
Two	32.8	35.2	29.2			
Three or more	23.3	23.3	27.2			
Children and youth, household members, number						
None	22.7	30.5	12.9	73.8	27.6	−1.30
One or two	49.5	52.3	39.6			
Three or more	27.8	17.2	21.3			
Gender of household head						
Male	77.1	68.4	84.4	102.2	0.5	−2.80
Female	22.9	31.6	17.8			
Educational attainment of household head						
None or primary	56.4	46.2	61.3	85.6	22.4	−7.91
Secondary education	32.3	36.4	24			
Tertiary education	11.4	17.4	0.3			
Location						
Urban	74.2	76.7	72.1	97.4	2.3	0.3
Rural	25.9	23.3	25.7			

Source: Calculations based on DANE-MESEP data.
Note: The figure is the result of the application of the Huppi and Ravallion decomposition (1991).
a. The categories of income have been defined using the average of the rankings of GDP and GDP per capita in 2012. High-income departments include Valle, Cundinamarca, Santander, and Antioquia. Middle-income departments include Atlántico, Caldas, Huila, Cesar, Bolívar, Boyacá, Tolima, Risaralda, Quindio, La Guajira, and Meta. The rest are defined as low-income departments.

Annex 4B Incomes and the MPI

Figure 4B.1 Income, by Source and Income Quintile, Colombia, 2002–13

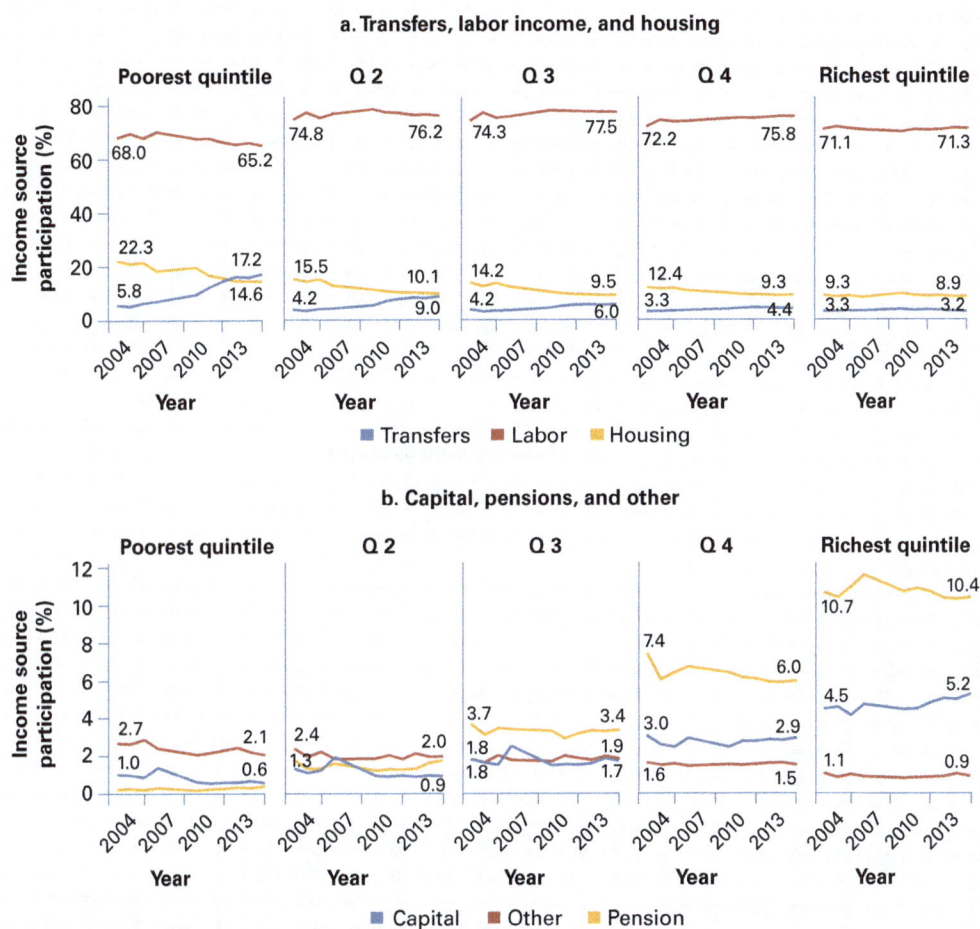

a. Transfers, labor income, and housing

Legend: ■ Transfers   ■ Labor   ■ Housing

b. Capital, pensions, and other

Legend: ■ Capital   ■ Other   ■ Pension

Source: Calculations based on DANE-MESEP data.
Note: Housing refers to imputed rents. Transfers include public and private transfers. MPI = multidimensional poverty index.

Figure 4B.2 Growth Incidence Curves of per Capita Income, Colombia, 2002–13

a. 2002–08

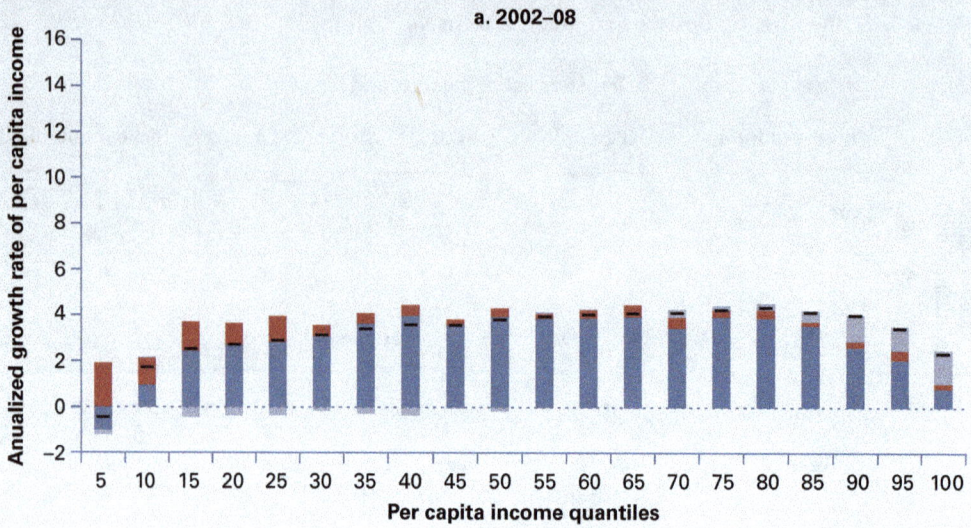

b. 2008–13

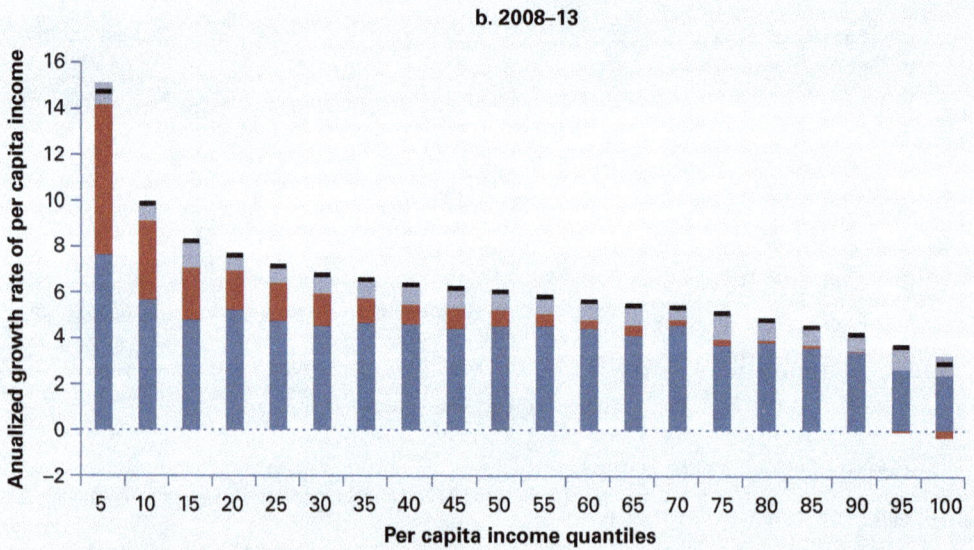

■ Labor income   ■ Transfers   ▫ Other nonlabor income   — Total

Source: Calculations based on DANE-MESEP data.
Note: Nominal values are deflated using the average consumer price index in Colombia by year.

Figure 4B.3 Income Source Contributions to Moderate and Extreme Poverty Reduction, Colombia, 2002–13

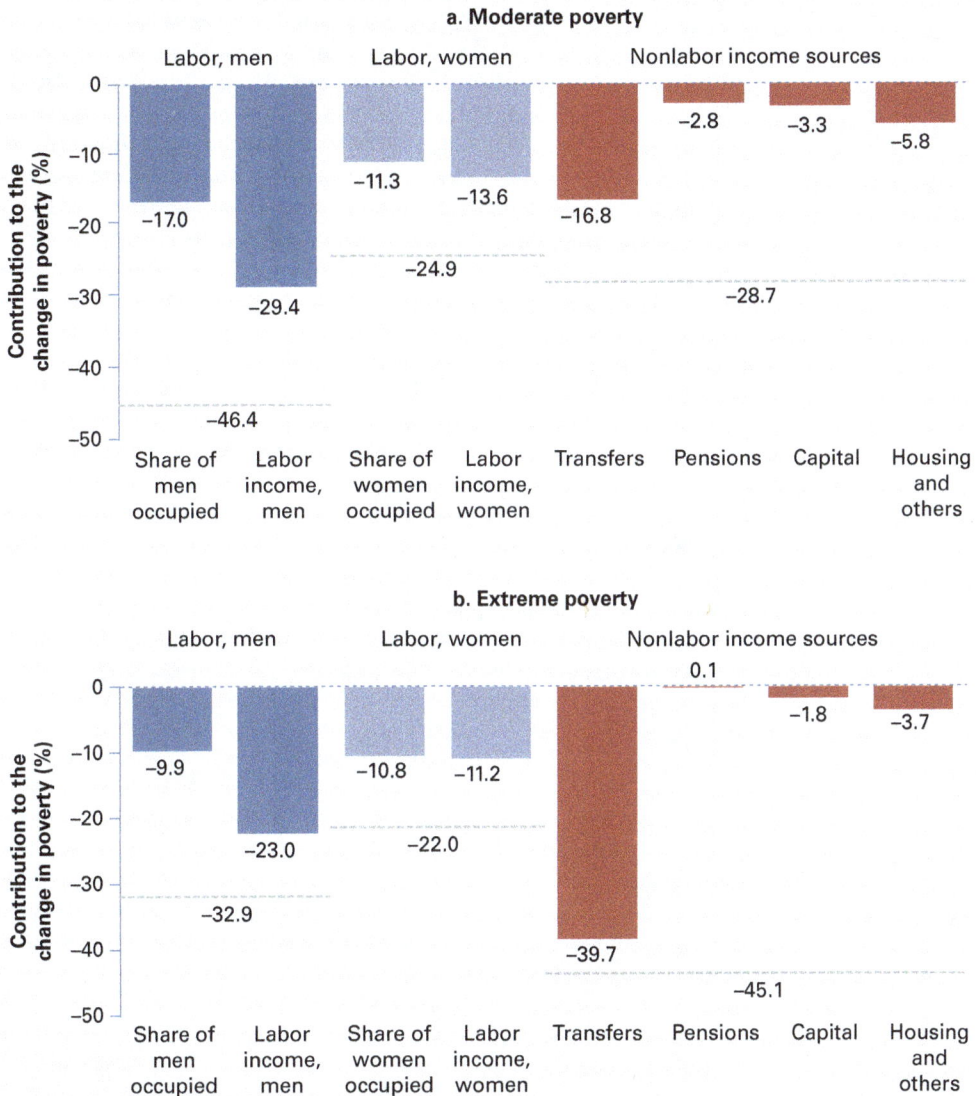

a. Moderate poverty

b. Extreme poverty

Source: Calculations based on DANE-MESEP data.

Note: For details on the underlying methodology, see Azevedo, Inchauste, and Sanfelice (2013). Other nonlabor income includes income from capital and housing and nonworker income. Share of occupied refers to gains attributable to increases in the number of employed household members. The data sets have been defined in real values using the average consumer price index, and the assumptions of rank preservation are based on households (see Azevedo et al. 2013).

Notes

1. This chapter builds largely on official poverty data and on the microdata collected by the Departamento Administrativo Nacional de Estadística (National Administrative Department of Statistics, DANE) of Colombia. For example, see Estadísticas por Tema: Pobreza y Condiciones de Vida (database), Departamento Administrativo Nacional de Estadística, Bogotá, https://www.dane.gov .co/index.php/estadisticas-por-tema/pobreza-y-condiciones. The poverty data have been developed jointly by the Misión de Empalme de las Cifras de Pobreza y Mercado Laboral (MESEP), the United Nations Economic Commission for Latin America and the Caribbean, and the World Bank. See Azevedo (2013).

2. For information on the Familias en Acción Program, see "Más Familias en Acción," Departamento para la Prosperidad Social, Bogotá, http://www.dps .gov.co/Ingreso_Social/FamiliasenAccion.aspx. See also endnote 27.

3. The Program for International Student Assessment (PISA) evaluates skills in mathematics, reading, and science among 15-year-old students in over 70 economies. See "Programme for International Student Assessment," Organisation for Economic Co-operation and Development, Paris, http://www.oecd.org /pisa/.

4. See "Plan Nacional de 2010–2014," National Planning Department, Bogotá, https://www.dnp.gov.co/Plan-Nacional-de-Desarrollo/PND-2010-2014 /Paginas/Plan-Nacional-De-2010-2014.aspx.

5. Cárdenas (2002) estimates that Colombia's armed conflict accounted for a loss of almost 2 percentage points in annual economic growth between 1980 and 2000. The associated costs have been estimated at around 9 percent of GDP in 2006.

6. This reflects the results of a Datt-Ravallion decomposition for 2002–13. For further details on the method, see Datt and Ravallion (1992).

7. World Bank calculations based on data of the WDI (World Development Indicators) (database), World Bank, Washington, DC, http://data.worldbank.org /data-catalog/world-development-indicators and SEDLAC (Socio-Economic Database for Latin America and the Caribbean), Center for Distributive, Labor, and Social Studies, Universidad Nacional de La Plata, La Plata, Argentina and World Bank, Washington, DC, http://sedlac.econo.unlp.edu.ar/eng/index.php.

8. Between 2008 and 2012, moderate poverty decreased by an average of nearly 2.3 percentage points a year, whereas, between 2002 and 2008, moderate poverty declined at a much slower 1.3 percentage points a year. The fall in the $1.25-a-day poverty rate in 2005 purchasing power parity (PPP) dollars was similarly impressive, dropping from 11.7 percent in 2002 to 6.6 percent in 2012.

9. In 2011, the government adopted this multidimensional measure of poverty. The MPI is a weighted average of 15 indicators (deprivations) clustered in five dimensions: education, childhood, employment, health, and housing. People are considered multidimensionally poor if they exhibit an MPI of 0.33 or more.

10. These estimates have been computed using the definition of the middle class proposed by López-Calva and Ortiz-Juárez (2014), who argue that the central characteristic defining the middle class is the vulnerability of falling again into poverty. See SEDLAC. The estimates of Angulo, Gaviria, and Morales (2013) for 2002–11 show similar trends and levels.

11. This is based on microdata harmonized using the regional $4.00-a-day poverty line (2005 PPP), which approximates the official moderate poverty line of about $4.06 (2005 PPP). See SEDLAC.

12. While male (female) participation in the labor force increased among the middle class and the vulnerable, it declined (remained practically stagnant) among the poor.

13. The Huppi and Ravallion decomposition (1991) allows for the identification of the household characteristics associated with poverty reduction as well as the sociodemographic changes related to these welfare gains.

14. The last census was conducted in 2005, and poverty rates are only available for department-level analysis. This limits the production of poverty maps and any deeper examination of disparities across the country.

15. In April 2014, World Bank President Jim Yong Kim announced a twin strategy for the World Bank going forward: (1) to end extreme poverty globally by 2030 and (2) to promote shared prosperity, that is, a sustainable increase in the economic well-being of the poorer segments of society, defined as the poorest 40 percent of the population (the bottom 40).

16. In 2010–13, the Gini (Theil) index declined by 2.1 (5.5) points, from 56.0 (64.1) to 53.9 (58.6). This four-year decline in inequality coincided with an acceleration in the average rate of poverty reduction.

17. While some level of inequality may be desirable, for example, to promote innovation and entrepreneurship, too much inequality may limit the prospects for economic development and additional poverty reduction. Ravallion (2007) reports that, while poverty generally tends to fall in growing economies, it does so at different rates depending on how inequality changes over time. In particular, poverty reductions are significantly slower in countries in which growth has been accompanied by rising inequality than in countries that have combined growth with narrowing inequality.

18. For instance, if one uses the changes in Brazil's income distribution during 2002–12 and Colombia's current per capita income growth, the result is a counterfactual that shows smaller reductions in poverty: 4.1 percentage points in addition to the observed reduction in moderate poverty and 1.3 percentage points in addition to the observed reduction in extreme poverty.

19. For more details on the asset-based framework, see the Overview.

20. Growth incidence curves display growth rates at each percentile of the consumption distribution and are a useful tool for examining whether growth is shared across the spectrum of the rich and the poor.

21. See the evolution of the shares of transfers across quintiles presented in annex 4B, figure 4B.1, and the contribution of transfers to income growth presented in annex 4B, figure 4B.2.

22. While transfers accounted for 5.7 percent of income among the bottom quintile in 2002, it represented 17.2 percent of this income in 2013. Among the third and higher quintiles of the income distribution, however, transfers rose only slightly and were a relatively negligible source of income throughout the period.

23. Despite the unequal distribution, pensions explained only 8.5 percent of the observed level of income inequality in 2010–13, while capital income explained only 4.3 percent.

24. These results are based on the linear decomposition in figure 4.6.

25. Hurtado, Lustig, and Meléndez (2013) carry out their calculations using surveys that capture household expenditures and incomes rather than the surveys used to produce the official numbers. Market income refers to wages and salaries, income from capital, and private transfers before government taxes, social security contributions, and public transfers.

26. Subtracting direct taxes and the employee contributions to social security from market income gives net income. Adding direct transfers results in disposable income; once indirect subsidies have been added and indirect transfers subtracted, the result is postfiscal income.

27. In 2012, Familias en Acción was redesigned and renamed Más Familias en Acción to improve targeting on vulnerable and poor populations. It is estimated that, in 2014, approximately 90 percent of the beneficiaries of Más Familias en Acción were considered poor or vulnerable (GEIH 2014).

28. This is demonstrated by the fact that these components have positive concentration coefficients. The concentration coefficient is similar to the Gini. It measures the association between two variables; only the cumulative distribution function can take a variable other than income as the parameter (see Van Kerm 2009).

29. The simulations do not account for any behavioral shifts in response to these changes.

30. The additional benefits of these programs include financial inclusion through exposure to savings accounts, a fall in the rate of teenage pregnancy, and crime reduction (Joumard and Londoño Vélez 2013a, 2013b).

31. The HOI is a scalar measure that synthesizes two factors: the average rate of coverage of a basic good or service among a population and a relative measure of equality of opportunity that is adjusted for differences in access to basic services among individuals in the population based on the circumstances of these individuals (Barros et al. 2009). Molinas Vega et al. (2012, 10) define the circumstances as "personal, family, or community characteristics that a child has no control over and that, for ethical reasons, society wants to be completely unrelated to a child's access to basic opportunities." The index calculation involves children because children are less likely to have any control over their circumstances.

32. For instance, higher educational attainment among household heads is associated with increases in total household income that are largest among the poorest quintile and decline as one moves up the income ladder (Zuluaga 2007).

33. A significant expansion in coverage was not observed between 2008 and 2012, though this is a relatively short time span.

34. The study concludes that health care coverage, but not pension coverage, acts as a disincentive to occupational transitions.

35. The study focuses on the part of the fiscal reform (Law 1607 of 2012) that relates directly to labor markets, the parafiscales, which include sources of funding for training, in-kind transfers, and employer contributions for health care.

36. World Bank (2013) and Global Financial Inclusion (Global Findex) Database, World Bank, Washington, DC, http://www.worldbank.org/globalfindex.

37. Global Financial Inclusion (Global Findex) Database, World Bank, Washington, DC, http://www.worldbank.org/globalfindex.

38. Thus, the transport cost from Bogotá to the Atlantic coast is $94 per ton and from Bogotá to Barranquilla on the Caribbean Sea is $88. By comparison, the transport cost per ton from Bogotá to Buenaventura on the Pacific coast for transshipment to the United States is $54 and from Buenaventura to Shanghai is $60; see Samad, Lozano-Gracia, and Panman (2012).

39. See "Floods in Brazil and Colombia: Inundated," *Economist*, London, January 13, 2011, http://www.economist.com/node/17906077; "Flooding in Colombia," ABColombia, London, May/June 2011, http://www.abcolombia.org.uk /subpage.asp?subid=402&mainid=23; "Colombia's Infrastructure: Bridging the Gaps," *Economist*, London, September 17, 2011, http://www.economist .com/node/21529036; "Colombia's Floods: That Damned Niña," *Economist*, London, December 10, 2011, http://www.economist.com/node/21541419.

References

Angulo, Roberto C., Yadira Díaz, and Renata Pardo. 2011. "Índice de Pobreza Multidimensional para Colombia (IPM-Colombia) 1997–2010." Archivos de Economía 009228, National Planning Department, Bogotá.

Angulo, Roberto C., Alejandro Gaviria, and Liliana Morales. 2013. "La década ganada: evolución de la clase media y las condiciones de vida en Colombia, 2002 and 2011." Documentos Cede 50 (October), Centro de Estudios sobre Desarrollo Económico, Universidad de los Andes, Bogotá.

Antón, Arturo, and Julio Leal. 2013. "Aggregate Effects of a Universal Social Insurance Fiscal Reform." IDB Working Paper IDB-WP-429, Intra-American Development Bank, Washington, DC.

Azevedo, João Pedro. 2013. "From Noise to Signal: The Successful Turnaround of Poverty Measurement in Colombia." *Economic Premise* 117 (May), Poverty Reduction and Economic Management Network, World Bank, Washington, DC.

Azevedo, João Pedro, María Eugenia Dávalos, Carolina Díaz-Bonilla, Bernardo Atuesta, and Raul Andres Castañeda. 2013. "Fifteen Years of Inequality in Latin America: How Have Labor Markets Helped?" Policy Research Working Paper 6384, World Bank, Washington, DC.

Azevedo, João Pedro, Gabriela Inchauste, and Viviane Sanfelice. 2013. "Growth without Reductions in Inequality." Background paper, Poverty and Gender Unit, World Bank, Washington, DC.

Barros, Ricardo Paes de, Francisco H. G. Ferreira, Jose R. Molinas Vega, and Jaime Saavedra Chanduvi. 2009. *Measuring Inequality of Opportunities in Latin America and Caribbean*. With Mirela de Carvalho, Samuel Franco, Samuel Freije-Rodríguez, and Jérémie Gignoux. Latin American Development Forum Series. Washington, DC: World Bank; New York: Palgrave Macmillan.

Basu, Kaushik. 2013. "Shared Prosperity and the Mitigation of Poverty: In Practice and in Precept." Policy Research Working Paper 6700, World Bank, Washington, DC.

Campos, Ana, Niels Holm-Nielsen, Carolina Díaz, Diana M. Rubiano, Carlos R. Costa, Fernando Ramírez, and Eric Dickson, eds. 2011. *Analysis of Disaster Risk Management in Colombia: A Contribution to the Creation of Public*

Policies. Bogotá: Global Facility for Disaster Reduction and Recovery, World Bank, Washington, DC.

Cárdenas, Juan Camilo, Hugo Ñopo, and Jorge Luis Castañeda. 2012. "Equidad en la Diferencia: Políticas para la Movilidad Social de Grupos de Identidad; Misión de Movilidad Social y Equidad." Documentos Cede 010319, Centro de Estudios sobre Desarrollo Económico, Universidad de los Andes, Bogotá.

Cárdenas, Mauricio. 2002. "Economic Growth in Colombia: A Reversal of Fortune." Archivos de Economía, National Planning Department, Bogotá.

CODHES (Consultoría para los Derechos Humanos y el Desplazamiento). 2010. "Tercer informe de verificación sobre el cumplimiento de derechos de la población en situación de desplazamiento." (December), Comisión de Seguimiento a la Política Pública sobre Desplazamiento Forzado, CODHES, Bogotá.

Cuesta, Jose, and Camilo Bohórquez. 2011. "Labor Market Transitions and Social Security in Colombia." Policy Research Working Paper 5650, World Bank, Washington, DC.

DANE (Colombia, Departamento Administrativo Nacional de Estadística). 2012. "Producto Bruto Interno, IV Trimestre y Total Anual." Press Release, DANE, Bogotá.

————. 2013a. "Principales Indicadores del Mercado Laboral." Press Release, DANE, Bogotá.

————. 2013b. "Boletín de Pobreza y Desigualdad." Press Release, DANE, Bogotá.

Datt, Gaurav, and Martin Ravallion. 1992. "Growth and Redistribution Components of Changes in Poverty Measures: A Decomposition with Applications to Brazil and India in the 1980s." *Journal of Development Economics* 38 (2): 275–95.

Escobar, Andrés, and Mauricio Olivera. 2013. "Gasto Público y Movilidad y Equidad Social." Documentos Cede 9 (February), Centro de Estudios sobre Desarrollo Económico, Universidad de los Andes, Bogotá.

Ferreira, Francisco H. G. 2012. "Inequality of Opportunity around the World: What Do We Know So Far?" *Inequality in Focus* 1 (1): 8–11.

Ferreira, Francisco H. G., and Marcela Meléndez. 2012. "Desigualdad de Resultados y Oportunidades en Colombia: 1997–2010." Documentos Cede 40 (November), Centro de Estudios sobre Desarrollo Económico, Universidad de los Andes, Bogotá.

Ferreira, Francisco H. G., Julian Messina, Jamele Rigolini, Luis F. López-Calva, María Ana Lugo, and Renos Vakis. 2013. *Economic Mobility and the Rise of the Latin American Middle Class*. Washington, DC: World Bank.

Higgins, Sean, and Claudiney Pereira. 2014. "The Effects of Brazil's Taxation and Social Spending on the Distribution of Household Income." In "Analyzing the Redistributive Impact of Taxes and Transfers in Latin America," ed. Nora Lustig, Carola Pessino, and John Scott, special issue, *Public Finance Review* 42 (3): 346–67.

Huppi, Monika, and Martin Ravallion. 1991. "The Sectoral Structure of Poverty during an Adjustment Period: Evidence for Indonesia in the Mid-1980s." *World Development* 19 (12): 1653–78.

Hurtado, Carlos, Nora Lustig, and Marcela Meléndez. 2013. "Gasto Social, Impuestos y Redistribución del Ingreso en Colombia." PowerPoint presentation,

World Bank and Government of Colombia's "Equity Day, Colombia," Bogotá. March 12.

IMF (International Monetary Fund). 2011. "Colombia: Staff Report for the 2014 Article IV Consultation." IMF Country Report 14/141, IMF, Washington, DC.

Jaramillo, Miguel. 2014. "The Incidence of Social Spending and Taxes in Peru." In "Analyzing the Redistributive Impact of Taxes and Transfers in Latin America," eds. Nora Lustig, Carola Pessino, and John Scott, special issue, *Public Finance Review* 42 (3): 391–412.

Joumard, Isabelle, and Juliana Londoño Vélez. 2013a. "Income Inequality and Poverty in Colombia, Part 1: The Role of the Labor Market." OECD Economics Department Working Paper 1036 (March), Organisation for Economic Co-operation and Development, Paris.

———. 2013b. "Income Inequality and Poverty in Colombia, Part 2: The Redistributive Impact of Taxes and Transfers." OECD Economics Department Working Paper 1037 (March), Organisation for Economic Co-operation and Development, Paris.

López-Calva, Luis F., and Eduardo Ortiz-Juárez. 2014. "A Vulnerability Approach to the Definition of the Middle Class." *Journal of Economic Inequality* 12 (1): 23–47.

Lustig, Nora, and Sean Higgins. 2012. "Commitment to Equity Assessment (CEQ): Estimating the Incidence of Social Spending, Subsidies, and Taxes; Handbook." Tulane Economics Working Paper 1219 (October), Department of Economics, Tulane University, New Orleans.

Lustig, Nora, Luis F. López-Calva, and Eduardo Ortiz-Juárez. 2013. "Declining Inequality in Latin America in the 2000s: The Cases of Argentina, Brazil, and Mexico." *World Development* 44: 129–41.

Lustig, Nora, and Marcela Meléndez. 2014. "The Impact of Taxes and Transfers on Inequality and Poverty in Colombia." Working paper, Commitment to Equity, Inter-American Dialogue, Washington, DC; Center for Inter-American Policy and Research and Department of Economics, Tulane University, New Orleans.

Molinas Vega, José R., Ricardo Paes de Barros, Jaime Saavedra Chanduvi, and Marcelo Guigale. 2012. *Do Our Children Have a Chance? A Human Opportunity Report for Latin America and the Caribbean.* With Louise Cord, Carola Pessino, and Amer Hasan. Report 65656. Directions in Development: Poverty. Washington, DC: World Bank.

Moller, Lars Christian. 2012. "Fiscal Policy in Colombia: Tapping Its Potential for a More Equitable Society." Policy Research Working Paper 6092, World Bank, Washington, DC.

OECD (Organisation for Economic Co-operation and Development). 2014. "PISA 2012 Results in Focus: What 15-Year-Olds Know and What They Can Do with What They Know." OECD, Paris.

OECD (Organisation for Economic Co-operation and Development), ECLAC (United Nations Economic Commission for Latin America and the Caribbean), and CIAT (Inter-American Center of Tax Administrations). 2014. *Revenue Statistics in Latin America 1990–2012.* Paris: OECD.

Ravallion, Martin. 2007. "Economic Growth and Poverty Reduction: Do Poor Countries Need to Worry about Inequality?" 2020 Vision Briefs BB08 (Special Edition), International Food Policy Research Institute, Washington, DC.

Samad, Taimur, Nancy Lozano-Gracia, and Alexandra Panman, eds. 2012. *Colombia Urbanization Review: Amplifying the Gains from the Urban Transition*. Directions in Development: Countries and Regions. Washington, DC: World Bank.

Sánchez, Fabio Torres, and Silvia Calderón. 2012a. "Riesgos Extensivos e Intensivos en Colombia: Análisis Histórico y Geográfico." Proyecto Fortalecimiento de la Gobernabilidad para la Administración del Riesgo Social en Colombia, World Bank, Washington, DC.

————. 2012b. "Pobreza y Desastres Naturales." Proyecto Fortalecimiento de la Gobernabilidad para la Administración del Riesgo Social en Colombia, World Bank, Washington, DC.

Santa María, Mauricio, Carlos Felipe Prada, and Ana Virginia Mujica. 2009. "Oportunidades, desafíos y barreras de la movilidad laboral en Colombia: reflexiones para la población en pobreza extrema y moderada." Working Paper 42, Fedesarrollo, Bogotá.

Schwab, Klaus, ed. 2012. *The Global Competitiveness Report 2011–2012*. Geneva: World Economic Forum.

Scott, John. 2014. "Redistributive Impact and Efficiency of Mexico's Fiscal System." In "Analyzing the Redistributive Impact of Taxes and Transfers in Latin America," eds. Nora Lustig, Carola Pessino, and John Scott, special issue, *Public Finance Review* 42 (3): 368–90.

SEDLAC (Socio-Economic Database for Latin America and the Caribbean), Center for Distributive, Labor, and Social Studies, Universidad de La Plata, La Plata, Argentina; World Bank, Washington, DC, http://sedlac.econo.unlp.edu.ar/eng/index.php.

Solo, Tova Maria, and Astrid Manroth. 2006. "Access to Financial Services in Colombia: The 'Unbanked' in Bogotá." Policy Research Working Paper 3834, World Bank, Washington, DC.

Van Gelder, Jean-Louis. 2013. "Paradoxes of Urban Housing Informality in the Developing World." *Law & Society Review* 47 (3): 493–522.

Van Kerm, Phillipe. 2009. "SGINI: Generalized Gini and Concentration Coefficients (with Factor Decomposition) in Stata." Working paper, CEPS/INSTEAD, Centre for Population, Poverty, and Public Policy Studies/International Networks for Studies in Technology, Environment, Alternatives, Development, Esch-sur-Alzette, Luxembourg.

World Bank. 2011. "High Food Prices: Latin American and the Caribbean Responses to a New Normal." Report 87932, Latin America and Caribbean Region, World Bank, Washington, DC.

————. 2012. "Colombia: First Programmatic Sustainable and Productive Cities Development Policy Loan Program." Program Document 71447, World Bank, Washington, DC.

————. 2013. "Shifting Gears to Accelerate Shared Prosperity in Latin America and the Caribbean." Poverty and Labor Brief, Report 78507 (June), Latin America and Caribbean Region, World Bank, Washington, DC.

————. 2014. "On the Road to Shared Prosperity: Investing into a More Equitable Latin America and Caribbean." Unpublished working paper, Poverty and Gender Group, World Bank, Washington, DC.

Yepes, Tito, Juan Mauricio Ramírez, and Leonardo Villar. 2013. "Infraestructura de transporte en Colombia." With Juliana Aguilar, Claudia Patricia Quintero, and Isabella Muñoz. Cuadernos de Fedesarrollo 46 (March), Fedesarrollo, Bogotá.

Yitzhaki, Shlomo, and Robert I. Lerman. 1985. "Income Inequality Effects by Income Source: A New Approach and Applications to the United States." *Review of Economics and Statistics* 67 (1): 151–56.

Zuluaga, Blanca. 2007. "Different Channels of Impact of Education on Poverty: An Analysis for Colombia." Discussion Paper ces0702, Center for Economic Studies, Katholieke Universiteit Leuven, Leuven, Belgium.

CHAPTER 5

Shared Prosperity and Opportunities in El Salvador

Megan Rounseville, Mateo Salazar, and Kinnon Scott

> Shared prosperity has different meanings: for the poor, it is a pretty phrase, hopeful; for the rich, it means communism; and, for the middle class, it means cost.
>
> Inequality consists of there not being opportunities for all.
>
> *Focus group participants*

Introduction

Salvadorans view the idea of shared prosperity through diverse lenses and differ in their beliefs about whether it can be achieved (ESEN 2014). The barriers to shared prosperity include historic inequality perpetuated through a lack of opportunities and a lack of access to economic resources, a state that is unable to promote growth and equity, a society that has no vision of appropriate goals, and a lack of solidarity across groups to create needed change. The concept of shared prosperity is prevalent within groups though not across them. There is consensus that the results of continued inequality are pernicious. Inequality is seen to act as a damper on the incentives for hard work and investment, and inequality in opportunity is at the root of the alarming levels of crime and violence in the country.

The past decade was a period of mixed progress in achieving shared prosperity and poverty reduction in El Salvador. The extreme poverty rate fell between 2000 and 2012, but the overall poverty rate changed little, and socioeconomic mobility was minimal.[1] Changes in poverty came about through more jobs, although not better jobs, and significant remittance inflows. Government direct transfers did not play a major role in poverty reduction. Economic growth was limited, and productivity showed only modest gains. However, some progress was achieved in nonmonetary indicators of welfare and in access to services. Low productivity in the tradables sector and the high levels of crime and violence are key constraints to economic growth. The fiscal situation is tight, and revenue collection accounts for only a small share of gross domestic product (GDP).

This chapter examines the empirical evidence on poverty and shared prosperity with the goal of identifying factors that may have led to advances in welfare and equity in El Salvador and highlighting areas where intervention could favor further progress. Trends in welfare are presented in the next section. The movement out of poverty is the focus of the following section: is the perception of a lack of mobility expressed by focus group participants reflected in the data? The subsequent section focuses on the drivers of poverty reduction and shared prosperity. The channels through which shared prosperity can be affected in the short and medium term are explored in the penultimate section, and the chapter ends with conclusions and recommendations.

Poverty, Shared Prosperity, and Inequality: Levels and Trends

Poverty

A substantial number of people escaped extreme poverty in El Salvador, but fewer moved out of poverty entirely (figure 5.1, chart a). Between 2000 and 2012, the extreme poverty rate was cut by almost 40 percent, declining from 19.0 to 11.3 percent; most of the change occurred between 2000 and 2004.[2] While the financial and price crisis of 2008–09 caused the poverty

Figure 5.1 Poverty Rates, El Salvador, 2000–12

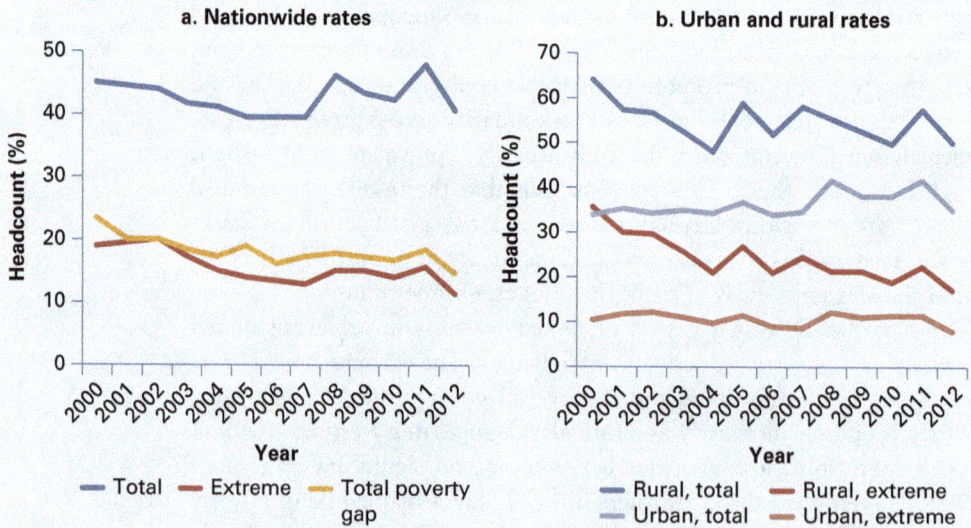

Source: Calculations based on data from Encuesta de Hogares de Propósitos Múltiples (Multipurpose Household Survey), 2000–12.

Map 5.1 Extreme Poverty, by Department, El Salvador, 2012

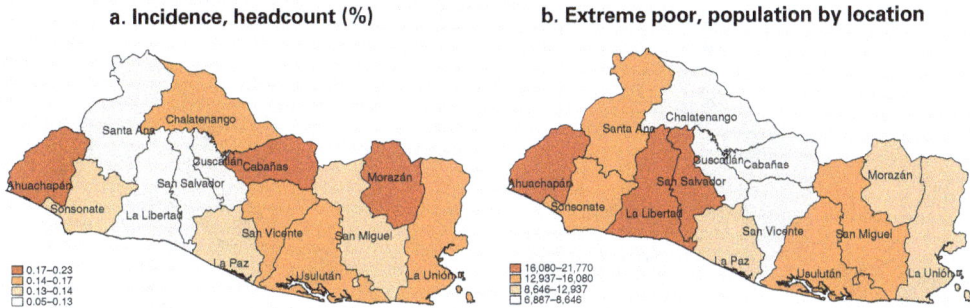

a. Incidence, headcount (%)

Legend:
- 0.17–0.23
- 0.14–0.17
- 0.13–0.14
- 0.05–0.13

b. Extreme poor, population by location

Legend:
- 16,080–21,770
- 12,937–16,080
- 8,646–12,937
- 6,887–8,646

Source: Calculations based on data from Encuesta de Hogares de Propósitos Múltiples (Multipurpose Household Survey), 2000–12.

rate to rise, the extreme poverty rate in 2012 was below the rate prior to the crisis.

In contrast, the overall poverty rate fell slowly after 2000. In 2012, 41 percent of the population was living in poverty, a decline of only 4 percentage points in 12 years. The poverty gap, however, declined more than the poverty rate, showing that welfare was improving. While the drop in overall poverty was small, it did reflect nearly a full recovery from the negative impacts of the financial crisis of 2008–09.

Despite its small size (8,000 square miles), El Salvador shows significant internal differences in poverty, and the nationwide rates mask substantial changes in rural areas (see figure 5.1, chart b). Poverty rates are higher in rural areas than in urban areas (50 and 35 percent, respectively). The gap narrowed appreciably over the 12-year period as the poverty reduction was largely confined to rural areas. Rural poverty rates fell sharply from 2000 to 2004: 15 percentage points in overall poverty and 17 percentage points in extreme poverty. However, rural poverty rates were volatile during 2004–12, and, by the end of the period, the poverty rate was not much different than it had been in 2004. Poverty varied by *departamento* in both the rate and the proportion of the poor residing in each department (map 5.1). Ahuachapán is the only department in which there was overlap between the high rate of overall poverty and the large population share of the extreme poor. Cabañas had a high rate of extreme poverty, but relatively fewer poor because of its smaller population, while La Libertad and San Salvador had low extreme poverty rates, but a large share of the extreme poor population.

Shared prosperity

The progress in shared prosperity mirrored the income gains made by the poor. The average income growth among people in the bottom 40 percent of the income distribution (the bottom 40) was 3 percent between 2004

Figure 5.2 Shared Prosperity, Central America and the Region, 2004–12

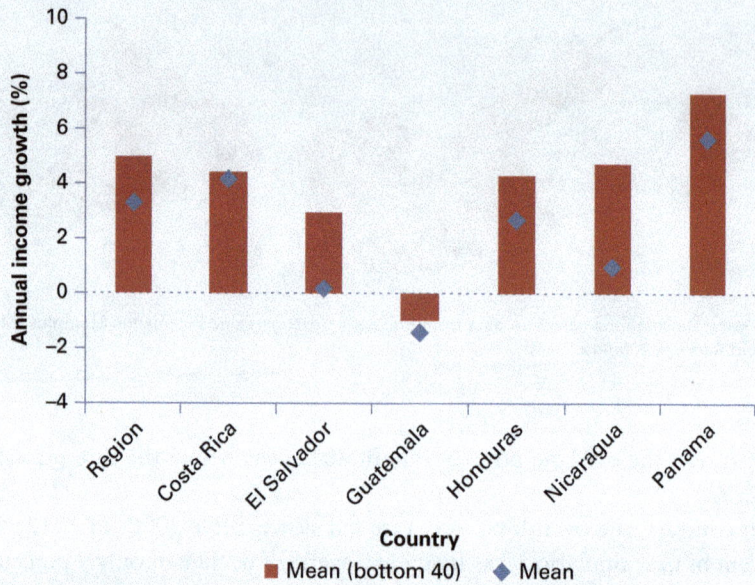

Source: Calculations based on SEDLAC (Socio-Economic Database for Latin America and the Caribbean), Center for Distributive, Labor, and Social Studies, Universidad Nacional de La Plata, La Plata, Argentina; World Bank, Washington, DC, http://sedlac .econo.unlp.edu.ar/eng/index.php.

and 2012. This was reflected in both the small decline in poverty and the shrinkage in the poverty gap. In contrast, the average income growth among the total population was constant in real terms. In circa 2004–12, the average in Latin America was 5 percent, compared with only 3 percent in El Salvador (figure 5.2). In Central America, only Guatemala's performance was worse than El Salvador's on this measure.

The differences in income growth of the bottom 40 across the country are striking (map 5.2). The most populous and most urban departments—La Libertad, San Salvador, and Santa Ana—also host the largest share of the bottom 40. Income growth among the bottom 40 was greatest in the department of San Salvador, at 4.3 percent, while growth in the other two departments was only slightly above the national average of 3.2 percent.[3] The departments that were the worst performers in mean income growth among the bottom 40 were Ahuachapán and Cabañas, which had relatively fewer of the bottom 40 (7 and 6 percent, respectively). Overall, the poorest did well in relative terms in El Salvador, but, in absolute terms, income growth was not sufficient to pull many of them out of poverty.

Inequality

Progress in shared prosperity has meant that income distribution has become more equitable over time. Between 2000 and 2012, as the incomes

Map 5.2 Bottom 40, by Department and Mean Income Growth, El Salvador, 2000–12

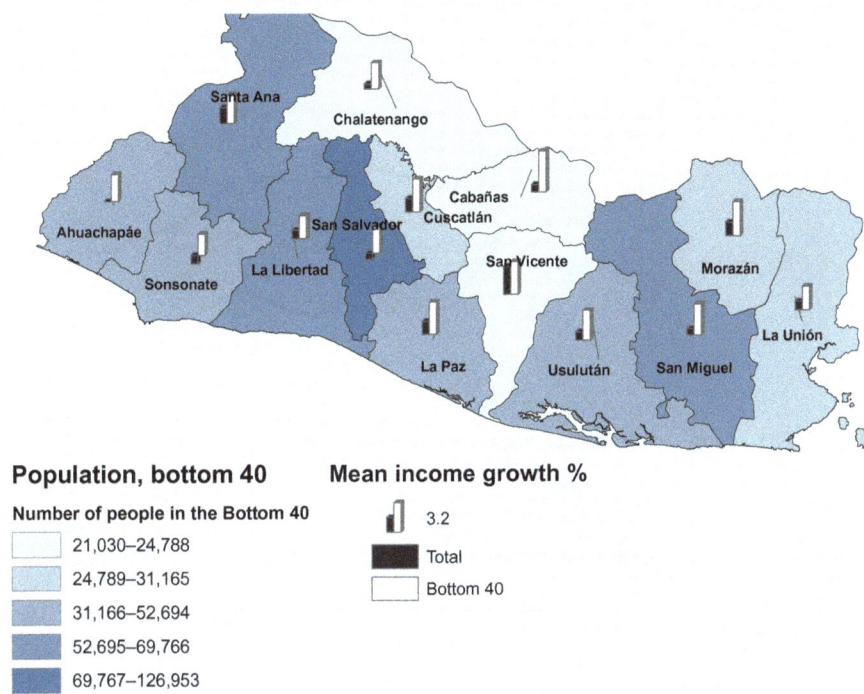

Population, bottom 40

Number of people in the Bottom 40

21,030–24,788
24,789–31,165
31,166–52,694
52,695–69,766
69,767–126,953

Mean income growth %

3.2
Total
Bottom 40

Sources: Calculations based on data from Encuesta de Hogares de Propósitos Múltiples (Multipurpose Household Survey), 2000–12. Shapefile: GADM Database of Global Administrative Areas, Environmental Science and Policy, University of California, Davis, CA, http://www.gadm.org/.

of the poorest rose at rates above those of the middle or upper ends of the income distribution, the Gini coefficient fell substantially, from 0.53 to 0.44 (figure 5.3). The decline in the rural Gini was more significant, reaching 0.37 in 2012, which reflected the rise in rural incomes. There was also a notable reduction in urban inequality. However, the trend flattened out in 2011–12.

Unlike populations in other Central American countries where inequality is mentioned as a main problem, Salvadorans do not identify inequality as one of the top problems in the country; it is a distant fourth.[4] In many ways, this reflects the fact that the country is more equitable than many of its neighbors. It also reflects the findings of recent qualitative research that shows the rich and the poor to be in agreement that income inequality is part of the natural order (ESEN 2014) (box 5.1). However, when asked explicitly if the income distribution in the country is fair, almost 70 percent of the population replied in the negative.[5] This varied by income group: 15 percent of the members of wealthier households (those who report they face no difficulty living within their means) find the distribution to be unjust, compared with 31 percent of respondents who reported they encountered extreme difficulty living within their means.

Figure 5.3 Trends in the Gini Coefficient, El Salvador, 2000–12

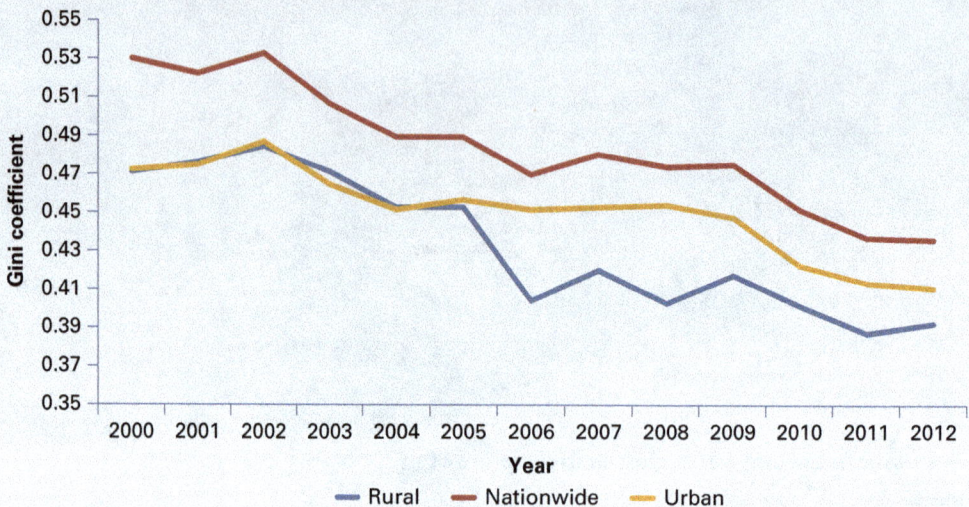

Source: Calculations based on data from Encuesta de Hogares de Propósitos Múltiples (Multipurpose Household Survey), 2000–12.
Note: The Gini coefficients do not precisely match the official statistics presented in DIGESTYC (2013).

Box 5.1 Inequality and Shared Prosperity: From Statistics to Experiences in San Salvador

A series of focus groups was conducted among various socioeconomic groups in San Salvador in 2014 to understand what inequality and shared prosperity mean in El Salvador.[a] The focus group participants were shown an aerial photograph of a neighborhood in San Salvador, where luxurious houses and green areas abutted a slum. Without using the word inequality, facilitators asked participants about the picture and about how they would compare their own well-being with others in Salvadoran society. The discussions that followed provided a lens into the inequalities participants faced.

- Participants defined inequality in terms of political power, economic resources, social capital, morals and values, culture, and educational attainment. Their experiences of inequality varied depending upon their own socioeconomic status.
- A predominant view was that one's place on the economic ladder was determined by birth and inheritance:

  It is the society itself that tries to establish [socioeconomic] stereotypes, while promoting [the idea that,] if you are poor, you stay poor, and, if you are rich, you will continue to be rich. (University student)

  [The rich] were born in golden cradles; so [their children], as my children would if I were a millionaire, keep the inheritance. (Man in low socioeconomic group)

- The middle class is the working class, the class everyone wants to be part of, including the wealthy. Participants of high socioeconomic status did not self-identify as wealthy; instead, they described themselves as middle class. They ascribed characteristics of selfishness, greed, and a lack of solidarity to the rich.

(continued)

Box 5.1 Inequality and Shared Prosperity: From Statistics to Experiences in San Salvador *(Continued)*

- Participants from low and high socioeconomic groups believe inequality is part of the natural order; they accept inequality as an inevitable aspect of life. In contrast, participants of midlevel socioeconomic status viewed inequality bitterly; they were frustrated that both the rich and the poor often found ways to evade paying their fair share.

- There was agreement across socioeconomic groups on the initial causes of inequality: a history that linked political power to economic power.

  Historically, there have been instruments of power that have ensured that certain families and certain sectors [of society] are the ones that benefit. (Vulnerable adult)

  Salvadoran society has always, ever since its beginnings, had this type of social inequality. (Woman in the high socioeconomic group)

- However, there was stark disagreement over why inequality is perpetuated within society. Opinions aligned according to one's own class. Participants in low and middle socioeconomic groups viewed mobility as a problem of opportunities.

  One works in the job that he has because he already knows that, in every direction, the doors are shut. . . ; opportunities are closed. (Man in low socioeconomic group)

  Participants in the high socioeconomic group thought that people living in poverty remain there because they make poor choices and do not exert themselves.

  What differentiates [poor people] is that there is no desire for improvement; opportunities exist, but there is no desire to improve. They don't want to take risks, they don't want to get out of their comfort zone, and they want everything to be fed to them. (University student)

- Participants across all socioeconomic classes believe that the predominance of crime, violence, and insecurity are strongly linked to the levels of inequality and lack of social mobility in the country.

- Participants agreed that the government should create the conditions for equal opportunities. Achieving shared prosperity would require social change among those who are currently unwilling to share, or a strong state able to enforce this solidarity through more effective tax collection and more efficient implementation of high-quality public services.

  If we all had access to better health care, to better systems, I think that then there wouldn't be so much discontent . . . , and we'd say "Yes, we will pay [taxes]." (Woman in the high socioeconomic group)

- While the participants viewed the government as the only means through which real change could occur, they also had little trust in the government's willingness to address inequality and the government's capacity to achieve lasting change.

  Government policy is not focused on really bringing people out of poverty, but rather on giving people leftovers so that they maintain them there [where they are]. (Woman in the high socioeconomic group)

  Here, you have to break the cycle of having poor that eat, rather than people who climb out of poverty, because, here, we have a government that feeds the poor and feeds them in the form of misery. (Man in the high socioeconomic group)

Source: ESEN 2014.

a. As part of Willingness to Share, a larger World Bank study, a series of focus groups across the economic spectrum were organized to learn how Salvadorans perceive inequality (see ESEN 2014). Nine focus groups were conducted that included the following participants: (1) men and (2) women in the low socioeconomic group, (3) men and (4) women in the medium socioeconomic group, (5) men and (6) women in the high socioeconomic group, (7) men and women university students, (8) men and women *ni-nis* (youth neither studying nor working), and (9) vulnerable men and women adults. The research was qualitative and was not statistically representative. The focus groups were also largely urban; thus, the study may have missed key rural perspectives.

Who Has Moved Out of Poverty in the Past Decade?

Intragenerational mobility

There is little evidence of intragenerational mobility in El Salvador. According to a synthetic panel analysis, only 7 percent of the poor in 2004 had moved out of poverty by 2007 and remained out of poverty in 2012, and, during the same years, only 5 percent had both moved into and moved out of poverty (a group defined here as the vulnerable) (figure 5.4).[6] In contrast, one-third of the population were among the chronic poor, that is, living in poverty in 2004, 2007, and 2012. Individuals who may be included among the nonvulnerable to poverty, that is, those who were nonpoor during all three years, represent 56 percent of the population. There was little downward mobility (nonpoor in 2004 and poor in both 2007 and 2012), partly because there was a decline in poverty overall, but also because the method used here underestimates downward mobility.

The majority of the chronic poor (that is, people who were poor in 2004, 2007, and 2012) were people who were in the poorest income quintile in 2004. Although incomes grew at a higher rate among the poorest quintile, the greatest mobility was exhibited by individuals who were in the second-poorest quintile in 2004 partly because they were closer to the poverty line

Figure 5.4 Intragenerational Mobility, El Salvador, 2004, 2007, and 2012

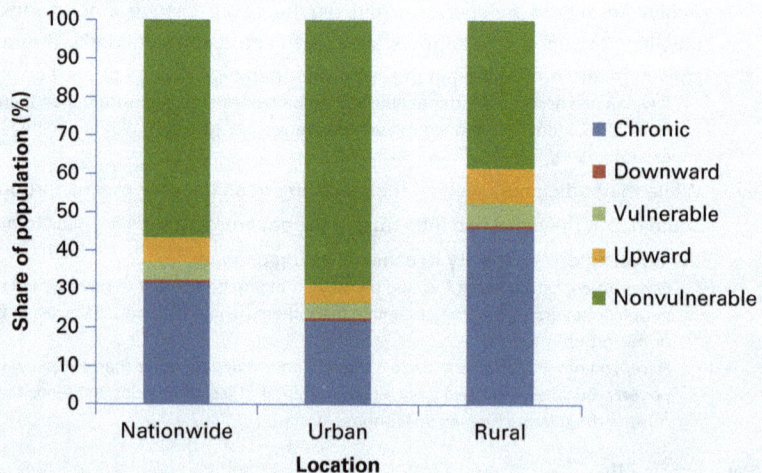

Sources: Calculations based on SEDLAC. The lower-bound estimate has been calculated using the synthetic panels of Dang et al. 2011.
Note: Data are based on the situation over three years: 2004, 2007, and 2012. Chronic = poor during all three years (income below $4 a day per person in purchasing power parity U.S. dollars). Upward = poor in 2004, but nonpoor in 2007 and 2012. Downward = nonpoor in 2004, but poor in 2007 and 2012. Vulnerable = people who moved both into and out of poverty during the period. Nonvulnerable = the nonpoor throughout.

Figure 5.5 Income Growth Rate, by Decile, El Salvador, 2000–12

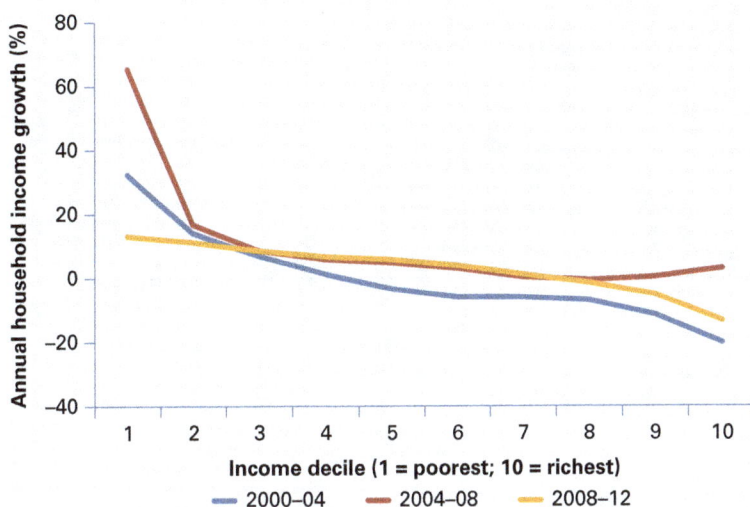

Source: Calculations based on data from Encuesta de Hogares de Propósitos Múltiples (Multipurpose Household Survey), 2000–12.

(figures 5.5 and 5.6). Only 4 percent of the poorest quintile was able to move out of poverty and remain out of poverty during at least one of the three years, while almost a quarter of the second-poorest quintile was able to do so. The latter group also showed the greatest share of people who moved in and out of the poor and nonpoor categories. The level of chronic poverty was also high among the poorly educated and people working in agriculture (43 and 52 percent, respectively). Nonetheless, individuals with only a primary education and individuals working in agriculture showed slightly higher rates of upward mobility than individuals in the lowest quintile: 8 percent of the two former groups moved out of poverty and stayed out of poverty during 2004–12.

A much larger change in income was required to move out of poverty than to fall into it. Successfully moving out of poverty was associated with substantial income growth, from 28 to 45 percent depending on location, while a much smaller fall in household income, around 10 percent, was sufficient to drop a household into poverty and keep it there (figure 5.7). Vulnerable households—those moving into and out of poverty—experienced substantial growth in income also, especially in rural areas, but the level of income growth was not adequate to protect them definitively from poverty. While the analysis here is not causal, the asymmetry between mobility and income growth highlights the issue of vulnerability and the need for social safety nets.

Figure 5.6   Poverty Mobility, El Salvador, 2004, 2007, and 2012

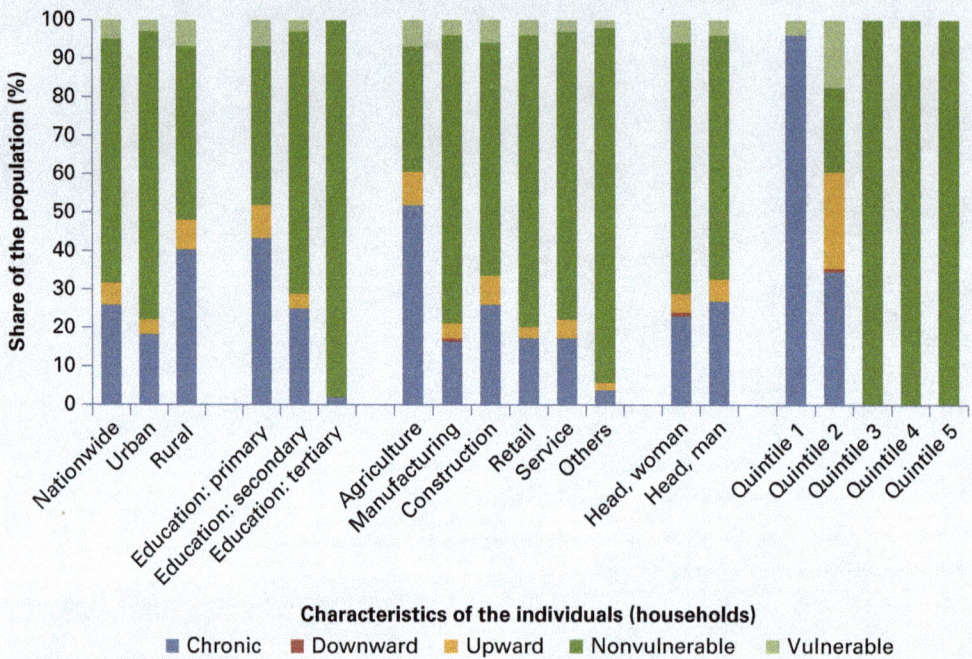

Characteristics of the individuals (households)

■ Chronic   ■ Downward   ■ Upward   ■ Nonvulnerable   ■ Vulnerable

Sources: Calculations based on SEDLAC. The lower-bound estimate has been calculated using the synthetic panels of Dang et al. 2011.
Note: Data are based on the situation over three years: 2004, 2007, and 2012. Chronic = individuals (households) who were poor during all three years (income below $4 a day per person in purchasing power parity U.S. dollars). Upward = poor in 2004, but nonpoor in 2007 and 2012. Downward = nonpoor in 2004, but poor in 2007 and 2012. Vulnerable = individuals (households) who moved into and out of poverty during the period. Nonvulnerable = the nonpoor throughout. Education, employment sector, and gender variables refer to the characteristics of the heads of household in 2004. The quintiles range from the poorest (1) to the richest (5).

Intergenerational mobility

In El Salvador, circumstances beyond the control of individuals limit access to the basic services needed to break the cycle of chronic poverty and promote intergenerational mobility (figure 5.8).[7] El Salvador has lower coverage rates and a lower human opportunity index (HOI) relative to the average in the Latin America and the Caribbean region in the completion of sixth grade on time and water and sanitation service access: only slightly more than 50 percent of children finished sixth grade on time in 2012, while only a third of children were living in households that had access to running water and sanitation (the lowest rates in Latin America).[8] El Salvador does well in enrollment rates. However, there is a larger gap in the completion of sixth grade on time. The completion of sixth grade on time is a proxy for school quality, not simply access.

The changes in access to basic services have been positive, although progress is uneven (see figure 5.8, chart b). The advances in electricity have brought El Salvador in line with regional averages. While the country lags

Figure 5.7 Household Income Growth, by Mobility Category, El Salvador, 2004, 2007, and 2012

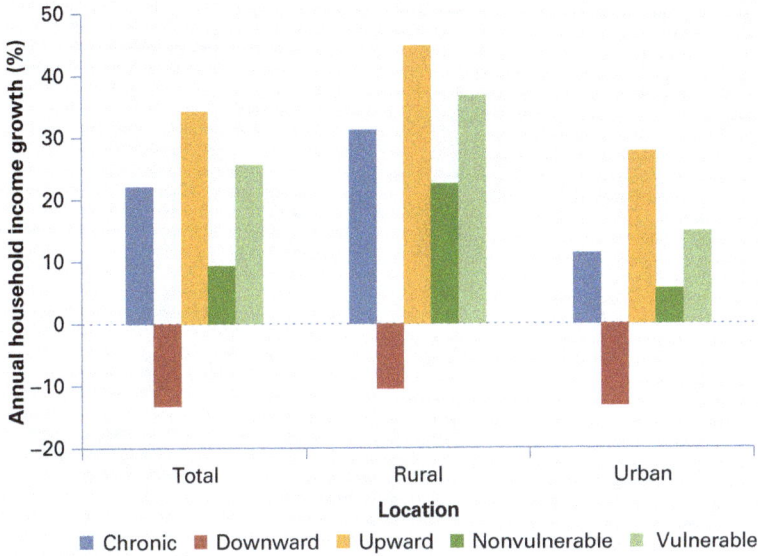

Sources: Calculations based on SEDLAC. The lower-bound estimate has been calculated using the synthetic panels of Dang et al. 2011.
Note: Data are based on the situation over three years: 2004, 2007, and 2012. Chronic = poor during all three years (income below $4 a day per person in purchasing power parity U.S. dollars). Upward = poor in 2004, but nonpoor in 2007 and 2012. Downward = nonpoor in 2004, but poor in 2007 and 2012. Vulnerable = people who moved into and out of poverty during the period. Nonvulnerable = the nonpoor throughout.

the region in the sixth grade completion indicator captured in the HOI, the shifts in this indicator were greater in El Salvador than in the region, leading to a convergence, albeit not in the short run. However, indicators on higher levels of education remain a concern. Secondary-school enrollment in El Salvador, at 67 percent, is low compared with the country's Central American neighbors and the region (75 and 87 percent, respectively). Meanwhile, secondary-school completion rates are low (40 percent), and there was no evidence of improvement in the latter part of the decade. Spending is below the level in similar countries both as a share of GDP and per student, and test scores are also low.[9] Water and sanitation indicators are low, and the recent improvement is negligible.

What Has Driven Poverty and Inequality Reduction?

Economic growth

In El Salvador, extreme poverty is quite sensitive to economic growth. Thus, although economic growth in the country in the past decade was the lowest in Central America, it still drove a reduction in extreme poverty. A

Figure 5.8 The Human Opportunity Index and Basic Service Access, El Salvador and the Region, 2000–12

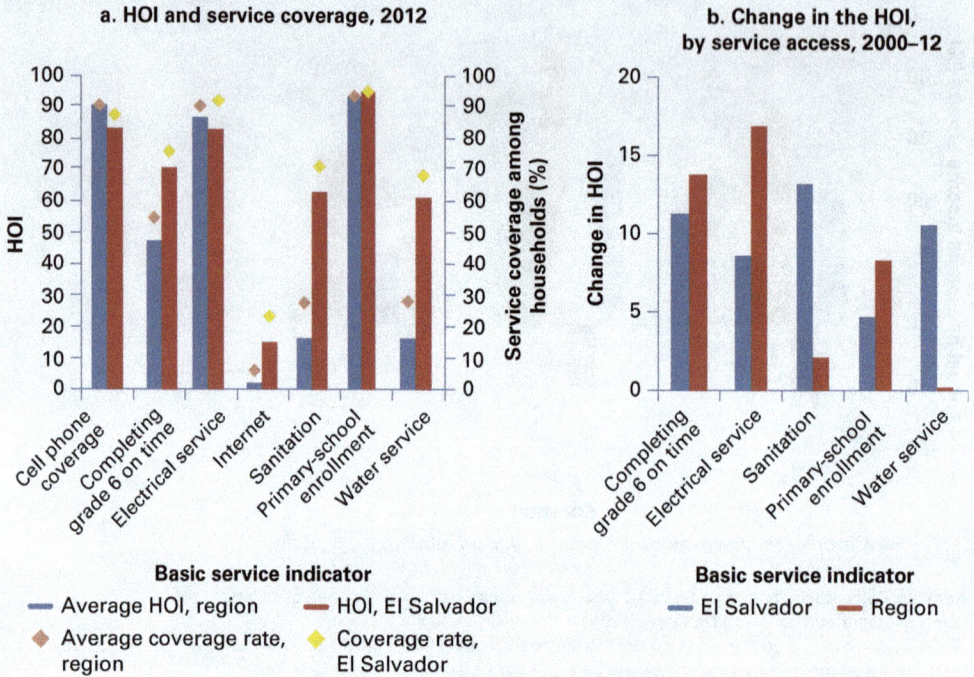

a. HOI and service coverage, 2012

b. Change in the HOI, by service access, 2000–12

Basic service indicator

— Average HOI, region   — HOI, El Salvador
◆ Average coverage rate, region   ◆ Coverage rate, El Salvador

Basic service indicator

— El Salvador   — Region

Source: Molinas Vega et al. 2012.
Note: Access to electricity = the household reports that it has access, regardless of the source of the access. Access to sanitation = there is a flush toilet on the property, and it is connected to a waste-removal system. Access to water = there is running water inside the dwelling. Access to the Internet = an Internet connection is available inside the home. Access to a cell phone = someone in the home has a cell phone that functions within the household. School enrollment = the school attendance rate among 10- to 14-year-olds in the home. Completion of grade 6 on time = children in the home avoided grade repetition up to and including the sixth grade. HOI = human opportunity index.

1 percent change in GDP was associated with a 2.2 percent change in extreme poverty (Cadena et al. 2013). Overall poverty levels, however, were much less responsive to growth.

The economic growth rate is projected to remain low (figure 5.9). An extensive growth analysis of El Salvador identifies two major constraints to growth: low productivity in the tradables sector and high rates of crime and violence (USAID 2011). The contribution to GDP growth of the growth in exports is low and was much lower after 2002 than in the preceding 10 years. The shift from agricultural exports to a model based on the *maquila*, an export manufacturing operation in a free trade zone, may be one factor constraining productivity because the maquila sector has limited productive links with the rest of the economy. Credit markets were not considered a binding constraint to growth in the past, but the downgrade in the investment rating of the country and the worsening fiscal situation may be

Figure 5.9 Annual per Capita GDP Growth Rate, Central America, 2000–12

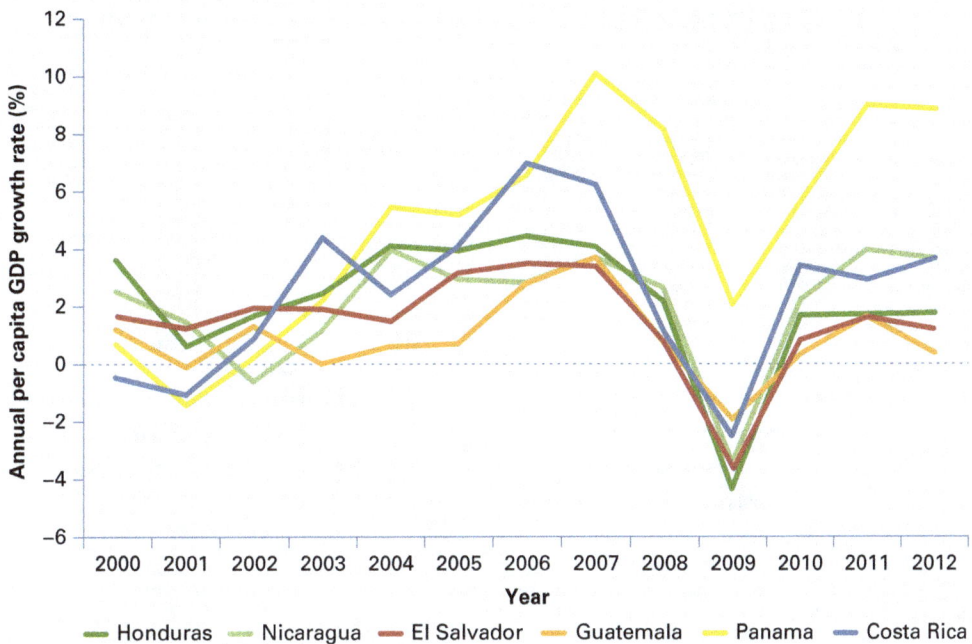

Source: Based on data from WDI (World Development Indicators) (database), World Bank, Washington, DC, http://data.worldbank.org/data-catalog/world-development-indicators.
Note: GDP = gross domestic product.

changing this; there is some evidence that small and medium enterprises are credit constrained. Additionally, several analyses highlight the need for the government to develop a policy environment that facilitates and promotes new economic activities (Hausmann, Rodrik, and Velasco 2005; Rodrik 2004; USAID 2011). The large cost of crime and violence has been found to be a major factor in raising the cost of goods and limiting El Salvador's ability to compete on world markets (Acevedo 2008; USAID 2011). (The issue of crime and violence is examined more fully below.)

While the negative growth at the peak of the 2008–09 fiscal crisis in the country has been reversed, the recovery has been slow. GDP growth is projected to be only 1.7 percent in 2014–16, below the low level of growth before the crisis.[10] Even with a high elasticity of poverty to growth, poverty reduction will be constrained by the slow growth. Thus, projections suggest economic growth alone will not be a major source of poverty reduction in the near future.

Labor

In rural areas, poverty has been reduced through a combination of increased employment and, to a lesser extent, higher earnings, primarily among men (figure 5.10). The labor effect on the reduction of overall poverty has been

Figure 5.10 The Decomposition of Poverty Reduction, El Salvador, 2000–12

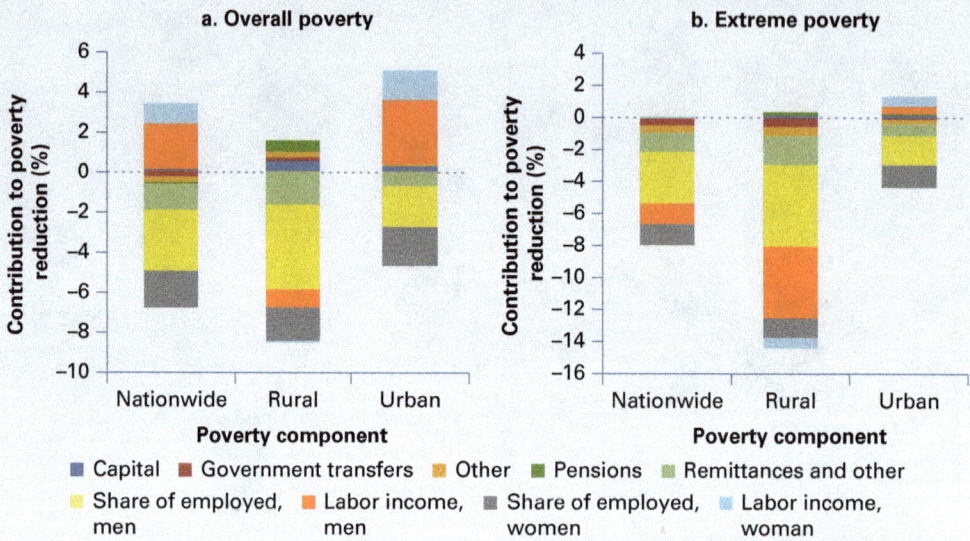

Source: Calculations based on data from Encuesta de Hogares de Propósitos Múltiples (Multipurpose Household Survey), 2000–12.

channeled through more employment rather than higher earnings: the change in the share of men employed accounted for a 4 percentage point decline in poverty over the period, compared with a less than 1 percentage point reduction in poverty because of higher earnings. In contrast, the effects of greater employment and higher earnings on the decline in extreme poverty were similar. The results in urban areas were somewhat different; there, the changes in labor income had a negative effect on poverty reduction. Given the small changes in poverty in urban areas over the period, however, these results may not be robust and should be viewed with caution.

Although slightly more jobs were created in urban areas than in rural areas (4.6 compared with 3.6 percent), the sharp decline in poverty in rural areas in 2000–04 was not mirrored in urban areas. However, the composition of the labor force in rural areas changed substantially during these years, while the composition in urban areas was static. In rural areas, there was a movement out of agriculture into construction and utilities, and there was a drop-off in self-employment and a rise in the number of employees.

Public and private transfers

Private remittances played a major role in poverty reduction. At $4.2 billion, they represented over 16 percent of GDP in 2012, a jump of more than tenfold since 1990 (figure 5.11). In 2000, 4 percent of households received remittances; by 2012, one household in every five did so. The remittances

Figure 5.11 Remittance Inflows, El Salvador, 1976–2012

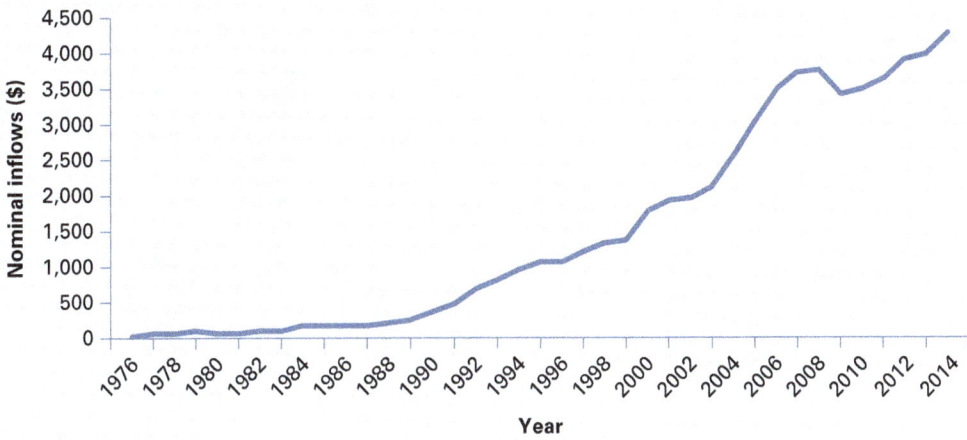

Source: Data from "Topics in Development: Migration, Remittances, and Diaspora," World Bank, Washington, DC, http://go.worldbank.org/0IK1E5K7U0.

sent per migrant also rose, up almost a third between 2000 and 2010. The remittances were not targeted only at poor households: the average per capita income of households receiving remittances was $8.90 (in 2005 dollars), compared with $3.10 among poor households.[11] The difference in incomes may have arisen because of the remittances, but a comparison of the non-income characteristics of households shows that individuals in remittance recipient households are more similar to the poor than not (figure 5.12). Even though a share of remittances goes to nonpoor households, the magnitude of the migrant group in the United States—estimated at 1.1 million in 2010—has helped reduce poverty in El Salvador.[12]

The reliance on remittances translates into a strong reliance on the U.S. economy: 88 percent of Salvadoran migrants reside in that country.[13] The sharp decline in remittances that occurred because of the 2008–09 financial crisis highlights the vulnerability associated with this dependence. However, the recovery in the United States led to a rise in remittances, which, by 2013, were above the precrisis level. Remittances also appear to become less important to poor households over time, in part because other sources of income of the poorest rose and in part because the per household amount fell (figure 5.13; see annex figure 5A.1 for data on the growth of remittances by decile).

While remittances play an important role in welfare, migration appears to have negative implications for child welfare. On the positive side, studies in El Salvador have demonstrated that remittances foster more schooling and a smaller supply of youth labor (Acosta 2006; Ambler, Aycinena, and Yang 2014). However, the scale of out-migration in El Salvador is such that 8 percent of all children have at least one parent who is living abroad; in

Figure 5.12 Remittance Recipients and Nonrecipients, the Poor, and the Nonpoor, El Salvador, 2012

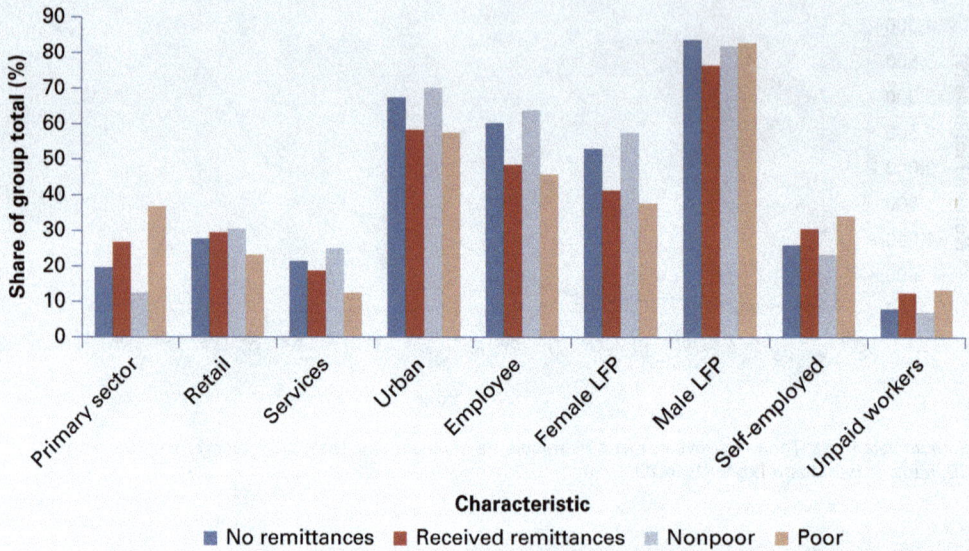

Source: Calculations based on data from Encuesta de Hogares de Propósitos Múltiples (Multipurpose Household Survey), 2012.
Note: The primary sector includes agriculture, fishing, and mining. Services include financial institutions, real estate agents, public entities, schools, health care providers, and other organizations. Labor force participation (LFP) refers to persons 25–65 years of age.

the department of Cabañas, the share is 12 percent; and, in La Unión, one child in seven has at least one parent who is outside the country. Many of these children live in extreme poverty: the correlation between a child living in extreme poverty and having a migrant parent is 0.60. Having an absent parent also appears to serve as a pull factor for child migration. La Unión, the department with the highest rate of migrant parents, also had one of the highest rates of unaccompanied minors going to the United States in 2014.

Government cash transfer programs have helped reduce extreme poverty in rural areas (see figure 5.10, chart b). The contribution has been small compared with private transfers; government cash transfers have lowered extreme poverty in rural areas by half a percentage point, or about one-third the corresponding contribution of remittances. *Comunidades Solidarias Rurales* (solidarity in rural communities), the main cash transfer program, has limited presence in urban areas. Moreover, government transfer programs are only a small part of all social programs and subsidies that benefit the poor. In 2011, the government spent $540 million on all social programs and subsidies, of which $201 million went to the two poorest quintiles.[14] Of this, only $27 million was in the form of transfers; thus, the analysis here clearly underestimates the effect of overall government spending on poverty.[15]

Figure 5.13 Ratio of Private Transfers to Total Income, by Decile, El Salvador, 2000–12

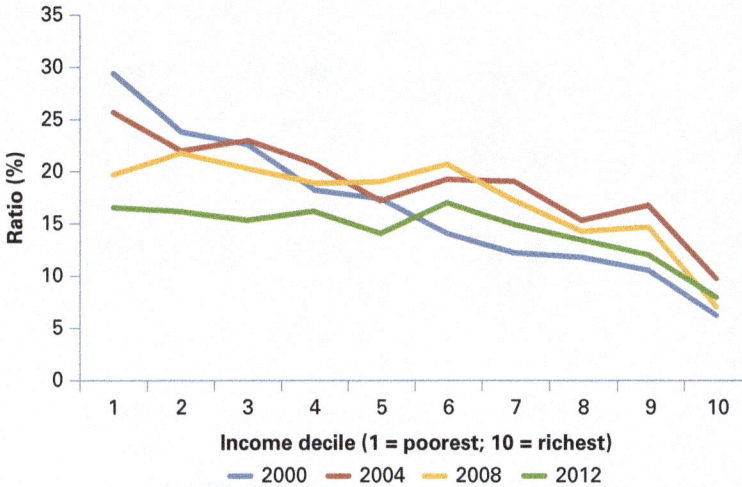

Source: Calculations based on data from Encuesta de Hogares de Propósitos Múltiples (Multipurpose Household Survey), 2000–12.

Changes in inequality

The decline in inequality during the period was driven largely by labor income in both urban and rural areas (figure 5.14). In contrast, remittances helped diminish inequality only in urban areas, while government cash transfer programs—these are the only programs captured in the household survey data—reduced inequality in rural areas. However, private and public transfers had only a limited effect on overall inequality.

Bringing about Change in Welfare and Shared Prosperity

Poverty and shared prosperity can be affected by policy in many areas of the economy and society. This section provides findings on particular areas, including fiscal policy; markets, especially labor markets; institutions; and one of the most troublesome issues in the country: crime and violence. The discussion represents a first step in the development of a framework for poverty reduction; additional research is needed to provide specific policy advice in each area.

Fiscal policy

Government spending on social programs has increased substantially in recent years and has served to reduce poverty. At 12.8 percent, government social spending as a share of GDP in El Salvador is above the spending in Guatemala, but well below the spending in Costa Rica and Honduras.

Figure 5.14 The Contribution of Income Components in Reducing the Gini Coefficient, El Salvador, 2000–12

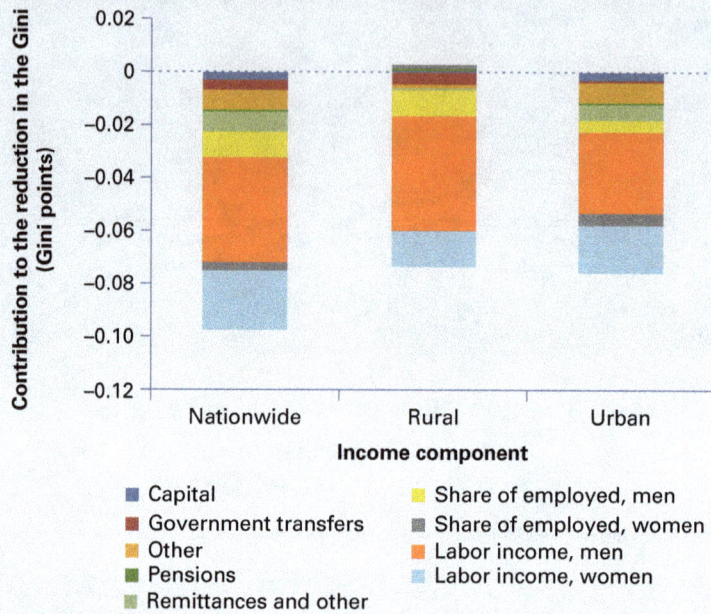

Source: Calculations based on data from Encuesta de Hogares de Propósitos Múltiples (Multipurpose Household Survey), 2000–12.

Compared with regional standards, spending on education and health care is below average, while spending on social protection is above average. Social protection spending in 2012 was 2.8 percent of GDP (compared with 1.1 percent in Costa Rica and 1.5 percent in Honduras). Spending on social assistance programs rose from 0.6 percent of GDP in 2007 to 1.0 percent in 2011.[16] Despite low coverage, the conditional cash transfer program has lowered poverty.[17] An evaluation of the temporary employment program also showed a positive welfare effect (Beneke de Sanfeliú 2014). While no specific research has been carried out to discover how overall social spending is affecting welfare in the country (beyond the specific cash transfer programs), the overall effect of social spending is expected to be poverty reducing through the associated investments in human capital.[18]

The poorest cannot always take advantage of the universal subsidies that exist. Indirect subsidies in water and electricity, for example, represent a larger share of GDP than the major social programs, but do not benefit the poorest segments of the population that have no access to public water and electricity (see below on access issues).[19] Even if poorer households have access, they use less of the services and thus receive less of the benefits of the subsidies. Subsidies are quite regressive: the bottom 40 receive only 28 percent of the value of all subsidies, while the top 40 receive 54 percent. In contrast, the bottom 40 receive 61 percent of the benefits of social spending (figure 5.15).

Figure 5.15   Incidence of Spending on Social Programs and Universal Subsidies, El Salvador

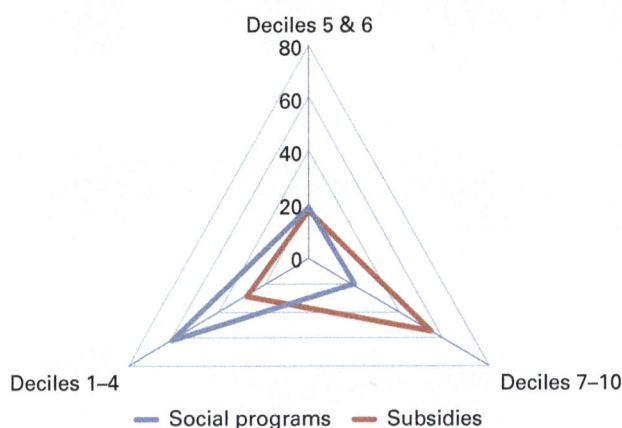

Deciles 5 & 6
80
60
40
20
0

Deciles 1–4   Deciles 7–10

— Social programs   — Subsidies

Source: Data of the Salvadoran Foundation for Economic and Social Development, cited in World Bank 2014.
Note: Subsidies include direct subsidies for liquefied petroleum gas and indirect subsidies for water, public transportation, and electricity.

The full impact of fiscal policy on poverty and inequality needs to be better understood. The fiscal situation is difficult: the deficit reached 4.2 percent of GDP in 2012–13, and the public debt rose to 57.0 percent of GDP after experiencing one of the highest growth rates in the region (World Bank 2014). El Salvador has the lowest tax effort—the tax revenue collected relative to the tax capacity—among 16 Latin American countries, which, combined with the recent rise in expenditure, suggests that the deficit will continue to increase (Fenochietto and Pessino 2013).[20] The fiscal difficulties, coupled with the low levels of predicted economic growth, mean that the resources for greater spending on social programs may be unavailable.

Markets

Labor markets are one of the critical channels of poverty reduction given that the primary asset of the poor is their labor. Recent years have exposed weaknesses in Salvadoran labor markets in job creation, unemployment, and earnings. New job creation has not always been accompanied by enhanced job quality.

Employment

While the country generated substantial numbers of new jobs in 2000–12, job creation, particularly in urban areas, has generally been in sectors in which there is low productivity growth (figure 5.16). Thus, for example, labor productivity rose 15 percent in the manufacturing sector, while only 7 percent of all new jobs were added in this sector. The agricultural sector,

Figure 5.16 Sectoral Employment and Productivity, El Salvador, 2000 and 2012

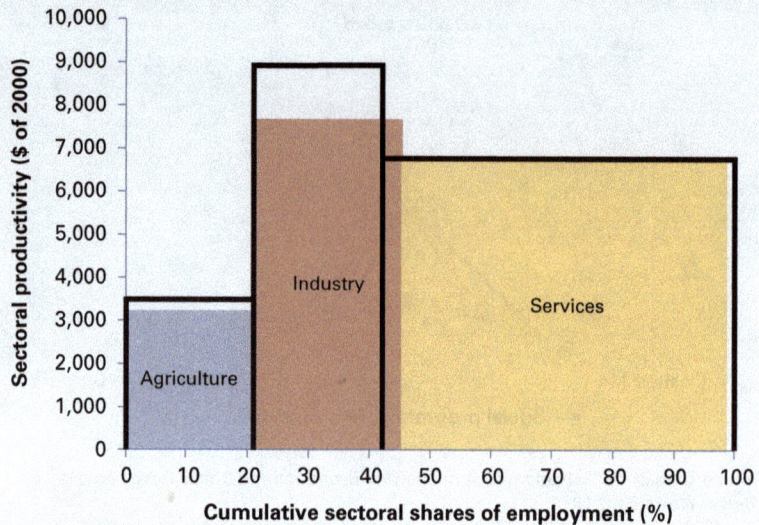

Source: Calculations based on data from WDI (World Development Indicators) (database), World Bank, Washington, DC, http://data.worldbank.org/data-catalog /world-development-indicators.
Note: The colored boxes represent the situation in 2000, and the outlined boxes represent the situation in 2012. Sector productivity is the ratio of the value added in the sector and the number of employees working in the sector.

where the poor are concentrated, has the lowest productivity, and gains have been minor.[21] The bulk of job creation has been in the services sector, where the gains in employment have not been accompanied by large advances in productivity.

Unemployment and underemployment

The unemployment rate in 2012 was 13 percent among the extreme poor and 9 percent among all poor (figure 5.17). Nationwide, unemployment rates have been falling slightly, although the rate is still 6 percent, slightly above the rate prior to the crisis. In addition, underemployment is a large and growing problem. According to a recent study (UNDP 2013), 46 percent of the labor force in 2012 earned less than the minimum wage or worked fewer than 40 hours a week, a share that has been rising since 2008. These trends in underemployment, coupled with the high unemployment levels among the poor, highlight the precariousness of employment in El Salvador and the continued vulnerability of much of the working population.

Institutions

Institutions matter for development. At their best, public institutions create and maintain an environment of stability, fairness, and transparency that allows productive and social investment. At the same time, public

Figure 5.17 Unemployment, El Salvador, 2000–12

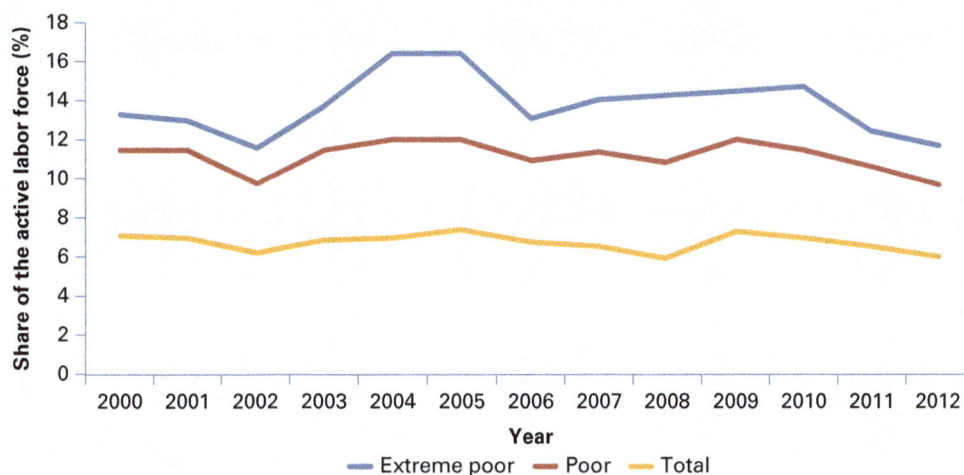

Source: DIGESTYC 2013; data from Encuesta de Hogares de Propósitos Múltiples (Multipurpose Household Survey), 2000–12.

institutions play an important role in human capital formation by providing quality services in education, sanitation, health care, and other key areas. Inequities in service provision, coupled with unfavorable perceptions of institutions, continue to affect development in El Salvador.

Basic services

The heterogeneity in income growth across the country is mirrored in the access to basic services (figure 5.18). Important gaps exist between the poor and nonpoor and across departments. Thus, for example, the poor have substantially less access to water and electricity services, although access to electricity is much closer to universal. Access to water shows enormous variation. For instance, in San Miguel, Santa Ana, and Usulután, the poor have less than half the access rate of the nonpoor. Despite a 91 percent coverage rate in electricity services nationally, there are still noticeable gaps across departments. The electricity access rates are lower in the east and west of the country, while in the far west, the poor–nonpoor gap is 18 percentage points.

The inequality in access to water and electricity raises concerns about the use of universal subsidies for these two services. The benefits of the subsidies accrue to the departments at varying levels, especially once population weights for the departments are taken into account. Meanwhile, it is often the nonpoor who obtain the greatest benefit from the subsidies; in many cases, the poor do without or provide their own services without the benefit of a subsidy. Given the substantial budget dedicated to the water and electricity subsidies ($52.6 million and $115.8 million, respectively) and the regressiveness of these expenditures, there may be room to improve access

Figure 5.18 Households with Access to Water and Electricity, by Poverty Status, El Salvador, 2012

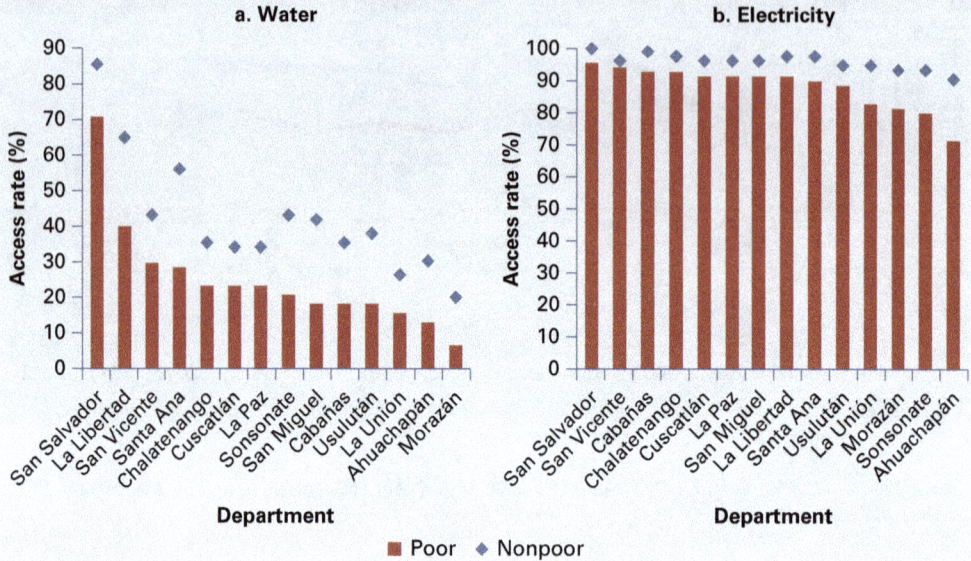

Source: Calculations based on data from Encuesta de Hogares de Propósitos Múltiples (Multipurpose Household Survey), 2000–12.
Note: Access to water = piped water on the property of the household, whether inside or outside the dwelling.

to services and social welfare by adopting a more targeted subsidy program or revising the universal subsidy.[22]

Competitiveness

On a global scale, institutional weaknesses influence the competitiveness of an economy. While weak institutions have not been found to exercise a binding constraint on economic growth, there is evidence that they play a negative role. The quality of the civil service bureaucracy ranks poorly in El Salvador relative to similar countries (USAID 2011). Similarly, in 2010, El Salvador ranked in the bottom 25th percentile globally in the rule of law (Kaufmann, Kraay, and Mastruzzi 2010).

The limited capacity of many local municipal institutions also affects the creation of employment and income sources. A series of studies of municipal competitiveness carried out in about 40 percent of all municipalities in El Salvador shows the variation that exists geographically along various dimensions of competitiveness (figure 5.19). Barriers to business development and, thus, job creation exist in many areas. Depending on the dimension, both the mean and the degree of heterogeneity vary across the country. In 2009–13, there was improvement in several indicators, but not in all: the cost of entry into business has risen, and, while illicit payments are not a substantial problem (the mean along this dimension is one of the

Figure 5.19 Municipal Competitiveness Indicators, El Salvador, 2009–13

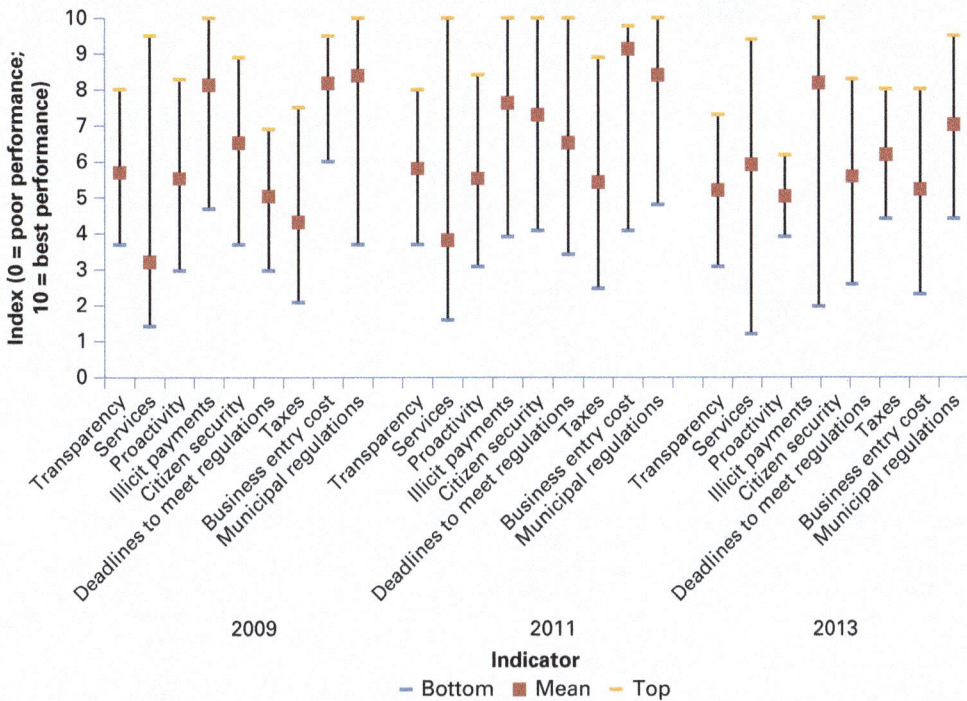

Source: USAID 2009, 2012, 2013.
Note: The 2013 indicators are not strictly comparable with the 2009 and 2011 indicators because (a) eight municipalities were added, (b) municipal regulations and the deadlines to meet regulations were changed, and (c) there are differences in the variables in each indicator.

highest, corresponding to better performance), the variance has increased, showing that this has become a problem in some municipalities. In parts of the country, there are clear barriers to employment and business creation that stem from capacity issues: efforts to improve the institutional capacity of municipalities may be an important element in enhancing labor market and welfare outcomes.

Perceptions and trust in government efficacy

Low levels of trust in government agencies revealed during polls shed doubt on the efficiency and efficacy of public institutions. There was less confidence in the government in 2012 than in 2004: the economic crisis and the rising crime rate seem to be taking a toll (figure 5.20). Trust or lack of trust in public institutions has the potential to affect the ability of these institutions to promote well-being, security, and growth. Respondents expressed the most confidence in the national government, but the level of confidence fell from 61 percent of respondents in 2004 to 55 percent in 2012. Trust in the police showed a substantial decline: in 2004, 64 percent of respondents

Figure 5.20 Trust in Government Institutions, El Salvador, 2004–12

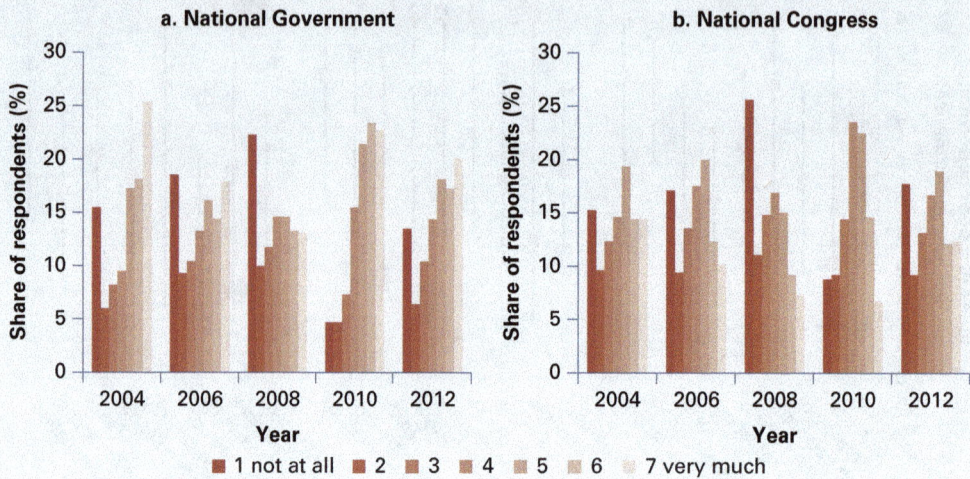

Source: Calculations based on data from "El Salvador," Latin American Public Opinion Project, Vanderbilt University, Nashville, TN, http://www.vanderbilt.edu/lapop/el-salvador.php.
Note: The questions were (a) "¿Hasta qué punto tiene confianza en el sistema de justicia?" (how much do you trust the justice system?), (b) "¿Hasta qué punto tiene confianza usted en el Congreso Nacional?" (how much do you trust Congress?), (c) "¿Hasta qué punto tiene confianza usted en el Gobierno Nacional?" (how much do you trust the national government?), and (d) "¿Hasta qué punto tiene confianza usted en la Policía Nacional?" (how much do you trust the national police?).

had some or a great deal of trust in the police, but, by 2012, the share had dropped to 49 percent. However, the small amount of data shows that trust is not perfectly correlated with perceptions of efficacy. The decline in confidence was reflected in a downswing in the perception that the government is successfully fighting poverty. Nonetheless, there was an increase in the perception that the government was improving citizen security (figure 5.21).

The average Salvadoran does not feel empowered to help bring about change in the country (figure 5.22). In 2008, almost a third of the population thought that the national government paid no attention to the needs of citizens; by 2010, the share had declined, but it had risen again by 2012. However, the rest of the population had shifted to a more positive view by 2012. The negative perceptions, coupled with the perception of limited institutional capacity, may make more difficult the government's task of bringing about the change needed to reduce poverty and promote shared prosperity.

Costs to society of crime and violence

Crime and violence in El Salvador play a significant role in hampering growth and fostering inequities. The rates of crime and violence are high. In 2011, El Salvador had the second highest homicide rate in the world, slightly behind Honduras (figure 5.23). In 2012, almost 25 percent of

Figure 5.21 Confidence in the Government to Achieve Poverty Reduction and Citizen Security, El Salvador, 2004–12

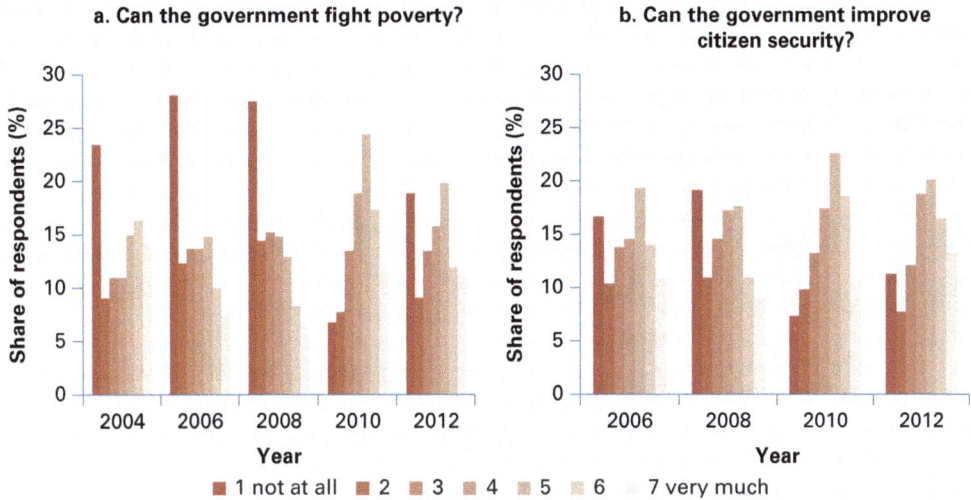

a. Can the government fight poverty?

b. Can the government improve citizen security?

■ 1 not at all   ■ 2   ■ 3   ■ 4   ■ 5   ■ 6   7 very much

Source: Calculations based on data from "El Salvador," Latin American Public Opinion Project, Vanderbilt University, Nashville, TN, http://www.vanderbilt.edu/lapop/el-salvador.php.
Note: The questions were (a) "¿Hasta que punto diría que el gobierno actual combate la pobreza?" (to what extent do you think the current government fights poverty?), (b) "¿Hasta que punto diría que el gobierno actual mejora la seguridad ciudadana?" (to what extent do you think the current government improves citizen security?).

Figure 5.22 Perceptions of Political Agency, El Salvador, 2008–12

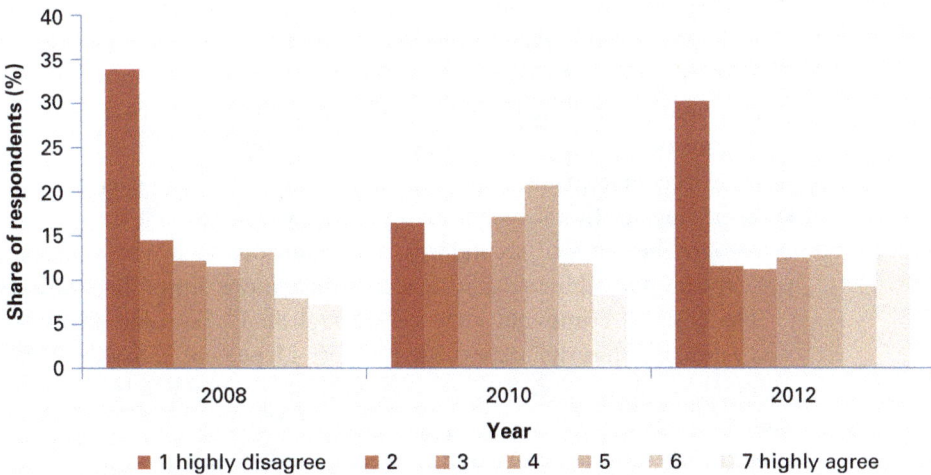

■ 1 highly disagree   ■ 2   ■ 3   ■ 4   ■ 5   ■ 6   7 highly agree

Source: 2008, 2010, and 2012 data from "El Salvador," Latin American Public Opinion Project, Vanderbilt University, Nashville, TN, http://www.vanderbilt.edu/lapop/el-salvador.php.
Note: The question was "A los que gobiernan el país les interesa lo que piensa como usted. ¿Hasta qué punto está de acuerdo o en desacuerdo con esta frase?" (Those who govern the country are interested in what people like you think. To what extent do you agree or disagree with this statement?)

Figure 5.23 Homicide Rates, Central America and Mexico, 1995–2013

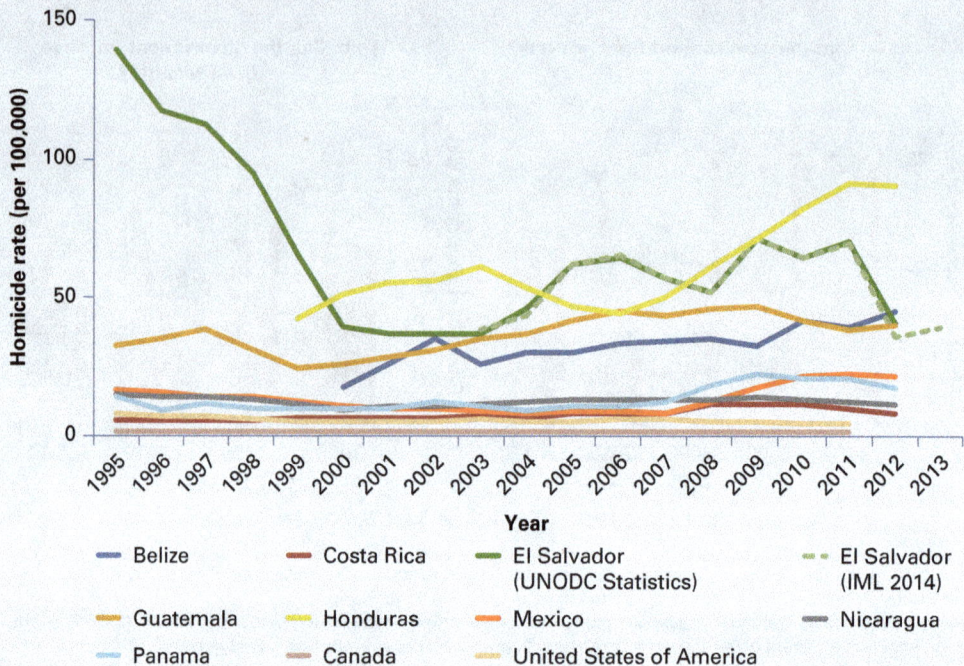

Legend:
- Belize
- Costa Rica
- El Salvador (UNODC Statistics)
- El Salvador (IML 2014)
- Guatemala
- Honduras
- Mexico
- Nicaragua
- Panama
- Canada
- United States of America

Sources: Dashed line: IML 2014. All other data: UNODC Statistics (database), United Nations Office on Drugs and Crime, Vienna, https://stats.unodc.org/.
Note: The IML and UNODC data are similar in 2005–11. UNODC data are not available for 2012–13. IML = Instituto de Medicina Legal.

Salvadorans reported they had been victims of a crime, and almost 60 percent listed crime and violence as the number one problem in the country. Recent analysis in El Salvador identifies crime and violence as a binding constraint on the economy that lowers the competitiveness of Salvadoran firms, affects investment, and raises costs (USAID 2011). Given the recent spike in violence (homicides were up 20 percent in the first six months of 2014 over the previous six months, and extortion levels were also on the rise), the need to address this issue is becoming more urgent (Segura 2014).

The costs of crime and violence are high in El Salvador. In 2008, it was estimated that they represented almost 11 percent of GDP (Acevedo 2008).[23] By 2011, the GDP forgone because of crime and violence was estimated at between 4.8 and 8.3 percent (USAID 2011). There is ample evidence of the effects of crime and violence on individuals and on businesses. Over 45 percent of men and 40 percent of women limit the places where they shop out of fear of crime and violence, and 15 percent have moved and more than 5 percent have changed jobs out of concern they may be victimized (figure 5.24). In 2010, over 85 percent of firms paid for security, 25 percentage points above the regional average, and slightly more than half of all firms identified crime, theft, and disorder as the major constraints to

Figure 5.24 Changes in Behavior because of Crime, El Salvador, 2012

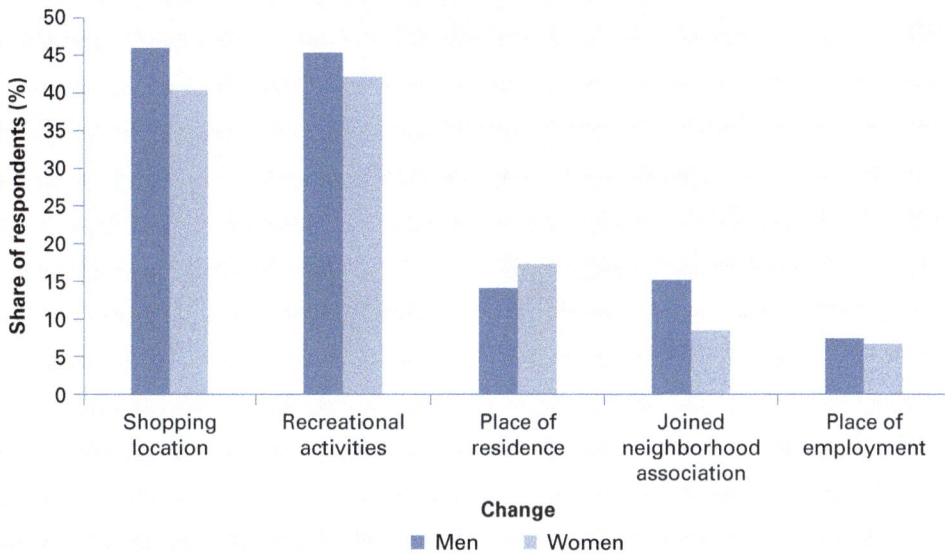

Source: Calculations based on 2012 data from "El Salvador," Latin American Public Opinion Project, Vanderbilt University, Nashville, TN, http://www.vanderbilt.edu/lapop/el-salvador.php.

doing business, which is also substantially higher than the regional average (figure 5.25). Although the costs to firms are similar to the regional average, the cost to the overall economy is higher in El Salvador given how widespread the losses are.

Crime and violence also affect migration, especially among children. While family reunification is a pull factor behind child migration, crime and violence are push factors (figure 5.26). There is a correlation between crime—proxied by the homicide rate—and the number of unaccompanied minors from El Salvador apprehended at the U.S. border in 2014. The correlation between homicide rates per 100,000 and unaccompanied minors per 100,000 of the population of the municipality of origin is 0.20 for El Salvador, which is slightly higher than the correlation for Honduras. There are other push and pull factors behind migration, but crime is clearly playing a key role in expanding the number of extremely vulnerable migrants from El Salvador.

The distribution of crime and violence is another source of inequality in El Salvador. Both the levels and the types of crime vary by geographical location, although there is little correlation between crime and poverty (figure 5.27). The departments of Cuscatlán and La Paz in the center of the country exhibit the highest crime rates, while the crime rate in the department of Morazán, in the east, is almost four times lower. Homicide rates are not correlated with the share of the population living in urban areas. In contrast, the incidence of rape is positively correlated with rural areas (a

Figure 5.25 Effects of Crime and Violence on Businesses, El Salvador, the Region, and the World, 2010

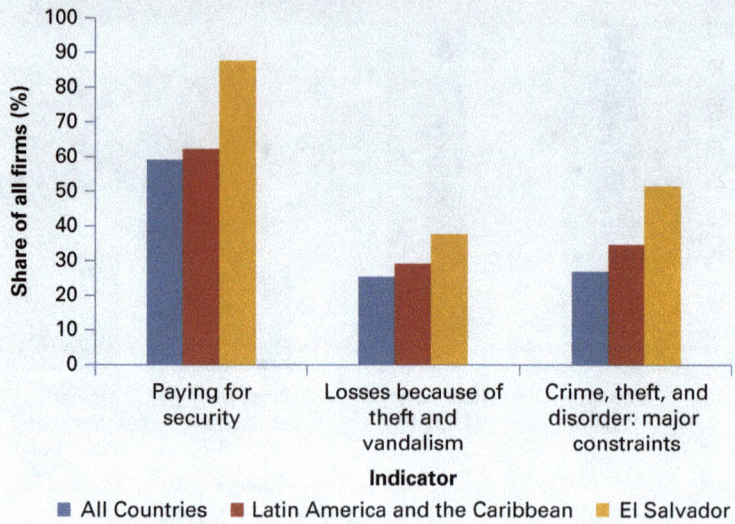

Source: Calculations based on "Crime," Enterprise Surveys (database), International Finance Corporation and World Bank, Washington, DC, http://www.enterprisesurveys .org/data/exploretopics/crime#2.

Figure 5.26 Correlation: Homicide Rates in El Salvador and Unaccompanied Child Migrants from El Salvador at the U.S. Border

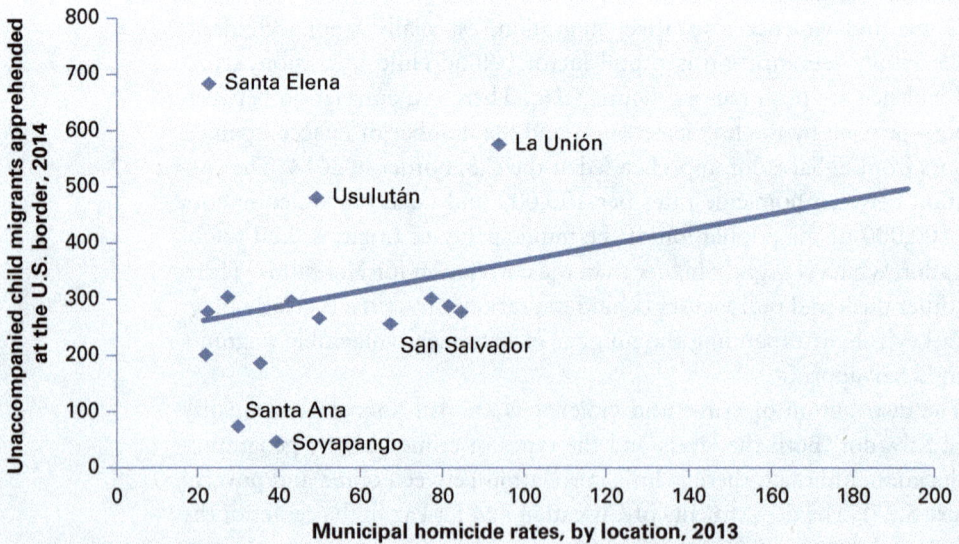

Sources: Homicide rates: World Bank estimates. Unaccompanied children: World Bank calculations based on data for January 1–May 14, 2014, in Stats and Summaries (database), U.S. Customs and Border Protection, Washington, DC, http://www.cbp.gov/newsroom/media-resources/stats?title=Border+Patrol.
Note: The data are per 100,000 inhabitants of El Salvador.

Figure 5.27 Crime Rates and the Poverty Rate, by Department, El Salvador, 2013

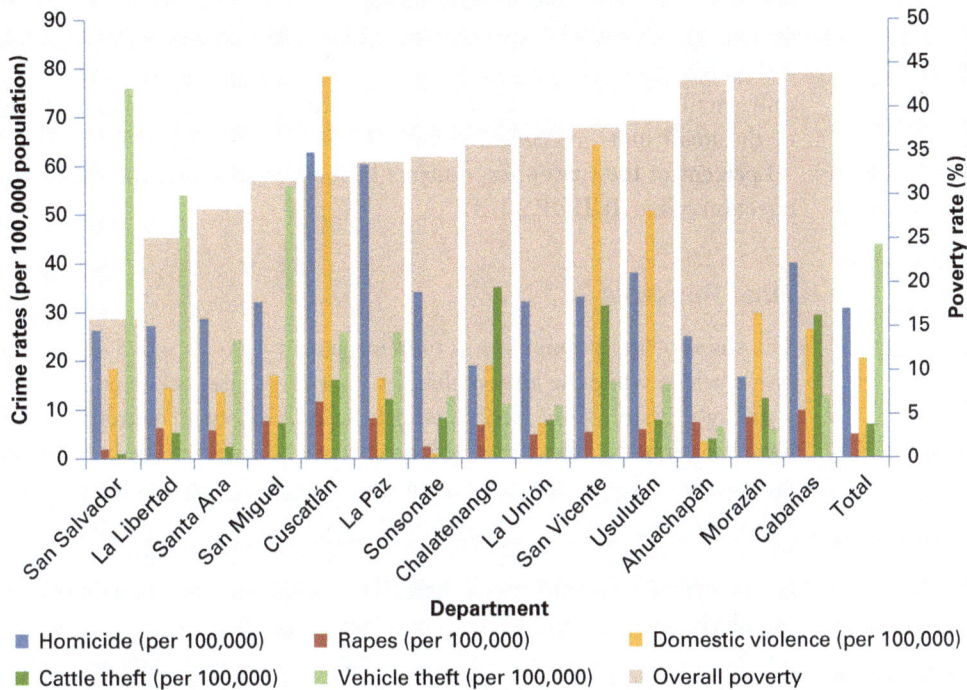

Legend:
- Homicide (per 100,000)
- Rapes (per 100,000)
- Domestic violence (per 100,000)
- Cattle theft (per 100,000)
- Vehicle theft (per 100,000)
- Overall poverty

Sources: El Salvador, Vice Ministry of Justice and Public Security, and World Bank 2013. Overall poverty rate: Encuesta de Hogares de Propósitos Múltiples (Multipurpose Household Survey), 2012.

0.61 coefficient of correlation), which highlights another problem involved in violence that has been overshadowed by the high homicide rates.[24] Meanwhile, criminals have been targeting the public transportation system in urban areas, which tends to be relied on particularly by the bottom 40 (USAID 2011). Municipalities have shown varying success in addressing violence and crime. The municipality of Alegría, in the west, for example, scored 8.3 (out of 10.0) on the citizen security subindex of the Municipal Competitiveness Index, while Talnique, in the center, only scored 2.6 (USAID 2013). The observed changes in economic behavior by individuals and firms will continue to hamper economic growth and poverty reduction unless crime and violence can be reduced.

The problem of crime and violence is not receding, despite the 2012 truce between the two main *maras* (organized gangs) and the government. There was a sharp drop in homicide rates—from 70 per 10,000 inhabitants in 2011 to 36 in 2012 and 39 in 2013—associated with the truce. However, there is serious concern that the homicide rate is now on another upward trend: the number of homicides rose in the first quarter of 2014 relative to the same period in 2013, from 551 to 794, which would represent a backslide toward pretruce levels (IML 2014).

There is conflicting evidence on the effect of the truce on other crimes. Robbery, extortion, and threats reported by individuals in surveys before and after the truce show almost identical levels of victimization: 22.8 percent in 2011 and 23.6 percent from May 2012 to April 2013 (IUDOP 2013). Moreover, the United Nations Office on Drugs and Crime has found only small declines in thefts, threats, and extortions.[25] This lack of change or the small shifts in crime and victimization may explain why more than 70 percent of the survey respondents believe the truce has had little or no effect on crime (IUDOP 2013).

Final Remarks

The share of the population in extreme poverty has dropped since 2000. Nonetheless, while the largest changes in poverty rates occurred almost 10 years ago, many of the people who have moved out of extreme poverty have not yet been able to move all the way out of poverty. The lack of social mobility revealed by the participants in focus groups conducted in 2014 is reflected clearly in data on poverty (see box 5.1). A large share of the population in El Salvador appears to be chronically poor. The lack of equitable access to services means that a share of the population is excluded from the benefits of development. Vulnerability remains high: the poor are more susceptible to unemployment and underemployment and the relatively small declines in income that can lead to long-term poverty.

Migration has been a coping mechanism among Salvadorans with limited opportunities and poor employment prospects, but this may now be curtailed. Remittances are an important source of income. It is estimated that almost 30 percent of the native-born Salvadoran population resides outside the country.[26] Surveys in recent years point to the continued expectation of emigration: as of 2012, almost one Salvadoran in four planned to emigrate within the next three years (figure 5.28). Emigration has served to boost incomes through higher earnings in the receiving country and through remittances, but has also provided an escape valve for the economy by keeping the supply of labor lower than it would have been in the absence of migration opportunities. However, greater border security and unusually high numbers of returnees may be placing limits on the role of migration.

The economy has added a significant number of jobs, which has helped reduce poverty. Nonetheless, the main effect of the labor market on poverty has been through more jobs, not better jobs. While a drop in unemployment has been observed and while job creation has been raising the number of available jobs to the precrisis level, productivity has not risen substantially. Indeed, the low productivity in the tradables sector is considered a binding constraint on growth. Median incomes have also fallen in many sectors. Addressing the factors that influence productivity must be at the crux of any effort to enhance welfare in El Salvador. Understanding the drivers of the somewhat more positive shifts in the rural labor market is also key:

Figure 5.28 Emigration from El Salvador, 2004–12

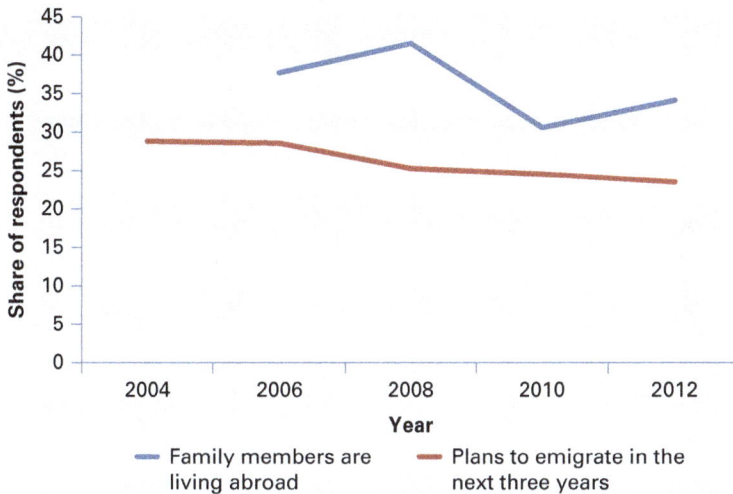

Source: Data sets from "El Salvador," Latin American Public Opinion Project, Vanderbilt University, Nashville, TN, http://www.vanderbilt.edu/lapop/el-salvador.php.

what has driven the movement away from self-employment and agricultural employment and how has this affected welfare and vulnerability?

Social programs have helped reduce poverty, albeit on a small scale. Universal subsidies for utilities and transportation, however, benefit the nonpoor disproportionately and exert severe pressure on the fiscal balance. Given the low economic growth projections in the short run and the expanding fiscal deficit, achieving a better balance in the spending on targeted social programs and subsidies may create additional fiscal space and have a greater impact on welfare.

The negative influence of crime and violence on well-being, especially in view of the newly rising trends in crime statistics since the truce, are a serious constraint in the country. The violence affects people's sense of security, changing behavior in daily life and increasing migration. Violence has also been shown to be correlated with the greater cost of doing business, thereby preventing investment and hampering the country's export capacity and competitiveness. Participants in the 2014 focus groups considered the persistent inequality in the country as one of the causes of the violence (see box 5.1). Thus, a key step in reducing crime and violence will be to address the inequalities in access to services, particularly education and jobs. Although El Salvador is a small country, there is substantial heterogeneity in the location of the poor, in the amount of progress in the effort to realize poverty reduction and shared prosperity, in the access to services, in the capacity of institutions, and in the types and levels of crime to which people are exposed. Leveling the playing field is an important component in improving welfare outcomes and building trust in the country.

Annex 5A Supplementary Data

There are striking differences between the poor and the nonpoor in terms of their human capital, employment status, and household characteristics. The average income of the nonpoor is close to four times that of the poor. On average, a person living in poverty has three years less schooling than a person not living in poverty and is more likely to be a rural resident, to be working in agriculture, and to have many more small children (resulting in higher dependency ratios). The poor are more likely to be self-employed and unpaid family workers, and women living in poverty are much less likely to be economically active than their nonpoor counterparts. Finally, more than 1 in every 10 of the nonpoor is working in a government job, while this is rarer among the poor.

Table 5A.1 Profile of the Poor, El Salvador, 2012

Attribute	Nonpoor	Overall poor	Attribute	Nonpoor	Overall poor
Household characteristics			*Labor force, %*		
Age of head, years	49.2	47.6	Employee	63.8	46.2
Per capita daily income, 2005 $	11.3	3.1	Employer	4.6	1.8
Education of head, years	7.5	4.3	Self-employed	23.4	34.4
Household size, members	3.4	4.5	Unpaid worker	6.6	13.1
Urban location, %	70.4	57.1	Women, active, age 25–65	57.8	37.8
Age 0–12, %	15.5	27.2	Men, active, age 25–65	82.3	82.8
Age 13–18, %	10.6	14.2	*Employment sector, %*		
Age 19–70, %	65.8	51.9	Construction	5.1	5.4
Age 70+, %	8.2	6.7	Domestic services	4.4	4.6
Employer, %			Manufacturing	16.3	14.2
Private, large	58.7	75.9	Primary sector	12.7	37.0
Private, small	41.3	24.1	Retail	30.2	23.6
Private employee	88.7	98.1	Services	25.3	12.3
Public employee	11.3	1.9	Utilities	5.9	3.0

Source: Calculations based on data from Encuesta de Hogares de Propósitos Múltiples (Multipurpose Household Survey), 2012; DIGESTYC 2013.
Note: The primary sector includes agriculture, fishing, and mining. Services include financial institutions, real estate agents, public entities, schools, health care providers, and other organizations. Large firms = firms with more than five workers. Small firms = fewer than five workers.

Table 5A.2 Remittance Recipients and Nonrecipients, El Salvador, 2000 and 2012

Attribute	2000		2012	
	Nonrecipient	Recipient	Nonrecipient	Recipient
Employment sector, %				
Construction	5.8	2.4	5.3	4.9
Domestic services	3.6	2.2	4.5	4.1
Manufacturing	18.1	14.9	16.2	12.6
Primary sector	22.2	32.0	19.3	26.4
Retail	26.7	32.4	27.9	29.1
Services	18.4	12.9	21.7	18.3
Utilities	5.3	3.3	5.1	4.7
Household characteristics				
Age of head, years	48.0	46.5	47.5	53.5
Per capita daily income, 2005 $	8.7	8.0	8.4	8.9
Education of head, years	5.5	5.4	6.7	5.1
Urban location, %	62.7	61.3	67.6	58.6
Male head, %	70.0	69.8	68.8	49.1
Per capita monthly income, 2005 $	263.5	244.7	255.3	270.1
Recipients and nonrecipients: share, %	95.9	4.1	80.2	19.8
Labor force, %				
Employee	55.1	53.8	59.9	48.3
Employer	4.6	7.3	3.5	5.0
Women, active, age 25–65	46.8	56.6	52.6	41.1
Men, active, age 25–65	80.8	92.6	83.8	76.4
Self-employed	26.5	31.9	26.3	30.8
Unemployed	7.2	4.9	2.2	3.8
Unpaid worker	6.6	2.2	8.1	12.0
Employer, %				
Private, large	62.8	63.0	62.9	73.1
Private, small	37.2	37.0	37.1	26.9

Source: Calculations based on data from Encuesta de Hogares de Propósitos Múltiples (Multipurpose Household Survey), 2012; DIGESTYC 2013.
Note: The primary sector includes agriculture, fishing, and mining. Services include financial institutions, real estate agents, public entities, schools, health care providers, and other organizations. Large firms = firms with more than five workers. Small firms = fewer than five workers.

Figure 5A.1 Rate of Growth of Private Transfers, by Decile, El Salvador, 2000–12

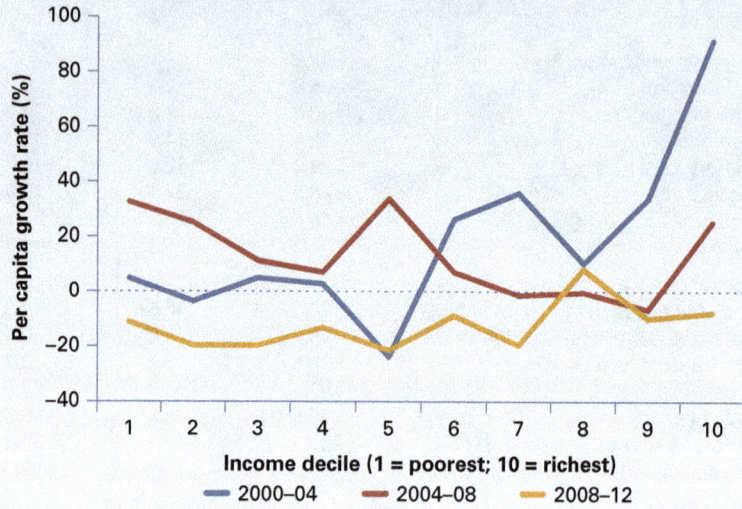

Source: Calculations based on data from Encuesta de Hogares de Propósitos Múltiples (Multipurpose Household Survey), 2000–12.

Table 5A.3 Change in the Employment Mix among the Nonpoor, El Salvador, 2004–12
percent

Department	Primary sector	Industry	Construction	Retail	Utilities	Services	Domestic services	Nationwide
Ahuachapán	32.4	41.2	−14.2	−3.8	−43.9	15.1	−4.6	3.2
Santa Ana	1.6	25.0	5.9	16.3	63.5	37.6	26.0	25.1
Sonsonate	14.5	−9.6	−45.3	−0.9	−13.3	69.2	12.8	3.9
Chalatenango	36.3	−10.1	54.3	29.7	25.3	17.9	9.2	23.2
La Libertad	12.2	6.7	−38.6	4.7	8.7	45.9	−38.1	0.2
San Salvador	61.8	−19.9	−21.5	−12.4	−24.5	8.3	−19.5	−4.0
Cuscatlán	147.4	44.3	31.7	68.6	8.6	46.4	−5.9	48.7
La Paz	44.0	−7.1	−25.7	28.7	37.0	63.8	−6.8	19.1
Cabañas	103.4	16.9	57.4	59.2	17.6	22.4	46.3	46.2
San Vicente	43.8	84.9	−11.1	36.8	60.0	41.8	69.1	46.5
Usulután	47.9	26.8	−29.8	58.3	9.3	28.8	1.6	20.4
San Miguel	2.3	−13.8	−11.8	21.6	20.1	−2.2	31.8	6.8
Morazán	86.5	121.5	12.1	58.8	27.5	117.6	38.6	66.1
La Unión	−19.0	47.6	−19.0	9.0	−32.1	4.4	−36.6	−6.5
Nationwide	43.9	25.3	−4.0	26.8	11.7	36.9	8.9	n.a.

Source: Calculations based on data from Encuesta de Hogares de Propósitos Múltiples (Multipurpose Household Survey), 2012; DIGESTYC 2013.
Note: The primary sector includes agriculture, fishing, and mining. Services include financial institutions, real estate agents, public entities, schools, health care providers, and other organizations. n.a. = not applicable.

Table 5A.4 **Change in the Employment Mix among the Poor, El Salvador, 2004–12**
percent

Department	Primary sector	Industry	Construction	Retail	Utilities	Services	Domestic services	Nationwide
Ahuachapán	32.2	99.1	32.3	131.3	47.2	154.1	−17.8	68.3
Santa Ana	3.3	38.1	24.8	25.6	78.6	54.4	51.6	39.5
Sonsonate	62.9	−11.3	47.0	2.2	50.5	84.0	63.0	42.6
Chalatenango	52.9	−1.2	−21.8	19.3	17.7	−5.6	−34.5	3.8
La Libertad	18.4	12.4	−12.7	17.1	41.6	121.0	20.8	31.2
San Salvador	87.3	3.2	−28.3	5.4	1.3	−5.9	23.6	12.4
Cuscatlán	1.5	15.6	−20.1	−0.2	441.4	126.0	147.2	101.6
La Paz	14.8	3.1	34.1	52.6	12.6	107.7	12.5	33.9
Cabañas	29.1	−0.2	35.8	30.5	−35.1	93.6	29.1	26.1
San Vicente	20.6	−12.4	−22.9	26.7	−6.1	103.6	−37.8	10.3
Usulután	69.6	3.1	−8.4	60.1	37.7	74.6	−44.5	27.5
San Miguel	−0.9	23.7	−24.9	14.9	63.6	14.0	10.2	14.4
Morazán	15.0	−8.2	−21.9	130.5	0.0	19.4	8.4	20.5
La Unión	35.0	54.5	−0.4	2.5	23.5	25.1	5.5	20.8
Nationwide	31.6	15.7	0.9	37.0	55.3	69.0	17.0	n.a.

Source: Calculations based on data from Encuesta de Hogares de Propósitos Múltiples (Multipurpose Household Survey), 2012; DIGESTYC 2013.
Note: The primary sector includes agriculture, fishing, and mining. Services include financial institutions, real estate agents, public entities, schools, health care providers, and other organizations. n.a. = not applicable.

Figure 5A.2 **Trust in Government Institutions, El Salvador**

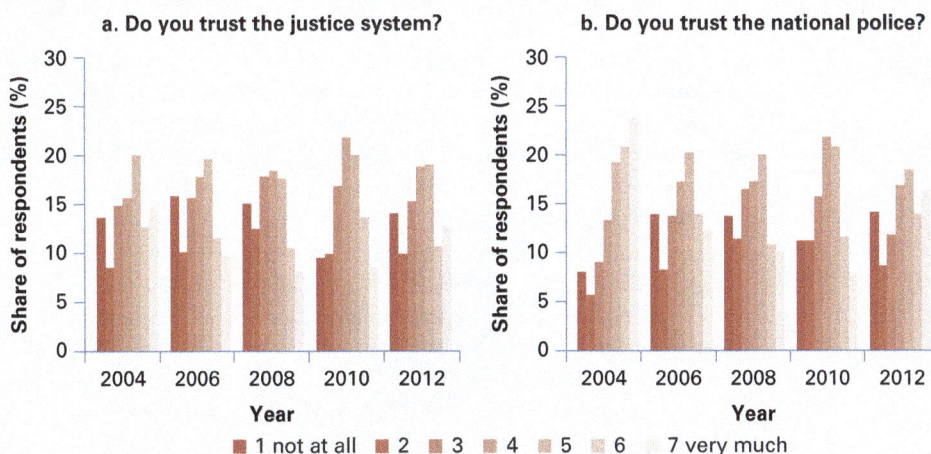

a. Do you trust the justice system?

b. Do you trust the national police?

■ 1 not at all ■ 2 ■ 3 ■ 4 ■ 5 ■ 6 □ 7 very much

Source: Calculations based on data from "El Salvador," Latin American Public Opinion Project, Vanderbilt University, Nashville, TN, http://www.vanderbilt.edu/lapop/el-salvador.php.
Note: The questions were (a) "¿Hasta qué punto tiene confianza en el sistema de justicia?" (how much do you trust the justice system?), (b) "¿Hasta qué punto tiene confianza usted en el Congreso Nacional?" (how much do you trust Congress?), (c) "¿Hasta qué punto tiene confianza usted en el Gobierno Nacional?" (how much do you trust the national government?), and (d) "¿Hasta qué punto tiene confianza usted en la Policía Nacional?" (how much do you trust the national police?).

Notes

1. Official statistics in El Salvador usually refer to poverty incidence measured at the household level. In this chapter, poverty rates are based on population, not households.

2. Based on the low international poverty line of $1.25 per person per day, the extreme poverty rate in El Salvador is estimated at 2.5 percent, below the average of 4.0 percent in the Latin America and Caribbean region.

3. Average income growth of the bottom 40 in each department refers to the income of those people who are counted among the bottom 40 nationwide and who live in the given department. Average income growth in each department is calculated by averaging across all residents, including those in the bottom 40 nationally who reside in the department.

4. Latinobarómetro Database, Latinobarómetro Corporation, Santiago, Chile, (2010 data set) http://www.latinobarometro.org/latContents.jsp.

5. Latinobarómetro Database, Latinobarómetro Corporation, Santiago, Chile, (2010 data set) http://www.latinobarometro.org/latContents.jsp.

6. In the absence of true panel data, the analysis is based on the synthetic panel technique of Dang et al. (2011). The methodology provides insights into trends among different types of households and individuals over time. Because the method uses a subset of households and an international poverty line of $4 a day (in 2005 purchasing power parity U.S. dollars), the overall poverty data do not match the official poverty data. Additionally, the lower-bound estimate is used because it requires fewer assumptions and is more conservative on the trends in upward mobility. However, it is also more conservative on the trends in downward mobility.

7. The characteristics of children (their circumstances), such as location of residence, gender (of the child and of the household head), parental educational attainment, household per capita income, number of siblings, and the presence of both parents in the household, act to restrict already low levels of access to basic services. This is captured in the human opportunity index (HOI), a measure of coverage that extracts a penalty for the inequity of coverage based on the correlation between circumstances and access. See Barros et al. (2009) for methodological details on the HOI.

8. The access to water indicator is narrowly defined here: individuals have access to water if the dwelling in which they live has piped water. In contrast, 83 percent of the population is considered to have access to water using the broader definition involving access to any improved water source. See WDI (World Development Indicators) (database), World Bank, Washington, DC, http://data.worldbank.org/data-catalog/world-development-indicators.

9. For additional details on spending, see Central America Social Expenditures and Institutional Review (project database), Human Development, Latin America and the Caribbean Region, World Bank, Washington, DC.

10. WEO (World Economic Outlook Database), International Monetary Fund, Washington, DC, http://www.imf.org/external/ns/cs.aspx?id=28.

11. See annex tables 5A.1 and 5A.2 for more details on the characteristics of poor and nonpoor households and remittance recipients and nonrecipients.

12. Although the overall amount of remittances in El Salvador is much higher than in Honduras, the amount remitted per migrant is much lower in El Salvador than in Honduras (around $3,000 and $5,500, respectively, in 2010).

13. See "Topics in Development: Migration, Remittances, and Diaspora," World Bank, Washington, DC, http://go.worldbank.org/0IK1E5K7U0.

14. Data of the Salvadoran Foundation for Economic and Social Development, cited in World Bank (2014).

15. The survey data used for the analysis allow only an estimate of the impact of transfers on poverty, but not on the impact of the rest of social spending on health care, education, and other social assistance.

16. The data on social spending are from Central America Social Expenditures and Institutional Review (project database), Human Development, Latin America and the Caribbean Region, World Bank, Washington, DC.

17. In 2012, the program covered only 16 percent of households in the poorest quintile. See Central America Social Expenditures and Institutional Review (project database), Human Development, Latin America and the Caribbean Region, World Bank, Washington, DC.

18. In 2012, the government spent 3.5 percent of gross domestic product (GDP) on education and 3.8 percent of GDP on health care services. See Central America Social Expenditures and Institutional Review (project database), Human Development, Latin America and the Caribbean Region, World Bank, Washington, DC.

19. In 2013, spending on social programs—conditional cash transfers, temporary income support, noncontributory pensions, agricultural programs, and school packages and school meals—reached $152 million, compared with the $168 million that went to water and electricity subsidies (data of the Salvadoran Foundation for Economic and Social Development, cited in World Bank 2014).

20. The *escalafón* (salary scale), which raised teacher salaries, is an example of new spending commitments that will affect fiscal sustainability.

21. See annex table 5A.1 for a description of the profile of the poor.

22. Data of the Salvadoran Foundation for Economic and Social Development, cited in World Bank (2014). Additional research on the effect of the subsidies on consumption patterns and in encouraging waste would also be useful.

23. This cost estimate includes the health costs (actual and loss of productivity); the costs of security and justice to the public sector, households, and firms; and the material costs (property losses) associated with crime and violence.

24. Thefts of livestock are also positively correlated with the share of the population living in rural areas, while vehicle thefts are positively correlated with the share of the population living in urban areas.

25. See UNODC Statistics (database), United Nations Office on Drugs and Crime, Vienna, https://stats.unodc.org/.

26. Estimates of the number of Salvadoran migrants in the United States are based on tabulations of U.S. census data. These data refer to foreign-born migrants and do not include people born in the United States who self-identify as Salvadorans. See Data Hub (database), Migration Policy Institute, Washington, DC, http://migrationpolicy.org/programs/data-hub/.

References

Acevedo, Carlos. 2008. "Los costos económicos de la violencia en Centroamérica." National Council of Public Security, Presidency of the Republic, San Salvador, El Salvador.

Acosta, Pablo. 2006. "Labor Supply, School Attendance, and Remittances from International Migration: The Case of El Salvador." Policy Research Working Paper 3903, World Bank, Washington, DC.

Ambler, Kate, Diego Aycinena, and Dean Yang. 2014. "Channeling Remittances to Education: A Field Experiment among Migrants from El Salvador." NBER Working Paper 20262, National Bureau of Economic Research, Cambridge, MA.

Barros, Ricardo Paes de, Francisco H. G. Ferreira, Jose R. Molinas Vega, and Jaime Saavedra Chanduvi. 2009. *Measuring Inequality of Opportunities in Latin America and Caribbean.* With Mirela de Carvalho, Samuel Franco, Samuel Freije-Rodríguez, and Jérémie Gignoux. Latin American Development Forum Series. Washington, DC: World Bank; New York: Palgrave Macmillan.

Beneke de Sanfeliú, Margarita. 2014. "Programa de Apoyo Temporal al Ingreso (PATI): Evaluación de Impacto." Salvadoran Foundation for Economic and Social Development, Antiguo Cuscatlán, El Salvador.

Cadena, Kiyomi E., Adriana Cardozo Silva, Leonardo Lucchetti, and Kinnon Scott. 2013. "Central America in the New Millennium: Six Different Stories of Poverty and Inequality." Unpublished report, World Bank, Washington, DC.

Dang, Hai-Anh, Peter Lanjouw, Jill Luoto, and David McKenzie. 2011. "Using Repeated Cross-Sections to Explore Movements in and Out of Poverty." Policy Research Working Paper 5550, World Bank, Washington, DC.

DIGESTYC (Dirección General de Estadística y Censos). 2013. "Encuesta de Hogares de Propósitos Múltiples 2012." DIGESTYC, Ciudad Delgado, San Salvador.

Encuesta de Hogares de Propósitos Múltiples (Multipurpose Household Survey). Various years. Government of El Salvador, Ministry of the Economy, General Directorate of Statistics and Census (DIGESTYC). http://www.digestyc.gob.sv /index.php/temas/des/ehpm.html.

El Salvador, Vice Ministry of Justice and Public Security, and World Bank. 2013. "El Salvador Delinquency Assessment." World Bank, Washington, DC.

ESEN (Escuela Superior de Economía y Negocios). 2014. "Proyecto Grupos Focales Disposición a Compartir: Informe Final del Estudio Cualitativo." ESEN, Santa Tecla La Libertad, El Salvador.

Fenochietto, Ricardo, and Carola Pessino. 2013. "Understanding Countries' Tax Effort." IMF Working Paper WP/13/244, International Monetary Fund, Washington, DC.

Hausmann, Ricardo, Dani Rodrik, and Andrés Velasco. 2005. "Growth Diagnostics." Working paper, Harvard University, Cambridge, MA. http://www6.iadb .org/WMSFiles/products/research/files/pubS-852.pdf.

IML (El Salvador, Instituto de Medicina Legal Dr. Roberto Masferrer [Institute of Forensic Medicine]). 2014. "Homicidios consolidado año 2013 según base de datos del instituto de medicina legal, cotejada y consensuada con la FGR y PNC." IML, San Salvador, El Salvador.

IUDOP (Instituto Universitario de Opinion Pública). 2013. "Los salvadoreños y salvadoreñas evalúan el cuarto año del gobierno de Mauricio Funes." *Boletín de Prensa* 27 (1): 1–16. IUDOP, Universidad Centroamericana José Simeón Cañas, San Salvador, El Salvador. http://www.uca.edu.sv/publica/iudop/archivos /boletin1_2013.pdf.

Kaufmann, Daniel, Aart Kraay, and Massimo Mastruzzi. 2010. "The Worldwide Governance Indicators: Methodology and Analytical Issues." Policy Research Working Paper 5430, World Bank, Washington, DC.

Molinas Vega, José R., Ricardo Paes de Barros, Jaime Saavedra Chanduvi, and Marcelo Guigale. 2012. *Do Our Children Have a Chance? A Human Opportunity Report for Latin America and the Caribbean*. With Louise Cord, Carola Pessino, and Amer Hasan. Report 65656. Directions in Development: Poverty. Washington, DC: World Bank.

Rodrik, Dani, 2004. "Rethinking Economic Growth in Developing Countries." Second Luca d'Aglian Lecture in Development Economics, Fondazione Luigi Einaudi, Turin, Italy, October 8.

SEDLAC (Socio-Economic Database for Latin America and the Caribbean), Center for Distributive, Labor, and Social Studies, Universidad de La Plata, La Plata, Argentina; World Bank, Washington, DC, http://sedlac.econo.unlp.edu.ar/eng/ index.php.

Segura, Edwin. 2014. "Homicidio: El Delito que más ha subido." *La Prensa Gráfica*, July 28. http://www.laprensagrafica.com/2014/07/28/homicidio-el-delito-que -mas-ha-subido.

UNDP (United Nations Development Programme). 2013. *Informe sobre Desarrollo Humano, El Salvador 2013: Imaginar un nuevo país, Hacerlo posible*. San Salvador: UNDP. http://www.sv.undp.org/content/dam/el_salvador/docs/povred /UNDP_SV_IDHES-2013.pdf.

USAID (United States Agency for International Development). 2009. "Índice de Competitividad Municipal 2009, El Salvador: Midiendo la Gobernabilidad Económica Local para Crear un Mejor Entorno Empresarial." August, USAID– El Salvador, San Salvador.

———. 2011. "Partnership for Growth: El Salvador, Constraints Analysis." July 19, USAID, Washington, DC. http://pdf.usaid.gov/pdf_docs/pnaeb762.pdf.

———. 2012. "Índice de Competitividad Municipal 2011, El Salvador: Midiendo la Gobernabilidad Económica Local para Crear un Mejor Entorno Empresarial." January, USAID–El Salvador, San Salvador.

———. 2013. "Índice de Competitividad Municipal 2013, El Salvador: Midiendo la Gobernanza Económica Local para Crear un Mejor Clima de Negocios." October, USAID–El Salvador, San Salvador.

WDI (World Development Indicators) (database). World Bank, Washington, DC. http://data.worldbank.org/data-catalog/world-development-indicators.

World Bank. 2014. "El Salvador: Fiscal Policy Options." February 3, World Bank, Washington, DC.

CHAPTER 6

Is Mexico on the Path to Shared Prosperity?

Kiyomi Cadena, Kinnon Scott, and Erwin R. Tiongson

Introduction

Mexico appears to have produced a mixed record of success in reducing monetary poverty and promoting shared prosperity. Monetary poverty has been stagnant the past 20 years, while the nonmonetary dimensions of poverty have improved. Volatile for most of the past 20 years and steadily deteriorating since 2007, monetary poverty is now back to its 1992 level. In terms of shared prosperity, that is, the growth of income among the bottom 40 percent of the income distribution (the bottom 40), Mexico compares unfavorably with other countries. However, based on the official multidimensional poverty measure, poverty has fallen in recent years. A variety of social indicators, including measures of deprivation along numerous dimensions, show significant improvement since 1990.

The disconnect between the improvement in nonmonetary dimensions of poverty and the lack of a corresponding improvement in income poverty is a key policy puzzle. The question thus becomes: is Mexico on the path to shared prosperity and extreme poverty reduction? The chapter draws on recent analyses to shed light on this puzzle.

The chapter is organized as follows. The next section describes the macroeconomic context. The subsequent section examines the evidence on the key trends in poverty and shared prosperity over the past two decades. To be consistent with the rest of this book, an income-based measure of poverty is used throughout, although the official poverty measure of Mexico is a multidimensional poverty index (MPI). The following section reviews the key drivers of these welfare trends. The penultimate section reviews the role of a range of polices that affect the ability of households to generate income and the options for improving fiscal policy, promoting inclusive markets, strengthening institutions, and mitigating risks. The final section offers pertinent remarks about the policy challenge.

The Macroeconomic Context

While Mexico has had periods of strong economic growth, average growth has been relatively low. It has lagged behind its peers in terms of economic growth. Between 1992 and 2013, annual growth averaged 2.6 percent, placing Mexico in the 32rd percentile of the countries of the world, 25th among upper-middle-income countries, and only in the 21st percentile among countries in Latin America and the Caribbean (figure 6.1). Per capita growth of gross domestic product (GDP) was even lower, averaging only 1.1 percent over the two decades. After the 2008–09 financial and price crises, average growth was lower, but Mexico's ranking improved, showing that the country was recovering slightly more rapidly than others: it's ranking in the region rose to the 35th percentile, 37th among upper-middle-income countries, and 38th among all countries.

Economic growth has been volatile. The 1994 and 2008–09 crises caused sharp declines in growth (5.8 and 4.7 percent, respectively) (figure 6.2). The economy was able to recover after both shocks, and, by 2010, the series of shocks that had led to the most recent recession had mostly faded: GDP

Figure 6.1 Economic Indicators, Rank among Upper-Middle-Income Countries, the Region, and the World, Mexico, 1992–2013

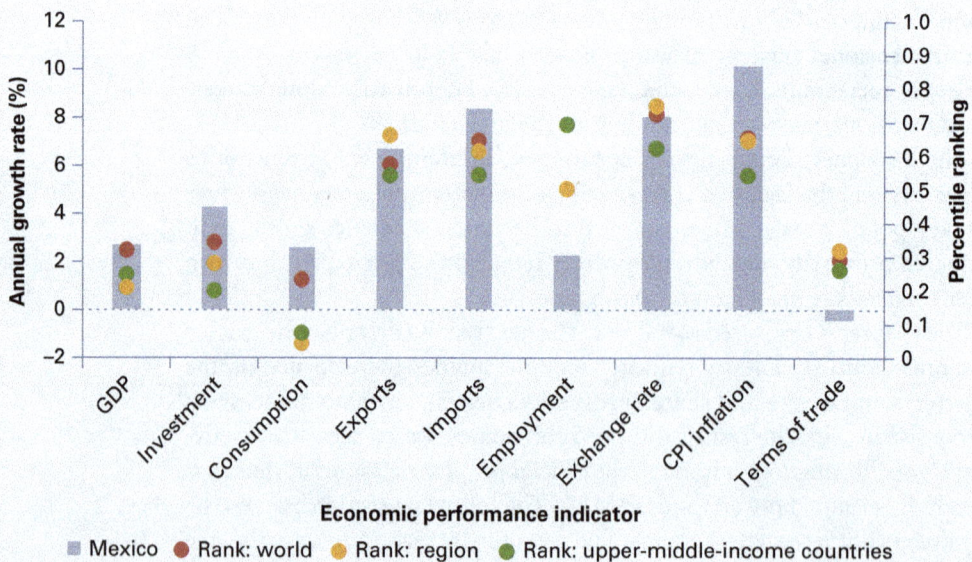

Legend: Mexico · Rank: world · Rank: region · Rank: upper-middle-income countries

Source: Data of WEO (World Economic Outlook) Database, International Monetary Fund, Washington, DC, http://www.imf.org/external/ns/cs.aspx?id=28.
Note: CPI = consumer price index; GDP = gross domestic product.

Figure 6.2 Annual GDP Growth Rate, Mexico, 1991–2013

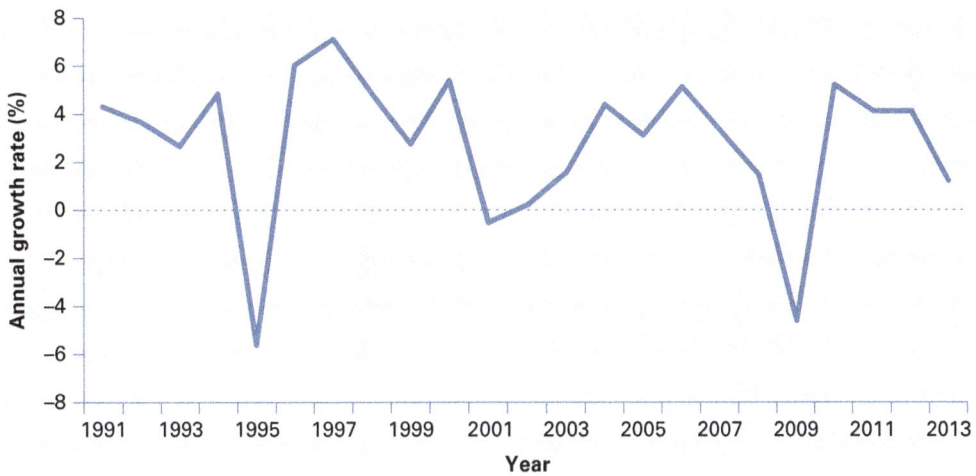

Source: Data of WEO (World Economic Outlook) Database, International Monetary Fund, Washington, DC, http://www.imf.org/external/ns/cs.aspx?id=28.

growth reached 5.1 percent in 2010. However, the pace of economic recovery has weakened. Growth was only slightly over 1 percent in 2013, and, while the economy is projected to grow at a somewhat more rapid rate in coming years, the rate is still expected to be low: 2.1 percent in 2015 and 2.7 percent in 2016.[1] Some of the slower growth has occurred because of the weakness in U.S. manufacturing and, as a consequence, a slowdown in Mexico's manufacturing sector, which represents 16 percent of Mexico's GDP.

Despite the sound macro and fiscal policies that helped limit the impact of the 2008–09 crisis on economic growth, the origins and nature of the crisis, compared with the crisis of 1994, have constrained the recovery. The two crisis periods had radically different origins. The 1994 Tequila crisis originated in Mexico and, while it spread to some other economies in Latin America, was essentially a localized event. In contrast, the recent financial crisis was global, originated in the developed world, and affected the world economy. It has thus generated more far-reaching and lasting consequences. Additionally, the international economic links that were drivers of economic recovery and poverty reduction in the 1990s have been a source of fragility and vulnerability during the recent recovery. The fact that the United States was Mexico's principal trading partner in 1994 (80 percent of Mexico's exports went to the United States) and that the U.S. economy generally did well during that period helped the Mexican economy recover quickly.[2] The strength of the U.S. economy in the 1990s provided an escape valve for workers who could not find good jobs in Mexico, and the remittances generated by this migration outflow also supported the local economy. In contrast, in the recent period, this same dependence (84 percent of Mexico's

Figure 6.3 Postcrisis Economic Performance, Mexico, 1995–99 and 2009–14

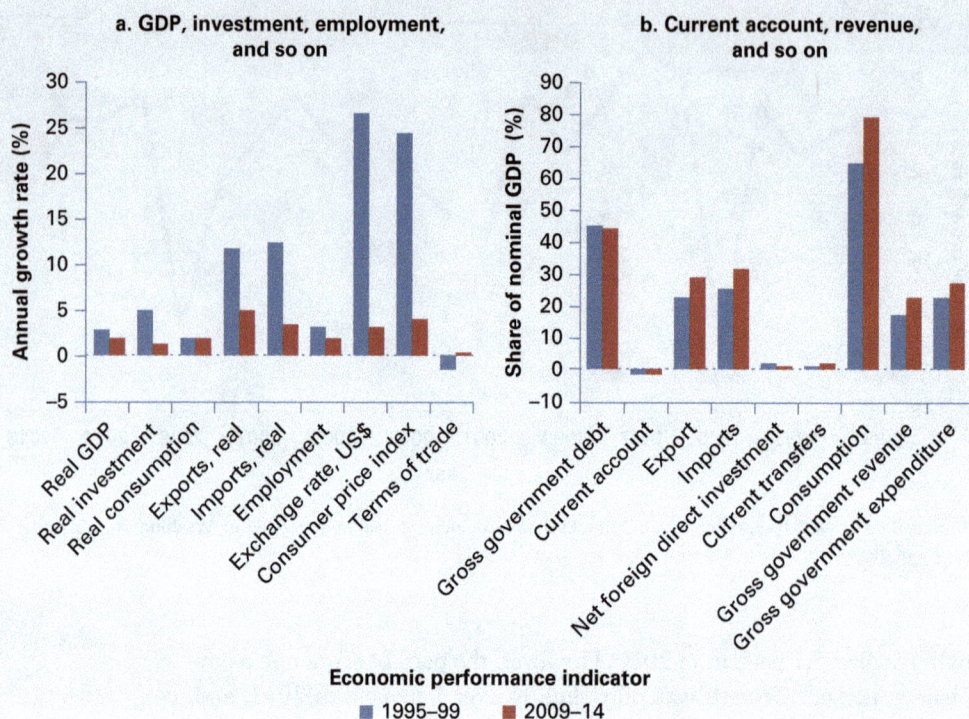

Source: Data of WEO (World Economic Outlook) Database, International Monetary Fund, Washington, DC, http://www.imf.org/external/ns/cs.aspx?id=28.
Note: GDP = gross domestic product.

exports now go to the United States) has been a source of vulnerability and fragility, which are reflected in falling exports, for example, along with the decline in immigration. Investment levels and employment growth have also been more sluggish during the current recovery. The global nature of the recent crisis helps explain the steadily lower GDP growth in Mexico in the post-2008 period compared with the post-1994 period (figure 6.3). The growth of real investment was dramatically slower in 2009–14 compared with 1995–99 (1.3 and 5.1 percent, respectively). Employment growth was likewise weaker; the elasticity of employment growth to GDP was 1.1 in 1995–99, compared with 0.9 in 2009–14 (see below).

Per capita real GDP growth rates have been flat in recent years, reflecting recent population growth that has offset the modest real GDP growth (figure 6.4). Trends in real GDP and real GDP per capita diverged sharply in 2005 and continue to diverge, reflecting a growing domestic population. Various factors led to the unexpected rise in the population growth rate in 2005–10 (after falling in previous years). First, the rate of decline in births faltered in the 2000s: in 1995–2000, the birth rate fell 2.0 percent, but only 1.7 percent in each of the following five-year periods. Second, the number

Figure 6.4 Index of Real GDP and GDP per Capita, Mexico, 1990–2013

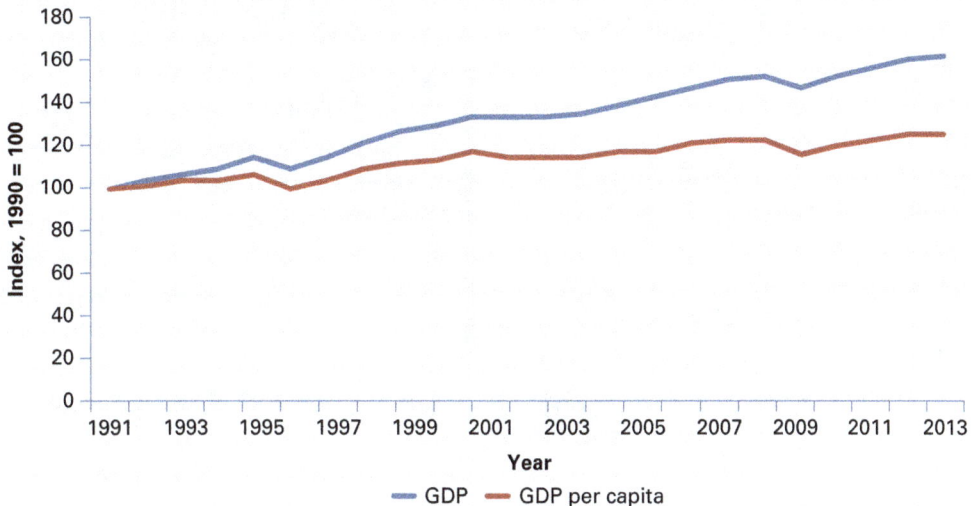

Source: Calculations based on data of WEO (World Economic Outlook) Database, International Monetary Fund, Washington, DC, http://www.imf.org/external/ns/cs.aspx?id=28.
Note: GDP = gross domestic product.

of Mexicans migrating to other countries also dropped. In 2000, 770,000 Mexicans immigrated to the United States. Since 2004, the total has fallen steadily, reaching 140,000 in 2010 and a net zero level in 2012 (Passel, Cohn, and Gonzalez-Barrera 2012).[3] The number of immigrants to Mexico has also risen; estimates place the number of undocumented immigrants at 140,000 per year.[4] While the share of immigrants in the Mexican population is quite low, it has doubled since 1990.[5]

Welfare Trends over the Past 20 Years

The wealth of data on Mexico facilitates an assessment of poverty over the past 20 years.[6] Given the sensitivity of the analysis of poverty and inequality to the choice of reference periods, data available for two decades provide a much better picture of the trends in welfare. Comparability issues often limit the ability to look at this wider picture: the MPI—Mexico's official poverty measure—can only be calculated back to 2008, for example. However, income poverty can be tracked over a full 20 years, thereby providing a longer view of income poverty and inequality, while highlighting the peaks and troughs of poverty in shorter reference periods.

The bad news: monetary poverty has not improved

Monetary poverty has not improved over the past 20 years: an income-based measure of poverty shows that the poverty rate was the same in 1992 and 2012 (figure 6.5).[7] This does not mean that income poverty was

Figure 6.5 Trends in Monetary Poverty, Mexico, 1992–2012

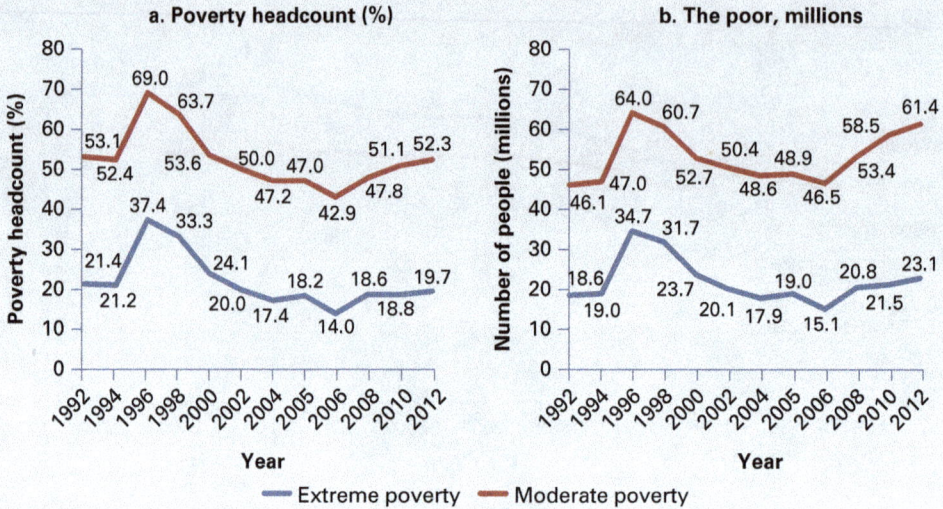

a. Poverty headcount (%)

y-axis: Poverty headcount (%)

Moderate poverty: 53.1, 52.4, 69.0, 63.7, 53.6, 50.0, 47.2, 47.0, 42.9, 47.8, 51.1, 52.3
Extreme poverty: 21.4, 21.2, 37.4, 33.3, 24.1, 20.0, 17.4, 14.0, 18.2, 18.8, 18.6, 19.7

b. The poor, millions

y-axis: Number of people (millions)

Moderate poverty: 46.1, 47.0, 64.0, 60.7, 52.7, 50.4, 48.6, 46.5, 48.9, 53.4, 58.5, 61.4
Extreme poverty: 18.6, 19.0, 34.7, 31.7, 23.7, 20.1, 17.9, 15.1, 19.0, 21.5, 20.8, 23.1

Year: 1992, 1994, 1996, 1998, 2000, 2002, 2004, 2005, 2006, 2008, 2010, 2012

— Extreme poverty   — Moderate poverty

Source: Data of *Consejo Nacional de Evaluación de la Política de Desarrollo Social* (National Council for the Evaluation of Social Development Policy, CONEVAL) using the traditional *Encuesta Nacional de Ingresos y Gastos de los Hogares* (Household Income and Expenditure Survey, ENIGH) 1992–2012.
Note: Estimates corresponding to 2006–12 rely on adjusted expansion factors from the 2010 population census.

stagnant throughout this period; in fact, it was quite volatile. As a result of the economic crisis of 1994, the overall (monetary) poverty rate rose from 52 percent to a peak of 69 percent in 1996. This was followed by 10 years of steady and significant declines: in 2006, the poverty rate reached a low, at 43 percent. The rate began to rise after 2006, however, and then the 2008–09 crisis pushed income poverty levels back full circle. Unlike the postcrisis period in the 1990s, there has not yet been a recovery in poverty rates. The extreme poverty rate followed a similar trajectory, although it is still below the 1992 level, and the last few years have witnessed a smaller increase relative to the overall poverty rate. Because of population growth, the pattern of income poverty implies that more people were living in income poverty in 2012 than in 1992.

Not only has economic growth been weak in recent years, but there has been a disconnect between growth and poverty reduction (see below). The elasticity of poverty to growth between 2006 and 2012 had the wrong sign: the economy expanded, but so did poverty. In 2000–06, however, the poverty elasticity to growth was strongly negative: a 1.0 percent upward change in economic growth led to a 6.6 percent decline in extreme poverty and a 3.6 percent decline in overall poverty.[8]

Shared prosperity—the growth in income among the bottom 40—exhibited a modest increase in Mexico, though a comparison with other countries is unfavorable. Between 2004 and 2012, the average income of the bottom 40 grew by 1.2 percent annually, double the corresponding

Figure 6.6 Income Beta Convergence, Mexico, 1990–2010

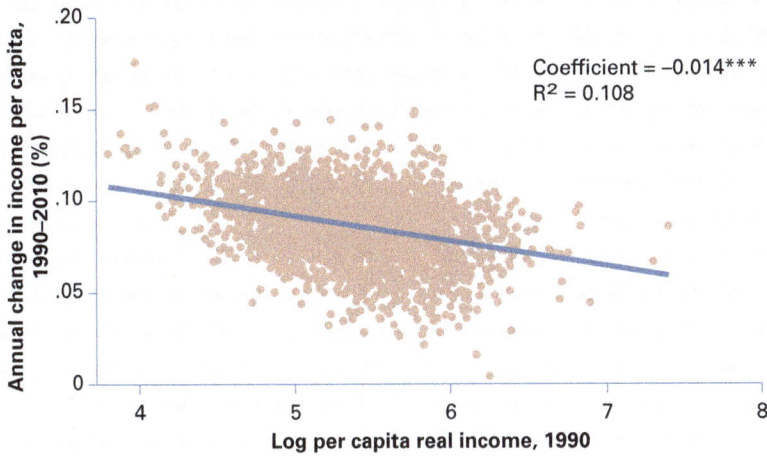

Coefficient = –0.014***
R^2 = 0.108

Source: Ortiz-Juárez and Pérez-García 2013.
Note: Coefficient refers to the annual convergence rate of –1.4 percent between 1990 and 2010.
*p < 0.1 **p < 0.05 ***p < .01

national average of only 0.6 percent. However, a comparison across 17 Latin American countries based on a harmonized income aggregate (to ensure comparability) shows that Mexico ranks near the bottom (16 out of 17) in income growth among the bottom 40 during the period (World Bank 2014). Most countries in South America benefited during this period from growth fueled by the commodity boom, which did not help Mexico. (In Mexico by 2010, commodity exports were at the same level as commodity imports.)[9]

The income growth story has varied across communities in Mexico. Monetary poverty levels show extreme heterogeneity across municipalities, where the rates ranged from below 20 to almost 100 percent in 1990.[10] Between 1990 and 2000, 42 percent of municipalities saw a fall in income poverty. In 2000–10, the ratio was even higher: almost three-quarters of municipalities experienced a decline in income poverty (Ortiz-Juárez and Pérez-García 2013). However, only 528 of 2,453 municipalities saw the poverty rate fall in both periods, while the rate rose in 167 municipalities over both periods.[11]

Between 1990 and 2010, poorer municipalities showed greater income growth than richer ones, thus providing evidence of beta convergence (figure 6.6). This is consistent with the growth incidence curves for municipalities over the same period (figure 6.7). The rate of convergence was stronger in 2000–10. Nonetheless, in aggregate, average municipal income growth over 1990–2010 was low. The convergence arose less because poorer municipalities showed sharp increases in income growth and more

Figure 6.7 Municipal Growth Incidence Curve, Mexico, 1990–2010

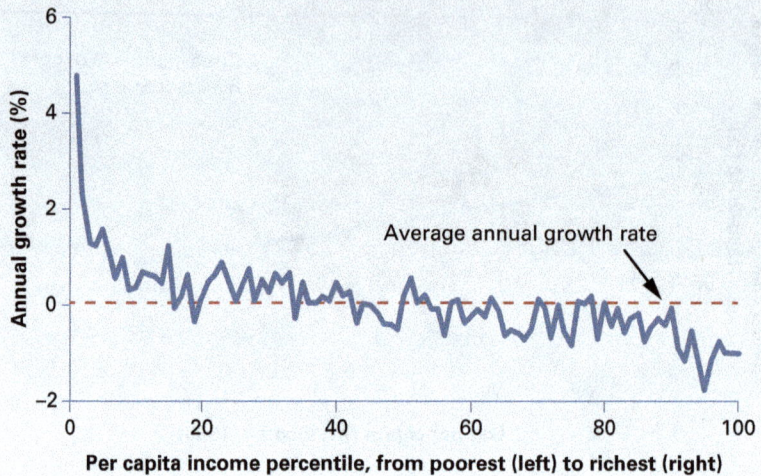

Per capita income percentile, from poorest (left) to richest (right)

Source: Dávalos et al. 2013.

because richer municipalities showed less growth; depending on the analysis, higher-income municipalities saw negative growth or growth at around 1 percent (Dávalos et al. 2013; Ortiz-Juárez and Pérez-García 2013). In contrast, nonmonetary measures of poverty improved over the two decades and also showed beta convergence (Ortiz-Juárez and Pérez-García 2013).

Despite some convergence on poverty, there remains great heterogeneity in the distribution of poverty (map 6.1; table 6.1). The southern states of Chiapas, Guerrero, and Oaxaca have the highest poverty rates. Yet, because of the distribution of the population, states such as the Federal District and Mexico with food poverty rates well below the corresponding rates of the poorest states have many more poor than any of the poorest states. Similarly, while poverty rates are much lower in urban areas than in rural areas, 41 percent of the extreme poor live in urban areas. At 48.3 percent, extreme poverty rates are almost three times greater among indigenous peoples than among the rest of the population.

There has been a slight decline in inequality

Trends in income inequality have mimicked some of the patterns in poverty over the past two decades (figure 6.8). Measured by the Gini coefficient, inequality widened after the 1994 crisis and then narrowed, though not steadily. In contrast to the trends in poverty, however, income inequality is narrower today than in 1994. According to Lustig, López-Calva, and Ortiz-Juárez (2013), the narrowing in inequality can be explained by two factors: a reduction in skills premiums and the expansion of targeted cash transfer programs, including the *Prospera* Program.[12] As with income, there is some evidence of beta convergence geographically (figure 6.9). Inequality ceased

Map 6.1 Extreme Poverty Headcount, Mexico, 2012

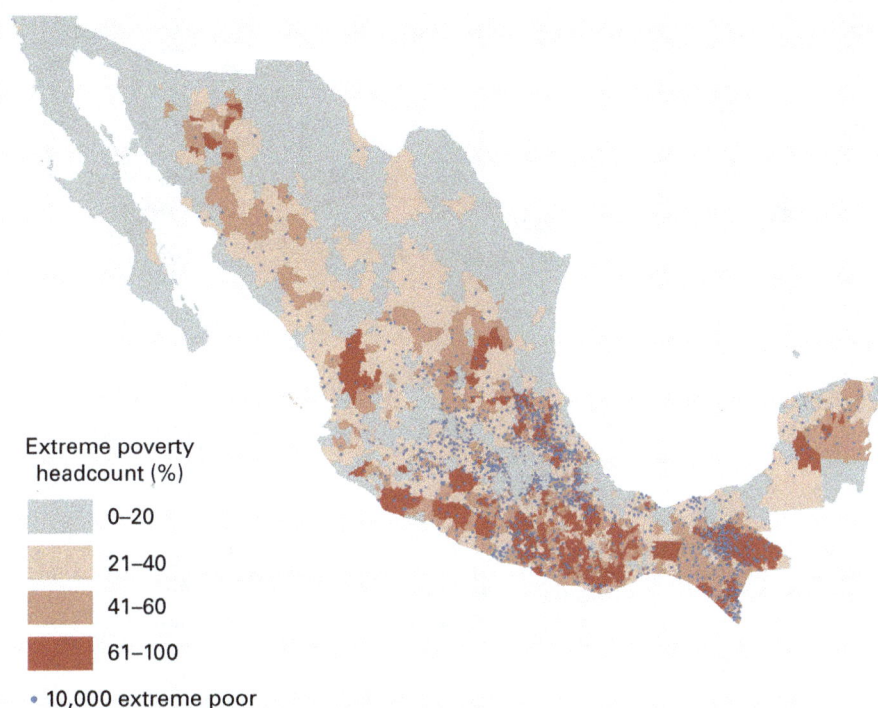

Extreme poverty
headcount (%)

☐ 0–20

☐ 21–40

☐ 41–60

☐ 61–100

• 10,000 extreme poor

Source: Data of CONEVAL based on the traditional ENIGH 2012.
Note: The data refer to CONEVAL's food poverty line (extreme poverty), which is based on an income measure.
The food poor are those people who do not have the purchasing power to acquire a basic food basket each
month.

Table 6.1 Food and Asset Poverty, by Area and Indigenous Status, Mexico, 2012

Indicator	Poverty headcount, %	Poor, number
Extreme poverty (food poverty)		
National	19.7	23,088,910
Urban	12.9	9,458,956
Rural	30.9	13,629,954
Indigenous people	48.3	3,927,481
Nonindigenous people	16.9	17,441,371
Moderate poverty (asset poverty)		
National	52.3	61,350,435
Urban	45.5	33,327,167
Rural	63.6	28,023,268
Indigenous people	80.3	6,531,690
Nonindigenous people	49.3	50,849,303

Source: Data of CONEVAL based on the traditional ENIGH 2012.

Figure 6.8 Trends in Income Inequality, Mexico, 1996–2012

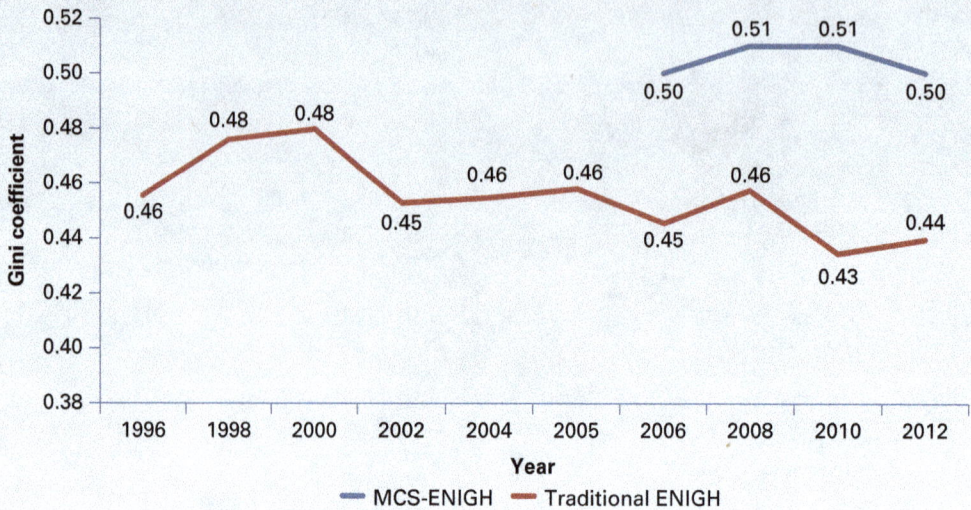

Source: Data of the *Instituto Nacional de Estadística y Geografía* (National Institute of Statistics and Geography, INEGI) based on the traditional ENIGH 1996–2012 and the *Modulo de Condiciones Socioeconomicas* (Socio-economic Conditions Module, MCS-ENIGH) 2006–12.
Note: The changes in inequality between 2010 and 2012 are not significant in either measure.

narrowing more recently, and there was no apparent change between 2010 and 2012. This may differ from other observed trends depending on the income series used in the analysis (see annex 6A).[13]

The evidence on socioeconomic mobility is mixed. A national survey shows that mobility is strong in the middle of the income distribution, but weak in the extremes (CEEY 2013; Serrano Espinosa and Torche 2010).[14] In 2011, half the people in the bottom and top income quintiles had started life in a household in the same quintile, compared with only 25–29 percent of the people in the middle quintiles (CEEY 2013). There is some evidence that overall mobility is lower in Mexico than in many other countries in Latin America (Ferreira et al. 2013).[15] Educational persistence is low in Mexico relative to other countries, and this contributes to low intergenerational mobility (Ferreira et al. 2013; OECD 2010). To the extent that low mobility leads to the misallocation of human resources, the fact that the perceptions of mobility among Mexicans are more pessimistic than actual mobility is cause for concern as is apparent from the evidence of the parental characteristics driving human capital accumulation among children (Campos-Vazquez and Velez-Grajales 2013; CEEY 2013).

The good news: nonmonetary measures of well-being have improved

Unlike income poverty, multidimensional poverty—using the official poverty measure in Mexico—fell over 2008–12 (table 6.2).[16] Extreme MPI

Figure 6.9 Municipal Beta Convergence in Inequality, Mexico, 2000–10

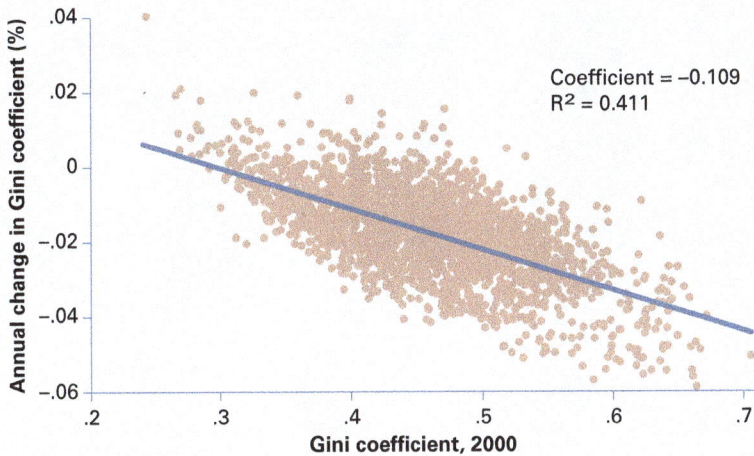

Coefficient = –0.109
$R^2 = 0.411$

Source: Ortiz-Juárez and Pérez-García 2013.

Table 6.2 Multidimensional Poverty Measurement and Social Deprivation Indicators, Mexico, 2010–12

Indicator, population	Percent			Number, millions		
	2008	2010	2012	2008	2010	2012
Poverty						
Poor	44.5	46.1	45.5	48.8	52.8	53.3
Moderate poor	33.9	34.8	35.7	37.2	39.8	41.8
Extreme poor	10.6	11.3	9.8	11.7	13.0	11.5
Vulnerable, social deprivations	33.0	28.1	28.6	36.2	32.1	33.5
Vulnerable, income	4.5	5.9	6.2	4.9	6.7	7.2
Social deprivation						
One or more deprivations	77.5	74.2	74.1	85.0	85.0	86.9
Three or more deprivations	31.1	28.2	23.9	34.1	32.4	28.1
Indicators, social deprivation						
Educational gap	21.9	20.7	19.2	24.1	23.7	22.6
Access to health care	40.8	29.2	21.5	44.8	33.5	25.3
Access to social security	65.0	60.7	61.2	71.3	69.6	71.8
Quality and room in the dwelling	17.7	15.2	13.6	19.4	17.4	15.9
Basic services in the dwelling	19.2	22.9	21.2	21.1	26.3	24.9
Food security	21.7	24.8	23.3	23.8	28.4	27.4
Well-being						
Income below the minimum poverty line	16.7	19.4	20.0	18.4	22.2	23.5
Income below the poverty line	49.0	52.0	51.6	53.7	59.6	60.6

Source: Data of CONEVAL based on the MCS-ENIGH 2008, 2010, and 2012.
Note: The estimates for 2008 suffer from comparability issues because they do not include some cooking fuels.

Figure 6.10 Trends in Nonmonetary Well-Being, Mexico, 1990–2010

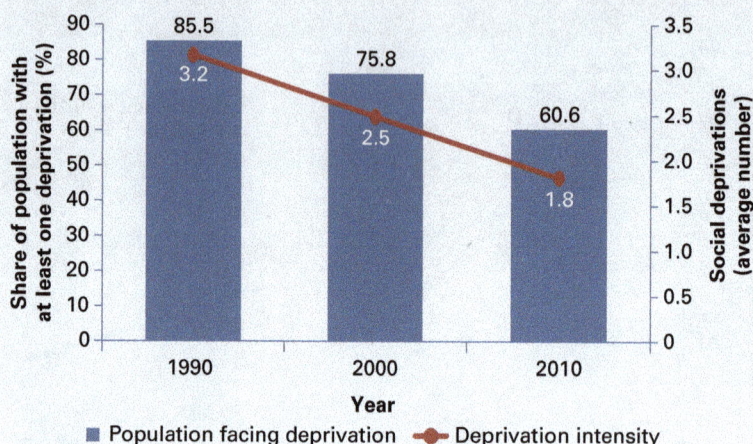

Source: Ortiz-Juárez and Pérez-García 2013.
Note: Estimates are based on the 1990, 2000, and 2010 (subsample) population
censuses. The shares are unweighted averages of the incidence of social deprivations
in municipalities. The maximum number of deprivations is six.

poverty decreased from 11.3 to 9.8 percent between 2010 and 2012. This decline reflected gains (fewer deprivations) in almost all the components of the measure. The average population experiencing three or more social deprivations dropped from 28.2 to 23.9 percent in 2012, and the share of the population facing social deprivations fell unambiguously in five of the six social areas in 2010–12. This mirrors the government's efforts to increase well-being through the implementation of programs to improve housing quality such as the Piso Firme (solid floor/foundation) Program and the expansion of social pensions among the elderly in rural areas through the 65 y Más program.[17] The largest improvement was in access to health care through the Seguro Popular program, which was introduced in 2003 and expanded beginning in 2010, when 8.2 million more people gained access.

Substantial progress has been achieved in nonincome poverty since 1990. The Índice de Privación Social (recortado) (adjusted social deprivation index), or IPS-8, an index of nonmonetary measures of welfare that includes education, water, sanitation, and electricity, along with housing-quality characteristics, shows that both the number of people facing deprivations and the average number of deprivations among those who are deprived have declined (figure 6.10; also see annex 6A). The incidence of social deprivations in municipalities fell from 85.5 to 60.6 percent in 1990–2010. Moreover, the average number of social deprivations dropped from 3.2 to 1.8 over the same period. The share of the population without access to electricity was slashed by 85 percent (figure 6.11). The educational

Figure 6.11 Trends in the Share of the Population Facing Social Deprivations, Mexico, 1990–2010

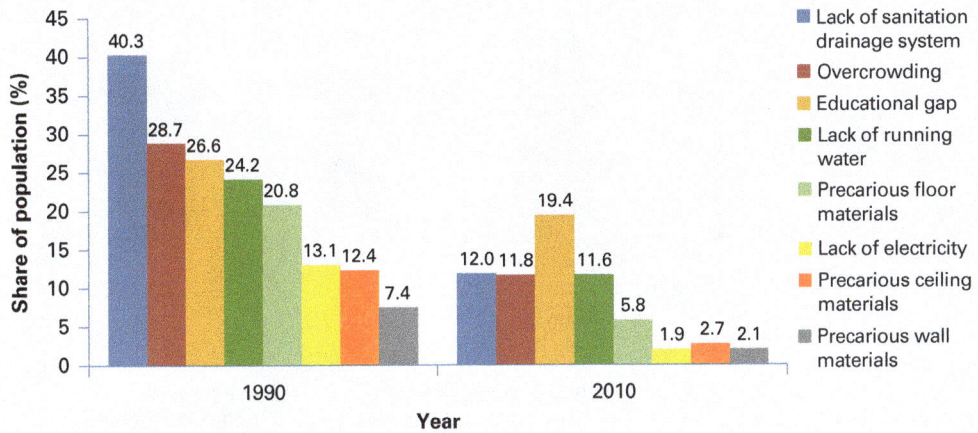

Source: Adapted from Ortiz-Juárez and Pérez-García 2013.
Note: Estimates are based on the 1990 and 2010 population censuses.

gap showed the least decrease among the indicators, but the reduction was still substantial, at 27 percent between 1990 and 2010.

Drivers of the Trends in Welfare

The improvement in the MPI without a parallel improvement in income poverty is a major policy puzzle. Progress in human capital, all else being equal, should translate into better employment opportunities, greater earnings, and, thus, less poverty. Access to schooling and health care, key inputs in the expansion of human capital, has improved; the changes in education have been occurring over the past 20 years (see table 6.2; figure 6.11). Yet, income poverty has increased during the past six years.

The recent rise in income poverty is linked to negative changes in labor income and remittances. Government programs have worked to mitigate these negative effects (figure 6.12). Mexico stands in sharp contrast to Latin America more generally in the role of labor income in poverty. Labor income has played an important role in moving households out of poverty in Latin America, accounting for over half of the poverty reduction, while a fifth of the reduction was accounted for by public and private transfers, and the remainder by a combination of demographic shifts and other nonlabor income (World Bank 2011). In contrast, in Mexico, changes in labor income are associated with a rise in poverty as are changes in household employment levels.[18] Demographic shifts that led to lower household dependency ratios, however, helped prevent poverty from increasing more quickly. Public transfers also played a strong mitigating role, especially in

Figure 6.12 The Decomposition of Changes in Income Poverty (Extreme), Mexico, 2006–12

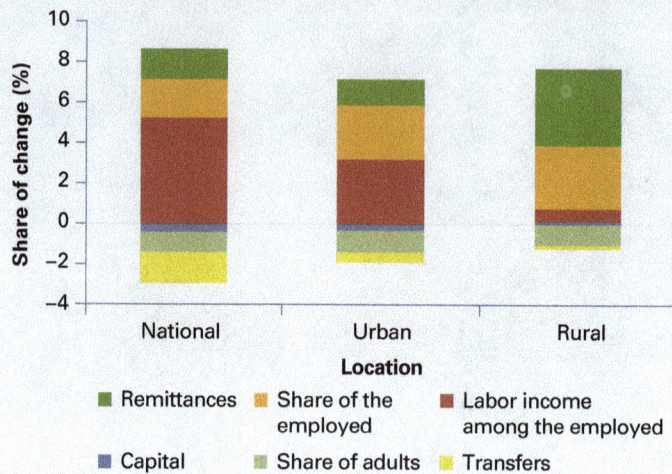

Source: Calculations based on the traditional ENIGH 2006–10.
Note: The estimates corresponding to 2006–10 rely on adjusted expansion factors from the 2010 population census.

urban areas. This section explores the limited role of labor income and the more positive role of social programs and public transfers in promoting welfare.

Social programs and a shift in household demographics helped improve well-being

The increases in income poverty and inequality would have been worse without the countereffects of government transfers between 2006 and 2012. In the absence of government transfers, the 2006–12 rise in extreme income poverty would have been 7.2 percentage points, higher than the observed change by 1.5 percentage points (see figure 6.12). Public and private transfers together lowered the Gini coefficient from 0.50 to 0.44.

Changes in social spending in the last two decades are behind the observed impact of public transfers on poverty. The last 20 years have seen significant increases in government spending. Overall spending has risen, but it is social spending that has witnessed the greatest expansion, almost doubling from slightly over 5 percent of GDP to more than 11 percent (see figure 6.19 below). Spending has also become more progressive. Improved targeting has enhanced the effectiveness of the welfare spending: in 1996, 56 percent of cash transfers were received by the bottom 40; by 2010, this share had climbed to 66 percent (López-Calva et al. 2013).

The other factor that helped to prevent poverty from rising even more was the change in household demographics: lower dependency ratios fostered poverty reduction by raising the proportion of household members who are of prime working age. This demographic shift was associated with a 1 percentage point reduction in poverty. In contrast to the impact of direct social spending, the shift was equally important in urban and rural areas.

The negative effects of labor market changes overwhelmed social policy effects

Changes in labor income and in the share of household members employed within a household are associated with an increase in income poverty over recent years. In particular, labor income and the share of employed boosted extreme poverty by 5.3 and 1.9 percentages points, respectively, between 2006 and 2012. This subsection explores the elements—both the usual suspects and new ones—that have affected labor markets.

First, there are not enough jobs. The labor market has been unable to absorb the expansion in domestic labor supply. There was a downward trend in the growth rate of the labor force prior to 2005. In 2005–10, however, the labor force grew by 12.0 percent, a rise relative to the 2000–05 growth of 9.8 percent.[19] The increase was driven by a decline in emigration and rising immigration flows. Migration has been an important feature of the economy: an average of 465,000 migrants have been going to the United States each year since 1992. While the 12 million Mexican immigrants in the United States represent about 30 percent of all immigrants in that country, the annual number of migrants to the United States from Mexico has fallen steadily since 2004 (from 670,000 in 2004 to 140,000 in 2010), while the number of migrants returning to Mexico has risen (from 670,000 in 1995–2000 to 1,390,000 in 2005–10 [Passel, Cohn, and Gonzalez-Barrera 2012]). The ratio of the active population to the working-age population was flat at 57 percent during 2005–12. In contrast, the working-age population as a share of the total population rose from 68.6 to 72.4 percent over the same period. A rough calculation indicates that, if migration had continued at the 2004 rate through 2005–10, the observed growth in the labor force would have continued to fall to around 8 percent, instead of increasing to 12 percent (see annex 6B).

Other factors tending to expand labor supply are the continuing inflows of workers from Central America and changes in the labor force participation of women. While precise data on migration are scarce, it is estimated that Mexico is host to some 725,000 Central American immigrants; annual inflows of undocumented migrants from the south are estimated at around 140,000 per year.[20] Overall, labor force participation rates have risen since 1992, although 2002–12 saw a smaller change relative to the previous decade (7.6 and 10.4 percent, respectively). Over the 20-year period, the growth in the labor force participation rates of the bottom 40 and the top 60 percent of the income distribution (the top 60) were similar, though the bottom 40 had consistently lower participation rates.[21] The female labor force participation rate increased from 34 to 44 percent over the two decades, although it is lower than the average rate among women in Latin America (51 percent in 2012).[22] The expansion in female labor force

Figure 6.13 Unemployment and Underemployment Rates, by Gender, Mexico, 2005–14

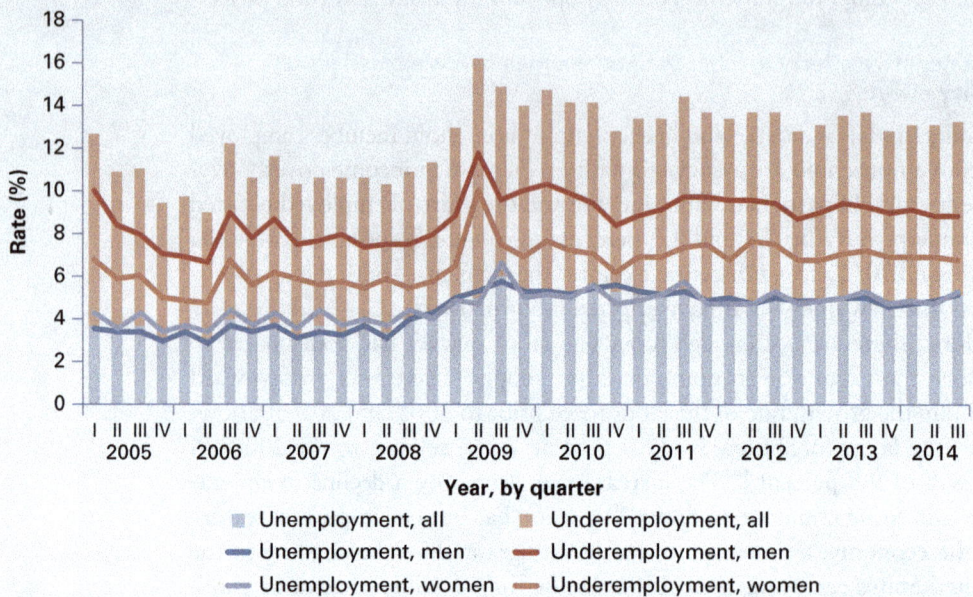

Source: Data of the Instituto Nacional de Estadística y Geografía (National Institute of Statistics and Geography, INEGI) based on the *Encuesta Nacional de Ocupación y Empleo* (National Employment and Occupation Survey, ENOE), 2005–13.
Note: Underemployment refers to people who want to work more hours and are able to do so.

participation boosted labor supply, although this was partially offset by a decline in the male participation rate from 84 to 79 percent over the same period. The change in labor force participation was much smaller over the last six years of the period (the years of rising income poverty): female rates rose from 41.7 to 44 percent, while the male rates fell only slightly, from 80.7 to 79.2 percent.

Unemployment and underemployment rates have been rising (figure 6.13). Unemployment and underemployment rose during the crisis. The growth of employment lagged the growth in the labor force described above. From 2008 on, a measurable divergence in the dynamics of the labor force and of employment yielded the expansion in unemployment and underemployment. During the recovery, the growth in the labor force matched the growth in employment, but the gap that had emerged earlier remains, and the economy has not yet been able to provide enough jobs to meet the needs of the labor force.

Second, there are not enough jobs that pay adequate wages. Among many employed workers, the wages they earn have not been sufficient to protect them from poverty. There are more low-paying jobs now than before the 2008–09 crisis: by the beginning of 2009, jobs paying between one and two minimum wages were the most prevalent (figure 6.14). There is also evidence of a reduction in the returns to education arising in part because of the

Figure 6.14 Labor Earnings Relative to the Minimum Wage, Mexico, 2005–13

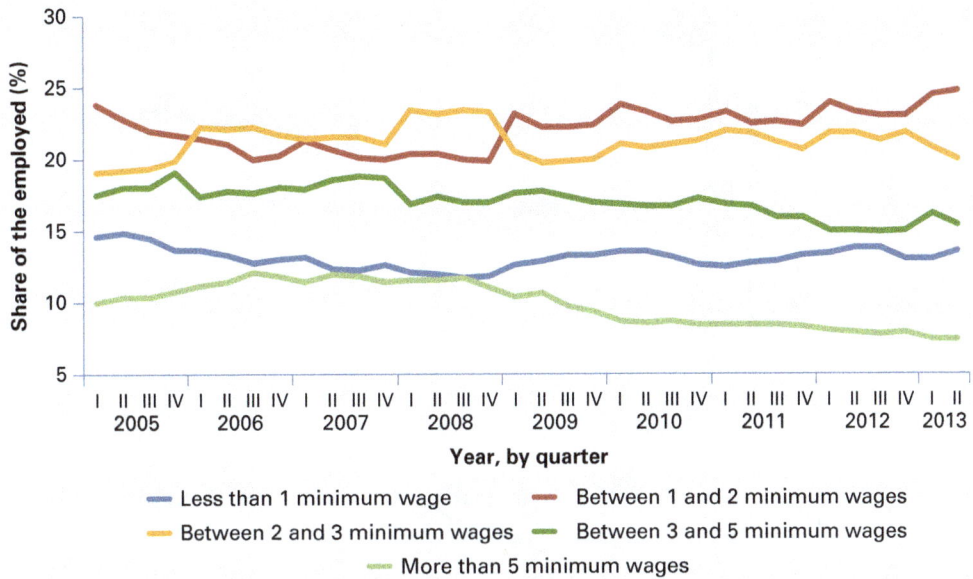

Source: Data of INEGI based on the ENOE, 2005–13.
Note: The not specified and no income categories have been excluded.

expansion in the share of the educated in the population and in part because of the differential quality of schooling available to the poor, leading to a likely drop-off in the average quality of the workforce (de la Torre et al. 2014). Since 2010, the labor income poverty index—the percentage of households that cannot pay for a basic food basket with labor income—has indicated there has been growth in poverty, which rose by 13 percent between 2010 and the first quarter of 2014 (figure 6.15). The real rate of increase is probably lower because the index tends to overestimate low incomes, but, even if one corrects for missing data, the trend remains upward (Campos-Vazquez 2013; Rodríguez-Oreggia and López Videla 2014).

Meanwhile, productivity was not increasing, and the small amount of job creation taking place was in lower-productivity sectors.[23] Some evidence of productivity growth exists in agriculture, but the level is low, and, overall, productivity has declined in services (figure 6.16). In a recent study of productivity and employment, Bolio et al. (2014) describe the two economies of Mexico: a modern, highly-productive sector that competes in the global market and a traditional sector consisting of small informal enterprises with low productivity. This traditional sector has been creating more employment in recent years, resulting in some reallocation of employment toward unproductive sectors. In its share of total employment, the traditional sector rose three percentage points, while productivity in the sector fell 6.5 percent. In the modern sector, productivity growth was positive. This trend

Figure 6.15 The Labor Income Poverty Index, Mexico, 2005–14

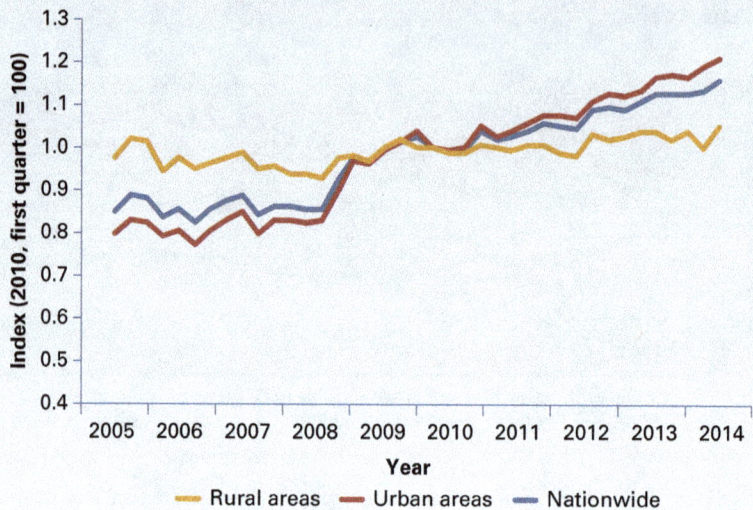

Source: Data of CONEVAL, 2014.

is reflected in labor shedding in the tradables sectors and a growing services sector characterized by many small, informal enterprises.

Third, the recent increase in crime and violence has affected economic growth and the creation of jobs. Levels of crime and violence have spiked in recent years (figure 6.17). After falling for a decade, homicide rates doubled between 2000 and 2010, from 12.3 to 21.5 per 100,000 population. Municipalities with higher levels of drug-related violence in 2007, when the spike in homicides occurred, experienced less growth in 2005–10 than others that had avoided the drug-related violence (Enamorado, López-Calva, and Rodríguez-Castelán 2014).[24] In 2010, 29 percent of firms identified crime and violence as a major constraint, and evidence exists that the violence has led to a stunting in firm creation.[25] Arias and Esquivel (2012) show that, for every 10 homicides, the share of employers relative to the size of the labor force falls 0.2 percent. Violence has also cut into enrollment in postprimary education, which may affect productivity as firms begin to face constraints in acquiring skilled labor (Marquez-Padilla, Pérez-Arce, and Rodríguez-Castelán 2015).

Changes in remittances are also associated with the recent rise in income poverty

The final factor associated with a rise in poverty in recent years is remittances. Like labor market movements in Mexico, which are affected by the strength or weakness of the U.S. market, the flow of remittances in Mexico reflects the health of the U.S. economy. Prior to the global financial crisis, remittances rose appreciably in Mexico, but the crisis caused the annual

Figure 6.16 Changes in Employment and Productivity, by Sector, Mexico, 2000 and 2011

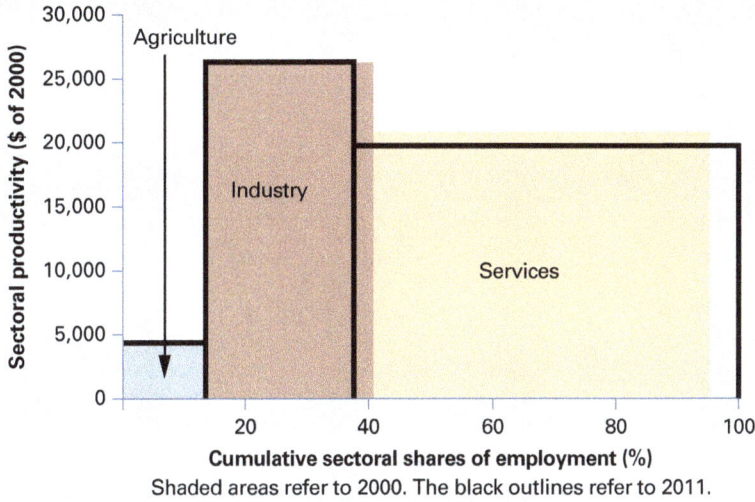

Shaded areas refer to 2000. The black outlines refer to 2011.

Source: Calculations based on data of WDI (World Development Indicators) (database), World Bank, Washington, DC, http://data.worldbank.org/data-catalog /world-development-indicators.
Note: Productivity is calculated as value added to gross domestic product per worker.

Figure 6.17 Homicides, Mexico, 1997–2011

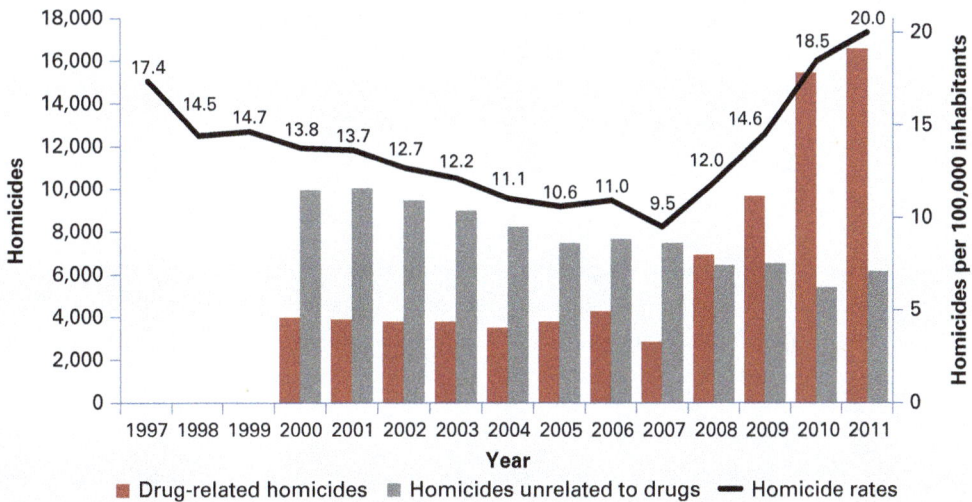

Sources: Population: Proyecciones de la Población 2010–2050 (database), Consejo Nacional de Población y Vivienda, Mexico City, http://www.conapo.gob.mx/es/CONAPO/Proyecciones. Homicides: Incidencia Delictiva (database), Sistema Nacional de Seguridad Pública, Mexico City, http://secretariadoejecutivo.gob.mx/index.php.
Note: Homicides unrelated to drugs = all homicides, less drug-related homicides.

Figure 6.18 Annual Growth in Remittances, Mexico, 2000–13

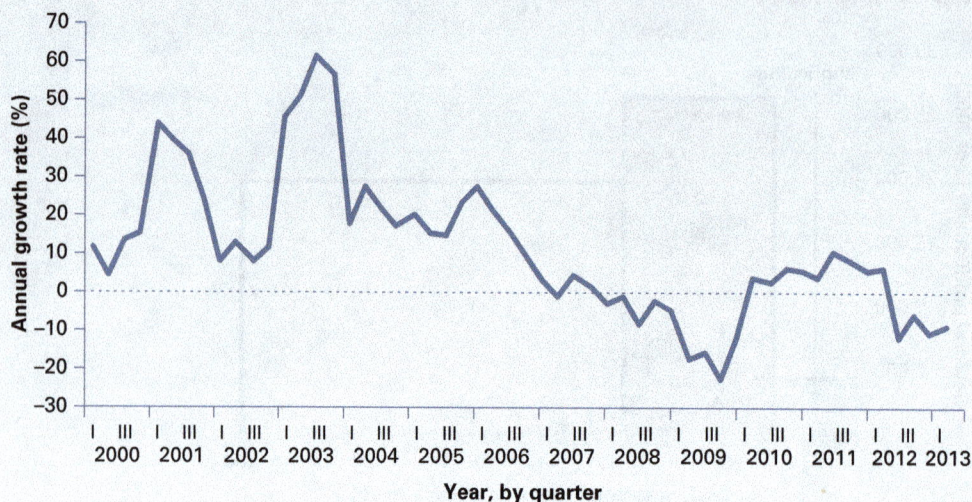

Source: Remesas (database), Banco de México, Mexico City, http://www.banxico.org.mx/ayuda/temas-mas-consultados/remesas.html.

growth rate to fall sharply, and it reached negative levels (figure 6.18). Although the annual growth of remittances was positive again in 2010, it was still far from the rates experienced in the first years of the decade. Additionally, among every quintile of the population, the share of households receiving remittances had dropped by 2012 relative to 2008.

The fall in remittances is linked to a rise in extreme poverty, particularly in rural areas. Between 2006 and 2012, changes in remittances accounted for a 3.8 percentage point increase in extreme poverty in rural areas and a 1.3 percentage point increase in urban areas.

Policy Channels for Poverty Reduction

A wide range of policies affect the welfare of households and the ability of households to generate income. This section explores the role of fiscal policy, markets, particularly labor and financial markets, institutions, and risks.

Improving fiscal policy

The last 20 years have seen significant changes in fiscal policy, especially in social spending (figure 6.19). While overall government revenues have been flat as a share of GDP, a noteworthy shift in spending patterns toward social sectors and programs has taken place. As noted above, social spending, which represented 5.5 percent of GDP in 1990, climbed to 11.0 percent in 2009.[26] It rose from 55 to 80 percent as a share of planned government

Figure 6.19 Federal Income, Tax Revenue, and Redistributive Spending, Mexico, 1990–2013

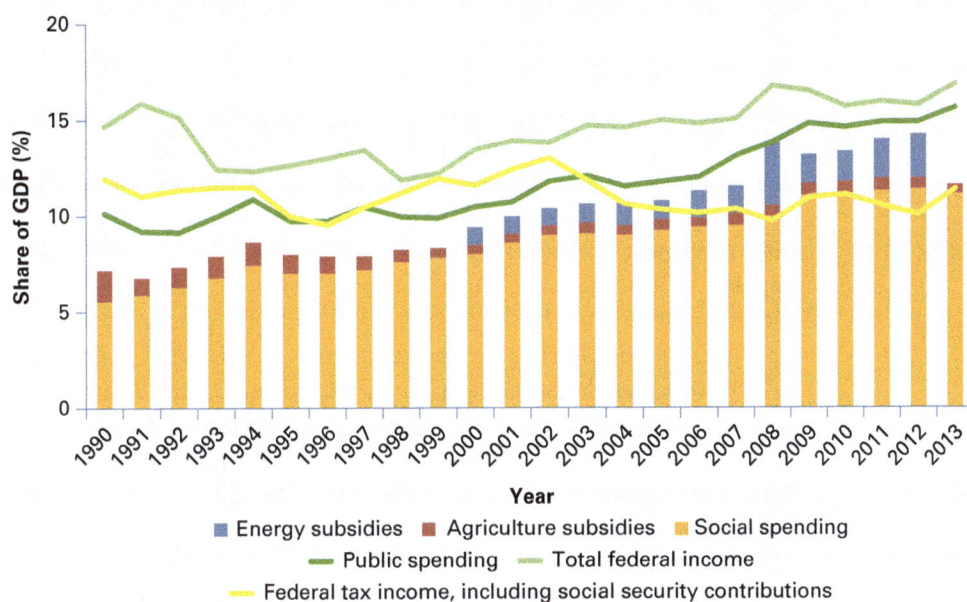

Source: Scott 2014.
Note: Public spending corresponds to budgeted public spending, excluding debt servicing and tax devolutions to states and state energy companies.

spending.[27] Tax revenues remained low, at between 10 and 13 percent of GDP, despite the increase in social spending.

Overall, fiscal policy has become more progressive (López-Calva et al. 2013; Scott 2014). As López-Calva et al. (2013) outline, fiscal policy had a negligible effect on poverty in 1996; in 2010, however, fiscal policy served to lower poverty by almost 3 percentage points (measured at $2.50 a day). Fiscal policy narrowed inequality by 3 percentage points in 1996; by 2010, the effect had risen to 5 percentage points. Scott (2014) finds that the net effect of fiscal policy in 2010 was to reduce poverty by 7.5 percent (1.4 percentage points) and 14.0 percent in rural areas (5.2 percentage points) and to reduce the Gini by almost 16 percent nationally (from 0.51 to 0.43), thereby generating a much larger impact on rural inequality than on urban inequality.

The recent fiscal reform is expected to reduce inequality because most of the increased revenues will come from higher taxes on the top 10 percent of the population. According to the Organisation for Economic Co-operation and Development (OECD 2015), the Gini coefficient before and after taxes and transfers was the same prior to the reform. However, with the approved reform, the Gini coefficient after taxes and transfers is expected to be lower, although it will remain high compared with the OECD average.

Mexico's two flagship social assistance programs, Prospera and Seguro Popular, both globally recognized for their impacts on poverty alleviation and human capital development, have driven improvements in nonmonetary poverty. The Prospera Program (formerly Oportunidades) has raised consumption among poor households and has had positive impacts on health, nutrition, and education.[28] Nonetheless, Farfán et al. (2011) show mixed effects in nutritional outcomes: the positive effects on rural children do not take place among urban children. In addition, there are concerns that the impact on employment—required to break the cycle of poverty—is not occurring. The recent move to add labor market and productive activities to Prospera is an attempt to address these issues. Meanwhile, Seguro Popular, which provides health insurance to people not covered by the social security regime, has expanded rapidly to cover practically all the targeted population (51.8 million people by the end of 2011).[29] Evaluations have shown that the program has boosted use among affiliates by 5 percentage points, decreased out-of-pocket expenditures by 25 percent, and reduced the incidence of catastrophic health expenditures by slightly more than 15 percent (Bosch, Belén Cobacho, and Pagés 2012; Frenk et al. 2006; Gakidou et al. 2006).

Other social programs have also performed well. The implementation of programs to improve housing quality such as Piso Firme and the expansion of a social pension program for the elderly, 65 y Más, have improved living conditions and lowered the vulnerability of households. Furthermore, enrollment rates at all levels of education have increased, and infant mortality rates continue to decline.

Despite significant successes, social spending is not entirely progressive. Scott (2013) shows that concentration coefficients for a range of programs highlight the disparities. Flagship social programs, along with *Procampo* (support for small agricultural producers), PET (a temporary employment program), and 65 y Más (noncontributory pensions), have promoted the positive change. Prospera has a concentration coefficient of –0.54, followed by PET at –0.48. However, subsidies for contributory pensions and higher levels of education and tax credits for education are regressive; contributions to social security show the most regressive effects.

The agenda on fiscal reform is neither comprehensive nor entirely favorable to the poor. Previous reforms, such as the reduction in indirect subsidies (mostly energy subsidies), improved efficiency at the cost of increasing poverty because the expansion in direct subsidies was not sufficient to offset the losses to the poor (Scott 2013). The overall progressivity of the fiscal system and its impact on poverty and inequality compare unfavorably with the systems in Argentina, Brazil, and Uruguay, which also spend a greater share of GDP per capita (López-Calva et al. 2013). Social protection programs still face challenges in coverage because of imperfect targeting and take-up among the poor. Mexico has been successful in targeting the flagship programs, but other social programs such as the *subsidio para el empleo* (employment subsidy program) are still regressive.[30] According to anecdotal evidence, even when programs are available for the poor, there may be a lack of take-up because of an absence of proper documentation or a lack of awareness. The human opportunity index (HOI), which captures how individual circumstances such as gender, place of residence, and educational attainment of the household head affect children's access to basic goods and services (higher values indicate more equitable access), shows that coverage is still far from universal and that basic service coverage is not equitable, despite substantial progress.

Promoting inclusive markets

By promoting inclusive markets, policy makers can improve the ability of the poor to use their assets and to increase the returns to these assets. There are many important markets that can affect poverty and shared prosperity. The focus of this subsection is labor and financial markets. Labor markets are critical; the main asset of the poor is their labor, and this market thus has tremendous potential to improve welfare. The lower levels of investment during the recent postcrisis period and the apparent disconnect between economic growth and job creation add to the need to focus on this market. Financial markets are also covered. These markets have traditionally excluded the poor; yet, access to financial services is fundamental to job creation and economic growth.

Labor markets

Employment rigidity affects labor markets in Mexico. In 2012, the country ranked 23rd among 183 countries in employment rigidity, an index comprised of measures of the difficulty of hiring (limited possible contractual arrangements) and firing.[31] High severance pay requirements, along with limited contractual arrangements, create strong disincentives to hiring and prevent labor markets from adjusting efficiently. These rigidities have, in all likelihood, only a limited effect in rural areas, but more impact in urban areas. The significant costs of hiring and firing result in a reduction of jobs in the formal sector, create disadvantages for women and youth that push up the associated unemployment rates, and constrain productivity because firms, especially small firms, adopt less technology or adopt it more slowly, cannot adapt to new environments, and invest less in training (Acemoglu and Shimer 2000; Djankov and Ramalho 2009; Feldmann 2009; Kaplan, Sadka, and Silva-Mendez 2008; Lopez-Acevedo 2002; Samaniego 2010; World Bank 2005, 2006). Unlimited severance payment leads to lengthy cases in the labor courts. More than half the cases before the Juntas de Conciliación y Arbitraje (Conciliation and Arbitration Boards) end in private settlements below legal mandates; legal fees absorb 30–40 percent of severance payments; and many workers do not bring suit for these reasons (Dávila Capalleja 1997; Kaplan and Sadka 2008; Kaplan, Sadka, and Silva-Mendez 2008).

The 2012 labor reform is designed to address several key issues of labor market rigidity that affect job creation. It provides for new types of contracts, including for trial periods and training, for seasonal and discontinuous jobs, and for jobs on an hourly basis. It also offers incentives for settling labor disputes more rapidly and caps the maximum payment in disputes. The goal of this greater flexibility is to boost formal sector employment and supply more opportunities for marginal workers to access the labor market through seasonal or hourly contracts. The risk is that existing jobs could thereby be shifted to a less permanent status to the detriment of workers; this will need to be monitored.

Other constraints to enterprise growth may also be limiting job creation. Mexico is characterized by a relatively small number of medium and large firms and a large pool of small or microenterprises that are not expanding: the economy has not generated firm growth that can establish a larger demand for labor. Financial constraints on small and medium enterprises exist. The ratio of private credit to GDP was 18.7 percent in 2011, placing Mexico in the bottom quarter of middle-income countries.[32] Recent evidence on the effect of the judicial system on firm size also suggests that judicial quality influences firm growth: states with higher-quality judicial systems have larger firms (Dougherty 2014). Although there has been discussion of the missing middle in Mexico, recent work casts doubt on this hypothesis, arguing that, while there is evidence of a bimodal distribution of employment, this is not so for firms (Hsieh and Olken 2014). Nor is there any clear indication that certain tax thresholds represent a binding constraint on enterprise development.

The small dip in informality rates seen in the mid-2000s was erased by the global financial crisis (figure 6.20). The informality is partly caused

Figure 6.20 Informality Rate, by Gender, Mexico, 2005–13

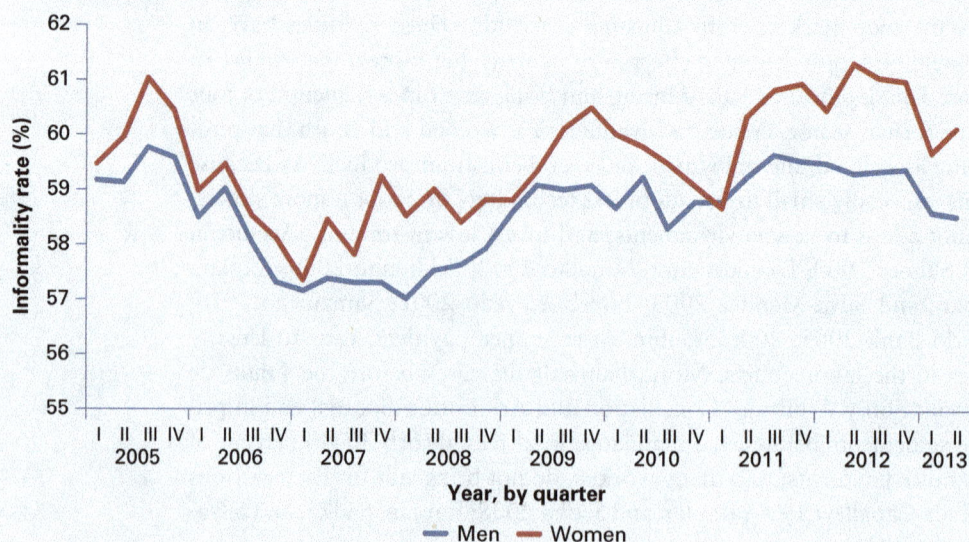

Source: Data of INEGI based on the ENOE, 2005–13.

Figure 6.21 Rigidity in the Employment Index, Regions and Selected Countries, 2012

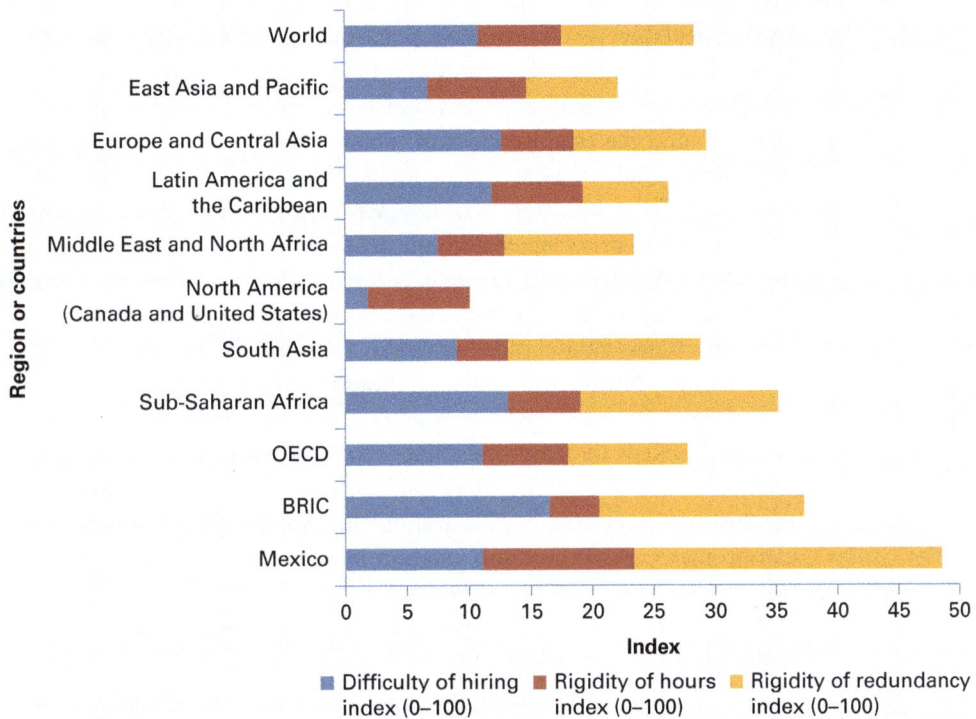

Source: Data of Doing Business (database), International Finance Corporation and World Bank, Washington, DC, http://www.doingbusiness.org/data.
Note: BRIC = Brazil, Russian Federation, India, and China; OECD = Organisation for Economic Co-operation and Development.

by rigidities in the labor market. Mexico had significantly higher scores on several indicators of rigidity in 2012 (figure 6.21). Nor are the high levels of informality that have characterized Mexico for so long expected to fall dramatically in the near future. Recent work shows that the structure of the economy is such that, with protected enclaves of employment, for every tradable job created in the economy, one formal job and one informal nontradable job are created (Pereira-López and Soloaga 2013). The evidence is mixed on whether the expansion of noncontributory pensions and health insurance affected the incentives for workers to seek formal jobs. For example, through Seguro Popular, informal workers can receive better health services than they could previously, which, in principle, can reduce the incentive to obtain health benefits through formal sector employment. There is some evidence of this, though the literature is inconclusive. Aterido, Hallward-Driemeier, and Pagés (2011) and Bosch and Campos-Vazquez (2010) find such a disincentive effect, albeit small. However, Azuara and Marinescu (2013) find only a small effect among less well-educated workers and no statistically significant disincentive effect in the overall population.

Financial markets

In the past 15 years, there have been significant changes in banking laws in an effort to promote use of the formal financial system. The creation of banks backed by retailers in the first part of the 2000s (Banco Azteca from Grupo Elektra was the first in 2002), the passage of an agent banking law in 2009 (whereby supermarkets and other retail stores provide financial services), and the establishment of mobile banking (2010) have increased the number and the coverage of financial service outlets throughout the country.[33] The centralization of payments by the government through the creation of a treasury single account in 2007 and the electronic payment of benefits to social program recipients have pulled an underserved segment of the population into the financial system. Between 2007 and 2010, over one million new households under Prospera and the *Programa de Apoyo Alimentario* (Nutritional Support Program) received payments through the banking system.[34] These new users are substantially different from the already banked: they are more likely to be women, have lower levels of education, and be new account holders (DAI 2010). The financial sector reforms of the present administration that are aimed at boosting lending can promote growth and job creation by expanding financial intermedia-tion and reducing credit constraints.[35]

Despite these policies, a significant share of the population relies on financial services outside the formal financial system (figure 6.22). Only 27

Figure 6.22 Financial Service Use, Mexico, 2011

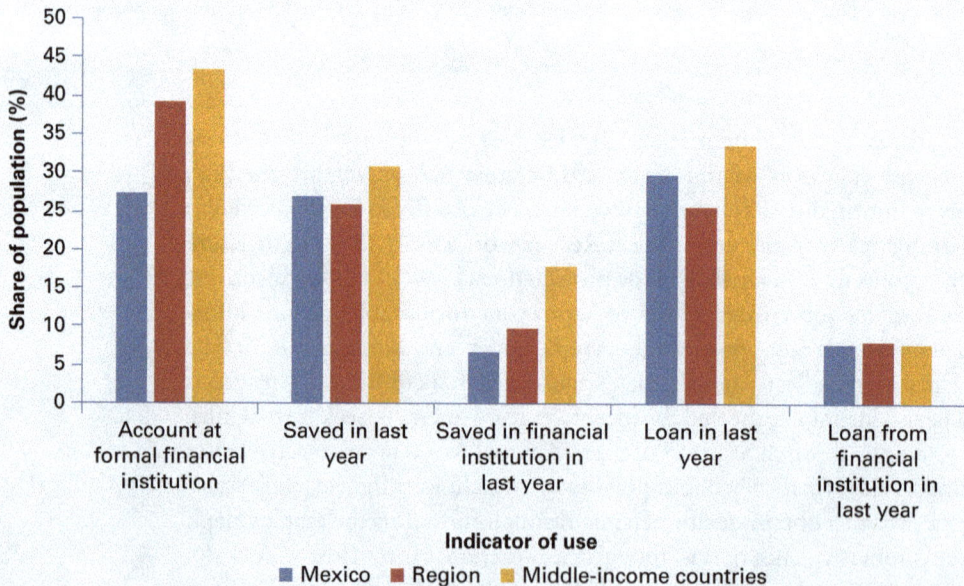

Source: Data of Global Financial Inclusion (Global Findex) Database, World Bank, Washington, DC, http://www.worldbank.org/globalfindex.

percent of all individuals 15 years of age or older had a bank account in 2011, compared with the average of 43 percent in middle-income countries. While the levels of savings in Mexico and other middle-income countries are similar (27 and 31 percent, respectively), only 7 percent of the population in Mexico saved money in a formal financial institution compared with 17 percent in middle-income countries. The incidence of borrowing in the financial sector is also low, though similar to the rates in the region and in middle-income countries: around 8 percent of borrowers borrow from formal financial institutions. A 2012 financial capability survey found that close to half the respondents reported they had used no financial services of any kind in the past year, and 42 percent had not used any financial service in the previous five years (Reddy, Bruhn, and Tan 2013). Households are vulnerable to financial risk: 70 percent of the respondents in the same survey reported they had regular or occasional shortfalls in meeting basic needs, such as housing and food, and one-third reported they would be unable to cover an unexpected major expense equal to a month's income.

Strengthening institutions

The improvements in access to services provide some evidence of the strength of institutions and their ability to deliver services. Over the past 20 years, there has been a significant expansion in services (see above). By 2010, access to sanitation had risen from 60 percent of the population to slightly less than 90 percent; electricity coverage became almost universal; and a lack of running water was affecting only half the share of the population affected in 1990. There have also been improvements in access to health care and education services.

The expansion of access to basic services has also become more equitable. The HOI showed improvement in 2000–10 (data do not exist for 1990). Between 2000 and 2010, the national values of the HOI increased from 58.6 to 70.1 (100 indicates full coverage) (Ortiz-Juárez and Pérez-García 2013). Circumstances play a smaller role in school enrollments and electricity access, and a larger role in sanitation and water access. Residence in urban or rural areas, per capita income, and parental educational attainment are the most relevant determinants of children's limited access to water and sanitation. However, the influence of circumstances was reduced between 2000 and 2012 in all areas of opportunity. Disparities in the HOI values for states showed a slight falloff over the last decade.[36] The states with the lowest HOI values in 2000 experienced larger improvements than states that began the period at higher values. This led to a narrowing in geographical opportunity gaps (figure 6.23). For example, the index in Oaxaca, among the poorest states, increased 49.8 percent, in Guerrero 37.2 percent, and in Chiapas 32.1 percent. In contrast, in states where the HOI had already been relatively high, the improvement was much smaller. For example, the HOI in Aguascalientes rose only 7.0 percent. Oaxaca started 2000 with an HOI of 30.0 percent, while Aguascalientes started at 80.0 percent.

Figure 6.23 The HOI, by State, Mexico, 2000 and 2010

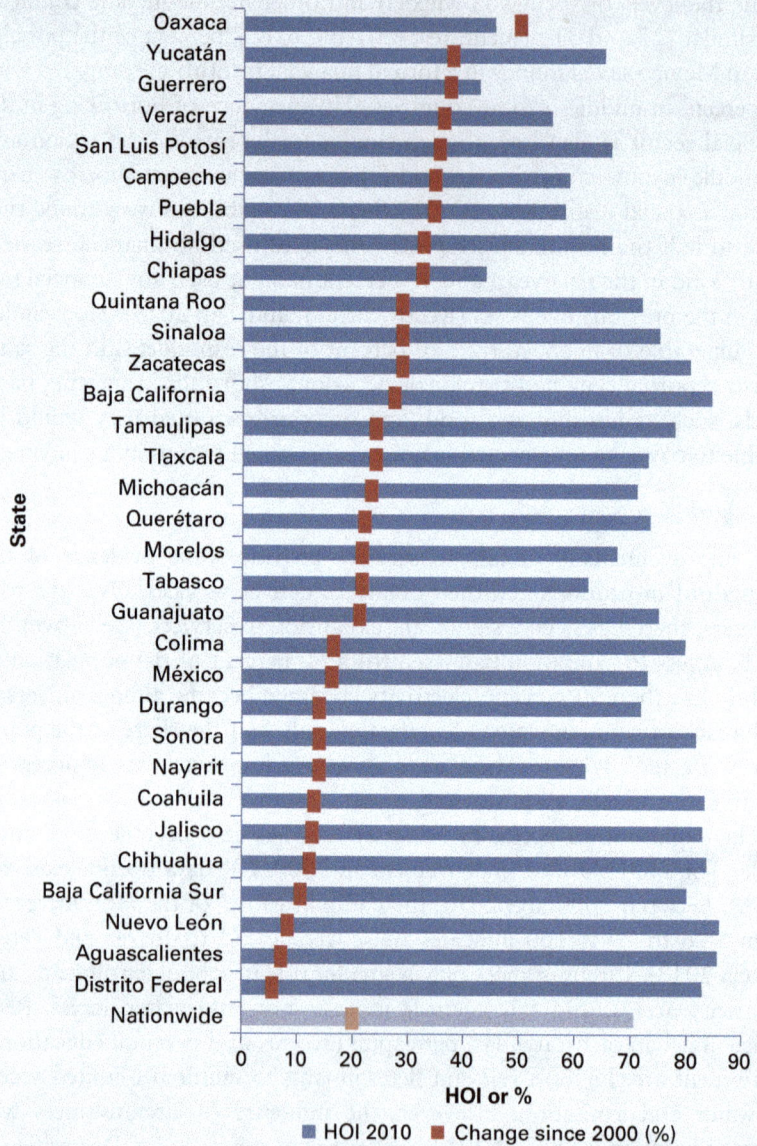

Source: Ortiz-Juárez and Pérez-García 2013.
Note: The circumstances used in this analysis are the gender of the child, gender of the
household head, urban or rural residence, incidence of physical or mental disabilities,
and educational attainment of the household head. HOI = human opportunity index.

However, improvements in human capital have not translated into higher
productivity, raising questions about the quality of educational services. In
a survey of firms, nearly a third of enterprises cited inadequate skills as an
obstacle to their performance.[37] About 43 percent of firms reported difficulty filling vacancies, substantially more than the 31 percent global average.

These difficulties do not apply to specialized occupations alone given that many low-skilled jobs are among the top 10 jobs that have been difficult to fill. In part, this may be because employers place a premium on soft skills (for example, discipline, ability to work in teams, and relating to others), along with the more traditional cognitive and technical skills. The seeming lack of skills raises questions about the quality of human capital accumulation.

The quality of services remains an issue. Despite rising access to education, Mexico still lags in educational achievement relative to other countries, including those in the region. Only 35 percent of Mexico's working-age population holds at least an upper-secondary educational certificate, which compares unfavorably with the 70 percent in Chile. The 2013 education census shows serious concerns about the quality of the education system: the census revealed poor school infrastructure and large numbers of employed teachers who were not actually working.[38] While enrollment rates are up, access to high-quality schooling is a concern. In 2012, Mexico had the lowest scores and passing rates in mathematics, reading, and science among the OECD countries and ranked 53rd among 65 countries in mathematics in the tests of the Program for International Student Assessment (PISA) (figure 6.24).[39] The country did see steady improvement in these scores from 2003 to 2009, but, by 2012, the positive trend had stopped or been reversed.[40] In addition, access to basic infrastructure within public schools is deficient. A substantial share of public schools suffer from lack of water, sanitation, and other features that are needed to support student achievement and avoid negative health consequences.[41] Private schools do not suffer from such deficiencies.

Mexico has embarked on efforts to improve the quality of its institutions and their ability to deliver services. The broad Social Development Law was passed in 2004 to increase the focus on evidence-based policy making by creating an obligation for the federal government to evaluate the social programs that it implements. In 2008, a constitutional reform around public expenditures and auditing established the incorporation of results-based budgeting for all three levels of government: federal, state, and municipal.[42] The emphasis is on ensuring that public spending matches priorities, that it is monitored and evaluated, and that this information is made public and used in program design and resource allocation. The overall goal is to improve the quality of public spending and service delivery. Additional reforms that strengthen the implementation of the results-based management approach include legislative reforms of the budgetary process (2006 and 2008), access to public information (2002 and 2010), and government accounting (2008).[43] The massive education reform, which was passed in 2012, seeks to enhance the quality of education. In particular, the reform proposes a standardized system for test-based hiring and promotion that would give the government the tools to make school staffing decisions based on objective teacher quality criteria. In the longer term, this is expected to raise the quality of public education and increase the skills of the labor force.

Figure 6.24 Quality of Education, 2012 PISA Results, OECD and the Region, 2012

a. Math scores, proficiency level 2

b. Reading scores, proficiency level 2

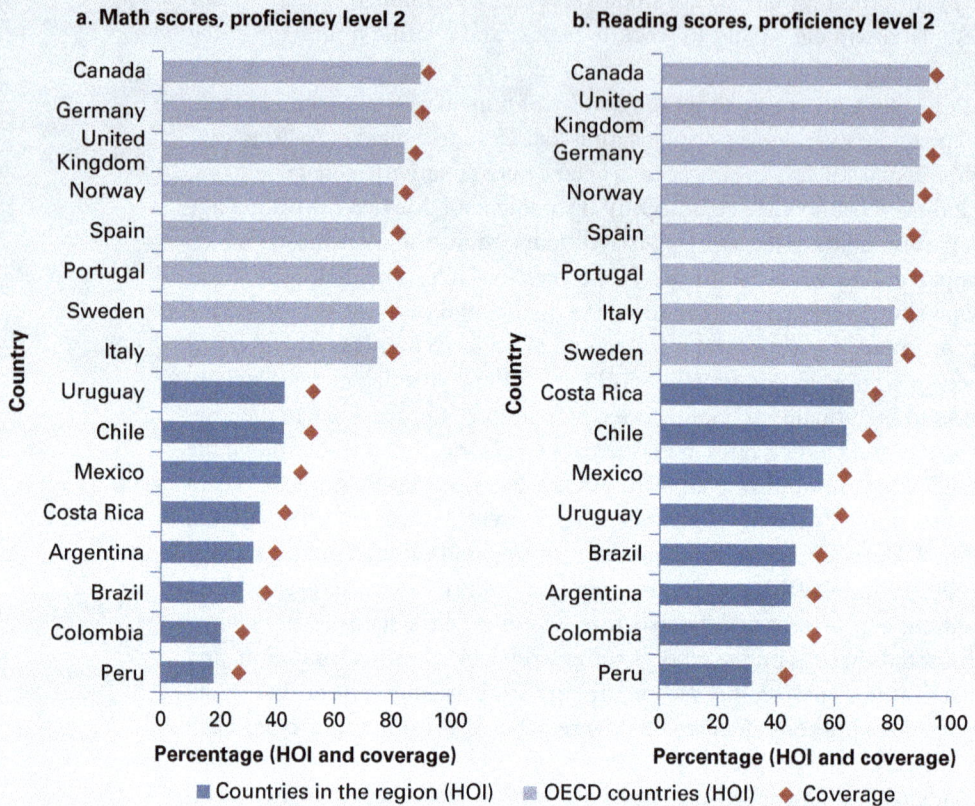

Source: Tabulations by Equity Lab, Team for Statistical Development, World Bank, Washington, DC, based on Program for International Student Assessment (PISA) data in OECD 2014.
Note: Coverage reports the percentage of each country's 15-year-olds who achieved a score of 2 or 3 on the PISA, while the human opportunity index (HOI) is the equity-adjusted coverage. The circumstances used to calculate equity adjustment in this analysis are the gender of the child, parental educational attainment, school location (region), the father's occupation, and a household wealth index (household assets). A score of proficiency level 2 is considered the minimum to apply the material successfully. The average among students in the OECD is proficiency level 3.

Mitigating risks

Along with crime and violence, natural disasters represent significant risks to the population of Mexico in terms of both fiscal risks for the country and welfare risks for households. Mexico is highly vulnerable to natural hazards: an estimated two-thirds of the population and GDP are at risk (de la Fuente 2010). The country is particularly at risk from earthquakes and hurricanes, although other hazards, such as droughts, volcanic eruptions, and other storms, affect significant shares of the population. The number of natural disasters and the number of people affected have risen over time (figure 6.25). Climate change is also expected to raise the frequency of extreme events, thereby increasing the risks to poor households given that the impacts of climate change tend to affect poorer households and poorer

Figure 6.25 Natural Disasters and Persons Affected, Mexico, 1940–2019

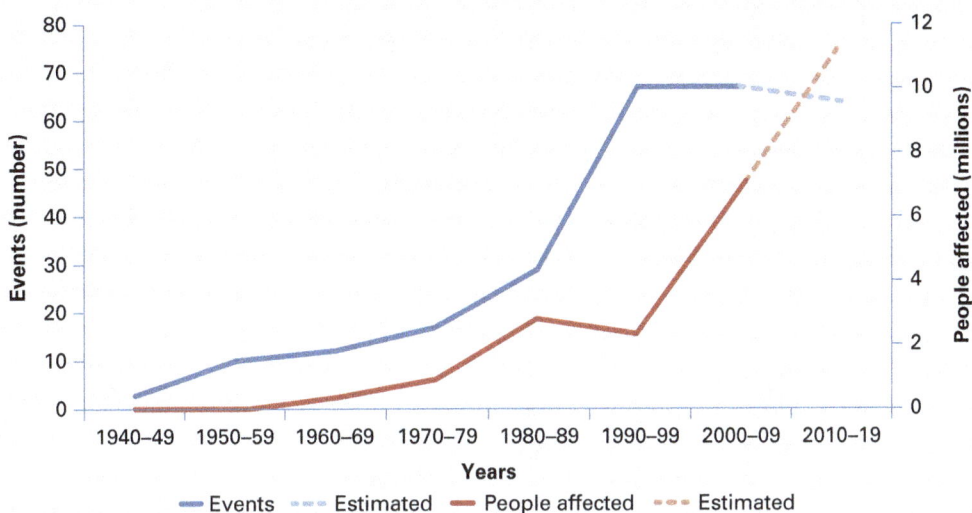

Source: EM-DAT (International Disaster Database), Centre for Research on the Epidemiology of Disasters, Université Catholique de Louvain, Brussels, http://www.emdat.be/database.

areas more heavily (Mearns and Norton 2009; Verner 2010). The costs of emergency response and reconstruction are high and variable: in 1999–2011, annual disaster spending was above $1.4 billion, while the costs in individual years ranged from $100 million to over $5 billion (World Bank 2012). The strong correlation between population density and the value of exposed infrastructure and construction highlights the poverty and fiscal challenges of natural hazards in the country (ERN 2011).

To address the fiscal risk of natural disasters, the government has taken an aggressive stance on disaster risk management.[44] As part of an integrated risk management strategy, it created the Fondo de Desastres Naturales (National Disaster Fund, FONDEN) in 1996 to address the costs of emergency response, recovery, and reconstruction. The mandate has involved a shift from a strictly postdisaster focus to a focus that also incorporates disaster prevention in part through build-back-better strategies. In 2005, FONDEN's mandate was expanded to include the design of a catastrophic risk coverage strategy, and, in 2006, the first sovereign bond for natural disasters was issued (for $450 million) against the risk of earthquakes. In 2009, a second bond was issued to cover earthquakes and hurricanes. In 2011, insurance contracts for $400 million were taken by FONDEN, and these were subsequently renewed.

Despite significant progress in addressing the fiscal risks of natural disasters, the ability of households to cope with natural disasters is limited. The vulnerability to natural hazards and poverty are strongly correlated in Mexico. Poorer households located in hazard-prone areas are more vulnerable, and poorer households are often located in areas more susceptible to natural hazard. Across municipalities, there is a significant correlation between marginalization and seismic and hydrological risks.[45] Mansilla (2008) finds that municipalities with larger populations of the marginalized experience sharply more severe housing damage and destruction during natural disasters relative to municipalities with fewer marginalized. The combination of poverty and vulnerability to risk translates into greater and more persistent disaster impacts on poorer households and communities (Báez and Santos 2006; Carter et al. 2007; de Janvry et al. 2006). In the case of Mexico, Rodríguez-Oreggia et al. (2013) show that natural disasters reduce human development and increase poverty. Over the five-year period covered by their analysis, the areas affected by natural disasters suffered, on average, a loss of two years of human development gains. Given the lack of access to social assistance programs and insurance, the vulnerability of households to natural disasters continues to be a significant source of risk in Mexico (de la Fuente, Ortiz-Juárez, and Rodríguez-Castelán 2015).

Final Remarks: The Policy Challenge

The question asked at the start of this chapter is whether or not Mexico is on the path to shared prosperity. The analysis here indicates that Mexico has taken important steps toward enhancing household welfare by improving access to services and basic infrastructure. However, parallel improvements in monetary poverty have not occurred. The analysis provides insights into the causes of this disconnect between nonmonetary and monetary poverty.

- Until 2012, Mexico was a victim of the global economic slowdown and, in particular, the slow recovery in the United States, its biggest market. The slowdown had multiple effects. It lowered investment and thus job creation. It also restricted a key source of income, remittances, and closed a major source of labor demand for Mexicans. The national labor market has been unable to absorb this expansion in labor supply. However, the stronger economic recovery of the United States relative to Europe may contribute to more growth and more poverty reduction in Mexico.
- Significant progress has been made in boosting the assets of the population generally and the poor in particular. Education levels, access to health care services, and access to basic infrastructure have all improved. Sharp differences in access related to children's circumstances remain and are limiting opportunities.
- There has been a disassociation between growth and employment creation. The quality of jobs has declined. Wages have fallen, and the informality rate has not been reduced. There needs to be an emphasis on raising the quality of jobs and addressing the factors constraining labor productivity.

- Fiscal policy can help reduce poverty and inequality, but, so far, Mexico has not been as successful as other countries in the region. The more effective targeting of resources and a reduction in spending on regressive programs may represent a means to achieve better welfare outcomes.

- The inadequate quality of services may be limiting the impact of recent expansions in government services. Access to services and social assistance has expanded dramatically, demonstrating the ability of the government to improve human capital and reduce vulnerability. However, converting these gains into household income generation has been a greater challenge. Prospera has raised health care and education among the poor, but program beneficiaries have not been able to take advantage of their newly acquired human capital in labor markets because there have not been enough jobs or earnings have been inadequate, given that the returns to education have also declined.

- Many markets function imperfectly. The energy and telecommunications sectors are clear examples of the deficiencies in competitiveness. Major reforms designed to address these issues are under way.[46] Labor markets continue to be characterized by rigidities that promote informality and depress demand. Financial markets are limited, and access to formal financial services are far from universal.

- Risk is affecting the economy in various ways, thereby exacerbating vulnerability and preventing households from lifting themselves out of poverty or remaining out of poverty. Crime and violence are a drain on the economy and are generating substantial direct and indirect costs. Despite a proactive approach to disaster-risk management, large swathes of the country are frequently subjected to natural disasters.

- Increasing productivity is a critical path to reducing poverty and promoting shared prosperity. The lack of job creation in higher-productivity sectors and the persistence of informal employment are barriers to income gains among poorer households. The main challenge is to remove the obstacles to the creation and expansion of high-productivity jobs and firms.

A serious package of structural reforms is ongoing in Mexico. Many of these reforms are designed to address the root causes of low productivity and the limited reduction of monetary poverty and to promote what the government calls democratizing the economy. The reforms focus on lowering the costs of key inputs to production and improving the efficiency and effectiveness of various sectors of the economy. In parallel, the government is supporting a wide range of social protection programs and has revised the Prospera flagship program to link the extreme poor to this wider range of programs more closely and thus address the multidimensional aspects of poverty.[47] The critical reforms are in the areas of fiscal policy, education, financial markets, labor markets, energy, and telecommunications.

It is too early to assess the effects of the package of reforms. However, the current administration's reform package has the potential to affect welfare and shared prosperity in a variety of ways. Several of the reforms will directly affect deprivations under the MPI, particularly deprivations in education, social protection, and food security. The ongoing education reform aims to address critical issues related to the access to and quality of education, thereby enhancing equity and labor skills.[48] The proposed universal pension would expand social security coverage and affect poverty by extending pensions to an additional two million elderly. The Cruzada Nacional contra el Hambre (National Crusade against Hunger), a flagship government welfare program, is designed to fill the constitutional right (Article 4) of the population to sufficient and nutritious food, a concern among the lowest population quintile and indigenous groups, which suffer from elevated levels of malnutrition (stunting is 25.6 percent among the former and 33.0 percent among the latter) (INSP 2012).

The quantity and quality of jobs could be affected by reforms in the financial sector, labor markets, and education. Financial sector reforms aimed at expanding lending are designed to boost growth and job creation by increasing financial intermediation and lowering credit constraints.[49] Reforms that attack the labor market rigidities affecting job creation—in 2012, Mexico ranked 23rd among 183 countries in employment rigidity (World Bank 2012)—could open up new employment.[50] Reforms that lead to higher quality in education will be critical to productivity and income gains. The expansion of the education system has been substantial, and education is a key area of government spending that makes the fiscal system progressive and reduces inequality. However, if it does not ensure education quality and the ability of the education system to create a skilled labor force, the expansion cannot live up to the promise.

Not all reforms are poverty reducing. Attention needs to be paid to mitigating negative impacts. Changes in the telecommunications and energy sectors have the potential to reduce the associated costs to households and businesses, but the immediate result of the recent fiscal reform has likely been to raise the cost and lower the consumption of particular goods.[51] The rise in the value of the poverty line has outpaced the increases in the overall consumer price index because fuel subsidies are being eliminated, and world food prices have gone up and remain high.[52] There is also the potential that labor market reforms will deepen the vulnerability of workers. Ensuring that the reforms contribute to shared prosperity and extreme poverty reduction will require that attention be paid to the mitigation of any negative or unexpected effects on welfare.

Annex 6A Data Sources

Numerous welfare indicators are used in Mexico, but not all of them provide coverage over the full 20-year period under review. Nor are there longitudinal data at the household level. To provide a picture of poverty and shared prosperity over the entire period, this chapter relies on a combination of measures and data sources.

The multidimensional poverty index

Mexico presently uses the MPI, a multidimensional measure of poverty that takes into account both income (monetary) poverty and multiple indicators of social deprivation (nonmonetary poverty).[53] The new measure reflects basic rights outlined in the Mexican Constitution and combines these social rights components with a more standard income component to create a broad, multidimensional indicator of welfare. The specific components measured by the MPI are (1) current income per capita; (2) gaps in educational attainment; (3) access to health care services; (4) access to social security; (5) the quality and available room in the dwelling, including the materials used in construction; (6) access to basic services in the dwelling such as electricity, drainage (sanitation), and water; and (7) access to food: moderate or severe food insecurity is a deprivation.[54] According to this new official poverty measure, individuals are considered poor if their incomes are below a well-being line (income poverty) and if they are deprived in at least one nonincome area. Moreover, individuals are considered to be among the extreme poor if their incomes are below the minimum well-being line and if they face three or more social deprivations.[55]

A long-term measure of nonmonetary poverty: the IPS-8

Because the official MPI measure was first implemented in 2008 and measurement occurs only every two years, relevant data are available for only three years, 2008, 2010, and 2012. Another indicator, the IPS-8, has been constructed to fill the gap and measure nonmonetary poverty over the longer term. The index measures welfare at the municipal level (not the household) based on a subset of the MPI deprivations derived from the population censuses of 1990, 2000, and 2010.[56] Because the data set represents municipal-level indicators, a longitudinal data set on municipalities has been constructed to show movements into and out of poverty, as well as evidence on convergence.

The monetary measure of poverty: income

Prior to the adoption of the MPI, the country used a purely monetary measure of poverty (income). A comparable income series exists that allows the study of shifts in poverty and inequality across households since 1992. The series is based on the Encuesta Nacional de Ingresos y Gastos de los Hogares-Tradicional (Income and Expenditure Survey, the traditional ENIGH) carried out by the Instituto Nacional de Estadística y Geografía (National Institute of Statistics and Geography, INEGI). The survey is conducted every two years.

Panel data on monetary poverty and inequality

Recent work under the auspices of the Consejo Nacional de Evaluación de la Política de Desarrollo Social (National Council for the Evaluation of

Table 6A.1 Measures of Poverty, by Data Source, Level of Disaggregation, and Availability, Mexico

Indicator	Source	Level of disaggregation	Years measure is available
Monetary poverty (income)	Traditional ENIGH	National, urban and rural areas, some states	1992, 1994, 1996, 2000, 2002, 2004–06, 2008, 2010, 2012
	Estimates based on the ENIGH	Nationwide, states, municipalities	1990, 2000, 2010
Multidimensional poverty index (MPI)	*Modulo de Condiciones Socioeconomicas* (Socioeconomic Conditions Module, MCS-ENIGH)	National, urban and rural areas, states	2008, 2010, 2012
	Estimates based on the MCS-ENIGH and the population census	Nationwide, states, municipalities	2010
Social deprivation index (IPS-8)	Population census	Nationwide, states, municipalities	1990, 2000, 2010

Social Development Policy, CONEVAL) and the World Bank takes advantage of small area estimation techniques and the fact that, in addition to the national population census every decade, Mexico carries out a sample census (the *Conteo*) midway between censuses to generate municipal monetary and nonmonetary measures of income (Ortiz-Juárez and Pérez-García 2013).[57] (The range of data sources available are illustrated in table 6A.1; box 6A.1 provides details on differences in income aggregates.) Because the municipal panel data set includes welfare measures on the nearly 2,500 municipalities in Mexico, it allows trends in poverty and shared prosperity to be tracked at a much finer level of disaggregation and over a longer period (20 years) than is usually the case. The data also provide a platform to examine issues of convergence and associated factors in welfare across the country. In addition, the longer-term view helps highlight areas of chronic poverty and areas of significant success. Investigating both can offer insights into how the country can reach the goal of *Mexico Incluyente* (inclusive Mexico), the term used in the National Development Plan, 2013–18.

Adjusted series for the social deprivation index, 1990–2010

In addition to the traditional monetary indicators of poverty and inequality that exist back to 1992, CONEVAL has created a series based on nonmonetary indicators using the population censuses of 1990, 2000, and 2010, the IPS-8. The IPS-8 is a variation of the social rights component used in the official methodology for the calculation of the MPI (CONEVAL 2009).

The adjusted IPS-8 includes eight social deprivation indicators: (1) educational gaps, (2) the quality of the floors in the dwelling, (3) the quality of the ceiling in the dwelling, (4) the quality of the walls in the dwelling,

Box 6A.1 Income Aggregates, Mexico[a]

In addition to the various welfare measures used in Mexico, income aggregates may differ across institutions. Some of these differences arise because of differences in the way in which the income aggregates are constructed. Others may arise because of reliance on separate surveys, especially given the introduction of the the Modulo de Condiciones Socioeconomicas (Socioeconomic Conditions Module, MCS-ENIGH) in 2008. Still others may arise because of the use of different reference periods.

The MCS-ENIGH incorporates two major changes in methodology relative to the traditional Encuesta Nacional de Ingresos y Gastos de los Hogares (Household Income and Expenditure Survey, ENIGH) (table B6A.1.1). First, it excludes imputed rent from the income aggregate. Adding or subtracting a component of income will either increase or decrease the total income of certain households. Second, it uses an adult equivalent scale to reflect economies of scale. Depending on the number of children in a household, the results may differ substantially from a simple per capita measure.

Table B6A.1.1 Differences between the Traditional ENIGH and the MCS-ENIGH, Mexico

	Income type (monetary and nonmonetary)		Components of total household income	Individual total household income
Survey (entity)	Labor income	Nonlabor income	Imputed rent	Methodology
MCS-ENIGH (CONEVAL)	Salaries of wage earners; income of self-employed (including self-consumption); other labor income	Transfers (public and private), capital	No	Adult equivalence scale
Traditional ENIGH (INEGI)	Salaries of wage earners; income of self-employed (including self-consumption); other labor income	Transfers (public and private), capital	Yes	Per capita

a. The SEDLAC harmonized data set (valuable in carrying out cross-country comparisons in the Latin America and the Caribbean region), which is not used in this chapter, also differs in the calculation of income aggregates. For the SEDLAC per capita income variable, labor income includes salaries for wage earners, income for the self-employed (including self-consumption), and other labor income; nonlabor income includes public and private transfers and other transfers; imputed rent is included. Also, income is calculated over the previous month, while the traditional ENIGH represents a six-month average. See SEDLAC.
b. CONEVAL = National Council for the Evaluation of Social Development Policy.
c. INEGI = National Institute of Statistics and Geography.

(5) the rooms available in the dwelling, (6) access to clean water, (7) access to sanitation, and (8) access to electricity. Other indicators such as access to health care and access to social security, which were included in the official MPI from 2008 to 2012, are not included in the IPS-8 because of data limitations.

The methodology is based on Alkire and Foster (2011) wherein the intensity of the social deprivation *(M)* is expressed by the following formula:

$$M = \frac{1}{nd} \sum_{i=1n}^{} \sum_{j=1}^{d} w_j \cdot \left(1 - \frac{x_{ij}}{z_j}\right) \qquad (6A.1)$$

where x_{ij} is the number of nonmonetary deprivations, j, that individual i faces; z_j is the minimum number (threshold) of the indicator (higher values are considered deprivations) for each deprivation j; d is the total number of deprivations j; and w_j are the weights of deprivation so that $j = \sum_{j=1}^{d} w_j = d$.

The main feature of M is that it measures the level of deprivation using two criteria: (1) a threshold that identifies individuals with deprivation in one component j (if $x_{ij} < z_j$) and (2) an interdimensional threshold (k) that indicates the minimum number of deprivations required to consider an individual poor. Thus, M reflects the proportion of individuals with social deprivations, multiplied by the intensity of the deprivation.

Annex 6B Migration and the Labor Force

The overall growth in the labor force between 2005 and 2010 was 12.4 percent, representing a total of nearly six million new people (table 6B.1). If the total number of migrants to the United States from Mexico had remained at the level of 2004, an additional 2.26 million people would have emigrated to the United States than actually did in 2005–10. The share of these who were of working age is not clear, but data on returnees show that one-quarter are children. Assuming that children and economically inactive adults are also migrating to the United States, this 2.26 million people probably overstates the working-age population still in Mexico that would have migrated in a previous period.

The change in returns is also dramatic. The only available data points are taken from the 2000 and 2010 population censuses, which ask about

Table 6B.1 Labor Force Growth Rates, Mexico, 2005–10

Indicator	2005	2006	2007	2008	2009	2010	Growth rate
Labor force	44,845,642	46,367,100	47,400,119	48,549,880	48,606,636	50,387,831	12.4
Labor force if outmigration remained at the previous level[a]	44,845,642	—	—	—	—	48,896,231	9.0
Labor force if outmigration and returnees remained at the previous level[b]	44,845,642	—	—	—	—	48,421,031	8.0

Sources: Migration data: Passel, Cohn, and Gonzalez-Barrera 2012. Labor force data: WDI (World Development Indicators) (database), World Bank, Washington, DC, http://data.worldbank.org/data-catalog/world-development-indicators.
Note: — = not available.
a. Assumes that migration to the United States remained at the level of 2004, that is, 2.26 million, of whom two-thirds were of working age.
b. Assumes that migration to the United States remained at the level of 2004, that is, 2.26 million people, of whom two-thirds were of working age. Also assumes there would be additional returnees, that is, 720,000 people, of whom two-thirds are of working age.

Figure 6B.1 Migration Patterns, Mexico, 1991–2009

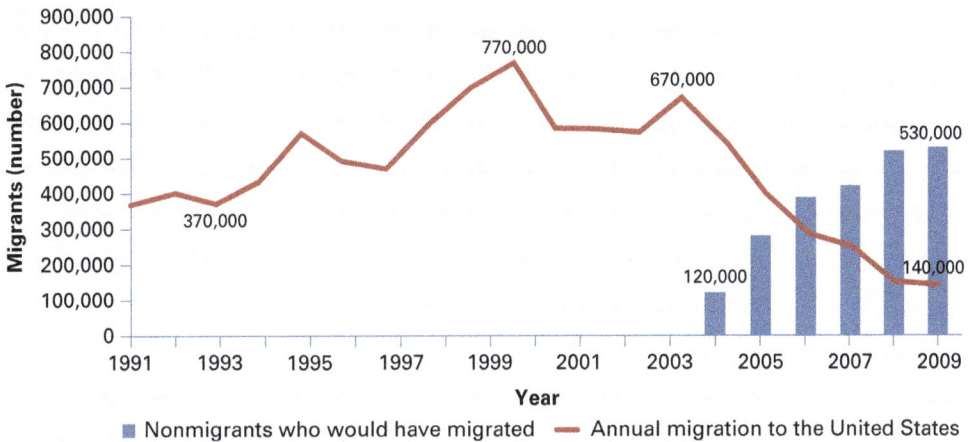

Source: Data on migration to the United States: Passel, Cohn, and Gonzalez-Barrera 2012.
Note: The blue bars represent people who did not migrate, but would have if the 2004 migration level had been maintained through 2005–10.

returns in the previous five years. According to this information, 670,000 people returned in 1995–2000, and 1.39 million people returned in 2005–10 (figure 6B.1). Of these, 300,000 were children.

If, from the labor force in 2010, one subtracts the people who would have been migrants if the 2004 migration pattern had held, the growth rate of the labor force would have been 9 percent, which is similar to the rate in 2000–05. (However, given that some fraction of the migrants were not of working age or were not economically active, only two-thirds of the flows are subtracted, not the full 2.26 million). If the individuals who would have been migrants if migration patterns had not changed and if the rate of returning migrants had held at the previous level (once more assuming only two-thirds were of working age), the growth in the labor force would have been 8 percent: 4 percentage points below the actual growth rate.

Notes

1. Other factors in the recent slowdown are constraints in the supply of natural gas to manufacturing firms, the decline in real public spending, and the drop-off in construction because of financial challenges facing larger construction firms. The data are from the Global Financial Inclusion (Global Findex) Database, World Bank, Washington, DC, http://www.worldbank.org/globalfindex.

2. WITS (World Integrated Trade Solutions) (database), World Bank, Washington, DC, http://wits.worldbank.org/WITS/.

3. The fall in net migration to the United States is consistent with recent evidence indicating that Mexican immigrant employment is more sensitive to the

business cycle than that of other groups in the United States and is more likely to be vulnerable during an economic downturn (Orrenius and Zavodny 2010).

4. See "Plan Nacional de Desarrollo 2013–2018," *Diario Oficial de la Federación,* Segunda Sección (May 20, 2013, 57).

5. See "Migración," Población, Hogares y Vivienda (database), Instituto Nacional de Estadística y Geografía, Aguascalientes, Mexico, http://www3.inegi.org .mx/sistemas/temas/default.aspx?s=est&c=17484.

6. See annex 6A for a full description of the various data series used in this chapter.

7. Before 2009, Mexico used three poverty lines: (a) food poverty (extreme poverty), (b) capabilities poverty, and (c) asset poverty (moderate poverty). The food poor are those people who do not have the purchasing power to acquire a basic food basket each month. The capabilities poor are those people who do not have the income necessary to cover a basic food basket, plus basic achievements in health care and education each month. The asset poor are those households that do not have sufficient income to cover the expenditures associated with capabilities realization, plus the costs of housing and transportation each month.

8. A Datt-Ravaillon decomposition relying on data in the harmonized Socio-Economic Database for Latin America and the Caribbean (SEDLAC) and an international poverty line of $4 per capita per day shows that, since 2003, only one-third of the reduction in poverty has been linked to economic growth, while redistribution explains the rest. See Datt and Ravaillon (1992) and SEDLAC, Center for Distributive, Labor, and Social Studies, Universidad Nacional de La Plata, La Plata, Argentina; World Bank, Washington, DC, http://sedlac.econo.unlp.edu.ar/eng/index.php.

9. Net commodity exports reached 10 percent of GDP in South America in 2010, while they were close to 0 percent in Central America and Mexico (Adler and Sosa 2011).

10. This is based on the small area estimates of income poverty for 2,453 municipalities reported by Ortiz-Juárez and Pérez-García (2013).

11. Comparable data do not exist for 2012; it is unclear how much change there might be at the municipal level. Four municipalities were dropped from the analysis because of data issues.

12. This program was launched in 1997 as the *Progresa* Program. The name was subsequently changed to the *Oportunidades* Program and, more recently, to Prospera. Before becoming Prospera, the program was a straight conditional cash transfer program. The new Prospera program adds preferential access to 29 other government programs to the conditional cash transfer benefit.

13. In the most recent period, 2010–12, there were three possible indicators. The Instituto Nacional de Estadística y Geografía (National Institute of Statistics and Geography, INEGI) official series (the traditional *Encuesta Nacional de Ingresos y Gastos de los Hogares* [Household Income and Expenditure Survey, ENIGH]) indicates a slight widening, from 0.435 in 2010 to 0.440 in 2012, though it is not statistically significant. The SEDLAC database also suggests that inequality widened between 2010 and 2012. In contrast, the new official series spanning 2008–12 based on official data of *Consejo Nacional de Evaluación de la Política de Desarrollo Social* (National Council for the Evaluation of Social Development Policy, CONEVAL), the *Modulo de Condiciones*

Socioeconomicas (Socioeconomic Conditions Module, MCS-ENIGH), indicates that the Gini coefficient fell slightly, from 0.51 to 0.50 between 2010 and 2012, though the change was statistically insignificant.

14. *Encuesta ESRU de Movilidad Social en México,* Centro de Estudios Espinosa Yglesias, Mexico City: the first round was carried out in 2006, and the second in 2012.

15. The comparison with other countries may be affected by the different time periods studied across countries.

16. Because of changes in methodology between 2008 and 2010, only the data on 2010–12 are strictly comparable.

17. Data of CONEVAL show that the population 65 years and older without access to social security declined from 28.8 to 26.5 percent in 2010–12, suggesting some positive impact of the program, although the change was not sufficient to show up in the multidimensional poverty index (MPI) measure. In 2012 and 2013, the program was expanded to cover all persons over 65 years of age (the program was formerly called *70 y Más*) without access to contributory pensions from the National Social Security Institute and the State Employees Social Security and Social Services Institute.

18. The decompositions lack robustness in explaining small changes in poverty; for this reason, an analysis of the full period is not included here.

19. Data of WDI (World Development Indicators) (database), World Bank, Washington, DC, http://data.worldbank.org/data-catalog/world-development-indicators.

20. See "Plan Nacional de Desarrollo 2013–2018," *Diario Oficial de la Federación,* Segunda Sección (May 20, 2013, 57). The fact that, for many Central American migrants, Mexico is a transit country adds to the difficulties of estimating migrant populations in Mexico.

21. Based on household survey data (ENIGH), labor force participation rates rose less slowly among the bottom 40 than among the top 60 (9.8 and 10.8 percent, respectively) between 1992 and 2002, but this was reversed in 2002–12, when the rate among the bottom 40 increased by 8.5 percent, compared with 7.0 percent among the top 60.

22. Data of WDI (World Development Indicators) (database), World Bank, Washington, DC, http://data.worldbank.org/data-catalog/world-development-indicators.

23. More generally, productivity is lower than official measures indicate. In an in-depth analysis of productivity in the services sector, Soloaga and Serrano (2013) find that the indicators are upward biased. This is because older, more formal firms are more likely to be included in the sample. Informal enterprises are excluded from most enterprise surveys. Meléndez (2013) discovers similar results in Colombia.

24. The levels of homicides unrelated to drugs did not have this effect (Enamorado, López-Calva, and Rodríguez-Castelán 2014).

25. Enterprise Surveys (database), International Finance Corporation and World Bank, Washington, DC, http://www.enterprisesurveys.org.

26. López-Calva et al. (2013) estimate social spending in 2010 at 8.6 percent of gross domestic product, but also document a strong increase: the absolute value of social spending rose 29.0 percent between 1996 and 2010.

27. This is derived from an alternative definition of budgeted government expenditure suggested by Scott (2014) that excludes debt servicing and tax devolutions to the states, but also state energy enterprises. Much of the analysis here draws on Scott (2014).

28. According to Araujo and Sandoval (2012), transfers from Oportunidades (now Prospera) resulted in a reduction of extreme poverty by 3.4 percentage points nationwide and 9.6 percentage points in rural areas. Several independent researchers have undertaken rigorous impact evaluations that demonstrate the positive impacts on health, nutrition, and education and shaped the program's design (Levy 2006, 2008; Skoufias 2005).

29. The data are from the Comisión Nacional de Protección Social en Salud (National Commission for Social Protection in Health).

30. Less than 5 percent of the subsidies go to the poorest household decile (Scott 2011).

31. See Doing Business (database), International Finance Corporation and World Bank, Washington, DC, http://www.doingbusiness.org/data.

32. WEO (World Economic Outlook) Database, International Monetary Fund, Washington, DC, http://www.imf.org/external/ns/cs.aspx?id=28.

33. The 2002 expansion of Banco Azteca into stores led to an increase in employment, income, and new businesses in the areas with the new branch offices (Bruhn and Love 2009).

34. Data of the Secretaría de Desarrollo Social (Secretariat of Social Development) on payment methods.

35. The proposed reforms include raising the competency of banks, bringing down the cost of credit, helping firms obtain credit, expanding credit to small and medium enterprises by increasing the lending of the national development bank, strengthening financial authorities in the effort to promote lending and improving regulations, and providing safeguards for consumers of financial services.

36. Ortiz-Juárez and Pérez-García (2013) estimate a nonparametric variant of the human opportunity index (HOI) to measure differences and changes across states between 2000 and 2010. The estimation was carried out for children between 5 and 15 years of age and relied on the following indicators of service access: the household is not overcrowded; the home has a finished floor, electricity, running water, a flush toilet, and access to sewage disposal; and school attendance. The circumstances considered were gender of the children, gender of the household head, rural or urban location, incidence of physical or mental disabilities, and educational attainment of the household head.

37. See "Mexico (2010)," Enterprise Surveys (database), International Finance Corporation and World Bank, Washington, DC, http://www.enterprisesurveys .org/data/exploreeconomies/2010/mexico.

38. Of the schools included in the census (23,000 in three states refused to participate), 69 percent lacked running water, and only slightly more than half had proper drainage (sanitation). See "Censo de Escuelas, Maestros y Alumnos de Educación Básica y Especial," Instituto Nacional de Estadística y Geografía and Secretaria de Educación Pública, Mexico City, http://www.censo.sep.gob .mx/. Of all people registered on school payrolls, 13 percent do not show up to work (INEGI and SEP 2014). In the state of Hidalgo, 1,440 teachers were

registered with the same birth date (December 12, 1912), meaning that they were 102 years old.

39. See "Figure 6: PISA Results for Mexico" (OECD 2013, 21), http://dx.doi .org/10.1787/eco_surveys-mex-2013-graph6-en.

40. Mathematics scores went from 385 in 2003, to 406 in 2006, 419 in 2009, and then down to 413 in 2012. The reading scores started at 400, went up for the next two testing periods to 425, and then, in 2012, were 424. In science, the scores moved from 410 in 2006, to 416, and then 415 in 2012 (OECD 2013, 2014).

41. Among public schools, 48 percent lack access to sewerage; 31 percent have no running water; and 11 percent do not have electricity (INEGI and SEP 2014).

42. *Diario Oficial de la Federación* (May 7, 2008).

43. See, respectively, *Ley Federal de Presupuesto y Responsabilidad Hacendaria 2006 and Reforma Constitucional,* Artículo 134, 2008; *Ley Federal de Transparencia y Acceso a la Información Gubernamental* 2002 and *Ley federal de Protección de datos Personales en posesión de los particulares*; and *Ley General de Contabilidad Gubernamental* 2008.

44. This description of the Fondo de Desastres Naturales (National Disaster Fund, FONDEN) is based largely on World Bank (2012).

45. The analysis of marginality is based on the index constructed by the *Consejo Nacional de Población y Vivienda* (National Population Council) and risk levels described in Cruz, de la Fuente, and Soriano (2011).

46. For details on these reforms, see "Decreto por el que se reforman y adicionan diversas disposiciones de los artículos 6o., 7o., 27, 28, 73, 78, 94 y 105 de la Constitución Política de los Estados Unidos Mexicanos, en materia de telecomunicaciones," *Diario Oficial de la Federación* (June 11, 2013), and "Decreto por el que se reforman y adicionan diversas disposiciones de la Constitución Política de los Estados Unidos Mexicanos, en Materia de Energía," *Diario Oficial de la Federación* (December 20, 2013).

47. The reformulation of the Oportunidades Program into Prospera incorporated new benefits in six areas: (a) education: scholarships for college education and technical careers; (b) health: more services and interventions under the basic package for enrollees in Seguro Popular; (c) nutrition: pregnant women and children under 5 years old receive food supplements; (d) financial inclusion: improved access to financial services such as loans, life insurance, and savings accounts; (e) labor markets: the Servicio Nacional de Empleo (National Employment Agency) has established training as a priority; and (f) productivity: priority access to 15 programs.

48. See "Decreto por el que se reforman los artículos 3o., 4o., 9o., 37, 65 y 66; y se adicionan los artículos 12 y 13 de la Ley General de Educación," *Diario Oficial de la Federación* (June 10, 2013).

49. The evidence is mixed. Hsieh and Olken (2014) find no evidence of credit constraints, although others find such evidence in Mexico and elsewhere. See De Mel, McKenzie, and Woodruff (2008) on Sri Lanka; McKenzie and Woodruff (2008) on Mexico; and Udry and Anagol (2006) on Ghana, although they focus on agriculture.

50. Doing Business (database), International Finance Corporation and World Bank, Washington, DC, http://www.doingbusiness.org/data.

51. The main food groups affected by the fiscal reform are high-calorie, low-nutrition foods (*comida chatarra*: junk food) and sugary drinks. According to the Encuesta Nacional de Salud y Nutrición 2012 (National Health and Nutrition Survey), close to 40 percent of adult women and about 27 percent of men are obese, and the share of overweight and obese adults has been steadily rising. Because of the obesity crisis in Mexico, there are possible health benefits from decreased consumption. Charcoal is the other item that has seen a reduction in use because of the new tax rates; for environmental reasons, a shift away from this fuel is likely beneficial. It is not clear what people are shifting to, however, nor how this is affecting household spending.

52. Although the world price of oil has fallen, which should mitigate some of the effects of the elimination of subsidies, the domestic price does not fully reflect these changes.

53. The MPI was adopted under the Ley General de Desarrollo Social of 2004 and first applied in 2008.

54. The MPI is calculated using the MCS-ENIGH, which differs from the data on monetary poverty produced using the traditional ENIGH.

55. For more on the methodology, see CONEVAL (2009).

56. See annex 6A for details on how the índice de privación social recortado (adjusted social deprivation index, IPS-8), has been constructed.

57. See Censos and Conteos de Población y Vivienda (database), Instituto Nacional de Estadística y Geografía, Aguascalientes, Mexico, http://www.inegi.org.mx /est/contenidos/proyectos/ccpv/default.aspx.

References

Acemoglu, Daron, and Robert Shimer. 2000. "Productivity Gains from Unemployment Insurance." *European Economic Review* 44 (7): 1195–1224.

Adler, Gustavo, and Sebastián Sosa. 2011. "Latin America's Commodity Dependence: What if the Boom Turns to Bust?" *iMFdirect* (blog), November 11. http:// blog-imfdirect.imf.org/2011/11/01/latin-americas-commodity-dependence-what-if-the-boom-turns-to-bust/.

Alkire, Sabina, and James Foster. 2011. "Counting and Multidimensional Poverty Measurement." *Journal of Public Economics* 95 (7–8): 476–87.

Araujo, María Caridad, and Carlos Sandoval. 2012. "La contribución del Programa de Desarrollo Humano Oportunidades a los ingresos de los hogares de México: un análisis de la Encuesta Nacional de Ingresos y Gastos de 2010." Inter-American Development Bank, Washington, DC.

Arias, J., and G. Esquivel. 2012. "A Note on the Side Effects of the War on Drugs: Labor Market Outcomes in Mexico." Unpublished working paper, cited in Ted Enamorado, Luis F. López-Calva, and Carlos Rodríguez-Castelán. 2014. "Crime and Growth Convergence: Evidence from Mexico." *Economic Letters* 125 (1): 9–13.

Aterido, Reyes, Mary Hallward-Driemeier, and Carmen Pagés. 2011. "Does Expanding Health Insurance beyond Formal-Sector Workers Encourage Informality?: Measuring the Impact of Mexico's Seguro Popular." IDB Working Paper 81001, Inter-American Development Bank, Washington, DC.

Azuara, Oliver, and Ioana Marinescu. 2013. "Informality and the Expansion of Social Protection Programs: Evidence from Mexico." *Journal of Health Economics* 32 (5): 938–50.

Báez, Javier E., and Indhira V. Santos. 2006. "Children's Vulnerability to Weather Shocks: Natural Disaster as Natural Experiment." Paper presented at the Latin American and Caribbean Economic Association's 11th Annual Meeting, Mexico City, November 3.

Bolio, Eduardo, Jaana Remes, Tomás Lajous, James Manyika, Morten Rossé, and Eugenia Ramirez. 2014. "A Tale of Two Mexicos: Growth and Prosperity in a Two-Speed Economy." McKinsey Global Institute, London.

Bosch, Mariano, María Belén Cobacho, and Carmen Pagés. 2012. "Taking Stock of Eight Years of *Seguro Popular* in Mexico." Inter-American Development Bank, Washington, DC.

Bosch, Mariano, and Raymundo M. Campos-Vazquez. 2010. "The Trade-Offs of Welfare Policies in Labor Markets with Informal Jobs: The Case of the 'Seguro Popular' Program in Mexico." Documento de Trabajo XII-2010, Centro de Estudios Económicos, Colegio de México, Mexico City.

Bruhn, Miriam, and Inessa Love. 2009. "The Economic Impact of Banking the Unbanked: Evidence from Mexico." Policy Research Working Paper 4981, World Bank, Washington, DC.

Campos-Vazquez, Raymundo M. 2013. "Efectos de los Ingresos No Reportados en el Nivel y Tendencia de la Pobreza Laboral en México." *Ensayos Revista de Economía* 32 (2): 23–54.

Campos-Vazquez, Raymundo M., and Roberto Velez-Grajales. 2013. "Female Labor Supply and Intergenerational Preference Formation: Evidence for Mexico." Documento de Trabajo VI-2013, Centro de Estudios Económicos, Colegio de México, Mexico City.

Carter, Michael R., Peter D. Little, Tewodaj Mogues, and Workneh Negatu. 2007. "Poverty Traps and Natural Disasters in Ethiopia and Honduras." *World Development* 35 (5): 835–56.

CEEY (Mexico, Centro de Estudios Espinosa Yglesias). 2013. "Informe, Movilidad Social en México 2013: Imagina tu futuro." CEEY, Mexico City.

Censos and Conteos de Población y Vivienda (database), Instituto Nacional de Estadística y Geografía, Aguascalientes, Mexico, http://www.inegi.org.mx/est /contenidos/proyectos/ccpv/default.aspx.

CONEVAL (Mexico, Consejo Nacional de Evaluación de la Política de Desarrollo Social, National Council for the Evaluation of Social Development Policy). 2009. "Metodología para la medición multidimensional de la pobreza en México." CONEVAL, Mexico City.

Cruz, Denisse, Alejandro de la Fuente, and Juan Soriano. 2011. "Riesgo de Desastres a Nivel Municipal en México: Diagnóstico General y Correlación con Pobreza." Background paper, World Bank, Washington, DC.

DAI (Development Alternatives Incorporated). 2010. "Encuesta sobre preferencias y necesidades de usuarios de productos y servicios financieros del Sector de Ahorro y Crédito Popular." Report, Bansefi, Mexico City.

Datt, Gaurav, and Martin Ravaillon. 1992. "Growth and Redistribution Components of Changes in Poverty Measures: A Decomposition with Applications to Brazil and India in the 1980s." *Journal of Development Economics* 38 (2): 275–95.

Dávalos, María Eugenia, Gerardo Esquivel, Luis F. López-Calva, and Carlos Rodríguez-Castelán. 2013. "Convergence with Stagnation: Mexico's Growth at the Municipal Level 1990–2010." Working paper, World Bank, Washington, DC.

Dávila Capalleja, Enrique Rafael. 1997. "Mexico: The Evolution and Reform of the Labor Market." In *Labor Markets in Latin America: Combining Social Protection with Market Flexibility*, edited by Sebastian Edwards and Nora Lustig, 292–327. Washington, DC: Brookings Institution Press.

de Janvry, Alain, Elisabeth Sadoulet, Pantelis Solomon, and Renos Vakis. 2006. "Uninsured Risk and Asset Protection: Can Conditional Cash Transfer Programs Serve as Safety Nets?" Social Protection Discussion Paper 0604, World Bank, Washington, DC.

de la Fuente, Alejandro. 2010. "Government Expenditures in Pre- and Post-disaster Risk Management." Background Note, World Bank, Washington, DC.

de la Fuente, Alejandro, Eduardo Ortiz-Juárez, and Carlos Rodríguez-Castelán. 2015. "Living on the Edge: Vulnerability to Poverty and Public Transfers in Mexico." Policy Research Working Paper 7165, World Bank, Washington, DC.

de la Torre, Augusto, Eduardo Levy Yeyati, Guillermo Beylis, Tatiana Didier, Carlos Rodríguez-Castelán, and Sergio Schmukler. 2014. "Inequality in a Lower Growth Latin America." Semiannual Report (October), Latin America and the Caribbean Region, World Bank, Washington, DC.

De Mel, Suresh, David McKenzie, and Christopher Woodruff. 2008. "Returns to Capital in Microenterprises: Evidence from a Field Experiment." *Quarterly Journal of Economics* 123 (4): 1329–72.

Djankov, Simeon, and Rita Ramalho. 2009. "Employment Laws in Developing Countries." *Journal of Comparative Economics* 37 (1): 3–13.

Doing Business (database). International Finance Corporation and World Bank, Washington, DC. http://www.doingbusiness.org/data.

Dougherty, Sean M. 2014. "Legal Reform, Contract Enforcement, and Firm Size in Mexico." *Review of International Economics* 22 (4): 825–44.

Enamorado, Ted, Luis F. López-Calva, and Carlos Rodríguez-Castelán. 2014. "Crime and Growth Convergence: Evidence from Mexico." *Economic Letters* 125 (1): 9–13.

ERN (Evaluación de Riesgos Naturales, América Latina). 2011. "Probabilistic Modelling of Natural Risks at the Global Level: The Hybrid Loss Excedance Curve." GAR 2011, Global Assessment Report on Disaster Risk Reduction, International Strategy for Disaster Risk Reduction, United Nations, Geneva.

Farfán, Gabriela, María Eugenia Genoni, Luis Rubalcalva, Graciela Teruel, and Duncan Thomas. 2011. "Oportunidades and Its Impact on Child Nutrition." University of California, Riverside, Riverside, CA.

Feldmann, Horst. 2009. "The Effects of Hiring and Firing Regulation on Unemployment and Employment: Evidence Based on Survey Data." *Applied Economics* 41 (19): 2389–2401.

Ferreira, Francisco H. G., Julian Messina, Jamele Rigolini, Luis F. López-Calva, María Ana Lugo, and Renos Vakis. 2013. *Economic Mobility and the Rise of the Latin American Middle Class.* Washington, DC: World Bank.

Frenk, Julio, Eduardo González-Pier, Octavio Gómez-Dantés, Miguel A. Lezana, and Felicia Marie Knaul. 2006. "Comprehensive Reform to Improve Health System Performance in Mexico." *Lancet* 368 (9546): 1524–34.

Gakidou, Emmanuela, Rafael Lozano, Eduoardo González-Pier, Jesse Abbott-Klafer, Jeremy T. Barofsky, Chloe Bryson-Cahn, Dennis M. Feehan, Diana K. Lee, Hector Hernández-Llamas, and Christopher J. L. Murray. 2006. "Assessing the Effect of the 2001–06 Mexican Health Reform: An Interim Report." *Lancet* 368 (9550): 1920–35.

Hsieh, Chang-Tai, and Benjamin A. Olken. 2014. "The 'Missing' Missing Middle." *Journal of Economic Perspectives* 28 (3): 89–108.

INEGI (Mexico, Instituto Nacional de Estadística y Geografía) and SEP (Mexico, Secretaria de Educación Pública). 2014. "Censo de Escuelas, Maestros y Alumnos de Educación Básica y Especial: Presentación de Resultados Definitivos." Press release 135/14 (March 31), Mexico City. http://www.inegi.org.mx/inegi /contenidos/espanol/prensa/boletines/boletin/Comunicados/Especiales/2014 /Marzo/comunica12.pdf.

INSP (Mexico, Instituto Nacional de Salud Pública, National Institute of Public Health). 2012. "Encuesta Nacional de Salud y Nutrición 2012: Resultados nacionales." INSP, Cuernavaca, Mexico.

Kaplan, David S., and Joyce Sadka. 2008. "Enforceability of Labor Law: Evidence from a Labor Court in Mexico." Policy Research Working Paper 4483, World Bank, Washington, DC.

Kaplan, David S., Joyce Sadka, and Jorge Luis Silva-Mendez. 2008. "Litigation and Settlement: New Evidence from Labor Courts in Mexico." *Journal of Empirical Legal Studies* 5 (2): 309–50.

Levy, Santiago. 2006. *Progress Against Poverty: Sustaining Mexico's Progresa-Oportunidades Program*. Washington, DC: Brookings Institution Press.

———. 2008. *Good Intentions, Bad Outcomes: Social Policy, Informality, and Economic Growth in Mexico*. Washington, DC: Brookings Institution Press.

López-Acevedo, Gladys. 2002. "Technology and Firm Performance in Mexico." Policy Research Working Paper 2778, World Bank, Washington, DC.

López-Calva, Luis F., Nora Lustig, John Scott, and Andrés Castañeda. 2013. "Gasto Social, Redistribución del Ingreso y Reducción de la Pobreza en México: Evolución y Comparación con Argentina, Brasil y Uruguay." CEQ Working Paper 17 (October), Commitment to Equity, Inter-American Dialogue, Washington, DC; Center for Inter-American Policy and Research and Department of Economics, Tulane University, New Orleans.

Lustig, Nora, Luis F. López-Calva, and Eduardo Ortiz-Juárez. 2013. "Declining Inequality in Latin America in the 2000s: The Cases of Argentina, Brazil, and Mexico." *World Development* 44: 129–41.

Mansilla, Elizabeth. 2008. "Afectación en Viviendas por Desastres y Marginación en México." Background paper, GAR 2009, Global Assessment Report on Disaster Risk Reduction, International Strategy for Disaster Risk Reduction, United Nations, Geneva.

Marquez-Padilla, Fernanda, Francisco Pérez-Arce, and Carlos Rodríguez-Castelán. 2015. "The (Non-) Effect of Violence on Education: Evidence from the 'War on Drugs' in Mexico." Policy Research Working Paper 7230, World Bank, Washington, DC.

McKenzie, David, and Christopher Woodruff. 2008. "Experimental Evidence on Returns to Capital and Access to Finance in Mexico." *World Bank Economic Review* 22 (3): 457–82.

Mearns, Robin, and Andrew Norton, eds. 2009. *Social Dimensions of Climate Change: Equity and Vulnerability in a Warming World.* New Frontiers of Social Policy Series. Washington, DC: World Bank.

Meléndez, Marcela. 2013. "Labor Productivity in the Services Sector in Latin America." Report, World Bank, Washington, DC.

OECD (Organisation for Economic Co-operation and Development). 2010. *Economic Policy Reforms: Going for Growth 2010.* Paris: OECD.

———. 2013. "OECD Economic Surveys: Mexico 2013." OECD, Paris. http://www.oecd-ilibrary.org/economics/oecd-economic-surveys-mexico_19990723.

———. 2014. "PISA 2012 Results in Focus: What 15-Year-Olds Know and What They Can Do with What They Know." OECD, Paris.

———. 2015. *OECD Economic Surveys: Mexico 2015.* Paris: OECD.

Orrenius, Pia M., and Madeline Zavodny. 2010. *Beside the Golden Door: U.S. Immigration Reform in a New Era of Globalization.* Washington, DC: American Enterprise Institute Press.

Ortiz-Juárez, Eduardo, and María Jesús Pérez-García. 2013. "Desigualdad, Pobreza y Política Social en México: Una Perspectiva de Largo Plazo." Consejo Nacional de Evaluación de la Política de Desarrollo Social and World Bank, Mexico City.

Passel, Jeffrey S., D'Vera Cohn, and Ana Gonzalez-Barrera. 2012. "Net Migration from Mexico Falls to Zero and Perhaps Less." *Hispanic Trends* (April 23), Pew Research Center, Washington, DC. http://www.pewhispanic.org/2012/04/23/net-migration-from-mexico-falls-to-zero-and-perhaps-less/.

Pereira-López, Mariana, and Isidro Soloaga. 2013. "Local Multipliers and the Informal Sector in Mexico: 2000–2010." Documento de Trabajo 5, Department of Economics, Universidad Iberoamericana, Mexico City.

Reddy, Rekha, Miriam Bruhn, and Congyan Tan. 2013. "Financial Capability in Mexico: Results from a National Survey on Financial Behaviors, Attitudes, and Knowledge." Report 82134, World Bank, Washington, D.C.

Rodríguez-Oreggia, Eduardo, Alejandro de la Fuente, Rodolfo de la Torre, Hector A. Moreno. 2013. "Natural Disasters, Human Development and Poverty at the Municipal Level in Mexico." *Journal of Development Studies*, 49 (3): 442–55.

Rodríguez-Oreggia, Eduardo, and Bruno López-Videla. 2014. "Imputación de ingresos laborales: una aplicación con encuestas de empleo en México." Working Paper 2014–21, Banco de México, Mexico City.

Samaniego, Roberto M. 2010. "Entry, Exit, and Investment-Specific Technical Change." *American Economic Review* 100 (1): 164–92.

Scott, John. 2011. "Gasto Público para la Equidad: Del Estado Excluyente hacia un Estado de Bienestar Universal." México Evalúa, Centro de Análisis de Políticas Públicas, Santa Catarina Coyoacán, Mexico City.

———. 2013. "Redistributive Impact and Efficiency of Mexico's Fiscal System." CEQ Working Paper 8 (January), Commitment to Equity, Inter-American Dialogue, Washington, DC; Center for Inter-American Policy and Research and Department of Economics, Tulane University, New Orleans.

———. 2014. "Mexico Policy Brief." Unpublished note (June 26), World Bank, Washington, DC.

SEDLAC (Socio-Economic Database for Latin America and the Caribbean), Center for Distributive, Labor, and Social Studies, Universidad de La Plata, La Plata, Argentina; World Bank, Washington, DC, http://sedlac.econo.unlp.edu.ar/eng /index.php.

Serrano Espinosa, Julio, and Florencia Torche, eds. 2010. *Movilidad social en México: Población, desarrollo y crecimiento.* Mexico City: Centro de Estudios Espinosa Yglesias.

Skoufias, Emmanuel. 2005. "PROGRESA and its Impacts on the Welfare of Rural Households in Mexico." IFPRI Research Report 139, International Food Policy Research Institute, Washington, DC.

Soloaga, Isidro, and Valeria Serrano. 2013. "Measuring Productivity in the Services Sector: The Case of Mexico." Report, World Bank, Washington, DC.

Udry, Christopher, and Santosh Anagol. 2006. "The Return to Capital in Ghana." *American Economic Review* 96 (2): 388–93.

Verner, Dorte, ed. 2010. *Reducing Poverty, Protecting Livelihoods, and Building Assets in a Changing Climate: Social Implications of Climate Change for Latin America and the Caribbean.* Report 55541. Directions in Development: Environment and Sustainable Development. Washington, DC: World Bank.

World Bank. 2005. *World Development Report 2006: Equity and Development.* Washington, DC: World Bank; New York: Oxford University Press.

———. 2006. *World Development Report 2007: Development and the Next Generation.* Washington, DC: World Bank.

———. 2011. "On the Edge of Uncertainty: Poverty Reduction in Latin America and the Caribbean during the Great Recession and Beyond." Poverty and Labor Brief (December), Latin America and the Caribbean Region, World Bank, Washington, DC.

———. 2012. "FONDEN: El Fondo de Desastres Naturales de México, una Reseña." World Bank, Washington, DC.

———. 2014. "Social Gains in the Balance: A Fiscal Policy Challenge for Latin America and the Caribbean." Poverty and Labor Brief, Report 85162 rev (February), Latin America and the Caribbean Region, World Bank, Washington DC.

WDI (World Development Indicators) (database). World Bank, Washington, DC. http://data.worldbank.org/data-catalog/world-development-indicators.

WEO (World Economic Outlook) Database. International Monetary Fund, Washington, DC. http://www.imf.org/external/ns/cs.aspx?id=28.

CHAPTER 7

Poverty and Shared Prosperity in Paraguay

*Santiago Garriga, Luis F. López-Calva,
María Ana Lugo, Alejandro Medina Giopp,
Miriam Müller, and Liliana D. Sousa*

Introduction

Isolated by nature and recovering from a period of historically slow growth, a high incidence of poverty, and persistent inequality during the 1980s and 1990s, Paraguay has faced many economic and social challenges at the beginning of the 21st century. By the year 2000, gross domestic product (GDP) per capita was only 50 percent of the Latin American average and 34 percent of the average among Paraguay's partners in the Southern Cone Common Market. High rates of poverty and inequality were an inherent characteristic of the country.

Yet, breaking with this past, Paraguay performed well and experienced a reduction in moderate and extreme monetary poverty between 2003 and 2013. The incomes of the bottom 40 percent of the income distribution (the bottom 40) grew at a more rapid pace than the average. This was the result of a period of substantial average growth, combined with a reduction in inequality.

This chapter explores whether the growth model behind these improvements and the consequent narrowing in inequality are consistent with the positive social dynamics involved in the construction of a more equitable society. It describes recent trends in poverty and inequality, the key drivers behind the progress, and the policy challenges in sustaining the recent welfare gains.

The analysis shows that higher labor earnings and employment levels, together with a slowdown in food price inflation and greater public transfers, are the main factors behind the positive welfare trends. High rates of economic growth opened new labor opportunities for the least well off

in more well-paid sectors and types of employment. The stable macroeconomic conditions helped restrain local food prices, halting the rise in the
cost of the basic food basket.

The country is now confronted by challenges that could threaten the sustainability of these advances. First, a large share of the population faces a
volatile economic environment in both rural and urban areas. Second, there
is still a stubborn lack of opportunity across population segments although
income inequality has narrowed and access to the principal services has
widened. Third, social policies are not sufficiently effective in offsetting the
inherited inequalities. The fiscal system is among the weakest in the region,
incorporating a regressive tax system and limited redistribution through
spending, combined with institutional and operational inefficiencies and
the lack of effective monitoring and evaluation that are enfeebling already
compromised social service delivery.

Trends in Poverty and Shared Prosperity

In 2003–11, economic growth was both substantial and volatile, and, while
moderate poverty declined, extreme poverty was more persistent, and
income inequality narrowed modestly. Per capita GDP grew by 33 percent,
despite a major dip during the 2009 drought and global financial crisis
when it fell by 5.2 percent relative to the previous year (figure 7.1). While

Figure 7.1 GDP per Capita, Poverty Rates, and Inequality, Paraguay, 2003–13

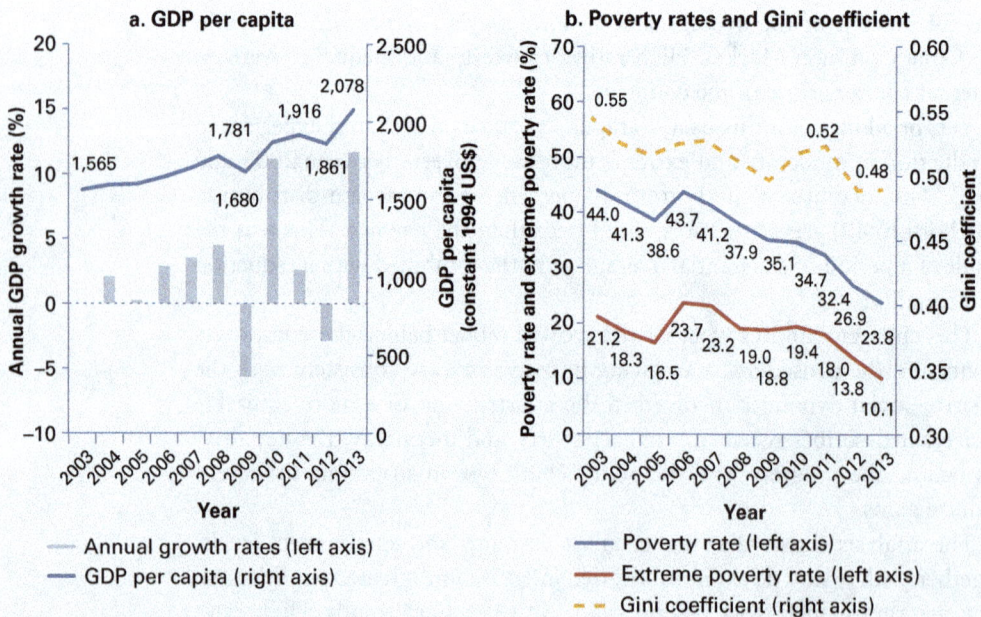

Source: Data of Banco Central del Paraguay and the General Directorate of Statistics, Surveys, and Censuses.
Note: GDP = gross domestic product.

Figure 7.2 Income Growth, the Bottom 40, Paraguay, 2003–13

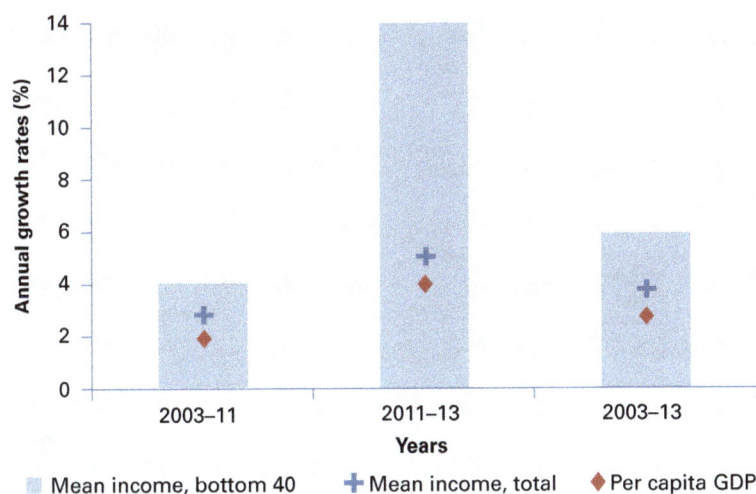

■ Mean income, bottom 40   ✚ Mean income, total   ◆ Per capita GDP

Sources: Mean income: Permanent Household Survey. Per capita GDP growth (in constant 1994 US$): Banco Central del Paraguay.
Note: GDP = gross domestic product.

the moderate poverty rate declined by 12 percentage points in this period, the extreme poverty rate fell by only 3 percentage points. In 2011, 32.4 percent of Paraguayans were still living in poverty, and 18.0 percent were living in extreme poverty. The income inequality rate has declined by merely 0.03 points since 2003 and, in 2011, was one of the highest rates in the region, at 0.53. The incomes of individuals in the bottom 40 rose at a rate slightly above the mean (4.0 and 3.3 percent, respectively), but this growth was not sufficient to reduce appreciably the high levels of extreme poverty and inequality (figure 7.2).

Since 2011, however, there have been substantial welfare improvements. By 2013, moderate poverty had fallen to 24 percent; extreme poverty had reached a historical low of 10 percent; and inequality had narrowed to less than 0.48 for the first time in 15 years (see figure 7.1). These changes reflect the fact that the rate of income growth was two and half times higher among individuals in the bottom 40 (the first two quintiles) relative to the average (14.0 and 5.6 percent, respectively) (see figure 7.2).

The size of the middle class and above was expanding and became the largest socioeconomic group in the country (figure 7.3). In 2003–13, the share of the population earning more than $10 per person a day rose by over 20 percentage points and, by 2013, represented half the population of the country.[1] The rate of growth of the middle class is similar in Paraguay and in the region, where the middle class also grew by 50 percent (Ferreira et al. 2013).

Yet, as at the beginning of the period, one in four Paraguayans was still economically insecure (the vulnerable), with a sizable probability of falling back into poverty. In a highly volatile environment such as Paraguay and in

Figure 7.3 Composition of the Population, by Socioeconomic Status, Paraguay, 2003–13

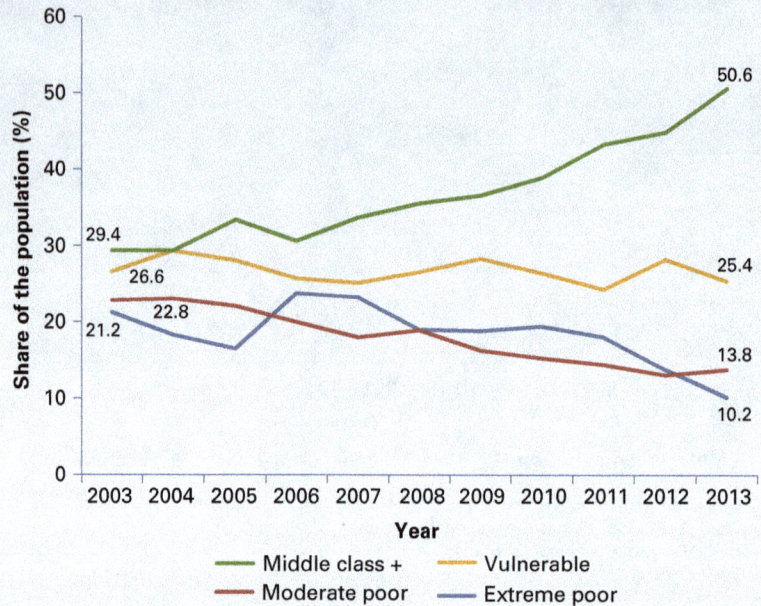

Source: Calculations based on 2003–13 data from the Permanent Household Survey.
Note: The official poverty lines have been used to calculate extreme poverty and total poverty. The threshold separating the vulnerable from the middle class and above is $10 a day (at purchasing power parity [PPP]). All values are expressed in Asunción prices. The values for 2012 are the average of 2011 and 2013 and do not include microdata from the Permanent Household Survey, which are preliminary.

view of the recent large improvements, seeking mechanisms to ensure that the gains of the period of growth are not reversed as soon as the winds shift is more important than ever.

There are signs of lasting structural change in the profile of poverty because the extent of deprivation in nonmonetary dimensions narrowed throughout the decade even during periods in which monetary poverty did not decline as much as in 2003–11 (figure 7.4). Unlike monetary indicators of poverty, which rely on cutoffs based on income or consumption, nonmonetary indicators of poverty measure the share of the population deprived of a key good or service according to defined standards. The share of Paraguayans who are deprived in at least four of seven key nonmonetary dimensions of well-being—education (two indicators), housing quality, access to water, access to sanitation, access to electricity, and assets—has gone down from one-third of the population to less than one-tenth.

Paraguay has made meaningful progress over the past decade in promoting women's empowerment and gender equality even if major challenges persist. Access to prenatal care and professional health care services at birth has widened, though it still lags relative to the regional average.

Figure 7.4 Multidimensional Poverty and Income Poverty Indicators, Paraguay, 2003–13

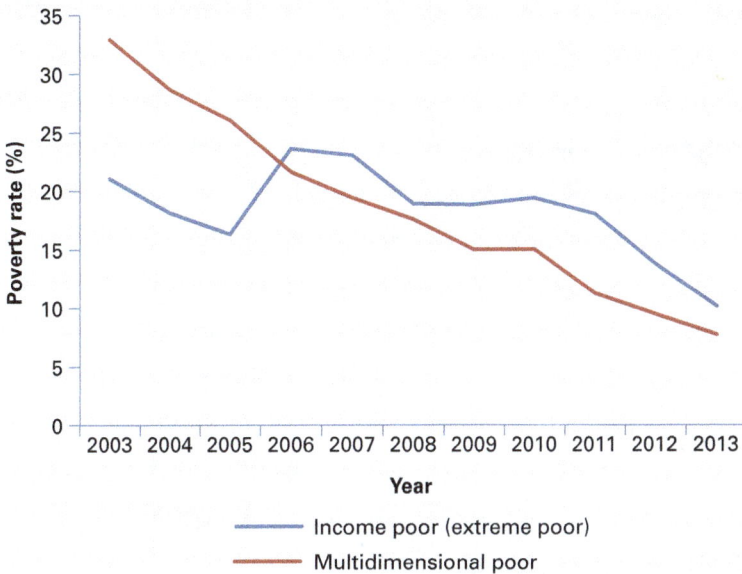

Source: Calculations based on data from the Permanent Household Survey.
Note: Income poor refers to the official extreme poverty rate. Seven dimensions were considered in determining multidimensional poverty: lack of assets (household does not possess two or more of the following items: television, telephone, means of transportation, or refrigerator); lack of electricity; lack of flush toilet or pit latrine; no household member has completed five years of schooling; any 7- to 15-year-old child in the household is out of school; the home is constructed with precarious wall materials; and the dwelling lacks running water.

The maternal mortality ratio showed clear progress in the past decade: 180 deaths per 100,000 live births in 2002 versus 100 deaths per 100,000 in 2010, 20 deaths per 100,000 higher than the regional average. Educational outcomes among girls (attainment and achievement) have improved, and girls now outperform boys in school. In recent years, there have also been key reforms in the legal framework on gender equality.

Drivers behind the Trends

Three factors explain the changes in poverty rates across 2003–11 and 2011–13: (1) changes in the position of the poverty line, (2) changes in distribution in terms of growth, and (3) changes in the shape of distribution, that is, the effects of redistribution. These three factors explain the stickiness of the extreme poverty headcount in 2003–11 and the impressive decline in poverty in 2011–13.

Between 2003 and 2011, while both growth and enhancements in the distribution contributed to the large reduction in poverty, food prices,

Figure 7.5 Per Capita Household Income Distribution, Paraguay, 2003, 2011, and 2013

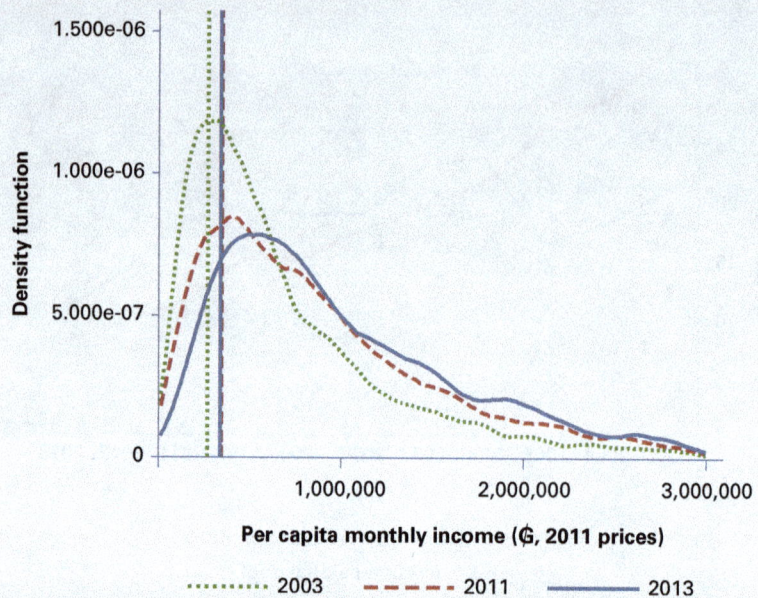

Source: Calculations based on data from the Permanent Household Survey for 2003, 2011, and 2013.
Note: The curved lines represent the density function of the distribution of per capita household incomes, expressed in constant 2011 guaranies. The vertical lines represent the respective extreme poverty lines. The deflator used for all lines is the general consumer price index derived by the Banco Central del Paraguay.

which are used to update the extreme poverty line, were rising at a higher rate than general prices in the economy and thus dampened the reduction in the extreme poverty rate. During this period, the distribution of incomes shifted to the right (representing income growth), while widening (representing narrowing inequality) (figure 7.5). At the same time, however, because of the rise in food prices, the extreme poverty line also moved to the right. Quantification of the effects of these three forces shows that growth and the improved income distribution contributed to a decline, by 9.48 percentage points, in poverty in 2003–11, while a rapid climb in the price of the food basket (relative to general prices) raised the poverty rate by 6.28 percentage points (figure 7.6). The net effect was less significant poverty reduction despite the sizable economic growth and the gains in redistribution.

In contrast, since 2011, the three forces have been trending in the same direction. The deceleration in the rise in food prices between 2011 and 2013 meant that, in real terms, the extreme poverty line was marginally lower in 2013 than in 2011. As a consequence, prices played a limited (though positive) role in the drop in the extreme poverty rate, whereas the better income distribution reflected in the widening of the distribution was behind 58 percent of the total change in the extreme poverty headcount

Figure 7.6 Changes in the Extreme Poverty Rate, Paraguay, 2003–11 and 2011–13

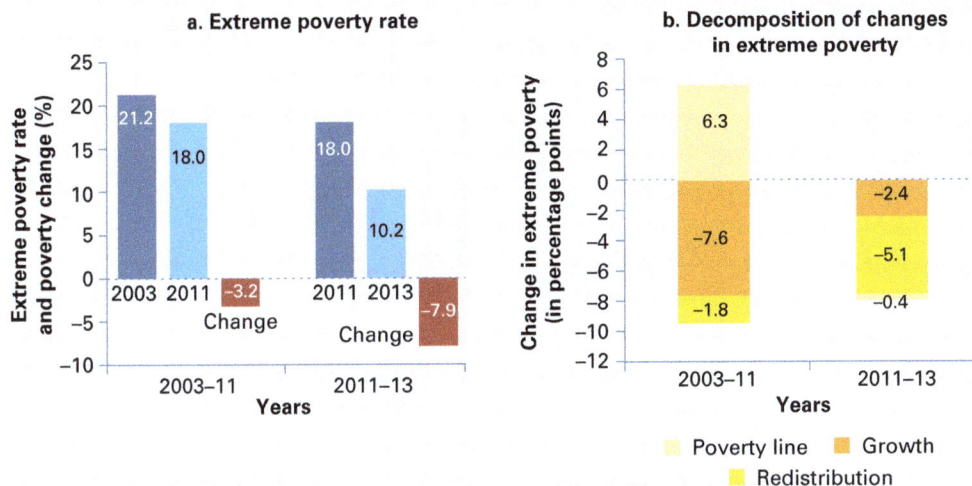

Source: Calculations based on data from the Permanent Household Survey for 2003, 2011, and 2013.

(5 percentage points out of close to 9). Average income growth (the shift to the right in the distribution) explains the remaining 42 percent of the fall (see figure 7.6). Additionally, given that a large share of the population is living in households with incomes near the extreme poverty line, even slight shifts in the poverty line can have noticeable impacts on observed poverty rates.

Disproportionate income growth among the less well off was a strong factor in the improvements in poverty. Growth incidence curves depict the annual per capita household income growth rates by percentile of the distribution (figure 7.7). Three features emerge. First, the annual growth rates are considerably lower between 2003 and 2011 than in 2011–13 (see the change in the values along the vertical axes). Second, the latter rates are considerably more progressive than the former. Finally, in contrast to the first part of the period, income growth was everywhere higher in rural areas than in urban areas during the more recent years.

Poverty reduction in rural areas is driven by both an increase in the number of people employed and higher average earnings among the employed (figure 7.8). Over a third of the fall in poverty was associated with households adding additional workers, both men and women. An additional third of the poverty reduction arose from greater earnings. Thus, about two-thirds of the rural poverty reduction was driven by better labor market outcomes.

Among the households most likely to have exited extreme poverty (the second through the fourth decile), the main source of labor income growth was wage increases, particularly in agriculture (figure 7.9). While self-employment in agriculture continues to be prevalent among the least well

Figure 7.7 Growth Incidence Curves, Paraguay, 2003–11 and 2011–13

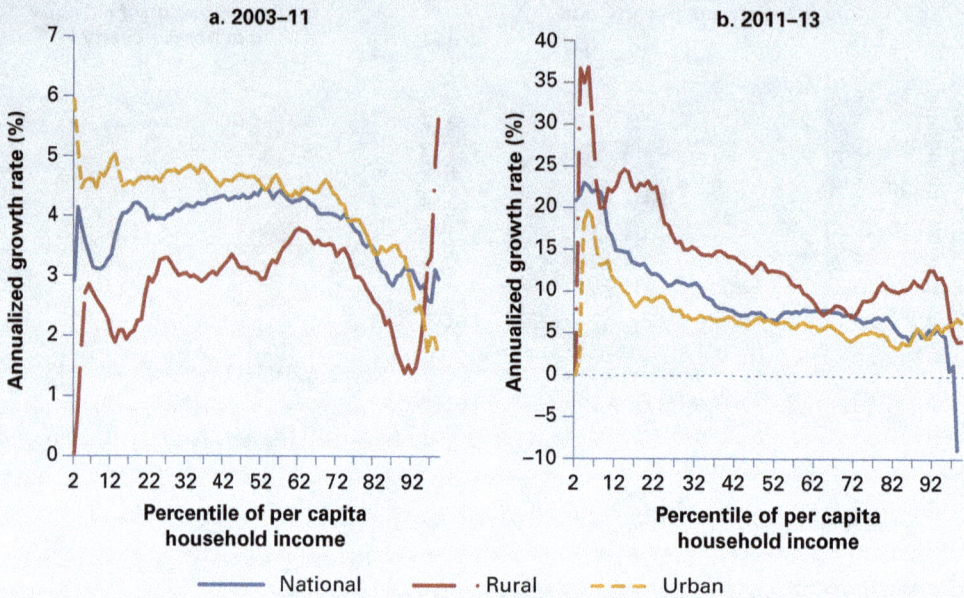

a. 2003–11

b. 2011–13

Source: Calculations based on data from the Permanent Household Survey for 2003, 2011, and 2013.
Note: Percentiles 1 and 99 are excluded from the charts.

off, there has been a shift toward off-farm wage jobs in agriculture in the past decade, suggesting that a gradual reallocation has occurred in rural labor from less-productive small farms to more-productive agribusiness. In addition, nonagriculture wage employment, such as construction and public services, has been offering alternative sources of income that tend to be more profitable than own-farm earnings. Among the bottom 40, the individuals more likely to take advantage of these opportunities in agriculture and nonagriculture wage employment have been men and women of primary working age (30–45 years) and those particularly (though not exclusively) in the Central Department and the group of eight departments classified in the survey as "rest of the departments."[2]

Nonlabor income, especially public transfers such as those associated with the Tekopora and Adultos Mayores programs, accounted for the remaining third of the decline in rural poverty. Adultos Mayores is a noncontributory pension transfer program for seniors (65 years of age or older) who are poor and do not receive any other pension or wage. The transfer amount is equivalent to 25 percent of the minimum wage. Tekopora is a conditional cash transfer program targeted at poor households with school-age children. It was designed for rural households, but was later extended to selected urban areas. It offers a sizable transfer (an average ₲200,000 a month, representing 20 percent of household income

Figure 7.8 Decomposition of Changes in Extreme Poverty Rates, by Rural and Urban Location, Paraguay, 2003–13

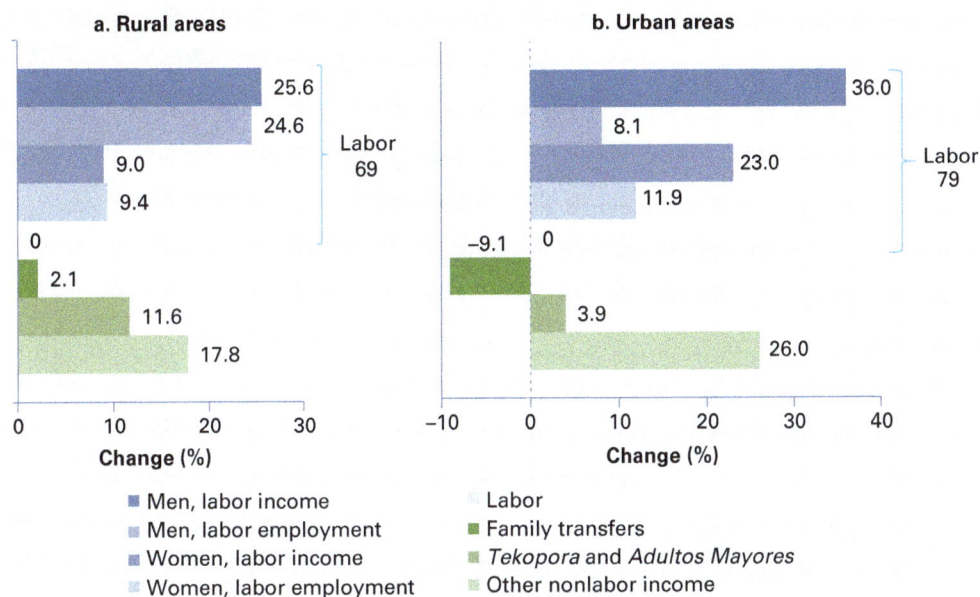

a. Rural areas

b. Urban areas

■ Men, labor income
■ Men, labor employment
■ Women, labor income
▨ Women, labor employment
▨ Labor
■ Family transfers
▨ Tekopora and Adultos Mayores
▨ Other nonlabor income

Source: Calculations based on the methodology described in Barros et al. 2006.
Note: The analysis represented in the figure, also known as a Shapley Decomposition, separates changes in poverty rates by income source. *Tekopora* and *Adultos Mayores* are public transfer programs (see the text).

Figure 7.9 Labor Income Growth and the Wage Employment Rate, Paraguay, 2003–13

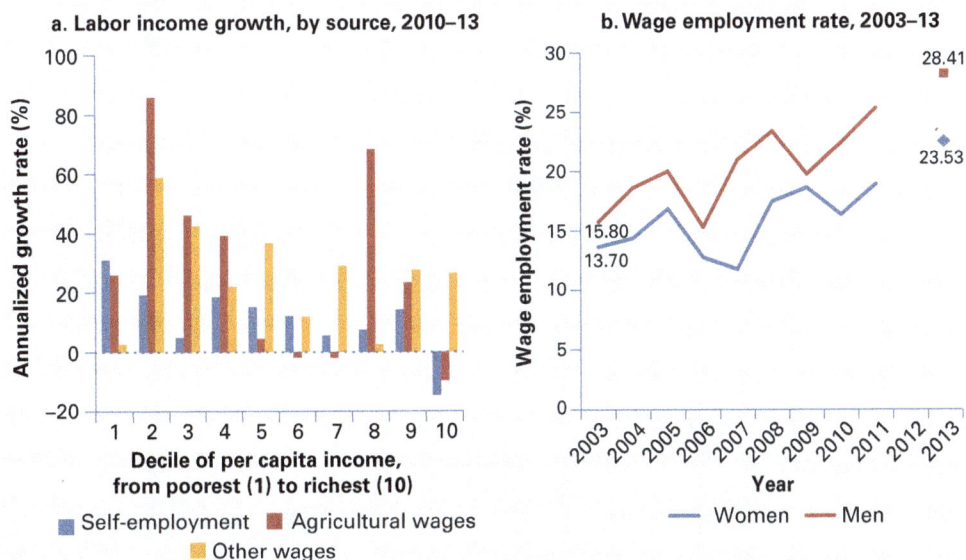

a. Labor income growth, by source, 2010–13

b. Wage employment rate, 2003–13

■ Self-employment ■ Agricultural wages
▨ Other wages

— Women — Men

Source: Calculations based on data from the Permanent Household Survey.

Figure 7.10 Tekopora Transfers and Changes in Extreme Poverty without Family Transfers, Paraguay, 2003–13

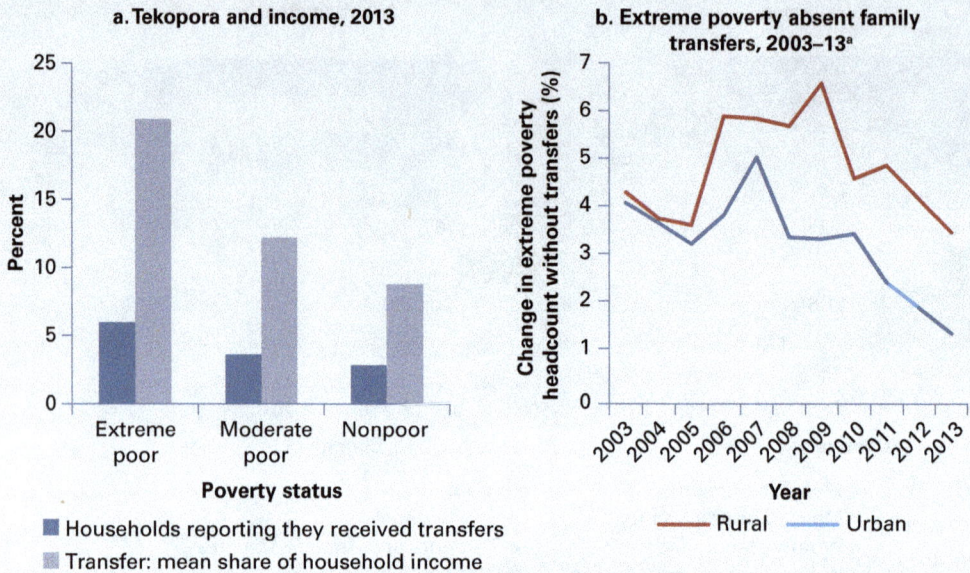

a. Tekopora and income, 2013

b. Extreme poverty absent family transfers, 2003–13[a]

Households reporting they received transfers

Transfer: mean share of household income

Rural — Urban

Source: Calculations based on data from the Permanent Household Survey.
a. The values for 2012 are the average of 2011 and 2013 and do not include microdata from the Permanent Household Survey, which are preliminary.

among extreme poor beneficiaries), but coverage is still fairly low. In 2013, according to household survey data, only 6 percent of extreme poor rural households and 4 percent of moderate poor households were receiving the transfer (figure 7.10, chart a).

Family transfers may not be an important driver behind the shifts in the incidence of poverty, but they have played an increasingly important role in alleviating poverty and as a mechanism enabling households to cope with adverse shocks (see figure 7.10, chart b). Without these transfers, the extreme poverty rate in rural areas would be 4 percentage points higher. The elderly and woman-headed households have received substantially larger household transfers, suggesting that internal migration was a household income diversification and coping mechanism.[3] Informal lending represents an important third mechanism that rural households have employed to cope with potential shocks. Despite a lack of access to formal financial markets (in 2011, only 3 percent of the bottom 40 reported they had bank accounts), 21 percent of rural residents reported they had loans, which had often been obtained from friends or family.

The drop by half in urban poverty is associated with significant enhancements in the urban labor market. In 2003–13, 79 percent of the fall in poverty was attributable to better labor earnings and higher employment levels (see figure 7.8). Higher earnings among both men and women were the primary drivers of urban poverty reduction, accounting for almost 60

Figure 7.11 Earnings among Workers with Incomplete Primary School and Employment, by Employer Type, Paraguay, 2003–13

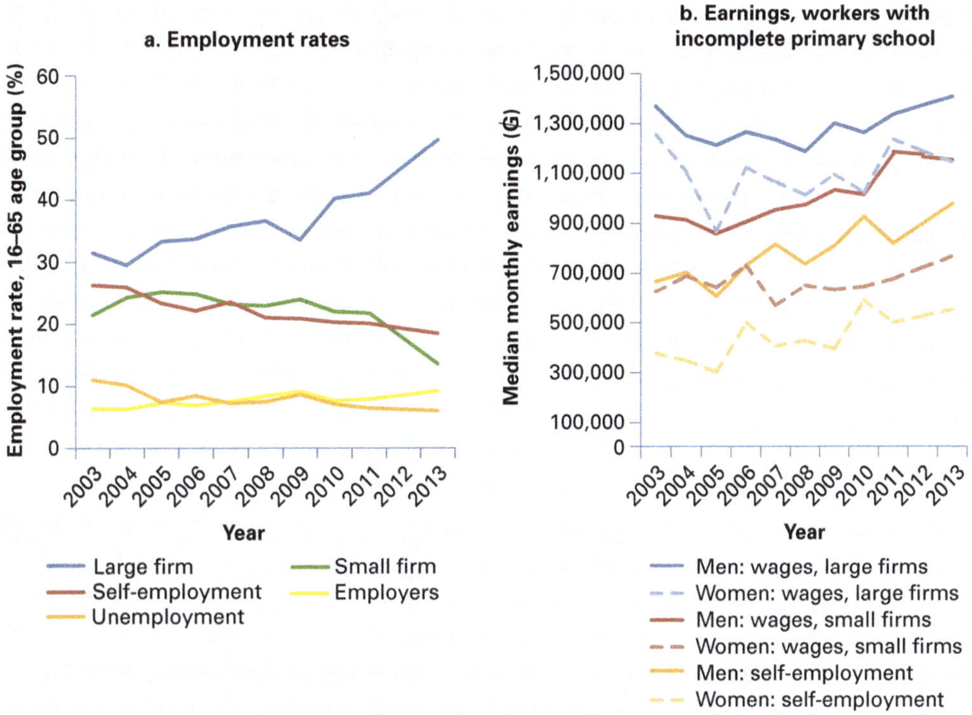

a. Employment rates

b. Earnings, workers with incomplete primary school

Legend (a): Large firm; Self-employment; Unemployment; Small firm; Employers

Legend (b): Men: wages, large firms; Women: wages, large firms; Men: wages, small firms; Women: wages, small firms; Men: self-employment; Women: self-employment

Source: Calculations based on data from the Permanent Household Survey.
Note: Employers include the self-employed who have finished secondary education. The values for 2012 are the average of 2011 and 2013 and do not include microdata from the Permanent Household Survey, which are preliminary.

percent of the overall change. The rise in labor incomes was associated with the boost in earnings among the self-employed and workers in small firms, as well as a surge in lower-skill jobs in the higher-paying large-firm sector (such as construction and public and private services) (figure 7.11). Among the bottom quintile, the more well educated, particularly men, and residents of the main metropolitan areas (Asunción and the Central Department) were more likely to be employed in higher-paying large firms and the public sector.[4] In addition to rising average earnings as a factor behind poverty reduction, the number of income earners in households grew as the unemployment rate declined and female participation expanded (the employment rate among women went up from 37 to 46 percent). In contrast to rural areas, household transfers among poor urban residents played only a limited role, possibly because remittances from urban to rural areas are often a diversification mechanism that extended families use to share income. Nonetheless, if urban families were not receiving household transfers, the incidence of extreme poverty in urban areas would be 20 percent higher (see figure 7.10, chart b).

Key Challenges

Paraguay has made substantial progress in the past decade in improving welfare and reducing inequality. There is reason for optimism especially because of the enhanced labor productivity in agriculture and the widening employment opportunities, which hints at the potential for long-lasting transformation.

Nonetheless, the country faces challenges that threaten the sustainability of these gains. This section focuses on two main potential obstacles. First, a large share of the population faces a volatile economic environment in both rural and urban areas. Second, a lack of opportunity persists among the poor, and the fiscal system is not effective in offsetting this inherited source of inequality. Addressing the first challenge requires enhancing the functioning of markets (mainly labor and credit markets) and of systems for managing risk. Addressing the second challenge involves establishing more equity in the fiscal system, in addition to ensuring that institutions are fair and efficient in the delivery of basic social services.

Volatility

Paraguay is a small landlocked agricultural country, and the economy is extremely volatile and regularly affected by shocks (World Bank 2014a). As a consequence, the welfare position of the poor in both rural and urban areas is threatened on a regular basis.

With the expansion of agriculture, which accounts for over 20 percent of total GDP, Paraguay's exposure to external shocks has increased in recent years. Shocks are largely driven by commodity price fluctuations, weather changes, and animal diseases (World Bank 2014a). The least well-off families in rural areas tend to be heavily reliant on the highly volatile agricultural sector. More than two-thirds of the extreme poor are largely self-employed in agriculture, where they cultivate a few crops for home consumption and markets. On average, 77 percent of labor income among these households is derived from activities in agriculture, cattle raising, or fishing (figure 7.12). In contrast, the share of agricultural income among nonpoor rural households is around 40 percent. Among many of these households, agriculture is fairly basic and characterized by insufficient irrigation systems, inadequate agricultural practices, and limited use of technology.

Because of limited access to financial markets and infrastructure, households enjoy few opportunities to diversify or insure against income volatility (World Bank 2014b). Thus, despite the volatility, fewer than 2 percent of agricultural workers purchased agricultural insurance in 2011 (Demirgüç-Kunt and Klapper 2012). Reliance on informal lending and household transfers are important strategies used by the rural poor to cope with these limitations. Through 2009, for instance, when the country was being affected by severe drought and the international financial crisis, household transfers to rural areas rose in importance; without this type of income, rural poverty would have been as much as 6.6 percentage points greater (or 20 percent greater than the observed poverty rate) (see figure 7.10).

Figure 7.12 Primary Sector Income and Rural Employment Sectors, by Poverty Status, Paraguay, 2013

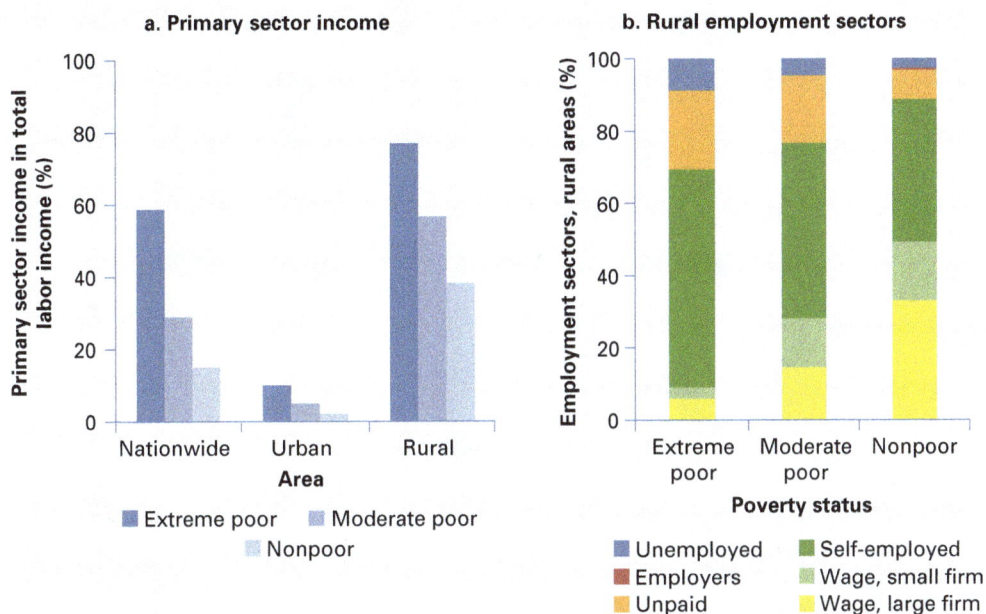

a. Primary sector income

b. Rural employment sectors

Legend (chart a): Extreme poor | Moderate poor | Nonpoor

Legend (chart b): Unemployed | Self-employed | Employers | Wage, small firm | Unpaid | Wage, large firm

Source: Calculations based on 2013 data from the Permanent Household Survey.
Note: The data refer to the 15–64 age group in the labor force. Employers in chart b include the self-employed who have finished secondary education.

Enhancing the resilience of households to volatility will require a combination of strategies to improve agricultural practice (through irrigation systems, crop diversification, and pest control), boost access to goods and financial markets, and expand the opportunities for workers to diversify their incomes through other activities or types of employment.

Vulnerability is not confined to rural areas. In urban areas, informal employment and unemployment are still prevalent among the least well off, who are therefore exposed to fluctuations in the economy and are largely untouched by minimum wage legislation. Though unemployment fell steadily throughout the past decade, it was exceptionally high among people living in poverty: the extreme poor are four times more likely and the moderate poor are two times more likely than the nonpoor to be unemployed (figure 7.13). In part, the rise in the unemployment rate among the extreme poor has reflected the lower propensity of the employed to be poor. As earnings and employment opportunities have expanded, many have exited extreme poverty so that the unemployed have come to represent a larger share of the extreme poor. Thus, because the proportion of the urban poor has fallen by half in recent years, from 10 to 5 percent, extreme poverty has become more closely associated with the lack of jobs.

Figure 7.13 Urban Unemployment and Employment Sectors, by Poverty Status, Paraguay, 2003–13

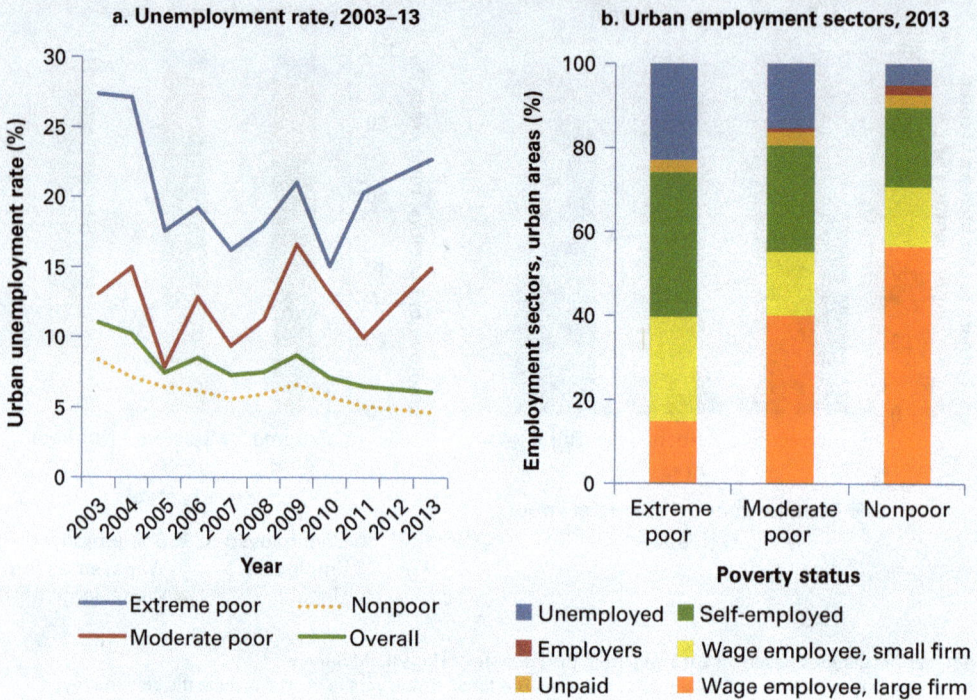

a. Unemployment rate, 2003–13

b. Urban employment sectors, 2013

Legend:
- Extreme poor
- Nonpoor
- Moderate poor
- Overall

- Unemployed
- Employers
- Unpaid
- Self-employed
- Wage employee, small firm
- Wage employee, large firm

Source: Calculations based on 2003–13 data from the Permanent Household Survey.
Note: The values for 2012 are the average of 2011 and 2013 and do not include microdata from the Permanent Household Survey, which are preliminary. Chart b: The data refer to the 15–64 age group in the labor force. Employers include the self-employed who have finished secondary education.

Self-employment (mostly in commerce and agriculture) and small-firm employment, which are relatively informal types of labor participation, are the dominant employment sectors among the urban poor (see figure 7.13). A third of the extreme poor are self-employed, and a quarter are employed in small firms, whereas a quarter of the moderate poor are self-employed, and 15 percent of the moderate poor are employees in small firms. Yet, wage employment in large (more well-paid) firms is far more common among the urban poor than among the rural poor, particularly among the urban moderate poor. Jobs in larger firms tend to be not only more well paid, but also less volatile, and they typically provide more job security and benefits. Specifically, 70 percent of urban workers in large firms have formal contracts, and 54 percent have access to pensions or a retirement system. Small firms rarely offer pensions or contracts (at 8 and 15 percent, respectively). The self-employed have limited access to pensions; pensions are nonexistent among the low-skilled self-employed; and only 6 percent of the skilled self-employed and employers have pensions.

Figure 7.14 Monthly Earnings as a Share of the Minimum Wage, by Employment Type, Paraguay, 2013

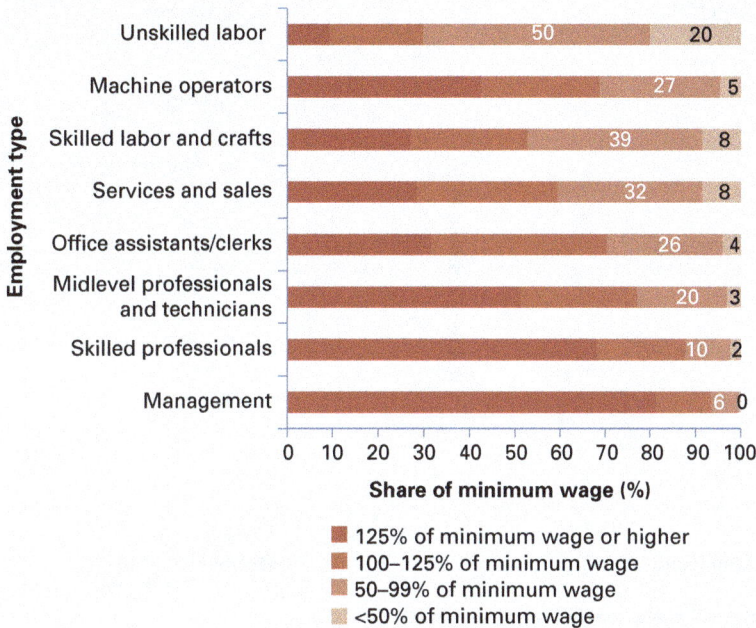

Source: Calculations based on 2013 data of the labor force survey, Encuesta Continua de Empleo, quarters 1–4.
Note: The data refer to the 15–64 age group in the labor force whose main occupations are reported as wage workers in private firms in urban areas who typically work over 30 hours per week and who did so during the reference week. Domestic workers and public sector workers are excluded.

To a large extent, low-skilled and unskilled labor—the workers most likely to be living in poverty—are unprotected by minimum wage legislation. Nearly two in every five full-time wage workers in the private sector earn less than the monthly minimum wage, including 70 percent of unskilled laborers (figure 7.14). Indeed, among unskilled laborers, one in five earns less than half the minimum wage. Over three-quarters of the workers in the most highly skilled occupations—management, skilled professionals, and midlevel professionals and technicians—earn more than the minimum wage.

The bulk of private sector employment associated with earnings below the minimum wage is found in microenterprises: 63 percent of wage workers who earn less than half the minimum wage work in firms with 5 or fewer employees, and another 14 percent in firms with only 6 to 10 employees. Similarly, 47 percent of workers who earn between 50 and 99 percent of the minimum wage work in firms with 10 or fewer workers.

Opportunities for all

Among the greatest structural barriers to equity that Paraguay faces today is the high and persistent level of inequality in opportunity across population

Figure 7.15 Access to Sanitation and Piped Water in the Home, Children, Paraguay, 2013

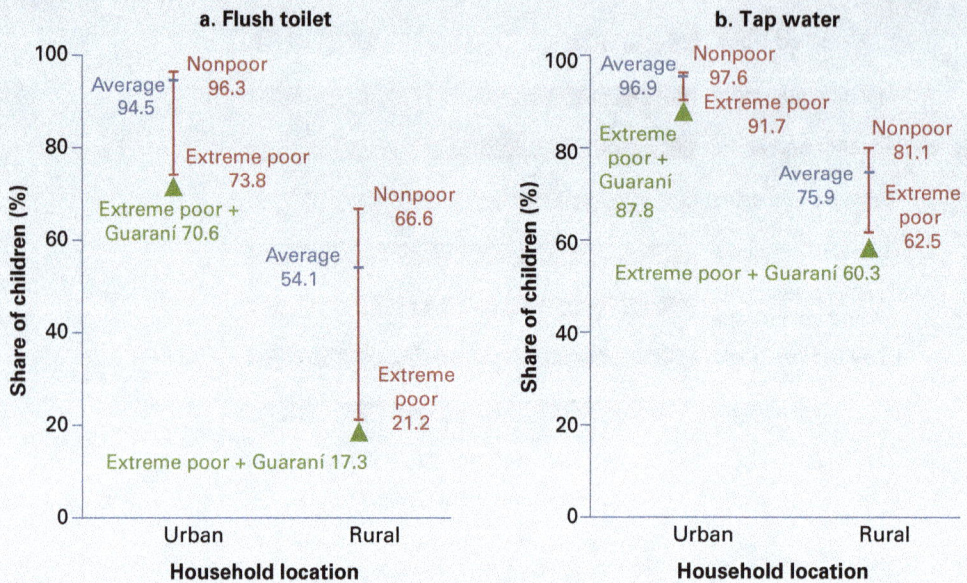

a. Flush toilet

- Average 94.5
- Nonpoor 96.3
- Extreme poor 73.8
- Extreme poor + Guaraní 70.6
- Nonpoor 66.6
- Average 54.1
- Extreme poor 21.2
- Extreme poor + Guaraní 17.3

Share of children (%) — Household location: Urban, Rural

b. Tap water

- Average 96.9
- Nonpoor 97.6
- Extreme poor 91.7
- Extreme poor + Guaraní 87.8
- Average 75.9
- Nonpoor 81.1
- Extreme poor 62.5
- Extreme poor + Guaraní 60.3

Share of children (%) — Household location: Urban, Rural

Source: Calculations based on 2013 data from the Permanent Household Survey.

groups. A society is equitable if socioeconomic achievement and access to opportunities are not dependent on the circumstances at birth over which individuals have no control, including family background. If inequality in one generation affects the life chances of children, it thereby transmits the existing inequitable pattern to the next generation. A growing literature shows that deficiencies in nutrition, education, and health at early stages in life can have long-lasting effects. In Paraguay, differences in living standards are substantial in many dimensions of well-being and are expressed at various points throughout the life cycle.

In Paraguay, access to basic services depends to a large extent on whether a child is born in a rural or urban household and, to a lesser though still considerable extent, on the socioeconomic status of the household. Half the children born in rural areas have access to flush toilets inside their homes; this is so among almost all children in urban areas, but particularly children in nonpoor households (figure 7.15). The situation is substantially worse among children born in extremely poor households: only one in five children in poor households has proper sanitation, and the share is slightly fewer if the household members only speak Guaraní at home.[5] A similar, though less pronounced situation is found with respect to access to water in the dwelling. Children born in rural areas have a 76 percent chance of having tap water in their homes, whereas, if they had been born in an urban area, their chances would increase to 97 percent. Chances are not much better in rural areas if the children are born in nonpoor households (81 percent).

Figure 7.16 Comparative Test Scores among Sixth Graders, Latin America and the Caribbean, 2006

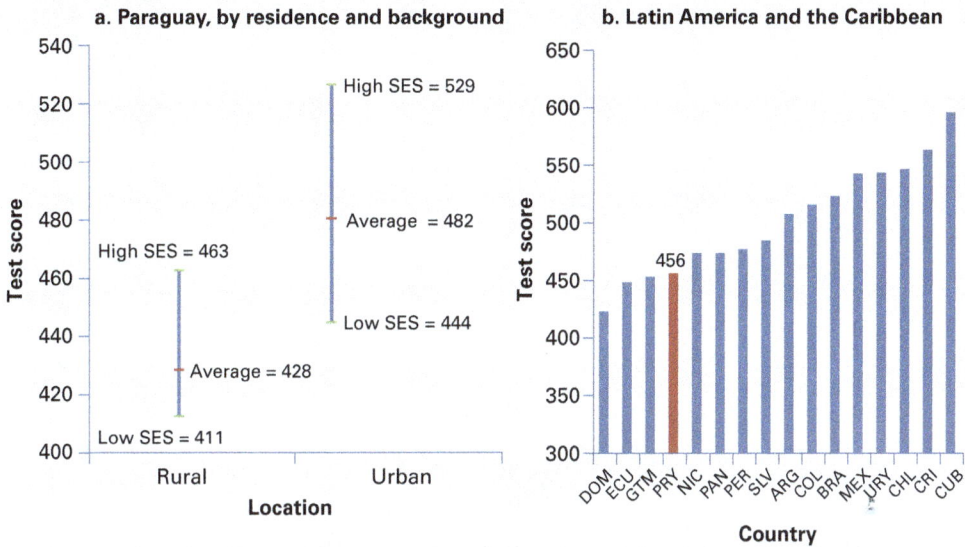

a. Paraguay, by residence and background

b. Latin America and the Caribbean

Source: Calculations based on data in Second Regional Comparative and Explanatory Study (database), Latin-American Laboratory for the Assessment of the Quality of Education, Regional Bureau for Education in Latin America and the Caribbean, United Nations Educational, Scientific, and Cultural Organization, Santiago, Chile, http://www.unesco.org/new/en/santiago/education/education-assessment-llece/perce-serce-databases/. *Note:* Chart a: SES = socioeconomic status. High SES = parents who have completed tertiary education. Low SES = parents who have, at most, completed primary education. Chart b: The state of Nuevo Léon stands in for Mexico (MEX).

While differences in school enrollment are less pronounced, the quality of schooling varies widely across groups, particularly between urban and rural areas. School quality in Paraguay at the elementary level is extremely low by Latin American standards. According to the Second Regional Comparative and Explanatory Study carried out by the United Nations Educational, Scientific, and Cultural Organization in 2006, Paraguay is among the bottom 5 countries of the 17 Latin American countries included.[6] Additionally, depending on where they live and the level of education of their parents, there are noticeable differences in the performance of Paraguayan children who reach sixth grade. Children in rural households of higher socioeconomic status perform only marginally better than children in urban households of low socioeconomic status (figure 7.16). Furthermore, the scores of children in urban households at the highest socioeconomic status in Paraguay are similar to the average score of children in Brazil, which was sixth among the countries studied. Meanwhile, a poor rural child is likely to score below the mean in any country in the sample, including the Dominican Republic, Ecuador, and Guatemala, the three countries at the bottom overall. In Paraguay, considerable differences are also found in the grade completion rate, another indicator of school quality. While the nonpoor

Figure 7.17 Overall Inequality and the Inequality of Opportunity, Paraguay, 2003–13

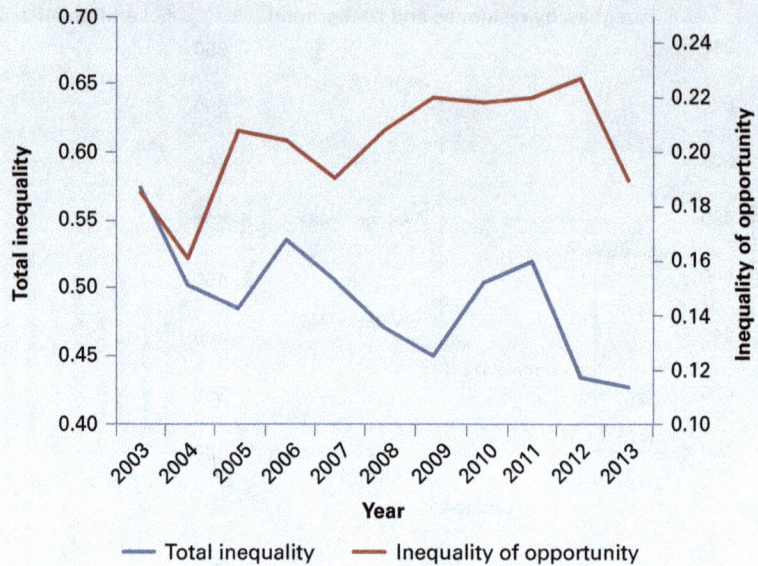

Source: Calculations based on data from the Permanent Household Survey (2003–13).
Note: Total inequality is measured by the mean log deviation. Inequality of opportunity is measured as between-group inequality relative to overall inequality, whereby groups are defined by the language spoken at home, the place of birth (rural versus urban, as well as region), and gender.

in urban areas show a completion rate of around 90 percent in sixth grade and over 70 percent in secondary education, the corresponding rates among the extreme poor in rural areas are below 55 and 20 percent, respectively.

When such children enter the labor market, the inequalities of opportunity they face remain. This inequality has been expanding in recent years. It is measured here by differences in mean income across groups based on circumstances not governed by choice or effort (such as the language spoken at home, rural or urban residence, or region of birth). Whereas total inequality fluctuated and, ultimately, narrowed between 2003 and 2013, the share of inequality accounted for by differences in the circumstances of individuals grew from 18 percent in 2003 to over 22 percent in 2012 before falling to 19 percent in 2013 (figure 7.17). Birth location and the language spoken at home are key factors associated with the observed inequality of opportunity in labor markets. This is in line with the finding that 75 percent of the people who remained in poverty in both 2003 and 2013 only spoke Guaraní at home. While the vast majority of the population is bilingual, the language of choice is highly correlated with economic outcomes. Additionally, gender has become a more important factor in explaining opportunity inequality. It did not appear as a factor in 2003, but had emerged as a contributor to between-group inequality by 2011.

Addressing income inequality and boosting intergenerational mobility require inclusive growth and the implementation of effective policies to foster gains among population segments that do not directly benefit from growth. Effective social service delivery and sustainable fiscal policy can play a crucial role in reducing inequality and providing access to opportunity.

According to a recent comparative study on the progressivity of fiscal systems in selected countries in Latin America and the Caribbean, tax collection in Paraguay, as in other countries in the region, is low relative to the average in the Organisation for Economic Co-operation and Development (OECD) and relies more heavily on consumer taxes (OECD, ECLAC, and CIAT 2014).[7] In 2010, tax revenue was only 16.5 percent of GDP, compared with an average of 34.0 percent in the OECD.[8] Lower tax revenue implies less fiscal space for social investments, such as improved education and infrastructure. Furthermore, while a quarter of the tax revenue in the OECD was derived from personal income tax, a typically progressive tax, the government of Paraguay did not enact personal income taxation until 2012 (Higgins et al., forthcoming). Instead, it relies on the value added tax, which accounted for 48 percent of tax revenues in 2010 (Higgins et al., forthcoming). This type of consumption tax is disproportionately paid by low-income consumers, who spend a higher proportion of their incomes on necessities.

Judged by comparable methodologies and harmonized data on the region, Paraguay appears to be the least effective among seven countries— Argentina, Bolivia, Brazil, Guatemala, Mexico, Paraguay, Peru, and Uruguay—at mitigating inequality through fiscal policy (figure 7.18).[9] While the Gini coefficients for market income earnings before taxes and transfers were similar in Paraguay and the other countries, they were indeed slightly higher in Paraguay after taxes and transfers. The provision of public education and public health services narrowed the effective income inequality somewhat, to 0.48. Though slightly lower than the initial Gini of 0.50, The decline of 0.02 points in Paraguay's Gini through fiscal policy was the smallest among the country Gini coefficients reported.

Though the Commitment to Equity analysis paints a stark picture of fiscal policy in Paraguay in 2010, several recent policy changes have addressed the shortcomings. Direct personal income taxation was introduced in 2012. Additionally, a tax of 10 percent on income from agriculture was adopted in 2013. These taxes should have the effect of reducing the regressivity of the tax system. On the other hand, these changes have been accompanied by a new value added tax on agricultural and livestock products and an expansion of the value added tax on most products, potentially decreasing the progressivity characteristic of the higher direct taxation. On the spending side, the government's *Sembrando Oportunidades* poverty reduction plan aims to fight poverty by targeting a quarter of a million families living in extreme poverty. The plan involves the expansion of cash transfer programs (such as the Tekopora, *Tekoha*, and *Propais II*) in terms of coverage and the amount of benefits. Adultos Mayores has also been expanded.

Figure 7.18 Comparative Redistribution Effectiveness of Fiscal Systems, Latin America and the Caribbean, 2009

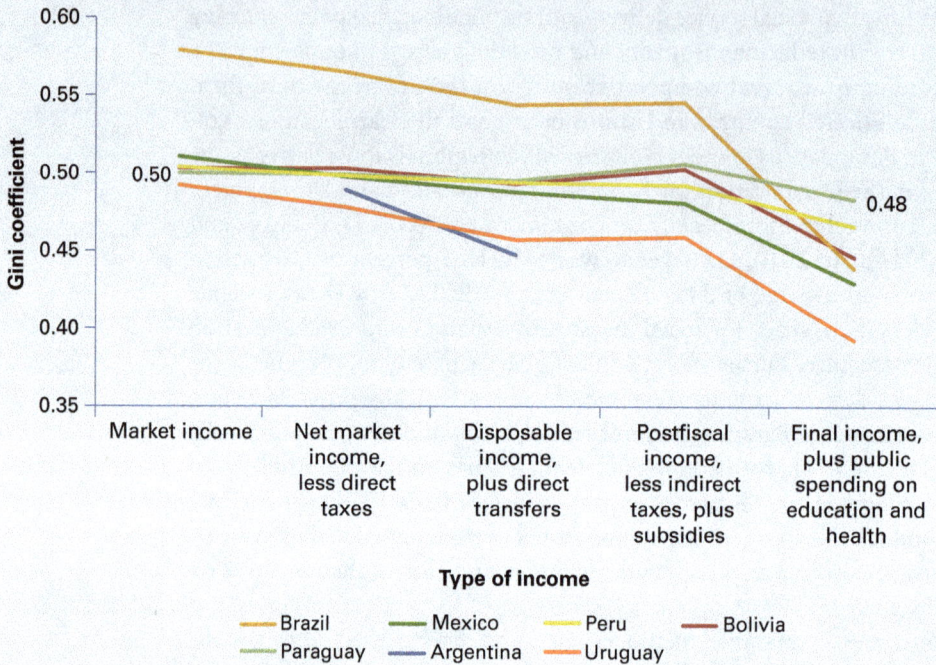

Sources: Bucheli et al. 2014; Higgins and Pereira 2014; Higgins et al., forthcoming; Jaramillo 2014; Lustig and Pessino 2014; Paz Arauco et al. 2014; Scott 2014.
Note: The Gini coefficients are calculated based on each of the five Commitment to Equity Project income definitions (see the sources). For Mexico and Paraguay, the data refer to 2010.

Moreover, the FONACIDE (the National Fund for Public Investment and Development or Fondo Nacional de Inversión Pública y Desarrollo) law passed in 2012 by Congress regulates the spending of extra revenue from electricity sales (to Brazil) on infrastructure projects, including investments in educational infrastructure.

Besides the fiscal measures, the other element of the explicit role of the government in reducing poverty and improving opportunities for all relates to the effective provision of essential social services. Though social expenditure has grown rapidly, from $95 per capita in 2003 to $584 in 2010, key basic social services, such as access to improved sewerage and running water, continue to be relatively inadequate (Guillén 2010). The paradox of greater social spending and stubbornly inadequate service delivery can be explained by at least three factors: (1) the ineffective allocation of resources, (2) institutional and operational inefficiencies, and (3) the lack of an effective monitoring and evaluation system.

Although the government's poverty strategy provides for a process for the allocation of resources to social programs that is based on socioeconomic indicators by geographical location, some resource allocations at the sectoral level are regressive. A recent study shows, for example, that public investment in education is not only low (and declining) in Paraguay compared with other Latin American countries, but also that investment in new classrooms is concentrated among schools serving the top quintile in the classroom availability index, while investments are lower where the need is most urgent, among poorer quintiles: almost half of the investment goes to the better 20 percent of schools, and only 7 percent to the lowest 20 percent (Wodon 2014).[10]

Social services are not delivered in a timely, regular, or coordinated manner, and there is insufficient quality control. These deficiencies can be addressed to some extent by improving the planning and implementation of public sector activities as part of the government budgeting process. Such coordination would allow public sector managers to track the social expenditures relevant to the delivery of goods and services more tightly. In addition, the recently strengthened Social Cabinet could play a key role in coordination among municipalities, departments, and social service delivery agencies, as well as ensuring that the proper quality control over the delivery process is in place. It is crucial to strengthen the civil service system, which is now characterized by high rates of turnover among personnel and the absence of a formal training system, resulting in substantial instability across public service positions and a shortage of professional skills.

Another obstacle facing service delivery is the lack of regular, efficient monitoring and evaluation of the timeliness, quality, and cost of projects. There is no integrated inventory of the beneficiaries of social programs and no national effort to integrate the few monitoring and evaluation initiatives that exist. With the exception of the evaluation of some programs by the Ministry of Finance as part of a pilot exercise, there is no viable system to measure the performance of public sector management units. This has negative consequences for accountability, the management of public programs, and the budget allocation process. Because there is no mechanism for the assessment of the quality of service delivery, identifying optimal policies and strategies is problematic.

Final Remarks

Paraguay has made substantial progress in the past decade in improving welfare and reducing inequality among the population. There are reasons for optimism, including the greater labor productivity in agriculture and the enhanced employment opportunities, suggesting that long-lasting transformation is possible. Nonetheless, the country faces challenges that may threaten the sustainability of the advances.

A key obstacle is the fact that a large share of the population faces a volatile economic environment. Both the rural and urban poor rely on irregular earnings streams, leaving them exposed to labor market and macroeconomic risks. While the urban poor have limited job prospects, leading to high rates of unemployment and self-employment, the rural poor disproportionately depend on agriculture for their incomes, exposing them to macroeconomic price fluctuations and local risks such as bad weather and agricultural pests. Large segments of the population that have escaped poverty therefore remain vulnerable to poverty and seem unable to join the ranks of the middle class.

A second major obstacle is the persistent lack of opportunity for all. Although income inequality has narrowed, some structural determinants of inequity remain. Inequalities persist across geographical areas, and access to good-quality basic services, such as education and safe water, is limited to more well-off population segments, especially in urban areas. A more equitable and efficient fiscal system can play a fundamental role in providing the essential safety nets to help people weather fluctuations in the labor market and offset the effects of inequality in the access of children to basic services.

Notes

1. The threshold that separates the vulnerable and the middle class is set at $10 per person a day (at 2005 purchasing power parity [PPP]), following the definitions in Ferreira et al. (2013).

2. These results are derived from a probit regression among adults in the bottom 40 on the probability of engagement in wage employment rather than self-employment, unemployment, unpaid work, or economic inactivity. Departments are added as dummy variables. The "rest of the departments" are Amambay, Caazapá, Canindeyú, Concepción, Cordillera, Guairá, Misiones, Ñeembucú, Paraguarí, and Presidente Hayes.

3. The comparison of transfers received by households with members over the age of 65 and woman-headed households with children involves controls for the variation in annual trends across rural and urban areas. These results are based on a log-linear regression of the total transfers received on household composition and year- and location-fixed effects.

4. This analysis is derived from a probit regression among adults in the bottom quintile on the probability of employment in large firms or in the public sector, as opposed to not working or working as self-employed, in a small firm, or as an unpaid worker.

5. Guaraní is an official language in Paraguay. Though it is an indigenous language (spoken by the Guaraní), it is also spoken by nonindigenous people, particularly in rural areas.

6. See Second Regional Comparative and Explanatory Study (database), Latin-American Laboratory for the Assessment of the Quality of Education, Regional Bureau for Education in Latin America and the Caribbean, United Nations Educational, Scientific, and Cultural Organization, Santiago, Chile, http://www.unesco.org/new/en/santiago/education/education-assessment-llece/perce-serce-databases/.

7. The countries in the study are Argentina, Bolivia, Brazil, Chile, Colombia, Costa Rica, the Dominican Republic, Ecuador, El Salvador, Guatemala, Honduras, Mexico, Nicaragua, Panama, Paraguay, Peru, Uruguay, and República Bolivariana de Venezuela.

8. Tax revenue in Paraguay in 2012, the most recent year for which data are available, has been estimated at 17.6 percent of GDP.

9. For several countries in the region, Higgins et al. (forthcoming) and Lustig, Pessino, and Scott (2014) report the Gini coefficient before and after taxes and transfers.

10. The classroom availability index represents "the number of classrooms available in a school normalized by the number of classrooms that should be available so that a value of 100 means that the school has exactly the number of classrooms it needs given its student population (all schools with an index value at or above 100 are not infrastructure poor)" (Wodon 2014, 10).

References

Barros, Ricardo P., Mirela De Carvalho, Samuel Franco, and Rosane Mendoça. 2006. "Uma Análise das Principais Causas da Queda Recente na Desigualdade de Renda Brasileira." *Revista Econômica* 8 (1): 117–47.

Bucheli, Marisa, Nora Lustig, Máximo Rossi, and Florencia Amábile. 2014. "Social Spending, Taxes, and Income Redistribution in Uruguay." In "Analyzing the Redistributive Impact of Taxes and Transfers in Latin America," ed. Nora Lustig, Carola Pessino, and John Scott, special issue, *Public Finance Review* 42 (3): 413–33.

Demirgüç-Kunt, Asli, and Leora Klapper. 2012. "Measuring Financial Inclusion: The Global Findex Database." Policy Research Working Paper 6025, World Bank, Washington, DC.

Ferreira, Francisco H. G., Julian Messina, Jamele Rigolini, Luis F. López-Calva, María Ana Lugo, and Renos Vakis. 2013. *Economic Mobility and the Rise of the Latin American Middle Class*. Washington, DC: World Bank.

Guillén, Stella. 2010. "El Gasto Social en Paraguay: una mirada detallada al periodo 2002–2010." Observatorio Fiscal, Centro de Análisis y Difusión de la Economía Paraguaya, Asunción, Paraguay.

Higgins, Sean, Nora Lustig, Julio Ramirez, and Billy Swanson. Forthcoming. "Social Spending, Taxes and Income Redistribution in Paraguay." *Public Finance Review*.

Higgins, Sean, and Claudiney Pereira. 2014. "The Effects of Brazil's Taxation and Social Spending on the Distribution of Household Income." In "Analyzing the Redistributive Impact of Taxes and Transfers in Latin America," ed. Nora Lustig, Carola Pessino, and John Scott, special issue, *Public Finance Review* 42 (3): 346–67.

Jaramillo, Miguel. 2014. "The Incidence of Social Spending and Taxes in Peru." In "Analyzing the Redistributive Impact of Taxes and Transfers in Latin America," ed. Nora Lustig, Carola Pessino, and John Scott, special issue, *Public Finance Review* 42 (3): 391–412.

Lustig, Nora, and Carola Pessino. 2014. "Social Spending and Income Redistribution in Argentina in the 2000s: The Rising Role of Noncontributory Pensions." In "Analyzing the Redistributive Impact of Taxes and Transfers in Latin America," ed. Nora Lustig, Carola Pessino, and John Scott, special issue, *Public Finance Review* 42 (3): 304–25.

Lustig, Nora, Carola Pessino, and John Scott. 2014. "The Impact of Taxes and Social Spending on Inequality and Poverty in Argentina, Bolivia, Brazil, Mexico, Peru, and Uruguay: Introduction to the Special Issue." In "Analyzing the Redistributive Impact of Taxes and Transfers in Latin America," ed. Nora Lustig, Carola Pessino, and John Scott, special issue, *Public Finance Review* 42 (3): 287–303.

OECD (Organisation for Economic Co-operation and Development), ECLAC (United Nations Economic Commission for Latin America and the Caribbean), and CIAT (Inter-American Center of Tax Administrations). 2014. *Revenue Statistics in Latin America, 1990–2012*. Paris: OECD.

Paz Arauco, Verónica, George Gray Molina, Ernesto Yáñez Aguilar, and Wilson Jiménez Pozo. 2014. "Explaining Low Redistributive Impact in Bolivia." In "Analyzing the Redistributive Impact of Taxes and Transfers in Latin America," ed. Nora Lustig, Carola Pessino, and John Scott, special issue, *Public Finance Review* 42 (3): 326–45.

Scott, John. 2014. "Redistributive Impact and Efficiency of Mexico's Fiscal System." In "Analyzing the Redistributive Impact of Taxes and Transfers in Latin America," ed. Nora Lustig, Carola Pessino, and John Scott, special issue, *Public Finance Review* 42 (3): 368–90.

Wodon, Quentin. 2014. "Analyzing School Infrastructure Needs, Costs, and Investments: A Case Study for Paraguay." World Bank, Washington, DC.

World Bank. 2014a. "Social Gains in the Balance: A Fiscal Policy Challenge for Latin America and the Caribbean." Poverty and Labor Brief, Report 85162 rev (February), Latin America and Caribbean Region, World Bank, Washington, DC.

———. 2014b. *Análisis de riesgo del sector agropecuario en Paraguay: Identificación, priorización, estrategia y plan de acción*. Report 92866. Washington, DC: World Bank.

CHAPTER 8

Steering toward Shared Prosperity in Peru

María Eugenia Genoni and Mateo Salazar

Introduction

Between 2004 and 2013, Peru made impressive strides in reducing poverty and improving social indicators. The total poverty rate fell from 58.7 to 23.9 percent of the population, and the extreme poverty rate declined by almost 12 percentage points, to 4.7 percent.[1] In the same period, 8.7 million Peruvians left poverty, and 3.0 million escaped extreme poverty. The Gini coefficient fell from 0.49 to 0.44, and the poorest 40 percent of the income distribution (the bottom 40) experienced larger income growth than the richest 60 percent (the top 60).

This remarkable performance was the result of solid growth in gross domestic product (GDP) in a context of macroeconomic stability. The combination of prudent macroeconomic policies, the ambitious structural reforms that started in the 1990s, positive terms of trade, and large foreign direct investment allowed Peru to emerge as one of the most stable and most rapidly growing economies in Latin America. Average growth was higher in 2002–13 than in any other decade in Peru's history. Real GDP increased at an average annual rate of 6.6 percent, and the economy almost doubled in size. The expansion of the labor market through greater participation and rising incomes explains approximately three-quarters of the reduction in extreme poverty and 80 percent of the reduction in inequality in Peru in recent years.

This has enabled Peru to advance the development agenda. However, the country still shows striking disparities. Extreme poverty is highly concentrated and persists in some areas of the country. Children's access to basic services is limited by, for example, location and the educational attainment of household heads, and this restrains their opportunity to reach their full potential. Informality is pervasive and significant, and access to financial markets is narrow. Although many people have exited poverty, most are vulnerable to the risk of falling back into poverty.

Over the last decade, growth has been strong and broadbased. The country has managed to keep inflation low, maintain a fiscal surplus, and reduce public debt to below 20 percent of GDP since 2012. International reserves represent a third of GDP and can serve as a buffer in case of external shocks.

Peru's growth performance is expected to remain robust during 2015. However, weaker commodity prices, the Federal Reserve's tapering in the United States, the economic slowdown in China, and the impact of El Niño may become tests of the Peruvian economy in the next couple of years. For the positive trends in poverty and inequality reduction to continue at the rates of the past decade, Peru needs to maintain the current pace of structural reform and improve competitiveness, but also close persistent development gaps within the country. The challenge is to strengthen the link between growth and equity so these reinforce each other and promote the virtuous circle of shared prosperity. The majority of the population remains vulnerable to the risk of falling into poverty; this has the potential to reverse the progress achieved over the course of the past decade. To prevent this from occurring, priority areas include closing gaps in infrastructure, increasing the quality of basic services such as education, and expanding market access among the poor and vulnerable. Improvement in the progressivity of the fiscal system is needed, as are coordination and implementation in public investments.

In April 2012, the World Bank announced a global strategy based on two goals: (1) eradicate extreme poverty worldwide by 2030 and (2) promote shared prosperity, that is, a sustainable increase in the well-being of the poorest segments of society, defined as the bottom 40. This chapter presents a review of Peru's progress in achieving these two objectives between 2004 and 2013.

The next three sections outline the progress in terms of poverty and shared prosperity during this period. The following section highlights four important channels for achieving a more equitable society that could enhance the capacity of Peru to accelerate shared prosperity: (1) maintaining equitable, efficient, and sustainable fiscal policy; (2) strengthening fair, transparent institutions that deliver high-quality public goods and service; (3) enabling an environment of well-functioning markets that are accessible to all; and (4) improving resiliency and risk management.

Outstanding Performance in Poverty Reduction

Peru achieved great success in lowering total and extreme poverty between 2004 and 2013. The share of the population living below the official extreme poverty line, which represents the minimum income necessary to meet basic food requirements in the country, dropped from 16.4 to 4.7 percent. The total poverty rate fell from 58.7 to 23.9 percent. Over the period,

Figure 8.1 Total and Extreme Poverty Rates, Peru, 2004–13

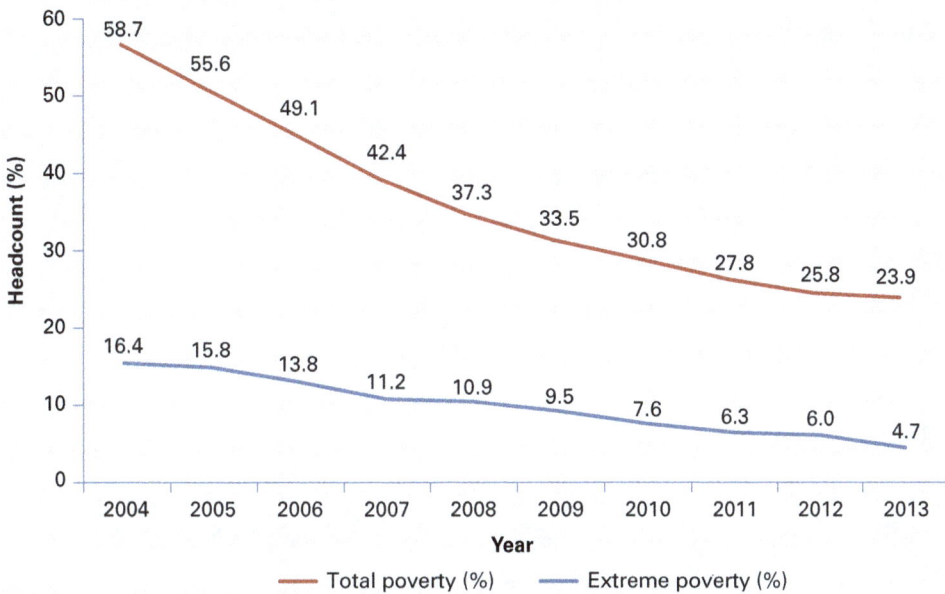

Source: Calculations based on data from the National Household Survey.
Note: The data are based on calculations using the official methodology for the estimation of poverty rates. The official poverty rates are monetary and based on a consumption aggregate.

8.7 million people rose out of poverty, and 3.0 million exited extreme poverty (figure 8.1; annex 8A, table 8A.1).

The reduction in extreme poverty has occurred more rapidly in some regions. Although the majority of regions saw declines in extreme poverty between 2004 and 2013, the declines were most dynamic in the regions of Huancavelica, Huánuco, and Puno (figure 8.2). In 2013, the extreme poverty rate was below 3 percent in 8 of the 25 regions.

In 2013, despite the progress, more than 1.5 million Peruvians were still living in extreme poverty, most of them in rural areas. Extreme poverty is largely a rural phenomenon in Peru. In 2013, about 16 percent of rural residents were still living in extreme poverty, compared with only 1 percent in urban areas (figure 8.3; annex 8A, table 8A.1). While over 77 percent of the poor in urban areas have been able to escape extreme poverty since 2004, the extreme poverty rate in rural areas has declined by 65 percent. The differences in these declines can also be seen in the respective shares of the population among the poor: the rural poor accounted for 76 percent of the total poor in 2004, but, by 2013, the share had risen to 83 percent.

Not only is extreme poverty highly rural, it is also concentrated in only a few districts. District poverty maps allow the identification of districts in which a large concentration of the extreme poor reside.[2] In 2012, almost

Figure 8.2 Changes in the Extreme Poverty Rate, by Region, Peru, 2004–13

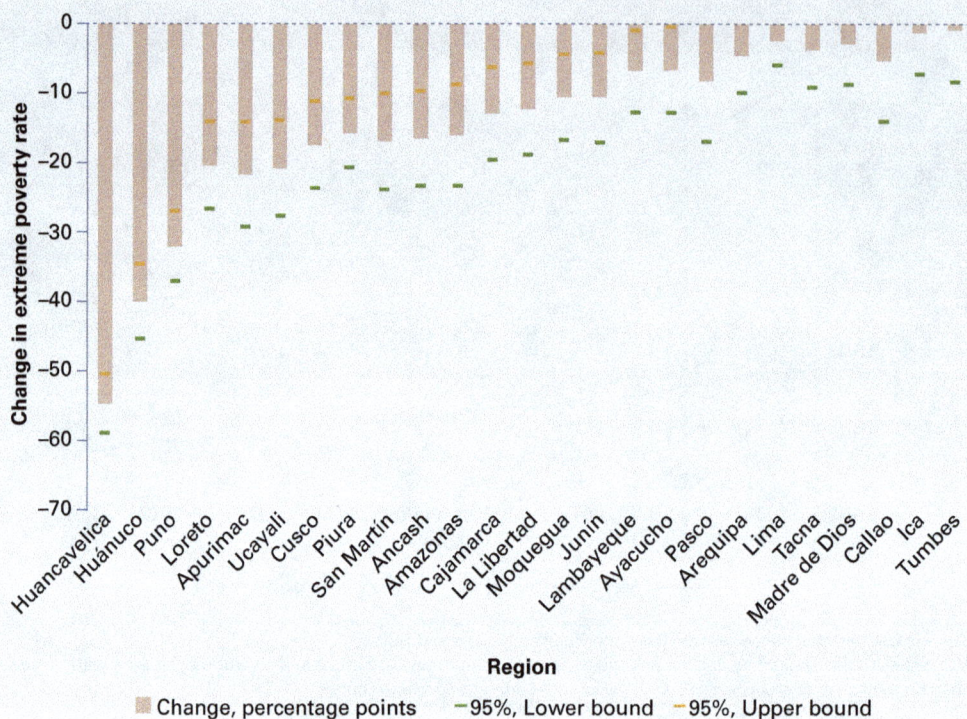

Change, percentage points   −95%, Lower bound   −95%, Upper bound

Source: Calculations based on data from the National Household Survey.
Note: The data are based on calculations using the official methodology for the estimation of poverty rates. The official poverty rates are monetary and based on a consumption aggregate.

half the extreme poor were concentrated in approximately 8 percent of the districts. A large portion of these districts are located in the regions of Apurímac, Cajamarca, La Libertad, and Piura.

A profile of the extreme poor highlights a combination of factors that may limit the ability of this population group to escape from poverty. In 2013, the average gap in educational attainment between household heads living in extreme poverty and other household heads was 4.6 years. Moreover, the extreme poor were significantly less likely to have access to basic infrastructure services; for instance, there was a 38.8 percentage point gap in access to safe water between the extreme poor and the rest of the population. There were also large differences in the labor market between people living in extreme poverty and the more well-off. Thus, compared with others, the extreme poor were more likely to work in the primary sector (78.5 percent) and to be self-employed or unpaid workers. The extreme poor were also more likely to be informally employed (working in smaller firms and without contracts) (annex 8B, table 8B.1). Indigenous origin is likewise correlated with extreme poverty.[3] Despite improvements in recent years,

Figure 8.3 The Extreme Poor in Urban and Rural Areas, Peru, 2004–13

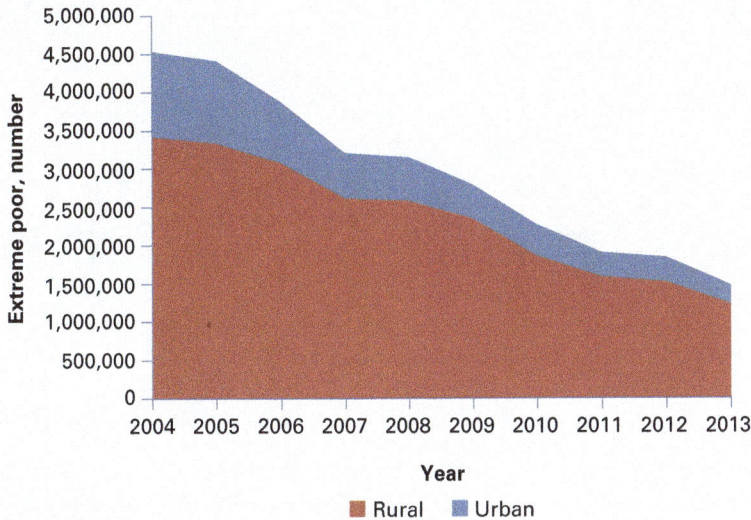

Source: Calculations based on data from the National Household Survey.
Note: The data are based on calculations using the official methodology for the estimation of poverty rates. The official poverty rates are monetary and based on a consumption aggregate.

the extreme poverty rate among the indigenous population was 9 percent in 2013, compared with 3.7 percent among the rest of the population.

From 2004 to 2013, Peru substantially reduced the share of the population that was poor in multidimensional and monetary terms simultaneously. Based on the extreme poverty line, this share fell from 28.1 to 11.5 percent during the period.[4] Moreover, the proportion of Peruvians who were simultaneously multidimensionally and monetarily poor declined by 8.2 percentage points. This reduction highlights the significant progress achieved in lifting people out of the multiple nonmonetary and monetary deprivations that make them more likely to remain in poverty (figure 8.4).

Extreme poverty affects two types of individuals in Peru: the chronic poor and people or households that have fallen into poverty because of temporary shocks. Using panel data for 2007 and 2010, one finds that only half of the extreme poor were the same people in these two years. Considering the group that was among the extreme poor in 2007, 60 percent had been able to leave extreme poverty by 2010 (figure 8.5, chart a). In 2010, only 51 percent of the extreme poor had also been among the extreme poor in 2007. (Box 8.1 compares this mobility in Peru and the region.) The remaining 49 percent were living above the extreme poverty line in 2007 (figure 8.5, chart b). This indicates that policies to move people out of extreme poverty may need to incorporate strategies to address temporary shocks as well as policies focused on fighting chronic poverty.

Figure 8.4 Households with Multiple Nonmonetary Deprivations, Peru, 2004 and 2013

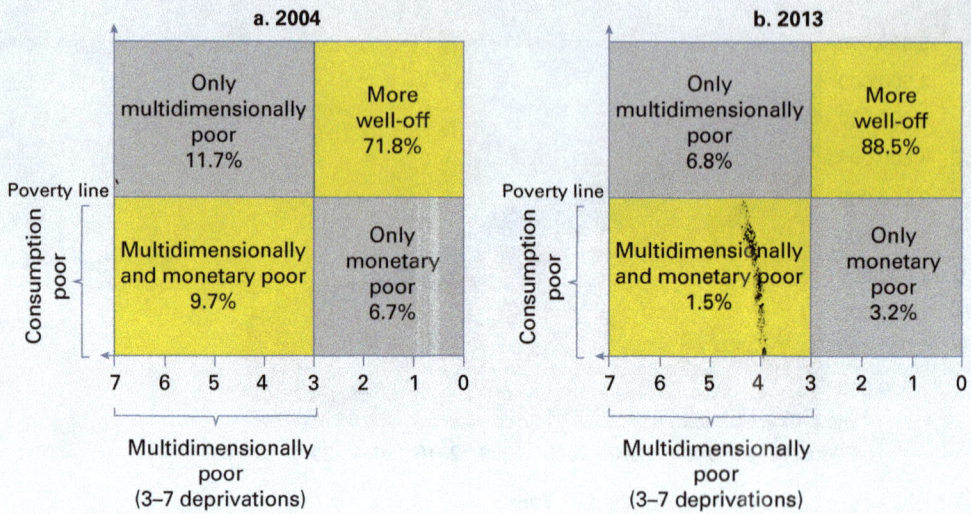

a. 2004

Only multidimensionally poor 11.7%	More well-off 71.8%	
Multidimensionally and monetary poor 9.7%	Only monetary poor 6.7%	

Poverty line

Consumption poor

7 6 5 4 3 2 1 0

Multidimensionally poor
(3–7 deprivations)

b. 2013

Only multidimensionally poor 6.8%	More well-off 88.5%	
Multidimensionally and monetary poor 1.5%	Only monetary poor 3.2%	

Poverty line

Consumption poor

7 6 5 4 3 2 1 0

Multidimensionally poor
(3–7 deprivations)

Source: Calculations based on data from the National Household Survey.
Note: More well-off refers to people who are not monetarily poor or multidimensionally poor. The official extreme poverty line is used to make the calculations. Individuals or households are multidimensionally poor if they are deprived in at least three of the following seven dimensions: (a) any school-age child (7 to 15 years of age) in the household is out of school, (b) no household member has completed five years of schooling, (c) the walls of the dwelling are precarious, (d) no access to tap water in the dwelling, (e) no flush toilet or pit latrine in the dwelling, (f) no electricity, and (g) the dwelling lacks at least two of the following: television, telephone, transportation, and refrigerator. See Castañeda et al. (2012).

Figure 8.5 Chronic Poverty, Peru, 2007 and 2010

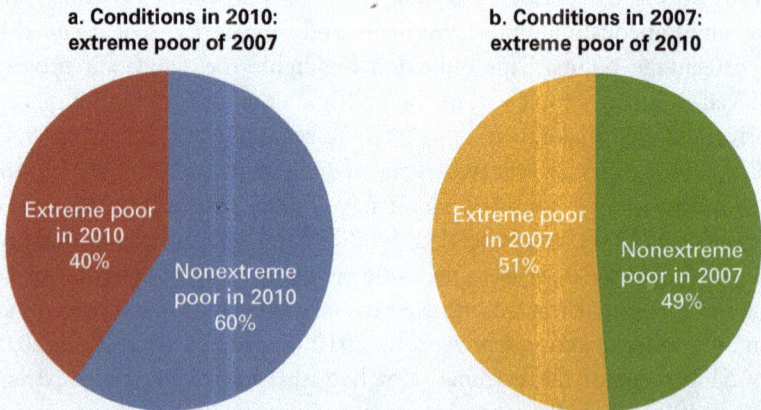

a. Conditions in 2010:
extreme poor of 2007

Extreme poor in 2010 40%

Nonextreme poor in 2010 60%

b. Conditions in 2007:
extreme poor of 2010

Extreme poor in 2007 51%

Nonextreme poor in 2007 49%

Source: Calculations based on data from the 2007–10 panel of the National Household Survey.

Box 8.1 Comparing Mobility Out of Poverty in Peru and the Region

Measured according to a poverty line of $2.50 a day, extreme poverty in Latin America and the Carib-
bean region declined by 10 percentage points, from 22.3 to 12.3 percent, between 2004 and 2012. The
reduction in Peru was more rapid than that seen in the region overall, falling from 25.2 to 11.6 percent
in these years. A similar trend is evident in moderate poverty rates, which fell 14 percentage points in
the region over the period, compared with 21 percentage points in Peru (figure B8.1.1).

Figure B8.1.1 Share of the Poor, Vulnerable, and Middle Class, Peru and the Region, around 2004 and 2012

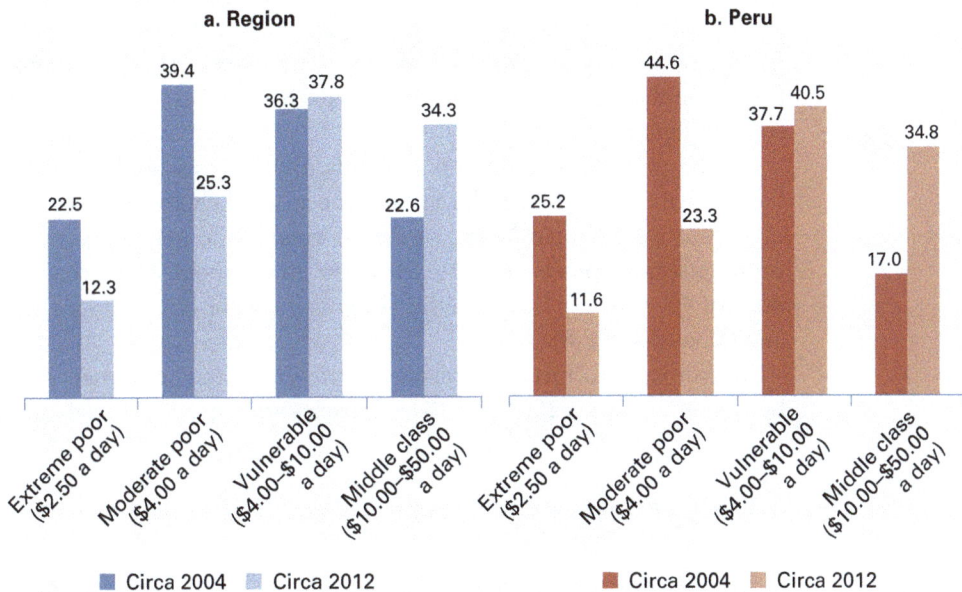

Source: Calculations based on data in SEDLAC.
Note: The SEDLAC database is a harmonized comparable dataset that relies on measures of poverty relying on
comparable income aggregates and poverty lines. Estimates of poverty, vulnerability, and the middle class at
the regional level are population-weighted averages of country estimates. Estimates for the region and for Peru
are based on income. The poor are defined as people living on less than $4.00 a day; the vulnerable are people
living on $4.00 to $10.00 a day; and the middle class is defined as people living on $10.00 to $50.00 a day (all in
2005 purchasing power parity U.S. dollars). To achieve an analysis based on the same set of countries each
year, interpolation has been applied if country data were not available in a given year.

In both Peru and the region in 2012, one in three people was in the middle class. The threshold for
the middle class of $10 a day per capita reflects a level of income at which the probability of falling
into poverty is less than 10 percent (Ferreira et al. 2013). By 2012, the number of people in the middle
class exceeded the number of poor, accounting for 34.8 percent of the Peruvian population, compared
with 34.3 percent in the region.

However, the largest portion of the population in Peru and the region is still vulnerable to the risk
of falling back into poverty. In Peru, 40.5 percent of the population has left poverty, but faces a non-
trivial probability of becoming poor again. In the region, 37.8 percent of the population remains
vulnerable.

Inequality Has Narrowed, but Remains Significant

Income inequality in Peru is still substantial, but has improved since 2004. Measured using the Gini coefficient, income inequality fell from 0.49 in 2004 to 0.44 in 2013 (figure 8.6; annex 8A, table 8A.1). The improvement in aggregate inequality masks important geographical differences. While the Gini coefficient in rural areas in 2004 and 2013 fell by only 1 point, urban inequality fell by 5 points. For the first time since 2010, inequality narrowed in rural areas in 2013.

The World Bank's indicator of shared prosperity—the growth rate of real income per capita among the bottom 40—shows that the poorest households have gained ground in the last few years. Between 2004 and 2013, average real per capita income grew 5.3 percent per year among the entire population, but at a higher annual pace, 6.7 percent, among the bottom 40 (figure 8.7).

The bottom 40 live in larger households, and the household heads tend to be less well educated. In addition, they are more likely to be self-employed or unpaid workers, participate in the informal economy, and work in the primary sector (annex 8B, table 8B.1). In 2013, about 21 percent of the bottom 40 were in Lima. Another 21 percent were in Cajamarca, Piura, and Puno (figure 8.8).

Within regions, there is significant variation in the performance of the bottom 40. Between 2004 and 2013, incomes among the bottom 40 in each

Figure 8.6 The Gini Coefficient, Urban and Rural Areas and Nationwide, Peru, 2004–13

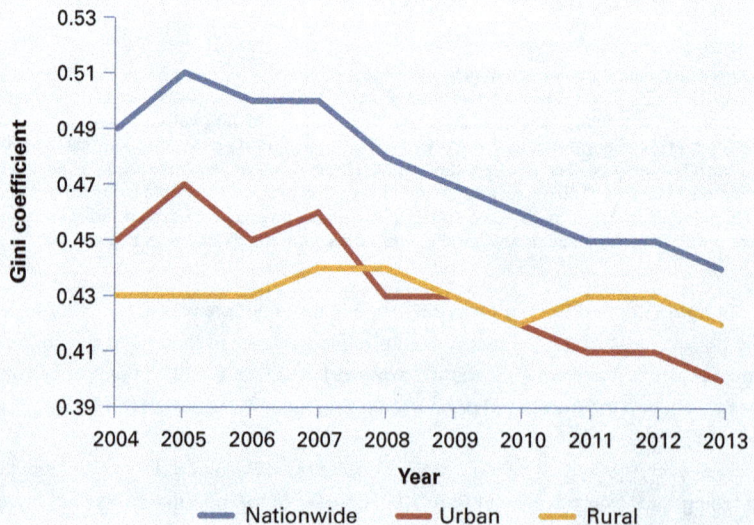

Source: Calculations based on data from the National Household Survey.
Note: The data are based on calculations using the official methodology. The Gini coefficients are based on an income-based aggregate.

Figure 8.7 Shared Prosperity: Mean Annual Growth in Average Income, by Region, Peru, 2004–13

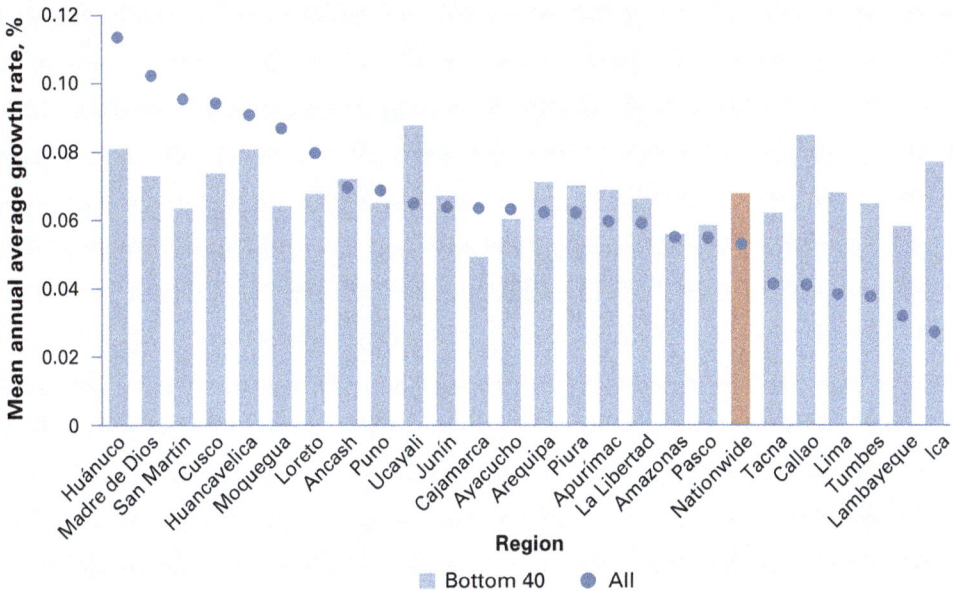

Source: Calculations based on data from the National Household Survey.

Figure 8.8 Distribution of the Bottom 40, by Region, Peru, 2013

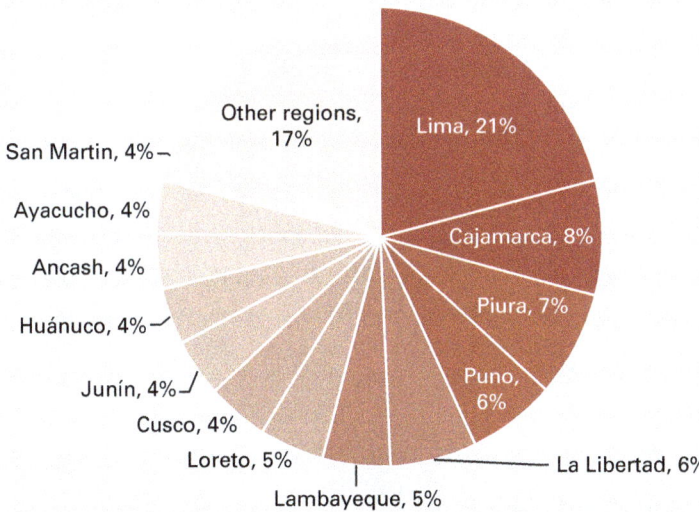

Source: Calculations based on data from the National Household Survey.
Note: The distribution of the bottom 40 is calculated using the distribution of total household income per capita.

region increased. However, there was significant variation in relative performance. For example, income growth among the bottom 40 in Huancavelica and Huánuco, two of the poorest regions in 2004, underperformed total income growth in these regions. In contrast, the bottom 40 in Apurímac, another poor region, showed much more rapid progress even though the average regional income lagged the national average (see figure 8.7).

Despite notable improvements in inequality indicators, Peru remains a highly unequal country. In 2012, the richest 1 percent of the population controlled almost 8 percent of all income. In contrast, the bottom 40 accounted for only 15 percent. In 2011, compared with Latin America and the Caribbean region, Peru presented one of the lowest Gini coefficients (after Argentina and Uruguay). However, the region and Peru are still lagging behind the relatively low levels of income inequality in other countries, particularly the members of the Organisation for Economic Co-operation and Development (OECD). The Gini coefficients in OECD countries that are not in Latin America and the Caribbean were between 0.24 and 0.41 in the late 2000s (World Bank 2013a).

Economic Growth: The Main Driver of Improvement

Peru's economy took off in 2000 and has since become one of the top performers in Latin America and the Caribbean. Between 2004 and 2013, GDP per capita rose by an average 5.4 percent a year. This is in sharp contrast with the relatively weak performance of previous decades (annex 8C, table 8C.1).[5] Moreover, the economy weathered the global financial crisis fairly well; although GDP growth slowed substantially, from 9.8 percent in 2008 to 0.9 percent in 2009, it rebounded rapidly, to 8.8 percent in 2010. Relative to the region, Peru was able to maintain positive GDP growth during the financial crisis (figure 8.9).

The strengthening of private consumption and investment is consistent with the more favorable environment necessary to reduce poverty. Between 2004 and 2013, internal demand was the main driver of GDP growth. Labor-intensive sectors, such as construction and services, were among the most dynamic during the period. The relationship between rapid growth and the reduction in poverty was strong. For each percentage point increase in GDP growth, poverty fell 1.3 percentage points. This elasticity was greater than that observed in previous years, indicating that growth was creating favorable conditions for poverty reduction. Poverty was more responsive to growth in urban areas than in rural areas; growth–poverty elasticity in rural areas of the Andean highlands and the Amazon rainforest was significantly below the national average (figure 8.10). This is consistent with the fact that the primary sector has not been as dynamic as other sectors in recent years.

The share of the working-age population has been increasing because of a demographic transition. Between 2004 and 2012, the share of the population 15–64 years of age rose from 62.3 to 64.5 percent. In the last decade,

Figure 8.9 GDP Growth, Peru, 2000–13

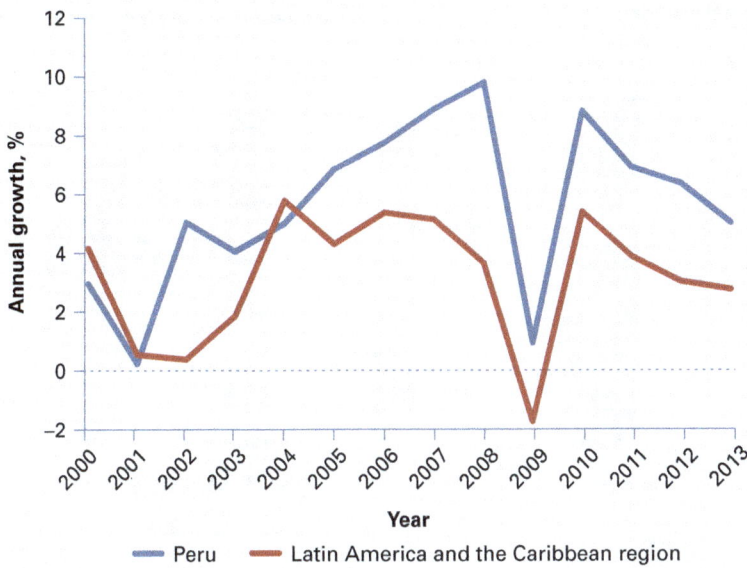

Source: WDI (World Development Indicators) (database), World Bank, Washington, DC,
http://data.worldbank.org/data-catalog/world-development-indicators.

Figure 8.10 Growth–Poverty Elasticity, by Geographical Region and Urban or Rural Area, Peru, 2004–13

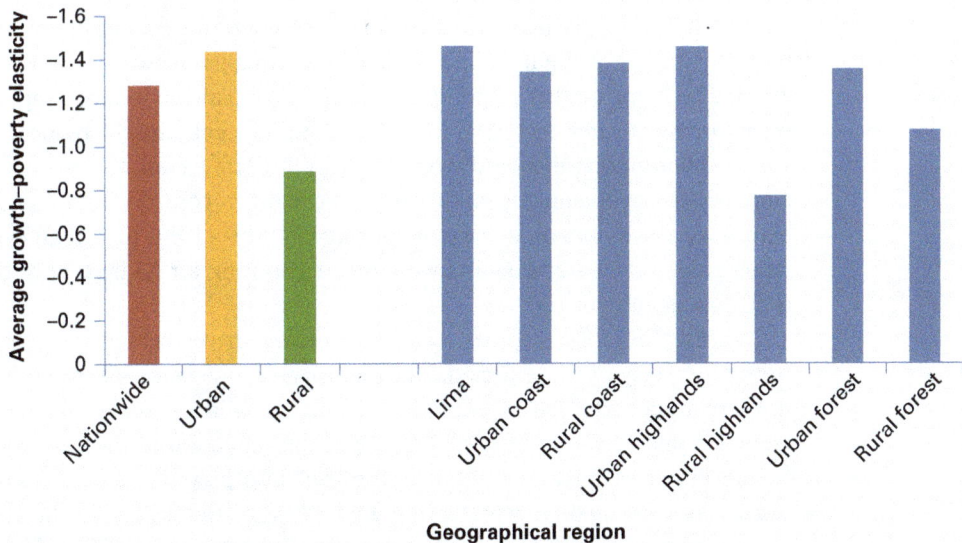

Source: Calculations based on data from the National Household Survey and data of the Central Reserve Bank of Peru.

Figure 8.11 Labor Market Performance, Peru, 2004 and 2012

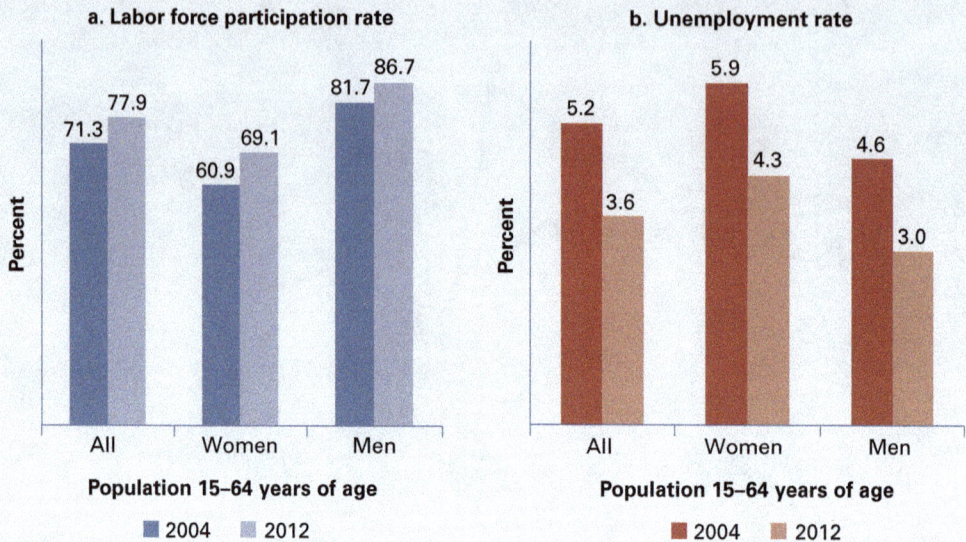

a. Labor force participation rate

71.3 · 77.9 · 60.9 · 69.1 · 81.7 · 86.7

All · Women · Men

Population 15–64 years of age

■ 2004   ■ 2012

b. Unemployment rate

5.2 · 3.6 · 5.9 · 4.3 · 4.6 · 3.0

All · Women · Men

Population 15–64 years of age

■ 2004   ■ 2012

Source: WDI (World Development Indicators) (database), World Bank, Washington, DC, http://data.worldbank
.org/data-catalog/world-development-indicators.
Note: The data for 2012 reflect the latest information for that year.

labor force participation expanded by 6.6 percentage points. This was driven in part by an 8.2 percentage point boost in labor force participation among women, 3 percentage points more than that among men. Indeed, female labor force participation explains 9 percent of the decline in extreme poverty and 17 percent of the decline in inequality between 2004 and 2013. The labor market responded well to this expansion in labor supply: unemployment rates decreased from 5.2 to 3.6 percent, and the reductions were similar among men and women (figure 8.11). Overall, the growth in employment opportunities among men and women contributed about 23 percent to the reduction in extreme poverty in 2004–13. It played an even larger role in the narrowing in inequality, accounting for 33 percent of the total change (annex 8D).

Increases in labor incomes were the primary driver behind the reductions in poverty over the period. The majority—53 percent—of the decline in extreme poverty can be explained by higher labor incomes. Similarly, labor income accounted for 47 percent of the reduction in the Gini coefficient. However, private and public transfers also played a key role in the reduction in inequality, representing 26 percent of the decline in the Gini coefficient between 2004 and 2013. Despite the importance of transfers in the reduction of inequality, they had a smaller role in the change in extreme poverty (annex 8D).

The gains were laudable, but Peru still lags developed nations. Sen's welfare index, an equity-adjusted GDP measure, can be used to compare Peru's

Figure 8.12 Growth Rates Needed to Achieve Sen's Welfare Index Benchmark in GDP per Capita and the Gini Coefficient by 2030, Peru

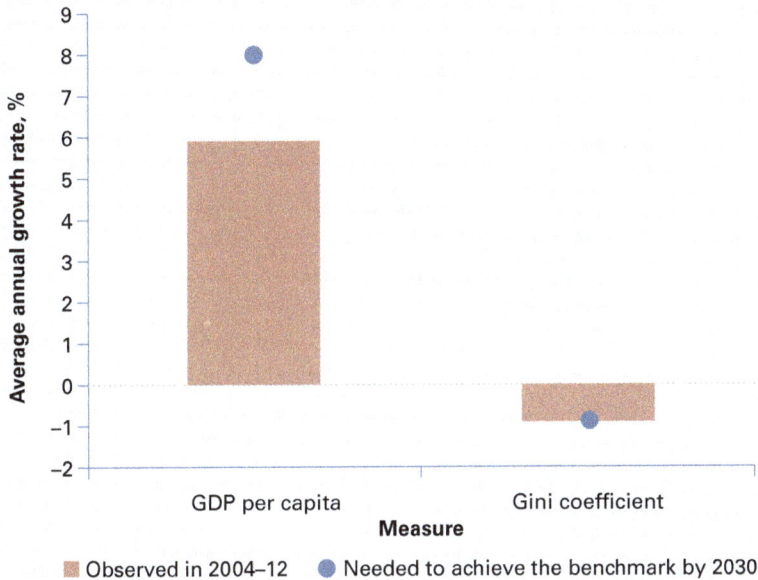

Source: Calculations based on data in SEDLAC.
Note: The benchmark refers to the population-weighted average of Sen's welfare index of the top 10 countries in 2000: Austria, Denmark, Ireland, Luxembourg, the Netherlands, Norway, Qatar, Singapore, Switzerland, and the United States. The benchmark of GDP per capita is $106.60 2005 international purchasing power parity U.S. dollars a day, and the Gini coefficient is 0.395.

performance to a benchmark group of countries to assess trends and convergence.[6] A substantial gap remains between Peru and these countries. If one assumes GDP growth remains at the levels of recent years (an average of 6.5 to 6.8 percent per year), it would take approximately 26 years to close this gap. This would require an 8.0 percent annual GDP growth rate to reach the level of welfare in benchmark countries by 2030. However, the prospects look more promising in income inequality. If the steady decline in inequality in Peru during the recent period continues, inequality can reach the Gini level of the benchmark countries by 2030 (figure 8.12).

Peru's growth performance is anticipated to remain robust in coming years. Domestic demand is expected to slow from 6.8 to 5.4 percent in 2013–14 because of a deceleration in consumption. Nonetheless, large mining projects such as those at Las Bambas, Cerro Verde, Constancia, and Toromocho will offset this trend in that operations there are projected over the next few years. As a consequence, exports should recover and increase in real terms. The fiscal stance is expected to remain positive, but with a tendency to soften starting in 2015. Total debt should decline and remain below 20 percent of GDP. The current account of the balance of payments is anticipated to remain at a manageable deficit of 4.3 percent of GDP, mainly financed through long-term capital flows. The current account deficit will improve progressively as new mining projects start up. However, weaker commodity prices, the tapering of the U.S. Federal Reserve, the impacts of natural phenomena such as El Niño, and the economic slowdown in China, which will affect the terms of trade, may pose a significant challenge.

Opportunities to Boost Shared Prosperity

The next challenge is to sustain the growth and social inclusion achieved in recent years. Economic growth will continue to be essential to improving welfare, but equity must also be fostered to enhance shared prosperity. This is the motivation underlying President Humala's national development and social inclusion strategy, Inclusion for Growth, which emphasizes the importance of promoting inclusion and increasing the welfare of excluded segments of the population as a central element in the growth process. Through the strategy, the government has set ambitious social targets that are to be realized by the end of the current administration in 2016. They encompass a significant expansion in the coverage of electricity, water, and sanitation infrastructure and voice and data services among rural households, the elimination of chronic malnutrition, and the implementation of universal access to preschool education. A new Ministry of Development and Social Inclusion was created at the end of 2011 to lead in the application of the strategy (World Bank 2012a).

Policies to reinforce the link between equity and growth will enhance shared prosperity in Peru. The country will be more equitable if all individuals have access to the opportunities and skills needed to generate income. This would allow more people to become productive and contribute to economic growth, while permitting both the poor and the nonpoor to share in the benefits of growth.

Four main channels are available to support the virtuous circle of economic growth and equity: (1) equitable and sustainable fiscal policy and fiscal stability; (2) accountable and efficient institutions and equitable service delivery; (3) well-functioning, inclusive, and equitable markets; and (4) resiliency and risk management to achieve social inclusion. Several policies can be used to take advantage of these channels.

Equitable and sustainable fiscal policy and fiscal stability

The economic growth process in Peru has been accompanied by fiscal discipline. During the past two decades, Peru has sustained primary surpluses in most years. In 2013, the primary surplus was 1.8 percent of GDP (annex 8C, table 8C.1). Sustained fiscal surpluses have reduced the public debt significantly. Between 2004 and 2013, the public debt fell 23 percentage points, to 19.2 percent of GDP. During the period, prudent fiscal policies kept inflation at an average annual rate of less than 3 percent, a historically low level. This has been important in maintaining the purchasing power of

Figure 8.13 Changes in per Capita Public Expenditures, by District Household Consumption, Peru, 2007–11

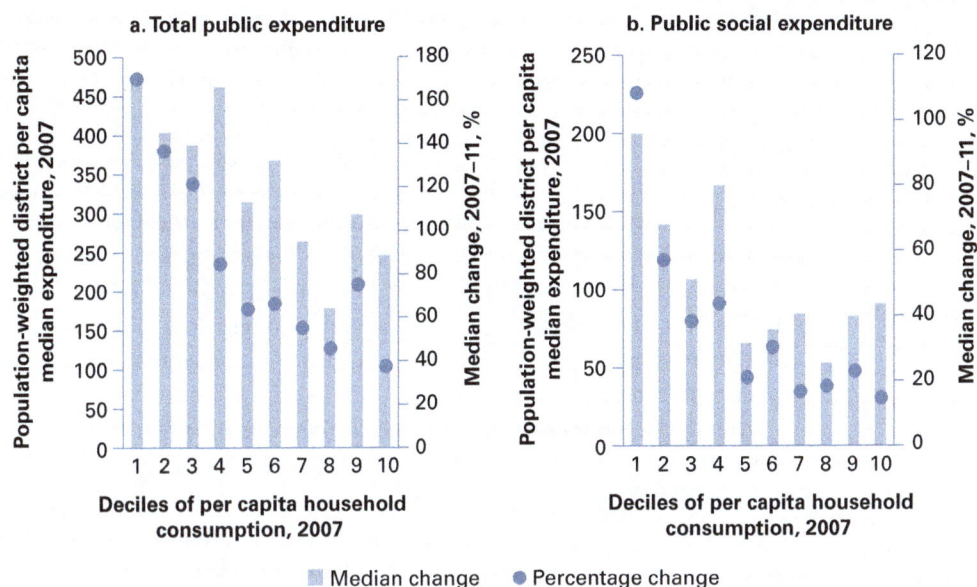

a. Total public expenditure

b. Public social expenditure

■ Median change ● Percentage change

Source: Calculations based on the 2007 poverty map of the National Statistics Office and data of the Ministry of Finance.
Note: Districts are grouped into deciles based on the estimated average per capita household expenditure in the 2007 poverty map. Spending amounts are expressed in S/. of 2007.

household incomes. Sustaining fiscal discipline will help ensure continuation of the recent positive trends in economic growth and poverty reduction.

Peru has substantial resources available to help narrow the large disparities observed in the nation. Revenues have benefited from economic growth. Current general government revenue rose from 17.4 to 21.7 percent of GDP between 2004 and 2013. Driven by an increase in the price of minerals, mining-related revenue has been a major contributor (World Bank 2012b). A key challenge in the effort to foster equity from the revenue side is the need to boost the relatively low level of tax collection. Widespread informality, the narrow tax base (because of the general design of taxes, tax evasion, and extensive exemptions and loopholes), and low average tax rates are behind the unsatisfactory collection rate (World Bank, forthcoming).

The greater revenue has made rising public expenditures possible. Current general government expenditures grew from 16.7 to 20.0 percent of GDP between 2004 and 2013 (annex 8C, table 8C.1). The relative increase in per capita public spending has been larger in the poorest areas (figure 8.13). Using district poverty maps, one may assess the extent to which the gains in government spending have been comparatively greater among residents of areas with more restrained levels of household consumption.

People living in districts in the bottom 40 percent of average household consumption showed larger increases in both total public spending and social public spending between 2007 and 2011. The poorest 10 percent of districts experienced the largest expansion in public expenditure in absolute and relative terms.

However, there is still a weak relationship between the level of public social spending and district poverty. A recent public expenditure review highlights the limited correlation between social spending and outcomes in education and health (World Bank 2012b). The weak relationship is driven by several factors. One important element is the fact that total social spending is low as a share of GDP in Peru compared with similar countries. The incidence analysis of Jaramillo (2013) indicates that the small impact of transfers on poverty is associated with low social spending. Another reason for the small impact on final outcomes may be the inefficiency of spending.

Overall, there is still significant space to improve the progressivity of the fiscal system and thereby enhance equity and boost shared prosperity. Using the Commitment to Equity methodology, one may compare market income (before taxes and transfers) and postfiscal income (after taxes and transfers).[7] This reveals that fiscal policy (without considering spending on in-kind transfers such as for health care and education services) has little to no noticeable redistributive impact. The Gini coefficient was 0.50 before taxes and transfers and 0.49 after taxes and transfers. Similar analysis on OECD countries highlights the larger redistributive role of the fiscal system: the Gini coefficient fell by approximately 14 points because of taxes and transfers.

Accountable and efficient institutions and equitable service delivery

In Peru, shared prosperity may be limited by large gaps in infrastructure in terms of the access to and quality of services. This infrastructure deficit has a negative impact on the investment climate and may compromise the ability of the country to grow to its full potential. In addition, inequalities in coverage across regions restrain the returns to other development initiatives such as investments in education, health care, and social programs.

Access to basic infrastructure services rose between 2004 and 2013 (figure 8.14, chart a). There was a significant expansion in the coverage of the cell phone network, and this had a positive impact on poverty reduction (Beuermann, McKelvey, and Vakis 2012). In addition, the share of households with comprehensive access to water, sanitation, electricity, and telephone services also went up substantially, rising nationwide from 30 to 64 percent (figure 8.14, chart b).

Substantial expansion in the access to water, sanitation, electricity, and telephones was observed in most regions. Apurímac, Ayacucho, and Huancavelica showed the largest increases in access to piped water, more than 35 percentage points between 2004 and 2013. Huancavelica exhibited the biggest improvement in the share of households with access to sanitation (sewerage), from 16 to 67 percent. Cajamarca had the largest gains in access

Figure 8.14 Access to Water, Sanitation, Electricity, and Telephone, Peru, 2004 and 2013

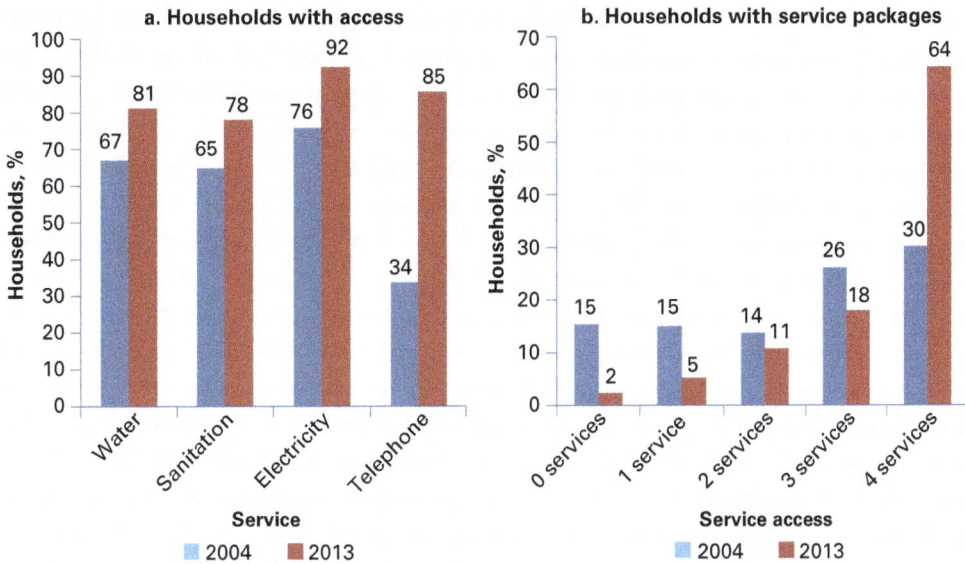

a. Households with access

b. Households with service packages

Source: Calculations based on data from the National Household Survey.

to electricity, from 33 to 76 percent. The expansion of telephone coverage, mainly driven by cell phone services, was led by Amazonas, Madre de Dios, and San Martin, at a growth of around 70 percentage points or more.

Disparities in access to services narrowed across regions in 2004–13 (figure 8.15). Most regions below the national average in access to water in 2004 had reduced the gap by 2013. The exceptions were Cajamarca and Ucayali. Huancavelica showed the largest decrease in the water gap, from 44 to 87 percent of the national average. Similar trends toward convergence were evident in sanitation and electricity. In the access to telephones, most regions had reached close to the national average by 2013.

Despite the improvements, poor and vulnerable households often still lack access to these basic services. In urban areas in 2013, 78 percent of households had access to water, sanitation, electricity, and telephone services, but, in rural areas, the share was only 20 percent (figure 8.16, chart a). Even within urban areas, less than half of households in the poorest income decile had access to all four services (figure 8.16, chart b). Escobal (2005) finds that infrastructure investment on roads, electricity, telecommunications, water, and sanitation in rural Peru has important complementary effects and that these produce a sustained impact on the growth of rural incomes. Thus, expanding access in a coordinated way by offering packages of services to communities may be a successful strategy for reducing poverty and boosting rural productivity, thereby contributing directly to equality and economic growth.

Figure 8.15 Index of Utility Coverage Rates, by Region, Peru, 2004 and 2013

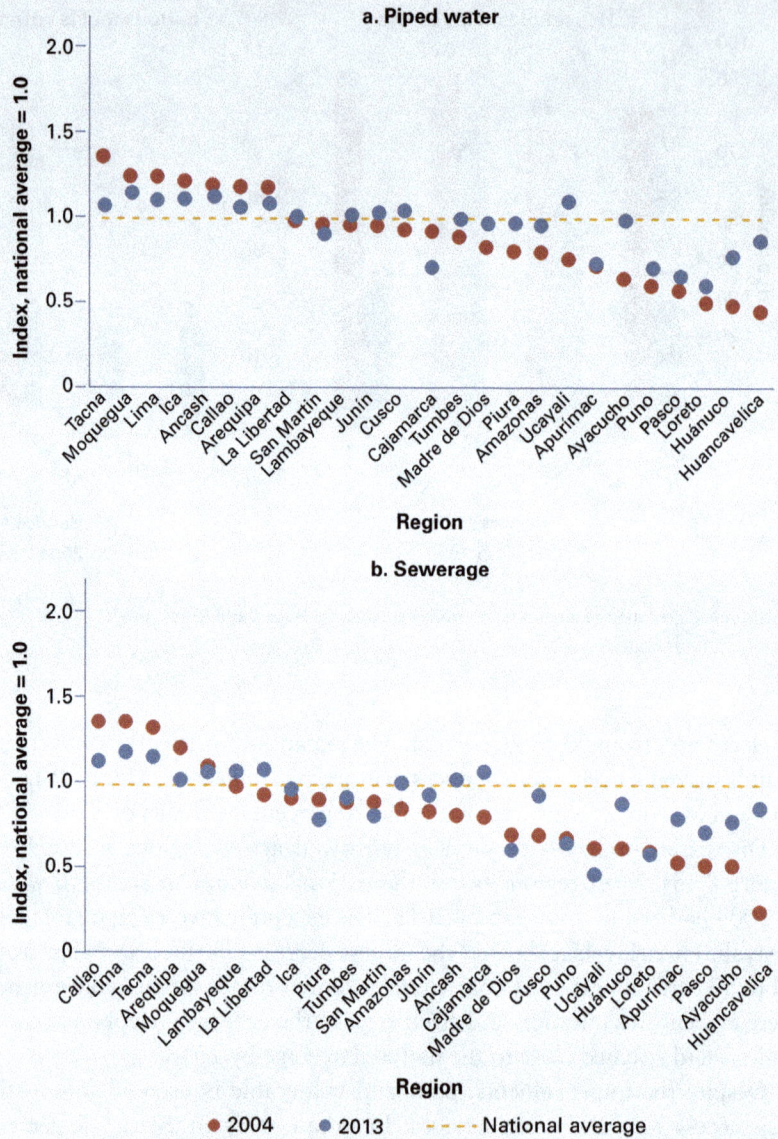

a. Piped water

b. Sewerage

● 2004　　● 2013　　- - - - National average

(continued)

The biggest disparities in coverage across regions are driven by differences in access to water and sanitation. In sanitation in 2013, 14 regions had a coverage rate that was less than 75 percent of the national average. In contrast, in electricity, the worst performers—Amazonas, Cajamarca, Huánuco, and Loreto—had coverage rates higher than 75 percent of the national average. At the national level, the access rates to sanitation were lower than the rates of access to water, electricity, and telephones. In 2013,

Figure 8.15 Index of Utility Coverage Rates, by Region, Peru, 2004 and 2013 *(Continued)*

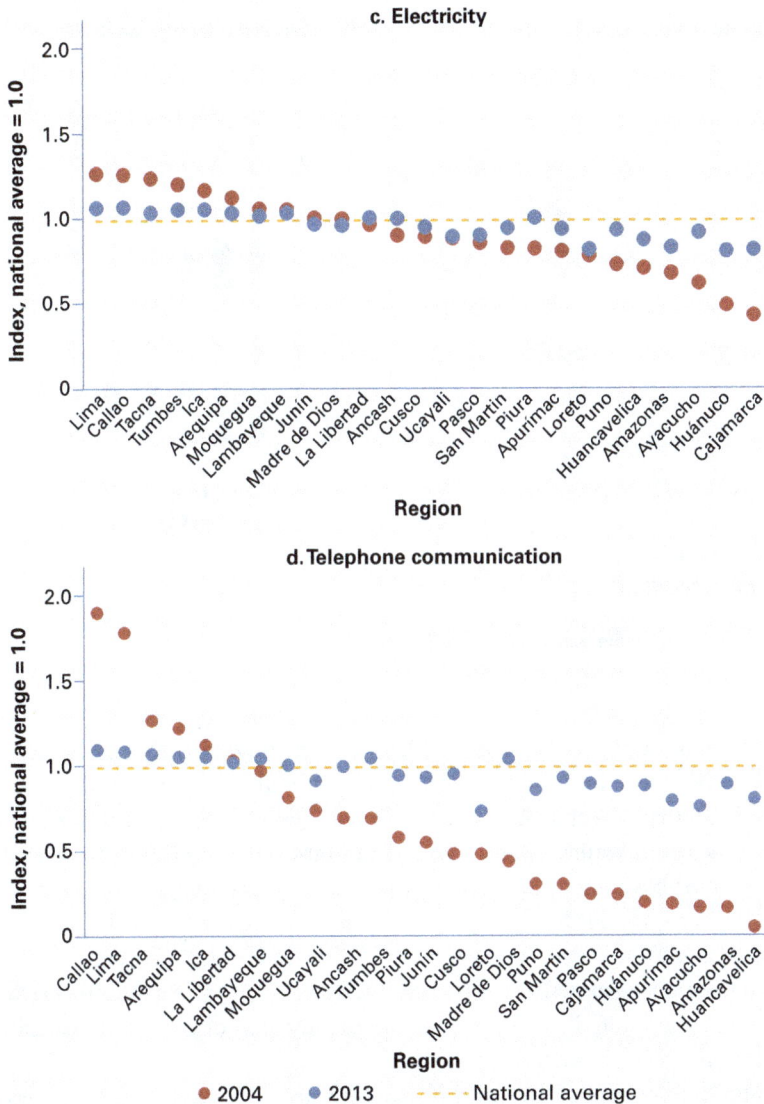

c. Electricity

d. Telephone communication

● 2004   ● 2013   - - - National average

Source: Calculations based on data from the National Household Survey.
Note: Gaps are calculated as the ratio between the share of households with access in the region and the share of households with access at the national level. Access to piped water includes access to water inside the dwelling or outside, but on the property. Access to sewerage includes septic systems and services connected to a network (inside the dwelling or outside, but within the property). Telephones include landlines and cell phones.

less than 50 percent of households in Loreto, Madre de Dios, and Ucayali had access to sewerage.

The characteristics of households are associated with the level of access of children to basic services and may be a factor in inequality in the future.

Figure 8.16 Access to Water, Sanitation, Electricity, and Telephone Services, Urban and Rural Areas, Peru, 2013

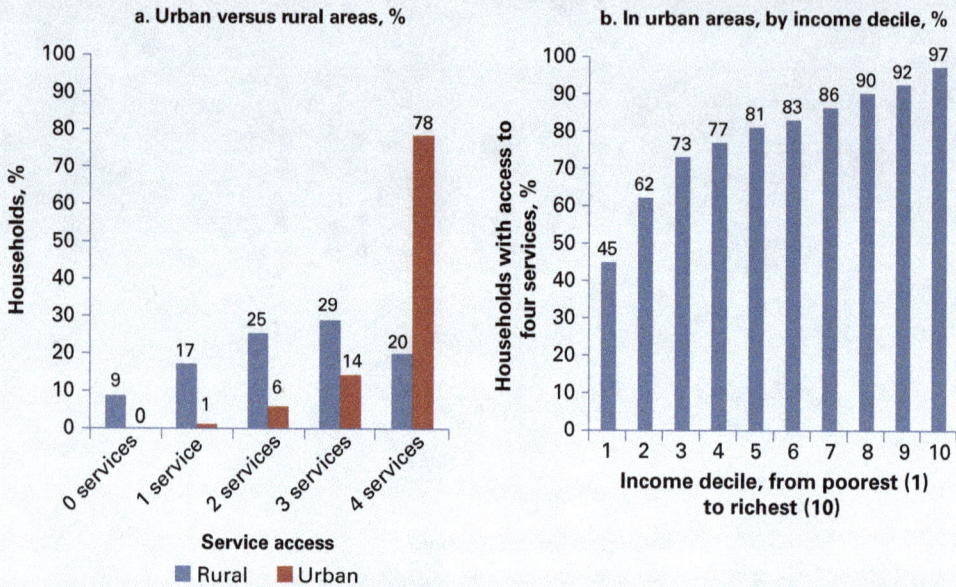

Source: Calculations based on data from the National Household Survey.

The human opportunity index (HOI) measures how characteristics such as area of residence and the gender and educational attainment of the household head may affect a child's access to basic goods and services, for example, education, water, electricity, and sanitation.[8] The HOI is an adjusted measure of coverage that extracts a penalty for any inequity in the coverage. In Peru, the HOI varies greatly by service area (figure 8.17, chart a). Thus, the HOI for water and sanitation is low (64) compared with the HOI for school enrollment (97). The low HOIs in water and sanitation reflect the relatively limited coverage, but also the unequal distribution associated with household characteristics.

The opportunity to live in a home with access to water and sanitation appears heavily correlated with urban or rural residence (figure 8.17, chart b). Children living in rural households are much less likely to enjoy access to water or sanitation. The place of residence explains 43 percent of the inequality in access to water or sanitation. Nonetheless, parental educational attainment and per capita income are also associated with a child's access to water and sanitation in the home; together, they explain another 43 percent of the inequality in the access to these services. Parental educational attainment is associated with most of the inequality in the access to education among children (40 percent).

Disparities in access are likewise associated with persistent disparities in important outcomes such as child nutrition. In 2013, 17.5 percent of

Figure 8.17 The Human Opportunity Index, Peru, 2012

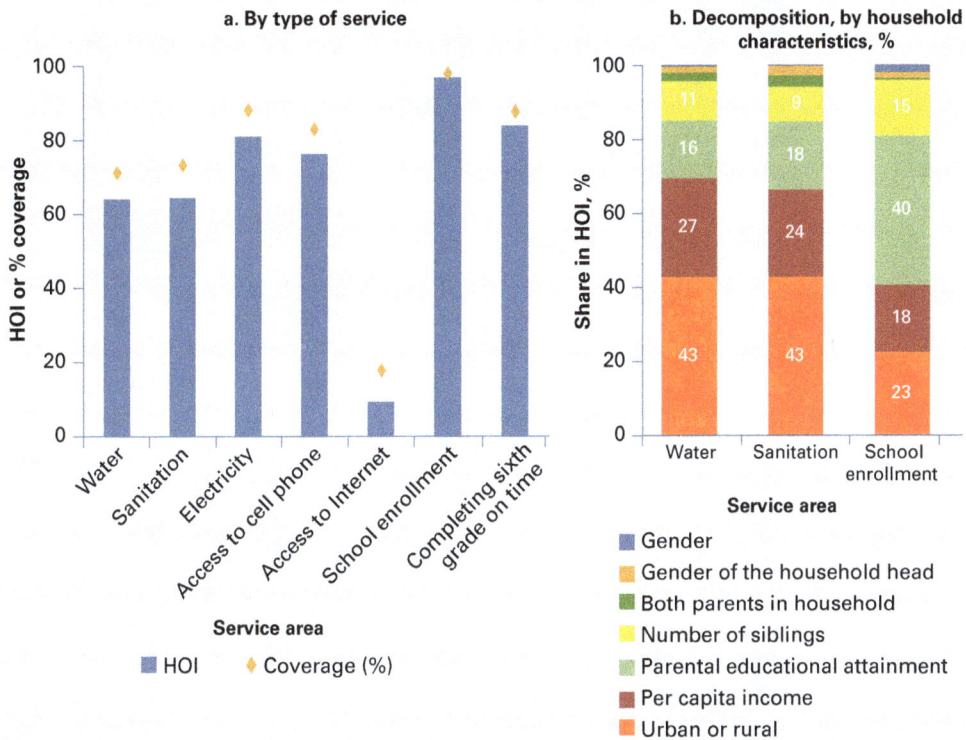

Source: Calculations based on data from the National Household Survey.
Note: HOI = Human Opportunity Index; for details on the HOI, see Barros et al. (2009).

under-5-year-olds were chronically malnourished, and 34 percent of children between 6 and 59 months of age suffered from anemia. The prevalence of chronic malnutrition was three times greater in rural areas compared with urban areas in 2013 (32.3 percent versus 10.3 percent, respectively). In addition, the share of children with anemia was 8.7 percentage points larger in rural areas than in urban areas (39.8 percent versus 31.1 percent, respectively). In 2013, 37.6 percent of under-5-year-olds in the poorest income quintile were chronically malnourished, compared with 2.3 percent of under-5-year-olds in the richest quintile. Similarly, approximately 4 in 10 children 6–59 months of age in the poorest income quintile had anemia, compared with 2 in 10 children in the same age-group in the richest quintile.

As coverage expands, increasing the quality of public services becomes a more daunting challenge. The index of the *Global Competitiveness Report 2011–2012* has Peru in 105th place among 142 countries in the overall quality of infrastructure, below many countries in Latin America and the Caribbean (Schwab 2012).[9] The inadequate supply of infrastructure is gauged as one of the top 5 barriers to doing business in Peru.

The issue of quality in education highlights, for example, the importance of integrated multisectoral approaches. Although primary-school enrollment is nearly universal in Peru, only 88 percent of children complete sixth grade on time (see figure 8.17, chart a). In addition, Peru fares less well than comparable countries on scores in the OECD's Program for International Student Assessment (PISA). In 2013, 75 percent of students at level 5 in mathematics did not possess the basic skills in mathematics of a level-2 student. Moreover, Peru's HOI for passing rates in mathematics in PISA was 18 percent in 2012, thus lagging Argentina, Brazil, Chile, Colombia, Costa Rica, Mexico, and Uruguay (World Bank 2014). The poor performance of students is worrisome for future growth because the need for a highly educated and competitive labor force is increasing in labor markets. *The Global Competitiveness Report 2011–2012* indicates that an inadequately educated workforce is another important barrier to doing business in Peru, which ranked 128th among 142 countries in the quality of the education system (Schwab 2012). However, poor student performance is not only the result of actions in the education sector, such as efforts to improve teacher quality. Many other factors, including access to safe water and early childhood nutrition, are also essential for learning.

The main challenge is ensuring that investments are prioritized and implemented effectively. Closing gaps in infrastructure is not about a lack of money; it is more about coordination and implementation. A recent public expenditure review on Peru (World Bank 2012b) highlights that investments are fragmented across an increasing number of small projects. Quality issues arise because of the lack of focus in expenditure on project preparation, which leads to significant delays in the implementation of projects. One important area that requires attention is the spending capacity of local governments, which have been acquiring greater responsibility in realizing public investments. However, this increased role has not been accompanied by greater management capacity. This is clear from the fact that a large share of capital spending remains undisbursed each year (World Bank 2012b).

Well-functioning, inclusive, and equitable markets

Given the centrality of labor markets in the reduction of poverty and the enhancement of shared prosperity, expanding access to the formal labor market is also a priority. Peru has one of the highest informality rates in Latin America and the Caribbean. This raises concerns about shared prosperity because it is a sign of the inefficient allocation of labor and public service use (Loayza, Servén, and Sugawara 2009). In addition, informality makes benefits tied to the labor market, such as health care and pensions, less progressive because it tends to exclude the poor (Jaramillo 2013).

The structure of dependent employment by firm size reflects the larger role of the informal sector in Peru and contrasts with the pyramidal structure observed in more developed countries (figure 8.18, chart a). In 2013, 7 in 10 employees were working in small firms (firms with fewer than

Figure 8.18 Dependent Workers, by Firm Size and Income Decile, Peru, 2004 and 2013

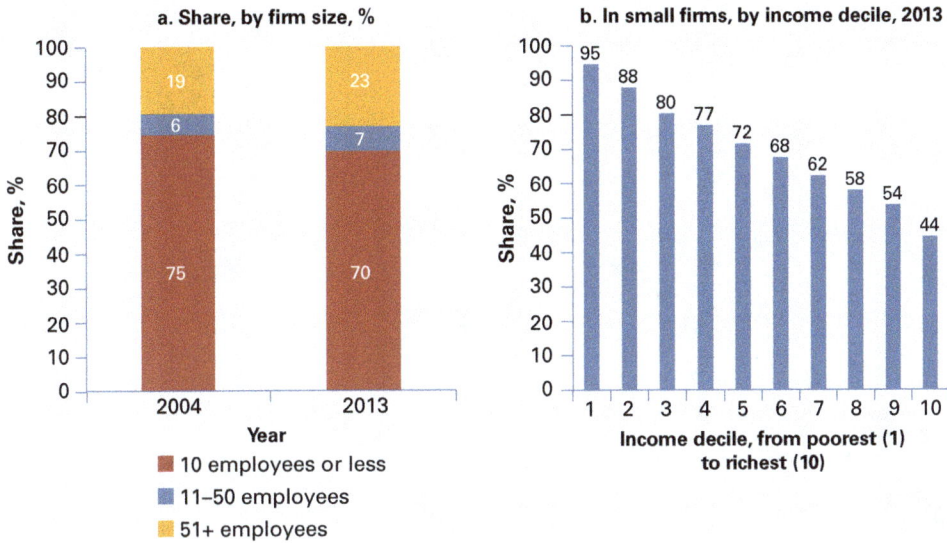

Source: Calculations based on data from the National Household Survey.

10 employees). Between 2004 and 2013, the share of employees in small firms fell by 5 percentage points, and this was accompanied by a rise in the share of employees in larger firms (those with 51 or more employees). The employees among the poorest segments of the population were significantly more likely to be working in small firms. For instance, in 2012, 95 percent of the employees in the bottom 10 percent worked in small firms. In contrast, only 44 percent of dependent workers in the top 10 percent worked in small firms (figure 8.18, chart b).

Starting from a low level of coverage, the share of workers affiliated with the pension system has grown substantially. Between 2004 and 2013, the share of workers who contributed to the formal pension system rose from 20 to 32 percent. However, the expansion in coverage among workers in the bottom 30 percent of the income distribution was below the national average (figure 8.19).

Expanding access to financial markets among the entire population is vital to economic growth and poverty reduction. Access to financial services can increase household security and productivity and the incentive to save. In the past decade, the financial sector has substantially expanded its presence in the country. As a result, one-third of the districts, representing 83 percent of the population, enjoyed some form of financial sector presence in 2013. The introduction of banking agents has helped grow the number of points of service, which, in 2013, reached 7 percent of the population in districts without other service points (figure 8.20) (World Bank 2013b).

Figure 8.19 Workers in the Pension System, by Income Decile, Peru, 2004–13

a. Share, %

b. Change in share, 2004–13, %

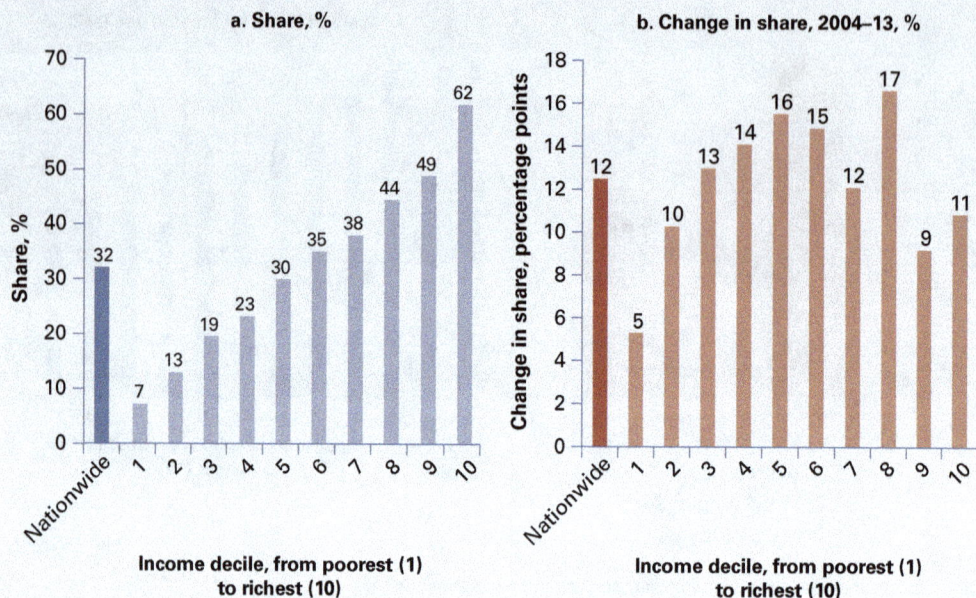

Income decile, from poorest (1) to richest (10)

Income decile, from poorest (1) to richest (10)

Source: Calculations based on data from the National Household Survey.

Figure 8.20 The Population with Financial Access Points in the District of Residence, Peru, 2013

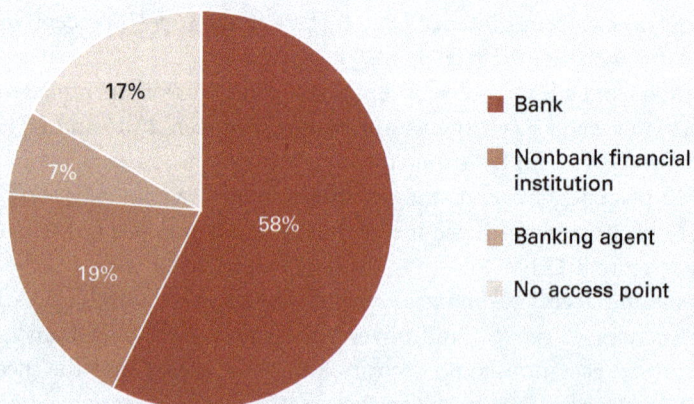

- Bank
- Nonbank financial institution
- Banking agent
- No access point

Source: Data of Superintendency of Banking, Insurance, and Private Pension Fund Administrators.
Note: Bank = a district with a bank branch. Nonbank financial institution = a district with no bank, but with a branch of a nonbank financial institution. Banking agent = a district with no bank branch or branch of a nonbank financial institution, but with a banking agent. For more, see World Bank (2013b).

Figure 8.21 Access to Financial Services, Bottom 40 and Top 60, Peru, 2011

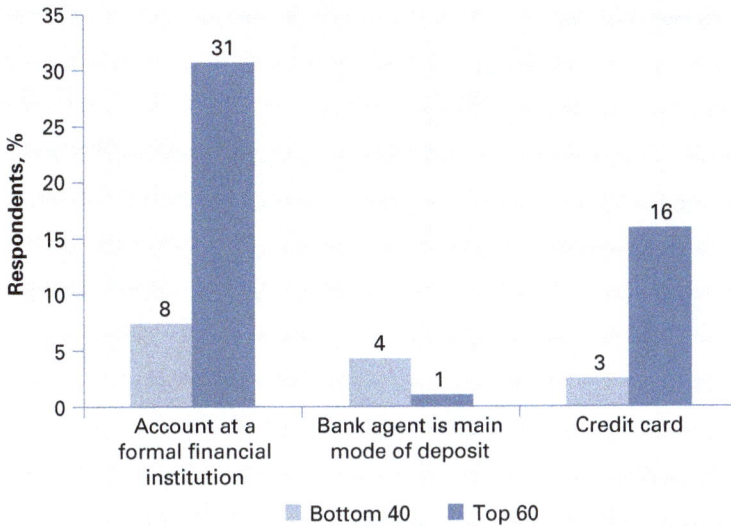

Source: Global Financial Inclusion (Global Findex) Database, World Bank, Washington, DC, http://www.worldbank.org/globalfindex.
Note: Account at a formal financial institution = respondents age 15+ years with individual or shared accounts at a bank, credit union, or other financial institution (for example, a cooperative or microfinance institution), or at a post office, including respondents who reported they had a debit card. Bank agent is main mode of deposit = respondents age 15+ years who have accounts at a formal financial institution and who report they usually rely on another person associated with their bank or financial institution to place cash in their accounts. Credit card = respondents age 15+ years who have credit cards.

Nonetheless, only 2 in 10 Peruvians over the age of 15 have accounts in formal financial institutions. In addition, there is a significant gap in access to financial services between the bottom 40 and the top 60 (figure 8.21). The recent expansion in the availability of banking agents may contribute to financial inclusion because such agents are more likely to be relied on by poorer individuals. The expansion of financial services to poor segments of the population with less educational attainment should be accompanied by policies to raise financial literacy, as well as by well-designed consumer protection initiatives, which can also lead to a greater use of financial services (World Bank 2013b).

Resiliency and risk management to achieve social inclusion

The majority of the population is vulnerable and at risk of falling into poverty. Panel data for 2007–10 indicate that this risk is not unsubstantial. In 2010, 2 in 10 of the poor had been living above the poverty line in 2007 (see figure 8.5). Poor households may be exposed to large, unusual shocks, but also to smaller, high-frequency events that may not allow them

Figure 8.22 Events Resulting in Household Income or Asset Loss during the Previous Year, Peru, 2013

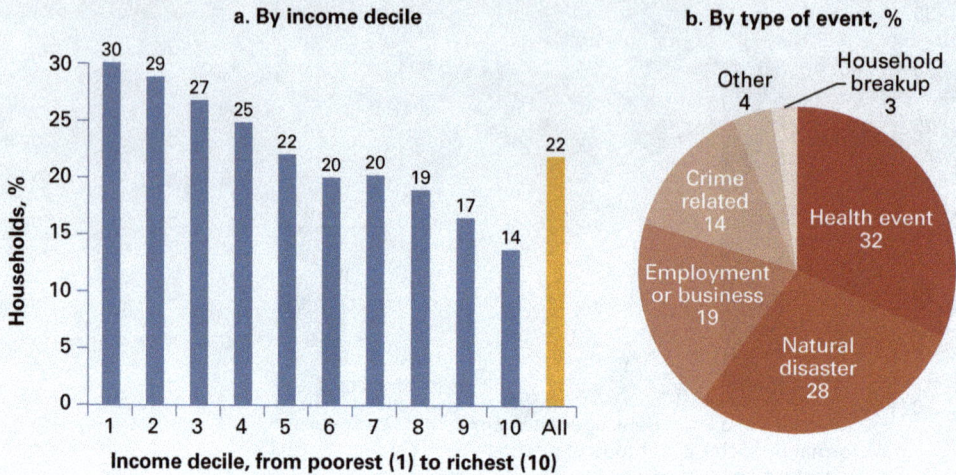

Source: Calculations based on data from the National Household Survey.
Note: The events resulting in the loss of income or assets were self-reported within the previous 12 months. Employment or business = an episode involving job loss or the loss of a family business by a household member. Health event = a household member was sick. Natural disaster = drought, flood, storm, infectious disease or epidemic, and so on. Crime related = a household member was robbed or assaulted. Household breakup = household head left the household.

to escape poverty. Limited risk management can push poor households to engage in undesirable coping responses that may have short- and long-term consequences for growth and equity. In their review, Báez, de la Fuente, and Santos (2010) find that disasters produce deleterious effects on nutrition, education, health, and many income generating processes. They also highlight that, in most cases, the poorest carry the heaviest burden from the impacts of disasters. Thus, risk management is central to sustaining the gains in reducing chronic poverty and the risk of falling into poverty.

The poor and vulnerable in Peru are more likely to experience episodes that result in the loss of income or assets. In 2013, 22 percent of households reported they had undergone an event that had caused a reduction in total household income or assets. The likelihood of reporting an event was larger among the poorest households. For instance, 30 percent of households in the poorest decile reported an incident in the previous year, while only 14 percent of the richest decile did so (figure 8.22, chart a).

In Peru, poor households are particularly vulnerable to weather-related events and natural disasters. The nature of the events reported ranged from the sickness of a family member (32 percent) or a natural disaster (28 percent) to loss of employment or family business (19 percent) (figure 8.22, chart b). For most of these events, the bottom 40 and the top 60 exhibit similar reporting rates. However, households in the bottom 40

Figure 8.23 Type of Events Reported, Bottom 40 and Top 60, Peru, 2013

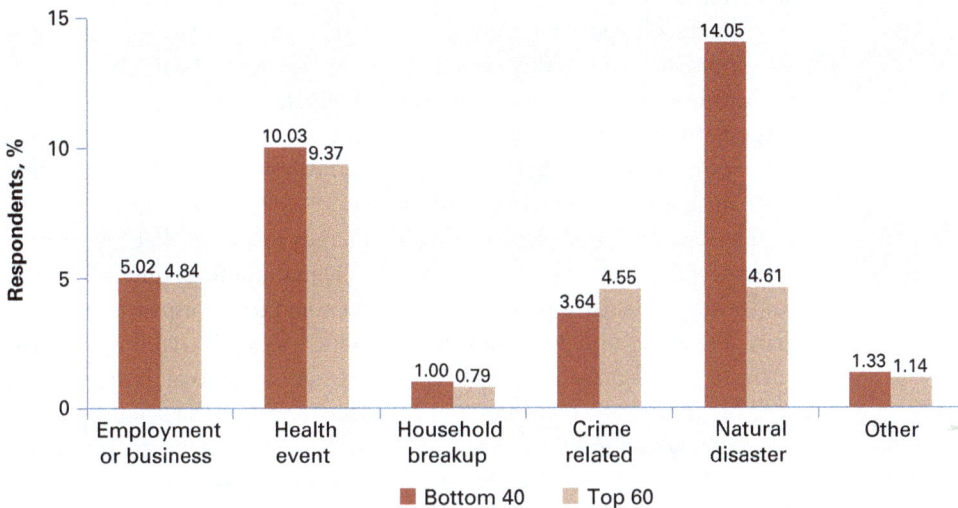

Source: Calculations based on data from the National Household Survey.
Note: The events resulting in the loss of income or assets were self-reported within the previous 12 months. Employment or business = an episode involving job loss or the loss of a family business by a household member. Health event = a household member was sick. Natural disaster = drought, flood, storm, infectious disease or epidemic, and so on. Crime related = a household member was robbed or assaulted. Household breakup = household head left the household.

were substantially more likely to report the effects of a natural disaster or weather-related crisis (figure 8.23).

Climate change threatens the progress that Peru has achieved in poverty reduction and in other social indicators. It may compromise the improvements in the human development index observed in Peru (UNDP 2013). The Country Note for Peru of the Global Facility for Disaster Reduction and Recovery specifies three priority goals in risk management: (1) take advantage of the decentralization process to develop the risk management capacity of local governments, (2) ensure that existing infrastructure and the productive sectors are resilient to disasters, and (3) reduce the risk of disaster by making major cities earthquake-resilient (World Bank 2010). Moreover, strengthening weather warning systems and social safety nets among the populations that are vulnerable and most likely to be affected could contribute to mitigating the impact of climate change and severe natural disasters.

Final Remarks

Economic growth and the reduction of inequality reinforce each other. This chapter presents the main trends in poverty and shared prosperity in Peru between 2004 and 2013. It shows that, driven by economic growth and stability, the progress has been impressive. The expansion of the labor market during the period explains approximately three-quarters of the reduction in extreme poverty and 80 percent of the reduction in inequality. However, it will take a long time for growth alone to allow Peru to reach the levels of development and equality seen in more well developed countries.

Although poverty has been reduced substantially in recent years, the largest share of the Peruvian population remains vulnerable to the risk of falling into poverty. This has the potential to reverse the progress achieved over the course of the past decade.

The chapter highlights four major themes in policy that are central to strengthening shared prosperity in Peru: (1) maintaining equitable, efficient, and sustainable fiscal policy; (2) strengthening fair, transparent institutions that deliver high-quality public goods and services; (3) enabling an environment of well-functioning markets that are accessible to all levels of society; and (4) improving risk management. This is well understood by the government, which is evident from the government's pursuit of an ambitious agenda of social inclusion. Even though growth prospects remain strong in Peru in 2015 and beyond, achieving gains in poverty and inequality reduction will require that efforts to allow the poor and vulnerable to participate in and contribute to the growth process are renewed and deepened. This is a central component in any attempt to consolidate the social and economic gains that Peru has realized over the past decade.

Annex 8A Poverty Rates and Gini Coefficients

Table 8A.1 Official Poverty Rates and Gini Coefficients, Nationwide and Urban and Rural Areas, Peru, 2004–13

Indicator	2004	2005	2006	2007	2008	2009	2010	2011	2012	2013
Total poverty (%)										
Nationwide	58.7	55.6	49.1	42.4	37.3	33.5	30.8	27.8	25.8	23.9
Urban	48.2	44.5	37.0	30.1	25.4	21.3	20.0	18.0	16.6	16.1
Rural	83.4	82.5	79.3	74.0	68.8	66.7	61.0	56.1	53.0	48.0
Extreme poverty (%)										
Nationwide	16.4	15.8	13.8	11.2	10.9	9.5	7.6	6.3	6.0	4.7
Urban	5.7	5.4	4.0	2.9	2.7	2.0	1.9	1.4	1.4	1.0
Rural	41.6	41.0	38.1	32.7	32.4	29.8	23.8	20.5	19.7	16.0
Income-based Gini										
Nationwide	0.49	0.51	0.50	0.50	0.48	0.47	0.46	0.45	0.45	0.44
Urban	0.45	0.47	0.45	0.46	0.43	0.43	0.42	0.41	0.41	0.40
Rural	0.43	0.43	0.43	0.44	0.44	0.43	0.42	0.43	0.43	0.42

Source: Calculations based on data from the National Household Survey.
Note: The official methodology for the estimation of poverty is based on a measure of consumption. The Gini coefficient is based on income.

Annex 8B Profile of the Poor and the Bottom 40

Table 8B.1 Average Characteristics of the Extreme Poor, the Poor, and Others, Peru, 2013
percent unless otherwise indicated

Characteristic	Extreme poor	Nonextreme poor	Poor	Nonpoor	Bottom 40	Top 60
Household						
Age of household head (years)	50.6	51.4	49.9	51.8	49.4	52.5
Woman household head	13.5	22.3	17.8	23.1	19.6	23.2
Education of household head (years)	4.2	8.8	5.8	9.4	6.5	9.7
Share of members age 0–12	34.9	21.3	31.7	18.9	29.9	17.5
Share of members age 13–18	14.3	12.0	14.3	11.5	14.4	10.9
Share of members age 19–70	43.6	60.6	48.3	63.4	50.1	65.4
Share of members age 70+	7.2	6.0	5.7	6.1	5.6	6.3
Household size (number)	6.1	4.9	5.9	4.6	5.5	4.6
Located in urban areas	16.7	78.3	50.5	83.2	57.0	85.8
Access to basic services						
Water	43.9	82.7	64.4	86.0	67.8	88.2
Toilet in the dwelling	46.7	79.7	60.4	83.8	65.1	85.6
Sewerage	11.9	69.7	37.8	76.1	44.9	79.5
Electricity	61.8	93.8	80.9	95.9	84.2	96.9
Telephone	51.9	90.6	73.6	93.5	78.1	94.9
Labor market (age 15–64)						
In labor force	75.6	74.5	74.2	74.7	71.2	76.4
Female labor force participation	65.6	66.4	63.9	67.1	61.8	68.8
Unemployed	2.3	4.1	3.7	4.1	4.5	3.8
Employer	1.9	4.6	2.3	5.2	2.5	5.5
Employee	16.1	52.4	35.5	55.4	33.8	59.1
Self-employed	43.8	32.3	40.0	30.6	41.6	28.5
Unpaid worker	38.3	10.7	22.2	8.7	22.1	6.9
Small firm (<11 workers)	96.7	69.0	86.6	65.1	87.4	61.8
No contract	53.0	35.2	48.8	32.0	46.5	30.9
Employment sector						
Primary	78.5	22.3	50.5	16.8	47.1	13.8
Manufacturing	6.5	10.7	9.5	10.8	9.8	10.8
Construction	3.5	6.7	6.1	6.7	5.3	7.2
Retail	5.6	20.4	12.7	22.0	15.1	22.1
Utilities	0.0	0.2	0.0	0.2	0.1	0.2
Services	5.8	39.7	21.2	43.5	22.6	45.9

Source: Calculations based on ENAHO (Encuesta Nacional de Hogares).

Annex 8C Macrodata

Table 8C.1 GDP and Fiscal Data, Peru, 2004–13

Indicator	2004	2013	Average, 2004–13
GDP (1994 S/., millions)	139,141	250,570	n.a.
Real GDP (variation, %)	4.98	5.02	6.61
GDP per capita (variation, %)	3.71	3.77	5.40
Primary fiscal surplus (% GDP)	1.0	1.8	2.45
Public debt (% GDP)	42.6	19.2	27.84
General government current revenues (% GDP)	17.4	21.7	20.07
General government nonfinancial expenditures (% GDP)	16.69	20.08	17.86
Inflation rate (annual change in consumer price index, %)	3.48	2.86	2.93

Source: Central Reserve Bank of Peru.
Note: GDP = gross domestic product; n.a. = not applicable.

Annex 8D Decomposition of Changes in Extreme Poverty and Inequality by Income Components

Figure 8D.1 The Reduction in Extreme Poverty, by Income Components, Peru, 2004–12

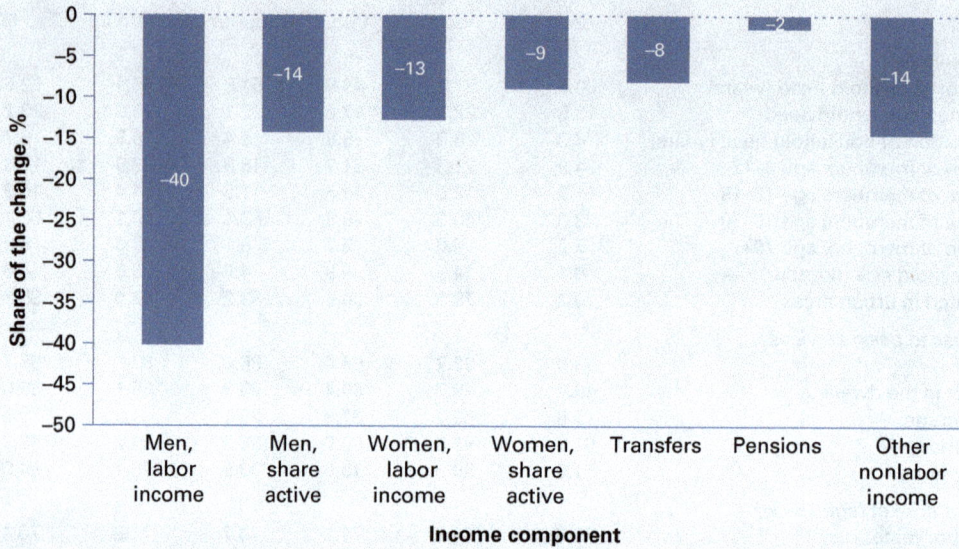

Source: Calculations based on data in SEDLAC.
Note: The figure shows the Shapley decomposition of the changes in poverty in 2004–12 by components of the income aggregate. See Azevedo, Sanfelice, and Nguyen (2012) on the technique.

Figure 8D.2 The Reduction in Inequality Measured by the Gini Coefficient, Peru, 2004–12

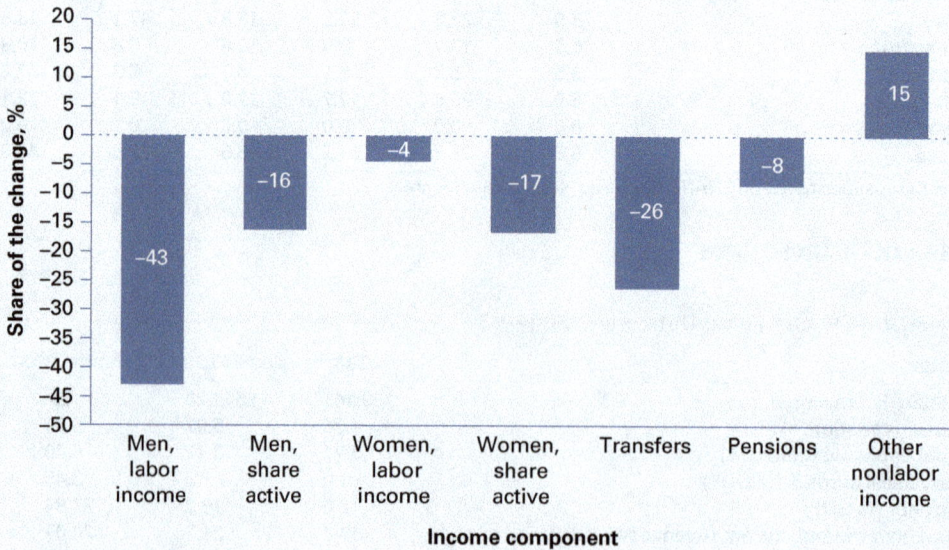

Source: Calculations based on data in SEDLAC.
Note: The figure shows the Shapley decomposition of changes in poverty in 2004–12 by components of the income aggregate. See Azevedo, Sanfelice, and Nguyen (2012) on the technique.

Notes

1. The majority of the numbers in this chapter are based on data of the Peruvian National Household Survey for 2004–13. The chapter takes advantage of the recently published comparable series of poverty rates and Gini coefficients for 2004–13. Poverty rates and Gini coefficients are estimated following the country's official, updated poverty methodology, which, with the technical support of the World Bank, was launched by the National Statistics Office in 2012. The methodology defines poverty as a monetary measure based on a consumption aggregate. The Gini coefficient is calculated using an income-based aggregate. For regional comparisons, the harmonized SEDLAC dataset has been utilized. (See SEDLAC [Socio-Economic Database for Latin America and the Caribbean], Center for Distributive, Labor, and Social Studies, Universidad Nacional de La Plata, La Plata, Argentina; World Bank, Washington, DC, http://sedlac.econo .unlp.edu.ar/eng/index.php.) The SEDLAC database involves the construction of comparable income-based aggregates and poverty lines for estimates of poverty rates across countries in the region as well as for the entire region.

2. Districts are third-level administrative subdivisions. They are subdivisions of the province, which is a subdivision of the region. In 2012, there were 1,838 districts, 195 provinces, and 25 regions.

3. Indigenous origin is defined based on mother tongue, which includes the Amazonic, Aymara, and Quechua languages.

4. Individuals or households are multidimensionally poor if they are deprived in at least three of the following seven dimensions: (a) any school-age child (7 to 15 years of age) in the household is out of school, (b) no household member has completed five years of schooling, (c) the walls of the dwelling are precarious, (d) no access to tap water in the dwelling, (e) no flush toilet or pit latrine in the dwelling, (f) no electricity, and (g) the dwelling lacks at least two of the following: television, telephone, transportation, and refrigerator. See Castañeda et al. (2012).

5. Average GDP per capita growth during the 1980s was negative. In the 1990s, macroeconomic stability was restored, but per capita GDP growth was still relatively restrained, averaging 1.4 percent over the decade.

6. Sen's welfare index is defined as GDP * (1 − GINI). The benchmark refers to the population-weighted average of Sen's welfare index of the top 10 countries in 2000: Austria, Denmark, Ireland, Luxembourg, the Netherlands, Norway, Qatar, Singapore, Switzerland, and the United States.

7. Commitment to Equity is an interagency initiative led by Tulane University and the Inter-American Dialogue, in cooperation with the World Bank, the Inter-American Development Bank, and the United Nations Development Programme. The Commitment to Equity framework is a diagnostic tool developed to assess the extent to which fiscal policies support a minimum living standard, human capital accumulation, and reductions in inequality (see Lustig et al. 2012).

8. The HOI takes values between 0 and 100 and is generally computed based on children age 0–16 years to remove the influence of individual effort and choice and focus on opportunities early in life (see Barros et al. 2009).

9. The index takes into account the quality of roads, railroads, ports, air transport, electricity, and telecommunications infrastructure.

References

Azevedo, João Pedro, Viviane Sanfelice, and Minh Cong Nguyen. 2012. "Shapley Decomposition by Components of a Welfare Measure." Unpublished working paper, World Bank, Washington, DC.

Báez, Javier E., Alejandro de la Fuente, and Indhira Santos. 2010. "Do Natural Disasters Affect Human Capital? An Assessment Based on Existing Empirical Evidence." IZA Discussion Paper 5164, Institute for the Study of Labor, Bonn, Germany.

Barros, Ricardo Paes de, Francisco H. G. Ferreira, Jose R. Molinas Vega, and Jaime Saavedra Chanduvi. 2009. *Measuring Inequality of Opportunities in Latin America and Caribbean*. With Mirela de Carvalho, Samuel Franco, Samuel Freije-Rodríguez, and Jérémie Gignoux. Latin American Development Forum Series. Washington, DC: World Bank; New York: Palgrave Macmillan.

Beuermann, Diether W., Christopher McKelvey, and Renos Vakis. 2012. "Mobile Phones and Economic Development in Rural Peru." *Journal of Development Studies* 48 (11): 1617–28.

Castañeda, Raul A., Anna Fruttero, Samantha Lach, Luis F. López-Calva, María Ana Lugo, Rogerio B. Santarrosa, and Jordan Solomon. 2012. "Poverty Dynamics in Brazil: Patterns, Associated Factors, and Policy Challenges." Policy report, World Bank, Washington, DC.

ENAHO (Encuesta Nacional de Hogares) (database). National Institute of Statistics and Informatics (INEI). Lima, Peru. http://www.inei.gob.pe/.

Escobal, Javier. 2005. "The Role of Public Infrastructure in Market Development in Rural Peru." PhD thesis, Wageningen University, Wageningen, Netherlands.

Ferreira, Francisco H. G., Julian Messina, Jamele Rigolini, Luis F. López-Calva, María Ana Lugo, and Renos Vakis. 2013. *Economic Mobility and the Rise of the Latin American Middle Class*. Washington, DC: World Bank.

Jaramillo, Miguel. 2013. "The Incidence of Social Spending and Taxes in Peru." CEQ Working Paper 9, Commitment to Equity, Inter-American Dialogue, Washington, DC; Center for Inter-American Policy and Research and Department of Economics, Tulane University, New Orleans.

Loayza Norman V., Luis Servén, and Naotaka Sugawara. 2009. "Informality in Latin America and the Caribbean." Policy Research Working Paper 4888, World Bank, Washington, DC.

Lustig, Nora, George Gray-Molina, Sean Higgins, Miguel Jaramillo, Wilson Jiménez, Veronica Paz, Claudiney Pereira, Carola Pessino, John Scott, and Ernesto Yañez. 2012. "The Impact of Taxes and Social Spending on Inequality and Poverty in Argentina, Bolivia, Brazil, Mexico and Peru: A Synthesis of Results." CEQ Working Paper 3, Commitment to Equity, Inter-American Dialogue, Washington, DC; Center for Inter-American Policy and Research and Department of Economics, Tulane University, New Orleans.

Schwab, Klaus, ed. 2012. *The Global Competitiveness Report 2011–2012*. Geneva: World Economic Forum.

SEDLAC (Socio-Economic Database for Latin America and the Caribbean), Center for Distributive, Labor, and Social Studies, Universidad de La Plata, La Plata, Argentina; World Bank, Washington, DC, http://sedlac.econo.unlp.edu.ar/eng /index.php.

UNDP (United Nations Development Programme). 2013. *Informe sobre Desarrollo Humano Perú 2013: Cambio climático y territorio, Desafíos y respuestas para un futuro sostenible.* Lima: UNDP.

World Bank. 2010. "Disaster Risk Management in Latin America and the Caribbean Region: GFDRR Country Notes, Peru." Global Facility for Disaster Reduction and Recovery, Washington, DC; Sustainable Development Unit, Latin America and the Caribbean Region, World Bank, Washington, DC.

———. 2012a. "Country Partnership Strategy for the Republic of Peru for the Period FY12–FY16." Report 66187-PE, World Bank, Washington, DC.

———. 2012b. "Public Expenditure Review for Peru: Spending for Results." Report 62586-PE, World Bank, Washington, DC.

———. 2013a. "Shifting Gears to Accelerate Shared Prosperity in Latin America and the Caribbean." Poverty and Labor Brief, Report 78507 (June), Latin America and the Caribbean Region, World Bank, Washington, DC.

———. 2013b. "Peru: Diagnostic Review of Consumer Protection and Financial Literacy." Report 84655, World Bank, Washington, DC.

———. 2014. "Social Gains in the Balance: A Fiscal Policy Challenge for Latin America and the Caribbean." Poverty and Labor Brief, Report 85162 rev (February), Latin America and the Caribbean Region, World Bank, Washington, DC.

———. Forthcoming. "Taxation and Equity in Peru: Selected Issues in Taxation Policy." Economic Policy Group, Poverty Reduction and Economic Management Department, Latin America and the Caribbean Region, World Bank, Washington, DC.

CHAPTER 9

Poverty and Shared Prosperity in Uruguay

*Oscar Barriga Cabanillas, Marina Gindelsky,
María Ana Lugo, Carlos Rodríguez-Castelán,
and Liliana D. Sousa*

Introduction

Uruguay is one of the most equitable countries in Latin America and the Caribbean and has traditionally been among the countries in the region with the lowest incidence of poverty. However, because it is a small open economy, Uruguay is regularly exposed to macroeconomic contagion that has ultimately disproportionately affected the poor and the vulnerable, who have tended to fall back into poverty over the last 25 years. Since the 2001–02 crisis, prudent macroeconomic management has reduced the country's exposure to risk and strengthened confidence in the country's institutions.

In the past 10 years, Uruguay has recovered from a crippling crisis. The economy has grown 6 percent annually; income inequality has been narrowed by 11 percent; and, according to a variety of metrics, poverty has been reduced by more than half. The growth has also been inclusive and pro-poor, allowing the poor to share in the benefits of the growth, thereby cutting into inequality. The mean per capita income of the bottom 40 percent of the income distribution (the bottom 40) has risen 9.4 percent a year since 2005 (the start of the postcrisis recovery), compared with 6.4 percent among the population as a whole.

By 2012, 12 percent of Uruguayans were living in moderate poverty, and fewer than 1 percent were living in extreme poverty. Income inequality is among the lowest in the region, though still higher than in any member countries of the Organisation for Economic Co-operation and Development (OECD). The substantive improvements in well-being, especially since 2007, are the result of a combination of favorable economic conditions and growth patterns that have led to greater employment opportunities, as well as key policy reforms in the labor market and in social protection to ensure that the less well off are able to contribute to the growth process and enhance their living conditions.

There are still notable challenges. The country remains exposed to internal and external risks that render some groups vulnerable to falling back into poverty. In addition, the expanded middle class requires higher-quality services, especially in education, and the demographic transition occasioned by the aging population may yet stress the sustainability of the fiscal system.

This chapter describes the recent trends in growth, poverty, and inequality in Uruguay and examines the main drivers of the welfare changes during the economic expansion in the country since 2007.

Trends in Growth, Poverty, and Shared Prosperity

The Uruguayan economy, like other Latin American economies, has been characterized by a high degree of economic growth volatility, which is linked to its productive structure, degree of openness, and vulnerability to major capital flows. Economic performance over 1990–2013 may be described in four phases (figure 9.1): expansion (1990–98), crisis (1999–2002), recovery (2003–06), and renewed expansion (2007–13). Growth volatility has declined over the past decade, and the country weathered the global financial crisis of 2008–09 relatively well.

Throughout much of the 1990s, global development policy was centered on promoting economic growth under the belief that this was the channel through which poverty could be reduced and welfare enhanced. In Uruguay during 1990–98, private consumption and investment were the main drivers of growth, while net exports detracted from growth. The economy expanded an annual average of 3.9 percent, and the moderate poverty rate in urban areas dropped about 41.0 percent.[1] However, income inequality widened slightly. Measured with respect to per capita income in urban areas, the Gini coefficient rose an average of 0.3–0.7 percent annually during the period.

Uruguay was heavily impacted by regional and global events around 2000, including the 1999 devaluation of the Brazilian real and the 2001–02 macroeconomic crisis in Argentina. Because of Uruguay's dependence on its main trading partners, its economy is closely tied to the fortunes of its neighbors.[2] The banking sector collapsed; reserves were depleted; sovereign debt crept upward; and annual inflation had soared again to double digits by 2002. Between 1998 and 2003, the economy shrank by 14.7 percent in real terms, and private consumption and investment contracted markedly, while net exports made a positive contribution to growth of 2.2 percentage points as imports declined appreciably. Moderate poverty surged, climbing to close to 40.0 percent in 2003, and extreme poverty had reached 4.7 percent by 2004 (figure 9.2).[3]

Figure 9.1 Real Growth of Gross Domestic Product, Uruguay, 1990–2013

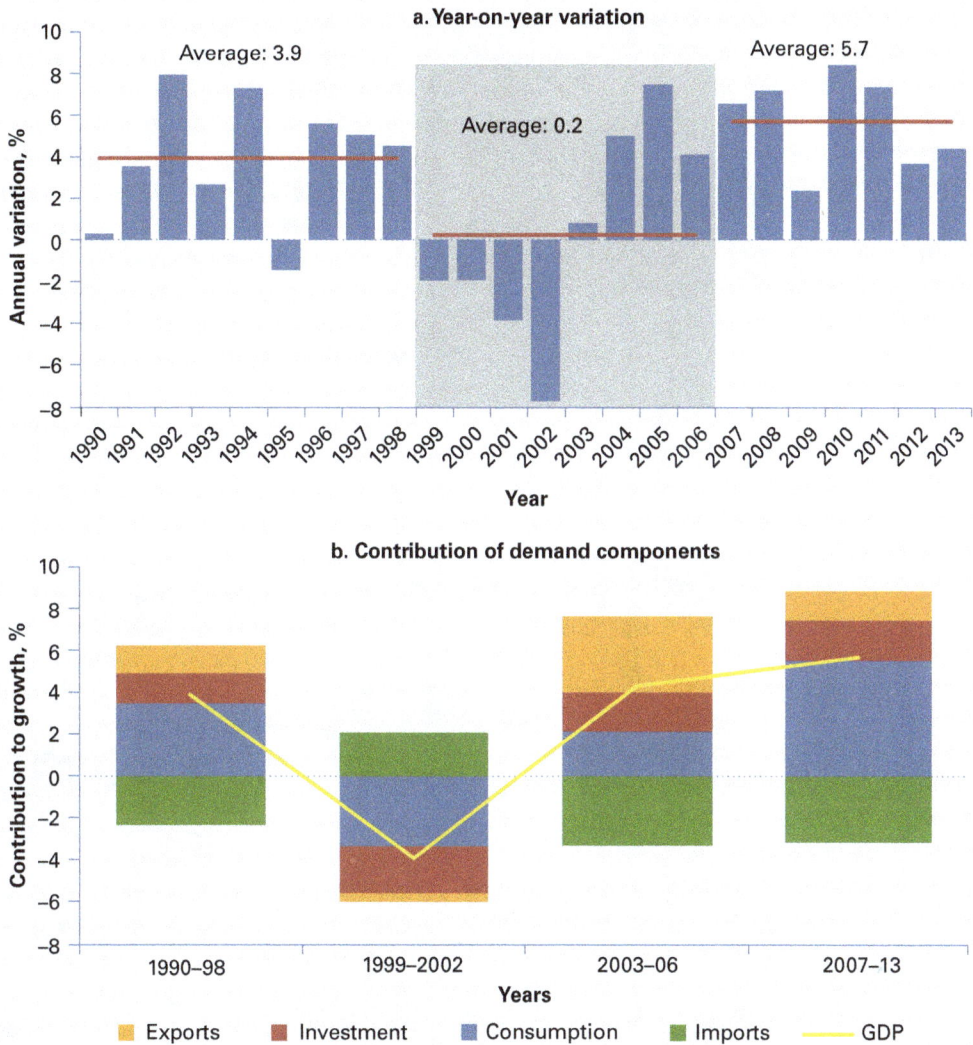

a. Year-on-year variation

Average: 3.9

Average: 5.7

Average: 0.2

b. Contribution of demand components

Exports   Investment   Consumption   Imports   ──── GDP

Sources: World Bank 2014a and data of the Banco Central del Uruguay.
Note: GDP = gross domestic product.

During the peak of the crisis, average per capita household income declined substantially; the growth rates were –9.5 percent during 2000–03.[4] However, the decline was less marked among the bottom 20 percent of the income distribution (figure 9.3). During this period, households in the middle of the income distribution were the most vulnerable.

After the 2001–02 crisis generated in Argentina, Uruguay faced a long road to recovery. However, the task was managed fairly well. Prudent macroeconomic policies, improvements in structural areas, and favorable

Figure 9.2 Trends in the Poverty Headcount, Uruguay, 2002–12

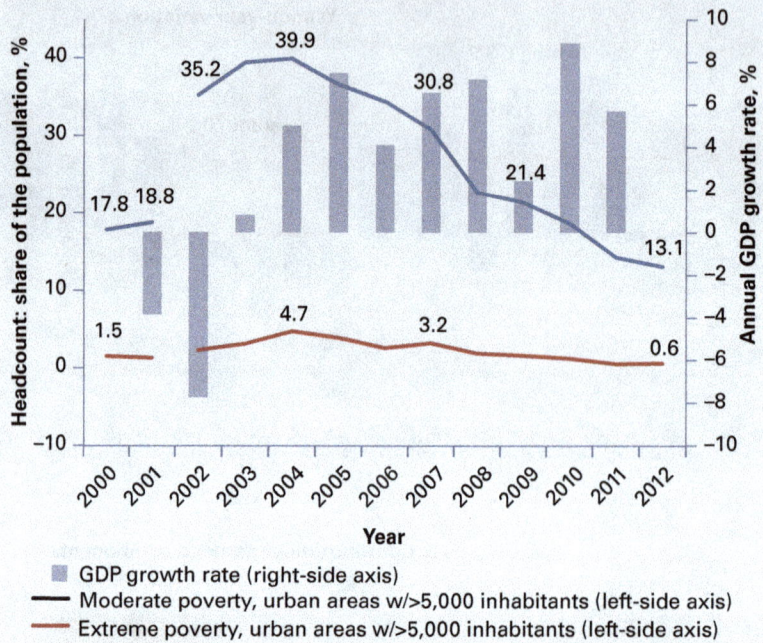

Source: INE 2013.
Note: Poverty rates correspond to Montevideo and urban areas with 5,000 or more inhabitants. The poverty headcount series is broken in 2002 because of a methodological survey change introduced by the National Statistics Institute. The poverty data for 2000 and 2001 are not comparable with the rest of the series. GDP = gross domestic product.

external economic conditions, such as buoyant demand for the country's main export products and a booming regional economy, all contributed to Uruguay's slow, but successful recovery. The real growth of gross domestic product (GDP) averaged over 5 percent beginning in 2003, and open unemployment fell from 17 percent in 2002 to close to 11 percent in 2006. Both private consumption and investment recovered, contributing to a substantial rise in imports that offset the positive contribution to growth of exports. The most rapidly growing sectors behind this growth were trade, transport, and communications. Additionally, increased coverage in social assistance programs softened the impact of the crisis on the welfare of the poor. The Asignaciones Familiares family allowance, initially a program for formal sector employees, was expanded in 2004 to include households with incomes at a threshold of three times the minimum wage. In 2005–07, the Plan de Atención Nacional a la Emergencia Social (PANES), a new cash transfer program, was implemented to offer more assistance to the poor.

By 2007, the share of the poor was still high, at 30.8 percent, though this was 9 percentage points lower than the peak in 2004. During the recovery, incomes across the distribution grew at a similar rate, around 4.8 percent,

Figure 9.3 Growth Incidence Curves of per Capita Household Income, Urban Areas, Uruguay, 2000–07

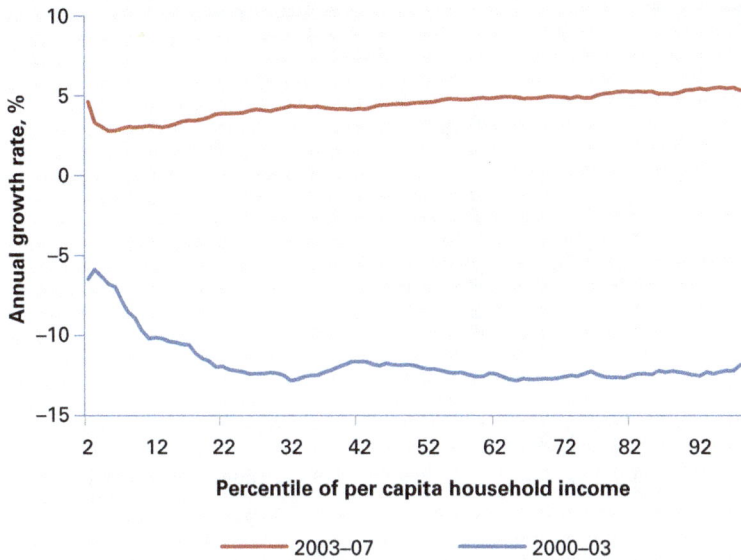

Source: Data of the 2000, 2003, and 2007 Continuous Household Survey.
Note: Poverty rates correspond to Montevideo and urban areas with 5,000 or more inhabitants.

although the rate was slightly lower among the lowest deciles. As a result, income inequality in Montevideo and urban areas with at least 5,000 inhabitants was almost unchanged.

The next phase, from 2007 to 2013, was an expansionary period, with average annual GDP growth rates of around 5.7 percent. The favorable external environment was characterized by strong external demand, high commodity prices, and high global liquidity. High commodity prices and abundant international liquidity contributed to strong investment in Uruguay; foreign direct investment averaged 5.0 percent of GDP and accounted for about a third of total investment. In addition, public investment rose appreciably as the government undertook significant investment projects. Rapid economic growth was accompanied by substantial job creation, and unemployment declined to historically low levels. Health care benefits and several other government transfers were monetized gradually and became part of calculated household income. Meanwhile, the successor of the PANES program, the Plan de Equidad (equity plan), lowered the incidence and intensity of poverty noticeably.

Thus, poverty rates declined rapidly after 2007. By 2012, only 12.4 percent of the population was living with a per capita income below the poverty line, about one-third the rate seven years earlier. The reduction in extreme poverty was even more dramatic in relative terms: the rate dropped

Figure 9.4 Growth Incidence Curves of per Capita Household Income, Uruguay, 2007–12

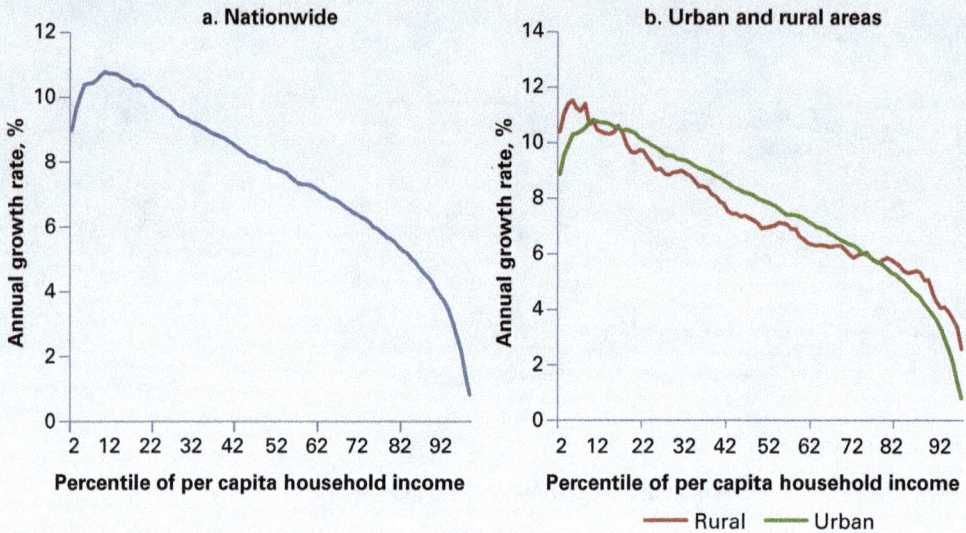

Source: Data of the 2007 and 2012 Continuous Household Survey.

to around 0.5 percent, less than one-sixth the rate seven years earlier (see figure 9.2).

The drop in poverty in 2007–12 was accompanied by strong income growth among the bottom 40. Between 2007 and 2011, the real per capita income of the bottom 40 rose by more than 9.7 percent annually, while mean income growth was closer to 6.0 percent (figure 9.4). In contrast, households in the top 20 percent of the income distribution experienced the smallest increase in income. A similar pattern was evident in both urban and rural areas.

The improvements at the bottom of the distribution were reflected in narrowing income inequality beginning in 2007 and the more rapid tightening starting in 2010 (figure 9.5, chart a). In 2007–12, the nationwide Gini coefficient fell an impressive 7 percentage points, from 0.45 to 0.38. This reduction was evident in urban areas and in rural areas (where the inequality gap has traditionally been smaller). Despite its strong standing regionally, however, Uruguay continues to exhibit greater inequality than any member of the OECD not in the region (figure 9.5, chart b).

As poverty fell, the size of the middle class rose steadily and currently represents the largest socioeconomic group in Uruguay. In 2002, 46 percent of the population was living on incomes of between $10 and $50 per person a day (in 2005 purchasing power parity [PPP] U.S. dollars), which is the World Bank monetary definition of the middle class (Ferreira et al. 2013) (figure 9.6).[5] Because of the noteworthy recovery after the crisis, more than 65 percent of the population belonged to the middle class by 2011. Another

Figure 9.5 Inequality, Uruguay, the Region, and the OECD, 2006–13

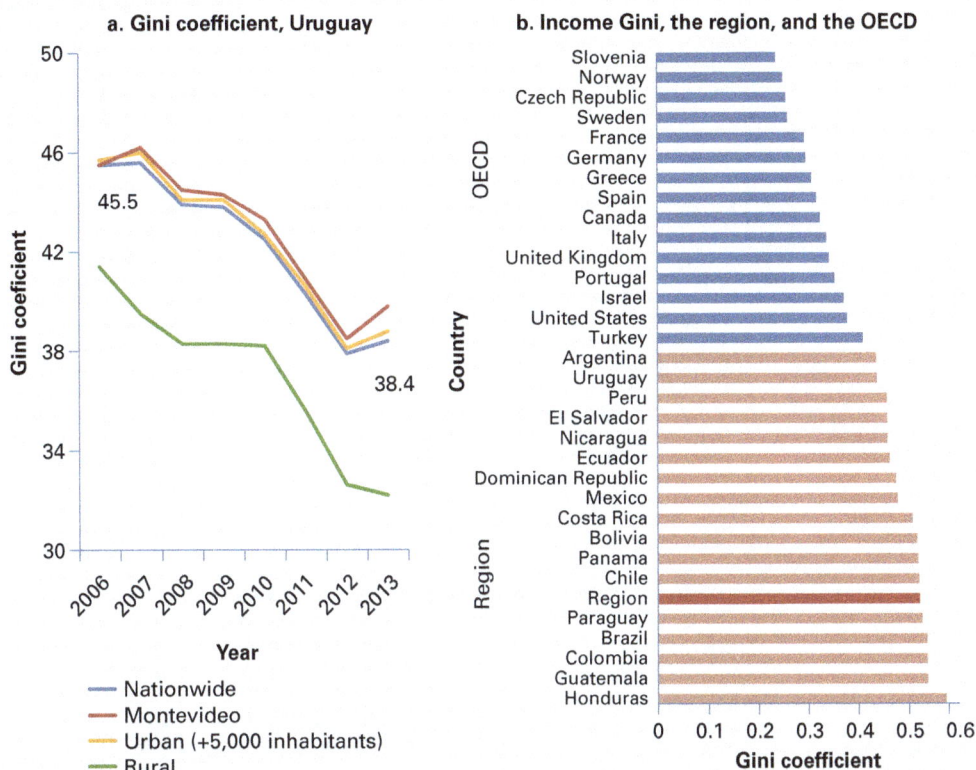

a. Gini coefficient, Uruguay

b. Income Gini, the region, and the OECD

Legend:
- Nationwide
- Montevideo
- Urban (+5,000 inhabitants)
- Rural

Sources: Chart a: Data of the 2006–13 Continuous Household Survey. Chart b: Uruguay and the region: data from SEDLAC (Socio-Economic Database for Latin America and the Caribbean), Center for Distributive, Labor, and Social Studies, Universidad de La Plata, La Plata, Argentina; World Bank, Washington, DC, http://sedlac .econo.unlp.edu.ar/eng/index.php; OECD countries: OECD.StatExtracts, http://stats.oecd.org/.
Note: OECD = Organisation for Economic Co-operation and Development.

16 percent, accounting for the second largest group in society, was the vulnerable, who have incomes above the official poverty line, but below the $10 a day threshold.

Drivers of the Reductions in Poverty and Inequality

Uruguay has made remarkable progress over the past decade in improving well-being and narrowing inequalities among the population. What are the main drivers behind the gains? This section explores the importance of both labor and nonlabor income sources in reducing poverty and enhancing the distribution of incomes. In particular, the advances in well-being are the result of a combination of favorable economic conditions and growth patterns that have led to greater employment opportunities, as well as key policy reforms in the labor market and in social protection to ensure that the less well off are able to contribute to growth and better living conditions.

Figure 9.6 Socioeconomic Groups, by Poverty Status, Uruguay, 2002–11

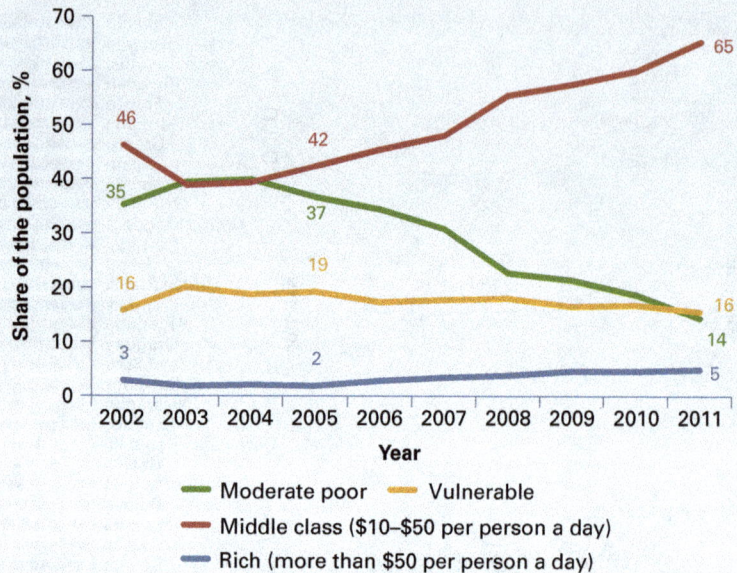

Source: Data of the 2002–11 Continuous Household Survey.
Note: Data correspond to Montevideo and other urban areas with 5,000 or more inhabitants. The moderate poverty line is equivalent to $8.57 per person per day (in 2005 purchasing power parity U.S. dollars) for people living in families of average size. Vulnerable represents people above the official poverty line, but below the middle class.

Declines in the share of the population that is living below a poverty threshold (the poverty line) can be decomposed into two parts: rising incomes (economic growth reflected in shifts in income distribution*)* and improvements in income distribution (income redistribution reflected in a narrowing of dispersion in income distribution) (see Datt and Ravallion 1992).

In Uruguay, economic growth is more significant than greater equality in the distribution of income in explaining the drop in urban poverty between 2003 and 2012; however, beginning in 2007, the narrowing of the inequality gap played an equally important role. In 2003–12, around 19.7 percentage points in the 26.4 percentage point decline in the moderate poverty headcount (from 39.4 to 13.1 percent) is explained by income growth, while the remaining 6.7 percentage points were the result of improvements in equitable income distribution (figure 9.7). Yet, this outcome arose from events over two distinct periods: in 2003–07, growth in the mean was the only driving force behind the observed drop in the share of the poor, whereas, over the next five years, in 2007–12, the almost 10 percent decline in the poverty headcount that was driven by economic growth was accompanied by a similar contraction associated with improved income distribution. Similar decompositions of the poverty reduction in the region

Figure 9.7 Decomposition of Shifts in Moderate Poverty, Urban Areas, Uruguay, 2003–12

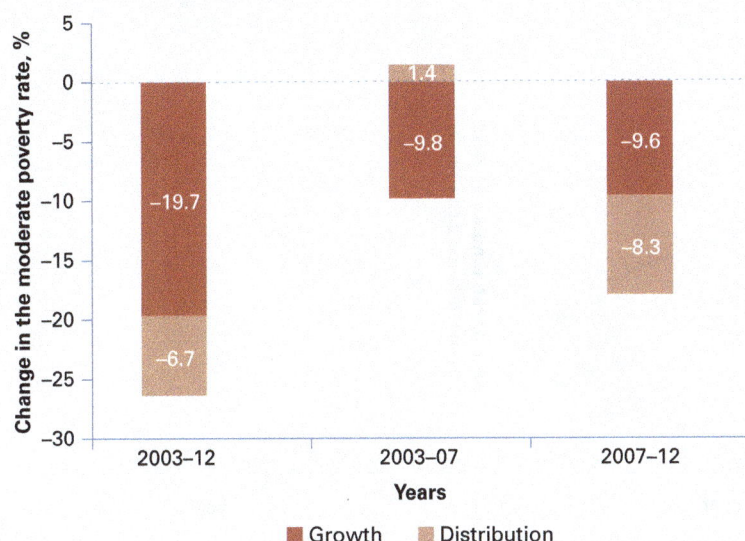

Source: Data of the Continuous Household Survey.
Note: The figure shows a Datt-Ravallion (1992) decomposition based on official moderate poverty lines. Data correspond to Montevideo and other urban areas with more than 5,000 inhabitants.

during these years reveal analogous trends: economic growth accounted for two-thirds of the drop in poverty between 2003 and 2012, while shifts in income distribution explain the remaining third.[6] As in Uruguay, changes in income distribution had a more substantial role in the region in 2007–12, representing nearly half of the reduction in poverty there.

The redistribution component should not be considered as representing the government's fiscal and social policies; rather, it reflects the fact that the incomes of less well-off households were rising at a more rapid pace than the incomes of the rest of the population because of increases in labor incomes (through higher earnings or higher employment rates) or upsurges in nonlabor incomes, including capital gains, private transfers, and public transfers.

Labor markets

Through greater earnings and the rising number of the employed, labor markets are fundamental in explaining the improvements in well-being in Uruguay. At the peak of the 2001–02 crisis, 17 percent of the economically active population was unemployed, and over 40 percent of the employed were not covered by social security. The situation began to improve significantly only after 2004. Unemployment fell rapidly and reached a record low of 6.1 percent in 2012, while labor informality (proxied by eligibility for

Figure 9.8 Unemployment and Formal Employment, Uruguay, 2006–12

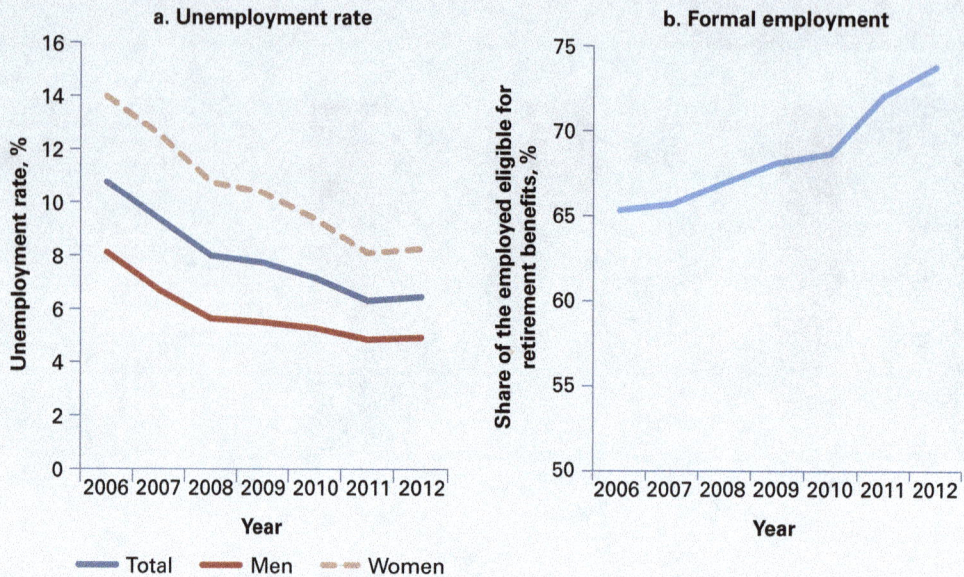

a. Unemployment rate

b. Formal employment

Legend: ——— Total   ——— Men   - - - Women

Sources: Chart a: National Statistics Institute. Chart b: Data of the 2006–12 Continuous Household Survey.

retirement benefits) also declined as a consequence of better macroeconomic conditions and the enhanced collection of social security contributions (figure 9.8). The higher employment rates and better employment outcomes were felt across the skills distribution: unemployment fell both among workers with only primary education or less and workers with only some secondary schooling (figure 9.9). Meanwhile, the shares of workers in wage employment (as opposed to self-employment or unpaid status) rose among both groups, from 38 to 41 percent among workers with primary education and from 53 to 56 percent among workers with some secondary schooling.

Employment declined during the crisis, especially in manufacturing, construction, transport, storage, and communications. During the recovery, employment expanded by about 4 percent annually. Employment growth accelerated in primary sector activities, the retail trade, and the hospitality industry, and recovered in manufacturing, construction, transport, storage, and communications. During the recent economic expansion, employment increased rapidly in construction and at a more moderate pace in transport, storage, and communications and in other services.

Utilities and transport, storage, and communications were the most rapidly growing sectors in terms of output in 2007–13 (table 9.1). The rise in the employment share of trade, tourism, and transport, combined with the dynamic growth of these sectors, meant that these sectors were the largest contributors to GDP and the largest sectors of employment, accounting for 29 percent of all employment in 2012.

Figure 9.9 Employment and Participation Rates, by Skill Level, Uruguay, 2007–12

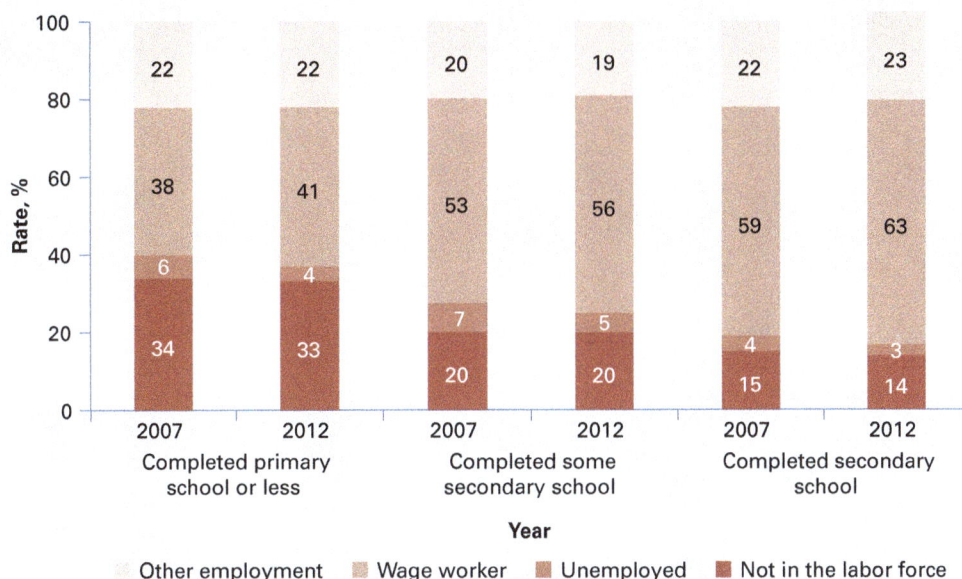

Source: Data of SEDLAC.
Note: Data refer to individuals age 15–70 years who reported they were not in school. Other employment = self-employment, employers, and unpaid workers.

Table 9.1 Sectoral Output and Employment Growth, Uruguay, 2003–13

average annual rate, %

	Output		Employment
Sector	2003–06	2007–13	2007–12
Gas, electricity, water	−9.4	15.5	6.7
Transport, storage, and communications	9.5	15	4.1
Trade and hospitality	4.2	7.2	4.6
Construction	6.3	4.9	1.1
Other services	0.5	3.8	4.0
Primary sector activities	6.6	3.5	−1.0
Manufacturing	7.7	3.1	0.2

Source: Based on data of the Banco Central del Uruguay.

The lack of growth in employment in the primary sector and in manufacturing resulted in a shift of low-skilled labor away from these sectors and toward construction, trade, and hospitality–transport. Among workers with only primary schooling, for example, the share of the employed in the primary sector fell by 1.7 percentage points between 2007 and 2012, while the share in manufacturing fell by 1.9 percentage points (figure 9.10, chart a). Even so, the primary sector continued to be the largest sector of employment among workers with only primary schooling or less, accounting for 20 percent of employment in 2012 (figure 9.10, chart b). In contrast,

Figure 9.10 Sector of Low-Skilled Employment, Uruguay, 2007–12

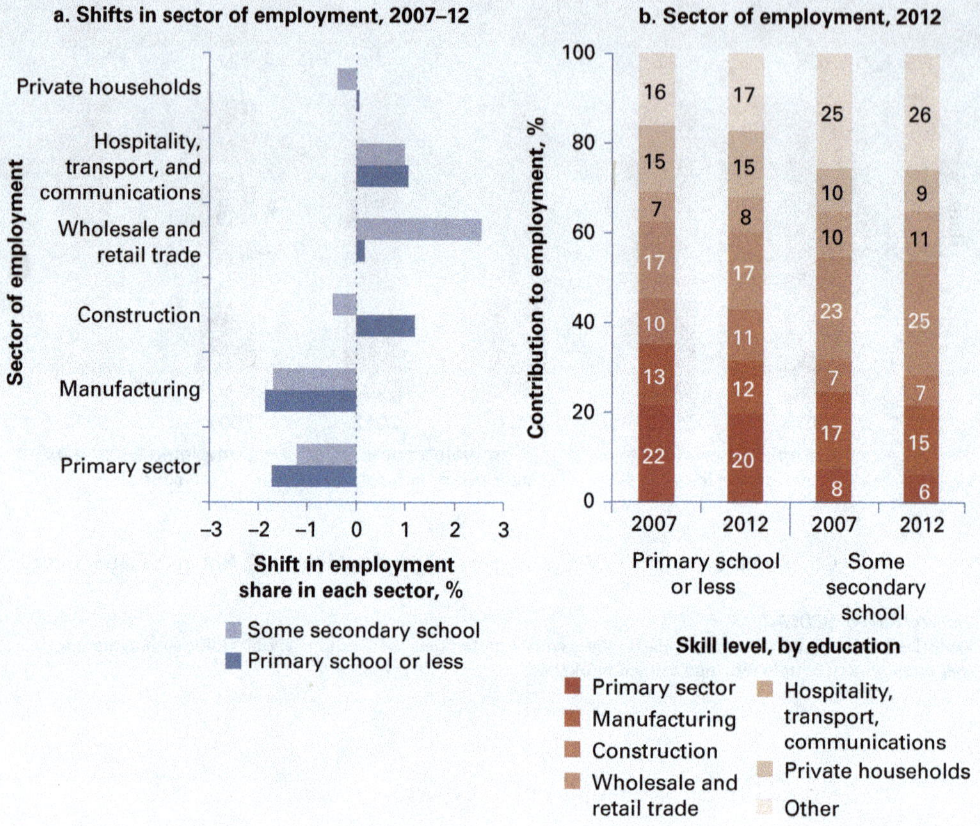
a. Shifts in sector of employment, 2007–12
Private households
Hospitality, transport, and communications
Wholesale and retail trade
Construction
Manufacturing
Primary sector
Sector of employment
–3 –2 –1 0 1 2 3
Shift in employment share in each sector, %
Some secondary school
Primary school or less
b. Sector of employment, 2012
100
80
60
40
20
0
Contribution to employment, %
16 15 7 17 10 13 22
17 15 8 17 11 12 20
25 10 10 23 7 17 8
26 9 11 25 7 15 6
2007 2012 2007 2012
Primary school or less
Some secondary school
Skill level, by education
Primary sector
Manufacturing
Construction
Wholesale and retail trade
Hospitality, transport, communications
Private households
Other

Source: Data of SEDLAC.
Note: Data refer to adults age 15 years or over who reported they were employed.

employment in construction and hospitality–transport grew at an annual rate of 1 percent among the lowest skilled workers, while trade was the largest employer of workers with some secondary schooling.

In addition to expanded employment opportunities, earnings rose throughout the decade. Real wages experienced a major and sudden drop during the 2001–02 crisis, losing about a fourth of their value. Real wages began recovering thereafter and, by 2009, had surpassed the precrisis level (figure 9.11).

Alves et al. (2012) argue that the recent narrowing in earnings inequality was driven largely by rising returns to education and declines in skill premiums. Indeed, earnings grew more quickly among the less skilled. Between 2007 and 2012, average monthly earnings increased by 27 percent among workers with only primary education or less and by 24 percent among workers with only some secondary schooling (figure 9.12). Meanwhile, the earnings of more highly skilled labor expanded by 10 percent among workers who had only finished secondary school and by 4 percent among

Figure 9.11 Real Wage Index, Uruguay, 2000–13

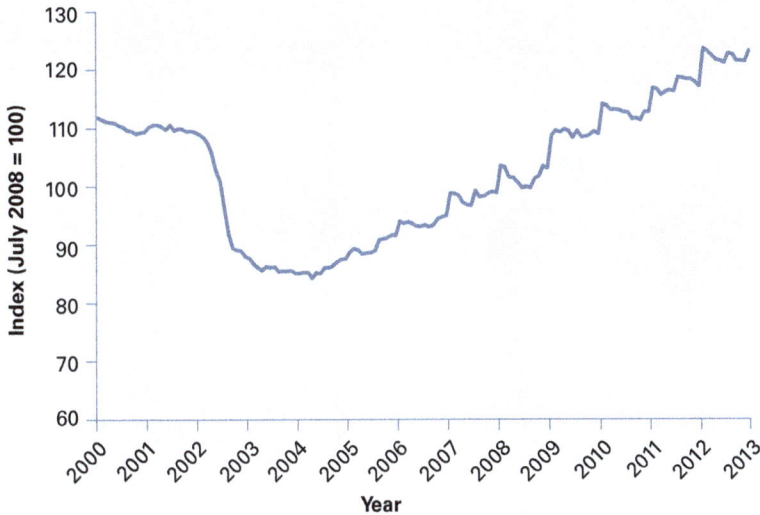

Source: Data of the National Statistics Institute.

workers with some tertiary education. Earnings growth rates were strong across the four skill groups between 2007 and 2009, but diverged thereafter. While the least skilled saw their earnings rise each year, workers with some tertiary education experienced annual reductions in mean monthly earnings on the order of 4 percent a year between 2010 and 2012. This drop in real returns to skills suggests that the skills premium was falling in Uruguay, while the binding minimum wage was leading to higher earnings among the lowest skilled.

The recent narrowing in earnings inequality occurred in a context of major institutional changes including increases in the minimum wage, which rose 200 percent between 2004 and 2010, the restoration of collective bargaining in 2005, and passage of a new law on wage negotiations in 2009 (Levy and Schady 2013).[7] In addition, there was an expansion in the rate of formality among private sector workers (Amarante et al. 2011).

The role of public spending

While labor markets played a fundamental role in the enhancement of living conditions in Uruguay, the introduction of income transfer schemes targeted at the bottom of the income distribution, as well as reforms in the personal income tax code, contributed toward a more equal society. Public spending in the country is generally prodigious and effective. It accounted for 21.7 percent of GDP in 2009. The three largest components of public spending were contributory pensions (8.5 percent of GDP), health care (4.7 percent), and education (3.7 percent) (Bucheli et al. 2014).

Prior to the 2001–02 crisis, the family allowance program Asignaciones Familiares provided monthly cash benefits to formal sector workers with

Figure 9.12 Growth in Labor Earnings, by Skill Level among Workers, Uruguay, 2007–12

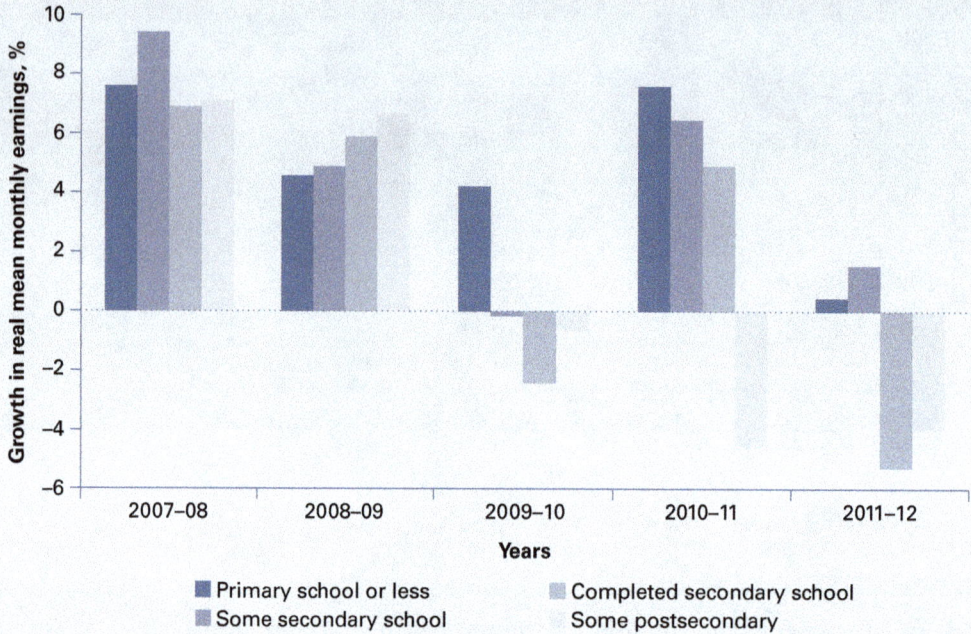

Source: Data of SEDLAC.
Note: Data refer to adults age 15 years or over who reported they were employed.

children (Amarante and Vigorito 2012). A social pension scheme for the elderly and disabled that was implemented in 1919 targeted the socially vulnerable. Though these transfers were protected during the crisis, they had limited impact on preventing people from falling into poverty because the value of the transfers was not raised. Asignaciones Familiares was expanded in 2004 to include households with incomes below $39 a month (three times the national minimum wage), but was still too low to have a significant effect on poverty (Amarante and Vigorito 2012).

Recognizing the need for more assistance for the poor and to facilitate social inclusion, PANES, an emergency social plan (see above), was carried out by the new Ministry of Social Development from April 2005 to December 2007 to target the bottom 20 percent of households living below the poverty line (8 percent of the total population). The plan had four main components: (1) a cash transfer, (2) a food card, (3) educational and social reinsertion programs, and (4) housing subsidies and public works. Of the households that were selected to participate, almost all obtained the cash transfer; 80 percent received the food card; and 20 percent participated in the latter two programs. PANES covered 83,000 households (5 percent of all households and 10 percent of the population), and the benefits represented an average of 30 percent of household incomes among the beneficiaries.

The program cost $80 million or 0.41 percent of GDP annually (Amarante and Vigorito 2012).

In 2007, PANES was refashioned into the Plan de Equidad Program (see above). The new program included tax and health care reforms, continued the $8–$16 per child cash family allowance transfers among households that did not receive more than the national minimum wage, maintained the food cards, expanded the coverage of early childhood services, and lowered the retirement age. By 2009, there were 364,000 beneficiaries, including 76 percent of all destitute children, 68 percent of children living in poverty, and almost all households in the poorest quintile. Under the program, noncontributory transfers accounted for an average of approximately 20 percent of household income among households in the bottom decile (Amarante et al. 2011). According to Dean and Vigorito (2011), the new transfer scheme significantly reduced extreme poverty, but had a limited effect on moderate poverty.

Despite the importance of current social programs, poverty persists in the country, particularly among households with low educational attainment, especially in Montevideo, and among households that are likely to be excluded from the transfer system. Moreover, even if they receive transfers, poor households with children are more likely to remain poor (Bucheli et al. 2014). This suggests that there is room for improvement in social spending.

On the revenue side, the progressive tax policy is estimated to have narrowed income inequality by 0.03 points of the Gini coefficient, a reduction of 6.0 percent after taxes (figure 9.13). Using the incidence analysis framework developed by Commitment to Equity, Bucheli et al. (2014) find that inequality prior to any taxation or public transfer (market income) was 0.49 in 2009.[8] Direct taxation, including personal income taxes and employment taxes, reduces inequality to 0.48, and public transfers further reduce the Gini coefficient to 0.46. Although indirect taxes, such as consumption taxes, are regressive or inequality increasing, inequality after these taxes have been taken into account (postfiscal income) remains at 0.46.

Bucheli et al. (2014) extend the analysis one step further. By adding the cost of publicly provided educational and health care services to the incomes of households that used these services, they estimate that the Gini coefficient would narrow to 0.39. This is the result of the greater take-up of these public services among lower-income households. It suggests that differences in service quality may also play a role given that households able to afford private services seem to opt out of public services at a higher rate.

Key Challenges

Vulnerability to external shocks

A small open economy, Uruguay is vulnerable to regional contagion effects, particularly from neighboring Argentina and Brazil. The correlation in GDP

Figure 9.13 The Gini Coefficient and Pre- and Postfiscal Incomes, Uruguay, 2009

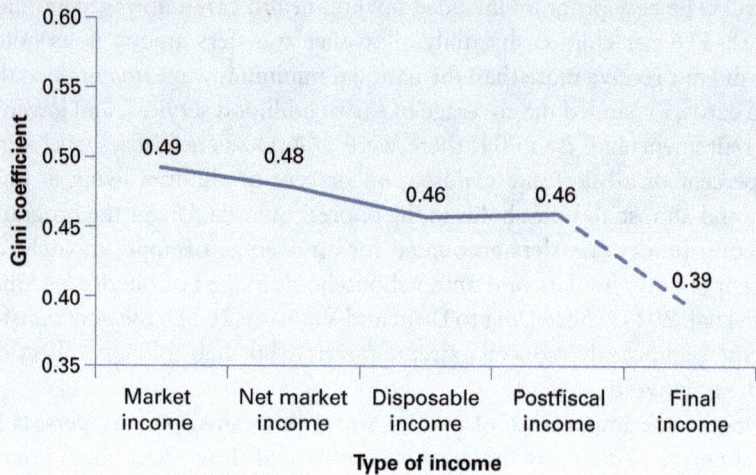

Source: Bucheli et al. 2014.

growth is 0.94 between Uruguay and Argentina and 0.83 between Uruguay and Brazil (IMF 2011). The correlation with the economic cycle in Argentina has likely declined in recent years as Uruguay has increased its trade with other partners. Argentina nonetheless remains one of the most important markets for service exports from Uruguay, albeit net tourism export revenues have declined markedly in recent years because of the difficult situation in Argentina. Uruguay has successfully diversified export destination markets; China and the Russian Federation have become important markets. China now accounts for more than 20 percent of Uruguay's merchandise exports (including reexports from free trade zones in China). Only 5.6 percent of merchandise exports went to Argentina in 2012–13, down from 14.5 percent in 1990–98. Brazil accounts for a much more significant share of Uruguay's exports, around 19.0 percent, and continues to be one of the main destinations of merchandise exports from Uruguay.

Barriga et al. (2014) have conducted a simulation exercise suggesting that, as a result of the policies implemented since the 2001–02 crisis, Uruguay is now in a better position to weather a severe crisis.[9] The predicted impact on poverty would be considerably smaller; inequality would not change significantly; and household incomes would only fall by 8 percent (figure 9.14). A large contributing factor in the greater resilience is the improved and expanded social safety nets, as well as the larger role of social transfers and nonlabor components in household incomes.

While the overall effect of a crisis on poverty would be relatively mild, the average per capita income of the vulnerable (those between the poverty line and the middle-class cutoff) would be 25 percent less in the event of a crisis (figure 9.15). The simulation predicts that younger individuals,

Figure 9.14 The Impact of a Crisis on Poverty and Inequality, Uruguay, 2011–14

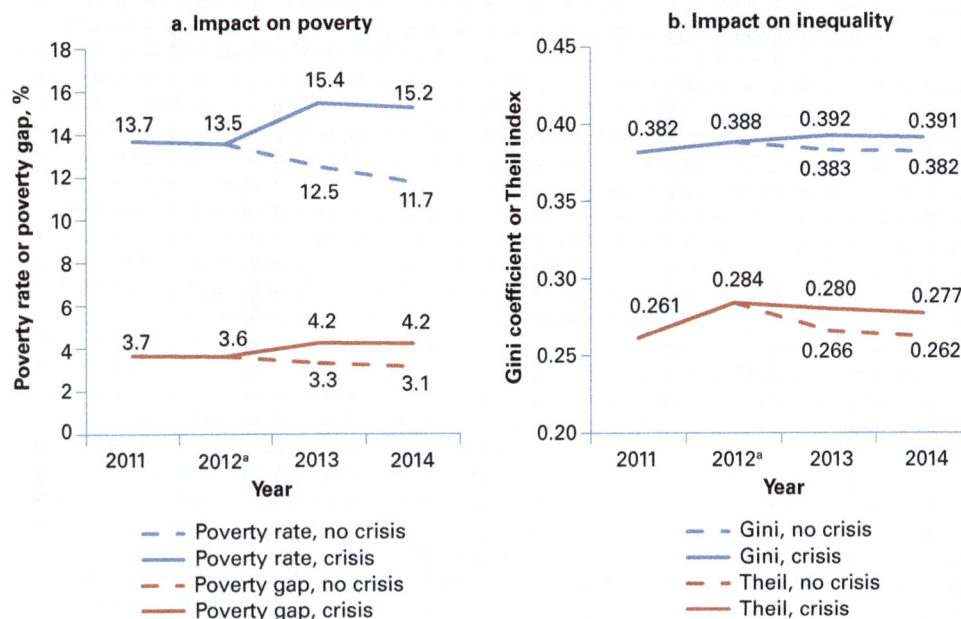

a. Impact on poverty

b. Impact on inequality

Source: Barriga et al. 2014.
a. Baseline year.

woman-headed households, larger households, and people who have not completed secondary education would be relatively more vulnerable to the risk of falling into poverty were a crisis to strike again. The likelihood of falling back into poverty is also higher in Montevideo than in rural areas; although this effect would be mostly driven by a lack of growth, changes in income distribution would also play a part.

Even in the absence of local economic shocks such as the Argentine crisis of 2001–02, it is important that government policy in Uruguay be designed with an eye toward protecting the gains in poverty and shared prosperity. Policy should reflect, for example, insight into how Uruguay might weather a slowdown in growth in the region. Though the simulation results of Barriga et al. (2014) are encouraging and suggest that Uruguay has successfully built up a resistance to regional contagion, they also highlight that some groups, particularly the less highly skilled and woman-headed households, are still vulnerable.

Service delivery

Education

Hanushek and Woessmann (2012) find that disparities in human capital can account for half to two-thirds of the income variations between Latin America and the rest of the world. In large part, this is driven by differences in both educational attainment and school quality.

Figure 9.15 Households in the Crisis Scenario in Year 2 (2014), Uruguay

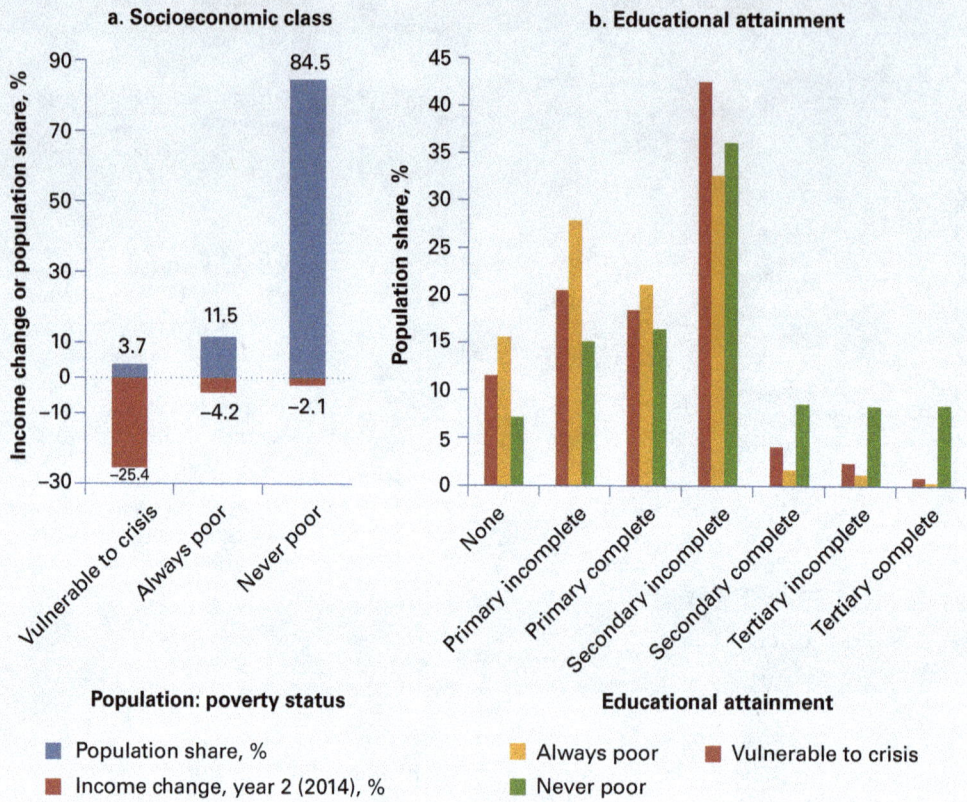

a. Socioeconomic class

b. Educational attainment

Population: poverty status

■ Population share, %
■ Income change, year 2 (2014), %

Educational attainment

■ Always poor   ■ Vulnerable to crisis
■ Never poor

Source: Barriga et al. 2014.

High secondary-school drop-out rates are a particular problem in Uruguay. School-age children whose parents have lower levels of educational attainment are significantly less likely to attend school (Ferreira et al. 2013). The performance of Uruguay appears to be about average for the share of 11- to 12-year-olds who are in third grade or higher, but below average in the share of 15-year-olds in seventh grade or higher for the parental group with less than primary educational attainment. Children of parents with no education have only a 60 percent chance of attending school by age 15. This is especially concerning given the desire in the country for inclusive growth and shared prosperity.

Many of these dropouts are not working either (figure 9.16). About 15 percent of all boys age 15–18 years and 17 percent of girls in the same age-group in 2012 were neither in school nor working. While the rate of youth neither in school nor working among girls in Uruguay is similar to the regional average, boys in Uruguay are significantly more likely to be out of school and out of work. This means these young people are not

Figure 9.16 15- to 18-Year-Olds Not in School and Not Working, by Gender, Uruguay and the Region, 2000–12

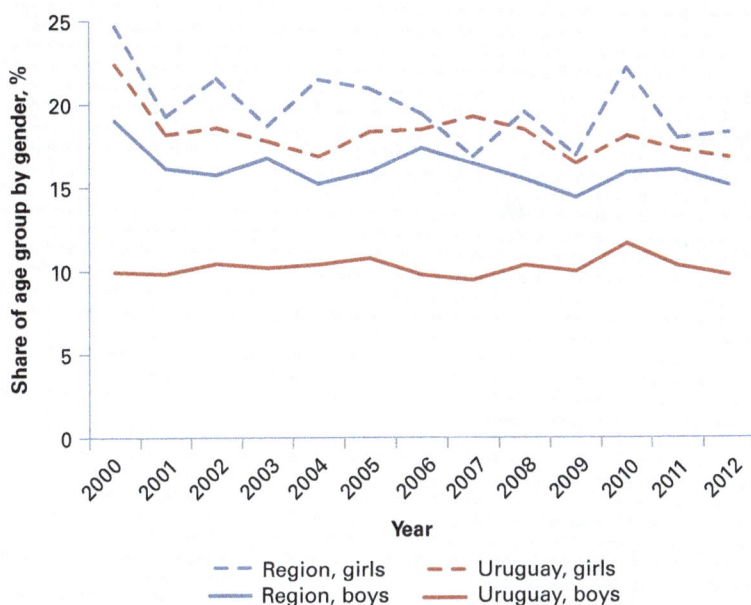

Source: Tabulations of Equity Lab, Team for Statistical Development, World Bank, Washington, DC, using data from SEDLAC and based on the methodology of De Hoyos, Popova, and Rogers 2015.

accumulating human capital through either formal education or on-the-job experience.

In addition, the quality of schooling in Uruguay is poor. Although test scores are better in Uruguay than in other countries in the region, they are well below the scores in OECD countries outside the region. Hanushek and Woessmann (2012) note that Uruguay has achieved the highest cognitive score in the OECD's Program for International Student Assessment (PISA), 4.30, among all Latin American countries.[10] In the student assessment tests in Uruguay in 2012, the share of 15-year-old students failing to achieve a score of 2 was 48 percent in science, 49 percent in mathematics, and 39 percent in reading.[11] Furthermore, the World Bank (2014b) finds that there is a significant disparity between the scores of students who attend public school and the scores of students who attend private school. In mathematics, for example, 79 percent of private school students achieved a grade of 2 or higher, double the rate of public school children, of whom only 35 percent scored 2 or higher. Similar gaps in achievement occur in science and reading. Because attendance at a private school is strongly correlated with parental earnings and educational attainment, this gap in test scores suggests that the provision of good-quality education is inequitable across socioeconomic groups. This will have significant impacts on inter-generational mobility and inequality and, potentially, the prospects for the nation's economic growth.

Expansion of health care and nutrition

Health care expenditure is around 4.6 percent of GDP and covers direct public health care for people living in poverty and a subsidy available to contributors to the Fondo Nacional de Salud, an in-kind transfer to health care providers. Nutrition benefits (0.3 percent of GDP) target families in extreme poverty by providing lunches. Social workers evaluate the (renewable) eligibility for the program, which lasts for up to 24 months. A food card program was launched in 2006 to offer households, pregnant women, and children under 18 years of age access to food and hygiene, conditional on school enrollment among children under 14, income below a threshold, and regular health care visits.

Health care indicators show that Uruguay outperforms the region in key areas, though there is room for improvement. Indicators of access to reproductive and health services are generally positive. In 2009, almost all births (99.7 percent) were attended by skilled health staff, which is better than the average among countries at the same income level (96.0 percent) and countries in the region (90.1 percent). Similarly, the maternal mortality ratio in 2010 of 29 per 100,000 live births was well below the regional average of 80. Adolescent fertility has also been declining; in 2012, it stood at 58.3 births per 1,000 15- to 19-year-old girls. Though lower than the regional average in 2011 of 68.1 births per 1,000, this is considerably higher than the world average (49.3 births per 1,000).

Final Remarks

Uruguay has demonstrated a remarkable ability to recover from a devastating crisis that not only damaged exports and production, but also led to several years of high inflation, macroeconomic instability, and soaring poverty rates. With prudent monetary and fiscal policies and a broad expansion of social protection programs, the government engineered a return to precrisis growth and poverty rates, while reducing inequality and fostering convergence across population groups, particularly with regard to the bottom 40, and both pro-poor and inclusive growth. Uruguay leads other countries in the region in many indicators of social inclusion and prosperity and exhibits lower levels of corruption, crime, and environmental degradation.

The substantive improvements in well-being, especially since 2007, are the result of a combination of favorable economic conditions and growth patterns that have led to more employment opportunities, as well as key policy reforms in the labor market and social protection that have ensured that the less well off have been able to contribute to the growth process and enhance living conditions.

Serious challenges must still be overcome. The country is exposed to internal and external risks that render certain population groups vulnerable to the risk of falling back into poverty. However, Uruguay has adapted well, as evidenced by the brevity of the drop in GDP associated with the recent global financial crisis. The government has demonstrated its willingness to respond to the needs of the population and has been efficient in developing organizational and administrative responses. Nonetheless, the expanded middle class is demanding better quality in services, especially in education. The quality of education is still significantly heterogeneous across the country and correlates highly with the socioeconomic status among students. Secondary-school drop-out rates are high, especially among the less well off. Improving education is thus crucial not only to ensuring the sustainability of economic growth, but also to enhancing economic mobility across generations. The demographic transition associated with the aging population may yet test the sustainability of the fiscal system.

Notes

1. Moderate poverty in urban areas dropped from 29.7 percent in 1990 to 17.8 percent in 2000. These rates are not comparable with the moderate poverty headcounts produced after 2001 because the methodology for measuring poverty was changed. See the note to figure 9.2.

2. At the beginning of the decade, Argentina and Brazil accounted for half of all Uruguayan trade. This situation has changed in recent years and China now tops the list, at 21 percent of the country's trade. About one-third of Uruguay's exports now go to Argentina and Brazil, and over half of tourism receipts and one-third of foreign direct investment originate from Argentina. These two countries affect Uruguay directly and indirectly by amplifying shocks from the rest of the world. (See IMF 2011.)

3. While the economy has certainly grown at a high rate and the country has been successful in reducing poverty and inequality, a more complete analysis of trends in the past decade requires an examination of the periods before and after the 2001–02 crisis to separate out growth spells, the impacts of the crisis, and the recovery. This is rendered difficult because of changes in household survey data both in methodology and coverage. Until 2005, the *Encuesta Continua de Hogares* (continuous household survey) excluded rural areas and towns of fewer than 5,000 inhabitants (around 20 percent of the total population), but, in 2006, it became representative at the national level (covering both urban and rural areas). This important methodological change was extrapolated only back to 2002; it would therefore be imprudent to compare poverty and inequality levels before and after that year. Additionally, because of the focus on urban areas prior to 2006, trends in crisis recovery can only be considered for urban areas.

4. These data correspond to Montevideo and urban areas with more than 5,000 inhabitants.

5. The thresholds correspond, respectively, to Ur$153 and Ur$765 per person a day in 2005 prices.

6. World Bank (2014b) and tabulations of Equity Lab, Team for Statistical Development, World Bank, Washington, DC, based on data of SEDLAC. The data

on the regional poverty decomposition are based on the per capita international moderate poverty line of $4 a day.

7. However, the direct impacts of these changes on earnings inequality are unclear. Some estimates suggest that the rise in the minimum wage had only a minor effect on the distribution of earnings because of the low starting point of the minimum wage and the lack of compliance (Borraz and Pampillón 2011). Likewise, the influence of centralized wage setting on earnings inequality has not been definitively established because of other confounding concurrent effects (Amarante et al. 2011).

8. Led by Nora Lustig, Commitment to Equity is a joint initiative of Tulane University, New Orleans, and the Inter-American Dialogue, Washington, DC. The website is at http://www.commitmentoequity.org/.

9. In this exercise, the benchmark scenario assumes that real GDP will continue to grow, though at a slightly slower rate; inflation will remain high; and there will be no drastic change in employment (though unemployment may begin to decline). However, under a scenario replicating a crisis similar in importance to the crisis of 2001–02, real GDP would contract significantly, though less than in 2001–02; inflation would reach double digits; and the share of trade in GDP would decline, leading to a rise in the unemployment rate.

10. Set to the program's test score scale, the cognitive score is the average test score in mathematics and science in all years in primary and secondary school. The highest score was 5.45 (Taiwan), and the lowest was 3.09 (South Africa).

11. A score of 2 is considered to represent the equivalent of a basic ability to apply the material to real-world situations.

References

Alves, Guillermo, Verónica Amarante, Gonzalo Salas, and Andrea Vigorito. 2012. "La desigualdad del ingreso en Uruguay entre 1986 y 2009." Documentos de Trabajo 03–12, Instituto de Economía, Universidad de la República, Montevideo, Uruguay.

Amarante, Verónica, Marisa Bucheli, Cecilia Olivieri, and Ivone Perazzo. 2011. "Distributive Impacts of Alternative Tax Structures: The Case of Uruguay." Documentos de Trabajo 09–11, Instituto de Economía, Universidad de la República, Montevideo, Uruguay.

Amarante, Verónica, and Andrea Vigorito. 2012. "The Expansion of Non-Contributory Transfers in Uruguay in Recent Years." Policy Research Brief 29, International Policy Centre for Inclusive Growth, United Nations Development Programme, Brasília, Brazil.

Barriga Cabanillas, Oscar, María Ana Lugo, Hannah Nielsen, Carlos Rodríguez-Castelán, and María Pía Zanetti. 2014. "Is Uruguay More Resilient this Time? Distributional Impacts of a Crisis Similar to the 2001/02 Argentine Crisis." Policy Research Working Paper 6849, World Bank, Washington, DC.

Borraz, Fernando, and Nicolas González Pampillón. 2011. "Assessing the Distributive Impact of More than Doubling the Minimum Wage: The Case of Uruguay." Documentos de Trabajo 17–11, Instituto de Economía, Universidad de la República, Montevideo, Uruguay.

Bucheli, Marisa, Nora Lustig, Máximo Rossi, and Florencia Amábile. 2014. "Social Spending, Taxes, and Income Redistribution in Uruguay." In "Analyzing the

Redistributive Impact of Taxes and Transfers in Latin America," ed. Nora Lustig, Carola Pessino, and John Scott, special issue, *Public Finance Review* 42 (3): 413–33.

Datt, Gaurav, and Martin Ravallion. 1992. "Growth and Redistribution Components of Changes in Poverty Measures: A Decomposition with Applications to Brazil and India in the 1980s." *Journal of Development Economics* 38 (2): 275–95.

Dean, Andrés, and Andrea Vigorito. 2011. "La Población de Menores recursos en Uruguay. Una Caracterización a Partir del Panel MIDES-INE-UDELAR." Unpublished working paper, Instituto de Economía, Universidad de la República, Montevideo, Uruguay.

De Hoyos, Rafael E., Anna Popova, and F. Halsey Rogers. 2015. "Out of School and Out of Work: A Diagnostic of *Ninis* in Latin America." Working paper, World Bank, Washington, DC.

Ferreira, Francisco H. G., Julian Messina, Jamele Rigolini, Luis F. López-Calva, María Ana Lugo, and Renos Vakis. 2013. *Economic Mobility and the Rise of the Latin American Middle Class*. Washington, DC: World Bank.

Hanushek, Eric A., and Ludger Woessmann. 2012. "Schooling, Educational Achievement, and the Latin American Growth Puzzle." *Journal of Development Economics* 99 (2): 497–512.

IMF (International Monetary Fund). 2011. "2011 Article IV Consultation." December, IMF, Washington, DC. https://www.imf.org/external/pubs/ft/scr/2011/cr11375.pdf.

INE (Uruguay, National Statistics Institute). 2013. "Estimación de la pobreza por el Método del Ingreso, Año 2012." April, División Estadísticas Sociodemográficas, INE, Montevideo, Uruguay.

Levy, Santiago, and Norbert Schady. 2013. "Latin America's Social Policy Challenge: Education, Social Insurance, Redistribution." *Journal of Economic Perspectives* 27 (2): 193–218.

SEDLAC (Socio-Economic Database for Latin America and the Caribbean), Center for Distributive, Labor, and Social Studies, Universidad de La Plata, La Plata, Argentina; World Bank, Washington, DC, http://sedlac.econo.unlp.edu.ar/eng/index.php.

World Bank. 2014a. "Macro Monitoring Notes: Uruguay." Country Management Unit for Argentina, Paraguay, and Uruguay, Poverty Reduction and Economic Management, Latin America and the Caribbean Region, World Bank, Washington, DC.

———. 2014b. "Social Gains in the Balance: A Fiscal Policy Challenge for Latin America and the Caribbean." Poverty and Labor Brief, Report 85162 rev (February), Latin America and the Caribbean Region, World Bank, Washington, DC.

9 781464 803574